INDIANA HISTORY

A Book of Readings

INDIANA HISTORY

A Book of Readings

Compiled and edited by
Ralph D. Gray

INDIANA UNIVERSITY PRESS
Bloomington & Indianapolis

The paper used in this publication meets the minimum requirements of American National Standard for Information Sciences—Permanence of Paper for Printed Library Materials, ANSI Z39.48-1984.

Manufactured in the United States of America

Library of Congress Cataloging-in-Publication Data

Indiana history : a book of readings / compiled and edited by Ralph D. Gray.
p. cm.
Includes index.
ISBN 0–253–32629–X. — ISBN 0–253–28191–1 (pbk.)
1. Indiana—History. I. Gray, Ralph D.
F526.3.I53 1994
977.2—dc20 94–5714

1 2 3 4 5 00 99 98 97 96 95 94

Dedicated to the memory of
Lee M. Gray (1902–1991)
and to two new kids on the block,
Dana Lynn and
Matthew Gray Boebinger

Contents

Preface

We have seen a considerable outpouring of quality publications dealing with the history of Indiana in the dozen or so years since *The Hoosier State* appeared in the early 1980s. Both the Indiana Historical Society and Indiana University Press have issued new monographs interpreting various aspects of the state's development, as have other presses within and without the state (many of which will be referred to in the pages that follow); in addition, two important surveys of Indiana history appeared in the 1980s, both from the prolific pen of Professor James H. Madison at Indiana University, Bloomington. In 1982 he completed volume five of the *History of Indiana* series (*Indiana through Tradition and Change, 1920–1945* [Bloomington and Indianapolis]), and four years later his synthesis of Indiana history, *The Indiana Way: A State History* (Bloomington and Indianapolis, 1986), appeared.

Other important developments related to the pursuit and enjoyment of Indiana history include the inauguration by the Indiana Historical Society of a popular history magazine, *Traces of Indiana and Midwestern History*, the completion in 1990 of *An Indiana Guide*, a useful companion for travelers throughout the Hoosier state, and the publication of two extremely helpful bibliographic guides to manuscript materials: *A Guide to the Manuscript Collections in the Indiana Historical Society and the Indiana State Library*, compiled by Eric C. Pomeroy and others, and *Religion in Indiana: A Guide to Historical Resources* (Bloomington, 1986), edited by L. C. Rudolph and Judith E. Endelman.

Obviously, both the resources for doing Indiana history and publication outlets for the results of that research have been increased over the last decade. Additional interest in state and regional history can also be documented. A large number of institutions of higher education offer survey and advanced courses in Indiana history, their counterpart courses at schools of continuing education via correspondence are heavily subscribed, and an increasing number of master's theses and doctoral dissertations explore themes in state history. Both the Indiana Historical Society and the Indiana Humanities Council offer research grants to individuals and institutions to further research and public discussion of state topics. Most recently, at least two scholarly presses have begun to publish monographs in series devoted to midwestern history and culture.

More than thirty scholars from colleges and universities and other research institutions throughout the state responded recently to a call for persons interested in state and local history, specifically Indiana history, to consider the needs and opportunities for new research and publications, for new questions to be posed and answered, in this field of inquiry. There have already been some tangible results from this brainstorming session, and the likelihood of significant new articles and monographs, reflecting new ways of looking at old problems, is strong.

The purpose of this volume is, as before, to provide both an overview of Indiana history, based upon primary and secondary accounts of significant events and personalities in the state, and a supplement to more traditional narrative and analytical surveys of Indiana history. Some of the selections below are new; some have been retained from the previous two-volume edition of this work. The same holds true for the introductory material, although the bibliographic entries have been updated.

I am particularly indebted to John Gallman, director of the Indiana University Press, for his interest and encouragement in this project. Not only did he act some ten years ago to save the first edition of *The Hoosier State* from imminent destruction, following a decision by its original publisher to discontinue its series of state histories, but he also provided the initial impetus for the current volume. I am grateful to the librarians and archivists who assisted me in obtaining materials to be considered for the new edition and to the many teachers and other readers over the years who have used this work and made useful comments regarding possible revisions in future editions. In particular I want to recognize James E. Farmer of Indianapolis, a journalist, author, and advisor to various state leaders, for his continuing interest in this project and several helpful suggestions. The Department of History at IUPUI has supported my efforts in studying, teaching, and writing about Indiana history in countless ways since I offered my first course in the subject in 1971. My final debt of gratitude is to my family for indulgence and encouragement as I pursued what is still an endlessly fascinating undertaking—reading about and exploring Indiana history.

Preface to The Hoosier State

There has been a renewed interest in the study of state and local history in recent years, stemming from such diverse stimuli as the growing fascination with the past sparked by the nation's bicentennial observation and the runaway popularity of Alex T. Haley's *Roots*. There is also a reaction building against the anonymity and temporariness of modern life styles. Although historical studies in general are "in crisis," according to a 1975 report to the Organization of American Historians, there is vitality and widespread appeal in community and state historical activities and studies. Such study has become more sophisticated and particularistic without being parochial, more analytical and specialized without being antiquarian.

The problem of readily available and inexpensive books and articles for the beginning student, however, still exists. The market for monographic state studies is not yet sufficiently broad in most cases to justify commercial publishing expenses, which means that the often abundant materials for community and state history have appeared mainly in expensive hardbound books and relatively small circulation journals or state agency publications. This book, intended as a partial corrective to the situation, makes available a sampling of the rich variety of sources that exist for the study of Indiana history. For the most part, I have selected recent secondary accounts and interpretations taken from journal articles or chapters in books; but I have occasionally used contemporaneous accounts and documents. I have even selected a few passages from works of fiction and poetry to help recapture the flavor and drama of Indiana's past.

Indiana is now well into the fourth quarter of its bicentennial period, having been admitted into the Union in December 1816. The first state to be created amid the westward rush following the War of 1812, its roots are the ones common to the other states of the area now known as the Old Northwest. But Indiana quickly developed a distinctive quality and character. By the end of the nineteenth century it was the most rural and homogeneous state of the region, with the highest number of Southern-born—and, conversely, the lowest number of foreign-born—citizens. Although the state is now both heavily industrialized—steel, automotive parts, pharmaceuticals—and urbanized, with most of its population living in cities between 10,000 and 100,000 in population, Indiana has retained its folksy, rural image.

Both the people, with their rural and southern orientation, and the land, devoid of any natural boundary except along the southern and southwestern edges, have contributed to Indiana's unique flavor. Because of the swampy terrain in parts of northern Indiana, that area encountered by the migrating hordes from New England, New York, and Pennsylvania after the southern third of the state had been settled, fewer remained there as permanent settlers than moved on westward into Illinois, Wisconsin, and Iowa. Consequently, the southern influence, so clearly recognized in the southern hills of Indiana, extended also into the flat, fertile plains of central and north-central Indiana. This contributed to the state's political and cultural orientation in the nineteenth century, its comparatively poor educational system—but, perhaps symbiotically, its rich tradition of oral and then written narratives—and its sympathy for slavery and the slaveholder. Although Indiana was unquestionably Unionist during the long, bloody struggle of the Civil War, "copperhead" influences were present, and Indiana was often a reluctant partner in the Reconstruction policies of the Republican party.

During the late nineteenth century, Indiana emerged as an important industrial state. This development, significantly boosted by the discovery in the latter 1880s of a huge but soon exhausted natural gas field, was first based on the processing of Indiana's large and diversified agricultural crop and livestock production. Subsequently, the location of giant steel-producing plants in northwestern Indiana, as well as the development of an indigenous automobile industry, magnified the state's role as a manufacturing center.

During this same period Indiana entered what has been called a "golden age" in terms of both politics and literature. Once the sixth largest state in the nation in terms of population and thus electoral votes, and with two evenly matched political parties, Indiana was the scene of political contests that were often fierce. And because both parties considered Indiana's "swing" vote essential, an unusually large number of Indiana politicians appeared on the national party tickets. Indeed, between 1868 and 1916 there were only three elections in which Hoosiers were not nominated by one or both of the two major parties. During those years one Hoosier, Benjamin Harrison, was elected president, and four Indiana men—Schuyler Colfax, Thomas A. Hendricks, Charles W. Fairbanks, and Thomas R. Marshall—were elected to the vice-presidency. Hoosier authors were also remarkably active and successful during this period, especially the so-called Big Four of Booth Tarkington, James Whitcomb Riley, Meredith Nicholson, and George Ade. And the literary output of the state has remained strong since that time.

In the twentieth century, Indiana has become known as the home of the world's richest automobile racing event, the Indianapolis 500, and of some of the nation's finest high-school and college basketball and football teams. It has a broadly based and diversified economy, which is contributed to almost equally by industrial business and agribusiness, and its blend of medium-sized urban and small-town communities share the landscape with still rustic rural countrysides. Many of the state's scenic historical and recreational sites have been preserved in an actively expanding state park and state memorial system. These include the sand-swept Indiana Dunes along the shores of Lake Michigan, the homes and studios of such artists and writers as T. C. Steele and Gene Stratton Porter, and the unsurpassed beauty of pristine forest land in such parks as Turkey Run and McCormick's Creek in central Indiana and Spring Mill and Clifty Falls in southern Indiana. Once evenly balanced politically—but always strongly conservative—Indiana has become more Republican in recent decades. It has also become more cosmopolitan, with a number of outstanding colleges and universities, lively civic and cultural groups throughout the state, and countless national and international business and professional organizations with headquarters in the state. Many economic, social, and racial problems remain, but the outlook is bright for "The Crossroads of America," which has been Indiana's motto since 1937 and is increasingly appropriate.

Ralph D. Gray

INDIANA HISTORY

A Book of Readings

Introduction

There are countless interpreters of Indiana, using many different modes of expression. The earliest include missionary and military reports for the preterritorial period, travel accounts by intrepid adventurers during the early nineteenth century, and letters, essays, and poems by residents or visitors, such as John Finley's "The Hoosier's Nest," an 1833 poetic tribute to the pioneers of Indiana that may have irretrievably attached that epithet to the people of Indiana. There were also attempts at formal histories of the state, beginning with John B. Dillon's typically long-titled work of 1843: *The History of Indiana from Its Earliest Exploration by Europeans to the Close of the Territorial Government in 1816 with an Introduction Containing Historical Notes of the Discovery and Settlement of the Territory Northwest of the River Ohio*. Since then the flow of poetry, essays, and histories about Indiana has been enormous, with some of the interpreters transcending local appeal and reaching national and international audiences. George Ade, Booth Tarkington, and James Whitcomb Riley are perhaps the best-known popular writers; Logan Esarey, Jacob Piatt Dunn, R. C. Buley, Donald F. Carmony, William E. Wilson, and John Bartlow Martin were among the most important historians of the state during the early and middle years of the twentieth century; more recently historians such as Darrel E. Bigham, Patrick J. Furlong, Dwight Hoover, James H. Madison, Robert M. Taylor, Lance Trusty, and others have made important contributions to our understanding of Hoosier life and culture.

It is the purpose of this brief introductory section to provide some general information about Indiana, its location and natural features, its people and their character. For fuller but still brief treatments and assessments, see especially John Bartlow Martin, *Indiana: An Interpretation* (1947 and 1992); Irving Liebowitz, *My Indiana* (1964); Howard H. Peckham, *Indiana: A Bicentennial History* (1978); and James H. Madison, *The Indiana Way* (1986), the most recent one-volume interpretation of the state.

INDIANA
The Land and the People

William E. Wilson

Professor William E. Wilson provides a good introduction to the Hoosier state, crisscrossed by the nation's main east-west highways and railways. After describing its geographical features, he reviews its geological past and its economic base and glances at its better-known nonagricultural products—writers and politicians. This selection is from the introductory chapter of Indiana: A History, *a fine interpretive history written for the state's sesquicentennial in 1966, when the author was a professor of English at Indiana University in Bloomington. He made a substantial contribution to the anniversary observance with this publication, while adding to his long list of books dealing with Indiana history. Professor Wilson's writings include* The Angel and the Serpent: The Story of New Harmony *(1964), the autobiographical* On the Sunny Side of a One-Way Street *(1958),* The Wabash *(1940), a volume in the Rivers of America series, and juvenile biographies of George Rogers Clark and Tecumseh, as well as a number of works of fiction.*

Indiana: A History *is one of the most recent histories of the state. Other useful introductions to this subject are in John D. Barnhart and Donald F. Carmony,* Indiana: From Frontier to Industrial Commonwealth *(2 vols., 1954); Charles Roll,* Indiana: One Hundred and Fifty Years of American Development *(2 vols., 1931); Jacob P. Dunn,* Indiana and Indianans: A History of Aboriginal and Territorial Indiana and the Century of Statehood *(5 vols., 1919); and John Bartlow Martin,* Indiana: An Interpretation *(New York, 1947; Bloomington, Ind., 1992). Meredith Nicholson, like Wilson, stresses the state's literary tradition in* The Hoosiers *(1900); see also R. E. Banta, ed.,* Hoosier Caravan: A Treasury of Indiana Life and Lore *(new ed., 1975), and A. L. Lazarus, ed.,* The Indiana Experience: An Anthology *(1977).*

The state of Indiana points southward 276 miles from the lower end of Lake Michigan toward the Gulf of Mexico and so stands athwart one third of the path that any east-west traveler must take on an overland journey across the United States. Because the fastest east-west interstate highways and the majority of railway trunk lines pass through the northern and central portions of Indiana and because modern tourists are intent mainly upon arriving anywhere other than where they are, and in the greatest possible hurry, the impression of Indiana left in the minds of such east-west transients is often incomplete and not altogether accurate. A flat land is what most of them remember, a flat land of rectangular fields planted mostly in corn, a flat land ornamented occasionally by small lakes and tree-shaded villages and scarred in one or two places by unprepossessing industrial areas.

Fewer travelers from outside the state cross Indiana in a north-south direction than those who make the east-west journey. One reason is that fewer direct highways run north and south through Indiana; another is that there are fewer places to come from or go to in a hurry on such routes. If there were more of these north-south tourists, the image of Indiana in outsiders' minds would be considerably altered. Corn would remain among the travelers' principal impressions; corn is everywhere in Indiana; but added to the flat land and the lakes and villages and industrial areas would be hills and ravines, caves and deep woodlands, and winding rivers.

Two thirds of the distance from Lake Michigan to the state's southernmost tip—or as far down as Terre Haute on the western border and Lawrenceburg on the eastern side—Indiana is monotonously 145 miles wide, even where it invades the southern loop of Michigan's waters and boldly approaches Chicago's lakefront. The state is thus straight-sided from the waist up because lawmakers and surveyors corseted it along meridian lines when Illinois was separated from Indiana Territory in 1809, with slight alterations in 1816 when Indiana became a state. Below the waistline—from Terre Haute and Lawrenceburg down to the tip of Posey County, where the Wabash River joins the Ohio—the width of the state varies with the temperamental meanders of these two rivers.

Every Hoosier schoolboy learns to say that Indiana is bounded on the north by Michigan, on the south by Kentucky, on the west by Illinois, and on the east by Ohio. In the main this is so, but a close look at a map shows that Kentucky bounds some of the east of Indiana as well as the south. The Wabash River definitely forms the western boundary of the state below Terre Haute, but the Ohio River, commonly called the southern boundary, is more eastern than southern along one third of its edging of Indiana. Most people, including most Hoosiers, forget that the Ohio flows in a sharp southwesterly direction and that when Hoosiers cross it to leave the state in many places above Jeffersonville they are headed east, not south.

The reason for such different views of Indiana as those of the east-west and the north-south travelers across the state is that Indiana is two distinct regions instead of one. Geologists like to think of it as three, but Hoosiers generally see their state divided by the Old National Road, now U.S. Route 40, and are likely to say, if asked where they are from, either "Northern Indiana" or "Southern Indiana." Within Indiana's boundaries, the Old National Road, surveyed by a Quaker named Jonathan Knight and cleared of outcropping geodes for its first traffic by 1832, is only a few miles longer than the state's width, entering Indiana from the east just below the 40th Parallel at Richmond, passing through the heart of Indianapolis, and departing for Illinois a short distance west of Terre Haute and the Wabash River.

Above this highway, Indiana is indeed a far-horizoned land, if not altogether flat. Here the great prairie begins its gradual upward tilt toward the Rockies a thousand miles away, and here, hardly distinguishable among lakes and marshes, is the watershed between the systems of the St. Lawrence and the Mississippi. This land is fabulously fertile for the growing of corn, wheat, oats, soy beans, and tomatoes, except in the Calumet area near Chicago, where a Colossus of comparatively recent industrial development stands astride a stretch of singing sand dunes along the shore of Lake Michigan.

The Calumet takes its name from the river Calumet, christened by the early French as the Chalumeau, which means a hollow reed of the sort that pipestems can be made of. It includes Gary, Hammond, East Chicago, and Whiting, each one contiguous to another and with a combined population close to half a million. Outside the Calumet there are two other large cities in the north, South Bend and Fort Wayne, each with metropolitan populations above 200,000; and there are a half-dozen smaller cities of 40,000 or more north of the Old National Road: Anderson Elkhart, Kokomo, Lafayette, Marion, and Muncie.

Below the Old National Road, the scenery of Indiana changes to hills, smaller farms, smaller towns, and fewer cities. Large man-made reservoirs are beginning to dot this area, but it is not naturally lake country. Here in the south, however, are most of Indiana's major rivers, among them the two-forked White and the two-forked Whitewater, the Blue, and the lower Wabash, and many rambling creeks. They flow toward all points of the compass, but eventually each fingers its way southward and in time its waters join those of the Ohio. Some of these rivers and creeks provide rich bottomlands in the Ohio Valley, and on the good land of the south corn, soy beans, and tomatoes prosper, but not in such great abundance as in the north. The southwestern corner of the state, known as "The Pocket," is famous for its melons as well as these other crops.

Here, on the Ohio, is the region's largest city, Evansville, a community of ups and downs in its growth throughout its century and a half of history, but with a metropolitan population in 1960 of 200,000. The only other large urban concentration in the south is the New Albany-Jeffersonville area on the Ohio, across from Louisville, Kentucky, with about 60,000 people in 1960. Vincennes, the state's oldest town continuously inhabited by white men, is in southern Indiana, as is Corydon, the first state capital. The population of Vincennes was less than 20,000 in 1960; Corydon is a village of a few thousand people.

Geology explains, in part, the difference between the two halves of Hoosierland. After the receding of the pre-Cambrian Sea, which once covered the whole area, three glaciers invaded what is now the state of Indiana. The first, called the Illinoian, moved down as far as the Ohio River and beyond it, except for one north-south strip that runs through the central part of the state and is known as the Crawford Upland. The second, called the Early Wisconsin, stopped about two thirds of the way down the stage at a line that is sometimes almost visible in the abrupt change of scenery that one witnesses as one drives along a north-south highway. The last, the Late Wisconsin, came only halfway down the state.

The result of the triple invasion of ice in the north was the leveling of hills and their crumbling into fine glacial subsoil, which in some of the farm land is many feet deep. In the once-glaciated and the unglaciated sections of the south, on the other hand, the hills remain tall and sometimes steep, and the land is not so fertile. Where there was no glaciation at all, there is almost no subsoil, and the bedrock is eroded into deep canyons and sharp ridges.

This unglaciated area, the Crawford Upland, which extends in a band down from Parke and Putnam counties to the Ohio River, is the most scenic of the state. It is the location of Marengo and Wyandotte caves—Wyandotte is the third largest in the United States—and of "Jug Rock" and "The Pinnacle" near Shoals, and its geological history accounts for the beauties of Shades, Turkey Run, McCormick's Creek, and Spring Mill, four of Indiana's score of state parks. In this unglaciated strip, as in the rest of southern Indiana, the hills generally run east and west, and streams and rivers have a difficult time wending their way south. Across the entire southern half of the state, there are seven bands of alternating upland and lowland, three such combinations occurring in southeastern Indiana, three in south-central Indiana, and one in the southwest. . . .

Indiana's farmers raise horses, beef and dairy cattle, and some sheep, although from pioneer days to the present mutton and lamb have never been widely popular in the Hoosier diet. But the four-legged creature that dominates the Indiana farm scene is the hog. In pioneer times, hogs were seldom fenced and were allowed to roam the woods and feast on mast. Later, with improved fencing, their diet changed to corn. By 1860 there were two hogs for every person in the state. Today, with roughly 60 per cent of Indiana urban and less than 40 per cent rural, hogs and human beings populate the state in about equal numbers, but Indiana still stands third in the nation in hog raising, outclassed in that endeavor only by Iowa and Illinois. A few years ago, Logan Esarey, an Indiana historian, nominated the hog as monarch of the state. "We may sing the praises of all the heroes of Indiana from LaSalle or George Rogers Clark to the present," wrote Professor Esarey eloquently, "but the prosperity of our state . . . has depended on Mr. Hog. In fat years and lean years . . . he has come up with his part, even though he does grunt about it considerably."

There are others, however, who argue that corn, and not the hog, is king in Indiana. After all, corn predates the hog in the state, and now that the supply of mast is depleted, the growing of corn must precede the raising of hogs. Corn was a staple of the Hopewellian mound builders' diet in prehistoric times before hogs were domesticated, and of the later Indians' diet before the white men came, and corn was always the first crop the white men planted after they arrived and settled. Although the land area of Indiana is comparatively small—36,291 square miles, less than two thirds of that of Iowa or of Illinois—Indiana ranks with Iowa and Illinois among the three top producers of corn as well as hogs in the United States. . . .

In the last one hundred years, Indiana has been more often Republican than Democratic in its politics, but from an outsider's view it has not always been easy to tell which party was in power, for both of them tend toward conservatism. Because of the remoteness of the state from the coasts, the interest of its people concentrates upon domestic problems more often than international affairs, and as a consequence some of the strongest isolationist sentiment in the nation has emanated from Indiana's politicians. In varying degrees of stridency the voice of "one-hundred-per-cent Americanism" has appealed to Indiana voters for the past fifty years. At the same time, the state has produced Eugene V. Debs, the most noted leader of the Socialist Party in American history, and men with broad international views of American destiny such as Albert J. Beveridge and Wendell L. Willkie. Since 1962, the governor and both senators have been Democrats. Seven presidential candidates have been either natives or, for considerable numbers of years, residents of Indiana, and three of them—Lincoln and the two Harrisons—were elected. Of eight candidates for the vice presidency, Colfax, Hendricks, Fairbanks, and Marshall were elected.

A few crusading Hoosiers from the beginning supported public education, and the once backward state now has one of the highest literacy rates in the nation. As early as 1825 Robert Owen was experimenting with new educational theories in his Utopian colony at New Harmony; soon thereafter, William Maclure established in that town the first trade school in the country; Evansville opened the first public high school in the West for both boys and girls in 1854; and for many of the early years of the present century the public school system of Gary was a subject of observation and study among American and foreign educators. There are four state supported institutions of higher learning in Indiana: Indiana University at Bloomington, Purdue University at West Lafayette, Ball State University at Muncie, and Indiana State University at Terre Haute. These public universities are supplemented by branches, or "centers," throughout the state and by thirty-five privately supported colleges and universities, including such nationally recognized institutions as DePauw, Wabash, Earlham, Butler, Hanover, and Notre Dame, which is the largest Catholic university for men in the United States.

This long tradition of emphasis on education may account, in part at least, for the third major preoccupation of Hoosiers after politics and schools; that is, literature. Since the publication of *The Hoosier School-Master* in 1871, Indianans have maintained a steady flow of books from the nation's publishers, not the least of which is the firm of Bobbs-Merrill at Indianapolis, now a subsidiary of Howard W. Sams and Company. The list of Indiana authors includes such widely varied talents and interests as those of Lew Wallace, James Whitcomb Riley, Booth Tarkington, Meredith Nicholson, Theodore Dreiser, George Ade, George Jean Nathan, Elmer Davis, and Eli Lilly. Riley is probably the only poet who ever became a millionaire by writing verse; Lilly is one of very few millionaires who ever became a writer with a genuine literary style.

Today the literary flood flows unabated in Indiana, although its so-called "Golden Age," when Riley, Tarkington, and Company were in their heyday, has passed. Each year Hoosier writers are honored with awards at an Indiana Authors' Day banquet, and in 1965 the Indiana Author's Day Committee had to consider 158 books published in the previous year by 135 natives and residents of the state. That means that about one out of every 20,000 adult Hoosiers got his name on the title page of a book in 1964; it is safe to guess that most of the other 19,999 will keep on trying.

Some Hoosiers who have made a place for themselves in the nation's history by following other avenues than politics, education, and literature are: James B. Eads, builder of the Eads Bridge across the Mississippi; Richard J. Gatling, inventor of the prototype of the machine gun; Elwood Haynes, a pioneer in the making of automobiles; Wilbur Wright, Virgil Grissom, and Frank Borman, pioneers in air and space; Alva Roebuck, co-founder of Sears, Roebuck; Bernard Gimbel, president of Gimbel Brothers; John T. McCutcheon, *Chicago Tribune* cartoonist; Hoagy Carmichael and Cole Porter, popular composers; Knute Rockne, Wilbur Shaw, Don Lash, and Mordecai (Three-Finger) Brown, of the sports world; Generals Burnside and Hershey, of the Civil War and World War Two; and George W. Whistler, civil engineer, the husband of "Whistler's Mother."

The Hoosier then, what is he? His character is not easy to describe, for his is a compound of many contradictory qualities. He is both sentimental and shrewd, provincial and sophisticated, suspicious and generous, nosey and self-contained, quick-tempered and kind, self-righteous and tolerant, egotistical and unpretentious. In another book about Indiana, I once wrote:

> The Hoosier's friendliness and hospitality are universally recognizable. He is easy to meet and quite ready to talk about himself. His eagerness to share his possessions as

well as his private life sometimes appears naïve to the outsider accustomed to the self-protective reticence and suspicion of more thickly populated regions. But the Hoosier is not naïve. He inherits his tradition of cordiality from lonely pioneer days when every stranger was at once a welcome friend and a helpless supplicant; yet from those same early days, he inherits a talent for quick and accurate appraisal of character. You may think that the Hoosier lays himself wide open on short acquaintance; but the chances are that he knows all there is to know about you long before he tells you a single thing about himself.

An adopted Hoosier, Irving Leibowitz, has said the same thing of Hoosiers more recently and more succinctly: "They are country smart and their kids are university educated."

Of late, the Hoosier has broadened his view of the world considerably by travel, by education, and by both adversity and success; but the foregoing quotations still define something basic and immutable in his character.

A POETIC QUESTION

William Herschell

This section includes a sample of Indiana dialect writing, as practiced earlier by novelist Edward Eggleston and poet James Whitcomb Riley. The selection below, one of the best-known poems—at least by title—about the state, is from the pen of William Herschell, a journalist who wrote in the vein of, but much less successfully than, James Whitcomb Riley. Herschell (1873–1939) is remembered for his bits of light verse, much of which first appeared in the columns of the Indianapolis News, *the newspaper for which he worked as a reporter and feature writer for thirty-seven years. A bronze plaque bearing the lines of Herschell's famous paean of praise to his native state rests in the rotunda of the Indiana State Capitol. For brief biographical details on Herschell, see R. E. Banta, ed.,* Indiana Authors and Their Books, 1816–1916 *(1949), and Arthur W. Shumaker,* A History of Indiana Literature *(1962).*

Ain't God Good to Indiana?

Ain't God good to Indiana?
    Folks, a feller never knows
Just how close he is to Eden
    Till, sometimes, he ups an' goes

From *The Smile-Bringer and Other Bits of Cheer* (1919), pp. 69–70.

Seekin' fairer, greener pastures
  Than he has right here at home,
Where there's sunshine in th' clover
  An' there's honey in th' comb:
Where th' ripples on th' river
  Kind o' chuckle as they flow—
Ain't God good to Indiana?
  Ain't He, fellers? Ain't He though?

Ain't God good to Indiana?
  Seems to me He has a way
Gittin' me all out o' humor
  Just to see how long I'll stay
When I git th' gipsy-feelin'
  That I'd like to find a spot
Where th' clouds ain't quite so restless,
  Or th' sun don't shine as hot.
But, I don't git far, I'll tell you,
  Till I'm whisp'rin' soft an' low:
Ain't God good to Indiana:
  Ain't He, fellers? Ain't He though?

Ain't God good to Indiana?
  Other spots may look as fair,
But they lack th' soothin' somethin'
  In th' Hoosier sky an' air.
They don't have that snug-up feelin'
  Like a mother gives a child;
They don't soothe you, soul an' body,
  With their breezes soft an' mild.
They don't know th' Joys o' Heaven
  Have their birthplace here below;
Ain't God good to Indiana?
  Ain't He, fellers? Ain't He though?

INDIANA
A New Perspective
Peter T. Harstad

The final selection here comes from the pen of Peter T. Harstad, a relative newcomer to the state of Indiana. Although he grew up in Minnesota, he is a native of Wisconsin and holds a

---

From "Indiana and the Art of Adjustment," in James H. Madison, ed., *Heartland: Comparative Histories of the Midwestern States* (1988), pp. 158–185.

Ph.D. degree in history from the University of Wisconsin. He had extensive experience in teaching and historical administration, particularly in Idaho and Iowa, before assuming the directorship of the Indiana Historical Society in 1984. Professor James H. Madison invited Harstad to contribute the chapter on Indiana to a volume devoted to comparative histories of twelve midwestern states. He responded with a thoughtful and perceptive analysis of his adopted state that brings a fresh perspective to the study and appreciation of the Hoosier state and its "art of adjustment" to the changing demands of the nineteenth and twentieth centuries. Other writings by Harstad include a biography, coauthored with Bonnie Lindemann, Gilbert N. Haugen: Norwegian-American Farm Politician *(1992), as well as several articles that focus on pioneer medicine and midwestern road and highway development.*

States are difficult to explain to American schoolchildren, who take them for granted, and they baffle foreign visitors, who have difficulty understanding that they are not subdivisions of the national government. What are the American states? A century ago an Englishman, James Bryce, traveled and studied in this country to answer this question and related ones. At the outset of his two-volume *American Commonwealth*, Bryce likened the nation and the states to a large building erected over a number of smaller ones, as had been the case with the Church of the Holy Sepulchre at Jerusalem. "First the soil is covered by a number of small shrines and chapels, built at different times and in different styles of architecture, each complete in itself. Then over them and including them . . . is reared a new pile with its own loftier roof, its own walls, which may perhaps rest on and incorporate the walls of the older shrines, its own internal plan." The simile works well enough for the original thirteen states, but its chronology is incorrect for Indiana and the other states of the heartland. Here the foundation of the Union and much of its superstructure predate the smaller units—a basic consideration in understanding nationalism in the Midwest. Indianans may, at times, be smug, but they do not think of their state as "complete in itself."

When Bryce wrote, the states were unequivocally within the Union and "subordinate to it." The Civil War had settled that. Yet Bryce saw the Union as "more than an aggregate of States," and the states as "more than parts of the Union." He perceived "two loyalties, two patriotisms," with the lesser jealous of the greater. "There are two governments, covering the same ground, commanding, with equally direct authority, the obedience of the same citizen." Understanding this double organization was, for Bryce, the "first and indispensable" step in understanding American institutions. . . .

Many questions arise about how Indiana got to be the way it was in [the early twentieth century]. Consideration of five topics suggests some answers: Indiana's window on the Great Lakes, the "southernness" of Indiana, adjustments to the natural environment, Indiana's place in the union, and the natural gas boom as a stimulant to industrialization.

Drafters of the Northwest Ordinance of 1787 intended to provide Great Lakes frontage for each of the "not less than three nor more than five" states to be created out of the area north of the Ohio River and east of the Mississippi. Eastern, southern, and western boundaries for the area that became Indiana are strongly suggested in the ordinance, but the northern boundary is mentioned only in reference to the possible subdivision of territory to its north: "Congress . . . shall have authority to form one or two states in that part of the said Territory which lies north of an east and west line drawn through the southerly bend or extreme of Lake Michigan."

By 1848, enabling acts had created five states out of the Northwest Territory, each of which had a window on the Great Lakes. It would have been easy enough to create one "horizontal" state with no Great Lakes outlet from what is now southern Indiana and the "Egypt" portion of southern Illinois. The lawmakers of 1787 headed that off in article five of the ordinance when they drew an interior line within the territory from "the Wabash and Post Vincents, due north to the territorial line between the United States and Canada." State-makers followed their lead. The southern extremity of this line became the Indiana-Illinois boundary when Indiana was admitted to statehood in 1816. The language of the ordinance urged vertical shapes for the southern subdivisions of the Northwest Territory (if it did not mandate them); the same is true of Great Lakes frontages. If, as historian Justin Winsor suggested, the lawmakers of 1787 envisioned windows on the Great Lakes to encourage settlers of the southern reaches of the Northwest Territory to look northward, the scheme worked. Along with the prohibition of slavery in article six of the ordinance, Indiana's and Illinois's windows on the Great Lakes deserve consideration as palliatives to southernness in those regions.

Although neither large nor blessed with a good natural port, Indiana's shoreline has had a continuing influence on the economy, history, and culture of the state. Without a Great Lakes port, it is unlikely that ore from the iron ranges of Minnesota would have been smelted on Indiana soil with Indiana coal beginning in 1908. Without iron and steel plants within its borders, there would have been less inducement for other heavy industries to locate in Indiana and less ethnic and cultural diversity in the state. Had Gary arisen on the other side of the Illinois border, developments in that state and in Indiana would have been different.

The result of a geographical legacy of the ice age and of a political adjustment of 1787 (upheld in 1816), Indiana's window on the Great Lakes provided perspectives and opportunities that were not inevitable.

As for Indiana's southernness, when William Henry Harrison looked out over the Wabash River from the veranda of his spacious Grouseland in Vincennes, he was at the latitude of the nation's capital—from whence came his appointment as governor of Indiana Territory. When he traveled the Ohio River along Indiana's southern border, he reached the approximate latitude of his ancestral home, Berkeley, on the James River in Virginia. The social structure of tidewater Virginia is what Harrison had in mind for Indiana. . . .

Through close demographic studies, modern scholars are providing more accurate insights into the nature and extent of Indiana's southernness than were previously possible. Whereas Marshall saw the old National Road as the northern extremity of southern preponderance in Indiana, Gregory S. Rose in a 1985 article finds the division to be "a transition zone across the state's middle section where counties were either slightly above or below the average nativity percentages." In 1850 southern-born settlers in Indiana "comprised 44.0 percent of the population that was born in the United States exclusive of Indiana, far above the average of 28.3 percent for the Old Northwest as a whole." Illinois came closest to this level with 34.8 percent. Here, then, is a sharp contrast between Indiana and the remainder of the Old Northwest: Indiana's population as of the middle of the nineteenth century was decidedly more southern in origin. Some of the people who migrated northward into Indiana did so, however, to escape certain features of southern civilization. That is most emphatically the case with the fugitive slaves, recently emancipated slaves, and free blacks who sought refuge in Indiana. The 1850 census indicates that of 11,000 Negroes living in Indiana, 1,426 were born in North Carolina, 1,172 in Virginia, 1,116 in Kentucky, 600 in Tennessee, 826 in Ohio, and the rest in Indiana or a scattering of other states and countries. Abraham Lincoln said that his family moved to Indiana from Kentucky "partly on account of slavery; but chiefly on account of the difficulty in land titles" in Kentucky. Other people who had no use for the institution of slavery were the Quakers from North Carolina who concentrated in east central Indiana. . . .

From early in Indiana history farmers and townsmen alike could benefit from access to cash markets beyond the state and region. What could be more logical in a state located between the Ohio River and the Great Lakes than construction of canals to link the major waterway? There appeared to be no greater hindrances than those already overcome with the completion of the Erie Canal in New York.

The Mammoth Internal Improvements Act of 1836 called for the alteration of Indiana's drainage system with canals, locks, aqueducts, and dams to make the major river systems navigable and to provide outlets to Lake Michigan and Lake Erie. The scheme, financed by a ten-million-dollar loan to the state, bogged down after the Panic of 1837. In the words of Paul Fatout the plan was "conceived in madness and nourished by delusion." Interest alone on borrowed money was ten times the state tax revenue. This time men and money succumbed to the environment.

The resulting political and fiscal embarrassment affected Indiana permanently. When Indianans adopted their second constitution in 1851, the document prohibited the state from contracting any debt except "To meet casual deficits in the revenue; to pay the interest on the State Debt; to repel invasion, suppress insurrection, or, if hostilities be threatened, provide for the public defense." An 1873 amendment prohibited the General Assembly from recognizing any liability or paying to redeem any stock of the Wabash and Erie Canal. These principles prevail to this day, a legacy from an attempt to alter the environment. If a visionary legislator forgets the debacle, a fiscally conservative colleague can promptly usher him or her to a Statehouse window and point to a segment of the never-completed Central Canal, which now serves as part of the water system of Indianapolis. . . .

It was up to a son of the heartland to steer the Union through its greatest crisis. Abraham Lincoln's early "textbook" on American history and government, *The Revised Laws of Indiana* (1824), is prefaced by ten key documents that trace the legal foundations of Indiana from the Declaration of Independence through to the constitution of 1816. Lincoln mastered and digested these documents and returned to them time and again, particularly the Northwest Ordinance and the United States

Constitution. The mature Lincoln coupled these two documents in a manner that bore directly upon the nature of the Union and gave his nationalism the flavor of the Old Northwest. He explained to an Indianapolis audience on September 19, 1859:

> The ordinance of 1787 was passed simultaneously with the making of the Constitution of the United States. It prohibited the taking of slavery into the North-western Territory. . . . There was nothing said in the Constitution relative to the spread of slavery in the Territories, but the same generation of men said something about it in this ordinance of '87, through the influence of which you of Indiana, and your neighbors in Ohio, Illinois, Wisconsin and Michigan, are prosperous, free men. That generation of men, though not to the full extent members of the Convention that framed the Constitution, were to some extent members of that Convention, holding seats, at the same time in one body and the other. . . . Our fathers who made the government, made the ordinance of 1787.

A subtle mind was telling Indianans that they were prosperous and free because the men who wrote the nation's constitution also prohibited slavery in Indiana. This argument he developed more fully and reasoned more closely at the Cooper Institute in New York City on February 27, 1860. He argued that the new congress under the constitution clinched his point in 1789 when it reaffirmed the ordinance. There was no question about the intent of the founding fathers—the central government was supreme and could impose conditions upon the territories and states.

After the Civil War broke out, some Indianans who accepted the supremacy of the national government challenged the Lincoln administration on other points. Governor Oliver P. Morton, a powerful executive, clashed frequently with the War Department about military leadership and support for Indiana troops in the field. Morton vexed his fellow Republican in the White House and strained the ties between Indianapolis and Washington. Yet there is little doubt that majorities in both political parties in Indiana supported Lincoln's concept of an indissoluble union. . . .

The discovery and use of natural gas, because of its timing, stimulated Indiana's industrial development out of all proportion to its long-term importance. The Civil War had accelerated forces of economic change, but industrialization had not progressed very far in Indiana by the mid-1880s. The biggest changes from the prewar years probably involved the greater use of steam power in small factories in the river towns and the replacement of animal power with steam power in some farm functions. Coal, a useful commodity in the age of steam, was in ample supply in southern and western Indiana, where it was mined as early as the territorial period.

The natural gas phenomenon was quite different and more dramatic. The events unfolded north of the Old National Road in that part of the state where Marshall claimed people were "always experimenting." As explained by State Geologist John B. Patton: "Discovery of natural gas in 1886 in what was to become the famed Trenton Field of northwestern Ohio and northeast-central Indiana triggered an industrial expansion that transformed sleepy county seat towns throughout the area into manufacturing centers that are still vital parts of Indiana's (and Ohio's) economy. . . ." Drillers found natural gas in 1876 at Eaton, near Muncie, but they did not know what to do with it. By 1886 that had changed; Ohioans had demonstrated its utility and had learned how to handle it in the eastern reaches of the Trenton Field.

A boom was on in Indiana by late 1886. The bringing in of a well was a spectacular event, especially when it was accomplished by dropping nitroglycerin down the drilled-out hole and igniting it. When the result was a roar of pressurized gas, belches of smoke, and flames taller than elms, Sunday afternoon audiences went home delighted. More than five thousand wells drilled in Indiana between 1886 and 1897 marked out the largest natural gas field then known in the United States. Burning fumes dotted the midnight landscape.

At Anderson a flaming archway spanned the street near the train depot. Gas was also pumped into White River and ignited so that a gigantic flambeau appeared to burn out of the water. In November 1887 a geologist estimated that fifteen billion cubic feet of gas had been wasted during the preceding six months in Indiana. Boom books and publicity campaigns attracted potential industrialists and investors. Towns vied with each other by offering various combinations of free factory sites, free fuel in perpetuity, and cash. Not since the flush times of the Mammoth Internal Improvements Act had there been so much optimism in Indiana.

In 1880 a few over 4,000 people were living in Anderson; in 1890 10,741. By Lamont Hulse's count, twenty-five new factories located there between 1887 and 1892 producing twenty-three hundred jobs. The boom was good for laborers and other city dwellers too because the towns offered free or very cheap gas for home heating, cooking, and lighting.

The Ball brothers, manufacturers of containers in Buffalo, New York, sought a good source of natural gas for manufacturing fruit jars. Before the days of pipelines, it was necessary to locate near gas wells. By offering five thousand dollars, free fuel, and free land, Muncie promoters induced the Ball brothers to locate there. Between 1890 and 1920 the Balls and other users of silica leveled Hoosier Slide, a 200-foot-high dune near Michigan City, by removing 13.5 million tons of sand. Manufacturers of plate glass, ceramic tile, and pottery located in Indiana; so did foundries, wire works, and metal fabricating plants.

Natural gas production peaked in 1900 with an estimated thirty-six billion cubic feet coming from the Trenton Field. It dropped off precipitously thereafter because of dwindling supply. Gas for domestic heating failed in Muncie in the winter of 1905. By 1906 production in the field declined to less than a quarter of that of 1900. The "down" side of the cycle is significant in the history of Indiana industrialism because it illustrates how Indianans adjusted to new circumstances. . . .

Jacques Barzun wrote that "whoever wants to know the heart and mind of America had better learn baseball." A corollary may follow that to know Indiana one must also understand both basketball and the Indianapolis 500. For reasons that defy analysis, for many years high school basketball has been played with greater intensity in Indiana than anywhere else, but the principles are similar to those operating throughout the heartland wherever small, vulnerable towns dot the landscape. From December through March, a minimum of five adolescent males or females (six of the latter in Iowa) have the potential of bringing victory and pride to their schools and towns. The game is played in a manner suggesting that individual and community destinies are being settled on the spot. "Hoosier hysteria" it is called in Indiana—an exciting and inexpensive celebration of youth, dexterity, and locale.

In contrast, the Indianapolis 500, a heavily capitalized sports event, is carried out with experienced, professional contenders. Its traditions date from the day Thomas R. Marshall laid the last brick (a gold one) in the track at Speedway. Some of these traditions stem from an older sport popular in the neighboring state to the south. While Kentuckians visit the paddocks to size up horses and to talk to the grooms and jockeys, the fans at Speedway visit the pits to view the machines and to talk to the crews and drivers. After time trials come Carburetion Day (another vestige of a bygone era), a huge parade, and finally Race Day itself, replete with celebrities, pageantry, pretty girls, and patriotism. The crowd joins in the singing of the "Star Spangled Banner." Then state patriotism gets its due with the strains of "Back Home Again in Indiana."

"Gentlemen, start your engines," comes the traditional command. After parade and pace laps, the race begins in earnest. The drivers know that, to win, they must respect the traditions of the track and push for the limits while adjusting the technologies of safety and speed to ever-changing situations. Bankers, housewives, and laborers—a cross section of the state and nation a third of a million strong—look on. All lose their cares during this Indiana rite of spring while men and metal compete for high stakes. Laborers who spend their lives in repetitive tasks such as cutting metal for the front supports of auto transmissions get particular satisfaction from observing the totality of the latest high-performance machines put to the test of the track. Few if any of the machines will be back next year because technology moves on. But the track will be here and so will many of the drivers. Three hours pass quickly while spectators discuss the race with friends, snack on fried chicken, and sip beverages. Something decisive is soon to take place. After two hundred laps the checkered flag comes down as the winner crosses the finish line—a narrow row of bricks left in place from the early years of the century. When the officials award trophies and purses amid network news coverage, Indianans know they have witnessed a world-class event in the heart of their state. Hoosiers love a good show and thrive on outside recognition.

On the way home spectators see a barefoot inebriate in the infield—an angular Anglo—beer in hand, smile on his face, mud up to his knees, and a red shirt on his back bearing the words, "It ain't bad to be a Hoosier."

But many perceived a deeper meaning to the events of the day. The Indianapolis 500 involves the accommodation of the technology of speed to that of safety. On the track, as well as in life, where men and women are put to the test and where conditions constantly change, there is need for continuity with what has gone before. Indiana is a state in the American heartland where this truism is widely understood and appreciated.

1. The First Inhabitants

Indiana, as its name implies, was the home of many different Indian cultures prior to the arrival of the first French explorers and missionaries in the second half of the seventeenth century; and during the next two centuries Indiana was home to both Indian and white peoples. The Indians of the pre-French period are known as *prehistoric*, while those Indians encountered by the successive waves of Frenchmen, Englishmen, and Americans are termed *historic*. Not only do no contemporary written records exist concerning the prehistoric tribes or nations, but there are no known links between these peoples and the historic Indians, the Delaware, Miami, Potawatomi, Wea, Piankashaw, and others living in the Ohio and Wabash valleys subsequent to 1650. Consequently, our knowledge of the prehistoric Indian peoples and their cultures is limited to that which comes from the archaeological evidence obtained from digs at Indian village sites and ceremonial or burial mounds. This evidence, fortunately, is quite considerable and continues to mount, largely through the efforts of archaeology departments at the state universities and at the University of Notre Dame, assisted by the Indiana Department of Natural Resources and the Indiana Historical Society.

Indians inhabited the region as long ago as 8,000 B.C., and in time, through the four separate cultural traditions that have been defined by archaeologists, made substantial cultural achievements. These included a settled town life, extensive trade and political networks, elaborate mortuary rituals, works of art, and practical items of work and war. The Indians of the Mississippian tradition, the last of the four groupings, either left or were driven out of the Ohio Valley by the seventeenth century, by which time European exploration and colonization in North and South America was well under way.

Spanish explorers and missionaries were the first to follow up on Columbus's discoveries and to build a New World empire. The French and the English moved more slowly, making only tentative moves during the sixteenth century. But both nations established footholds in North America in the early seventeenth century, the British in the Chesapeake Bay and Massachusetts Bay areas, the French in the St. Lawrence Valley.

Samuel de Champlain founded Quebec in 1608, and soon Frenchmen were exploring the sources of the river, then the Great Lakes area and beyond, always searching for trade (particularly in furs), territory, and religious converts. Sometime after the middle of the seventeenth century, the first French explorers reached what is now Indiana. Father Marquette may have passed through the region in 1675 while en route from the Illinois country to the upper reaches of Lake Michigan. But the first documented European visit to Indiana came in 1679. In that year Robert Cavelier de la Salle led a small exploring party across the then rather inhospitable marshlands in the northwestern corner of the state.

Subsequently, the French established three bases in what is now Indiana, all located along the historic waterway passage connecting Lake Erie and the Ohio River via the Maumee and Wabash rivers. Although a French settlement at present-day Fort Wayne perhaps antedated the establishment of a post at Fort Ouiatenon in 1717, now located a few miles below Lafayette, it was not until five years later that a similar fortified trading post, Fort Miamis, was erected at the former site. The third French post in Indiana, established along the lower Wabash in the early 1730s, was Vincennes. The French developed a substantial fur trade with various Indian tribes at all three locations during the middle years of the century, but they faced growing competition from the English for the furs and the good will of the Indians after 1750. Within little more than a decade, the French were removed from the Wabash Valley and indeed from all of North America.

At the beginning of the eighteenth century, France, according to historian Louise P. Kellogg, "had the most magnificent opportunity that has ever been offered to a colonizing power." The Mississippi Valley stretched out before her, inviting "occupation and exploitation"; but the French were unable to secure their tenuous hold on the valley or even to remain as an imperial power in the New World.[1] Indiana, remote from both centers of French colonial authority—Quebec and, after 1700, New Orleans—played a minor role in the imperial rivalry between France and Great Britain, which culminated in the "Great War for the Empire" of 1754–1763. But the fate of the French in Indiana as well as elsewhere in America was dependent on the outcome of that rivalry.

Indian Achievements

Centuries before the first Europeans arrived in America, the interior of North America, including the area that became Indiana, was populated by various "prehistoric" peoples. Archaeological studies, particularly in this century, have revealed much about the misnamed "Indians" who roamed the forests and plied the waterways of the mid-continent, and who made significant contributions to the economy and culture of those who followed. Far from being nomadic savages living off the bounty of the land, the evidence clearly indicates a number of different cultural developments, major agricultural and commercial achievements, and in time a highly developed town life. For reasons which have yet to be fully explained, the prehistoric Indians had left the Indiana area and had been replaced by other "historic" Indian tribes from the north and east by the time the first Frenchmen reached the area in the mid-seventeenth century.

1. Louise Phelps Kellogg, "France and the Mississippi Valley: A Résumé," *Mississippi Valley Historical Review*, XVIII (June 1931), 3.

INDIANA'S PREHISTORIC CULTURES

James H. Kellar

Professor James H. Kellar, a leading archaeologist in Indiana, summarized the current knowledge of Indiana's prehistoric peoples and their achievements in an early chapter of Indiana to 1816: The Colonial Period *(1971), by John D. Barnhart and Dorothy L. Riker. Professor Kellar of Indiana University, now retired, formerly directed the Glenn A. Black Laboratory of Archaeology in Bloomington and served as archaeologist for the Indiana Historical Society. His writings include* An Introduction to the Prehistory of Indiana *(1973), to which the reader is referred for a fuller discussion of this theme and for bibliographic suggestions. See also B. K. Swartz,* Indiana's Prehistoric Past *(1973), and the older but still useful book by Eli Lilly,* Prehistoric Antiquities of Indiana *(1937). See too the chapter on Indiana archaeology in James H. Madison,* Eli Lilly: A Life, 1885–1977 *(1989).*

All too frequently in an understandable but ethnocentric concern for our own lives and time and their immediate antecedents, it is . . . forgotten that what is presently Indiana had been occupied for many millenniums prior to the appearance of Europeans. The contributions of these earlier occupants, the American Indians, are inescapable to even the most casual observer, although their cultures have long since been obliterated.

The name of the state and its capital city are obvious reminders of Indian occupation, as are the names of four of the immediately adjacent states [and several Indiana counties, rivers, and places]. The native people also made incalculable contributions to the economy of Indiana. The millions of acres of field corn, the leadership in the production of popcorn, the contract tomato crop in the north, and the tobacco harvest in the south all involve plants originally domesticated by the Indian. The same is true of the turkey, the raising of which contributes to the agricultural wealth of the state. Pumpkins, squash, beans, and peppers are other common plant products first utilized by the native inhabitants.

American Indian themes recur in our music and literature and television programming. The last, unfortunately, relies upon the Indian-European conflict for some of its story line, with the result that the contrived events rarely have much real relationship to actual happenings. And the early documentary history, as well as some of the recent, would have been markedly different had there been no human antecedents to contest the European claim to what we have erroneously called a "virgin wilderness."

Unlike the historical record for nearly five centuries of European-derived influence there are no coexistent written sources to document the several thousand years of Indian occupation. Therefore, it is generally impossible to obtain an understand-

From John D. Barnhart and Dorothy L. Riker, *Indiana to 1816: The Colonial Period* (1971), pp. 13–16, 28–30, 35–36, 42–46, 49–50, 52.

ing of individual lives and specific events, or to identify ethnic groups and the languages spoken. It is possible, however, to reconstruct something of the broad picture of cultural change and development through time and comprehend some of the conditions which produced these by reference to the surviving unintentional prehistoric record. This record includes a great variety of manufactured objects (artifacts), remains of plants and animals used by man, human burials, and the man-induced changes in the natural landscape. Careful archaeological excavations in contexts where these occur and the systematic study of the results provide the data whereby an otherwise silent past is permitted to speak.

There are literally thousands of such localities in Indiana and it is a rare river terrace that provides no such evidence. The most common items are the ubiquitous projectile points manufactured from chalcedony or chert. These are often found in association with other materials, such as animal bone, fire-cracked rock, and sometimes bits of pottery, all of which serve to identify the camps and villages of early peoples. Burial mounds are widely distributed, and there are a few hilltop "forts," some geometric earthworks, Indian cemeteries, and "workshops."

Archaeologists working with such materials in the eastern United States have developed a number of generally understood interpretative frameworks; one of these emphasizes what presently appears to be the dominant prehistoric cultural continuities. The continuities are perceived of in terms of four broadly defined cultural *traditions*.

The *Big Game Hunting Tradition* (to about 8000 B.C.) has reference to the earliest well-documented New World populations whose distinctive projectile points have been found in direct association with some of the large Late Pleistocene mammals which are now extinct.

The *Archaic Tradition* (8000 B.C. to 1000 B.C.) makes reference to early groups small in size and seasonally mobile who depended upon hunting, fishing, and plant collecting as the basis for subsistence. There is evidence to suggest that this tradition represents a continuation from the preceding with changes resulting from an increasing ability to utilize a variety of natural resources. This ability was undoubtedly given impetus by the slow changes in the environment as the effect of the "ice age" (Pleistocene) was superseded by conditions approximating those of the present.

The *Woodland Tradition* (1000 B.C. to A.D. 900) is generally defined by the presence of pottery, the surface of which has been impressed with cords and/or fabrics, and the development of burial ritualism as exemplified by burial mounds and other earthwork features.

The *Mississippian Tradition* (A.D. 800 to Historic Period) ultimately led to settled "town" life in some areas and greater residential stability in others based upon the intensive utilization of domesticated plants. The presence in the South of flat-topped mounds upon the surfaces of which were erected important structures and a distinctive ceramic complex are definitive characteristics for this tradition. . . .

This interpretive framework applies generally to the whole of eastern North America, of which Indiana is a small and, from the perspective of natural areas, an artificially defined part. Since human populations do move and it takes time for ideas to be transmitted from one group to another, it is to be expected that developments in one area need not occur at the same time as in another or, for that matter, be expressed in precisely the same way once they are present. For example, in Indiana, the "classic" *Mississippian Tradition* sites appear considerably later than in other areas to the west and, even then, only in a very restricted area. Also, cultural expressions in northern Indiana consistently differ from those in the south at every time period. Such situations are undoubtedly accentuated by obvious and subtle differences in the natural conditions encountered by prehistoric man. . . .

The beginning of the *Woodland Tradition* is marked by the appearance of fire-hardened pottery containers. This introduction constitutes a technical achievement of no small importance, not only for the vessels produced but also as regards the intellectual endeavor represented. Ceramics are one of the very few native products in which there is a transformation of raw materials into something totally different. Selected clays, tempering, and water are combined and, after drying, sufficient heat is applied to induce a physical reaction with the result being a hard insoluble substance.

Ceramics are also important for the prehistoric archaeologist. Each step of the pottery-making process is susceptible to considerable variation: the choice of clays and the tempering medium, the methods used to form the container, the shape of the vessel itself, types of surface decorations, the presence of handles or other appendages, the temperature of the firing process. All of the foregoing separately and in combination can produce an almost unending variability. However, as with ourselves, what was produced was controlled by group style preferences; these were not universal but differed at particular times and places. Pottery sherds are the most frequently recovered artifact on many sites. This, combined with their systematic variability, permits the establishment of a ceramic chronology to which other associated cultural materials can be related. Wherever pottery has been produced almost invariably archaeologists have used it to establish time scales and, initially at least, to differentiate cultures of the past. . . .

The *Early Woodland Tradition* groups, in common with their immediate predecessors, were fundamentally reliant upon hunting, fishing, and collecting for their means of subsistence. The major differences are in the presence of pottery and, in southwestern Indiana, a markedly decreased reliance upon the river mussel as a source of food.

The earliest pottery recognized is a type referred to as *Marion Thick*. It or related material is present in southern Indiana and northward in the Wabash drainage into the lake region. As the name indicates, it is very heavy, often being over an inch in thickness. The outer surface, sometimes the inner, too, is impressed with heavy cords patterned to suggest that a woven fabric might have been used. . . .

The middle period of the *Woodland Tradition* is typically the time during which ritualism as perceived through burial practices reaches a climax. It, in a sense, constitutes the culmination of trends begun in the Archaic and given additional impetus during the early Woodland period. This is reflected in many ways. Burial mounds are widely dispersed over eastern North America from southern Canada to the Gulf of Mexico and the Appalachians to the Plains. Even more widely spread trade patterns are apparent: obsidian from Wyoming, grizzly bear teeth from the Rocky

Mountains, copper from the upper Great Lakes region, pipestone and flint from Ohio, hornstone from Indiana, mica from the southern Appalachians, and marine shells from the Gulf of Mexico region. Also, a few distinctive artifacts and decorative styles occur sporadically in distant sites: copper "pan pipes," bicymbal-shaped copper ear spools, "monitor" type stone pipes, clay human figurines, and some techniques of pottery decoration, i.e., dentate stamping, as well as vessel form. All of these contribute to a picture of considerable social interaction at about the beginning of the Christian Era. . . .

The definition of Late Woodland is based largely upon negative qualities; that is, those special features of culture which served to underscore our contemporary view of life during the Middle Woodland period become markedly attenuated or disappear. Earthwork complexes were no longer in use, though a few mounds continued to be constructed. However, these served as general cemeteries in many instances, rather than as repositories for the select few. The trade for exotic raw materials was substantially terminated and such items as mica, obsidian, copper, and marine shells occurred rarely, if at all. Craft specialization suggested by the work produced from these materials, as well as the effigy stone pipes, was no longer apparent. The material culture was often remarkably uniform and lacking in stylistic variation and evidence of experimentation. There was overall a sense of monotony, of sameness, and of local isolation.

A number of explanations have been proposed to account for what amounts to a significant change in the cultural orientation of the Woodland populations. However, most of these are unsatisfactory because they are not susceptible to testing. For example, one proposal is that the limited technological base was ultimately insufficiently productive to support the native institutions responsible for maintaining the inferred ceremonial practices. Another suggestion is that the system itself became so complex and highly developed that further elaboration of the pattern was not feasible. A third hypothesis and one which offers some opportunity for testing is that the Middle Woodland populations were displaced by intruders; the so-called hilltop forts, at least two examples of which are located in Dearborn and Clark counties, are cited as evidence for a struggle for control. This explanation is obviously allied with much earlier statements regarding the demise of the "mound builders," but it rests on the assumption that the intruders were American Indians, as were those intruded upon. A fourth suggestion, and one for which evidence can be marshaled, is ecological in nature. Plant cultivation is present during Middle Woodland, though it does not appear to have been intensively practiced, and it is possible that maize production provided the extra subsistence margin required for the indicated ceremonial development. Being near the northern limits of effective maize cultivation, slight climatic shifts could drastically alter the productivity of the then available seed. And a slight decrease in average temperatures is indicated beginning about A.D. 400, which accords reasonably well with the time when Middle Woodland begins to exhibit "decline." Interestingly, the cultural pattern maintains continuity farther to the south where the natural change would have had much less impact. . . .

The *Mississippian Tradition* climaxes in what is the most complex of the several

North American cultural developments. Unlike the Woodland apogee which is confined to a limited and somewhat esoteric segment of culture, that during Mississippian is reflected at many levels from the commonplace to the specialized. Also, elements of the development persisted into the period of early European settlement and limited insights were gained by direct observation, specifically in the southeastern states.

The basic tradition was dependent upon the intensive cultivation of maize, beans, and squash, as well as other lesser seed crops and tobacco, which in combination with resident plants and animals, provided an abundant and richly varied food supply. Settlements were permanently established and some evidence of intentional long-range planning is apparent in house distributions, the preservation of open areas within the towns, and the placement of community structures. Some of the larger towns extended over hundreds of acres and must have had populations of several thousand. The raw materials exploited differed little from those available and used for millenniums by the American Indian, but the artifacts produced from bone, stone, and shell and the ceramics were varied and occur in great numbers. The emergent picture is one in which marked social stratification is present and elements of social control are vested in institutions having a religious-political function. Undoubtedly, the town exercised a hegemony over nearby farmsteads. . . .

The outstanding "classic" Mississippian site in Indiana, Angel Mounds, is located a few miles east of Evansville in the flood plain of the Ohio. A summary description of its physical remains serves to convey something of its importance.

The site extended over an area slightly in excess of a hundred acres and was shielded from the mainstream of the Ohio River by a narrow island. The residents undoubtedly were afforded some protection by this natural feature and, additionally, more than a mile of high bastioned stockade made of logs covered with clay daub covered the mainland approaches. A three-terraced flat-topped mound measuring 650 by 300 by 44 feet had been constructed near the approximate center of the settlement; a large structure reserved for a highly esteemed person or group undoubtedly occupied the broad platform. A number of smaller truncated pyramids were erected for yet other community structures. Just west of the large mound was an open plaza. Around this plaza and throughout the village substantial houses were constructed. These were generally square to rectangular in plan and ranged from about sixteen feet to thirty feet on a side. Construction was accomplished by setting upright posts in a trench and then covering the frame with cane mats and these with daub. These houses followed consistent orientations in various segments of the community. While only a portion of the site has been excavated, projections from this suggest that about two hundred dwellings would have been present at any one time. The population estimate based on the number of houses produces a figure of at least one thousand residents. Food reliance was upon cultivated plants, game, fish and mussels, and wild plant products.

The Mississippian occupants of Angel Mounds were skilled craftsmen. They produced a good quality shell-tempered pottery having many vessel forms undoubtedly to serve specific functions. Though most of it is without surface decoration, some painted wares were manufactured. Using stone, bone, and shell, numerous tools necessary for daily life were manufactured in quantity as were other artifacts for personal adornment. . . .

Ideally, we should now be in a position, after summarizing ten thousand years of Indiana prehistory, to relate all of this to the Indian occupants of record. Actually, this is for the moment at least, impossible. The explanation for this inability is simple. Various bands of the Miami and Potawatomi occupied the greater portion of the state. Other residents included the Delawares, Shawnee, and a few members of other ethnic groups. These were without exception late migrants into the region. For example, it is not until the late seventeenth century that the Miami apparently moved southeast from Wisconsin and Illinois. The Potawatomi came at about the same time or a bit later. The Delawares did not arrive until the middle of the following century. And at least some of the Shawnee seemed to have wandered over nearly all the eastern United States in the early historic period before returning to what may have been their earlier Ohio Valley homeland. The obvious fact is that the known Indian occupants came into Indiana from the outside and even though they might have lived here earlier, there is no way to relate a fully prehistoric site or culture to a specific ethnic group under these circumstances.

The First Europeans

THE FAILURE OF FRENCH POLICY

George Rawlyk

French presence in the interior of North America was comparatively short. Given the administrative difficulties it was experiencing at home and in the colonies, coupled with the competitive disadvantages under which the French labored while struggling with Great Britain for control of the Ohio and Mississippi valleys, France was unable to remain as a New World power after the mid-eighteenth century. The commercial and military empire of the French fell victim to the more populous and more powerful English empire. Even the long-standing alliances between the French and the Indians had been weakened by English penetration and competition on the frontier. When it came to a military solution to the problem, the French, by a narrow margin, did not prevail.

George Rawlyk, a Canadian scholar, here reviews the colonial policy of France and analyzes its mistakes in strategy that he believes led to the loss of France's colonial empire. Its quest for military superiority through dramatic confrontation with the English in the upper

From "The 'Rising French Empire' in the Ohio Valley and Old Northwest: The 'Dreaded Junction of the French Settlements in Canada with those of Louisiana' " in John B. Elliott, ed., *Contest for Empire* (1975), pp. 45–50, 51–52, 52–57.

Ohio Valley, rather than by a more prosaic but effective buildup of trade relations with Indians in the interior, led to an immediate English response. The resulting French and Indian War brought about the removal of France from all of North America and left the French-Canadian people in only a small portion of Canada.

A good survey with a full bibliography of France's colonizing efforts in North America is William J. Eccles, France in America *(1972); see also Louise P. Kellogg,* The French Regime in Wisconsin and the Northwest *(1925), and* The French, the Indians, and George Rogers Clark in the Illinois Country *(1972). The best collection of primary documents on New France is still Reuben G. Thwaites, ed.,* The Jesuit Relations and Allied Documents *(73 vols., 1896–1901).*

Despite the American propaganda barrage concerning the "Rising French Empire" and despite the widespread fear of "French Encirclement," few inhabitants of pre-Conquest New France manifested any real interest in westward imperial expansion. There was more than enough empty space for them to fill in the St. Lawrence Valley. It is not surprising, therefore, that until nearly the middle of the eighteenth century the Ohio Valley was almost totally ignored by the French authorities. It is true, of course, that after 1701 the French had theoretically adopted a new policy of territorial expansion designed to exclude the Anglo-Americans from the interior of North America. This policy was implemented by creating Louisiana and by constructing fortifications in the Illinois country. The Ohio Valley, however, was almost completely bypassed. In fact, the upper reaches of the Ohio were not even explored by the French until Léry's expedition did so in 1729. At this same time, it should be pointed out, La Vérendrye was already planning his explorations in search of the "western sea."

In 1721 the British Board of Trade finally responded to news about French expansion south of the Great Lakes by urging the building of fortifications on the Great Lakes and in the Allegheny passes. But little of consequence was actually done by the British to block the French. In 1726 Fort Oswego was built on Lake Ontario but nothing was done about the Allegheny passes, and the Ohio Valley was as much ignored by the British as it was by the French.

In view of this record of inactivity in the Ohio Valley, it seems both remarkable and ironic that, in the short space of ten years from 1744 to 1754, French interest and behavior in the Ohio country, together with the growing Anglo-American fear of French encirclement, would play such a key role in precipitating hostilities between France and England. The apparent change in French policy seemed to many contemporaries to have been very dramatic. Yet a closer examination of developments in the Ohio country during this period reveals not so much a sudden change in policy as a logical extension of the policy which for decades had guided French activities in North America.

This policy recognized that the fur trade remained the economic pillar of New France. Centered at Montreal, this trade accounted for two thirds of all French-Canadian exports during the first half of the eighteenth century even though agriculture and industry were receiving considerable governmental assistance. The French policy also, it should be pointed out, recognized the relative paucity of settlers in the French North American colonies. Consequently, it was realized that the success of French colonial enterprises in North America was based on a careful cultivation of the various Indian nations. By this means the French had succeeded in obtaining both furs and much-needed allies. It is interesting to note that the French governmental authorities actively participated in implementing this policy. Forts Frontenac, Niagara, and Detroit were maintained as King's posts; goods were sold below cost there in order to entice the Indians away from English posts such as Fort Oswego. Every year a portion of the profits earned from the sale of *congés* and post leases was spent on presents for the Indians to keep them loyal and passive. And before the outbreak of the War of the Austrian Succession in 1744, this policy had, it seems clear, helped guarantee the neutrality or pro-French stance of most of the Indians inhabiting the region south of the Great Lakes.

Nevertheless, such a policy had some obvious weaknesses; one of these was the dangerous French dependence on an uninterrupted flow of trade goods with which to purchase the continued friendship of the Indians. During the War of the Austrian Succession, from 1744 to 1748, this flow was seriously blocked by British naval supremacy in the North Atlantic. As early as 1745, French colonial officials predicted that their Indian allies would automatically turn to Anglo-American traders once the French were not able to satisfy their needs. The commandant of Detroit pointed out in July, 1745, that the English at Fort Oswego were spreading rumors to the Indians traveling to Montreal that the French would soon be short of trade supplies. Within two years the English had made good this threat, and the French post commanders found themselves confronted by a serious dilemma. Their efforts to buy the active assistance of the Indians in the Illinois country for attacks on the Anglo-Americans, who had penetrated the region in force after 1743, had collapsed because they had nothing with which to make payments to their allies. In disgust and out of need, the Indians began to turn to the very people the French detested and feared—the Anglo-Americans.

Despite these real threats to French policy, some of the French colonial officials, at least in their letters, showed confidence and optimism. Obviously they were eager to impress the minister of Marine that they were still in control of events. However, by the summer of 1747 they could no longer avoid the harsh realities of the new situation. It had become clear to the distraught French post commanders at Detroit and in the Illinois country that a general Indian uprising against the French was being planned. The Anglo-American traders at Sandusky and the area of the Greater Miami River had been extremely active in 1746 and 1747 in drawing many of the Indians away from the French. They had fully exploited the scarcity of French goods and also the Anglo-American victory at Louisbourg in 1745. If the so-called "French Gibraltar of North America" could be captured by a motley collection of Yankees and if the British fleet could virtually drive the French navy from the North Atlantic, the Indians could expect little assistance from their traditional allies. Not only did the Anglo-American traders drive home this point about the shattered French prestige and power, but they also cleverly played on fears of the Ottawa, Potawatomi, Hurons, Chippewa, and Miami, concerning imminent raids by the Iroquois, who were known to be sympathetic to the English. In addition, the Anglo-Americans gave presents to the Indians in an attempt to win them over. These policies were so successful that by the middle of 1747 the Hurons near Detroit were preparing a surprise attack on that settlement. Other tribes, it was hoped, would join in and sweep the upper country and the Illinois country free of the French. Only a fortuitous discovery of the plan by the Baron de Longueuil, the commandant of Detroit, enabled the French to prepare for the uprising and to summon help.

The so-called "Conspiracy of 1747" was nipped in the bud largely because of the arrival of a shipment of trade goods at Detroit, together with an impressive military escort. Once the Indian attack plan was aborted, most of the Indians made loud declarations of loyalty to the French. And soon the correspondence of the colonial administrators regained its earlier sense of optimism.

Nevertheless, this incident had a significant impact on the French and on their policy. As might be expected, the French officials recognized that one of the principal causes of the unrest had been the Anglo-American activities among the Indians. And, furthermore, the refusal of the traditional French-Indian allies to help suppress the uprising persuaded at least the Marquis de La Galissonière, the governor of Canada from 1747 to 1749, that never again should the French allow themselves to be caught in a position where they were forced to rely on the co-operation of Indians: "I think that one of the best ways of forestalling in the future any similar disorder would be to settle a good number of husbandmen at Detroit. Thus that post would be in a condition to subsist almost entirely of itself and to defend all the posts which are nearby." At this point, La Galissonière introduced for the first time the contention that the real threat to the Illinois country came from uncontested Anglo-American access to the Ohio Valley: "I think that is the only way of preventing the English from establishing themselves on the Ohio River, an establishment quite capable of interrupting our communication with the Mississippi which is almost necessary to both colonies."

Here, then, is a statement of the fundamental impact which the "Conspiracy of 1747" had on French policy in North America. Most of the Indians had indicated in no uncertain terms that their support would go to whichever power exhibited the greater military and commercial strength and prestige. Prestige in this sense rested on the ability to maintain a firm grip on trade in the interior, an ability which the French could no longer be certain of exercising in the face of growing British seapower. Unable, therefore, to rely in the future on being able to outbid the English for the cooperation and support of the Indians, the French were compelled to consider the alternative—barring the Anglo-Americans from the interior of the continent altogether. The Comte de Raymond, commanding officer at Fort des Miamis, suggested that this be done through diplomatic channels. More realistically, La Galissonière focused his attention on what could actually be done to plug the Anglo-American conduit to the interior—the Ohio Valley. The geophysical characteristics of the region, it was argued, were such that the existing troops of New France were capable of blocking the Ohio Valley without depending on the Indians for support. . . .

La Galissonière's proposals earned what some would consider to be undeserved praise, both from his contemporaries and from most historians. In a way, of course, his proposals were strategically shrewd. Yet they were neither as realistic nor as original as La Galissonière's admirers would like to believe. The proposals were unrealistic because

France had never before succeeded in mounting a sustained immigration and settlement program in North America. They were also unrealistic because the Indians would never have tolerated a major settlement program. One of the few advantages which the French had over the English in North America was that their frontier posts were never transformed into major settlements. Some of them, to be sure, supported small-scale European communities; but these were always designed merely to add to the military strength and security of the post. The Indians had made clear their attitude towards settlement; the English understood this and so did most of the French. Thus, La Galissonière's grandiose proposals were at odds with reality. . . .

Throughout the Ohio Valley and the Illinois country and beyond, the Indians were very restless and were giving every indication of conspiring once again to try to drive the French from that territory. The new center of the anti-French movement was La Demoiselle's Miami village on the Great Miami River. By 1750 the Anglo-Americans had established a trading post there called Pickawillany, and they had quickly become the predominant influence in the new Indian intrigue. Early in 1750 reports began to circulate among various French post commanders and officials about the possible imminent Miami and Shawnee attacks. . . .

Given the circumstances and his instructions, Governor La Jonquière [La Galissonière's successor] did his best to strengthen the French position in North America. Fort Rouillé (Toronto) was established in 1750 in order to intercept the Indian trade flowing to Fort Oswego. The post at Michilimackinac was strengthened and forts were built at Sault Ste. Marie and at the foot of the Niagara portage. Diplomatic negotiations in 1750 and 1751 secured the neutrality of the Cayuga and Onondaga; these tribes had, following La Galissonière's activities in 1749, feared that the French were eager to force the withdrawal of all Indians from the Ohio Valley. La Jonquière reassured them, promising that "The French, who will go to the Beautiful river, will carry wherewith to supply the wants of those who are there, and will be careful not to disturb them." Only those who proved hostile to the French, declared the governor, would be in danger of expulsion. Finally, in an effort to determine more precisely what was happening in the Ohio country, the governor sent Captain Philippe de Joncaire with a small party to that region.

Despite these efforts, which remained within the limits set by La Jonquière's instructions, the reports sent back by Joncaire and other French officers in the interior indicated that a passive policy would not work. During 1751, at least nine Frenchmen and two slaves were killed in isolated incidents south of Lake Erie. Rumors were circulating of conferences attended by Illinois, Miami, Delawares, Shawnee, Iroquois, and Anglo-American traders. Tension increased when a bad harvest created a scarcity of provisions. Joncaire sadly reported that "the Indians of the Beautiful river are all English."

Faced with this rapidly deteriorating situation, La Jonquière was receptive to any plans offering firm measures against the hostile Indians of the Ohio Valley, especially those at Pickawillany. . . . But once again the plan had to be abandoned. . . .

La Jonquière never had another opportunity to suppress the Indians of the Ohio country. Following an unrelated dispute with Rouillé, he resigned his offices, and before he could return to France, he died, in March, 1752. His replacement, the

Marquis Duquesne, was still in France, and so the administration of the colony fell temporarily into the hands of Longueuil, the governor of Montreal.

During his brief term in office, Longueuil attempted to continue La Jonquière's efforts to suppress the Indian unrest in the interior. He proposed sending a force of four hundred French troops to Detroit that summer, to be followed in the spring of the following year by a slightly larger force. Sometime in 1753, according to the plan, the approximately eight-hundred-man force would then overpower and overawe the hostile Miami and drive out the Anglo-Americans. This plan, in its strategic thrust, was quite similar to La Jonquière's plan of 1751. It differed, of course, in one fundamental way! Longueuil explicitly excluded the Indians from participating. The uncooperative behavior of the Indians domiciled at Detroit in 1751 may have persuaded him not to use any Indians. Or it may have been that Longueuil, expecting the Indians to join the French expedition once they saw its size, deliberately excluded any mention of them because he did not want to alienate his superior.

While Longueuil labored hard to try to put his plan into effect in the summer of 1752, a force of 250 Chippewa Indians from Michilimackinac, under the command of Charles-Michel Mouet de Langlade, had taken the initiative and had attacked and destroyed Pickawillany. La Demoiselle, the Miami chief who had caused so much trouble for the French, was permanently removed from the scene by the simple expedient of boiling and eating him. The terror of a smallpox epidemic contributed further to the collapse of the Indian unrest in the Ohio and Illinois country.

Even before the news of the Langlade expedition had reached him, Rouillé was expressing his displeasure with the extent to which La Jonquière and Longueuil had ignored his orders to avoid entanglements with the Indians. The minister of Marine was determined that the new governor of New France should clearly understand his wishes and conscientiously carry them out. Duquesne was, therefore, warned to ignore the advice of these French Canadians who wanted him to continue the policy of La Jonquière and Longueuil.

Consequently, when Duquesne arrived in New France, he was committed to implementing a military policy independent of Indian allies. He immediately made plans to occupy the upper Ohio Valley in force in order to bar English access to the country and the Indians beyond. An expedition was organized, and in 1753, over two thousand Frenchmen (300 Troupes de la Marine and 1,700 Canadian militia) advanced into the area south of Lake Erie and into the upper reaches of the Ohio Valley. Forts were erected and garrisoned, roads were built, and when the Anglo-Americans tried to protest or resist, they were packed on their way.

This was more than the English colonial governments had bargained for, but most were not keen to finance countermeasures. Nevertheless, a small military force under the command of George Washington, financed by the Virginia House of Burgesses, set out early in 1754 in an effort to force the French to withdraw. The result was rather an ignoble defeat for Washington—but a defeat with major consequences. The mother countries began to participate directly in these affairs, with the result that the Seven Years' War between France and England began, to all intents and purposes, not in 1756 but rather in 1754 in the forested mountain country of the upper Ohio Valley.

What, then, can be said about French policy in the Ohio-Illinois country? La Jonquière, influenced by Canadians such as Longueuil and Bigot, had tried to preserve French authority in the region by forcing the Indians to co-operate. This policy depended on the active assistance of allied Indians. It was a policy rooted in the belief that an exercise of French power and prestige would draw the Indians away from the Anglo-American traders who had already penetrated the territory. But the French ministry of Marine was adamantly opposed to this policy. Maurepas and Rouillé both believed that the expulsion of the Anglo-American traders was the major objective. This could be achieved, they thought, by mounting exclusively French military operations against the traders; no Indian allies would be necessary. As far as they were concerned, the "Conspiracy of 1747" had underscored the fact that the Indians were not to be trusted.

Superficially, the latter policy seemed to be the more effective of the two. Duquesne's expedition, mounted without the help of Indians, had evidently impressed the native inhabitants of the Ohio Valley. Moreover, it had succeeded in sealing the English out of the Ohio country. Thus, it may be argued that the success of the expedition seemed to justify Rouillé's arguments.

Yet Duquesne's accomplishments were not won in isolation nor were they achieved without great cost. The 1752 attack on Pickawillany and the smallpox epidemic had made Duquesne's task that much easier. Yet it must not be forgotten that Duquesne lost four hundred men to disease just in building his road to the Ohio from Lake Erie. This huge cost in human lives confirmed the worst fears of the French Canadians who had opposed the expedition. But most important of all, Duquesne's efforts, by not only claiming but also occupying the upper Ohio Valley, directly threatened the English colonies in North America and helped spark the "Great War for the Empire." La Jonquière's attempts to secure the Illinois country by pacifying the restless Indians through intrigue, diplomacy, and the help of allied Indians probably would not have provoked Great Britain into war. The French Canadians, as has been pointed out earlier, had little interest in the Ohio Valley, except for the few who resented the Anglo-Americans' use of it as a base from which they threatened the Illinois and upper country.

Thus, the metropolitan French perception of the Ohio Valley and the Illinois country had, by 1749, led to the adoption of a policy directed towards the military occupation of the region. Although this was a policy which ran counter to the wishes of many influential French Canadians, it was, nevertheless, only a variant of the policy which had guided French activities in North America for decades. That policy had enabled the French to expand into and exploit the interior of North America without occupying it with settlements. Instead, the French had relied on the respect and cooperation of the Indians. The imperial objectives of France and the commercial objectives of New France were compatibly expressed within the framework of this policy. However, when the commercial disruption caused by the War of the Austrian Succession undermined the co-operation of the Indians, it also undermined the faith of French administrators in the wisdom of that policy. And, consequently, the policy was modified. Reliance on the Indians was discouraged, settlement of the interior was favored, and military operations against the Anglo-Americans were promoted.

Some French Canadians, at least, realized the basic dangers involved in such a policy. It represented, among other things, the abandonment of the traditional French-Canadian approach to North American realities. Metropolitan France was imposing its special brand of ignorance on the affairs of New France. The Conquest owed more to this policy than it did to historical inevitability. As Professor William J. Eccles has observed, "Ineptitude in the French military command and government at home, and the fortunes of war, gave Britain dominion over the vast French territory." It was, it should be pointed out, a close thing. Had Montcalm not adopted such foolish tactics at Quebec on September 13, 1759, the British army might have been destroyed and New France, including the Illinois country, at least, might have remained French territory. But for how long? Historians, of course, must deal with what happened and not with what might have happened. By 1760 the "Dreaded Juncture of the French Settlements in Canada with those of Louisiana" had been dealt a fatal blow. The French-Canadian nation would have to be satisfied with the somewhat restrictive provincial boundaries of Quebec rather than those of a transcontinental Gallic country.

THE FRENCH FORT AT VINCENNES

August Derleth

Vincennes, the oldest urban settlement in Indiana, was established as a French outpost on the lower Wabash River in the early 1730s. The youthful Sieur de Vincennes had overcome many difficulties in carrying out this mission, but his promising career as a French administrator ended with his death at the stake in 1736 during the Chickasaw wars. The village bearing his name, however, survived, despite general neglect by the British after 1763; and it became the site of stirring conflict during the middle years of the American Revolutionary War. Furthermore, with the formation of an Indiana Territory in 1800, Vincennes was designated the territorial capital.

From this place Governor William Henry Harrison oversaw the development of the territory and directed United States relations with various Indian people then living there. In time these relations deteriorated into open hostilities. During the War of 1812 the territorial capital was moved to Corydon, but Vincennes continued as an important commercial and cultural center of southwestern Indiana. At the present time Vincennes has a population of approximately 20,000. And it treasures many visible links with its heritage: the Old Cathedral, erected in 1825 on the site of the original French church; the George Rogers Clark National Memorial; Grouseland, the fine Federal-style mansion of Governor Harrison; the Elihu Stout print shop, the first in the territory; and Vincennes University, the oldest one in the West.

From *Vincennes: Portal to the West* (1968), pp. 4–9, 12–23. Copyright © 1968. Used by permission of
the publisher, Prentice Hall/A Division of Simon & Schuster, Englewood Cliffs, N.J.

August Derleth, an extremely prolific writer and interpreter of the Old Northwest with over a hundred books, most notably his Sac Prairie and Wisconsin Saga series, is one of the best and most recent historians of Vincennes. In the passages below, Derleth describes both the founding of Vincennes and its final years under French control. For additional material on early Vincennes, see Clarence W. Alvord, The Illinois Country, 1673–1818 *(1920), Louise P. Kellogg, ed.,* The French Regime in Wisconsin and the Northwest *(1925), and Leonard Lux,* The Vincennes Donation Lands *(1949).*

On September 30, 1725, the Company of the Indies sent to Périer, the new Governor of Louisiana, a letter proposing that—since Kaskaskia and Cahokia, with Fort de Chartres, held the Mississippi side of the country of the Illinois, and the post among the Ouiatenon to the north, an anchor ought to be established in the southeast corner, where the Wabash bent toward the Ohio, thus securing the area—either along the Wabash itself or at the mouth of the Tennessee River.

"M. Périer will reflect well on this subject," the official wrote, "and consider if, by giving eight or ten soldiers to the said Sieur de Vincennes, with the missionary destined for the Ouabache, he will not find himself in condition to assure, by the Indians, the communication between Louisiana and Canada, and to prevent the English from penetrating into our colony, without obliging the Company to construct a fort on the lower Ouabache, of which the expense of the establishment and the support of the garrison make an object of consequence."

To facilitate this venture, Vincennes was confirmed as a halfpay lieutenant attached to Louisiana, though he was not formally detached from Canada. He was then a young man just as old as the century—26. It was hoped that he could persuade a large body of Indians to settle at the place he chose to establish a post wherever he thought best at the bend of the Wabash, since the King and his ministers seemed to be reluctant to send into the American provinces any substantial number of colonists. The King, however, did instruct the Governor of Canada to release Vincennes for the purpose of establishing the fort on the Wabash.

Delays, notwithstanding orders and instructions, were integral to life in the wilderness. It took a year before Governor Périer got around to sending a load of goods to supply the still non-existent post on the Wabash, but the boat set out from New Orleans so late that it encountered ice and had to turn back. And the next spring Vincennes fell ill, and remained in poor health until midsummer. In the meantime, the Company of the Indies stipulated that the new post was to be manned by ten soldiers and two officers. The Company fixed upon three hundred livres as sufficient for the construction of the fort, and 1,170 livres as pay for the men during the initial year of their occupation of the post. As for presents for the Indians, the Company estimated that 800 livres ought to be enough.

Périer immediately objected to the niggardliness of the allowance. But such parsimony was all too typical of the official approach to the problem of establishing posts and maintaining good relations with the Indians. Périer made clear that the Company was allowing only half enough money to build the fort, and scarcely a fourth of the sum that would be needed if the French were to compete on anything like an equal basis with the British for the favor of the Indians.

When he recovered, Vincennes was in no hurry to select a site for the post on the

Wabash. He went back to live for a while with the Miami at Ouiatenon, but there is some reason to believe that he had already made a tentative selection of the Wabash site, though the building of the fort waited upon a more favorable occasion. At some time during 1727 Vincennes and a small group of soldiers made their way down the Wabash and fixed upon a site for the new post—not at the mouth of that river, after all, but approximately a hundred and fifty miles up river from the junction of the Wabash and the Ohio. The post was first called Poste des Pianguichats, after Indians found in the vicinity—one of the numerous branches of the Miami, who had made themselves at home among the remains of the settlement left by the first inhabitants of the area, the Mound Builders, long since vanished.

The site chosen for the post lay along the Wabash in relatively low, flat terrain, with some knolls and low hills bounding it. Vincennes obviously had an eye for settlement, not alone for the building of an isolated fort, for which he might have found a less pregnable position. The chosen site appeared to him to be a fertile one, a site to which French settlers could be drawn; it was a country of many trees—beech, pawpaw, persimmon, sycamore, maple, linden, pecan, red gum, tulip, aspen, ash, cottonwood, elm, wild plum, oak, black locust, and some juniper—one that afforded its wild life, which included elk, raccoons, opossums, wolves, foxes, and porcupines, all manner of natural food—nuts, persimmons, wild strawberries, mulberries, wild apples, and other food commonly found in the wilderness of the continent's heartland. It was a country which, already supporting much game as well as a great variety of fish in its streams—sturgeon, catfish, pike, perch, bass, suckers, mullets and pickerel being the most common—would certainly fit well into the plans of the French governors for the strengthening of French control by enduring settlement.

Despite the characteristic lack of vigor with which the King and his ministers pressed colonization of the region, Vincennes, when he returned from his stay among the Miami, persisted. Limitations notwithstanding, he had built a fort by early 1732, and on March 7 of that year he wrote to one of the officials of the Marine in France a letter typical of many that he was to write:

> I begin by informing you that the Wabash is composed of five nations who compose four villages of which the least has sixty men carrying arms, and all of them could furnish from six to seven hundred men if it were necessary to assemble them for the welfare of the service and for their own welfare. On account of the nearness of the English, it has been impossible for me to bring together all these nations because there has always been a lack of merchandise in this place. The fort which I have built is about eighty miles in the Wabash country up the river by which the English have been able to descend and open up commerce with these nations. The place is very suitable in which to build a great settlement which I would have done if I had had troops enough. In regard to the commerce which one can carry on here, a traffic in skins could go on all year to the extent of 30,000 skins.

The Indians, however, wooed by both the French and the English, were troublesome:

> I have never had a greater need of troops in these places than at the present time. The

savages, the Illinois, as well as the Miami and others are more insolent than they have ever been, especially since the Foxes were defeated. The little experience which I have acquired in the twenty years that I have been among them, causes me to fear some evil trick on the part of these nations and above all, of my own who, seeing a settlement which I had begun, did not seem to wish it to be continued. Since for three years nothing has happened. Except, Monsieur, the migration of all the nations not only of the lakes but also of other places.

Vincennes had no illusions about the "friendship" of the Indians, knowing that that friendship had its price, which the British were far more successful in meeting than were the French, who were forever deprived of merchandise for trade and gifts by the shortsighted insularity of the officials of whom Vincennes and other French commanders addressed repeated representations.

You do me the honor to indicate to me that I send you a statement of the work done and to be done. There is only one fort and two houses within and it will be necessary very soon to build a guard house with barracks in which to lodge the soldiers. Nothing else is possible in this place with so few troops. I need thirty men with an officer. I am more embarrassed than ever, in this place, by the war with the Chickasaws, who have come twice since spring. Only two days ago the last party took away three people and since the French took up tomahawks against them I am obliged every day to put up a defense. I hope, that of your goodness, you will indeed wish to give your attention to this place and to my difficulty for myself as well as for the little garrison which I have. This is the favor which he awaits, from you, who has the honor to be, with profound respect, M., your very humble and very obedient servant, Vincennes.

Vincennes's superiors did little to alleviate his needs. . . . Nevertheless, Vincennes did everything in his power to establish a settlement as well as a fort at the site. In 1733, having built a house apart from the fort, he married the daughter of Philippe Longpré of Kaskaskia, and lost no time in fathering two daughters, Marie Therese and Catherine. Despite the shortage of goods, he kept the local Indians friendly. But, though the land was fertile, and the Indians—when they were impelled to do so, raised maize, beans, squash, and other vegetables, and found the country replete with wild game as the river was with fish—colonists could not readily be lured to a site so deep in the wilderness. . . .

By late 1735, Governor de Bienville, exasperated by reports from the outposts of the colony, concluded that the only solution lay in war with the Chickasaw. He needed a pretext for making war and did not have far to look for one. In the course of a recent war with the Natchez Indians, some of the Natchez had escaped from French soldiers and taken refuge with the Chickasaw south of the Ohio; Bienville now demanded that the Chickasaw surrender the fugitives. The Chickasaw, who had been interfering for a long time with the movements of French traders, soldiers and settlers and who, like the Chickasaw north of the Ohio, were trading with the British, refused to give up the Natchez, as the Governor of Louisiana had foreseen. When his ultimatum was rejected, Bienville had the pretext he wanted.

He had his plans made. . . . On the night of March 24, the war party moved into position near the village, French and Indian allies deploying themselves in the most advantageous manner. They waited out the night and attacked at dawn. Unfortunately, it was unlikely that so large a party of French soldiers and Indians could have gone unnoticed in enemy territory. The Chickasaw were well aware of their presence—not only those in the village under attack but also those in the central encampment of Chickasaw. Furthermore, the movement of the soldiers toward the village could scarcely have been unobserved.

The battle had only begun, when several hundred Chickasaw poured in from the woods around the village. Their appearance so dismayed and frightened some of the attacking forces that the Miami fled at once. The French, the Iroquois and the Arkansas Indians were left alone. The battle raged intensely for a while, but the Chickasaw were much superior in numbers, and the French, with their allies, suffered a disastrous defeat.

Artaguiette died in action. Those members of his attacking party who were not slain or could not manage to escape were taken prisoner. One of them, Rickarville, who made his escape months later with the help of British traders among the Chickasaw, said that the prisoners were taken into the Chickasaw village and burned at the stake in an orgy that lasted from three in the afternoon until midnight.

Among the prisoners who were put to the stake was François Bissot, Sieur de Vincennes, who had established the fort and the settlement along the lower Wabash and given the latter his name. . . .

[Following Vincennes' death, Governor Bienville appointed Louis de Bellerive de St. Ange, the son of his venerable commander in the Illinois country, to command the Wabash post. A loyal and dedicated man, St. Ange arrived in Vincennes late in 1736 to take up his new duties, trying to rebuild both the fort and the strained Indian alliances.]

St. Ange went ahead with badly needed repairs to the fort left by Vincennes. It needed to be strengthened, and it needed stone facing. He took steps toward replacing the Indians who had left the area for the north, and at his urging a small band of Indians settled not far away at the site of Russellville, Illinois. But it was clear to St. Ange that what the post at Vincennes needed primarily was not Indians but French settlers, and this problem he could not resolve without help from the government, for the settlers were reluctant to come unless they could own the land they settled.

Bienville, however, still nursed his plan to remove the post to the mouth of the Ohio and was of little help. Yet, in 1742, the Piankeshaw remaining at Vincennes—no doubt with the consent of the Miami nation of which they were part—surrendered the territory trapped by the French to the French. It was a larger territory than that occupied by Vincennes, one embracing more than a million and a half acres lying north and east of Vincennes, though Congress later reduced the amount for Vincennes to five thousand acres, which were given to the Borough of Vincennes and later became known as the "Vincennes Common."

Settlement at Vincennes became more attractive. The government at New Orleans did little to cooperate with St. Ange. Bienville was replaced in 1743 by Governor Vaudreuil, who promised to make the French fur trade once more a flourishing business. He expected to send more traders among the Indians in the colony and intended by this means to increase the influence of the French, thus weakening that of the British. In the face of the niggardliness with which the French government served the colonies' needs, however, this goal was sheer naïveté. . . .

By 1743, however, when Vaudreuil came to the governorship, St. Ange had established himself. Indeed, the post was for a while called "St. Ange" or "St. Anne," though to Bienville it remained the fort of the Piankeshaw and to the traders it was more commonly known as the "little Weas" or "Little Wiaut," both names meaning "Little Ouiatenon" after the Ouiatenon Indians, to which the Piankeshaw were believed to belong. But the name "Vincennes" was even more widely and persistently applied to the post and to the settlement, such as it was.

The settlement was slow to grow. The Piankeshaw village had been called "Chip-pe-co-ke," which meant "scrub brush," but it was now largely deserted. Though the surrender of the Indian lands in 1742 was intended to stimulate settlement by the French, the post at Vincennes was referred to as late as 1746 as "quite inconsiderable," having "about 40 men and 5 negroes," whose occupation was "hunting and the culture of wheat and tobacco." St. Ange was anxious for the settlement to grow, for he wanted to counter Vaudreuil's plan for a fort at the mouth of the Ohio, where, he had been informed, the soil was rich, buffalo were plentiful and the French could deliver goods by water far more inexpensively than the British could carry them over the mountains.

Settlement was expedited by gifts of the commandant at the post, particularly of titles to land. Very probably Vincennes issued no land grants, as the land was in his time still claimed by the Indians. But St. Ange did so, though because of lack of registration no record has been left. The earliest record of a deed is of one issued to François Racine dit Beauchêne, though this deed was lost and was validated by the Federal government long after it was given. The first deed on the legal records of Vincennes was issued in April 1750 to François Filiatreau. None seems to have been for any very great land area; most of the French interested in settling wanted grants of areas about 150 feet square—enough space for a house, perhaps a summer kitchen, an outhouse, a storage building for pork, a place to keep chickens, a stable, perhaps a garden plot and an orchard. And, because the early settlers were engaged in trading, they preferred their land to be located on or near the fort, whereas those French settlers who hoped to engage in farming preferred their land to run back from the shore of the Wabash and liked to own areas of "two by forty arpents," which came to somewhat more than 68 acres. . . .

During much of the decade that followed St. Ange's assumption of command at Vincennes, England and France were at war because of France's part in the War of the Austrian Succession. . . . All this conflict had little effect on Vincennes, save that a few volunteers from that post went to take part in the defense of Fort Duquesne. After the cession of the land by the Indians twelve years before, Vincennes had begun slowly to grow. French-Canadians came to settle there, taking up land on three sides of the fort and back from the Wabash.

With the country around the fort relatively calm and quiet, St. Ange turned his attention to the development of the settlement. The fort itself was improved and repaired. St. Ange undertook to build a chapel next to the fort; he named it "St. Francis Xavier" in honor of the Jesuit priest, Father Francis Xavier de Guinne, who visited the settlement from time to time. He laid out and opened two streets—Busseron Street and Rue de St. Honoré, which led away from the front gates of the fort.

There remained the constant danger of Indian attack, particularly as information reached the fort that the British were patching up all their quarrels with the Indians, including the wavering Iroquois, with whom Benjamin Franklin and other delegates from New England, Pennsylvania, Maryland and New York had conferred at the behest of the British government. They had drawn up a plan of union—a patent indication that the British meant to use their Indian allies against the French. But nothing in the way of unusual depredations by the Indians against the French took place. The settlement was accustomed to learning that an occasional traveler had been set upon and robbed—perhaps killed—by marauding Indians, and British traders were beginning to appear within range of the fort's command, but no event of an untoward nature took place. . . .

On February 10, 1763, the Treaty of Paris ended the French and Indian War. By its terms France ceded to Great Britain all its claims to Canada and the territory east of the Mississippi except for the city of New Orleans. Throughout the years of hostilities—and though the British had seized a French fort as close as that at Ouiatenon above Vincennes—the post commanded by St. Ange took part in no engagement.

Nor were the British in any haste to take over Vincennes. They were principally engaged from May through November of 1763 in dealing with the destructively successful uprising of Indians led by the Ottawa chief, Pontiac, who scourged the region from Niagara west to Detroit, which withstood a seige of five months until Pontiac lifted it in November. Under Pontiac, the Indians had destroyed Fort Sandusky, Fort St. Joseph, Fort Miami, Fort Ouiatenon, Fort Venango, Fort Le Boeuf, Fort Presque—the fort at Vincennes escaped.

Not until the rebellion led by Pontiac had been crushed did the British think again of Vincennes. In May 1764 St. Ange was ordered to take command at Fort de Chartres and to hold it until the British called upon him to turn it over to them. On May 18 he delivered a farewell address to the garrison and people of Vincennes, and, turning the post over to Major Joseph Antoine Drouët, Sieur de Richardville, who was assisted by François de Coindre, he departed for Chartres, leaving behind him close to seventy families, most of them French-Canadians.

2. The Era of the American Revolution, 1763-1789

Although the British, according to the terms of the Treaty of Paris of 1763, acquired the Illinois country, a vast interior region previously controlled by France, they did not immediately occupy their new territory. Indeed, British policy as expounded in the Proclamation of 1763 was to discourage colonial settlement in the trans-Appalachian area until Indian title to the land was extinguished. This policy, coupled with the limited success of an Indian uprising known as Pontiac's Rebellion, meant that Britain's hold on the Wabash Valley was at best a nominal one for several years. Of the three former French posts in Indiana, the British were driven out of Forts Miamis and Ouiatenon during the Indian war of 1763–1765, and they never had occupied the post at Vincennes. There, after the French commandant Louis de St. Ange departed in 1764, the small French settlement that remained handled its own affairs until renewed British interest in the West during the 1770s. But the British hold was still tenuous until after the Revolutionary War was under way and George Rogers Clark was able to make an initial conquest of the area for Virginia in 1778. He did this merely by dispatching a representative there after he had taken Forts Kaskaskia and Cahokia along the Mississippi River. The loss of Vincennes, however, prompted Lieutenant Governor Henry Hamilton, the officer in charge at Detroit, personally to lead a small British force down the Wabash and retake the fort, thereby setting the stage for Clark's heroic reconquest of Vincennes, the surrender coming on February 25, 1779.

The significance of what Clark did has been debated for many years. Many historians now question the older view that Clark's exploits had direct impact on the negotiations in Paris leading up to the peace settlement of 1783, particularly the generous boundaries the United States obtained in the West. Nevertheless, Clark's dramatic achievement had and continues to have powerful influence on the minds of the people in the nation, especially those in the Old Northwest. The selections in this chapter relate to the classic confrontation between Clark and Hamilton, between a young frontiersman and an aristocratic officer, with both a contemporaneous and a recent analysis of these men.

In 1787, less than a decade after Clark first embarked on his western country mission, the United States adopted a monumental piece of legislation concerning the procedures by which the newly acquired land in the Ohio Valley would be governed and the processes leading to eventual statehood for the area on the basis of complete equality with the original states. This legislation, known as the Northwest Ordinance, also guaranteed to all inhabitants of these lands certain basic rights and freedoms prior to statehood, including a sometimes ignored prohibition of slavery and involuntary servitude.

For further reading on Clark, Hamilton, and the American Revolution in the West, see George M. Waller, *The American Revolution in the West* (1976), Lowell H. Harrison, *George Rogers Clark and the War in the West* (1976), and John D. Barnhart, *Henry Hamilton and George Rogers Clark in the American Revolution* (1951). See also an older account of Clark by an enthusiastic champion of his, James A. James, *The Life of George Rogers Clark* (1928), and the pioneering history by Indianapolis banker and politician William H. English, *Conquest of the Country Northwest of the River Ohio, 1778–1783 and Life of Gen. George Rogers Clark* (2 vols., 1896).

A Historian's View

Professor Bernard Sheehan, a specialist in early American history, has explored the relationship between, first, Indians and Europeans and later, Indians and Americans. A professor of history at Indiana University for many years, Sheehan's major publications include Savagism and Civility: Indians and Englishmen in Colonial Virginia *(1980), and* Seeds of Extinction: Jeffersonian Philanthropy and the American Indian *(1973). In the selection below, Sheehan draws upon his deep knowledge of this relationship as he analyzes the myths surrounding George Rogers Clark's heroics in the capture of various points in the Old Northwest, as well as those associated with an aristocratic, "hairbuying" British officer, Lieutenant Governor Henry Hamilton, from whom Clark accepted an unconditional surrender of Fort Sackville at Vincennes on February 25, 1779.*

It may be noted that the Kaskaskia-Cahokia-Vincennes captures by Clark were intended as the preliminary to an assault on Detroit, the keystone of British occupation in the West, but that the Detroit expedition was never mounted. This has led to a considerable controversy over the long-range significance of Clark's actions in the Illinois country, but the scholarly debate cannot detract from the inspired leadership of Clark, the epic heroism of the youthful commander and his men, or the completeness of their victories in 1778 and 1779.

As Professor Sheehan argues, however, it is possible that the "savage" label and charges of inhumanity and cruelty have been laid at the wrong door. Like Professor John D. Barnhart, who had in the late 1940s discovered a journal written by Hamilton in 1778 and 1779 that provided the basis for a reexamination of the man's career in North America, Sheehan viewed Hamilton as a man of sensitivity, artistry, and honor who was both fascinated and repulsed by the often brutal life style of the native Americans. The historian also considers Clark to be the very antithesis of Hamilton and much more like the Indians against whom he was fighting than his British counterparts.

In their later lives, both Clark and Hamilton faced enormous difficulties. Immediately after the end of the American Revolutionary War Clark continued in the military defense of the frontier, but his successes were limited and his personal fortune declined. For a short while he lived in Clarksville, part of the 150,000 acres provided to Clark and his soldiers and the first

American settlement in the entire Northwest Territory. But he was held personally liable for debts incurred in the service of his country, and he lost his lands and his reputation. Ten years before his death in 1818, while living in Kentucky with a relative, Clark fell and severely injured a leg, which subsequently had to be amputated. Similarly, Hamilton, during and after his release from prison in Williamsburg, Virginia, largely occupied himself writing long narratives about his experiences in both the Seven Years' and the American Revolutionary wars and defending himself against charges of incompetence and inhumanity.

THE CHARACTERS OF HENRY HAMILTON AND GEORGE ROGERS CLARK COMPARED

Bernard W. Sheehan

It would be difficult to find two more dissimilar characters of the revolutionary generation than Henry Hamilton and George Rogers Clark. The Anglo-Irish gentleman and the Virginia Indian fighter seemed destined to clash when they met on the Illinois frontier. Hamilton had already become infamous as the promoter of Indian attacks on the American settlements and the supposed buyer of white scalps. Not even Simon Girty, the "white savage," could equal the iniquity that attached to Hamilton's reputation; indeed, not until recent times have historians managed to restore a semblance of balance to the memory of his career in America. In contrast, Clark emerged a hero from the Revolution, and his renown has remained high since.

The issue between Hamilton and Clark in the 1770s was the American Indian. To be sure, for the outcome of the war and the establishment of independence, both men were minor characters. The conflict in the West gained significance only in hindsight. George Washington won the war east of the mountains, employing an army of conventional design and training, with no more than grudging attention to the unseemly conflict that occupied the frontier regions. The western hostilities were important, however, because they brought into the fray the Indian tribes that weighed heavily in the thinking of Americans about themselves. As the behavior of both Hamilton and Clark testifies, Americans and Englishmen were deeply torn over the problem of the Indian. At the same time that they scorned the native way of life as the savage antithesis of civility, they felt strangely attracted to it. In addition, the Americans came to believe that the alliance between the British and the "merciless Indian savages," to use Jefferson's phrasing from the Declaration of Independence, united the foes of liberty with the enemies of civilization. Thus the Hamilton-Clark

From " 'The Famous Hair Buyer General': Henry Hamilton, George Rogers Clark, and the American Indian," *Indiana Magazine of History*, LXXIX (March 1983), 1–5, 11, 13–15, 16–18, 22–23, 25–26, 27–28. Reprinted by permission of the Editor, *Indiana Magazine of History*.

conflict touched the deepest strains of American commitment during its revolutionary trial.

The question of employing the native warriors in the War for Independence arose at the outset of the conflict, but after the emission of much pious rhetoric from both sides, most of the Indians joined the crown. At first the Continental Congress seemed inclined to promote Indian neutrality, perhaps on the assumption that the natives were more likely to support the British, but local American commanders had already recruited warriors. Besides, rumor had it that the British ministry had formed a plan to unite the tribes against the rebellion. By 1776, on grounds that their involvement was inevitable, the Congress abandoned attempts to keep the Indians neutral and tried with little success to engage them on the American side. British policy had originally been negative, designed to keep the warriors from joining the Americans, but by 1777 military necessity and the prevalent conviction that the Americans had taken the first steps led to the systematic promotion of Indian attacks on the frontier.

The piety exuded by both sides over the misbehavior of their enemies in allying themselves with the "savage" Indians was more than partisan propaganda. There had been a long history of native participation in the American extensions of European wars, hence much experience of native warfare. There had been time for the development of deep feelings. In the end, no doubt, most Englishmen and Americans would have agreed that since the Indians would be fighting "for somebody . . . they may better be fighting for us than against us." All agreed, however, that the very presence of the Indians in the conflict tainted the cause of those allied with them and presented the other side with the necessity of fighting for the very survival of civilization. . . .

Hamilton showed the influence of the romantic vision of nature prevalent in the late eighteenth century. He had been brought up in County Cork in the midst of a landscape of power and terrible beauty; thus, as he said of north Wales, he recognized "Nature . . . in his rude and awful Majesty." While in America he found time to indulge an artistic bent and left a small cache of line drawings of Indians and scenes that obviously struck his imagination. He seemed particularly affected by waterfalls, of which four drawings remain: two of Niagara and one each of the falls of the Passaic and the Falls of Chaudiere on the Ottawa. In each, great rushes of water plunge with vast energy throwing up clouds of spume and spray and conveying an image of tremendous potency. Along the shore foliage and broken trees in forbidding confusion complete an impression of almost Gothic menace. In one Niagara picture the infinitesimal human figures clash with the sweep and strength of the surrounding scene. Hamilton's landscape art reveals an avid observer who held a certain awe for the force of nature.

The native people entered into Hamilton's drawings in dissimilar ways. The nine extant Indian portraits disclose a genuine concern for native personality. Faces are vividly drawn, some stolid, others more animated, but all are depicted with strength of character. One has the impression that Hamilton found inner resources in these native people and that his renderings strove to give them concrete and tactile realization. In contrast, the native figures that appear in Hamilton's landscapes are overwhelmed by the settings. The two minute Indian hunters who lounge on the edge of a high, precipitous cliff serve mainly to heighten the sheer force of the scene. Others are no more than minimal shapes, human no doubt, but with no function other than to magnify the power of the natural surroundings. In his view of the falls of the Passaic River, however, Hamilton attributes to the native figures a violence of their own entirely compatible with the surrounding turmoil. Two Indians (the figures are unclothed and hence seem to be Indian) appear at the base of the falls, one in the pool and the other on shore, in the midst of a violent altercation. Hamilton's caption reads: "Here a Savage jealous of his wife, threw her into the River, and in her attempting to get to shore cut off her arm with his Tomahawk." . . .

From his experience in the Seven Years' War Hamilton had learned how "deplorable" Indian fighting could be. The British, especially, remembered the debacle after the capture of Fort William Henry. When Hamilton fell into French hands at the battle of Sainte Foy in April, 1760, he asked to be taken to the officer in charge. That gentleman, perceiving the danger, exchanged coats with Hamilton so that the scarlet trim on his British uniform would not be seen by the Indians. "Shortly after this," Hamilton later recorded, "we prisoners were marched ostentatiously thro the Indian encampment, not without a very unpleasant feeling, the Savages employed some in scraping and dressing Englishmen's scalps, others whetting their knives and Tomahawks—" Hamilton knew that the Indians had already scalped many of his colleagues who had been wounded. He also suspected that not all French officers could be depended upon to protect British prisoners. Rumor had it that the French turned over many prisoners to their "savage" allies who then tortured and killed them. . . .

In its popular form the case against Hamilton rested on accusations that he encouraged the Indians to bring in scalps and rewarded them for these grisly totems of their success. Most of the evidence derived from rumor and hearsay. Some was plainly fraudulent, as, for example, the testimony of John Dodge, but there were eyewitnesses who told believable stories of what they had seen at Detroit. Daniel Sullivan and John Leith had both visited the fort and had brought back vivid accounts of Hamilton's dealings with the Indians. Leith's story in particular portrayed the misery of the Indians' prisoners and the importance that the British and Indians attached to scalps in the war against the frontier, but neither Leith nor Sullivan had actually seen Hamilton pay for the scalps. That accusation had no more than rumor for support, though it remained virtually universal.

In fact, the popular contentions were not far from the mark. Hamilton accepted scalps from the Indians without, it would appear, very close scrutiny as to their origins. If he did not actually pay for them with a formal bounty, he certainly did reward the natives for their services and success against the frontier settlements. . . .

Hamilton's principal antagonist in the West, George Rogers Clark, faced a different sort of problem in his dealings with the native people. Unless he managed to take Detroit and sweep the British from the Northwest, Clark stood little chance of gaining the Indians' loyalty; thus, his attitudes toward them diverged in many ways from Hamilton's. For him the natives were not potential allies but implacable enemies who tormented his brethren in the frontier settlements. In addition, Clark was free of that eighteenth-century scientific attraction to the natives that informed Hamilton's thinking about them. (And, it might be added, that played so prominent a part in the musings of Clark's mentor, Jefferson, and in the later career of his younger brother, William.) Clark was far more the coarse-grained frontiersman, intelligent but ill-educated, extraordinarily resourceful but ultimately dependent on drink, an Indian fighter who despised his enemy but who often imitated native ways. In this last sense the contrast with Hamilton breaks down. For Clark, the Indian could not have been an intellectual issue; nevertheless, he struggled, as did so many in the border settlements, with the lure of native habits. All the more ironic, then, that he should have seen in Hamilton's relations with the Indians evidence of the lieutenant-governor's betrayal of civil order. . . .

By 1777, when Clark formulated his plan to subdue the northwest Indians, the issue of native participation had been settled. Most of the tribes had already come in on the British side or were likely to do so soon. Hence the American reaction could be expected. The native people had chosen the wrong side in a struggle that for the Americans was certain to determine the future of mankind. People like Henry and Jefferson, the two Virginia governors with whom Clark dealt, counseled the severest treatment of the tribes who opposed American interests. They could only be a treacherous and dangerous people. They "must be managed," wrote Henry, "by working on their Fears," a sentiment echoed by Jefferson to the effect that if the Indians could not be taught to keep faith, they must be taught to fear. Later in the conflict Jefferson recommended to Clark the "total suppression of Savage Insolence and Cruelties," by which he no doubt meant the "extermination" or removal of tribes who persisted in resistance.

Clark's own formula for treating with Indians fully conformed to the governors' sentiments. He proposed to discard the notion "that soft speeches was best for Indians." It had, he thought, caused untold mischief. He preferred what he called the French and Spanish method, harsh speech and the threat of immediate action. Elaborate festivities with much ceremonial talk and expensive gifts (more the French and Spanish than the English usage) only fostered illusions in the Indians' minds and led to greater demands and ultimately to another outbreak of conflict. Blunt language and speedy retribution would keep the peace. He told one native group that if they continued to support the British "they would see their great father as they called him given to the Dogs to eat." The Indians, he believed, must be convinced that "we are always able to crush them at pleasure, and determined to do it when Ever they misbehave." . . .

It should be noted that Clark's practice did not always conform to his principles. He did, for example, adopt the traditional manner of speaking to Indians, which demanded a heavily allusive mode of speech and the kind of simple vocabulary thought to be suitable for primitive people. In conference with Black Bird, a Chippewa chief, Clark delivered his usual account of the establishment of English settlements in America and the reasons for the Revolution. Black Bird, in turn, "assumed the Airs of a Polite Gen . . . and attempted to speak as much in the European manner as possible." Thus the discussion occupied the better part of the day with Clark doing his best to avoid the "Similes" he used with other Indians. Black Bird, it appears, accepted the new dispensation that Clark attempted to introduce into Indian-white relations. Most other Indians did not, in which case Clark adopted the traditional forms of speech that white men assumed were compatible with the Indian manner.

The truth of the matter was that Clark made a conscious effort at imitating the Indians. It was not merely that he led frontiersmen whom a contemporary observer described as "a wild, ungovernable race, little less savage than their tawny neighbours," men who in fact engaged in "similar barbarities." Clark cultivated the image. He argued that the only way to fight Indians was "to excell them in barbarity." The French inhabitants of Kaskaskia had gotten the message. They were convinced that Clark and his followers "ment to strip the women and children or take the Bread out of their mouths or . . . make war on the women and Children or the Church." Clark finally reassured them but not before recording his pleasure that the French should entertain "a most horrid Idea of the Barbarity of the Rebels," that they should believe them "more savage than their Neighbours the Indians."

Clark and his men followed the frontier habit of dressing in a partial imitation of the Indians. Governor Fernando de Leyba of St. Louis described their entrance into town. "The commanding colonel arrived . . . in a hunting shirt and breechcloth, naked of foot and limb and with his bed, food, and gun on his shoulder. The troops had no other equipment than breechcloth, powder horn, gun, and knapsack." They were, as Leyba noted, "bandits in appearance." The reason was clear. When Clark and his little army reached the falls of the Ohio on their way to attack Kaskaskia in 1778, they abandoned their baggage "except as much as would equip us in the Indean [*sic*] mode." In 1780 on his trip east to lead an attack against the Shawnees, Clark and his men disguised themselves as Indians in order to make their way safely through the wilderness; and, of course, most of the men who followed him into Ohio for that campaign dressed in "hunting shirts and breech clouts, some linen & others buckskin." . . .

Hamilton's decision to give up Vincennes on February 24, 1779, presented Clark with an opportunity to visit a proper vengeance on the enemies of civilization. Hamilton remained the arch-criminal. Though Clark had probably not invented the phrase, his reference to the lieutenant-governor as "The Famous Hair Buyer General" established the moral justification and the propaganda theme for his western strategy. Actually the description had been used a year earlier in a letter to Clark from James Willing, the notorious filibusterer. Willing's reference, however, was to Philipe de Rocheblave, the British representative at Kaskaskia who had learned the art of frontier fighting from Charles Langlade during the French and Indian War. Clark knew Rocheblave's reputation, and upon entering Kaskaskia he promptly loaded the gentleman with irons, confiscated his property, and locked him in a hog pen. Rocheblave was soon released from his shackles, and Governor Henry later directed that his property should be returned, but not before Clark had made his views clear and offered a preview of his behavior once the principal villain fell into his hands.

When Hamilton realized the futility of continued fighting and asked Clark in the traditional manner for terms, he received an unexpected response. In Clark's mind he deserved no terms at all. One does not offer terms to the allies of savages who have forsaken the rules of civilization. In reply to Hamilton's request for an explanation, Clark spoke frankly: now that he had within his grasp the greatest part of the Indian partisans from Detroit, he "wanted an excuse to put them to Death or other ways treat them as I thought proper that the Cries of the Widows and Fatherless on the Frontiers that they had occationed now Required their Blood from my Hands. . . ." Hamilton tried a feeble defense, but Clark was not listening. He ended the conversation with a burst of passion: "my blood glows within my veins to think on the crueltys your Indian parties have committed. . . ." Of course Clark was often unrestrained in his speech. He acted and spoke boldly, and one can assume that he did not always mean all that he said. He did finally offer Hamilton and his men terms, very broad ones it is true, but terms nonetheless; yet, there would seem no reason not to take him at his word. Circumstances led him to make concessions, even to moderate his views of Hamilton, but he never ceased to think of him as the "Hair Buyer" or to believe that Indian warfare, abetted by the British, constituted a breach of civil order.

How deeply Clark felt became evident after Hamilton's surrender. He first permitted the British and French captives who had taken no part in Indian depredations to leave for Detroit; then, despite the formal capitulation, Clark ordered all the prisoners who had accompanied Indians on their raids to be put in irons—neck, hands, and feet. Only after a vigorous protest by Hamilton was the order left unexecuted. Without the intervention of the townspeople, a number of the French partisans would have been hanged. Hamilton believed that his own life had been threatened, and on one occasion he fled from his quarters. In time Clark softened. Hamilton's gentlemanly bearing and apparent rectitude led Clark to grant him and his men the freedom of the fort, but he did not change his views on Hamilton's ultimate guilt. Consequently, on March 8, 1779, the lieutenant-governor and twenty-six of his followers were dispatched under guard to Williamsburg to face the wrath of the Kentucky frontier posts on the way and, at the end of their journey, the stern justice of Thomas Jefferson. . . .

On the day that Hamilton reached Williamsburg, the Virginia Council, in an order written probably by Jefferson, made public its determination concerning the treatment that the lieutenant-governor and his aide might expect. The council accused Hamilton of "inciting the Indians to perpetuate their accustomed cruelties" and of offering "standing rewards for scalps, but . . . none for prisoners." To implement his policy, he had called a great Indian council to gather at the mouth of the Tennessee River. The Americans found substantiation for their case in one of Hamilton's proclamations left by the warriors with the bodies of frontier patriots after one of their raids. In addition, the council accused [Phillip] DeJean and [William] La Mothe of aiding Hamilton in inciting this frontier crime wave. After listing the usual British and Indian atrocities against the western settlements, Jefferson took the occasion to expand his indictment to cover the British handling of prisoners. On this issue "the conduct of the British officers, civil and military, has in its general tenor, through the whole course of this war been savage and unprecedented among civilized nations." In making his case, of course, Jefferson seized upon every possible item to put the British in the worst light. In stretching the argument to include the "general tenor" of

British attitudes, he had done a great deal more. He had, in fact, revealed how profound he believed the argument between Britain and America had become. Hamilton symbolized this contest between liberty and tyranny, civilization and savagery.

In his discussion with General Phillips, Jefferson became enmeshed in the issue of Hamilton's capitulation. Believing, as did Jefferson, that Hamilton had placed himself beyond the law, Clark had demanded unconditional surrender, but he had not possessed sufficient force to insist. As a result, Hamilton had obtained terms and had marched out of Vincennes with military honors. The terms, however, did not touch upon the later treatment of the prisoners, nor did they prohibit confinement in the common jail or the wearing of irons. Jefferson interpreted this absence of specific limitations as a license to impose the kind of punishment he believed Hamilton richly deserved. Phillips argued Hamilton's innocence of the charges and maintained that in any case he could not, because of the formal submission with terms, be dealt with so severely. Opinion at the Continental Congress supported Jefferson's view. So also on first consideration did General Washington, but Washington sought professional advice and found that Jefferson's cogent reasoning flew in the face of international usage and would very likely provoke British retaliation. Hence Jefferson changed his policy but not his opinions. . . .

In the deepest sense, of course, Hamilton and Jefferson held identical views of the native people. Both believed that Indians were "savages," that their mode of life was the antithesis of civilization. Hamilton's nagging anxieties over his complicity in the attacks on the frontier, his repeated and futile efforts to conform native warfare to British standards, disclosed the importance he attached to the differentiation between civilization and "savagery." His anxieties dissolved at least partially, however, when he confronted real Indians. True enough, the romantic strain in his approach to the continent and its inhabitants led to an emphasis on the violence inherent in "savagery," but his portraits of individual Indians transcended that generalization. They revealed a genuine interest and even sympathy for the native people. One should not be surprised, therefore, that Hamilton became an adept practitioner of forest diplomacy and so readily donned native costume or joined the war dance. The American continent had made its mark on Hamilton and left him deeply divided in his loyalties.

Not so George Rogers Clark. He never doubted where his loyalties lay. They resided with the revolutionary cause and the frontier people he strove so mightily to defend. And he knew his enemies. These were the "savage" Indians and the conscienceless British who aided their bloody assaults on the white settlements. How then can one explain his curious affinity for native ways? Was it merely that he suffered the fate of all Indian-haters: he became what he despised? This is very likely true, though in Jeffersonian terms the process might have been described differently. An account of Clark's career in the West read like living proof of Jefferson's perception that civilization and "savagery" constituted opposite images of each other. As the frontiersman plunged into the wilderness and left civil ways behind, he risked transformation into the "savage" who opposed him. In defense of civility he became a "savage." Jefferson saw the first point, the defense of civility, but missed the second; hence, he failed to recognize that his friend Clark might have been an even more dangerous enemy of human nature than the "Famous Hair Buyer General."

A Participant Writes

The brief account below, written by George Rogers Clark (1752–1818), describes his travels en route to the lower Wabash and certain aspects of the battle and subsequent surrender of Fort Sackville, the British name for their post at Vincennes. The Clark report and a report by Lieutenant Governor Henry Hamilton were published jointly in Milo M. Quaife, ed., The Capture of Old Vincennes: The Original Narratives of George Rogers Clark and of His Opponent Gov. Henry Hamilton *(1927).*

Clark's account was written in 1791 at the urging of James Madison. Some years earlier, in a letter to George Mason, Clark had reported in detail on his campaign in the West, but all copies of the 1779 sketch were lost. The second report, 128 pages long, now rests in the Draper Collection at the Wisconsin Historical Society in Madison. Because various awkward passages render Clark's unedited prose difficult to understand, when Professor Quaife prepared the 1791 report for publication originally in the Lakeside Classic Series in 1920, he modernized its spellings, punctuation, and paragraphing; but the language—"for the most part"—is Clark's own. The Hamilton report, written in 1781, covered his "proceedings" from 1776 through June 1781. It relates the basic facts about his Vincennes expedition and his subsequent imprisonment at Williamsburg, Virginia. This report, written by a well-educated British officer and reprinted a number of times, appears unchanged in the Quaife edition.

Professor Quaife was a distinguished scholar of Michigan, Wisconsin, and the Old Northwest. His major publications include, with Sidney Glazer, Michigan: From Primitive Wilderness to Industrial Commonwealth *(1948), and a number of edited works. For a recent concise and accurate description of the fall of Fort Sackville, see the National Park Service booklet written by Robert C. Alberts,* George Rogers Clark and the Winning of the Old Northwest *(1975). See also the more general work by Jack Sosin,* The Revolutionary Frontier, 1763–1783 *(1967), and the older but comprehensive collection edited by James A. James,* George Rogers Clark Papers, 1771–1781 *(1912).*

OUR MARCH UPON VINCENNES

George Rogers Clark

We now saw that we were in a very critical situation, cut off as we were from all intercourse with the home government. We perceived that Governor Hamilton, by the junction of his northern and southern Indians, would be at the head of such a force in the spring that nothing in this quarter could withstand him. Kentucky must fall immediately and it would be fortunate if the disaster ended here. Even if we should immediately make good our retreat to Kentucky we were convinced that it

---

From Milo M. Quaife, ed., *The Capture of Old Vincennes: The Original Narratives of George Rogers Clark and of His Opponent Gov. Henry Hamilton* (1927), pp. 118–122, 124–127, 131–132, 134–135, 138–140, 142–146, 149–150. Some footnotes in Quaife's edition have been omitted.

would be too late even to raise a force sufficient to save that colony, as all the men in it, united to the troops we had, would not suffice, and to get succor in time from the Virginia and Pennsylvania frontiers was out of the question. We saw but one alternative, which was to attack the enemy in his stronghold. If we were successful we would thereby save the whole American cause. If unsuccessful, the consequence would be nothing worse than if we should not make the attempt. We were encouraged by the thought of the magnitude of the consequences that would attend our success. The season of the year was also favorable to our design, since the enemy could not suppose that we would be so mad as to attempt a march of eighty leagues through a drowned country in the depth of winter. They would, therefore, be off their guard and would not think it worth while, probably, to keep scouts out. If we could make good our advance to Vincennes we might probably surprise and overcome them, while if we should fail, the country would be in no worse situation than if we had not made the attempt. This and many other similar reasons induced us to resolve to attempt the enterprise, which met with the approbation of every man among us.

Orders were immediately issued for making the necessary preparations. The whole country took fire and every order, such as preparing provisions, encouraging volunteers, etc., was executed with cheerfulness by the inhabitants. Since we had an abundance of supplies, every man was equipped with whatever he could desire to withstand the coldest weather. Knowing that the Wabash would probably overflow its banks to a width of five or six miles and that it would be dangerous to build vessels in the neighborhood of the enemy, I concluded, both to obviate this and to convey our artillery and stores, to send around by water a vessel strong enough to force her way, as she could be attacked only by water (unless she should choose otherwise) since the whole of the lowlands was under water and she might keep away from any heights along the river. A large Mississippi boat was immediately purchased and completely fitted out as a galley, mounting two four-pounders and four large swivels, and manned by forty-six men under the command of John Rogers.[1] He set sail on February 4, with orders to force his way up the Wabash as high as the mouth of White River, and there secrete himself until further orders; if he should find himself discovered he was to do the enemy all the damage he could without running too great risk of losing his vessel. He was not to leave the river until he had abandoned hope of our arrival by land, but he was strictly enjoined to so conduct himself as to give rise to no suspicion of our expected approach. . . .

Everything being ready on the fifth of February, after receiving a lecture and absolution from a priest, we crossed the Kaskaskia River with one hundred and seventy men and at a distance of about three miles encamped until February 8. When we again resumed the advance the weather was wet and a part of the country was covered with several inches of water. Progress under these conditions was difficult and fatiguing although, fortunately, it was not very cold considering the time of year. My object now was

1. John Rogers was a cousin of Clark. He saw service in the earlier years of the Revolution, and in 1778 became second lieutenant in Captain Helm's company on Clark's Kaskaskia expedition. As noted here, Clark placed him in command of the war galley sent against Vincennes. After its capture Rogers was sent to convey the British prisoners to Williamsburg.

to keep the men in good spirits. I permitted them to shoot game on all occasions and to feast on it like Indians at a war dance, every company taking turns in inviting the other to its feast. A feast was held every night, the company that was to give it being always supplied with horses for laying in a sufficient store of meat in the course of the day. I myself and my principal officers conducted ourselves like woodsmen, shouting now and then and running through the mud and water the same as the men themselves.

Thus, insensible of their hardships and without complaining, our men were conducted through difficulties far surpassing anything we had ever experienced before this to the banks of the Little Wabash, which we reached on February 13. There are here two streams three miles apart, and the distance from the bank of one to the opposite bank of the other is five miles. This whole distance we found covered with some three feet of water, being never less than two, and frequently four feet in depth. I went into camp on an elevation at the bank of the river and gave the troops permission to amuse themselves. For some time I viewed with consternation this expanse of water; then accusing myself of irresolution, without holding any consultation over the situation or permitting any one else to do so in my presence, I immediately set to work. I ordered a pirogue to be constructed at once and acted as though crossing the water would be only a bit of diversion. Since but few of the men could find employment at a time, pains were taken to devise amusement for the rest in order to keep up their spirits. However, the men were well prepared for the undertaking before us as they had frequently waded farther than we must now, although seldom in water more than half-leg deep. . . .

On the seventeenth I dispatched Mr. Kennedy with three men to cross the River Embarrass, which is six miles from Vincennes, charging him to procure, if possible, some boats in the neighborhood of the town, but chiefly to obtain some information if he could do so in safety. He went, and on reaching the river found that the country between it and the Wabash was flooded. We proceeded down below the mouth of the Embarrass, vainly attempting to reach the banks of the Wabash. Finding a dry spot we encamped late at night and in the morning were gratified at hearing for the first time the morning gun of the British garrison. We resumed our march and about two o'clock in the afternoon of the eighteenth gained the banks of the Wabash three leagues below the town and went into camp.

I now sent four men across the river on a raft to find land if possible, proceed to the town, and purloin some canoes. Captain McCarty set out with a few men the next morning with a little canoe he had made for the same purpose. Both parties returned unsuccessful; the first was unable to make land, and the Captain was driven back by the appearance of a camp. I immediately dispatched the canoe down the river to meet the galley, carrying orders for it to proceed day and night. Meanwhile, determined to have as many strings to my bow as possible I directed the men to build canoes in a sheltered place. I had not yet given up hope of our boat arriving; in case she should, these canoes would augment our fleet; should she not come before they were ready, they would answer our purpose without her.

Many of our volunteers began for the first time to despair and some to talk of returning but our situation was now such that I was past all uneasiness. I merely laughed at them; without persuading or ordering them to desist from such an attempt I told them

I would be glad if they would go out and kill some deer. They departed puzzled over my conduct. My own men knew that I had no idea of abandoning an enterprise for want of provisions so long as there were plenty of good horses in our possession and I knew that our volunteers could be detained without the use of force for a few days, by which time our fate would be determined. I conducted myself in such a manner as to lead every one to believe I had no doubt of success. This kept up their spirits, and the hunters being out, they had hope of momentarily obtaining a supply of food, besides the expectation of the arrival of the galley. I perceived that if we should not be discovered for two days we would effect the passage of the river.

On the twentieth the water guard decoyed a boat ashore having five Frenchmen and some provisions on board. These men were on their way down-river to join a party of hunters. They informed us that we had been discovered and that the inhabitants were well disposed toward us. They said the fort had been completed and greatly strengthened, and that the number of men in it was about the same as when Mr. Vigo left Vincennes. In short, they gave us all the information we desired, even telling us of two boats that were adrift up the river, one of which Captain Worthington recovered.

Having now two small boats, early on the morning of the twenty-first, abandoning our baggage, we began crossing over the troops and landing them on a small elevation called the Mamel. While engaged in searching for a passage Captain J. Williams gave chase to a canoe but could not take it. The men we had captured said it was impossible for us to make the town that night or at all with our boats. Recalling what we had done, however, we thought otherwise, and pushing into the water marched a league, frequently in water to our armpits, to what is called the upper Mamel. Here we encamped our men, still in good spirits from the hope of soon putting an end to their fatigue and realizing their desire to come into contact with the enemy.

This last march through the water was so far superior to anything our prisoners had conceived of that they were backward about saying anything further. They told us the nearest land was the Sugar Camp, a small league away on the bank of the river. A canoe was sent off to it and returned with the report that we could not pass. I now went myself and sounding the water found it as deep as my neck. I returned with the thought of having the men transported to the Sugar Camp in the canoes, which I knew would consume the entire day and the ensuing night since the boats would pass but slowly through the bushes. To men half starved the loss of so much time was a serious matter and I would now have given a good deal for a day's provisions or for one of our horses. . . .

Now came the real test of our ability. The plain between us and the town was not a perfect level, and the sunken ground was covered with water full of ducks. We observed several men out on horseback shooting ducks about half a mile away and sent off several of our active young men to decoy and capture one of them in such a manner as not to alarm the rest. The information we obtained from this person was similar to that received from those we had taken on the river, with the exception of the news that the British had that evening completed the wall of the fort and that there were a large number of Indians in the town. Our situation was now sufficiently critical. We were within full view of a town which contained upward of six hundred men, counting soldiers, inhabitants and Indians, with no possibility of retreat open to us in case of defeat. The crew of the galley, although numbering less than fifty men, would have constituted a reinforcement of great importance to our little army. But we would not permit ourselves to dwell on this. We were now in the situation I had been laboring to attain. The idea of being taken prisoner was foreign to almost all of our men. In the event of capture they looked forward to being tortured by the savages. Our fate was now to be determined, probably within the next few hours, and we knew that nothing but the boldest conduct would insure success. I knew that some of the inhabitants wished us well, while many more were lukewarm to the interest of the British and Americans alike. I also learned that the Grand Chief, the son of Tobacco, had within a few days openly declared in council with the British that he was a brother and friend of the Big Knives. These circumstances were in our favor. Many hunters were going back and forth and there was little probability of our remaining undiscovered until dark. Accordingly I determined to bring matters to an issue at once, and writing the following address to the inhabitants sent it off by the prisoner we had just taken:

To the Inhabitants of Vincennes—

Gentlemen: Being now within two miles of your village with my army determined to take your fort this night, and not being willing to surprise you, I am taking the measure of requesting such of you as are true citizens and desirous of enjoying the liberty I bring you to remain quietly in your houses. If there are any that are friends of the King of England I desire them instantly to repair to the fort and there join his troops and fight like men; and if any that do not repair to the garrison shall hereafter be discovered they may depend upon being severely punished. Those, on the other hand, who are true friends to Liberty may expect to be well treated. I once more request that they keep out of the streets, for every person found under arms upon my arrival will be treated as an enemy. . . .

The garrison was now completely surrounded and the firing continued without intermission (except for about fifteen minutes shortly before dawn) until nine o'clock the following morning. Our entire force, with the exception of fifty men kept as a reserve in case of some emergency, participated in the attack, being joined by a few young men. I had acquainted myself fully with the situation of the fort and town and had detailed information concerning each of them. The cannon were on the upper floors of strong blockhouses located at each angle of the fort eleven feet above the ground, and the portholes were so badly cut that our troops lay under their fire within twenty or thirty yards of the walls. The enemy did no damage except to the buildings of the town, some of which were badly shattered, while their musket fire in the dark was employed in vain against woodsmen who were sheltered behind the palings of the houses (the gardens of Vincennes were close to the fort and for about two-thirds of the way around them were fenced with good pickets firmly set in the ground and about six feet high. Where these were lacking breast-works for the troops were soon made by tearing down old houses and garden fences, so that the troops within the fort enjoyed but little advantage over those outside; and not knowing the number of the enemy, they thought themselves in a worse situation than they actually were), river banks, and ditches, and did us no damage except for the wounding of a man or two.

Since we could not afford to lose any of our men, great pains were taken to keep them sufficiently sheltered and to maintain a hot fire against the fort in order to intimidate the enemy as well as to destroy them. The embrasures for their cannon were frequently closed, for our riflemen finding the true direction would pour in such volleys when they were open that the artillerymen could not stand to the guns. Seven or eight of them were shot down in a short time. Our men frequently taunted the enemy in order to provoke them into opening the portholes and firing the cannon so that they might have the pleasure of cutting them down with their rifles. Fifty rifles would be leveled the instant the port flew open, and had the garrison stood to their artillery most of them, I believe, would have been destroyed during the night as the greater part of our men, lying within thirty yards of the walls, and behind some houses, were as well sheltered as those within the fort and were much more expert in this mode of fighting. The enemy fired at the flash of our guns, but our men would change their positions the moment they had fired. On the instant of the least appearance at one of their loopholes a dozen guns would be fired at it. At times an irregular fire as hot as could be maintained was poured in from different directions for several minutes. This would be continually succeeded by a scattering fire at the portholes and a great uproar and laughter would be raised by the reserve parties in different parts of the town to give the impression that they had only fired on the fort for a few minutes for amusement, while those who were keeping up a continuous fire were being regularly relieved. . . .

[The next day the] firing immediately recommenced with redoubled vigor on both sides and I do not believe that more noise could possibly have been made by an equal number of men. Their shouting could not be heard amid the discharge of the muskets, and a continual line of fire around the garrison was maintained until shortly before daylight, when our troops were withdrawn to positions that had been prepared for them sixty to one hundred yards from the fort. Scarcely could a loophole be darkened by the garrison when a rifle ball would pass through it, and for them to have stood to their cannon would have entailed the useless destruction of their men. In this respect the situation of the two parties was much the same. It would have been imprudent in either to have wasted men unless some decisive stroke should require it.

Thus the attack continued until nine o'clock on the morning of the twenty-fourth. . . .

Toward evening a flag of truce appeared with the following proposals.[2] I was greatly at a loss to conceive what reason Governor Hamilton could have for wishing a truce of three days on such terms as he proposed. Many said it was a stratagem to

2. Hamilton's proposal, as recorded in Major Bowman's journal, was as follows: "Lieutenant Governor Hamilton proposes to Colonel Clark a truce for three days during which time he promises there shall be no defensive works carried on in the Garrison on condition Colonel Clark shall observe on his part a like cessation of any offensive work, that he wishes to confer with Colonel Clark as soon as can be and further proposes that whatever may pass between them two and any other person mutually agreed upon to be present, shall remain a secret till matters be finally concluded—as he wishes that whatever the result of their conference may be (it may redound) to the honor and credit of each party—If Colonel Clark makes a difficulty of coming into the fort Lieutenant Governor Hamilton will speak to him before the Gate."

obtain possession of me. I thought differently and had no idea that he entertained such a sentiment, as an act of that nature would infallibly ruin him. I was convinced he had some prospect of succor or of extricating himself from his predicament in some way. Although we had every reason to expect a reinforcement in less than three days that would at once put an end to the siege, I did not think it prudent to agree to the proposal. . . .[3]

We met at the church about eighty yards from the fort, Governor Hamilton, Major Hay, Superintendent of Indian Affairs, Captain Helm, who was his prisoner, Major Bowman, and myself, and the conference began. Governor Hamilton produced articles of capitulation containing various provisions, one of which was that the garrison should be surrendered on being permitted to go to Pensacola on parole. After deliberating on every article I rejected the whole proposal. Hamilton then desired me to make some proposition. I told him I had no offer to make other than I had already done, that they surrender themselves as prisoners unconditionally. I observed that his troops had behaved with spirit, and without viewing us as savages they could not suppose they would be treated the worse in consequence. If he chose to comply with my demand, the sooner he should do so the better, as it was in vain for him to make any counter proposition. He must know by this time that the fort would fall and that both of us must regard all blood that might still be spilled as murder on the part of the garrison. My troops were already impatient and begging for permission to storm the fort. If such a step were taken many of course would be cut down, and the consequences of an enraged body of woodsmen breaking into the fort must be obvious to him. It would be beyond the power of an American officer to save a single man.

Various arguments were exchanged for a considerable period of time. Captain Helm attempted to moderate my fixed determination, but I told him he was a British prisoner and it was doubtful whether he could with propriety speak on the subject. Governor Hamilton then said that Captain Helm was liberated from that moment and might act according to his pleasure. I told the Captain I would not receive him on such terms; that he must return to the fort and await his fate. I told the Governor we would not begin hostilities until a minute after the drums should give the alarm. We took leave of each other and parted, but I had gone only a few steps when the Governor stopped me and politely asked if I would be kind enough to give him my reasons for refusing any other terms than those I had offered to the garrison. I told him I had no objection to giving him my real reason, which simply was that I knew the greater part of the principal Indian partisans of Detroit were with him and I desired to be free to put them to death or treat them in any other way I might think proper. I said that the cries of the widows and the fatherless they had occasioned upon the frontiers now required their blood at my hands and I did not choose to be so timorous as to disobey the absolute command of their authority, which I regarded

3. [Clark's] answer is recorded in Major Bowman's journal as follows: "Colonel Clark's compliments to Mr. Hamilton and begs leave to inform him that Colonel Clark will not agree to any other terms than that of Mr. Hamilton's surrendering himself and Garrison Prisoners at discretion. If Mr. Hamilton is desirous of a conference with Colonel Clark he will meet him at the Church with Captain Helm."

as next to divine. I said I would rather lose fifty men than to surrender the power properly to execute this piece of business. If he chose to risk the massacre of his garrison for their sakes it was his own affair and I might perhaps take it into my hand to send for some of those widows to see it executed. . . .

On the morning of the twenty-fifth arrangements were made for receiving the garrison, and about ten o'clock it was surrendered with due formality and everything was immediately arranged by me to the best possible advantage. On first viewing the interior of the fort and its stores I was astonished at its being surrendered in the manner it had been. However, it was a prudent and lucky circumstance which probably saved the lives of many men on both sides since on the preceding night we had inclined to attempt to undermine it and I found it would have required great diligence on the part of the garrison to have prevented us from succeeding. I found, too, on further examination, that our information concerning the interior arrangements was so good that in all probability the first hot shot after the arrival of our artillery would have blown up the magazine. This would at once have put an end to the siege since the situation of the magazine and the quantity of powder it contained were such that its explosion must have destroyed the greater part of the garrison.

An Enlightened Western Policy

The Land Ordinance of 1785 and the Northwest Ordinance of 1787 represent two remarkable achievements of the Confederation Congress. The first document provided for an elaborate and sophisticated system of land survey and sale, the basis of which is still used. It established the congressional township which consisted of thirty-six one-square-mile sections and was laid out in a carefully surveyed and numbered gridiron pattern across the Old Northwest and then much of the rest of the country. Shortly afterwards, in an equally enlightened ordinance that replaced a 1784 plan suggested by Thomas Jefferson, the Confederation Congress established a system of government for the territory "North West of the river Ohio." In broad outline, the Northwest Ordinance provided for a three-step process by which three to five states, equal in all particulars to existing states, would emerge. After an initial phase of an appointed government, the territory was authorized an elected territorial legislature and a delegate to Congress as soon as its population reached 5,000 voters (adult white males). Stage three—statehood—required a minimum population of 60,000 people, not just voters. This legislation, which also contained the famous and precedent-setting prohibition of slavery, as well as a bill of rights, has been acclaimed as a document, in Theodore Pease's words, "secondary only to the Constitution of the United States."

A number of publications appearing in or near to the bicentennial year of the Northwest Ordinance have served to explicate the document, analyze the circumstances surrounding its adoption and implementation, and highlight anew its continuing significance. See the essays collected in *Pathways to the Old Northwest: An Observance of the Bicentennial of the Northwest Ordinance* (1988), *The Northwest Ordinance, 1787: A Bicentennial Handbook* (1987), edited by Robert M. Taylor, a special issue of the *Indiana Magazine of History* (March 1988) devoted to articles on the Northwest Ordinance, and the monograph by Peter S. Onuf, *Statehood and Union: A History of the Northwest Ordinance* (1987). See also, for further information on the ongoing legacy of the Land Ordinance of 1785, Malcolm J. Rohrbough, *The Land Office Business: The Settlement and Administration of American Public Lands, 1789–1837* (1966); Hildegard Binder Johnson, *Order upon the Land: The U.S. Rectangular Land Survey and the Upper Mississippi Country* (1976); and George W. Geib, "The Land Ordinance of 1785: A Bicentennial Review," *Indiana Magazine of History*, LXXXI (March 1985), 1–13.

THE NORTHWEST ORDINANCE, 1787

Theodore Calvin Pease

Professor Pease, a student of Midwestern and especially Illinois history during his long tenure as professor of history at the University of Illinois, both clarifies the background and explains the reasons for his admiration of the Ordinance in the article below. It is a revised version of an address he delivered to an American Historical Association meeting in Philadelphia, December 1937. Pease was also the author of The Story of Illinois *(1925) and* The Frontier State, 1818–1848 *(1918), and he edited a number of documentary collections.*

Meeting in Philadelphia at this season [1937], the American Historical Association appropriately commemorates the 150th anniversary of the Philadelphia convention and of the framing of the Constitution of the United States. While the members of the Mississippi Valley Historical Association join in that commemoration, they naturally remember that another document, secondary only to the Constitution of the United States, is especially intrusted to their historical charge. They remember that on the thirteenth day of July, 1787, the Congress of the Confederation passed an ordinance for the government of the Northwest Territory. . . .

In appraising the place of this document in American history, as it is most fitting to do at this time, it is not essential to seek after novelty or rush frantically in search of unconventional interpretations. All students of western history are familiar with the particulars necessary for a valuation of the ordinance; one of them as well as another may set these forth.

That this is possible is due in great measure to the fact that a generation after the Northwest Ordinance was framed, its authorship became an honor to be contended

---

From "The Ordinance of 1787," *Mississippi Valley Historical Review,* XXV (September 1938), 167, 168, 170–180.

for. One may pass over the enthusiastic Ohio panegyrist who in 1837 assured his audience that the ancient Romans would have ascribed its composition to the nymph, Egeria! Daniel Webster, in his debate with Robert Y. Hayne, inserted a set eulogy on Nathan Dane as the true author. With other historical partisans ready to press the claims of Thomas Jefferson, of Edward Carrington, of Rufus King, and of Manasseh Cutler himself, large quantities of evidence were collected, preserved, and criticized, so that the main facts connected with the ordinance have long since been set aside to cool.

In appraising its place in American history, the most ardent patriot, the most earnest nationalist need have no misgiving about stating the last iota of the truth concerning it. The importance of that document in American history is past arguing. The devil's advocate may be allowed to say everything that can be said in its disfavor, and when he has done his worst, its sanctity will still prevail beyond all doubt. Historical truth is not singular but diverse; of the infinite number of things which may be said of any historical event or situation, a given number are always sure to be equally true. For instance, there is the saying that under the Ordinance, the United States became one of the most successful colonizing nations of all history; there is Andrew C. McLaughlin's interpretation of the document, along with the Constitution of the United States, as the creation of a system of imperial order toward which the men of the Thirteen Colonies had striven for a quarter of a century, both inside and outside the British Empire. These things are true and many more. . . .

It must also be admitted that the statesmen who labored the passage of the Ordinance do not appear always to have been highminded or disinterested. The great prohibition of slavery, hastily interpreted not to be retroactive, bore, it is true, the original imprint of the humanitarianism of the great Virginians. But for its insertion in the final Ordinance, cavillers have alleged, and with a show of evidence, that smug New England prejudice went hand in hand with the enlightened self-interest of southerners who did not wish slave grown tobacco from northwest of the Ohio to compete with the produce of the Old South.

Further one must admit that if, under the similar Southwest Ordinance, the annals of the Southwest Territory were vacant, in the Northwest Territory personality clashed on personality, governors and governed found no good to speak of each other, and the Ordinance put into practice brought not peace but a sword. One should also recall the corollary that the states formed out of the Northwest Territory did not, in fond memory of the government of their infant years under the Ordinance, inscribe its provisions unaltered in their state constitutions. Quite the reverse. As has already been said, the Ordinance, in the first stage of territorial government, assigned the whole of the legislative, executive, and judicial functions to the governor and judges appointed from above; and hemmed in with property qualifications the offices themselves, and the suffrage grudgingly doled out in the second state of territorial government. In sharp contrast, the first state constitutions of Ohio, Indiana, and Illinois established manhood suffrage and made governors mere figure heads, with scarcely power to do more than draw the meager salaries constitutionally assigned to them; those constitutions rendered courts and judges subject to the election and recall of the legislative representatives of the people. . . .

Having said all these things in dispraise of the Ordinance, one might well ask whence its sanctity, whence its greatness, whence its abiding place of honor in American institutions? The answer is not difficult. Once again one should remember that historical truth is not single and simple but manifold and complex. In the 1820's, the Ordinance was a sacred thing. Representatives of the Northwest Territory in Congress averred that to their constituents it was a pillar of cloud by day and a pillar of fire by night. It could be invoked as a sacred oracle to prohibit the extension of slavery into a state of the Northwest. Friends and partisans of the statesmen who had framed it could contend eagerly over the honor of authorship. "It approaches," said Judge Timothy Walker of Ohio, "as nearly to absolute perfection as anything to be found in the legislation of mankind; for after the experience of fifty years it would perhaps be impossible to alter without marring it." The answer must be that, with all its defects and shortcomings, the Ordinance embodied the policy, the theory of government and the ideal which, in the large, had worked, and worked so brilliantly in the first expansion of the American political system beyond the Alleghenies and to the Mississippi River. A colonizing system so successful that men scarcely recognized it for such, a balance of local autonomy and central authority so exact that it seemed inevitable—those were the things which gave the Ordinance its prestige and its sanctity. Seeing it as the adaptation of an ideal of government to a situation, it can best be appraised in the light of earlier national attitudes toward the West and its settlement.

One might begin with the policy of France in the Old Northwest as it developed from the latter half of the seventeenth century. It would be more true than false to say that with the exception of the settlements in the American Bottom and at Detroit, the French government never wished nor expected an extensive colonization of the West by Frenchmen. . . .

Actually, the French policy in the occupation of the West appears to have been a fine drawn scheme of diplomacy in which the very aptitude of the Indian in that form of politics could be used to involve him in elaborate and far-reaching spider webs of entangling alliances. Once enmeshed, the tribes had perforce to further the ends of French policy, even to lifting the tomahawk against any of their fellow prisoners who struggled to free themselves. French commandants in the West were not so much commanders of frontier garrisons around which settlements might spring up, as military and diplomatic representatives accredited to certain tribes. The commandants at Miamis, Ouiatenon, Vincennes, and St. Joseph were really the French residents near the Miami Confederacy, the Wea, the Piankeshaws, and the Pottawotomie. . . .

When the English, in the negotiations of the Treaty of 1763, bargained for the extension of their frontier to the Mississippi River, they scarcely contemplated any general settlement of the region. Originally, they had entered into the war with the idea of protecting the western frontiers of their colonies against French encroachment. In placing the boundary between the two nations in America at the Mississippi, they intended solely to keep their subjects so far apart that there would be no opportunity for future disputes. When they declared that they would probably never deforest or settle those regions, they were undoubtedly speaking at least as sincerely as diplomats ever do. Actually, Pontiac's insurrection made them acutely aware of French habitants in the West encouraging the Indian resistance. They hastened as soon as they could to occupy the Mississippi line, in the hope of bringing the French frontiersmen to heel; and were disappointed at finding that the French authorities did not take away their inhabitants when they departed. Until 1774 they made no provision for their government, other than autocratic military rule. As Louise P. Kellogg has shown, they seriously considered concentrating all French inhabitants in one village in order to deal with them in easier fashion.

On their own frontiers, however, the English had a somewhat different problem. In the backwoods of their colonies, they had a population recruited from a half dozen nationalities, including half a dozen economic classes, pressing westward with a blind urge which seems subconscious and biological. Anyone who has worked in the sources of the western movement can visualize for himself rough, barbarous families, far more prolific than the red men, now venting on the Indians cruelties as savage as those of the Indians themselves; now pressing in foolhardy fashion to establish their cabins and cornfields close to hostile villages; now fleeing in equally blind panic back to the frontiers. Sometimes they were savages, sometimes cowards, sometimes heroes, but always a force to be reckoned with from their antlike instinct to reproduce their species and to leave their children in a better station of life than they had been. A recurrence of this population in generation after generation, farther and farther west on the advancing frontier has been a commonplace of American history for almost half a century; and the control, the management, the repression of this element, to say nothing of the land speculators who exploited it, was one of the problems respecting the western country that confronted Great Britain.

The un-wisdom with which the British ministry dealt with it is written large across the history of the American Revolution. . . .

The answer to the Quebec Act is the American Revolution, the settlement of Kentucky, the occupation of the Illinois country and the Ohio Valley in the name of Virginia, and the Old Dominion's grandiloquent attempt to extend her frontiers west and northwest to encompass the whole land. Actually, her conquest was but partial. Inspired by land companies possessing speculative titles in the region, Virginia's sister colonies acidly called attention to her neglect of the tasks assigned her in the common cause. In 1781, her great soldier, George Rogers Clark failed in his last attempt on Detroit. With her chance to gain possession of the whole Northwest forever gone, Virginia was perforce compelled to bargain away to the Confederation her title to the fringe of her military occupation along the Ohio and the Mississippi. In doing this, she stipulated a guarantee of her right to Kentucky and that none of the land companies who had banded together and had stirred up the landless states to oppose her wider claims should profit one acre by her cessions.

But the problem of the West remained the most serious one. The Treaty of 1783 had given the United States the title to the Northwest, but only a paper title. Spain or Great Britain or possibly even France might well be expected to wrest the region from the United States, seemingly too feeble to maintain her hold on it by diplomacy or by the sword, or even to begin its economic exploitation. The frontiersmen, treated as step-children by the older states of Kentucky and Tennessee, deprived of all stable government northwest of the Ohio, slipping into anarchy, their trade outlets to the south and to the north controlled by Spain and England, stood on a pivot between older states to which they were tied by blood and by old political habit and the great empires to the north and to the south which seemingly could offer much more in their economic development.

To the rescue of the West two great Virginians stepped forward, each by the method to which his hand naturally turned. While Washington, the man of action, plunged into the wilderness he had known since his boyhood, to search out trade routes by which the two sides of the Alleghenies might profitably carry on commerce with each other, Jefferson, the man of contemplation, thought of political means and of political ideas which might bind the men of the western waters to the men of the Atlantic seaboard. The problem seemed to be two-fold. On the one hand, without strong government, the West might either drift into allegiance to Great Britain or Spain or else by some act of lawlessness involve the infant confederacy in a disastrous war with one power or the other. Central control there must be. On the other hand, if the tidewater was to play the same step-mother's role toward the western settlers that Great Britain had played to the tidewater settlers in the days before the Revolution, the West was as good as gone. If the land speculator buying up his land in vast tracts from a government too lazy to sell it retail, insisted on exacting an exorbitant wholesaler's profit from the men who must till it in the sweat of their brows, an economic revolution must inevitably accompany the political one.

In seeking a solution, Jefferson, even as he had deftly woven the ideas and aspirations of revolutionary America into the Declaration of Independence, brought together things both old and new that might solve the problem. His work during the winter and spring of 1784 as a member of the Congress of the Confederation was as significant as that of any other period of his life. There can be little doubt that the initiative was his in the framing of the Ordinance of 1784. Adapting an earlier suggestion to his end, on the map of the western country, he drew a checkerboard of states from one hundred to one hundred and fifty miles in dimension. The states were plotted in the idea that river systems and large bodies of water were economic unities, rather than boundaries of political division. In each one of these divisions, once the Indian title had been extinguished and the lands put on sale, he imagined a little community of free men meeting together to devise themselves a government. Because little time could be spared to this task from the harsh struggle of wresting a living from the wilderness, because law books would be few and statesmen fewer, he imagined them adopting the constitution and the laws of some one of the thirteen states. Thus he imagined them governing themselves, sending an observer to the government of the Confederation, and finally, once they had attained a population comparable to that of a state, gaining admission to the Confederation on full equality with the older states.

Asking himself what security there could be that the people in this community would remain in due subordination to the central government, or what security they could themselves expect for their admission to the Union in the fullness of time, he recognized immediately that no such system could possibly rest on coercion or force. The most bigoted strong-government man would admit the impossibility of the government's ever using military force to secure obedience in the west country; but the political theory which Jefferson and his fellows had taught in the American

Revolution pointed to compact as the true origin of all free government, pointed to free and unforced covenant or agreement as the highest and most sacred sanction for political power known among men. Therefore, to invest the Ordinance of 1784 with the highest sanctity and authority, he inserted in it articles of compact between the people of the older states and the people of the newer West, to bind them forever into political unity, and to serve as the guarantee of the bargains implied on either side. As a great idealist, he inserted also the great prohibition of slavery, north as well as south of the Ohio, only to see it struck out, as he bitterly commented, because of one man's illness in his own Virginia delegation.

Fitting exactly into his larger project, was the Ordinance of 1784 for the sale of lands, later in the Ordinance of 1785 destined to be expanded into the land policy of the United States. Again in his draft land ordinance he borrowed from ideas already current, but he also invented and coordinated. But the underlying concept is a great system of rectangular surveys so simple that a plain man may see for himself where his land lies and its metes and bounds. It is moreover a system in which the government will trouble to sell at retail in tracts so small that a half dozen families may at least club together to buy without paying tribute to a land speculator. Superimpose on this system a series of treaties extinguishing Indian titles, and Jefferson's concept for saving the West by political wisdom stands revealed. . . .

But what of the significance of the Ordinance in the more distant perspective of history? Some months ago one of the most prized members of this association was promoting before a congressional committee an undertaking of vital interest to the Mississippi Valley Historical Association. As he unfolded a plan of action reaching to the year 1949 a congressman asked him if he expected the United States to last so long. The author of this paper admits that he was deeply impressed only by the patient good humor of his fellow member's answer. His own temptation would have been to quote the greengrocer in Shaw's play, "Ah, the world will go on, ma'am: don't you be afraid of that. It ain't as easy to stop it as the earnest kind of people think."

But admitting for the moment that the political civilization of the United States may in the distant future be submerged beneath communism, fascism, race worship, technocracy, or whatever fashions in government that future may bring forth, the fact remains that very often time permits political ideals to outlive the death of the civilization that produces them. The Athenian democracy of Pericles lies buried under more than a score of centuries; it has suffered the drums and tramplings of twenty conquests; it is overlaid by the strata of twenty tyrannies. But there survives that funeral oration of Pericles in which he commemorated men whose lives their country's freedom had made so precious that for that country they freely laid down their lives. That endures and men this night may hearten themselves by it in lands where they must go into their innermost chambers to meditate on it.

And a precious part of the world's heritage in distant ages to come, whatever may have befallen the United States, will be the ideas that men may not permanently by their brothers be held in political subordination and clientage; and that the highest and most sacred guarantee, the most practical and stable cement of states and governments is the free and unforced covenant and agreement of man and man.

3. Harrison, Tecumseh, and Territorial Politics

Indiana was part of the Northwest Territory from its organization in 1787 until the establishment of a separate Indiana Territory in 1800. The events of paramount importance during this time were the establishment of a government headed by Arthur St. Clair; the eventual defeat of the Indians in Ohio in 1794, after two unsuccessful tries; and the passage of the territory into second stage government in 1798.

Young William Henry Harrison was with General Anthony Wayne as he carefully plotted his moves leading to the decisive Battle of Fallen Timbers. Following that battle came the establishment of Fort Wayne at the strategic three-river site of former settlements of both the French and the Indians; and then came the Treaty of Greenville (1795), which provided for the removal of the Miamis and other Indians westward. Thus Indiana became the area of the next major Indian-white confrontation, culminating in the Battle of Tippecanoe (1811) and the war that followed.

Shortly after the Treaty of Greenville, when the Northwest Territory advanced governmentally into the semirepresentational stage, William Henry Harrison became the first territorial delegate to Congress from the nation's first territory. Appointed to this position in 1798, he served during the 1799–1800 session. Although delegates were not allowed to vote on legislation, they handled all the other duties of congressmen. Interestingly, Harrison is credited with a role in two major pieces of legislation during his brief tenure as delegate: the (Harrison) Land Act of 1800, and the establishment of a separate Indiana Territory. President John Adams then appointed Harrison territorial governor, a post the transplanted Virginian held through three reappointments by Presidents Jefferson and Madison.

During Harrison's tenure as governor of the Indiana Territory from 1800 to 1812, he had the dual responsibility of governing the huge area and of maintaining peaceful relations with the Indians while getting title to as much of the land as necessary. Initially, the Indiana Territory comprised all of the former Northwest Territory except for essentially what was to become the state of Ohio in 1803. But in 1805 the Michigan Territory, and in 1809 the Illinois Territory, which included everything west of the Indiana-Illinois boundary, were given their own governments. Despite the enormity and incongruity of Harrison's tasks, the new governor performed satisfactorily in all areas. By a series of treaties, he obtained title from various Indian tribes to most of the southern third of Indiana, in addition to other portions of land where white men had already settled. When Tecumseh and his brother, known as the Prophet, decided that the Treaty of Fort Wayne (1809) had gone too far, and planned an organized resistance to further encroachments, Harrison took the initiative and the opportunity afforded by Tecumseh's temporary absence from the scene in the fall of 1811 to win an ultimately decisive victory over the Prophet at Tippecanoe.

In the meantime, Harrison had established a government at the settlement at Vincennes, thriving by that time, where he built for himself an imposing brick mansion, Grouseland, which still stands. And he developed into a capable, even astute, frontier politician. There were many issues dividing the small but growing number of pioneers who came to Indiana during its territorial period. However, the political differences tended to be more personally focused as differences between the aristocratic Harrison's followers, who had settled for the most part in southwestern Indiana, and the anti-Harrison people, who were concentrated in the eastern and southeastern sections of the territory. Perhaps surprisingly, slavery in the supposedly slave-free land "North West of the river Ohio" was one of the major issues; others involved matters of local self-government; the location of the territorial capital, especially after the 1809 loss of Illinois from Vincennes jurisdiction; and personality conflicts between Harrison and the eventual leader of the anti-Harrison bloc, long-time territorial delegate Jonathan Jennings.

The War of 1812, despite the early conflict at Tippecanoe, which was continued by the same parties, had little direct impact on the territory. For defenses against Indian raids, a number of blockhouses were erected across the southern tier of Indiana, especially after the bloody massacre at Pigeon Roost late in 1812; but few battles were fought in the region. Governor Harrison resigned his political office early in the war and distinguished himself again as a successful military commander through his invasion of upper Canada. At the Battle of the Thames, his most important victory in the war, Harrison once again confronted Tecumseh, now an ally of the British; but the resourceful Indian leader was killed during the battle.

At war's end, the country resumed its westward march more vigorously than ever before. Soon Indiana had the required minimum population for statehood. In a rapid series of events in 1815 and 1816, including a constitutional convention at the new territorial capital of Corydon in June 1816, Indiana became the nineteenth state of the Union on December 11, 1816.

For information on the territorial period in Indiana, see especially Dorothy B. Goebel, *William Henry Harrison* (1926), and John D. Barnhart and Dorothy L. Riker, *Indiana to 1816: The Colonial Period* (1971). See also Logan Esarey, ed., *Messages and Letters of William Henry Harrison* (2 vols., 1922), Hubert H. Hawkins, ed., *Indiana's Road to Statehood* (1964), and Gayle Thornbrough, ed., *The Correspondence of John Badollet and Albert Gallatin, 1804–1836* (1963). More recently, in a pair of biographies of the famous Shawnee brothers, R. David Edmunds has suggested a greater role for Tenskwatawa (The Prophet) in organizing an Indiana resistance to white encroachment upon their lands. See *The Shawnee Prophet* (1983) and *Tecumseh and the Quest for Indiana Leadership* (1989).

Contrary Patterns in Territorial Life

The Indiana territorial period lasted sixteen years. During most of this time peace prevailed, and Governor William Henry Harrison was primarily involved in administering the area and in obtaining land cessions from the Indians. Although partisan politics was absent, since there were few if any Federalists in the territory, there was much political rivalry based on support for or disapproval of Harrison and his Virginia coterie. In time this opposition was led by Jonathan Jennings, Indiana's territorial delegate from 1809 to 1816, when he became the first governor of the state.

There were, however, a number of issues that divided the growing number of territorial pioneers and enlivened public discussion. They included the court system and the administration of justice, the formation of new counties, advancement into second- and third-stage government, popular participation in political affairs, Indian affairs, and the tormenting issue of slavery. According to the two authors represented below, John D. Barnhart and Jacob P. Dunn, the dominant features of territorial life were, paradoxically, a remarkable growth in democratic practices and the continuation of slavery under another name. At the same time that property qualifications for suffrage were being removed, and election rather than appointment to the upper house of the territorial legislature was being approved, along with popular election of the territorial delegate to Congress, legislative sanction designed to perpetuate slavery under long—even interminable—contracts was also being granted.

In 1805 the Indiana legislature adopted an act permitting slaves to be brought into the territory and, if over the age of fifteen, bound for service "for any term of years."[1] Slaves under fifteen were to be registered and to serve to the age of thirty-five if male, thirty-two if female. Under the terms of this act, which remained in force until 1810, indentures of twenty to forty years in duration were common, and Professor Thornbrough discovered two indentures calling for terms of service of ninety years, and two more of ninety-nine years. After 1810 no new slaves could be brought into the territory and held under indentures; but the existing agreements were not affected. Clearly, the prohibition of slavery set forth in the Northwest Ordinance was not absolute. But in the view of historian Jacob P. Dunn, the inclusion of a slavery prohibition clause in the Indiana Constitution of 1816 marked the state's "redemption from slavery." For further analysis of this issue see Paul Finkelman, "Slavery and the Northwest Ordinance: A Study in Ambiguity," *Journal of the Early Republic*, VI (Winter, 1986), 343–370.

Professor Barnhart has examined the concurrent growth of democratic practices and their widespread influence in Indiana and surrounding states in his book *Valley*

1. Emma Lou Thornbrough, *The Negro in Indiana: A Study of a Minority* (1957), p. 9.

of Democracy: The Frontier versus the Plantation, 1775–1818 (1953). A professor of history at Indiana University for many years, he is also the author of a number of articles concerning the sources of migration into the Midwest. Mr. Dunn, in addition to his history of the state to 1816, *Indiana: A Redemption from Slavery* (1888), also wrote *Indiana and Indianans: A History of Aboriginal and Territorial Indiana and the Century of Statehood* (5 vols., 1919).

DEMOCRATIC INFLUENCES IN TERRITORIAL INDIANA

John D. Barnhart

The population of Indiana Territory was approximately twenty-five thousand in 1810, when Indian difficulties were soon to check migration for a short time. The trails as well as the nativities of the early settlers indicate that this population came largely from south of the Ohio River and practically all over trails through Pennsylvania and the Southern states.

The experiences of this frontier population in establishing its social and political institutions form an interesting and significant chapter in the development of frontier democracy. The forces which handicapped the influence of the frontier in the South were absent or so weak as to be unable to control the formation of government and society. Largely lacking were the numerous planters and their slaves. Undemocratic state governments with their policies which favored land speculation, slavery, and aristocracy were not in control. Climate and other geographic forces did not make possible an agricultural regime based upon staple products such as cotton, rice, indigo, or tobacco.

A few aspired to be country gentlemen in imitation of the planter class, farms were often called plantations, a few colored slaves and workers were held as house servants, and land speculation existed on every hand, but more often it was the activity of the small landholder rather than of the rich who dealt in thousands of acres. The little coterie of able men who gathered around Harrison at Vincennes came to be called the Virginia Aristocrats. Negro servants were held by some of them. Aristocratic manners, characteristic of the plantation South or of the old country, had been carried into this frontier region. General James Dill, a native of Ireland and a Harrison appointee, attended court as a prosecuting attorney in the costume of a gentleman of the Revolutionary period, knee breeches, silver buckles, and cue, "a mild protest against the leveling tendencies of the age" and of the frontier.

But the character of society was not determined by these forces. The larger number of citizens were small landowners and squatters. Until the land was surveyed and

From "The Democratization of Indiana Territory," *Indiana Magazine of History,* XLIII (March 1947), 8–11, 13–17, 20–22. Reprinted by permission of the Editor, *Indiana Magazine of History.*

placed on sale, nearly all were squatters. When the sales were opened, those who had the money bought small pieces of land. Since the credit system held sway from 1800 to 1820, many a poor man got together enough money to make the first payment and then hoped that industry and good fortune would enable him to meet the succeeding payments before it was too late. The arrears of interest and principal indicate that many had been too optimistic. But the point is that the Indiana frontier was a poor man's home and its development in the formative period was shaped by frontier influences.

The law which created Indiana Territory re-established the same nonrepresentative type of government which existed in the first stage of the Northwest Territory. William Henry Harrison, the governor of the new territory, had gained experience in the former where he served for short periods as secretary and delegate to Congress. He avoided many of the arbitrary acts of St. Clair, but his policies and appointments as governor attracted to him many of the more conservative leaders and antagonized a few vigorous men and a growing number of the newer settlers. Although the secretary, John Gibson, spent his life along the frontier from Pittsburgh to Vincennes, he had little influence upon the government, and the judges were not noted for their sympathy with the ways of the frontiersmen. From the beginning, however, there was much interest taken in the acts of government, and neither the efforts of the people to make the government more democratic nor the governor's critics were suppressed. An almost immediate and continuous movement was begun to make the government not only responsive to the wishes and needs of the people, but also to place it in their hands.

The causes of this movement might be classified as the conditions which produced discontent and the developments which gave the people the opportunity to participate in their own government. Some of them were the lack of unity in a territory which included remote settlements occupied by people of different origins, connections, and interests, as well as the uncertainty of land titles, the activity of land speculators, and the claims of the Indians to large parts of the territory. But the desire of the people for greater self-government, the political ambitions of various individuals, the efforts to legalize slavery, and the difference of opinion as to the best methods of attracting settlers to the country were also involved. Perhaps this latter point has not received enough attention. Persons of aristocratic tendencies placed much emphasis upon the importance of securing men of wealth, family, and education. The closest source of such settlers was the planter class of Kentucky and other Southern states. The planters owned slaves, hence the efforts to legalize slavery. On the other hand, the democratic masses from the South, many of whom had there suffered political, social, and economic discriminations, and settlers from the North were not enthusiastic about the pretensions of the aristocrats to superior talents and they were not willing to pay the price of their coming,—the admission of slavery. It was the old contest of a white man's society with democratic features against the planters' social order with its aristocratic characteristics. Often the contest degenerated into petty quarrels in which every act of the governor was attacked and defended with spirit and acrimony, but if one sees only these disputes, the trees have obscured the forest.

The territorial history of Indiana falls rather naturally into five divisions. There was the unrepresentative stage of territorial government which lasted four years, the early part of the second stage before the separation of Illinois Territory in 1809, the shorter term between the division of the territory and the resumption of Indian warfare, the three years of warfare from the Tippecanoe campaign in 1811 to the end of Harrison's campaign in 1813, and finally the successful struggle for statehood, 1814–1816. . . .

The first period of territorial government came to an end when Harrison reversed his position on the advisability of passing into the second or semi-representative stage of government in 1804. Petitions, he stated, were presented to him asking for representative government. To ascertain the wishes of a majority, he called an election on September 11, at which time the majority of those voting, favored the change. The governor proclaimed the second stage and called an election of representatives for the lower house of the territorial assembly.

Whether the change represented the wishes of the majority or not, a violent newspaper controversy broke out, in which Harrison's critics soon made known their opposition. "A Freeholder of Knox County," who was probably William McIntosh, criticized Harrison's sponsorship of the Vincennes Convention as well as a recent meeting in Vincennes for the purpose of petitioning for the second stage. He asserted that the advance should have come spontaneously and not have been forced by the governor. The meeting to which he referred had adopted an address in which objection was made to the limited legislative powers of the governor and judges, to the power of Congress to countermand their action, to the unsuitability of the laws of other states for Indiana Territory, and to a lack of a voice in any act of the territorial or national government. In extravagant language, the address referred to the first stage of territorial government as the most abominable and tyrannical system ever organized for freemen. The second stage was described as imperfect but as an improvement. It also asserted that the expenses would not be too heavy, that a delegate in Congress was needed, and that able men could be found to serve in the legislative assembly. "Gerald," who was probably Benjamin Parke, asserted that the petitions induced a strong belief that a majority of the freeholders wanted the change in government, while "A Citizen," probably McIntosh, denied this, and a "Plough Boy" defended the governor. Name calling and heat were soon substituted for reasoning, the writers revealed each other's identity, and Parke obviously tried to provoke McIntosh into challenging him to a duel, but the latter asked Parke if calumny was Harrison's last defense.

For a time, however, Harrison and his supporters kept things well in hand. President Thomas Jefferson requested Harrison to choose for him the five members of the upper house of the legislature and Benjamin Parke, Harrison's close friend, was elected delegate to Congress.

The territorial legislature functioned with reasonable wisdom, thus denying the allegation that the territory lacked the necessary men of talents. Two of the measures which seem to demonstrate the good sense of its members were the substitution of a single county court for the earlier complicated system, and the codification of the laws. More important was the gradual assertion and execution of the wishes of the people in a territorial government that was only partially representative. . . .

The territorial legislature soon reflected the sentiment of the people. The second session of the second General Assembly which began on September 26, 1808, indicated a growing appreciation of its powers and of the popular will in contrast to the wishes of the governor and his supporters. The legislative council petitioned Congress that its members should be popularly elected, and the lower house petitioned the division of the territory and the popular election of the delegate to Congress. The representatives may have exceeded their authority to be certain that a federal officer should not have a seat in the legislative council. After a number of petitions opposing slavery were received and after General W. Johnston delivered a very able report against the admission of slavery, the representatives voted unanimously to repeal the territorial act concerning the introduction of Negroes and mulattoes into the territory, but the repeal was rejected by the upper house. The lower house also petitioned that the veto power and other controls over the legislature be restricted. Jesse B. Thomas was chosen to be the delegate to Congress after he pledged himself to work for the division of the territory. It has been pointed out that the election of Thomas was due to a union of the antislavery forces east of the Wabash with the proslavery forces west of the Wabash in opposition to the Harrison party, without recognizing clearly that this union indicated that slavery was not the leading issue. It was Harrison's first serious defeat and from it stemmed the events which gave the popular party control of the legislature after the division of the territory.

Congress responded to these demonstrations of the popular will by providing for the popular election of the councilors and the delegate to Congress, and for the division of the territory by the creation of Illinois Territory. The Harrison group was now face to face with a growing popular party which already included a majority of the people in the new Indiana Territory and which received the opportunity to control the entire legislative branch of the government as well as the delegate to Congress. Harrison remained quite popular, perhaps in part because he was public spirited and above much of the petty politics which accompanied the larger struggle.

The changes in the structure of the territorial government caused a long and acrimonious contest in 1809 which revealed a democratic spirit and procedure in advance of its time. The regular election for members of the legislature was held on April 3, 1809, before official word was received of division. Additional members were made necessary by division and new members and the delegate to Congress were elected on May 22. Throughout the early months of the year, the partisan controversy was waged in the columns of the *Western Sun*, through handbills, and in public meetings. Even after the last election, there were charges and counter charges, explanations for what had happened, and an anti-climactical campaign for and against the reappointment of Governor Harrison. The election resulted in the choice of Jonathan Jennings as delegate to Congress in which position he became the leader of the anti-Harrison forces. The upper house of the territorial legislature was chosen for the first time by the voters. The legislative results of the election and the protests of the Harrison leaders leave no doubt of the significance of the results. . . .

When the elections for the new legislature were called in 1810, there was only a slight revival of the contest of the preceding year. Outside of Knox County the popular party was successful, and in Knox, General W. Johnston, who was not a Harrisonite, was elected as one of the representatives. This legislature wrote the victory of the popular party into law. New counties were formed, members of the legislature were apportioned, the date for the election of the congressional delegate was set, the indenture law was repealed, and the law requiring servants of color to fulfill the contracts under which they entered the territory was also repealed. Nothing is more revealing than Harrison's failure to use his absolute veto upon any of these acts. No longer was his influence dominant. His friends could not browbeat a critic into silence, and he was willing to give up the struggle if peace could be restored.

But some of his followers and many of his opponents were unwilling to make peace. The people were unwilling to give up the democratic advances and, indeed, wanted to make their government more democratic. The violent storm in the press, however, ceased and something very much like a calm ensued. Jennings endeavored to persuade Congress to declare ineligible for election to the legislature officers appointed by Harrison, to remove the territorial capital from Vincennes, to grant manhood suffrage, and to provide for the election of sheriffs in place of appointment by the governor. He even wrote about filing impeachment charges against the governor. Two petitions were sent to Congress late in 1811 complaining of Harrison's interference in elections and asking that officials of the United States be prohibited from interfering improperly in elections. When Harrison vetoed a bill to move the capital from Vincennes, the people of Jefferson County petitioned that the veto power be taken from him.

Congress, in response to the wishes of the petitioners, extended the franchise to free white adult males who paid taxes, and made ineligible to seats in the territorial legislature the officers appointed by Harrison except the justices of the peace and the officers of the militia. Jennings was reelected in April, 1811, again defeating Thomas Randolph, in fact he served for the remainder of the territorial period. The territorial legislature transferred the conduct of the elections from the sheriffs to the judges of the court of common pleas, provided that polls be opened in each township in contrast to one in each county, and changed the method of voting from *viva voce* to written ballots. It is quite possible that the change in the number of polling places enfranchised more persons than the Congressional act extending the right of suffrage. The seat of government was soon moved from Vincennes to Corydon where the governor's political friends were much less numerous. This measure, however, was not so important as the broadening of the franchise and the election law.

The advance to the second territorial stage of semi-representative government, the division of the territory, the election of delegates to Congress who were representatives of the opposition, the winning of control of the territorial legislature, the repeal of the acts which encouraged the violation of the prohibition of slavery, the extension of the franchise, the democratization of the territorial government, and the subduing of Harrison and his more aggressive supporters constituted a democratic victory of significant proportions. In a very real sense the democratic forces won their victory in the territorial period in contrast to the earlier territories in the Ohio Valley where the popular advance came when state constitutions were adopted. Only the election of the executive, the escape from Congressional supervision of local affairs, and full participation in national affairs, all of which could be secured only when the territory became a state, remained to be won. In Indiana Territory the popular victory was complete except for these. The people had gone as far as they could in creating a democratic government, the final step would complete the victory. That step was statehood.

SLAVERY IN THE INDIANA TERRITORY

Jacob Piatt Dunn

Naturally the interest of the people was absorbed in the convention. It was the great event of the period. But more than all else they were anxious to know just what would be done in regard to slavery. An estimable lady of Lawrenceburgh, who preserves her faculties unimpaired at the advanced age of eighty-five years, informs me that she remembers clearly the day when the news of the final action reached that place, and that the message which passed from mouth to mouth was, "She has come in free! She has come in free!" Other matters were not of so much importance, and there was a quiet faith that they had been properly cared for. And yet after all this controversy, and all the care of the convention, the slavery question was not yet definitely settled. As to the effect of the Constitution on future importations there was no question, but as to its effect on pre-existent slavery and servitude there remained a wide divergence of opinion. In the eastern counties it was generally considered that slaves and servants were emancipated, and masters acted on that theory, though still feeling themselves charged with the care of keeping their old servitors from want. One master told his negro man and woman that they were free, and might do whatever they liked. If they desired it, he would give them a cabin and bit of land and they might take care of themselves; or, if they preferred, they might continue to live with him, and he would give them a wage allowance and care for them. After a protracted consideration of the subject they concluded to remain. Another master made a similar proposal to his negro woman, but she replied, "No, damn you! I'll go to Cincinnati and soon be as rich as any of you." And sure enough she did locate at Cincinnati, opened a little eating-house, and acquired a competence. This difference of sentiment was due only to the spirit of the negroes, for they were all treated kindly.

In the western counties a few masters removed their slaves from the State, and some of these were afterwards released by the courts of Southern States, as we have seen. The great majority, however, simply continued to hold their slaves in Indiana. The idea which commonly obtained was that the Constitution could have no effect on preëxisting slavery; that the property in slaves was a vested right, secured by the Ordinance, and

---

From *Indiana: A Redemption from Slavery* (1888), pp. 430–435, 442–444.

could not be impaired. Even the courts in that section proceeded on this theory. The first case in which the question was involved came to trial on October 5, 1816, before David Raymond, president judge of the first circuit. It was a replevin suit brought against Thomas Jones by Mason Pecongar *alias* The Owl, an Indian who had adopted civilized life and settled near Vincennes, for the recovery of a colored girl and a cross-cut saw. The jury found for the plaintiff as to the girl, but a new trial was granted and the case was continued. It was settled out of court, for no further mention of it occurs in the records. In 1817, Bob and Anthony, held as slaves by Luke Decker, Jr., brought suit for their freedom in Orange County. They were sons of Dinah, a female slave brought by Luke Decker, Sr., from Virginia, prior to 1787. They gained their freedom, but not until the case had been fought for five years in various courts, and after the question involved had been decided by the Supreme Court in another case, which we will examine presently.

The masters of indented negroes in this section also held to their servants, probably from an enlargement of that quality of the mind which gives one a vague sense of ownership in anything he has once owned. In fact many of them were not sufficiently versed in the intricacies of the law to perceive any distinction between their cases and those of the ancient inhabitants. If this point of vested rights was of any importance, they had their slaves before the adoption of the Constitution as well as the older settlers. Of course there was understood to be a reservation of rights to the ancient inhabitants by the Ordinance, but what did that amount to? The property of a freeborn American less sacred than that of a Frenchman? Perish the thought! This was the line of argument of the statesman from "Egypt" with the *lucus a non lucendo* name, Mr. John Grammar, who said in the Illinois legislature, on a proposition to emancipate indented slaves: "I will show that are proposition is unconstitutionable, inlegal, and fornenst the compact. Don't every one know, or leastwise had ought to know, that the Congress that sot at Post Vinsan garnisheed to the old French inhabitants the right to hold their niggers, and haint I got as much rights as any Frenchman in this state? Answer me that, sir."

It must be confessed, too, that no very strict regard was paid to the rights of indented negroes. An illustrative instance is recorded by Sol Smith, the great theatrical pioneer of the Mississippi valley, who was even more famous and popular in his day than his namesake Sol Smith Russell is now. In 1819 he served for a time as an apprentice at Vincennes, and in describing his experience there he thus refers to his master's wife: "This lady had been 'raised' in Kentucky, and having been in the habit of commanding slaves, and the laws of Indiana not permitting her to own any of those convenient appendages to a household, she made use of her husband's apprentices in place of them. She had one negro—his name was Thompson—who had been brought from Kentucky under indentures. He was to be free at the age of twenty-one, and he was now at least thirty-five! Mrs. ___ made him believe he was but fourteen, and that he had yet seven years to serve. Thompson used to ask us boys in the office if we didn't think he was fifteen years of age. Of course we could not encourage him in such abolitional ideas. So he served on in blessed ignorance, and whether he has yet arrived at the desired age of twenty-one I am not informed." There may be some slight exaggeration in this, for Sol Smith was not a man to let a story be spoiled for lack of a little color; but in its general tenor it would have applied to many cases in Indiana. The negroes were ignorant, and there were few persons who were willing to incur the enmity of their neighbors by interfering in their behalf. Hence there arose, as G. W. Johnston had reported in 1808, "the most flagitious abuse" of the indenture system.

It should be borne in mind that there was nothing secret or clandestine about slaveholding in the western counties. It was the common opinion that the Constitution had no effect on preëxistent slavery. Indented negroes and other slaves were advertised and sold publicly, and it is hardly necessary to say that this would not have occurred, for lack of purchasers, if there had been any serious question as to the titles to them. The custom continued with so little interruption that in the census of 1820 there were still reported one hundred and ninety slaves in Indiana,—only forty-seven less than there were in 1810. One hundred and eighteen of these were held in Knox County, thirty in Gibson, eleven in Posey, ten in Vanderburgh, and the remainder scattered in Owen, Perry, Pike, Scott, Sullivan, Spencer, and Warrick. In the other twenty-four counties no slaves were reported. . . .

If the writer has done his work properly, the reader now realizes that the slavery of Indiana, small as was its actual extent, was the chief agency in the moulding of our infant growth. It made political parties that otherwise would never have existed. It put men in office who but for it might have lived in obscurity. It excluded men from office who but for it would have been on our lists of public men. It put laws on our statute books, and erased them. It put articles in our first Constitution. It was the tap-root of our political growth,—the great central matter of controversy to which all other questions were subordinate. It drew broad party lines here when national party lines were practically blotted out; and when those lines were drawn, leaders of the dominant party were excused for offenses that would otherwise have ended their political careers, while leaders of the opposition suffered for the merest trifles. In short, it made a quarter of a century of our political history, and, at the end of that time, left the people of Indiana more strongly opposed to the institution of slavery than they ever could have been without it. It had some effect, too, in the councils of the nation, long after it had been disposed of; for when in the debate on the California bill, in June, 1850, the question arose as to slavery in the territory acquired from Mexico, the refusals of Congress to admit slavery to Indiana served as precedents against it.

More than this, if our work is well done, justice has been given to an almost forgotten generation of Indiana men. It has at various times been loosely stated that this man from the North, or that man from the South, saved Indiana from slavery. Not so. The men of Indiana did that. We honor Randolph, and Grayson, and Jefferson for their sentiments, as we do also Coit, and Dane, and King, but these men did not exclude slavery from Indiana, and, if we may believe the testimony that has been cited, they did not intend to do so. That we owe a debt of gratitude to the Congress that made the Ordinance, and to those that persisted in maintaining it as it was framed, is evident; but our gratitude cannot flow to either side of the line between North and South. If we consider the benefits derived from the Ordinance, we see benefactors from Virginia and Massachusetts standing side by side. If we look to the congressional action on petitions, we see that every Congress, regardless of politics, declined to amend the Ordinance. If we look to the composition of the congressional committees that acted on the petitions, we find them divided as evenly as possible between the North and the South, usually with an Indiana man in the balance; and of their six reports, three favoring the admission of slavery and three opposing it, we find two favoring and one opposing by chairmen from the North, and one favoring and two opposing by chairmen from the South; in no instance do we find a minority report. If we look to the sentiment of the nation at the climax of the struggle in Indiana in 1807, we find Congress almost a unit for the abolition of the slave-trade, and yet we find no effort in Congress, from any section, to nullify the indenture law, as the anti-slavery men of Indiana had asked them. If we look to the influence of literature, we find nothing from the North that had more effect in Indiana than Jefferson's "Notes on Virginia." At this day, when it seems fashionable to belittle Mr. Jefferson at all opportunities, we commend to the people of Indiana the consideration of how much of the great anti-slavery report of General W. Johnston, and the revolution of sentiment connected with it, may be justly attributed to the influence of the words of Thomas Jefferson. Nor is this suggestion thrown out for the purpose of bringing him into prominence to the disadvantage of his contemporaries from the North. It is merely to restore, for our own purposes, the historical balance which the reaction of recent years has falsified. Nothing can now detract from the influence he had in determining our early controversies, and nothing should obscure his just credit in our remembrance of it. We do not go beyond the bounds of our State to give praise for the final solution of our local slavery question, for Congress put the solution upon the men of Indiana and they worked it out on Indiana soil. For the privilege of solving it, under the Ordinance, without the interference of Congress, our thanks go abroad, but to no section. As to this we write, as was inscribed on our contribution to the great monument to the greatest of Americans: INDIANA KNOWS NO NORTH, NO SOUTH, NOTHING BUT THE UNION.

A Classic Confrontation

The most famous and significant confrontation of the territorial period occurred between Governor Harrison and the great Shawnee leader Tecumseh. After General Anthony Wayne, with whom Harrison had served in the 1790s, defeated the Indians at Fallen Timbers in northwestern Ohio, the next great clash between reds and whites came in Indiana. It was part of Harrison's duties as governor to act as Indian agent and arrange for land cessions. After several previous treaties transferring, at least in the eyes of the United States, land from the Indians to the Union, Harrison entered into new negotiations in 1809 at Fort Wayne. The resulting treaty with Delaware, Potawatomi, Miami, and Eel River tribes conveyed more than 2,800,000 acres of land to the United States, an event which prompted Tecumseh and his brother to begin stiffer resistance to white encroachment. Tecumseh personally explained his views to Harrison in a tense series of conferences in Vincennes during August 1810, after which Harrison increased his military preparations. Talks occurred again in late September 1811, when Tecumseh returned to Vincennes before continuing south in search of new recruits for the Indian confederation he hoped to organize.

At this time Harrison recorded his respect for Tecumseh as "one of those uncommon geniuses, which spring up occasionally to produce revolutions and overturn the established order of things. If it were not for the vicinity of the United States, he would perhaps be the founder of an Empire that would rival in glory, that of Mexico or Peru."[1] Harrison also made plans to act quickly during Tecumseh's absence and attack his base of power at Prophetstown. This led to the battle of Tippecanoe, fought on November 7, 1811.

Professor Marshall Smelser of the University of Notre Dame, a careful student of the early national period of American history, is the author of *The Democratic Republic, 1801–1815* (1968), a volume in the New American Nation series published by Harper & Row. The article from which the passages below were taken was based on an address delivered to the Society of Indiana Pioneers in 1963.

TECUMSEH, HARRISON, AND THE WAR OF 1812

Marshall Smelser

Indiana Territory had only twenty-five thousand citizens in 1810. When one reflects that the populations of Ohio and Kentucky combined were more than twenty-five times as great, it will be easily understood that the War of 1812 in the Old Northwest was more their war than it was Indiana's. Indiana was only a beachhead in the wilderness. The history of the war as it concerns Indiana is more biographical than geographical, more dramatic than analytic. This paper will treat it that way—as a high tragedy involving two able natural leaders. Like all tragedies, the course of its action gives the feeling that it was inevitable, that nothing could have been done to prevent its fatal termination. The story is the drama of the struggle of two of our most eminent predecessors, William Henry Harrison of Grouseland, Vincennes, and Tecumseh of the Prophet's town, Tippecanoe.

It is not easy to learn about wilderness Indians. The records of the Indians are

1. Quoted in John D. Barnhart and Donald F. Carmony, *Indiana: From Frontier to Industrial Commonwealth* (2 vols., 1954), I, 129.

From "Tecumseh, Harrison, and The War of 1812," *Indiana Magazine of History*, LXV (March 1969), 25, 28, 30–31, 33, 35, 37–39.

those kept by white men, who were not inclined to give themselves the worst of it. Lacking authentic documents, historians have neglected the Indians. The story of the Indian *can* be told but it has a higher probability of error than more conventional kinds of history. To tell the tale is like reporting the weather without scientific instruments. The reporter must be systematically, academically skeptical. He must read between the lines, looking for evidence of a copper-colored ghost in a deerskin shirt, flitting through a green and bloody world where tough people died from knives, arrows, war clubs, rifle bullets, and musket balls, and where the coming of spring was not necessarily an omen of easier living, but could make a red or white mother tremble because now the enemy could move concealed in the forest. But the reporter must proceed cautiously, letting the facts shape the story without prejudice.

. . . [O]ur story is a sad and somber one. It shows men at their bravest. It also shows men at their worst. We are dealing with a classic situation in which two great leaders—each a commander of the warriors of his people—move inexorably for a decade toward a confrontation which ends in the destruction of the one and the exaltation of the other. Tecumseh, a natural nobleman in a hopeless cause, and Harrison, a better soldier than he is generally credited with being, make this an Indiana story, although the last two acts of their tragedy were staged in Ohio and in Upper Canada. To understand why this deadly climax was inevitable we must know the Indian policy of the United States at that time; we must know, if we can, what the Indians thought of it; and we must know something about the condition of the Indians.

The federal government's Indian policy was almost wholly dedicated to the economic and military benefit of white people. When Congress created Indiana Territory, the United States was officially committed to educate and civilize the Indians. The program worked fairly well in the South for a time. Indiana Territory's Governor Harrison gave it an honest trial in the North, but the problems were greater than could be solved with the feeble means used. The management of Indian affairs was unintelligently complicated by overlapping authorities, a confused chain of command, and a stingy treasury—stingy, that is, when compared with the treasury of the more lavish British competitors for Indian favor. More to the point, most white Americans thought the Indians should be moved to the unsettled lands in the West. President Jefferson, for awhile, advocated teaching agriculture to the Indians, and he continued the operation of federal trading posts in the Indian country which had been set up to lessen the malevolent influence of private traders. These posts were successful by the standards of cost accounting, but they did nothing to advance the civilization of the Indian. Few white people wished the Indians well, and fewer would curb their appetites for fur and land just to benefit Indians.

The conflict between whites and Indians was not simple. The Indians were neither demons nor sculptured noble savages. They were not the single people Tecumseh claimed but were broken into fragments by language differences. Technologically they were farther behind the Long Knives—as the Indians called the frontiersmen—than the Gauls who died on Caesar's swords were behind the Romans. But they had a way of life that worked in its hard, cruel fashion. In the end, however, the Indian way of life was shattered by force; and the Indians lost their streams, their corn and bean fields, their forests.

Comparatively few white residents of the United States in 1801 had ever seen an Indian. East of the Mississippi River there were perhaps seventy thousand Indians, of whom only ten thousand lived north of the Ohio River. They were bewildered pawns of international politics, governed by the French to 1763, ruled in the name of George III of England to 1783, and never consulted about the change of sovereigns. As Governor Harrison himself said, they disliked the French least, because the French were content with a congenial joint occupation of the wilds while the white Americans and British had a fierce sense of the difference between mine and thine. The governor admitted the Indians had genuine grievances. It was not likely, for example, that a jury would convict a white man charged with murdering an Indian. Indians were shot in the forest north of Vincennes for no reason at all. Indians, Harrison reported, punished Indians for crimes against Long Knives, but the frontiersmen did not reciprocate. But the worst curse visited on the Indians by the whites was alcohol. Despite official gestures at prohibition, alcohol flowed unchecked in the Indian territory. Harrison said six hundred Indian warriors on the Wabash received six thousand gallons of whiskey a year. That would seem to work out to a fifth of whisky per week per family, and it did not come in a steady stream, but in alternating floods and ebbs.

Naturally Indian resentment flared. Indian rage was usually ferocious but temporary. Few took a long view. Among those who did were some great natural leaders, Massasoit's disillusioned son King Philip in the 1670s, Pontiac in the 1760s, and Tecumseh. But such leaders invariably found it hard to unite the Indians for more than a short time; regardless of motive or ability, their cause was hopeless. The Indians were a Stone Age people who depended for good weapons almost entirely on the Long Knives or the Redcoats. The rivalry of Britain and the United States made these dependent people even more dependent. Long Knives supplied whisky, salt, and tools. Redcoats supplied rum, beef, and muskets. The Indians could not defeat Iron Age men because these things became necessities to them, and they could not make them for themselves. But yielding gracefully to the impact of white men's presence and technology was no help to the Indians. The friendly Choctaw of present Mississippi, more numerous than all of the northwestern tribes together, were peaceful and cooperative. Their fate was nevertheless the same as the fate of the followers of King Philip, Pontiac, and Tecumseh.

The Indians had one asset—land. Their land, they thought, belonged to the family group so far as it was owned at all. No Indian had a more sophisticated idea of land title than that. And as for selling land, the whites had first to teach them that they owned it and then to teach them to sell it. Even then, some Indians very early developed the notion that land could only be transferred by the unanimous consent of all tribes concerned rather than through negotiations with a single tribe. Indian councils declared this policy to the Congress of the United States in 1783 and in 1793. If we follow James Truslow Adams' rule of thumb that an Indian family needed as many square miles of wilderness as a white family needed plowed acres, one may calculate that the seventy thousand Indians east of the Mississippi needed an area equal to all of the Old Northwest plus Kentucky, if they were to live the primitive life of their fathers. Therefore, if the Indians were to live as undisturbed primitives, there would be no hunting grounds to spare. And if the rule of unanimous land cessions prevailed, there would be no land sales so long as any tribal leader objected. Some did object, notably two eminent Shawnee: Tecumseh, who believed in collective bargaining, and his brother, the Prophet, who also scorned the Long Knives' tools, his whisky, and his civilization. Harrison dismissed the Prophet's attack on land treaties as the result of British influence, but collective conveyance was an old idea before the Shawnee medicine man took it up. The result of the federal government's policy of single tribe land treaties was to degrade the village chiefs who made the treaties and to exalt the angry warrior chiefs, like Tecumseh, who denounced the village chiefs, corrupted by whisky and other gifts, for selling what was not theirs to sell. . . .

By the time he found his life work Tecumseh was an impressive man, about five feet nine inches tall, muscular and well proportioned, with large but fine features in an oval face, light copper skin, excellent white teeth, and hazel eyes. His carriage was imperial, his manner energetic, and his temperament cheerful. His dress was less flashy than that of many of his fellow warriors. Except for a silver mounted tomahawk, quilled moccasins, and, in war, a medal of George III and a plume of ostrich feathers, he dressed simply in fringed buckskin. He knew enough English for ordinary conversation, but to assure accuracy he was careful to speak only Shawnee in diplomacy. Unlike many Indians he could count, at least as far as eighteen (as we know by his setting an appointment with Harrison eighteen days after opening the subject of a meeting). Military men later said he had a good eye for military topography and could extemporize crude tactical maps with the point of his knife. He is well remembered for his humanity to prisoners, being one of the few Indians of his day who disapproved of torturing and killing prisoners of war. This point is better documented than many other aspects of his character and career.

The Prophet rather than Tecumseh first captured the popular imagination. As late as 1810 Tecumseh was being referred to in official correspondence merely as the Prophet's brother. The Shawnee Prophet's preaching had touches of moral grandeur: respect for the aged, sharing of material goods with the needy, monogamy, chastity, and abstinence from alcohol. He urged a return to the old Indian ways and preached self-segregation from the white people. But he had an evil way with dissenters, denouncing them as witches and having several of them roasted alive. . . .

One of the skeptics unconverted by the Prophet and unimpressed by the divinity of his mission was Indiana Territory's first governor, William Henry Harrison, a retired regular officer, the son of a signer of the Declaration of Independence, appointed governor at the age of twenty-eight. Prudent, popular with Indians and whites, industrious, and intelligent, he had no easy job. He had to contend with land hunger, Indian resentments, the excesses of Indian traders, and with his constant suspicion of a British web of conspiracy spun from Fort Malden. The growing popularity of the Prophet alarmed Harrison, and early in 1806 he sent a speech by special messenger to the Delaware tribe to try to refute the Prophet's theology by Aristotelian formal logic. Harrison was not alone in his apprehensions. In Ohio the throngs of Indian pilgrims grew larger after the Prophet during the summer of 1806 correctly predicted an eclipse of the sun (forecast, of course, in every almanac) and took credit for it. A year later, when reports indicated the number of the Prophet's followers was increasing, the governor of Ohio alerted the militia and sent commissioners to investigate. They heard Blue Jacket deny any British influence on the Indians. At another meeting later at Chillicothe Tecumseh denounced all land treaties but promised peace. The governor of Ohio was temporarily satisfied, although Harrison still thought the Prophet spoke like a British agent and told the Shawnee what he thought. But in the fall of 1807 there was no witness, however hostile, who could prove that either Tecumseh or the Prophet preached war. On the contrary, every reported sermon and oration apparently promised peace. An ominous portent, however—at least in Harrison's eyes—was the founding of the Prophet's town on the Tippecanoe River, in May, 1808.

The Prophet visited Harrison at Vincennes late in the summer of 1808 to explain his divine mission to the incredulous young governor. Privately, and grudgingly, Harrison admitted the Prophet had reduced drunkenness, but he persisted in his belief that the Shawnee leader was a British agitator. The Prophet went to Vincennes again in 1809 and boasted of having prevented an Indian war. Harrison did not believe him. There is good evidence that in June, 1810, Tecumseh tried unsuccessfully to persuade the Shawnee of the Maumee Basin to move west in order to clear the woods for war. When Harrison learned this he sent a message to the Prophet's town. The "Seventeen Fires," he said, were invincible. The Redcoats could not help the Indians. But if the Indians thought the New Purchase Treaty made at Fort Wayne in 1809 was fraudulent, Harrison would arrange to pay their way to visit the President, who would hear their complaint. Tecumseh privately said he wished peace but could be pushed no farther. These rumblings and tremors of 1810 produced the first meeting of our two tragic protagonists.

Tecumseh paddled to Vincennes with four hundred armed warriors in mid August, 1810. In council he denounced the New Purchase Treaty and the village chiefs who had agreed to it. He said the warrior chiefs would rule Indian affairs thereafter. Harrison flatly denied Tecumseh's theory of collective ownership and guaranteed to defend by the sword what had been acquired by treaty. This meeting of leaders was certainly not a meeting of minds. A deadlock had been reached. A cold war had been started. During the rest of 1810 Harrison received nothing but bad news. The secretary of war suggested a surprise capture of the Shawnee brothers. Indians friendly to the United States predicted war. The governor of Missouri reported to Harrison that the Prophet had invited the tribes west of the Mississippi to join in a war, which was to begin with an attack against Vincennes. The Indians around Fort Dearborn were disaffected and restless. A delegation of Sauk came all the way from Wisconsin to visit Fort Malden. Two surveyors running the New Purchase line were carried off by the Wea.

In the summer of 1811 Tecumseh and about three hundred Indians returned to Vincennes for another inconclusive council in which neither he nor the governor converted the other. Tecumseh condescendingly advised against white settlement in the New Purchase because many Indians were going to settle at the Prophet's town in the fall and would need that area for hunting. Tecumseh said he was going south to enroll new allies. It is important to our story that Tecumseh was absent from Indiana in that autumn of crisis. Aside from this we need note only that on his southern tour he failed to rouse the Choctaw, although he had a powerful effect on the thousands of Creek who heard his eloquence.

At this point it is important to note Governor Harrison's continuing suspicion that Tecumseh and the Prophet were British agents, or at least were being stirred to hostility by the British. British official correspondence shows that Fort Malden was a free cafeteria for hungry Indians, having served them seventy-one thousand meals in the first eleven months of 1810. The correspondence also shows that Tecumseh, in 1810, told the British he planned for war in late 1811, but indicates that the British apparently promised him nothing.

The year 1811 was a hard one for the Indians because the Napoleonic wars had sharply reduced the European market for furs. The Indians were in a state that we would call a depression. And we should remember that while Tecumseh helped the British in the War of 1812 it was not because he loved them. To him the British side was merely the side to take against the Long Knives.

In June and July of 1811 Governors William Hull of Michigan Territory and Harrison of Indiana Territory sent to the secretary of war evaluations of the frontier problems. Hull's was narrowly tactical, pessimistic, and prophetic of the easy conquest of Michigan if the British navy controlled Lake Erie. Harrison's, although in fewer words, was broadly strategic and more constructive: the mere fact of an Indian confederation, friendly to the British and hostile to the Long Knives, was dangerous; the Prophet's town (hereafter called Tippecanoe) was ideally located as a base for a surprise downstream attack on Vincennes, was well placed as a headquarters for more protracted warfare, and was linked by water and short portages with all the northwestern Indians; the little known country north of Tippecanoe, full of swamps and thickets, could easily be defended by natives, but the power of the United States could be brought to bear only with the greatest difficulty. Early in August, 1811, Harrison told the War Department he did not expect hostilities before Tecumseh returned from the South, and that in the meantime he intended to try to break up Tecumseh's confederacy, without bloodshed if possible. On their side, the Indians told the British they expected some deceitful trick leading to their massacre.

The military details of the Battle of Tippecanoe need not be exhausted here. Harrison's forces moved up the Wabash and arrived at Tippecanoe on November 6, 1811. When Harrison was preparing to attack, he was met by emissaries from the Prophet. Both sides agreed to a council on the next day. The troops encamped with correctly organized interior and exterior guards. Here the story diverges into two versions. White writers have said the Indians intended to confer, to pretend falsely to agree to anything, to assassinate Harrison, and to massacre the little army. They allege the Prophet had promised to make the Indians bullet proof. A Kickapoo chief later said to British officers that a white prisoner the Indians had captured told them Harrison intended to fight, not to talk. At any rate, the shooting started at about four in the morning, an unfortunate moment for the Indians because that was the hour of "stand to" or "general quarters" in the white army. Curious Indians in the brush were fired on by sentries. The Indians then killed the sentries. It was then, and only then, the Indians said, that they decided to fight. The battle lasted until mid morning, when the Indians ran out of arrows and bullets and fled. A detachment of Harrison's troops then burned the deserted village and the winter corn reserve of the Shawnee. Two days later the troops withdrew. The depth of the cleavage between Indians and whites is shown by the fact that the Potowatomi Chief Winnemac, Harrison's leading Indian adviser, came up the river with the troops but fought on the side of his bronze brethren. Harrison had 50 Kentucky volunteers, 250 United States infantry, and several hundred Indiana militia, who had been trained personally by him. Reports of losses vary. Indians admitted to losing 25 dead, but soldiers counted 38 dead Indians on the field. This was the first time in northwestern warfare that a force of whites of a size equal to the redmen had suffered only a number of casualties equal to those of their dusky enemies. Heretofore whites in such circumstances had lost more than the redmen had lost. Estimates of Indians in the fighting range from 100 to 1,000. Six hundred would probably be a fair estimate.

As battles go, Tippecanoe cannot be compared with Fallen Timbers in 1794 or Moraviantown in 1813, but it was politically and diplomatically decisive. Its most important effect was to divide the tribes in such a way as to make Tecumseh's dream fade like fog in the sun.

The Battle of Tippecanoe

The Battle of Tippecanoe has a significance far beyond that of territorial Indiana. In many ways it represents the beginning of the War of 1812, and its fame lived on to color and influence politics in America during the 1830s and 1840s. The ticket of "Tippecanoe and Tyler Too" was successful in 1840, after Harrison, "Old Tip," had made a strong showing in the 1836 race. President Madison mentioned the "warfare just renewed" in the West when he asked Congress for a war declaration against the British in June 1812.[1]

For all its fame, however, the Battle of Tippecanoe was a costly victory for the United States and the immediate reaction to it carried considerable criticism of Harrison for the heavy losses sustained. Harrison had fewer than 1,000 under arms at Tippecanoe; his casualties totaled 188, including 62 dead. Neither the number of Indian combatants nor the extent of their losses is known, but the estimates range from nearly equal in both cases to considerably fewer in both. The basis for considering Tippecanoe a victory for Harrison at all stems from the fact that he and his troops held the battlefield afterwards and they destroyed Prophetstown the following day before returning home.

One of the more unusual aspects of this clash between soldiers and Indians is that

1. James D. Richardson, ed., *Messages and Papers of the Presidents* (20 vols., 1897), II, 488.

firsthand reminiscences of it exist from both sides. The two selections below contain, first, the recollections of Judge Isaac Naylor, at the time of the battle a twenty-one-year-old volunteer rifleman. Subsequently a lawyer and circuit court judge, Naylor lived in Crawfordsville, Indiana, from 1833 until his death in 1873. The second selection is by Shabonee or Shabonier, a Potawatomi chief (1775–1859) who fought both at Tippecanoe and at the Battle of the Thames (1813), where Tecumseh was killed. A prominent spokesman for the Indians, but known as a peace advocate after 1815, Shabonee became acquainted with Solon Robinson, an agricultural journalist and promoter who founded Crown Point in Lake County in the 1830s. Many years later Robinson published *Me-Won-I-Toc* (1864), a collection of Indian stories which included Shabonee's recollection of the Battle of Tippecanoe.

For additional information about the battle, see Logan Esarey, ed., *Messages and Letters of William Henry Harrison* (2 vols., 1922); Dorothy Goebel, *William Henry Harrison* (1926); and John D. Barnhart and Donald F. Carmony, *Indiana: From Frontier to Industrial Commonwealth* (2 vols., 1954); a good, brief account of the battle is by Gayle Thornbrough, "Tippecanoe," *American Heritage*, II (Autumn 1950), 16–19.

AN EYEWITNESS ACCOUNT OF TIPPECANOE

Judge Isaac Naylor

I became a volunteer of a company of riflemen and, on September 12, 1811, we commenced our march towards Vincennes, and arrived there in about six days, marching one hundred and twenty miles. We remained there about one week and took up the line of march to a point on the Wabash river, where we erected a stockade fort, which we named Fort Harrison. This was two miles above where the city of Terre Haute now stands. Col. Joseph H. Daviess, who commanded the dragoons, named the fort. The glorious defense of this fort nine months after by Capt. Zachary Taylor was the first step in his brilliant career that afterward made him President of the United States. A few days later we took up our line of march for the seat of the Indian warfare, where we arrived on the evening of November 6, 1811.

When the army arrived in view of Prophet's Town, an Indian was seen coming toward General Harrison, with a white flag suspended on a pole. Here the army halted, and a parley was had between General Harrison and an Indian delegation who assured the General that they desired peace and solemnly promised to meet

From Isaac Naylor, "An Eyewitness Account of the Battle," *The Battle of Tippecanoe: Conflict of Cultures*, ed. Alameda McCollough (1973), pp. 10–13. This account was first published as "The Battle of Tippecanoe, as described by Judge Isaac Naylor, A Participant—A Recently Discovered Account," *Indiana Magazine of History*, II (December 1906), 161–169. Reprinted by permission of the Editor, *Indiana Magazine of History*.

him the next day in council to settle the terms of peace and friendship between them and the United States.

Gen. Marston G. Clark, who was then brigade major, and Waller Taylor, one of the judges of the general court of the Territory of Indiana, and afterward a senator of the United States from Indiana (as one of the General's aides), were ordered to select a place for the encampment, which they did. The army then marched to the ground selected, about sunset. A strong guard was placed around the encampment commanded by Capt. James Bigger and three lieutenants. The troops were ordered to sleep on their arms. The night being cold, large fires were made along the lines of encampment and each soldier retired to rest, sleeping on his arms.

Having seen a number of squaws and children at the town, I thought the Indians were not disposed to fight. About ten o'clock at night, Joseph Warnock and myself retired to rest, he taking one side of the fire and I the other—the members of our company being all asleep. My friend Warnock had dreamed, the night before, a bad dream which foreboded something fatal to him or to some of his family, as he told me. Having myself no confidence in dreams, I thought but little about the matter, although I observed that he never smiled afterwards.

I awoke about four o'clock the next morning, after a sound and refreshing sleep, having heard in a dream the firing of guns and the whistling of bullets just before I awoke from my slumber. A drizzling rain was falling and all things were still and quiet throughout the camp. I was engaged in making a calculation when I should arrive home.

In a few moments I heard the crack of a rifle in the direction of the point where now stands the Battle Ground House, which is occupied by Captain DuTiel as a tavern. I had just time to think that some sentinel was alarmed and fired his rifle without a real cause, when I heard the crack of another rifle, followed by an awful Indian yell all around the encampment. In less than a minute I saw the Indians charging our line most furiously and shooting a great many rifle balls into our camp fires, throwing the live coals into the air three or four feet high.

At this moment my friend Warnock was shot by a rifle ball through his body. He ran a few yards and fell dead on the ground. Our lines were broken and a few Indians were found on the inside of the encampment. In a few moments they were all killed. Our lines closed up and our men in their proper places. One Indian was killed in the back part of Captain Geiger's tent, while he was attempting to tomahawk the Captain.

The sentinels, closely pursued by the Indians, came to the line of the encampment in haste and confusion. My brother, William Naylor, was on guard. He was pursued so rapidly and furiously that he ran to the nearest point on the left flank, where he remained with a company of regular soldiers until the battle was near its termination. A young man, whose name was Daniel Pettit, was pursued so closely and furiously by an Indian as he was running from the guard line to our lines, that to save his life he cocked his rifle as he ran and turning suddenly around, placed the muzzle of his gun against the body of the Indian and shot an ounce ball through him. The Indian fired his gun at the same instant, but it being longer than Pettit's the muzzle passed by him and set fire to a handkerchief which he had tied around his head. The

Indians made four or five most fierce charges on our lines, yelling and screaming as they advanced, shooting balls and arrows into our ranks. At each charge they were driven back in confusion, carrying off their dead and wounded as they retreated.

Colonel Owen, of Shelby County, Kentucky, one of General Harrison's aides, fell early in the action by the side of the General. He was a member of the legislature at the time of his death. Colonel Daviess was mortally wounded early in the battle, gallantly charging the Indians on foot with sword and pistols according to his own request. He made this request three times before General Harrison would permit it. This charge was made by himself and eight dragoons on foot near the angle formed by the left flank and front line of the encampment. Colonel Daviess lived about thirty-six hours after he was wounded, manifesting his ruling passion in life—ambition and a patriotism and ardent love of military glory. During the last hours of his life he said to his friends around him that he had but one thing to regret—that he had military talents; that he was about to be cut down in the meridian of life without having an opportunity of displaying them for his own honor, and the good of his country. He was buried alone, with the honors of war, near the right flank of the army, inside the lines of the encampment, between two trees. On one side of the tree the letter 'D' was plainly visible many years. Nothing but the stump of the other tree remains. His grave was made here to conceal it from the Indians. It was filled up to the top with earth and then covered with oak leaves. I presume the Indians never found it. This precautionary act was performed as a mark of special respect for a distinguished hero and patriot of Kentucky.

Captain Spencer's company of mounted riflemen composed the right flank of the army. Captain Spencer and both of his lieutenants were killed. John Tipton was elected and commissioned captain of his company in one hour after the battle, as reward for his cool and deliberate heroism displayed during the action. He died at Logansport in 1839, having been twice elected senator of the United States from Indiana.

The clear, calm voice of General Harrison was heard in words of heroism in every part of the encampment during the action. Colonel Boyd behaved very bravely after repeating these words: 'Huzza! My sons of gold, a few more fires and victory will be ours!'

Just after daylight the Indians retreated across the prairie toward their own town, carrying off their wounded. This retreat was from the right flank of the encampment, commanded by Captains Spencer and Robb, having retreated from the other portions of the encampment a few minutes before. As their retreat became visible, an almost deafening and universal shout was raised by our men. 'Huzza! Huzza! Huzza!' This shout was almost equal to that of the savages at the commencement of the battle; ours was the shout of victory, theirs was the shout of ferocious but disappointed hope.

The morning light disclosed the fact that the killed and wounded of our army, numbering between eight and nine hundred men, amounted to one hundred and eight. Thirty-six Indians were found near our lines. Many of their dead were carried off during the battle. This fact was proved by the discovery of many Indian graves recently made near their town. Ours was a bloody victory, theirs a bloody defeat.

Soon after breakfast an Indian chief was discovered on the prairie, about eighty yards from our front line, wrapped in a piece of white cloth. He was found by a soldier by the name of Miller, a resident of Jeffersonville, Indiana. The Indian was wounded in one leg, the ball having penetrated his knee and passed down his leg, breaking the bone as it passed. Miller put his foot against him and he raised up his head and said: 'Don't kill me, don't kill me.' At the same time five or six regular soldiers tried to shoot him, but their muskets snapped and missed fire. Maj. Davis Floyd came riding toward him with dragoon sword and pistols and said he would show them how to kill Indians, when a messenger came from General Harrison commanding that he should be taken prisoner. He was taken into camp, where the surgeons dressed his wounds. Here he refused to speak a word of English or tell a word of truth. Through the medium of an interpreter he said that he was coming to the camp to tell General Harrison that they were about to attack the camp. He refused to have his leg amputated, though he was told that amputation was the only means of saving his life. One dogma of Indian superstition is that all good and brave Indians, when they die, go to a delightful region, abounding with deer, and other game, and to be a successful hunter he should have his limbs, his gun and his dog. He therefore preferred death with all his limbs to life without them. In accordance with his request he was left to die, in company with an old squaw, who was found in the Indian town the next day after he was taken prisoner. They were left in one of our tents. At the time this Indian was taken prisoner, another Indian, who was wounded in the body, rose to his feet in the middle of the prairie and began to walk towards the wood on the opposite side. A number of regular soldiers shot at him but missed him. A man who was a member of the same company with me, Henry Huckleberry, ran a few steps into the prairie and shot an ounce ball through his body and he fell dead near the margin of the woods. Some Kentucky volunteers went across the prairie immediately and scalped him, dividing his scalp into four pieces, each one cutting a hole in each piece, putting the ramrod through the hole, and placing his part of the scalp just behind the first thimble of his gun, near its muzzle. Such was the fate of nearly all of the Indians found dead on the battle-ground, and such was the disposition of their scalps.

The death of Owen, and the fact that Daviess was mortally wounded, with the remembrance also that a large portion of Kentucky's best blood had been shed by the Indians, must be their apology for this barbarous conduct. Such conduct will be excused by all who witnessed the treachery of the Indians and saw the bloody scenes of this battle.

Tecumseh being absent at the time of the battle, a chief called White Loon was the chief commander of the Indians. He was seen in the morning after the battle, riding a large white horse in the woods across the prairie, where he was shot at by a volunteer named Montgomery, who is now living in the southwest part of this state. At the crack of his rifle the horse jumped as if the ball had hit him. The Indian rode off toward the town and we saw him no more. During the battle The Prophet was safely located on a hill, beyond the reach of our balls, praying to the Great Spirit to give victory to the Indians, having previously assured them that the Great Spirit would change our powder into ashes and sand.

We had about forty head of beef cattle when we came to the battle. They all ran off the night of the battle, or they were driven off by the Indians, so that they were all lost. We received rations for two days on the morning after the action. We received no more rations until the next Tuesday evening, being six days afterwards. The Indians having retreated to their town, we performed the solemn duty of consigning to their graves our dead soldiers, without shrouds or coffins. They were placed in graves about two feet deep, from five to ten in each grave.

General Harrison, having learned that Tecumseh was expected to return from the south with a number of Indians whom he had enlisted in his cause, called a council of his officers, who advised him to remain on the battlefield and fortify his camp by a breastwork of logs, about four feet high. This work was completed during the day and all the troops were placed immediately behind each line of the work when they were ordered to pass the watchword from right to left every five minutes, so that no man was permitted to sleep during the night. The watchword on the night before the battle was 'Wide awake, wide awake.' To me it was a long, cold, cheerless night.

On the next day the dragoons went to Prophet's Town, which they found deserted by all the Indians, except an old squaw, whom they brought into camp and left her with the wounded chief before mentioned. The dragoons set fire to the town and it was all consumed, casting up a brilliant light amid the darkness of the ensuing night. I arrived at the town when it was about half on fire. I found large quantities of corn, beans and peas. I filled my knapsack with these articles and carried them to the camp and divided them with the members of our mess, consisting of six men. Having these articles of food, we declined eating horse flesh, which was eaten by a large portion of our men.

CHIEF SHABONEE'S ACCOUNT OF TIPPECANOE

Shabonee

It was fully believed among the Indians that we should defeat General Harrison, and that we should hold the line of the Wabash and dictate terms to the whites. The great cause of our failure, was the Miamies, whose principal country was south of the river, and they wanted to treat with the whites so as to retain their land, and they played false to their red brethren and yet lost all. They are now surrounded and will be crushed. The whites will shortly have all their lands and they will be driven away.

In every talk to the Indians, General Harrison said:

> Lay down your arms. Bury the hatchet, already bloody with murdered victims, and

From J. Wesley Whickar, ed., "Shabonee's Account of Tippecanoe," *Indiana Magazine of History*, XVII (December 1921), 353–360. Reprinted by permission of the Editor, *Indiana Magazine of History*.

> promise to submit to your great chief at Washington, and he will be a father to you, and forget all that is past. If we take your land, we will pay for it. But you must not think that you can stop the march of white men westward.

There was truth and justice in all that talk. The Indians with me would not listen to it. It was dictating to them. They wanted to dictate to him. They had counted his soldiers, and looked at them with contempt. Our young men said:

> We are ten to their one. If they stay upon the other side, we will let them alone. If they cross the Wabash, we will take their scalps or drive them into the river. They cannot swim. Their powder will be wet. The fish will eat their bodies. The bones of the white men will lie upon every sand bar. Their flesh will fatten buzzards. These white soldiers are not warriors. Their hands are soft. Their faces are white. One half of them are calico peddlers. The other half can only shoot squirrels. They cannot stand before men. They will all run when we make a noise in the night like wild cats fighting for their young. We will fight for ours, and to keep the pale faces from our wigwams. What will they fight for? They won't fight. They will run. We will attack them in the night.

Such were the opinions and arguments of our warriors. They did not appreciate the great strength of the white men. I knew their great war chief, and some of his young men. He was a good man, very soft in his words to his red children, as he called us; and that made some of our men with hot heads mad. I listened to his soft words, but I looked into his eyes. They were full of fire. I knew that they would be among his men like coals of fire in the dry grass. The first wind would raise a great flame. I feared for the red men that might be sleeping in its way. I, too, counted his men. I was one of the scouts that watched all their march up the river from Vincennes. I knew that we were like these bushes—very many. They were like these trees; here and there one. But I knew too, when a great tree falls, it crushes many little ones. I saw some of the men shoot squirrels, as they rode along, and I said, the Indians have no such guns. These men will kill us as far as they can see. "They cannot see in the night," said our men who were determined to fight. So I held my tongue. I saw that all of our war chiefs were hot for battle with the white men. But they told General Harrison that they only wanted peace. They wanted him to come up into their country and show their people how strong he was, and then they would all be willing to make a treaty and smoke the great pipe together. This was what he came for. He did not intend to fight the Indians. They had deceived him. Yet he was wary. He was a great war chief. Every night he picked his camping ground and set his sentinels all around, as though he expected we would attack him in the dark. We should have done so before we did, if it had not been for this precaution. Some of our people taunted him for this, and pretended to be angry that he should distrust them, for they still talked of their willingness to treat, as soon as they could get all the people. This is part of our way of making war. So the white army marched further and further into our country, unsuspicious, I think, of our treachery. In one thing we were deceived. We expected that the white warriors would come up on the south bank of the river, and then we could parley with them; but they crossed far down the river and came on this side, right up to the great Indian town that Elskatawwa had gathered at the mouth of the Tippecanoe. In the meantime he had sent three chiefs down on the south side to meet the army and stop it with a talk until he could get the warriors ready. Tecumseh had told the Indians not to fight, but when he was away, they took some scalps, and General Harrison demanded that we should give up our men as murder[er]s, to be punished.

Tecumseh had spent months in traveling all over the country around Lake Michigan, making great talks to all the warriors, to get them to join him in his great designs upon the pale faces. His enmity was the most bitter of any Indian I ever knew. He was not one of our nation, he was a Shawnee. His father was a great warrior. His mother came from the country where there is no snow, near the great water that is salt. His father was treacherously killed by a white man before Tecumseh was born, and his mother taught him, while he sucked, to hate all white men, and when he grew big enough to be ranked as a warrior she used to go with him every year to his father's grave and make him swear that he would never cease to make war upon the Americans. To this end he used all his power of strategy, skill and cunning, both with white men and red. He had very much big talk. He was not at the battle of Tippecanoe. If he had been there it would not have been fought. It was too soon. It frustrated all his plans.

Elskatawwa was Tecumseh's older brother. He was a great medicine. He talked much to the Indians and told them what had happened. He told much truth, but some things that he had told did not come to pass. He was called "The Prophet." Your people knew him only by that name. He was very cunning, but he was not so great a warrior as his brother, and he could not so well control the young warriors who were determined to fight.

Perhaps your people do not know that the battle of Tippecanoe was the work of white men who came from Canada and urged us to make war. Two of them who wore red coats were at the Prophet's Town the day that your army came. It was they who urged Elskatawwa to fight. They dressed themselves like Indians, to show us how to fight. They did not know our mode. We wanted to attack at midnight. They wanted to wait till daylight. The battle commenced before either party was ready, because one of your sentinels discovered one of our warriors, who had undertaken to creep into your camp and kill the great chief where he slept. The Prophet said if that was done we should kill all the rest or they would run away. He promised us a horseload of scalps, and a gun for every warrior, and many horses. The men that were to crawl upon their bellies into camp were seen in the grass by a white man who had eyes like an owl, and he fired and hit his mark. The Indian was not brave. He cried out. He should have lain still and died. Then the other men fired. The other Indians were fools. They jumped up out of the grass and yelled. They believed what had been told them, that a white man would run at a noise made in the night. Then many Indians who had crept very close so as to be ready to take scalps when the white men ran, all yelled like wolves, wild cats and screech owls; but it did not make the white men run.

They jumped right up from their sleep with guns in their hands and sent a shower of bullets at every spot where they heard a noise. They could not see us. We could see them, for they had fires. Whether we were ready or not we had to fight now for the battle was begun. We were still sure that we should win. The Prophet had told us that we could not be defeated. We did not rush in among your men because of the fires. Directly the men ran away from some of the fires, and a few foolish Indians went into the light and were killed. One Delaware could not make his gun go off. He ran up to a fire to fix the lock. I saw a white man whom I knew very well—he was a great hunter who could shoot a tin cup from another man's head—put up his gun to shoot the Delaware. I tried to shoot the white man but another who carried the flag just then unrolled it so that I could not see my aim. Then I heard the gun and saw the Delaware fall. I thought he was dead. The white man thought so, too, and ran to him with his knife. He wanted a Delaware scalp. Just as he got to him the Delaware jumped up and ran away. He had only lost an ear. A dozen bullets were fired at the white man while he was at the fire, but he shook them off like an old buffalo bull.

Our people were more surprised than yours. The fight had been begun too soon. They were not all ready. The plan was to creep up through the wet land where horses could not run, upon one side of the camp, and on the other through a creek and steep bank covered with bushes, so as to be ready to use the tomahawk upon the sleeping men as soon as their chief was killed. The Indians thought white men who had marched all day would sleep. They found them awake.

The Prophet had sent word to General Harrison that day that the Indians were all peaceable, that they did not want to fight, that he might lie down and sleep, and they would treat with their white brothers in the morning and bury the hatchet. But the white men did not believe.

In one minute from the time the first gun was fired I saw a great war chief mount his horse and begin to talk loud. The fires were put out and we could not tell where to shoot, except on one side of the camp, and from there the white soldiers ran, but we did not succeed as the Prophet told us that we would, in scaring the whole army so that all the men would run and hide in the grass like young quails.

I never saw men fight with more courage than these did after it began to grow light. The battle was lost to us by an accident, or rather by two.

A hundred warriors had been picked out during the night for this desperate service, and in the great council-house the Prophet had instructed them how to crawl like snakes through the grass and strike the sentinels; and if they failed in that, then they were to rush forward boldly and kill the great war chief of the whites, and if they did not do this the Great Spirit, he said, had told him that the battle would be hopelessly lost. This the Indians all believed.

If the one that was first discovered and shot had died like a brave, without a groan, the sentinel would have thought that he was mistaken, and it would have been more favorable than before for the Indians. The alarm having been made, the others followed Elskatawwa's orders, which were, in case of discovery, so as to prevent the secret movement, they should make a great yell as a signal for the general attack. All of the warriors had been instructed to creep up to the camp through the tall grass during the night, so close that when the great signal was given, the yell would be so loud and frightful that the whole of the whites would run for the thick woods up the creek, and that side was left open for this purpose.

"You will, then," said the Prophet, "have possession of their camp and all its equipage, and you can shoot the men with their own guns from every tree. But above all else you must kill the great chief."

It was expected that this could be easily done by those who were allotted to rush into camp in the confusion of the first attack. It was a great mistake of the Prophet's redcoated advisers, to defer this attack until morning. It would have succeeded when the fires were brighter in the night. Then they could not have been put out.

I was one of the spies that had dogged the steps of the army to give the Prophet information every day. I saw all the arrangement of the camp. It was not made where the Indians wanted it. The place was very bad for the attack. But it was not that which caused the failure. It was because General Harrison changed horses. He had ridden a grey one every day on the march, and he could have been shot twenty times by scouts that were hiding along the route. That was not what was wanted, until the army got to a place where it could be all wiped out. That time had now come, and the hundred braves were to rush in and shoot the "Big chief on a white horse," and then fall back to a safer place.

This order was fully obeyed, but we soon found to our terrible dismay that the "Big chief on a white horse" that was killed was not General Harrison. He had mounted a dark horse. I know this, for I was so near that I saw him, and I knew him as well as I knew my own brother.

I think that I could then have shot him, but I could not lift my gun. The Great Spirit held it down. I knew then that the great white chief was not to be killed, and I knew that the red men were doomed.

As soon as daylight came our warriors saw that the Prophet's grand plan had failed—that the great white chief was alive riding fearlessly among his troops in spite of bullets, and their hearts melted.

After that the Indians fought to save themselves, not to crush the whites. It was a terrible defeat. Our men all scattered and tried to get away. The white horsemen chased them and cut them down with long knives. We carried off a few wounded prisoners in the first attack, but nearly all the dead lay unscalped, and some of them lay thus till the next year when another army came to bury them.

Our women and children were in the town only a mile from the battle-field waiting for victory and its spoils. They wanted white prisoners. The Prophet had promised that every squaw of any note should have one of the white warriors to use as her slave, or to treat as she pleased.

Oh how these women were disappointed! Instead of slaves and spoils of the white men coming into town with the rising sun, their town was in flames and women and children were hunted like wolves and killed by hundreds or driven into the river and swamps to hide.

With the smoke of that town and the loss of that battle I lost all hope of the red men being able to stop the whites.

I fought that day by the side of an old Ottawa chief and his son, the brother of my wife. We were in the advance party, and several of those nearest to me fell by the bullets or blows of two horsemen who appeared to be proof against our guns. At length one of these two men killed the young man and wounded the chief, and at the same time I brought him and his horse to the ground. The horse ran, before he fell, down the bluff into the creek, quite out of the way of the whites. The man's leg was broken and he had another bad wound. I could have taken his scalp easily, but Sabaqua, the old chief, begged me not to kill him. He wanted to take him to his wife alive, in place of her son whom the white brave had killed.

I was willing enough to do this for I always respected a brave man, and this one was, beside, the handsomest white man I had ever seen. I knew him as soon as I saw him closely. I had seen him before. I went to Vincennes only one moon before the battle as a spy. I told the governor that I came for peace. This young man was there and I talked with him. He was not one of the warriors but had come because he was a great brave. He had told me, laughingly, that he would come to see me at my wigwam. I thought now that he should do it. I caught a horse—there were plenty of them that had lost their riders—and mounted the white brave with Sabaqua behind him to hold him on and started them off north. I was then sure that we should all have to run that way as soon as it was light. The Indians were defeated. The great barrier was broken. It was my last fight. I put my body in the way. It was strong then, but it was not strong enough to stop the white men. They pushed it aside as I do this stick. I have never seen the place since where we fought that night. My heart was very big then. Tecumseh had filled it with gall. It has been empty ever since.

The Nineteenth State

Following the War of 1812, a wave of settlement swept across the New West like pent-up flood waters bursting through a dam. Indiana's population jumped from 35,000 or 40,000 prior to the war to more than 147,000 in 1820, 685,000 in 1840, and over 1,350,000 in 1860. Other western states were growing rapidly too. Beginning with Indiana, a total of six new states entered the Union in the six years between 1816 and 1821.

The statehood movement had been present in Indiana since at least 1811, when the first petition for statehood was submitted to Congress. But this sentiment was not a unanimous one, primarily for monetary reasons. Nevertheless, when a second request was approved by the territorial legislature in December 1815, Congress responded with an enabling act on April 19, 1816, which authorized a constitutional convention. Convened in June at Corydon, which had been the territorial capital since 1813, the delegates quickly agreed to proceed with drawing up a constitution. The Indiana constitution was advanced for its time, particularly the education article, which called on the state to provide "as soon as circumstances will permit . . . for a general system of education, ascending in a regular gradation, from township schools to a state university, wherein tuition shall be gratis, and equally open to all."[1] The constitution reflected the prevailing Jeffersonian philosophy concerning republican institutions and limited executive authority, and it required annual elections and meetings of the General Assembly. Given the prevailing concern for the economy in 1816, as described below, it is not surprising that circumstances never permitted the establishment of the comprehensive educational system envisioned, and this article was substantially modified in the new constitution of 1851.

The selection below, taken from the first volume of a multivolume *History of Indiana* planned in the late 1950s as part of the state's sesquicentennial observation, was written by John D. Barnhart and Dorothy L. Riker. Professor Barnhart of Indiana University did not live to complete this work, and Ms. Riker, an experienced editor and writer at the Indiana Historical Society, agreed to finish the book and see it through the press. The passages below, taken from the final chapter of the prestatehood volume, describe the process by which Indiana Territory became the state of Indiana and some of the more significant provisions in the constitution of 1816. Professor Barnhart was a lifelong student of the history of Indiana and the Old Northwest. His major publications include *Valley of Democracy: The Frontier versus the Plantation in the Ohio Valley, 1775–1818* (1953) and, with colleague Donald F. Carmony, *Indiana: From Frontier to Industrial Commonwealth* (2 vols., 1954). Among the many volumes edited and coedited by Dorothy L. Riker are *The John Tipton Papers* (3 vols., 1942), *The Executive Proceedings of the State of Indiana, 1816–1836* (1947), *Messages and Papers Relating to the Administration of James Brown Ray, Governor of Indiana, 1825–1831* (1954), and *Indiana Election Returns, 1816–1851* (1960). She also coedited, with Gayle Thornbrough, *Readings in Indiana History* (1956).

STATEHOOD ACHIEVED

John D. Barnhart and Dorothy L. Riker

Though there was some opposition among the citizens of Indiana Territory to the formation of a state government in 1816, it was minor. The advance to statehood was considered as the normal procedure, the capstone of the territorial structure; the only question was whether the people were ready for it at this particular time. Statehood promised to bring to a victorious conclusion the long struggle of the anti-Harrison or Jennings party to democratize the territorial government and to do away with slavery. Citizens of the new state would be able to elect their highest officials rather than have them appointed by the federal government; they would make their own laws without the possibility of an absolute veto by a governor they did not choose. In addition to local self-government, they would be able to participate in

1. Quoted in Hubert H. Hawkins, ed., *Indiana's Road to Statehood* (1964), p. 87.

From John D. Barnhart and Dorothy L. Riker, *Indiana to 1816: The Colonial Period* (Indianapolis: Indiana Historical Bureau and Indiana Historical Society, 1971), pp. 439–463 passim.

national affairs, and they were very conscious at this time of the importance of national policies respecting the Indians, defense, and the disposal of the public lands. And considering the situation realistically, as politicians are wont to do, it would mean more offices to be filled.

News of the passage of the Enabling Act by Congress on April 19 reached Vincennes on May 2 and was published in the Vincennes *Western Sun* two days later. This left only nine days before the date stipulated in the act of the election of delegates to the convention. However, since passage of an enabling act in some form was almost a foregone conclusion, those interested in becoming delegates had no doubt communicated orally, if not in writing, their willingness to serve. Jennings wrote from Washington as early as February 7 that he "should be gratified to be in the convention," and about the same time William Hendricks was writing in Indiana that in his opinion "no country ever presented more candidates for its population, than does Indiana, to lay the foundation of our proposed State fabrick." . . .

The Enabling Act had apportioned the delegates according to the suggestion made by the territorial Assembly in its memorial to Congress, except Harrison County was given five instead of four delegates. The total number was forty-three apportioned among the thirteen counties in existence prior to the 1815 General Assembly. Clark, Franklin, Harrison, Knox, and Washington Counties each had five; Gibson and Wayne, four; Dearborn and Jefferson, three; and Perry, Posey, Switzerland, and Warrick, one each. . . .

Eleven, or possibly twelve, of the delegates were born in Virginia, seven in Pennsylvania, six in Kentucky, five in Maryland, two each in New Jersey and Connecticut, one each in North and South Carolina and Delaware, four in Ireland, and one each in Switzerland and Germany. Although only six were natives of Kentucky, twenty-seven had lived there prior to coming to Indiana. Only nine of the members had not lived previously below the Mason-Dixon Line.

The youngest member was twenty-eight, the oldest fifty-eight; sixteen were in their thirties, twenty-one in their forties, and five were in their fifties. Eleven of the delegates had served in the territorial legislature; two were judges of the General Court; thirteen had served as county judges, three as prosecuting attorneys, three as sheriffs, and at least half had been justices of the peace; over half had some legal training. Eight were field officers in the militia; five had been on the Tippecanoe campaign. Three were Baptist preachers, one a Methodist preacher, and two were physicians.

Historian John B. Dillon described the convention as composed

> mainly of clear-minded, unpretending men of common sense, whose patriotism was unquestionable and whose morals were fair. Their familiarity with the Declaration of American Independence—their territorial experience under the provisions of the Ordinance of 1787—and their knowledge of the principles of the Constitution of the United States, were sufficient, when combined, to lighten materially their labors in the great work of forming a Constitution for a new State.

Another student of the convention wrote, "None of them [the delegates] were truly great men; many of them men of limited education, and very few of them learned men. Nearly all . . . were frontier farmers, having a general idea of what they wanted, but willing that the more learned members should put it in shape."

When the convention assembled at Corydon on June 10, 1816, Jennings was chosen as president and William Hendricks, who was not a delegate, as secretary. . . .

The first order of business after the selection of a presiding officer and secretary was the adoption of the rules for governing the convention. That its work was to be conducted in a businesslike fashion is indicated by Rule XI, "Whilst the president is putting a question, or addressing the convention, none shall walk across the room; nor when a member is speaking enter on private discourse, or pass between him and the chair," and Rule XVII, "Every member shall particularly forbear personal reflections, nor shall any member name another in argument or debate." Rule XXII would seem to disprove the accusation that the constitution was pushed through the convention without time for debate: "No resolution, section or article, in the constitution, shall be finally agreed upon until the same shall have been read on three several days, unless a majority of two-thirds may think it necessary to dispense with this rule." The convention sat as a committee of the whole a short time each day, and in regular session another brief period. The remainder of the time was spent by the various committees in their work. There is no evidence of any long speeches being made, but there was ample time for discussion. . . .

The legislature was given sufficient powers and responsibilities to make it the dominant branch of state government, but was held in restraint by the division of power and the system of checks and balances. It was to consist of a senate and a house of representatives possessed of all the authority usually exercised by such bodies. Representation was to be apportioned on the basis of an enumeration of adult white males which was to be made every five years. The representatives were to be elected annually. The senators were to serve for three years, but their terms were to be so arranged that one third of the body would be elected every year. The two houses possessed powers of legislation, appropriation, impeachment, some power of appointment, and control of their own members and procedure.

The provisions regarding the executive branch of government (Art. V) were drafted by a committee of which John K. Graham was chairman. In the state governments which came into existence during and immediately after the Revolution, the provisions regarding the executive reflected a reaction against arbitrary authority; such executives were almost powerless and only gradually did they gain in stature. This process was well under way at the time Indiana framed her first constitution. The Indiana article was drawn largely from the Kentucky constitution. The governor and lieutenant governor were to be elected for three-year terms and were eligible for re-election but could hold the office for only six of any nine years. The governor was to be the commander in chief of the military and naval forces of the state; he was given limited appointive powers, had authority to remit fines and forfeitures and grant reprieves and pardons, could call the legislature into special session, and could veto bills which he did not approve. If a majority of the members of each house repassed a bill over his veto it became law. This veto was therefore weaker than many state executives exercise today. A secretary of state, a treasurer, and an auditor were to be elected by joint ballot of both houses of the legislature and their duties were to be fixed by law. At one point in the debate an amendment was offered to make the office of the secretary of state appointive by the governor with the advice and consent of the Senate, but it was defeated. . . .

A most unusual portion of the constitution was Article IX which committed the state to the encouragement of learning on the grounds that the general diffusion of knowledge and the advantages of education were essential to the preservation of free government. "As soon as circumstances will permit," the legislature was to provide "for a general system of education, ascending in a regular gradation, from township schools to a state university, wherein tuition shall be gratis, and equally open to all." Unfortunately the qualification at the beginning of the section enabled the legislature to avoid its responsibility in this matter until after a new constitution was adopted in 1851. It was a noble vision, the attainment of which was prevented by the lack of wealth and the indifference of the people until the frontier period was past. The fines collected for breaches of the penal law and the fees paid for exemption from militia duty were to be devoted to the support of county seminaries. Ten per cent of the proceeds of the sale of lots in county-seat towns was to be set aside for the use of public libraries. A penal code was to be formed on the principles of reformation and not of vindictive justice. The legislature was to found one or more farms as asylums for the aged, infirm, and unfortunate. On the whole the article embodies a rare recognition (in a frontier state) of the public's social responsibilities. . . .

The work of the convention was completed in nineteen days, at a total cost of $3,076.21. Each member was allowed $2.00 per day for each day's attendance plus $2.00 for each twenty-five miles traveled to and from the seat of government. The secretary and assistant secretaries received $3.50 per day; doorkeeper and assistant doorkeeper $2.00 per day. Mann Butler of Louisville was allowed $200 for printing and stitching the constitution and journal; $41.50 for books, stationery, etc.; $27.50 for tables, benches, etc.; and $40 for overseeing the printing, stitching, and distribution of the constitution and journal.

Transition from the old to the new government was provided in Article XII and was relatively simple, at least on paper. The President of the convention was directed to issue writs to the county sheriffs calling for an election to be held under territorial laws on August 5, 1816, to choose a governor, lieutenant governor, a representative in Congress, members of the General Assembly, sheriffs, and coroners. The Enabling Act had stipulated that Indiana was to have one representative in Congress until after the census was taken in 1820, while Section 9, Article XII of the constitution had outlined the first apportionment of members of the Assembly among the counties of the state. There were to be twenty-nine representatives and ten senators.

The time between the close of the convention and the election was only five weeks. Printing presses were available by this time not only at Vincennes, but at Brookville, Lexington, Corydon, and Vevay, and possibly elsewhere. Fourth of July gatherings would have offered opportunities also for prospective candidates to make themselves known. A spirited campaign for the governorship was waged between Jonathan Jennings and Thomas Posey, with the former receiving 5,211 votes as against 3,934 for Posey. In the race for lieutenant governor only 7,474 votes were cast, of which Christopher Harrison of Salem received 6,570, and the remaining votes were divided between John Vawter, Abel Findley, John Johnson, Davis Floyd, and Amos Lane. For representative in Congress William Hendricks defeated Allan D. Thom and George R. C. Sullivan by a decisive majority. Sullivan withdrew from the contest two days before the poll in the hope of throwing his support to Thom, but the announcement did not reach most of the counties until after the election.

Looking at the returns for the General Assembly, it will be noted that one-third of the successful candidates had served in the constitutional convention, while eleven of the thirty-nine had served in the territorial legislature. In the returns for sheriffs, in seven counties those who had been holding the office under appointment from the territorial governor were elected.

The first General Assembly under the state government met on November 4, the governor and lieutenant governor were inaugurated on November 7, and the following day the Assembly elected James Noble and Waller Taylor as members of the United States Senate. Hendricks was sworn into office and seated in Congress on December 2 and the two senators on December 12. A resolution admitting Indiana to the Union "on an equal footing with the original States in all respects whatever" was adopted by Congress and approved by President Madison on December 11, 1816. This date has generally been regarded as marking the birthday of the state, although the federal laws were not formally extended to the new commonwealth until March 3, 1817.

No provision had been made in the Enabling Act or in the constitution whereby the Indiana electorate could participate in the presidential election of 1816. The General Assembly therefore chose three presidential electors on November 16, and they met shortly thereafter and cast their votes for James Monroe for president and Daniel Tompkins for vice-president. When the two houses of Congress met the following February to count the electoral votes, the question was raised whether or not Indiana's votes should be counted, since they had been cast prior to her admission into the Union. After Representative Hendricks made a forceful presentation of the case for his state, the decision was made to include Indiana's three votes. . . .

The framing of the constitution under which Indiana began its existence as a state was the culmination of the struggle of the pioneers to escape the undemocratic government of the territorial period. The men who took the initiative from Governor Harrison and who successfully struggled to liberalize the Northwest Ordinance continued to labor for self-government until they had formed a democratic state. As a part of this contest they reiterated the prohibition of slavery and halted the further introduction of indentured servitude. White manhood suffrage and the equal apportionment of representation, unchecked by a strong gubernatorial veto, placed the power in the hands of popularly chosen representatives.

The true significance of the constitution is seen when it is compared with the early fundamental law of the southern states with their property qualifications for office holding and voting, unequal representation, and protection of slavery, which tended to produce an aristocratic social structure. From these states came most of Indiana's pioneers, but when in their turn they founded a state government they took the opportunity to eliminate the undemocratic features of these older documents.

4. Life on the Indiana Frontier

During the pioneer period in Indiana, approximately the years between the two constitutions of 1816 and 1851, very significant changes were occurring in practically all walks of life. Most apparent were the demographic changes. Both the central and northern portions of the state were settled, partly by the northward movement of Hoosiers into the fertile flatlands that virtually characterize all but the southern third of Indiana, and partly by the northern and western migration of people from the upper South, Ohio, and the middle Atlantic states. But prior to 1850 the number of foreign immigrants was small.

In 1825 the General Assembly held its first meeting in the new state capital of Indianapolis, the new "city of Indiana" located and laid out for that purpose only four years earlier near the geographical center of the state. Even the regions surrounding the swampy and marshy wetlands in the north were settled during the 1830s and after; most of Indiana's present number of counties were established by 1840, and by 1860 all ninety-two had been organized.

The primary economic activity of Indiana's first generation was, of course, agriculture. Most pioneer farmers eked out a living from the soil, provided most of life's essentials through their own and their family's sweat and skills, bemoaned the lack of adequate transportation to town and market, and worried about the Indians. Work-related tasks such as barn raisings, corn huskings, and road building were turned into social affairs for entertainment; politics and religion also provided diversions from the usual routine of work from dawn to dusk.

By 1850 the state had become a major supplier of the national granaries, ranking high particularly in the production of corn (4th), wheat (6th), and oats (8th); Indiana was also a major producer of hogs and sheep. Although some mills and factories existed in the state, these activities were "neither an important nor typical part of the scene during the first half of the nineteenth century."[1] Rather, the economy was characterized by the curious combination of self-sufficiency and cooperation common to frontier conditions, and the average family faced a bewildering variety of daily tasks that were required to obtain the necessities of life. Hard work, long hours, and constant activity were the rule. The development of the state fair in the 1850s reflected not only the growing maturity of the state's agriculture, but also the usefulness of an exchange of information and a social outlet.

Other activities and interests were essential too, to provide access to market for the crops produced and to tend to the whole person—his educational, religious, and cultural development. In spite of the advanced concept of state responsibility for a "general system of education"—including elementary, secondary, and higher—that

1. John D. Barnhart and Donald F. Carmony, *Indiana: From Frontier to Industrial Commonwealth* (2 vols., 1954), I, 345.

was written into the first constitution of 1816, circumstances never did permit its implementation before the plans were adopted for a reduced system in the 1851 constitution. Instead, the public schools of the pioneer period remained a local responsibility, often unmet, that was supplemented in places with private schools operated by churches or individuals. Indiana also became the home of a number of private, usually church-related, colleges during the early nineteenth century, in addition to the two state-supported colleges, now Vincennes University (1806) and Indiana University (1820).

Among the obstacles to the development of a free public school system were the public's denial of the usefulness of education, its aversion to the additional tax burden, and the preference of some for church or private schools. In the late 1840s, however, a concerted campaign for improved public schools in Indiana, spearheaded largely by Professor Caleb Mills of Wabash College, finally resulted in much-needed constitutional and legislative reforms. Although the 1851 constitution did not provide for free higher education, it did—together with the Free Public School Law of 1852—authorize the establishment of a free public school system. But little progress was made during the 1850s because of controversies and lawsuits challenging the authority of the state to levy taxes for educational purposes; finally, during the 1860s and after, the basis for a system of free elementary and secondary schools was laid.

Pioneer Indiana was also the scene of one of the best-known Utopian communities in America, Robert Owen's New Harmony. The village itself, located on the lower Wabash several miles south of Vincennes, had been established by Father George Rapp in 1814. He and his followers prospered in the area during the decade they remained; but the Rappites returned to Pennsylvania in 1824–1825, after Robert Owen, a Scottish industrialist and reformer, had agreed to the purchase of New Harmony. The communal society Owen founded was much less successful than George Rapp's had been, but many of the intellectuals attracted to the town by Owen's advanced ideas concerning society, education, equality, and the rights of labor remained in Indiana after the New Harmony experiment collapsed in 1827, thereby enriching the quality of life in the state. The same may be said of Robert Owen's five children, who played important roles in the scientific, educational, political, and military history of the state during the next half-century.

A major concern of Hoosiers in the early nineteenth century was transportation. The growing populace needed improvements in and additions to the natural routes of travel provided by rivers and streams, buffalo traces, and Indian trails. In the 1820s a major north-south connection known as the Michigan Road was laid out from Madison on the Ohio River through Indianapolis and South Bend and on to Michigan City at Lake Michigan. The leading east-west thoroughfare in the 1830s, the National Road, traversed the state from Richmond in the east to Terre Haute in the west, via Knightstown, Indianapolis, and Brazil. The state's transportation network was further enriched by canal construction during this decade and by the appearance of the railroad in the state in the 1840s. Unfortunately, the state became involved in a disastrous Mammoth Internal Improvement program in 1836, in which it decided to use state funds and credit to underwrite an ambitious, eight-project plan designed to crisscross the state with improved roads, canals, and railroads at a cost of some $10,000,000. The Panic of 1837 intervened, followed by a severe depression from 1839–1843. Some of the state's money was embezzled, and none of those projects of the 1830s was completed by the state, which was now saddled with an enormous debt and still in need of improved transportation. In time the projects themselves were taken up and completed by private concerns, and the state slowly extricated itself from debt. But the episode profoundly affected the people at the time and has had a continuing impact.

Moreover, long before the end of the canal age in Indiana, the railroad began to appear in the state. Barely 200 miles of track were in operation in the state in 1850, the major line being a connection between the thriving river town of Madison on the Ohio and the still struggling political capital at the center of the state. By 1860, however, more than 2,000 miles of track had been laid and put into operation. A selection below describes the three-step process by which the general enthusiasm for railroads, often unreasonably high, led to legislative authorization and sometimes resulted in actual lines being built.

Indian relations, and the eventual removal of most of the Indians living in Indiana, is another aspect of pioneer Indiana. In the Treaty of St. Mary's, or the New Purchase Treaty, concluded in 1818, the Delaware Indians agreed to leave central Indiana within three years. Their departure actually occurred one year sooner, in 1820, when they moved into the trans-Mississippi West. The transplanted Indians included the first wife and children of William Conner, a prominent Indian trader and settler in central Indiana. In the 1830s a major Potawatomi removal occurred, the forced-march route from Indiana into Missouri being designated another "trail of tears." In the 1840s a third and final large-scale removal involving the Miamis in the Fort Wayne area took place. Although some Indians remained on land granted to them in previous treaties, the Indians as a threatening presence had disappeared. That fear, as well as a contemptuous attitude of some whites toward all Indians, had precipitated the now famous massacre at Fall Creek, in north central Indiana, in 1824. The basic facts regarding this event are presented by George Chalou, "The Fall Creek Massacre," *Prologue: The Journal of the National Archives*, IV (Summer 1972), 109–114; this frontier tragedy also provided Jessamyn West, an Indiana-born author, with the basis for her powerful, best-selling novel, *The Massacre at Fall Creek* (1974).

The readings that follow, written both by pioneer contemporaries and by writers and historians afterward, describe various aspects of pioneer life in Indiana. The state is indeed fortunate in the number and quality of its reporters on pioneer life. In addition to the works represented in the selections below, particular notice should be given to the Pulitzer Prize–winning book by Professor R. Carlyle Buley, *The Old Northwest: Pioneer Period, 1815–1840* (2 vols., 1950); and to such primary sources as Emma S. Vonnegut, trans. and ed., *The Schramm Letters: Written by Jacob Schramm and Members of His Family from Indiana to Germany in the Year 1836* (1935); Hugh McCulloch, *Men and Measures of Half a Century: Sketches and Comments* (1888); and Sandford C. Cox, *Recollections of the Early Settlement of the Wabash Valley* (1860).

For additional information on the economic and cultural activities of the Indiana pioneers, see John D. Barnhart and Donald F. Carmony, *Indiana: From Frontier to Industrial Commonwealth* (2 vols., 1954); Logan Esarey, *A History of Indiana* (2 vols., 1915, 1918); and Paul Wallace Gates, *The Farmer's Age: Agriculture, 1815–1860* (1960).

Pioneers

THE SETTLERS

L. C. Rudolph

A good summary statement about the heavily southern origins and often indolent nature of the first Hoosiers has been written by the Reverend L. C. Rudolph. In the first section of his book on the early history of Presbyterianism in Indiana, he has written eloquently and understandingly about "the settlers" and the hardships of their life on the frontier; but he also discusses their optimism, their willingness to share meager resources, and their good humored acceptance of the limitations imposed on them by circumstances. There is also a brief passage concerning the problems of travel in an area with almost no roads worthy of the name.

Rudolph, a former member of the Louisville Presbyterian Theological Seminary faculty, became acquisitions librarian at the Lilly Library on the campus of Indiana University at Bloomington. In addition to Hoosier Zion, *he has written about the origins of Methodism in the United States in his biography* Francis Asbury *(1966). For more information on pioneer life in Indiana, see R. Carlyle Buley,* The Old Northwest: Pioneer Period, 1815–1840 *(2 vols., 1950); see also the reminiscences of Oliver Johnson, as recorded by his son, Howard Johnson, in* A Home in the Woods *(1951, reprinted 1978).*

Most of Indiana's earliest settlers were from the southern backwoods. It has been customary to think that southern Indiana was settled from the south while northern Indiana was settled from the north and east, the National Road being a rough division. After a painstaking check of census data, Elfrieda Lang concludes that early Indiana was even more southern than most scholars had supposed. Miss Lang's calculations show that in Indiana the southern population moved right on into the north. Indiana was insulated from the northern and eastern population streams by swampy land that blocked the way to the more desirable Wabash country. The lake port at Michigan City was backed by sand dunes, and the persistent "Kankakee Pond" extended from the Illinois line to South Bend. The Yankees bypassed Indiana because they could not, or thought they could not, get in. As [Richard L.] Power

From *Hoosier Zion: The Presbyterians in Early Indiana* (1963), pp. 4–11.

concludes, "Paradoxically, although the state lay directly in the path of the westward-moving thousands, thousands moved westward and never saw it."

On the other hand Indiana was open to the south. From the Cumberland Gap the watercourses ran northwest. The famous Wilderness Road led to Kentucky and to the Ohio River at points below Cincinnati. Limestone formations and the best soils ran in nearly perpendicular belts northward from the Ohio. These corridors connected Indiana with the Appalachian back country, the great reservoir of land-hungry pioneers.

From these Appalachian valleys came Indiana's early settlers. To be sure, a few members of the seaboard plantation stock migrated to the Old Northwest: Charles Willing Byrd, William Henry Harrison, Edward Coles, and the father of Edward Eggleston are examples. There were also population islands, like the French at Vincennes, the Swiss-French wine producers at Vevay, English settlements near Evansville, and the Owen settlement at New Harmony. The towns at the commerce centers quickly attracted and developed a merchant class. But for every handful of these gentry there was a woodsfull of marginal settlers. They may have been Scotch, Scotch-Irish, German, English, or even French in their origin, but they had been pioneering for one or more generations before reaching the Ohio. Their pioneering had been done in the back country of Virginia and especially in North Carolina. The view that the main current into Indiana came from North Carolina is supported by careful students of the population movements.

As a rule the southern settlers were poor. The better lands of Kentucky soon commanded a higher price than new settlers could pay, so they pressed on into Indiana. Though there were few navigable streams reaching back more than forty miles from the Ohio, the settlers pressed across the great river, settled along the available streams, and then assaulted the forest directly. The hills of southern Indiana were not yet exploited or eroded, and the natural drainage provided healthful living sites. Moving to the woods of Indiana meant an outlay of several hundred dollars if one held a Yankee farmer's standard of comfort and equipment. There had to be money for horses, a wagon, boat transport, land, cabin, barn, and subsistence, both for the trip and until the first crop could be harvested. The great body of southern pioneers had no such standard. They strapped the articles which they felt must be moved upon the backs of their family and animals and set off "jinglety bang." Many had absolutely nothing to lose and were going "no where in perticklar." If they had any money and avoided getting cheated by land sharks, they bought land. If they had no money, they "squatted," hoping to buy later when their situation improved. If their situation did not improve, they became part of that useful group of shifting pioneers who sold their improvements for what they could get and moved on to "squat" and tame more wilderness.

In the woods of Indiana these southern settlers became specialists in subsistence living. Most of them had been "patch farmers" in the back country, and that was what the occasion seemed to demand. There was the perpetual matter of wresting food, clothing, and shelter from the forest and taking care of the family. That was all time permitted. They soon learned that keeping such demands on their time to the minimum allowed more rest for tired and often sick bodies. Their first shelter was likely to be a half-faced camp, a sort of pole pen with an open side before which a fire burned, followed by a rough log cabin. Either may merit description by a traveler as a "pen," a "miserable hole," or a "dirty hovel." William Faux found little to please him on his American tour in 1819, and Indiana frontier cabins were no exception:

> Saving two comfortable plantations, with neat loghouses and flourishing orchards, just planted . . . I saw nothing between Vincennes and Princeton, a ride of forty miles, but miserable log holes, and a mean ville of eight or ten huts or cabins, sad neglected farms, and indolent, dirty, sickly, wild-looking inhabitants. Soap is nowhere seen or found in any of the taverns east or west. Hence dirty hands, heads, and faces every where. Here is nothing clean but wild beasts and birds, nothing industrious generally, except pigs, which are so of necessity . . . Nothing happy but squirrels; their life seems all play, and that of the hogs all work.

But even such a warm friend of the West as Richard L. Mason recorded in his travel account that same year, as he passed from Louisville through newly settled country to Vincennes, that accommodations were poor and charges high, the people impolite, and their private shelter woefully inadequate to protect them from the severe weather. In time, if the settler stayed and prospered, he might improve the first round-log shelter as a kitchen and attach it by a sort of breezeway to a new and larger hewn-log house.

When the demands of subsistence living allowed it, the southern settler did not think leisure a sin. It was a constant scandal to the Yankee population that the Hoosier made little hay, planted few fruit trees, built few barns, and seemed content with the most scrubby breed of livestock. Neither the zeal of the Yankee nor the thrift of the peasant German marked him. Crawford County farmers climbed the beech and the oak trees in spring to observe the amount of bloom. If they thought the bloom forecast enough beechnuts and acorns to fatten their shoats, they planted little corn.

A host of early writers undertook to characterize the settlers. Some, plainly resentful, called them ignorant, coarse, lazy, lawless. Those accustomed to deference because of prestige or money found the frontiersmen unimpressed by either. Hoosiers did not call a traveler "sir," they called him "stranger." Samuel J. Mills and Daniel Smith, reporting on their travels through the "Territories," declare, "the character of the settlers is such as to render it peculiarly important that missionaries should early be sent among them. Indeed, they can hardly be said to have a character." On the other hand, some have become romantic about the frontier and its settlers. John E. Iglehart is moved by strong passages from Frederick Jackson Turner's essays, especially: "Western democracy was no theorist's dream. It came stark and strong from the American forest." . . . State patriots and historians for local anniversary occasions are also prone to idealize the pioneers.

The way of the frontier farmer was most often hard. He was sick or his horse was lame or the squirrels were eating the corn. But things were about to be different. Every farmer seemed prepared to draw from his pocket a lithographic city and grant the merest acquaintance the favor of taking a few building lots. In spite of present difficulties boundless optimism seemed the mood, and it went with a fierce frontier loyalty that was not anxious for outside counsel. Akin to this was the brashness, buoyancy, and confidence of public figures or candidates—a willingness to support all claims with a fight. The frontiersmen called it a "pushing" spirit and R. Carlyle Buley has attributed to it the ability of young Hoosier doctors to undertake difficult cases without a qualm, and of untried lawyers to plead their cases with unwarranted, flowery eloquence.

The early Indiana settler was willing to share what he had. If there was to be preaching, he would make his house a sanctuary and send out the word—"give out preachin." If travelers needed shelter, they were welcome to the cabin with the rest. In fact, some have charged the Hoosier settler with hospitality beyond his facilities. "Traveled over a fertile country four miles to Steenz, making a distance of thirty-four miles. At this dirty hovel, with one room and a loft, formed by placing boards about three inches apart, ten travelers slept. There were thirteen in the family, besides two calves, making in all, with my friend and self twenty-three whites, one negro and two calves." Problems of dressing or undressing for bed in such large and mixed companies seem to have troubled eastern travelers much more than Hoosiers. For understandable reasons, the settler was willing to share what he had—short of his money. This was too scarce. In the new settlements almost all trade was carried on by barter of goods and service. If the store account could be paid in tow linen, "sang" (ginseng), hides, or "chopping," no cash was forthcoming. When a whole acre of bottom land, trees and all, might be had for less than two dollars, parting with silver was parting with one's best hopes for a farm. This has a real bearing on church subscriptions. Cash was not for trade or pledge; it was for land.

Only if he lived beside a heavily traveled road might the woodsman make some charge for accommodations. When he did so, he would most likely add one room to his cabin, hang out a sign to "keep public," and dignify the whole by the name of tavern. The tavern-keeping settler is by no means the typical citizen of Indiana's frontier, however—there were few roads of any importance. "Zane's trace across Ohio had no real parallel in Indiana, and the settlers stuck to the navigable streams with unfailing persistence." The earliest major road in Indiana was the Vincennes Trace or the "Buffalo Trace," from Louisville to Vincennes. It amounted to a westward extension of the Wilderness Road and became the chief land route for southerners bound for Illinois.

In frontier usage the word "route" should usually be substituted for "road." As late as 1823 the route from Vincennes to Indianapolis was laid out by dragging a log with an ox team through the woods, prairies, and marshes. Specifications for roadbuilding were very loose, and there was no effective system of maintenance beyond corduroying crucial stretches with fallen logs. A road was a general indication of direction to which one returned between mud holes. There might be bridges or ferries over major streams, and there might be lodging of a sort along the way. Indiana's roads, or lack of them, called forth some purple passages from early travelers. Baynard Hall, a Presbyterian clergyman and the first principal of the new Indiana Seminary at Bloomington in 1823, commented on the roads only thirty miles north of the Ohio:

> The autumn is decidedly preferable for travelling on the virgin soil of native forests. One may go then mostly by land and find the roads fewer and shorter; but in the early

spring, branches—(small creeks)—are brim full, and they hold a great deal; concealed fountains bubble up in a thousand places where none were supposed to lurk; creeks turn to rivers, and rivers to lakes, and lakes to bigger ones; and as if this was too little water, out come the mole rivers that have burrowed all this time under the earth, and which, when unexpectedly found are styled out there—"lost rivers!" And every district of a dozen miles square has a lost river. Travelling by land becomes of course travelling by water, or by both: viz., mud and water. Nor is it possible if one would avoid drowning or suffocation to keep the law and follow the blazed road; but he tacks first to the right and then to the left, often making both losing tacks; and all this, not to find a road but a place where there is no road,—untouched mud thick enough to bear, or that has at least some bottom.

A critic with fewer clerical inhibitions inscribed in the register book of a tavern at Franklin:

The Roads are impassable—
Hardly jackassable;
I think those that travel 'em
Should turn out and gravel 'em.

SENATOR SMITH'S REMINISCENCES

Oliver H. Smith

The record of Indiana's historic past has been enriched by a number of contemporaneous writings. One of the most valuable is Early Indiana Trials and Sketches *by Oliver H. Smith, an attorney, politician (a Democrat, then a Whig), and railroad promoter of central Indiana during the antebellum period. A native of Pennsylvania, Smith came to Indiana in 1817 at the age of twenty-three, and he began his legal career in 1820. Elected to the Indiana General Assembly in 1822, and to Congress in 1826, Smith served a single term in the United States Senate from 1837 to 1843, after which he moved to Indianapolis and devoted himself to railroading. His book began as a series of newspaper articles in 1857 that recalled various incidents associated with Indiana's earliest years of statehood, particularly its robust and personalized system of justice. Because of the popularity of Smith's first installments in the Indianapolis newspaper, he expanded the series to include a number of "sketches" and other material. These were collected and published in book form in 1858, the year before Smith's death.*

The selections below are representative of Smith's prose—straightforward, vibrant, and laced with humor and frankness. From his sketches come information on the art of frontier politics, an early Indiana legislature and its members, the important role played by circuit-riding ministers on the frontier, the difficulties of travel in the days before railroads and automobiles, the hardiness and ingenuity of individual settlers, and much more.

Early Condition of Indiana.

While my mind is on Indiana, the reader will excuse me for deferring my sketches

From *Early Indiana Trials and Sketches* (1858), pp. 116–117, 76–77, 80–81, 97, 28–29.

of the House of Representatives, the Senate, the Supreme Court and other matters at Washington, to a more convenient season. And, as these sketches seem to be looked upon as a part of the history of early Indiana, while I make no such pretensions, and refer the public to the authentic history of the State by my valued friend John B. Dillon, Esq., State historian, I may be excused for stating some matters that will be only interesting to the citizens of our State who would like to compare Indiana as she was, with Indiana as she is. I shall not even attempt the comparison, but leave the reader to make it for himself.

At the time I came to the State in March, 1817, there was not a railroad in the United States, nor a canal west of the Alleghany mountains. The telegraph had not been discovered, fire was struck by the flint and steel, the falling spark was caught in "punk" taken from the knots of the hickory tree.—There was not a foot of turnpike road in the State, and plank roads had never been heard of; the girdled standing trees covering the cultivated fields, the shovel-plow the only cultivator, no roads west of Whitewater, not a bridge in the State; the traveling all done on horseback, the husband mounted before on the saddle, with from one to three of the youngest children in his arms—the wife, with a spread cover reaching to the tail of the horse, seated behind, with the balance of the children unable to walk in her lap. We young gentlemen retained the luxury of a single horse; not a carriage nor buggy in all the country. After some years Mr. Lovejoy brought a buggy without a top, to Connersville, from New England. I borrowed it to ride to Wayne county, but I gave up the buggy and took my horse, for fear the people would think me proud, and it would injure my election to Congress.

The finest farms around Connersville in one of the most beautiful countries in the world, cleared, with orchards and common buildings, were $5 to $10 per acre. I bought the fine farm of one hundred and sixty acres, adjoining Connersville, the same now the residence of my friend Hon. Samuel W. Parker, of John Adair, of Brookville, for $9 per acre, in three annual installments without interest. The brick two-story dwelling in which I lived when I was elected to Congress, in the heart of Connersville, twenty-six feet front, well finished, with back kitchen, lot 26 by 180, good stable, I bought of Sydnor Dale for $325,—which was considered a high price at the time. The excellent farm over the river one mile below town, in 1828, I bought of William Denman for $5 per acre, in payments. There was very little money in the country, and produce was equally low in proportion. I bought the finest qualities of stall-fed beef, and corn-fed hogs, for family use, at a cent and a half per pound; corn ten cents, wheat twenty-five cents per bushel, wood delivered and cut short at the door at a dollar per cord; boarding at common houses, with lodging, from a dollar to two dollars a week, and at the very best hotels two dollars and a half. The first year I traveled the circuit, my fees fell short of two hundred dollars; and the second, when they increased to three hundred, I felt as safe as a Stephen Girard. All my wants were supplied, I owed nothing, and had money in my pocket.—No white man had settled more than five miles west of Connersville at that time. . . .

An Early Legislature in Indiana.

In August 1822, I was elected to the Legislature from Fayette, and late in November mounted my pony and started for Corydon, the temporary seat of government. My way led by Madison, then a small village. Late in the evening of the third day from home, I rode up to a little frame house, about the center of the town, to which I was directed as the only hotel. My horse was taken at the steps by a slim, flaxen-haired youth of a hostler. I had a first-rate supper, a sweet, clean bed, a good breakfast, and left on my journey in the morning, the landlord, as I supposed, being from home. The next Monday the House of Representatives met in the old court-house at Corydon. John F. Ross, the clerk, called the roll; "County of Jefferson," when to my surprise, my flaxen-headed hostler stepped forward, in the person of Gen. Milton Stapp, in after years Lieutenant Governor, and one of the most distinguished men of the State. The roll calling progressed, as I stood by the side of the General he bowed and smiled. The "County of Vanderburgh and Warrick:" I saw advancing a slender, freckled-faced boy, in appearance eighteen or twenty years of age. I marked his step as he came up to my side, and have often noticed his air since. It was Gen. Joseph Lane, of Mexican and Oregon fame in after years. The house was composed mostly of new members, and was said to be the greenest ever convened in the State, myself included. We had, however, a few who would pass even at the present day. Gen. Stapp, Isaac Howk, Horace Bassett, John Dumont, Isaac Julian, Pinkney James, Gen. Burnett, William A. Bullock, Lucius H. Scott, Dennis Pennington, Benjamin V. Beckes, Dr. Sylvanius Everts, Nathaniel Hunt, and others. The session lasted six weeks, and perhaps no Legislature ever met and adjourned in the State, doing less harm.—There were a few measures, however, in which I took an active part, that may bear mentioning. The poll-tax system was first established, the exemption in favor of widows, of personal estate to the value of one hundred dollars, from the debts of deceased husbands; and the act giving a representation to "the new purchase," to strengthen the middle and northern parts of the State, in passing the law for the removal of the seat of government from Corydon to Indianapolis. This latter act was warmly contested, debated weeks and finally passed by a very close vote. The first constitution provided that "Corydon in Harrison county, shall be the seat of government of the State of Indiana, until the year eighteen hundred and twenty-five, and until removed by law." It further provided, "the General Assembly may, within two years after their first meeting, and shall in the year eighteen hundred and twenty-five, and every other subsequent term of five years, cause an enumeration to be made, of all the white male inhabitants above the age of twenty-one years; the number of Representatives shall at the several periods of making such enumeration be fixed by the General Assembly, and apportioned among the several counties." The question was whether it was competent for the Legislature to take the census and make the apportionment at any intermediate time, or whether it could only be done at the expiration of every five years. We carried the bill in favor of the first construction, and the seat of government was removed years sooner than it would otherwise have been. We had little important business before us; Gov. Hendricks was inaugurated, and Judge Parke elected to revise the laws.

An Electioneering Operation.

An incident occurred in the election of Treasurer of State that may be instructive to candidates. Daniel C. Lane was the incumbent.—There was no tangible objection against him as an officer, but it was rumored that he could see a short rich man over the head of a tall poor man. His competitor was Samuel Merrill, then of Vevay, afterward for years Treasurer of State, and President of the State Bank. The day for the election was not fixed. I was among the warm friends of Mr. Merrill. Our prospects for his election were very poor—chances as ten to one against us. Mr. Lane, as was the custom, began his course of entertainments, and, as his house was small, he only invited to his first dinner the Senators and the Speaker of the House of Representatives, Gen. Washington Johnston,—intending, no doubt, to feast the members of the House on some other evening before the election.

Next morning the House met, and a few of us understanding each other passed around among the uninitiated, and soon had them in a perfect state of excitement against Lane. The time had now come, and I introduced a resolution inviting the Senate to go into the election instanter. The resolution was reciprocated, and down came the Senate. The joint convention was immediately held, and Mr. Merrill was elected by a large majority, the Senators voting for Mr. Lane and the members of the House for Mr. Merrill, who made the State a first-rate officer. The Legislature adjourned, and I returned home through the woods. This ended my legislative career in the State, as I was never afterward a candidate.

Electioneering.

I have sketched the most important trials that were had during my two years as circuit prosecuting attorney, which ended with the spring term of 1826, when I became a candidate for Congress and resigned. Amos Lane was appointed my successor. The most of the sketches that will be given are of after occurrences.

My competitor for Congress in 1826, the Hon. John Test, was one of the first men in the State, had been on the court bench, was a fine lawyer, a good speaker, and had represented the district three full terms. The contest on my part looked at first almost hopeless. Stump speaking was just coming in fashion. The people met our appointments by thousands. The judge had his high character to aid him, and I brought to my aid a strong voice, reaching to the very extremes of the largest crowds. The judge went for the graduation of the public lands, and I went for home gifts to actual settlers. My position was the most acceptable to the masses. We met in Allenville, Switzerland county, on one occasion. The whole country was there. The judge was speaking, and for the first time introduced the new subject of railroads. He avowed himself in favor of them, and said he had voted for the Buffalo and New Orleans road, and then rising to the top of his voice, "I tell you, fellow-citizens, that in England they run the cars thirty miles an hour, and they will yet be run at a higher speed in America." This was enough. The crowd set up a loud laugh at the expense of the judge. An old fellow, standing by me, bawled out, "You are crazy, or do you think we are all fools; a man could not live a moment at that speed." The day was mine. The judge had ruined his prospects by telling such an improbable story at that day. On another occasion the judge was speaking in favor of the tariff in the highest terms. The people knew but little about it, but what they had heard was decidedly against it; few knew the meaning of the word, and fewer what it was like. One old fellow said he had never seen one, but he believed "it was hard on sheep."

Perils of a Congressional Campaign.

There was fun in those days. We had no parties then, and there was some life in a contest—very different from after times, when the candidates had to be engrafted into the party stock, and drew all their life and strength from the party to which they belonged.

On one occasion in after years I was speaking at a battalion muster in Ripley county, and had spoken over two hours. I noticed an old man leaning against a tree in front of me. As I closed he roared out, "Mr. Smith you have made one of the best speeches I ever heard, I agree with all you have said. Will you answer me one question before you leave the stand." "Most certainly." "Will you vote for General Jackson?" "No, sir, I shall vote for Henry Clay." "Then you can't get my vote." The question was between Jackson and Clay, and not between myself and [my] competitor as to who should go to Congress, with the old man then. The contest grew warm, and more and more doubtful. My stock was rising, and with it my spirits. My district covered one-third of the state.

I had not, as yet, visited the county of Allen, some hundred miles north of Randolph. There were no roads, nothing but Indian paths, to travel at that day through the wilderness. In the early part of May I turned the head of my pony north for Fort Wayne. The streams were high and the path for miles under water in places. I rode in that campaign a small brown Indian pony, a good swimmer, a fine pacer, and a fine traveler. The first day after I left the settlements at the Mississinewa, I reached the Indian station at Francis Godfroy's. The chief was [away] from home, but one of his wives came out at an opening in the picketing, and pointed toward Fort Wayne; the chief was there. She could not speak a word of English. I pointed to the stable, then to my horse, then to my mouth, then laid my head on my hands, shut my eyes, and commenced snoring. She seized the reins of the bridle; I dismounted and passed through the pickets into the house. My faithful pony was fed. Night came on at length; supper was announced, by motions; corn bread, venison, and sassafras tea, a bear skin on the floor for a bed, and sound sleeping followed. Breakfast of the same over, and I was about starting alone, when there came up an Indian that could speak a little broken English. I agreed with him for a guide for two dollars for a day to get me over the Salamonia and Wabash rivers. We were soon on our horses, and off went my guide at full speed on his pony, and was soon out of sight. I overtook him, however, at the Salamonia. In we went, he leading. The ponies swam beautifully; and away we started for the Wabash.

Itinerant Preachers.

I should be false to the history of Early Indiana were I to pass by in silence the itinerant Methodist preachers who contributed so much to the establishment of good order, quiet, intelligence, morality and religion among the first settlers, and without intending to give offense to others, I venture the remark, that early Indiana, nay, more, Indiana to-day, owes more to the itinerant Methodist preachers than to all other religious denominations combined.

Their system carried their churches into every settlement, and where two or three were gathered together, there was a Methodist preacher or exhorter in the midst. They were at the bed-side of the dying man on their knees, and at the grave their voices were heard in songs of praise. Other denominations waited for the people to come up from the wilderness to worship, while the itinerant Methodist preacher mounted his horse, and sought out their cabins in the woods, held his meetings there, carrying the Gospel, and leaving the Bible and Hymn Book as he went.

A Sheriff Outwitted.

In early times, before the first land-sales of the beautiful Whitewater valley, where Connersville, Liberty, Cambridge City, Centerville and Richmond now stand, there lived upon the east bank of Whitewater, a mile above Connersville, a most remarkable woman by the name of Betty Frazier. She was a small, tough-looking, rather swarthy woman; her husband, George Frazier, was a poor cripple, and with their children was entirely supported by Betty. They had settled upon a small fraction of government land, intending to purchase at the sales. The land-office was at Cincinnati, and General James Findlay was the Receiver. The spring of the year, after a severe winter, had come; the sales were to take place the next winter, and Betty had the season before her to raise the money to pay for her land. She commenced with a young stock of hogs, caring for them daily, driving them to the best mast, and preparing a good patch of corn for the fattening process. She had one horse only to tend her crop, and to ride to Cincinnati when she drove her hogs down to sell, and buy her land.

One day about mid-summer she saw a horseman ride up to her cabin in full uniform. She met him at the bars: "Well, General Hanna, how do you do?" "Very well, Mrs. Frazier." "What on earth has brought you all the way from Brookville to my poor cabin?" "I am very sorry to tell you, Mrs. Frazier, that I am the sheriff, and have an execution against your property." "Well, General, I always submit to the law; come with me to the stable and I will give you my only horse as the best I can do." There were no "exemption laws" then. Betty and the General proceeded to the stable. It was a strong log building with a single door, no window, overlaid with a solid platform of logs, and filled above with hay for the horse. The door fastened outside with a large wooden pin in a log. "There, General, is the horse—take him." The General stepped in and commenced untying the horse. Betty immediately fastened the door outside, driving the pin into the hole to its full length, and left the General to his reflections while she attended to her household affairs. Time passed away; night came on; but no relief to the captured General. Morning came, and with it came Betty. "Well, General, how did you sleep last night." "Not very well. I am ready to compromise this matter; if you will let me out and show me the ford over Whitewater (the river was muddy and high), I will leave you and the horse and return the execution 'no property found.' " "Upon honor?" "Yes, upon honor." Betty opened the door. The General mounted his horse and silently followed Betty down to the river side. "There, General, you will go in just above the big sycamore, and come out at that haw-bush you see." The General started; at the second step both horse and rider were under water out of sight, and the chapeau of the General was seen floating down the river. Still, he being one of the pioneers, and his horse a trained swimmer, gallantly stemmed the current, and exactly struck the haw-bush, his horse swimming to the very shore, while Betty stood on the bank screaming—"I guess the Brookville officers will let me alone now till I have sold my pigs and bought my land." The General rode on dripping wet to his brigade that mustered that day. But the end was not yet. Time rolled on; the pigs grew to be well fatted hogs. Betty mounted her pony; the little boys started the hogs for Cincinnati; they had ten days to get there before the land-sales; the distance was about seventy miles. Nothing unusual occurred on the road until they arrived at New Trenton, at Squire Rockafellow's. The night was stormy; the snow fell deep; next morning found Betty at the usual hour on the pony, well wrapped, with *an infant a few hours old in her bosom*. She arrived with her hogs at Cincinnati the day before the sale, sold them for cash, and the late General Findlay told me that she stood by his side on the box and bid off her land, with her infant in her arms. Surely "Truth is stranger than fiction."

Cultural Centers of the 1820s

Among the newcomers to Indiana in the 1820s were the followers of Robert Owen, the industrialist-reformer who established his shortlived experiment in communal living in 1825. Although the Owenite community failed in 1827, a number of the remarkable and talented people who had come to New Harmony remained and exerted a continuing influence on the educational, scientific, and humanitarian developments in Indiana for decades. Among a number of important "firsts" at New Harmony are the first public library in Indiana, the first workingmen's institute, the first kindergarten, and sponsorship of the first geological survey of the state, a service performed by David Dale Owen.

At the time of the New Harmony experiment in southern Indiana, the William Conner farm, an important cultural center of a different sort, was developing in central Indiana. Conner, originally a fur trader and Indian agent with his brother John (who later founded Connersville in southeastern Indiana), had established himself on the White River (above what became Indianapolis) to continue working with the Indians. Following the Treaty of St. Mary's, Conner's Indian wife and her children departed for the West with the migrating Delaware in 1820. The home Conner built for his new wife in 1823, and where the Conners lived until 1837, has become the Conner Prairie Settlement and Museum, a "living history" restoration of pioneer life now operated by Earlham College. It is located a few miles south of Noblesville. Conner, his achievements, and the current use of his home and its surroundings are described below. The best sources on the history of New Harmony, including both the Rappite and Owenite phases, are William E. Wilson, *The Angel and the Serpent:*

The Story of New Harmony (1964); George B. Lockwood, *The New Harmony Movement* (1905), and Karl J. R. Arndt, *George Rapp's Harmony Society, 1785–1847* (1965). Arndt has also collected, translated, and edited thousands of Rappite documents for his *Indiana Decade of the Harmony Society, 1814–1824* (2 vols., 1976–1978). See also Richard W. Leopold, *Robert Dale Owen: A Biography* (1940), and Arthur E. Bestor, Jr., *Backwoods Utopias: The Sectarian and Owenite Phases of Communitarian Socialism in America, 1663–1829* (1950). For additional information on William Conner, see Charles N. Thompson, *Sons of the Wilderness: John and William Conner* (1937), and John Lauritz Larson and David G. Vanderstel, "Agent of Empire: William Conner on the Indiana Frontier, 1800–1855" *Indiana Magazine of History*, LXXX (December 1984), 301–328.

ROBERT OWEN'S NEW HARMONY

Roger D. Branigin

Roger D. Branigin, an attorney and businessman from Lafayette, Indiana, at the time of his election as governor of Indiana in 1964, was a native of Johnson County. There he acquired what became a lifelong fascination with the legal, social, and political history of his home state. During his tenure in office, he was instrumental in developing a restored New Harmony that now serves as a mecca for tourists interested in the cultural history of America and, in conjunction with the University of Southern Indiana nearby, as a center for the study of communal societies in general. Branigin's own extensive collection of Indiana law and history books, as well as his personal papers, have been deposited in the library at Franklin College, Franklin, Indiana, his alma mater. In 1971, during the Robert Owen Bicentennial Conference in New Harmony, the former governor delivered an address reflecting upon Robert Owen's impact upon Indiana, part of which is reprinted below. His observations were intended, he said, not as history but as "the remarks of a friendly observer." They serve, the former governor's modesty notwithstanding, as a fine overview of Owen and the Owenite society at New Harmony, and the continuing influence of both upon the state.

For additional information on New Harmony, including both the Rappite community established there in 1814 by Father George Rapp and the society established there by Robert Owen in 1825, see in particular the article by Donald E. Pitzer and Josephine M. Elliott, "New Harmony's First Utopians, 1814–1824," Indiana Magazine of History, *LXXV (September 1979), 224–300, and Donald F. Carmony and Josephine M. Elliott, "New Harmony, Indiana: Robert Owen's Seedbed for Utopia,"* Indiana Magazine of History, *LXXVI (September 1980), 161–187. Professor Pitzer is director of the USI Center for Communal Societies, and Mrs. Elliott is a lifelong resident and student of New Harmony. Donald F. Carmony, a professor at Indiana University and an authority on early Indiana history, edited the* Indiana Magazine of History *for many years.*

Robert Owen came to America and to Indiana in the waning days of 1824. He was

From Roger D. Branigin, "Robert Owen's New Harmony: An American Heritage," in *Robert Owen's American Legacy: Proceedings of the Robert Owen Bicentennial Conference*, ed. Donald E. Pitzer (Indianapolis: Indiana Historical Society, 1972), pp. 14–24.

fifty-three years old and showed no diminution of the extraordinary zeal and the boundless energy which had marked his course as industrialist, educator, philosopher, and reformer. He had lived through the turbulent years of the French Revolution, the collision of the industrialists and reformers in Britain's Industrial Revolution, and the "alarming" advance of the trade union movement. None of these swayed Owen from his primary purpose, the establishment of a new system of education and social amelioration. To prove the soundness of his views, he needed a new workshop, not contaminated by the industrialists and the clergy. His decision to look abroad may have been accelerated by the alienation of his English friends who were shocked by his denunciation of the established churches. . . .

Indiana was indeed a wilderness. The state had just selected its new capital, Indianapolis. It was called "the village at the end of the road," and was a bold move from the more civilized town of Corydon, the seat of government for a brief nine years. The land offices were doing a brisk business, reflecting in part the ease of selection of land laid off on the so-called Jeffersonian system of survey. Towns were being laid out with or without adequate survey, mill sites and ferry franchises were in demand, and the sound of the axe and the anvil punctuated the silence of the forests. The Erie Canal was being readied for the first Albany-Buffalo barge in the fall. Solid citizens, adventurers, vagabonds, merchants, traders, and just plain people were making their way to the new country by raft or boat or wagon, seeking cheap land, excitement, opportunity, and bringing their religion and their politics with them. The Wilderness Road, the Ohio, the Maumee, and the Wabash, the Great Lakes, and the Indian traces all led to the new Eden. There were shipyards at Madison, vineyards at Vevay, and all manner of craftsmen at the Falls—smiths, wool carders, cabinetmakers, chandlers. The Michigan Road was being planned northward from Madison. The Wabash trade route was clear of danger and busy. Activity was high at the great portage, Fort Wayne. . . .

Across the way some forty miles from New Harmony, Abraham Lincoln worked the land and cleared the woods with his cousin, Dennis Hanks. Lincoln was then fifteen years old. Many men have speculated upon the course of history if the young Lincoln had met with the dreamers and the scholars of New Harmony. Tradition has it that he lacked the necessary parental consent and the $100 tuition charged of outsiders who studied in the progressive New Harmony schools. Lincoln's poet biographer Carl Sandburg ventures to say that Lincoln did know about New Harmony and once told Dennis Hanks that he marvelled at the thousands of books and the men there who knew everything. Almost forty years later, Lincoln did come to know Owen's son, Robert Dale, who implored the President to issue an emancipation order. "It . . . stirred me like a trumpet call," Lincoln later recalled.

The Rappite decade along the lower Wabash ended in 1824. The Harmonists used their savings and their newly found wealth to begin building in Beaver County, near Pittsburgh, beautiful new brick structures for their society and to dream again the hopes and the promises of Father George Rapp. They would call their new home Economy. They left, at New Harmony, comfortable dwellings which were ultra modern compared to the rude cabins of the frontiersmen. The homes were sturdy, warm in winter and cool in summer, varmint-free, with better facilities for cooking and for rest than the lean-tos of the woods. By 1825, New Harmony was almost uninhabited and ready to receive its new landlord from across the Atlantic.

And what manner of man was this Robert Owen, poised to embark on his noble experiment? He was, it would appear, a bundle of opposites—gentle and unyielding, kindly and opinionated, thrifty and generous, a practical dreamer, a scholarly industrialist, a visionary, a reformer, a good father, a poor judge of character, a pantheist who was sometimes a better Christian than his Christian critics. Ralph Waldo Emerson once said "whoso would be a man, must be a nonconformist." The essayist was not speaking of Robert Owen, but he could have been. Owen was, indeed, a nonconformist who harbored no fears of the establishment and held no man in awe. And he was a scholar—of the sort William Shakespeare had in mind in describing Cardinal Wolsey as "a ripe and good one; exceeding wise, fair-spoken, and persuading." His remarkable competence in business and his skills in management and finance were matched by a broad scholarship in educational, scientific, and cultural fields. His writings, a bit pedantic at times, bear witness.

He was not a politician. Politics is the art or science of government, and practical politics involves the art of compromise. There was but little compromise in the marrow of Owen's bones. He was endowed with a personal magnetism rare among men, and yet he could repel as readily as convince. In one of his better-known declarations (for he could be oracular upon occasion) he proclaimed that society's chief ills were armies, churches, lawyers, doctors, and exclusive universities. No man wise in the ways of compromise and practical politics would have invited so many entrenched enemies into the arena for one encounter.

In truth, Robert Owen was an enigma. Few masters of business affairs concerned themselves with the welfare of the people or with the solution of social problems as did the cotton spinner of New Lanark. His conclusions were not influenced by the church for he had early lost all belief in existing religion. He had a creed, a belief, pantheistic though it was, and had carved out for himself a peculiarly personal philosophy: "The great secret in the right formation of man's character is to place him under the proper influences from his earliest years," he wrote. "Character is formed by circumstances over which man has no control and thus he is not a proper subject for praise or blame." . . .

There was a bit of Phineas T. Barnum in Robert Owen and more than a touch of Samuel Johnson—and so, in the elaborate arrangement he made for the grand move upon America, he planned big. It began with a stay in New York during the winter to advertise his program. Then he made two dazzling appearances in the Hall of Representatives in the Capitol of the Young America. On February 25, 1825, and again on March 7, Owen lectured on his plans for the creation of a new social system to audiences that included Presidents James Monroe and John Quincy Adams together with members of their Cabinets, the Supreme Court, and both Houses of Congress. Only a first rate Madison Avenue public relations man of our day could have arranged such performances before two presidents of the United States and their retinue. Later, in December 1826, Owen had a six-foot-square architect's model of the ideal community edifice which he planned to built at New Harmony displayed at the United States Patent Office and at the White House. He would suffer attack from New Harmony critics because he would not produce the model for the membership.

Almost immediately after these auspicious and exciting proceedings in the nation's capital, Owen left for New Harmony. Hopes were never higher, expectations were never greater. On April 20, 1825, he addressed the community, and his words reflected the enthusiasm and the assurance of success which possessed everyone. Within a week a constitution for the government of the society was presented by Mr. Owen and adopted without dissent. With the legal and social machinery ready, success of the enterprise was thought to be automatic. With parting injunctions and good wishes, Owen departed for the East in early June, and in mid-July returned to New Lanark.

The New Moral World had been launched. By the spring of 1826, the educational experiments of Owen and his partner, the distinguished Philadelphia scientist and patron of the arts, William Maclure, were under way. Plans were being readied for milling, cotton manufacture, weaving and tanning, soap making, and dyeing. Production never quite kept up with plans and hopes. The pottery was idle for want of workers, and while there were some bakers, butchers, farmers, tanners, a brewer, a tinner, coopers, and a smith, the unmanaged economy barely dragged on.

Before the year's end, Owenite societies were organized in other communities: Yellow Springs in Ohio, Blue Spring near Bloomington, and at places as distant as New York, Pennsylvania, and Tennessee. But almost all of them withered and died before the collapse of the social experiment at New Harmony in April, 1827.

At the close of 1825 there may have been as many as a thousand people resident in New Harmony. Many of the idle, the vicious, and the curious had already departed, having worn out their welcomes in a community of dedicated people. Things weren't going well, but spirits were still high because of the master's return from England in January, 1826.

In a speech on January 12, Owen announced to the residents of New Harmony what was to be his greatest American achievement. He had convinced William Maclure and an illustrious group of his scientific and educational colleagues of Philadelphia to join the experiment on the Wabash. At that very moment, Pestalozzian educators Madame Marie D. Fretageot and William S. Phiquepal, naturalists Thomas Say and Charles Lesueur, as well as Maclure and Owen's son Robert Dale, were on board the *Philanthropist* making their way to New Harmony. The arrival of the famous "Boatload of Knowledge" on January 24 established New Harmony (farther west than any American college) as the intellectual center of the West. And in the years that followed, the list of scholars grew to include such men as Joseph Neef, Gerard Troost, Josiah Warren, and the younger Owens themselves.

Within a fortnight of Owen's announcement of the coming of the scholars, the Preliminary Society adopted a constitution for the Community of Equality which many accepted—but differences over religion caused some defections; enough to form a new community, Macluria. Shortly, there was another with the unpronounceable name of Feiba Peveli, forerunner of the postal zip code. Everything seemed in proper course for success. Robert Owen's report in May, 1826, was a happy appraisal of progress made and vision of hope for the future. But despite the bright and exciting things going on, success just never came. In succession came dispute, dissension, litigation, and finally disintegration.

It should offend none, upon an occasion such as this, if we should look with a critical eye upon the works of a great man whose memory we gather to honor. . . . To speak of the unhappy collapse of the New Harmony experiment is to begin reflections upon the rich and last contributions of Robert Owen to our American heritage. There is a tendency, upon occasions of celebration, to overlaud the works of men. There should be no danger here for there are still flowers growing from the seed this restless spirit sowed here almost a century and a half ago. A distinguished Vice-President of the United States [Thomas R. Marshall] said in his memoirs:

> No movement of purely human origin is ever entirely a success or completely a failure. Out of the New Harmony experiment . . . grew up the idea not only of coeducation but of a system whereby every child in the state was to have a chance for a liberal education. From it came also the wise and beneficial laws . . . with reference to woman and her property . . . and the traveling library.

To the traveling library he attributed the literary fecundity and facility of speech of Hoosiers of the last century.

The Indiana constitution of 1851—our basic law today—bears the Owen imprint. The product of a New Harmony craftsman, Robert Dale Owen, its article on education provides that

> Knowledge and learning, generally diffused throughout a community, being essential to the preservation of a free government; it shall be the duty of the General Assembly to encourage by all suitable means, moral, intellectual, scientific and agricultural improvement, and to provide by law for a general and uniform system of common schools, wherein tuition shall be without charge, and equally open to all.

This dream has come to pass. And the introduction to America of the Pestalozzian principles of education, a particular fancy of Robert Owen, affected the course of all American education. It was to insure the faithful transmission of the system fashioned by Pestalozzi and Fellenberg that Owen had attracted Phiquepal, Madame Fretageot, Neef, and other teachers to the experiment. Their influence upon generations of educators is incalculable. . . .

One of the great residual bequests which Robert Owen made to America was the assembly in New Harmony of that remarkable collection of scholars, scientists, and imaginative men and women. Their influence upon our culture, our lives, our manners and ideals is difficult to measure. . . . Foremost among all those brought here were Robert and Caroline Dale Owen's distinguished children. They have given to America, in almost unending line the leaven to make it great: Robert Dale, the dreamer of dreams; William, the practical planner; David Dale, the insatiable collector; and Richard, the great humanist and scholar. They are all recorded in the Hoosier's Hall of Fame, and none without good reason.

Last then, Robert Owen left us New Harmony, still preserved from the disc of the bulldozer and the ball of the wrecker. Here dwells the spirit of the mind and the heart.

And tonight, if you would listen, you may hear the impassioned plea of the orator, the sweet notes of the harpsichord, the laughter and gayety of the dance, the magic voice of the actor, the even tones of the schoolmaster—perhaps the light laughter of lovers—and if Robert Owen had left just this, it would have been enough.

WILLIAM CONNER'S FARM

Lorna Lutes Sylvester

Indiana Territory was just over two years old in August, 1802. Carved from the Northwest Territory in May, 1800, the new area included all but a sliver of the present state of Indiana, all of Illinois and Wisconsin, about half of Michigan, and a tiny section of Minnesota. The territory's white population of approximately 6,500 lived mainly in Kaskaskia, Cahokia, Mackinac, Detroit, Clark's Grant, Vincennes, and a few other "scattered and isolated islands" of settlement "entirely surrounded by a wide sea of green forest."

By 1802 settlements in the area eventually to become the state of Indiana formed a narrow crescent beginning in the lower Whitewater Valley in the east, south along the Ohio River, and up the Wabash to Vincennes in the west. Except for the sizable Vincennes Tract, surrounding the town of Vincennes; the 150,000 acre Clark's Grant, opposite the falls of the Ohio; the wedge shaped Gore in the east, which would be added to Indiana Territory in 1803; and isolated patches of land granted to the whites by the Treaty of Greenville in 1795, the future Hoosier State in 1802 was entirely Indian country. Here and there roamed the Piankashaw, Miami, Shawnee, Wea, Kickapoo, Potawatomi; and in the territory's midsection, between the two forks of White River, were the peaceful Delaware. The estimated Indian population ranged from 5,000 to 25,000; whites numbered about 2,500. The country which is now central and northern Indiana was, in 1802, "a continuous primeval wilderness. . . . There were no roads other than Indian trails and buffalo traces, no boats except the softly gliding Indian canoes, no towns other than straggling Indian villages, no inns between the white settlement. . . . It was veritably the haunt of wild beasts and savage men." Two missionaries to the Delaware on White River further attested to the isolation of the area in 1802, "the Delaware towns, of which there are nine in all, lie from four to five miles apart, and are scattered along the river. After these towns come other settlements of Indian nations as for instance, the Nanticoke, Schawanos and others. After that there is nothing but meadowland as far as the eye can reach, until the banks of the Wabash."

In this wilderness in the Delaware Indian country, about four miles south of the present site of Noblesville, Indiana, "on a beautiful moonlight night, August 12, 1802

From "Conner Prairie Pioneer Settlement and Museum," *Indiana Magazine of History*, LXV (March 1969), 1–2, 4–7.

. . . with only the aid of a French Canadian," William Conner completed the construction of a double log cabin which was to serve as a home for his Indian wife and children and also as a trading post. Located on the eastern side of the west fork of White River at a point where the stream made a horseshoe bend, the cabin soon became a landmark in the area. For several years Conner's trading post was the central market place for Indians in the vicinity, and hundreds of furs left there for Cincinnati via Conner's Trail to John Conner's store a few miles below Brookville, Indiana.

John and William Conner were brothers who had come to the Delaware country from Detroit during the late eighteenth century. Both had married Delaware women—William's wife being Chief Anderson's daughter, Mekinges—both had been licensed traders to the Indians even before building their respective posts, and both were to be extremely influential in the development of Indiana Territory and the Hoosier State. They served as guides on military and diplomatic missions, were interpreters and advisers for many of the treaties removing Indian title to the land in eastern Indiana Territory, fought in the War of 1812, served in the state legislature, helped select the site of Indianapolis, founded towns, and operated numerous businesses in addition to the fur trade.

The Conner brothers had spent most of their lives in an Indian environment. Their parents, Richard and Margaret Conner, were adopted members of the Shawnee tribe, Margaret having lived with the Shawnee from childhood. John, William, their brothers, and their sister were raised among the Christian Delaware in the Moravian mission towns in Ohio and Michigan. At the end of the Revolutionary War the Conner family was living near Detroit where Richard Conner had acquired vast acres of farm land. Before the turn of the century, however, John and William left their father's farms for the Indian country in what was to become the state of Indiana. While John eventually chose to locate in the Whitewater Valley near the border between Indian and white territory, William and his wife, Mekinges, settled in their double log cabin on the west fork of White River near the Delaware towns. Here scores of Indians came to trade their beaver, fox, raccoon, mink, otter, muskrat, and other pelts for the Hudson Bay blankets, trade axes, knives, beads, and similar paraphernalia which Conner stocked. Here Mekinges cared for their six children. From here William left to serve with General William Henry Harrison as guide, interpreter, and soldier during the War of 1812. And to this primitive log cabin in 1820 came Governor Jonathan Jennings and ten commissioners appointed to select a site for the permanent seat of government in the four year old state of Indiana.

The location selected was at the confluence of Fall Creek and White River approximately fifteen miles south southeast of the Conner cabin. By the Treaty of St. Mary's (New Purchase Treaty) at St. Mary's, Ohio, in 1818, the United States had removed Indian title to the land in central Indiana in which the Conner cabin and the capital site were located. Both the Conner brothers had been extremely influential as interpreters and advisers in securing Indian agreement to this treaty. Indeed, according to two of the United States commissioners, Jonathan Jennings and Lewis Cass, the Conners "had it in their power to have prevented any purchase of Indian title to land on the waters of the White river. . . ." The Treaty of St. Mary's was particularly significant for William, for by it the Delaware agreed to leave Indiana for lands provided by the federal government west of the Mississippi River. According to tribal law an Indian wife must remain with her people, thus Mekinges and the six children would leave with them. Conner himself could have accompanied his wife—some white men married to Indian women did so—but William chose to remain in Indiana.

The Delaware had been given until 1821 to leave the state, but during the late summer of 1820 most of the tribe gathered at the Conner cabin preparatory to departure. They left for the West in August or September, accompanied by Mekinges and her children. Approximately three months later, on November 30, 1820, Conner married Elizabeth Chapman, stepdaughter of John Finch who had moved to the west fork of White River in the summer of 1819. Conner had first met Elizabeth on a trip to Connersville earlier in 1819. According to one writer, whose wife was a great granddaughter of John Conner, William was attracted to her even at this time, and the attraction became mutual after Elizabeth moved to the White River country with her stepfather. The fur trader and his new wife moved into the double log cabin which he had built for his Indian family eighteen years before.

Three years later, however, Conner built a new home for Elizabeth—a two story, brick structure, one of the first such buildings in the New Purchase area. Located approximately one mile south of the cabin site and back from the river, the brick house sat on a small hill overlooking rich river bottoms and the semicircular sweep of White River itself. According to one historian the house was considered "elegant" and "remarkably handsome" at the time of its construction, and he describes it as follows:

> A center hall divides the house, disclosing at one end the broad sweep of the prairie farm and providing at the other the usual mode of entrance from the land which leads to the main road. On entering the yard the old well first meets the eye. . . . Spacious rooms with a fireplace in each, open from the hall, and from it a graceful stairway leads to the second floor, where there is a similar arrangement of rooms with a fireplace in each. . . . Adjoining the dining room on the south side of the hall is an old-fashioned kitchen containing a spacious fireplace with an oven on one side. A staircase . . . leads to a loft-like room above the kitchen.

William and Elizabeth Conner lived in this home until 1837 when they moved to a 150 acre farm adjoining Noblesville, Indiana. The circuit court of Hamilton County—formed in 1823—also held its early sessions in the brick house, as did the Board of County Commissioners.

Conner's interests in the new state of Indiana were by this time myriad. In 1823 in conjunction with Josiah F. Polk he platted and founded the town of Noblesville which soon became the county seat of Hamilton County. After John Conner's death in 1826 William maintained the operation of his brother's store in Indianapolis, his mills in Hamilton and Fayette counties (including wool carding, gristmill, sawmill, and distillery), his two farms and two town lots. William also served as a member of the Association for the Improvement of Common Schools in Indiana, as commissioner to lay out a road from Indianapolis to Fort Wayne, and as a charter member of the Indiana Historical Society. He still saw occasional service as an interpreter in treaty negotiations with the Indians. He also served in the state House of Representatives for three terms (1829–1830, 1831–1832, 1836–1837) and accompanied the Indiana militia as a guide during Black Hawk's War in 1832.

When Conner and his wife Elizabeth moved from their brick home on White River to Noblesville in 1837, he liquidated many of his businesses. Until approximately the time of his death in 1855, however, he maintained his interest in internal improvements in Indiana—roads, canals, and railroads—operated a saw- and gristmill about four miles north of Noblesville, conducted a general store on the west side of the public square in that town, and managed nearly three thousand acres of land which he owned in Hamilton, Cass, Wabash, and Marion counties. When Conner died at the age of seventy-eight, he was survived by his wife, nine of their ten children, and a burgeoning state which owed more to his resourcefulness, enterprise, and energy than most of its citizens would ever realize.

Not until May, 1855, about three months prior to his death, did Conner become sole owner in fee simple of the land on White River on which he had built his first cabin and brick home. He had settled there while the area was still Indian country, but when the land passed to the federal government by the Treaty of St. Mary's, the Conner homestead should have been reserved to him, as similar acreage was to other individuals in like situations. Conner, however, when assured that the government would make adjustments later, agreed to postpone his claim. "Later" proved to be thirty-seven years and many legal maneuverings in the future.

After Conner's death the land on White River had a number of owners, and during the twentieth century the house was allowed to deteriorate. This neglect and the passage of time almost erased the original dignity and simplicity of the Conner homestead. In 1933, 110 years after its construction, Eli Lilly, then president of the Indiana Historical Society, purchased the brick house and surrounding acres. After careful and painstaking restoration of the original structure the house was opened to the public on a limited basis. Guests there could see the Jacob Cox portraits of William and Elizabeth Conner as well as furnishings and memorabilia of the Conners and of the period in which they lived. In 1964, after further restoration, Mr. Lilly presented the Conner Prairie Settlement to Earlham College to be operated as a permanent historical museum.

Visitors to Conner Prairie today enter the settlement through a pioneer museum which houses a 150 year old dugout canoe, exhibits depicting frontier farming and the life of William Conner, and a collection of early farm implements, a gift of the Purdue Agricultural Alumni Association. From the museum, guides—dressed in apparel typical of the early 1800s—conduct tours through a log barn, containing a covered wagon and other farm equipment of the period, and a log cabin and log trading post representing the double cabin and trading post which Conner had during the early nineteenth century. As the tour is routed, next come a log distillery and springhouse and a board and batten loom house, which contains all the equipment needed by the pioneer housewife to card, spin, and weave her cloth. (The log buildings in Conner Prairie Settlement were moved there from Brown County, Indiana; the loom house came from the south edge of Carmel, Indiana.) In these buildings Conner Prairie guides demonstrate the uses of the items on display. Visitors can see how an early flintlock rifle was loaded and how candles were dipped, how flax or wool was carded, spun on the old spinning wheels, then woven into cloth on the large looms. In the kitchen of the brick house meat will probably be roasting on the fireplace spit, and possibly bread will be baking in the unique beehive oven. Only in the old distillery—which was plugged by the State Alcoholic Beverages Commission—will there be no demonstrations.

And as the present day guests step out of the old brick house onto the front veranda—added at the time of the restoration in the 1930s—they may well agree with an earlier visitor to the Conner home who wrote, "I never beheld a more delightful scene than when I looked down . . . on a field of three hundred acres of waving corn, some two feet high, with fifteen or twenty merry plowmen scattered over it at work." This writer entered the house "out of nature's forest, only broken by the occasional cabins and small patches of cleared land of the early settlers." Today's visitor enters from the hurried and harried activity of the twentieth century, but the peace, dignity, simplicity, and beauty of William Conner's homestead has endured for almost 150 years and is still there to touch him.

ESTABLISHING THE PUBLIC SCHOOLS

Val Nolan, Jr.

Caleb Mills is recognized as the father of the public school system in Indiana. Not only did he campaign effectively for constitutional reform and new educational legislation during the late 1840s and early 1850s (described in the pages below), he also served a term as Superintendent of Public Instruction, an elected office, and as such helped establish the system for which he had labored very diligently over a number of years. For too long, in Mills's opinion, the easterners' jibe that "Hoosier" was a synonym for "ignorant" was too nearly true to be humorous; and the college professor was moved into action when he read the 1840 Census and its alarming report that Indiana ranked at the bottom of the northern free states in literacy, and was even surpassed by several southern slave states.

The Constitution of 1851, while moving away from the first constitution's attempt to set up a system of free higher education, did authorize the establishment of a free public school system at the lower levels. The Free Public School Law of 1852 embodied the General Assembly's first attempt to carry out its new constitutional mandate, but litigation over the right of the state to tax its citizens for educational purposes delayed the actual establishment of an adequate school system until after the Civil War. Gradually, however, during the late nineteenth century, both elementary and secondary school programs were started, and these were supplemented by a growing network of private colleges throughout the state and by two new state schools—Purdue University, the state's land grant institution established for agricultural and

From "Caleb Mills and the Indiana Free School Law," *Indiana Magazine of History*, XLIX (March 1953), 81–90.

mechanical training in 1870, and the Indiana State Normal School, now Indiana State University, authorized in 1865.

The contributor of the following piece is Val Nolan, Jr., professor of law at Indiana University in Bloomington. For further information on Mills and nineteenth-century schools, see Charles W. Moores, Caleb Mills and the Indiana School System *(1905), and Richard G. Boone,* A History of Education in Indiana *(1892, reprinted 1941). See also Carl F. Kaestle,* Pillars of the Republic: Common Schools and American Society, 1780–1860 *(1983).*

Historians have long assigned to Caleb Mills the leading role in Indiana's free school movement of the middle 1800's, a movement that culminated over one hundred years ago in the passage of the state's first truly systematic free school law. Mills' most enduring claim to generalship in the victory lies in his six widely-read "Educational Messages" written under the nom de plume "One of the People." Why he preferred to conceal his identity, and how and when his secret eventually became public are facts not revealed in the rather meager biographical materials. A recently discovered letter from Mills to John Barron Niles is interesting therefore, both because in it Mills divulges his identity as "One of the People" and because it reveals how thoroughly Mills was a fighter and not simply a philosopher of the revolution. A brief narrative will place the letter in its setting.

Despite the truly memorable educational article in its Constitution of 1816, Indiana approached mid-nineteenth century with its ideal of free popular education still a lofty concept rather than a reality. Most common schools, where they existed at all, were locally maintained and therefore cheaply administered and poorly taught, their doors open for brief periods each year only to those who could afford and were willing to pay tuition. County seminaries, on their level, were no better; and Indiana University reached only a few. Private academies and colleges brightened a little the gloom of the state's educational picture (some were good, and the mere existence of private schools indicated considerable interest in education); but they were not, of course, free. The harvest of such apathetic cultivation is not surprising. The 1840 census revealed that one of seven of Indiana's adults could not read or write, and its illiteracy rate exceeded that of all northern and of three slave states.

"Among all those who saw the calamitous ignorance of the people and were ambitious of better things for the State . . . was one whose contributions to the question were sufficiently definite and sound to be recognized as the chief factor in its solution." On the day following the opening of the 1846 session of the General Assembly, *The Indiana State Journal* carried "An Address to the Legislature" over the signature "One of the People." The writer pointed to Indiana's lamentable inadequacy in the vital field of education, then passed to concrete consideration of particular evils and of remedies. Public funds at that time devoted to schools came largely from the federal land grant of one section in each congressional township. The money derived from these sections was not consolidated and then distributed equally throughout the state; instead each township kept whatever it could realize from its own section. Thus the very communities that most needed public assistance and could least afford to support schools from local funds, *i.e.*, communities where land values were low and farms poor, in fact received the least help from the land donation; prosperous townships got the highest incomes from their more valuable lands. Such inefficient use of the funds must be rectified, said the Address, by equal state-wide distribution. Furthermore and even more significant, the really basic support for free schools must be raised by taxation. Finally, only if higher schools improve will well-trained teachers be available; therefore let the county seminaries and the state university be reorganized. Sell all the physical facilities of the seminaries and of the university; distribute the interest on the proceeds to one private seminary in each county and to every college whose governors will agree to maintain certain stipulated standards, to train teachers, and to devote the money received to provide prospective teachers with free tuition.

Eight days after the address appeared, Governor James Whitcomb in his annual message to the legislature urged that body to revise the entire school system and place it under the charge of a state superintendent. The General Assembly passed no such statute, but it indicated its interest by adopting a joint resolution calling upon the friends of education in Indiana to meet at Indianapolis in a convention to consider the school problem.

Mills' second address, to the 1847 legislature, expanded upon many of the points already made, called taxation a necessity not only as a money raising device but also as the most effective way to insure public interest in education, and explored problems of requisite buildings, adequate salaries for teachers, books, and integrated school superintendence. Probably at least partly in response to the messages, the General Assembly ordered a referendum to determine the public will on a free school bill introduced at the session; the referendum vote was in favor of the bill. The third address analyzed this vote by counties, pointing to the close correlation between a county's high illiteracy rate and its hostility to the bill. The 1848 legislature to which the third message was addressed passed a new school law adopting taxation as a means of support of common schools and equalizing the periods of instruction in all schools in each congressional township. But this step forward was largely vitiated by a local option provision whereby each county could decide for itself whether to operate under the new system. The act also failed to consolidate the school funds and to require equal distribution. The fourth address was therefore a criticism of this statute, which had meanwhile been rejected by twenty-nine counties.

"One of the People" directed his fifth appeal, in the form of four letters in *The Indiana Statesman*, to the men who assembled in Indianapolis in October, 1850, to draft a new constitution for the state. Like so many in his time and since, he sought to incorporate the details of the particular project close to his heart in the fundamental law of the state, where it would be relatively secure from future legislative tampering. The only real novelty of this address, which reiterated all the familiar arguments, was a proposal to divide the permanent public education money into three parts, the Common School, the Literature, and the University Funds. The interest from the Literature Fund was, in addition to being used to subsidize private academies, to be spent to establish and increase common school libraries, a recently recognized instrument of public instruction.

It was after his fifth address that Mills wrote Niles and revealed himself as "One of the People." How the Wabash College professor and the influential lawyer delegate had become acquainted can be conjectured: Mills graduated from Dartmouth College in 1828, Niles in 1830. Mills' reference to "scenes of bygone years" has just that touch of nostalgia which supports the inference of an undergraduate acquaintanceship. Obviously Mills expected sympathy from the well-educated Niles, himself a former teacher of chemistry in the medical department of the Indiana Medical College of La Porte.

John B. Niles Esq.,
(Constitutional Convention)
Indianapolis, Ind.
[Postmark Crawfordsville, Dec. 10.]

Wabash College
Dec. 7, 1850

John B. Niles Esq.
My Dear Sir:

You may perhaps be surprised to receive a letter from me. It would be pleasant to sit down and chat over scenes of bygone years, but we revolve in such different orbits that it is utterly impossible to calculate when two such bodies will be in conjunction. Were it certain that the convention would not complete their labors by Christmas & that the portion of the constitution pertaining to Education would not be disposed of before that time, I think I should confer upon myself the honor of a lobby membership for a few days. But I presume that period would be too late for the accomplishment of the principle object of such a visit and therefore I will venture to propose a conference on the subject of constitutional provision for popular Education. I presume you feel a deep interest in this subject & are prepared to favor any plan that bids fair to accomplish the object in the most effectual manner. There is a strong disposition among timid polititions & demagogues to skim along the surface and ask what will be popular, disregarding whatever is essential to their success, providing it is not grateful to the more ignorant or selfish of the dear people. Presuming that you do not sympathize with such & are willing & desirous to embody in the fundamental law of the commonwealth educational provisions of an enlightened and liberal character, I will proceed to communicate to you what I wish to be considered a *secrete*, vis, that the Educational Addresses to the Legislature, under the signature of One of the people, for the last *four years*, and the *fifth* published in the Indiana Statesman, addressed to the Constitutional Convention came from me. They have been extensively circulated and read, & have done something to awaken & increase the interest in fact in popular education. I presume you have read the one addressed to the Body, of which you are a member. I flatter myself that the plan suggested in that address, will commend itself to your favorable regard, and if so, I wish you would give it the benefit of your influence and support when the subject of Education comes up for discussion. Now is the time to strike, and in the right spot. Can you not make a *great speech* on the subject and show shallow heads that academies and colleges are as indispensable to a good educational system as common schools? Show them that these higher institutions are the intellectual reservoir from which proceed the controlling influences of society. Whence proceed inventions and improvements in every department of human industry, but from awakened, cultivated intellects? Will you carefully read the several nos. if you have not already done it & suggest any difficulties & modifications & thus give me an opportunity to explain, obviate & demonstrate the soundness & wisdom of the scheme. No one, who has *seen* the operation of free schools in New England, will question for a moment, the wisdom, nay, the necessity of a partial support at least by taxation, & the undesirableness of a fund so large as to superseed the necessity of taxation. This point being established, where is the necessity of a public fund larger than I have shown we should have from the three sources indicated. Let the Literature fund derived from the fines & forfeitures, bank tax & saline funds be consolidated & appropriated for the encouragement of academi[e]s, common school libraries & apparatus. New York has appropriated $90,000 annually & for a series of years on the plan suggested securing the raising an equal sum by the recipiants of the grant. The fine and forfeiture funds, bank tax and saline funds would go but a little way in sustaining the common schools of the state, not amounting to 25 cents per head on all the children in the state; but for the purpose proposed, they would be sufficient, abundantly sufficient to secure a library of 150 or 200 vols such as you will see in the state library room, to every school district in the state. What a glorious point gained to secure such a result. Such a library would educate parents as well as children [and] prove of untold value to every neighborhood. I hope you will both take hold of it yourself and endeavor to enlist others in its support. I have urged Jernigan to do what he can with the members of his acquaintance and hope you will stand up and support the Educational Committee should they propose it. Could you not get a dozen of your most intelligent & influential members to unite & push it thro' with a rush. In respect to the University plan, I see no objection at all. The funds are all in the possession & under the *sole & exclusive control* of the State on my plan. It proposes to alienate not a dollar but to make every dollar tell on cultivated mind[s]. It proposes nothing but what is just, liberal & wise. You can see at a glance that the influence of its operation would be most happy & efficient. It would do more to expose imposition & elevate the standard of collegiate education than anything that could be done. The adoption of the plan suggested in its threefold division would both bless & honor us as a state. The facts & statistics embodied in that address & its predecessors, would furnish you with unanswerable arguments. I will send you a copy of the second & third for perusal. I should rejoice to see that plan, or something substantially like it, incorporated into the organic law of the state. Let me hear from you at an early date & know the result of your recruiting service. Could you not return by this place & spend a day with us? Yours truly

Caleb Mills

P.S. Let this all be "*sub rosa*."

While Niles may have given his silent support, or may have subscribed to Mills's views but not thought the matter one to be embodied in detail in a constitution, certain it is that he never made a "great address." Nor was the article reported by the committee on education and passed after amendment by the convention in any sense an embodiment of Mills's plan. True, the new constitution called for "a general and uniform system of Common Schools, wherein tuition shall be without charge, and equally open to all"; a perpetual Common School fund was established and the office of Superintendent of Public Instruction created. But county seminaries were abolished, with no attempt to find a substitute in private institutions, and Indiana University was left unscathed. All details of the school system to be effected under the new government were left to the legislature.

To the 1851 General Assembly, then, Mills directed his last appeal, calling attention to the peculiar significance any law passed at this time must have as a sort of interpretation of the spirit of the new constitution. Buttressing his call for immediate action by presenting even more depressing data from the recent 1850 census, Mills asked for a law embodying those details of his plan which were still permissible under the new constitution. Fundamentally, the statute must provide three essentials; freedom, competence, and supervision.

The legislature's response must have been gratifying, for the comprehensive School Law of 1852 was a long step in the march to organize in the state a system of uniform public-supported schools. A taxing provision contained no such escape clause as ruined the 1849 act; and school funds were to be consolidated and equally distributed. Administrative organization too was revamped; the congressional township was abolished as an administrative unit and local control of schools given to civil townships, under the supervision of a state Board of Education presided over by the Superintendent of Public Instruction. Other sections of the law taxed for the purpose of establishing township libraries, regulated the examination and licensing of teachers, and sought to provide for the erection of school buildings. The influence of Mills, or at least the general conformity of the act to many of Mills's most important suggestions, is clearly apparent.

The fate of the statute in the courts is another and more discouraging story. But despite the fact that Supreme Court decisions during the next few years "almost destroyed the school system," legislative tenacity and a change of the judicial heart eventually gave Indiana a workable school law. In the long war for effective free schools ultimate victory was Caleb Mills's.

Transportation Problems and Plans

One of the major problems confronting the pioneers of Indiana was the development of a satisfactory system of transportation that would serve not only to bring people and needed supplies to the frontier, but also offer an outlet to markets for farmers and others. Overland routes such as those resulting from road or even turnpike construction proved not to be effective in meeting the growing demand for cheaper and reliable travel and transport facilities. Given the importance of water transportation, especially by rivers in the area, it was a natural step to consider ways to improve existing water transport. This had led to the creation of a canal movement in the United States in the years immediately following the end of the War of 1812, a movement symbolized and greatly strengthened by the remarkable success of the Erie Canal that spanned the state of New York. Completed in 1825, this 363-mile-long canal touched off efforts by states throughout the country to build canals that would similarly transform their economies. The selection below describes Indiana's ambitious attempts to build a comprehensive canal system, beginning in a comparatively modest way in 1827 but expanding the plans significantly in 1836, when the Mammoth Internal Improvement Act was adopted. The spectacular failure of the "System of 1836" not only bankrupted the state and changed forever methods of financing state projects, but it also helped pave the way for the subsequent railway age.

For additional information on the early transportation history of Indiana, see Paul Fatout, *Indiana Canals* (1972), Logan Esarey, *Internal Improvements in Early Indiana* (1912), Elbert Jay Benton, *The Wabash Trade Route in the Development of the Old Northwest* (1903), R. Carlyle Buley, *The Old Northwest: Pioneer Period, 1815–1840* (2 vols., 1950), and Philip D. Jordan, *The National Road* (1948). For a broader perspective, see George Rogers Taylor, *The Transportation Revolution, 1815–1860* (1951), and Ronald E. Shaw, *Canals for a Nation: The Canal Era in the United States, 1790–1860* (1990).

THE WABASH AND ERIE CANAL

Ralph D. Gray

The canal era dawned slowly over the broad expanse of still heavily wooded land that was the Hoosier state during the 1820s and early 1830s. Other states were already feverishly involved in various internal improvements by this time. New York had completed its monumental Erie Canal in 1825 and only ten years later, because of the press of traffic, had undertaken a major enlargement program. Pennsylvania had begun extensive canal and railroad building projects, also in the 1820s, and most other states up and down the Atlantic coast were similarly involved. In the West, beyond the Appalachians, Ohio had set the pace, embarking as early as 1825 upon an extensive public works program which included not one but two Lake Erie-to-Ohio River canals. But if Indiana was slow to catch the internal improvements fever, she contracted an unusually severe case of it in the mid-1830s. In December, 1834, when Governor Noah Noble addressed the Indiana General Assembly of 1834–1835, he declared that "no good reason can be assigned why we should longer hesitate to follow the successful examples of other States." Indiana should, he con-

---

From Ralph D. Gray, "The Canal Age in Indiana," in *Transportation and the Early Nation* (Indianapolis: Indiana Historical Society, 1982), pp. 113–134 passim.

tinued, "borrow [the] money at a fair rate of interest," devote it to "some well selected objects of paramount public utility," and thereby "enrich both" the government of the state and its people.

An immediate legislative response to the governor's proposal was delayed by disagreements over specific projects and routes, but the following year, amid near universal popular applause and support from both sides of the aisle in the new Statehouse, a bill providing for "a general system of internal improvements" was adopted. Often referred to as the Mammoth Internal Improvement program, the act of 1836 committed the state to eight turnpike, canal, and railroad projects estimated to cost well in excess of $10 million. Quite clearly the improvement fever had reached Indiana, resulting in a major transformation of the state—its economy, its political orientation, and its societal and cultural dimensions.

A canal age in Indiana had threatened to begin early in the nineteenth century when, on August 24, 1805, the first territorial legislature issued a charter to the Indiana Canal Company, its ostensible purpose being to construct a passage around the falls in the Ohio River near present-day Jeffersonville. However, as John Badollet remarked afterwards to Albert Gallatin, "that undertaking . . . was in my humble opinion the basis on which a plan of gigantic Speculation was intended to rest," and subsequent developments confirmed this judgment. The canal company's sponsors, among them the redoubtable Aaron Burr, were more interested in their authority to issue paper money and establish a bank than in digging a navigation channel, and several writers have concluded that this venture was intended to help finance the so-called Burr Conspiracy. This association, of course, did not invalidate the significance of the canal project itself, and subsequent attempts to build a much-needed Ohio Falls Canal were made in 1817–1819, and again in the early 1820s, but they proved futile. The first canal efforts in Indiana ended, in Paul Fatout's words, "after much sound and fury signifying nothing capable of floating a boat." In the meantime, Kentucky was bestirring herself and making plans to build the short bypass waterway on her side of the river. Aided by a sizable federal stock subscription granted in 1826, Kentucky, to the continuing good fortune of its major Ohio River port, completed the Louisville and Portland Canal in 1829.

By [this] time . . . , Indiana was becoming deeply involved with its own major improvement project, a Lake Erie-Wabash River connection, and with several other canal, as well as railroad, projections. The first and obvious waterway project was, of course, along the historic "Wabash trade route," obstructed only in the Fort Wayne area by the necessity for a portage between the Maumee and Little Wabash rivers. The importance of this route, used by early French explorers of the Mississippi Valley, [had been] recognized in the Ordinance of 1787, which declared the waterways and necessary portages between the St. Lawrence and Mississippi rivers to be "common highways, and forever free," and in the writings of George Washington, who dreamed of connecting the Ohio River with the eastern seaboard not only via an extended "Potowmack" canal but also by way of a St. Lawrence-Lake Erie route.

An early definite prediction of the Wabash and Erie Canal was made in 1816 by Robert B. McAfee in his *History of the Late War in the Western Country*, where he pointed to the short portage—only seven or eight miles—between the head of navigation on the Maumee [and] the nearest navigable branch of the Wabash. "A canal at some future day," he confidently asserted, "will unite these rivers." Three years later a government surveyor, James Riley, ran a line of levels over the portage and concluded that a canal there was not only practicable but destined for greatness. Indiana's first governor, Jonathan Jennings, although a resident of distant Clark County on the Ohio, had already endorsed the concept of a state-sponsored system of roads and canals, including the Maumee-Wabash connection. Such talk excited the admiration of others, including De Witt Clinton, famed for his promotion of the Erie Canal in New York. He exclaimed to a supporter of the Indiana canal in 1818: "I have found the way to get into Lake Erie and you have shown me how to get out of it. . . . You have extended my project six hundred miles.". . .

Construction of the Wabash and Erie Canal began, with appropriate ceremony, at Fort Wayne on February 22, 1832. According to the terms of the land grant, construction had to begin by March 2, 1832, so the state met its deadline with nine days to spare. Soon the first thirty-two miles of the line between Fort Wayne and Huntington were under contract, and within two years over one thousand men, chiefly Irish laborers, were at work with pick and shovel, cart and team. Jesse L. Williams, a youthful veteran of the Miami and Erie Canal in Ohio, was chief engineer, beginning an association which lasted throughout the entire life of the Wabash and Erie. Despite occasional labor problems, including a series of "Irish wars," the canal was opened from Fort Wayne, and general enthusiasm for internal improvements all over the state rose perceptibly. Few anti-improvement candidates for the state legislature stood a chance of election, and the broad internal improvements sentiment across the land in the prosperous boom years of 1835 and 1836 was soon translated into legislation. In Indiana the 1835–1836 General Assembly was designated the "General System" legislature by one editor at the start of its sessions, and it eventually responded with the previously mentioned act for a "general system of internal improvements."

By its terms the Wabash and Erie Canal was to be extended and completed to Terre Haute, some seventy-five miles below Lafayette, and two other canals, linked to one another and to the Wabash and Erie, were to be built, one in the central and southwestern part of the state, one in the southeastern area. Railroads and turnpikes were to serve other portions of Indiana. This so-called Mammoth Internal Improvement act had enjoyed firm bipartisan support, and it was almost universally hailed within as well as without the state. It cannot be said that Indiana adopted its ambitious but ultimately disastrous program without due deliberation or that it was an unpopular measure. Calvin Fletcher, an Indianapolis attorney and businessman not given normally to overstatement, believed that "this grand project will exalt Indiana among the nations of the earth."

The canal portions of this "system," in addition to providing for the Wabash and Erie extension, authorized the Whitewater Canal between Cambridge City on the National Road and Lawrenceburg on the Ohio River, via Connersville, Laurel, Metamora, and Brookville, and further authorized the Central Canal, to extend from a point to be determined along the Wabash and Erie near Peru all the way south to the Ohio River at Evansville via Indianapolis, Worthington, and Petersburg. Extensions linking both the Whitewater and Wabash and Erie canals with the long Central Canal, the latter project being known as the Cross-cut Canal from Terre Haute to Worthington, were also laid out, but of these projects only the Whitewater was completed as planned. Both the Cross-cut and the southern sections of the Central Canal were incorporated later into an expanded version of the Wabash and Erie line in 1847, thereby linking Terre Haute and Evansville by water just shortly before a railroad between the two cities was completed. . . .

There is [need] only to summarize the history of the Wabash and Erie Canal after adoption of the Butler bill of 1847. When the three-man board of trustees officially assumed control of the canal and its appurtenances in July, 1847, the enterprise was entering its most prosperous period as well as the time of its most virtuous leadership. The bondholder-elected trustees—nonresident Charles Butler and resident Thomas H. Blake of Terre Haute—were indefatigable in their labors, scrupulously honest in their dealings, and totally dedicated to making the canal a financial and commercial success. High standards of performance were set for all employees, and close attention was paid both to new contract lettings and land sales on the lower divisions of the property and to efficient maintenance and operation of the canal on its upper divisions, in the belief that these were essential ingredients of successful canal management. New bookkeeping procedures and new, more modern office practices were instituted, and for a time it appeared that the trustees' conviction that honest and efficient employees and management, together with strict measures of economy and plain hard work, would be rewarded.

Income from rents, tolls, and land sales was promising during the late 1840s and early 1850s—the peak year for the canal as a whole was in 1852—and slowly but steadily, despite repeated outbreaks of cholera and other epidemics among the canal laborers, the waterway inched its way through the southwestern counties of Indiana to the Ohio River at Evansville. It was clear to most observers, however, that already the canal's days were numbered; the southern extension, on which more than $2 million was spent in construction, returned less than half that much in tolls and rents during its seven partial years of operation. To the board, the reason for this was clear; it did not lie in long interruptions to navigation caused by floods and by vandalism (and there were many examples of both); rather it stemmed from the inattention, if not the perversity, of the state legislature in authorizing railroads to parallel virtually every mile of the canal during the 1850s.

To the trustees, these acts violated the spirit of the 1847 agreement, and again morally obligated the state to assume direct responsibility for the entire state debt, since by its positive action the value of the canal, and hence one half of the bondholders' investment, had been destroyed. A petition specifically requesting this was submitted to the legislature in 1857, 1867, and again in 1871. The first two brought simple responses that it was "inexpedient" for the state to consider "purchase" of the canal; the third petition, however, resulted in a constitutional amendment forever prohibiting the state from recognizing obligations dating from the 1847 agreement.

By then, of course, only scattered sections of the canal were in use, and not long afterwards, in 1874, the trustees formally surrendered their trust and closed the books on the enterprise. The bottom lines revealed the extent of financial loss—a total of $8,259,244.03 had been spent on the Wabash and Erie Canal over the years, a total of $5,477,238.41 had been received as income. Based on these figures, many historians have agreed with Alvin F. Harlow's assessment of the failure, that it was "the most colossal, the most tragic failure in all canal history. . . ." Even Harlow, however, recognized the canal's contributions to the development of the state, adding that, "pitiable as it was, it played a tremendous part in the making of Indiana and the Middle West.". . .

Among the contemporaries who commented on the importance of the Wabash and Erie Canal to Indiana was Calvin Fletcher of Indianapolis. Immediately following the Fort Wayne celebration of its opening from Lafayette to Lake Erie, he wrote an editorial for an Indianapolis newspaper describing the novelty of sending wagons westward (to Lafayette) with cargoes intended for eastern markets via the new waterway, and suggesting that "the immense influence the opening of this canal will have on three-fourths of the whole State is incalculable." Even so, he must have been surprised when in 1844 as many as four hundred wagons a day arrived at Lafayette with canal cargoes. It was reported that "long trains of wagons [waited] by the hour . . . for their turns to unload" their farm products. These wagons had come as far as "100 miles to the millers and [merchants] on the canal . . . where elevators rose and factories multiplied. . . . " In time the canal ports of Fort Wayne, Huntington, Wabash, Peru, Logansport, Delphi, and Lafayette all "attained a substantial commercial importance." Corn shipments at Toledo, gathered from the Wabash and Maumee valleys, grew following the opening of the Wabash and Erie Canal from approximately 5,000 to 500,000 bushels a year, and by 1851 reached 2,775,149 bushels. . . .

For their time and their place, the two Indiana canals [that] were completed and in operation for some twenty to forty years—the Whitewater and the Wabash and Erie canals—had a positive impact upon their regions, served to stimulate agricultural and urban growth, and helped develop the towns, the millsites, the population, and the trade which the railroads of a later time dominated so completely.

BEGINNING THE RAILROAD NETWORK

Victor M. Bogle

The railroad was introduced into the United States in 1830—with the initial Baltimore and Ohio Railroad charter dating from 1827—and almost immediately there was talk of building railroads in all parts of the country. Indiana had its share of early railroad boosters but, as Professor Bogle points out, very little was done in the way of actual construction until the 1850s. The planning and promoting of lines in the 1830s and 1840s, however, was important

---

From "Railroad Building in Indiana, 1850–1855," *Indiana Magazine of History*, LVIII (September 1962), 211–224, 226–227, 230–231.

in that a more realistic appraisal of which routes to build was possible afterwards. Three factors influenced the layout of the state's rail network: market requirements, existing transportation (largely natural waterways), and the location of the state capital. By 1850, in Professor Bogle's phrase, "the building era of Indiana's railroads had arrived" (p. 217), with three-quarters of the railroad mileage constructed in the 1850s completed and in operation by 1855. By that time, too, the first "union station," a depot used in common by all the railroads serving Indianapolis, had been constructed in the capital city.

For more information on the history of railroading in Indiana, see Emma Lou Thornbrough, Indiana in the Civil War Era, 1850–1880 *(1965); Wylie Daniels,* The Village at the End of the Road *(1938); and George W. Hilton,* Monon Route *(1978). See also the delightful anecdotal article about the early days of the Monon by Thomas Carter Perrin, "The New Albany-Salem Railroad—Incidents of Road and Men,"* Indiana Magazine of History, *XV (December 1919), 342–362; and the excellent general account by George Rogers Taylor,* The Transportation Revolution, 1815–1860 *(1951).*

With increasing frequency these days back-page stories in Indiana newspapers indicate that rail service is to be discontinued on sections of the Pennsylvania, the New York Central, and the Monon—or that a few of the remaining giant corporations are negotiating to bring about the ultimate in railroad consolidation. Most Hoosiers who grew up before World War II can recall when railroads were somehow different, if not more important, than they are now. Some may already be looking back nostalgically to days when the steam locomotive and sleek diesel were dramatic symbols of commercial progress, or when a train ride was the standard means for making a trip to Chicago, New York, or Denver. A moment's reflection will prompt the realization that these are but signs of a new chapter in the railroad history of the state, and that, if it is not the concluding chapter, certainly it is one falling near the close of a long and fascinating story.

The phases of Indiana's 130 years of railroad history can be capsuled into a few simple statements. From the late 1820's until around 1850 there was much *talking* but not much *building*. From 1850 to the early 1870's the basic network was established, very much along the lines projected by the earliest promoters. During the latter decades of the past century, consolidation of major lines took place, and many branch and feeder lines were built to supplement the basic network. Since World War I consolidation has continued while the network has retrenched due to competition from other forms of transportation. With minor modifications, this summary might be applied to the history of railroads in most of the states between the Appalachians and the Mississippi River. But such generalizations obviously ignore the unique and multitudinous steps which Indiana and other states have pursued in fitting themselves into the nation's railroad pattern.

The present study is concerned primarily with railroad developments in the state of Indiana during the period 1850–1855 when, after a somewhat lengthy prelude, the rail network of the state finally began to take shape. In a sense this presentation is a "progress report" on a more ambitious research project designed to encompass the story of Indiana's railroads from their origins to their current operations. Because of the abbreviated scope of this report, developments preceding and following the first half decade of the 1850's have been dealt with in a cursory manner only; and although a judicious effort has been made to base conclusions on defensible data, this study must naturally suffer from a lack of perspective because of incompleted research. It is hoped, nevertheless, that what is presented here will serve as a sample of the kind of study that railroad history in the state and nation gives rise to and, in fact, demands.

The decade of the 1850's began with little actual railroad construction accomplished in Indiana. The eighty-six-mile connection between Madison and Indianapolis—the state's pioneer railroad—had been in operation between its terminal towns since 1847, but even this pre-1850 success had not come easily. The dream of a railroad between these points went back to the agitation of the early 1830's when the Indiana General Assembly granted charters to mushrooming "rail road" companies all over the state—even before anybody was sure just what a "rail road" was. The Madison and Indianapolis Railroad has deservedly received much attention from Indiana's historians for its initial achievements; but the fact that it required fifteen years for Indiana to build its first operable railroad is certainly indicative of the times.

There may be, on the other hand, a tendency to dismiss too lightly the period of the 1830's and 1840's as a background for later construction. A study of the projected routes outlined in the hundred or more separate railroad charters issued from 1832 to 1850 reveals that these fragmentary lines, prompted largely by local interests, did make some sense when plotted on a composite map of the state. Of the more than four thousand miles of railroad authorized in these early charters, most lines were designed to connect geographic points which, in the perspective of 125 years ago, should have been connected. In fact, some of the routes were of such intrinsic importance that companies to construct railroads over them were authorized again and again after earlier charters became obsolete. The route from the Falls of the Ohio River to Lake Michigan, over which the New Albany and Salem Railroad company eventually completed its road, was one which figured in many separate pre-1850 charters. Another route was that of the Buffalo and Mississippi (later the Northern Indiana) Railroad company; it meandered over the northern tier of counties toward Chicago, sending its projected tributaries in all directions to catch infant villages along the way. Still other routes consistently regarded as important were those from Evansville to Terre Haute, from Richmond to Terre Haute, from Lafayette to Indianapolis, from Peru to Indianapolis, from Lawrenceburg to Indianapolis, and from the Ohio Falls area to Indianapolis. Once railroad building began in earnest in the early 1850's, these routes were among the first started.

The general assembly was usually quite lenient in the time it allotted companies to complete their roads, but legislative authority alone was not enough to get them built. In many instances in which a company was little more than a flare-up of "rail fever," the project normally died soon. Apparently this was the fate of such unbuilt roads as the Levenworth [*sic*] and Bloomington (1834), the Charlestown and Ohio (1835), the Perrysville and Danville (1836), and perhaps 40 percent of all those chartered in the 1830's and 1840's. It is impossible to determine how many other companies were stillborn before they even reached the charter stage, but it is likely that at one time or another through the thirties and forties almost every settlement in the state at least dreamed of an all-important rail connection.

Stripped of certain emotional overtones which accompanied the formation of the early railroad projects, the problem the planners and promoters tried to solve with their schemes was an economic one. Paraphrased in a single word, it was *markets*. They wanted means to dispose of their surplus commodities and facilities to obtain products their own economy was not advanced enough to provide. In simplest terms, this meant they must somehow attach their locality to a point or points where the advantageous exchange could take place. When the railroad fever first hit the Hoosier State, waterways were the accepted mode of transporting bulky materials over long distances. The initial purpose of the railroad was to supplement the waterway system. Since the state's population was weighted toward the Ohio River, towns along its banks had a strong priority as terminals for the earliest chartered roads. Of the hundred or so authorized before 1850, twenty-five were to have points on the Ohio as one of their terminals. Almost this many more were to touch the Wabash and Erie Canal, while others were to tie in the northern portion of the state with the natural waterway supplied by the Great Lakes. A few of the more ambitious routes, most notably the one to be followed by the New Albany and Salem Railroad, attempted to link all three of these east-west waterways.

If it had not been for the establishment of the state's capital near the geographic center of the state, this plan of using railroads chiefly as a means of linking waterways probably would have prevailed somewhat longer. The location of the capital town itself came to be an important factor in railroad planning. To plan a railroad of any significant length and not somehow have it reach the promising capital became almost infeasible. Though by 1850 Indianapolis was little more than the political center of the state—noticeably behind Madison, New Albany, and other communities in industrial advancement—this town was ideally situated for the kind of transportation revolution now beginning. It served as a magnet to draw to a central point what otherwise might have been dangling lines. The foresight, promotion, and sheer good luck which combined to create Indianapolis into the rail hub of the state make up one of the intriguing stories in Indiana's history.

By the close of the 1840's Indiana was recognized as a valuable hinterland for any established marketing center which could arrange to tap it. The larger Ohio River towns, and some of the not-so-large ones, early visualized themselves in this highly profitable role. Promoters in Evansville, New Albany, Jeffersonville, and Lawrenceburg consciously or unconsciously worked toward this end. Madison, having the first success in getting a railroad into the interior, actually came closest of the river towns to being a regional distribution center. Ultimately, however, it was larger, out-of-state cities which exerted the real gravitational pull: Cincinnati and Louisville to the southeast; Cleveland and Toledo to the northeast; and the phenomenal Chicago to the northwest. There may have been an awareness on the part of Indiana's early railroad promoters that anything they might accomplish would eventually fall as gain to commercial interests in distant cities, but there is little to indicate that by the early 1850's they were seriously disturbed about it.

Although there was no sharp break between rail developments of the late 1840's and those of the beginning 1850's, the new decade did promise certain advantages over the previous period. The state had gotten over most of the financial shock resulting from the internal improvements fiasco of the late thirties, and relatively prosperous times were back again. Along with a large increase in the state's population there had undoubtedly been a commensurate increase in property values and investment capital. Also, managerial and technical talent had no doubt evolved as a result of the trial-and-error experiences of the recent past. Still another important stimulant was the example of the Madison and Indianapolis Railroad. Its success proved that railroads could be built and operated in Indiana; here was the encouragement needed to goad planners of other roads into action.

At the beginning of the 1850's many earlier charters were still legally in effect, but no more than ten of the companies authorized to construct railroads showed serious inclinations to start building. These companies were surveying their routes and attempting to accumulate sufficient funds to begin construction. At least two of the railroads were at the track-laying state; before the year 1850 closed, the Indianapolis and Bellefontaine Railroad company laid down twenty-eight miles of track between Indianapolis and Pendleton, and the New Albany and Salem completed its track thirty-five miles to Salem.

The year 1851 brought further proof that the building era of Indiana's railroads had arrived. The vigorous Terre Haute and Indianapolis Railroad company almost completed trackage over its seventy-three-mile route within this single year; the Northern Indiana Railroad company opened a twenty-five-mile stretch from the Michigan state line, near White Pigeon, to South Bend; the Indianapolis and Bellefontaine company moved its line sixteen miles farther east to the village of Chesterfield; and the New Albany and Salem finished an additional twenty-mile section beyond the original terminus of Salem to the village of Orleans. Two other companies began laying track; the Peru and Indianapolis had the twenty-one-mile section from Indianapolis to Noblesville ready for use in March and the Jeffersonville road, heading northward to Columbus, completed twenty-seven miles of track to Vienna, in Scott County, before the year's end.

The following three years (1852, 1853, 1854) showed the same kind of tangible results. Early in 1852 the Northern Indiana company joined with the Michigan Southern Railroad company to open a route curving through the northwestern corner of the state into Chicago. During 1852 the Lafayette and Indianapolis company, blessed with ideal terrain, built its entire seventy-three-mile line, and by the close of the year the Jeffersonville company had finished its road to Columbus and added an eleven-mile section to Edinburg. Meanwhile, the twenty-five mile Martinsville and Franklin Railroad was opened for business in November.

In January 1853 the Indianapolis and Bellefontaine company celebrated the opening of its track to Union (now Union City) on the Indiana-Ohio state line and joined with finished roads in the neighboring state to give Indiana its first rail link to major cities on the eastern seaboard. The Indiana Central Railroad company opened its line from Indianapolis to Richmond in the fall of 1853; and a few weeks later, after more than two decades of false starts, the Lawrenceburgh and Upper Mississippi Railroad company finally got its road completed between Indianapolis and Lawrenceburg. Largely as a result of the growing rivalry of the older Madison and Indianapolis company and the newer Jeffersonville company, another feeder line was completed in December in southern Indiana; this was the twenty-three-mile Columbus and Shelbyville.

The New Albany and Salem Railroad, longest of all the pioneer roads, moved forward methodically and completed its 288-mile route across the state from New Albany to Michigan City by the middle of 1854, thus realizing the dreams of early promoters to tie by rail the Ohio River and Lake Michigan. During 1854 two other companies managed to open service between key terminal points; the Peru and Indianapolis did this in the spring, and the Evansville and Illinois (from Evansville to Terre Haute) in the following November.

Also during the same three-year period other important lines were either in the advanced planning or early construction stage. These were: the Ohio and Mississippi, from Lawrenceburg to Vincennes (actually a segment of the Baltimore to St. Louis trunk system); the Cincinnati, Logansport and Chicago, which was to join the rail complex in western Ohio to roads converging on Chicago; and the Lake Erie, Wabash and St. Louis (known later as the "Wabash"), destined to run from Fort Wayne along the Wabash Valley into Illinois. These roads, all designed to span the state from east to west, would eventually comprise a significant part of Indiana's rail network, but their completion did not occur until some months after the period directly considered in this report.

By the close of the year 1854 over fourteen hundred miles of railroad had been completed and were in operation in Indiana. . . .

No systematic study has yet been made of the eighteen completed roads' financial statements, but fragmentary evidence indicates that the average cost per mile was well over $15,000. This includes the costs of right of way, surveying, preparing the roadbed, rolling stock, and station facilities. Therefore, a conservative estimate of the investment in Indiana's completed roads by 1855 is more than $21,000,000—roughly twice the estimated cost of the whole projected internal improvements system of the 1830's and 1840's. Some companies, such as the Lafayette and Indianapolis, had little difficulty in preparing a roadbed and thereby cut initial engineering costs to a minimum. Other roads, confronted with rough terrain and numerous streams to bridge, were obliged to spend considerably more. Obtaining sufficient capital to finish a road once construction began was a sore problem with several of the roads. Others arranged adequate financing of the entire line before beginning construction.

No really standard procedure was followed in raising the necessary funds to construct these railroads of the early 1850's, but certain common features did prevail. Usually the charter specified the amount for which the road could be capitalized; depending on its length this might vary from $150,000 to more than $1,000,000. Since the charters governing the roads constructed in the 1850–1855 period had been issued some years before, when practical information on costs was unavailable, the capitalizations specified in these charters obviously were little more than guesses. On the other hand, increases in capitalization were apparently obtained with ease. From evidence thus far studied, it appears that the capital to be raised by selling stock in a new company was intended to cover about 50 percent of the railroad's total cost. The other half was to be procured from the sale of bonds, frequently with an interest rate as high as 10 per cent.

A "typical" case of the procedure followed in planning and building one of the early Indiana railroads might be depicted as follows. A number of persons in a region of the state decided that they should have a railroad. A mass meeting was then held in a courthouse where articles of association were drawn up, the more affluent or vocal members of the area were designated officers of the company, and an application for a charter was forwarded to the state government. The charter, running anywhere from a few summary statements to several dozen paragraphs, included information about the route, time allowed for building, amount of capitalization, gauge of track, permissible arrangements with other railroad companies, and directors of the newly formed corporation.

Once the charter was approved, solicitation began for the sale of stock. This was one of the crucial phases in the destiny of the new company, for if officials failed to sell enough initial stock to build up momentum for their enterprise, the venture halted right there. A strong appeal was made to residents at all points along the proposed line to purchase or to make pledges for stock. In exchange for stock certificates the buyer might give cash, real estate, equipment of various sorts, or his promise to contribute so many days labor. When enough stock was thus distributed to indicate to officials that the project was likely to succeed, the president and his agents began their campaign to sell bonds to larger investors, usually at an attractive discount, and a man was selected to supervise the engineering. Hereafter the president spent much of his time in eastern commercial capitals peddling bonds and seeking bargains on rails and other needed equipment. This was another crucial point in the affairs of the project. If times were good and the president could make a convincing case for his railroad, money from the sale of bonds poured in and the road was brought to completion with a minimum of delay; if times were bad and money tight, the project slowed up or was indefinitely postponed.

The eighty-four-mile Bellefontaine line (Indianapolis to Union) may serve as an example of railroad financing in the 1850's. The road's 1848 charter authorized a capitalization of $1,000,000 with a stipulation that this amount might be increased at the pleasure of the company. The line was completed early in 1853 at a reported cost of about $1,300,000. A little over half of this initial indebtedness was in the form of stock; the remainder was divided between 7 per cent foreign bonds and 10 per cent domestic bonds. During its first six months of operation (July–December, 1853), the Bellefontaine had gross earnings of $118,000. Almost $40,000 of this amount went for running expenses, $27,000 for paying interest on bonds, and $31,000 for paying 4 per cent dividends on stock; a little less than $20,000 was designated as "surplus." Since the Bellefontaine's connections were excellent, earnings could be expected to increase dramatically within the next few years. In the case of other roads not so favorably located, the margin of surplus profits left little for maintenance, improvements, and removal of bonded indebtedness.

Income for the completed or partially completed roads consisted of receipts from the transport of passengers, freight, mail, and baggage. . . .

Approximately half of the gross receipts of most early Indiana railroads came from the transport of freight. Freight rates were so flexible during this period that no accurate estimate on charges as they applied to various commodities can yet be given, but considerable data exists about the types and quantities of freight carried on several of the roads. During the months when the road was running only to the nearest town to which track had been laid down, the usual pattern was a flow of farm commodities from the smaller terminal to the larger and a simultaneous flow of finished goods from the larger to the smaller. For example, during a three months' period when the Peru road was operating only between Noblesville and Indianapolis, Noblesville shipped southward to Indianapolis 1,000 barrels of flour, 218 barrels of eggs, and over 21,000 pounds of bacon; in turn Indianapolis shipped northward 25 plows, 126 barrels of salt, 36 kegs of powder, and 20,000 feet of lumber. This pattern was soon altered if the rural terminal became a junction point for one or more other roads. It then served as a trans-shipment center where all kinds of goods from a wider region were accumulated for shipment to more distant markets.

Although corn and wheat were among the most important items of freight transported by the Indiana railroads to Cincinnati and other eastern cities, hogs were probably the most important single commodity. During the weeks of late fall and early winter carload after carload of "porkers" was gathered from outlying areas and sent to the slaughtering centers. In the early 1850's the Madison and Indianapolis road probably carried the bulk of this traffic, transporting as many as thirty or forty loads in a single day, but the Lafayette, the Bellefontaine, and the Lawrenceburgh lines also had their share. Some of the longest and most heavily loaded freight trains during these years were those carrying rails and other building equipment for roads under construction. Again this was the type of business from which the Madison road benefited greatly, since its southern terminus was a principal landing point for heavy river shipments from both east and west. But in the long run the Madison road paid dearly for helping to supply its future competitors. . . .

By 1855 most completed roads had telegraph service extended along their routes, but it is not clear from available reports just what this facility contributed to the operation of the railroads. Most companies also were granted contracts for carrying mail over the area of their routes. Although mail was thus speeded to distant points, postal service to smaller communities which had been regular stops on stage lines was sometimes slowed. Express service, operated principally by the Adams Company, became an important adjunct of the railroads. Express cars were included in some of the larger trains, and the company's agents were kept busy transferring more valuable freight at important junctions.

Confining the account of railroad developments to a description of track laying and scheduled train service would seriously distort the history of Indiana's early railroad building. The classic iceberg example is certainly applicable here, for what is concealed below the surface may be immeasurably more important than what is visible; for example, the number of railroad proposals of the early 1850's almost defies enumeration. Distinguishing between projects which were more and those which were less serious in intent requires the utmost vigilance from the later investigator. Just about everybody wanted to build railroads whether the building made sense or not. "There seems to be a kind of Railroad mania abroad," remarked the editor of the *Indiana Journal* in the spring of 1853. "In almost every newspaper within our own and adjoining States, we find some new Road projected. The last one is from Covington through Pinhook to Lafayette! There are at least a dozen talked of from the Atlantic to the Pacific."

As yet no attempt has been made in the present study to determine precisely how many separate companies were chartered in the 1850's to build railroads in Indiana, but a day by day survey of the *Indiana Journal* reveals scores of newly projected roads. A conservative estimate of their proposed mileage would be over thirty-five hundred—more than double the amount of track laid during the 1850–1855 period. The peak of railroad optimism and agitation was reached in 1853; during this year alone at least twenty-five new roads, with a total distance of over seventeen hundred miles, occasioned some degree of discussion or action. If all the railroads created on paper had materialized, the cost for the times would have been astronomical. The more serious-minded planners, faced with the prospects of a tightening money market, began to realize this, and there was a sharp decline in new proposals during the latter months of 1854 and on into 1855. "Railroad talk" certainly continued, but it came to center upon a few favored projects, most notably the Evansville Straight Line Railroad, promoted as Indiana's link in the vital transportation chain binding the South to the Union.

Pioneer Agriculture

THE FARMING SEASONS

Logan Esarey

The selection below comes from Logan Esarey's delightful little book The Indiana Home, *which might be considered the distillation of Esarey's experiences and learning in and about Indiana over a lifetime. The book is a collection of Professor Esarey's unpublished lectures, notes, and papers as arranged by a junior colleague, Professor R. Carlyle Buley, and published posthumously in 1943. In the passage below, taken from the chapter entitled "Farm Life in the*

From *The Indiana Home* (1953; 4th ed., 1976), pp. 86–99. Copyright © 1953, 1976 by Indiana University Press. Reprinted by permission.

Fifties," Esarey describes the never-ending round of chores and the seasonal activities of the Hoosier farmer in the prosperous last decade before the Civil War.

The author, to a degree at least, lived the life of a pioneer farmer during his youth. He was born in 1873 in a log cabin in Perry County, a rugged rural area in southern Indiana where primitive methods and practices were slow in being abandoned, and he remained in the county until 1903. In the introduction to a 1970 reprint of Esarey's major book, A History of Indiana *(2 vols., 1915, 1918), Professor Donald F. Carmony, a student of Esarey at Indiana University, stated: "When Esarey wrote or talked about butchering, sheep-shearing, blacksmithing, grist milling, churning, drying fruits, making maple sugar and syrup, tanning, spinning, weaving, and the like, he drew upon information gained from personal experience and observation. When he explained the use and importance of the ax, frow, broadax, cross-cut saw, sickle, maul, cradle, wedge, and walking plow, he was describing tools which he, himself, had used." For a fuller appreciation of his character and career, see R. Carlyle Buley's tribute, "Logan Esarey, Hoosier,"* Indiana Magazine of History, *XXXVIII (December 1942), 337–381.*

The farmer's most important job in early spring was breaking for corn. The work began as soon as the ground was thawed. A side or turning plow was in general use, though a few of the more conservative farmers still used a big shovel plow, especially if oxen were used. During this decade [1850s], there was about one yoke of oxen in Indiana for each farm. The big gentle, lazy, liquid-eyed oxen were still in favor among the farmers. An ox team would break about an acre per day while horses or mules could break as much as two acres. All good farmers hoped to have their corn land, except the new ground, broken and harrowed by May 10. Planting was more rapid. The field was "laid off" with a one-horse shovel plow into squares about three and a half or four feet and the corn dropped by hand in the intersections and covered with hoes. The dropping was often done by women, but men or grown boys handled the hoes. A planting crew usually consisted of one man and a horse to lay off the rows, and two droppers and two coverers with hoes. They planted about eight acres per day. Corn drills—not check rowers—were on the market but they were not favored because the farmers perferred to plow the corn both ways. Corn planting was finished by the middle of May and the new ground by the last of the month. If planting was finished in good time everybody had a holiday, usually spent in fishing.

There followed a busy month cultivating or plowing corn. All farmers hoped for a rain as soon as the planting was done and then two or three weeks of dry weather. Just as soon as the corn was up enough to show the row the alert farmer went over it with a "harrey" (harrow), removing the front tooth and straddling the row. Then at week or ten-day intervals he plowed it with a one-horse double-shovel plow. It is still undecided whether the crop should be "laid by"—that is, given the final plowing—with a shovel or a side (turning) plow. The latter left the corn ridged high and braced it against wind and storm. If a dry summer followed, however, it was just too bad. If two or three weeks of wet weather followed the planting, the weeds and grass "got the jump" on the corn and it had to be "barred" out. This meant weary days with the hoe. In any case the good farmer went over his cornfields after they were "laid by," or perhaps after harvest, and cut out all the weeds. This was done by the Fourth of July at latest, and we must now leave our cornfields for "harvest."

By the last of June the sun was riding high at its summer solstice, the wheat fields on the southern slopes were taking on a golden glow and the heavily whiskered heads were bending with the weight of the ripening grain. The farmer took down his grain cradle, sharpened the scythe, tightened the nib and mended the weak or broken fingers. Like the logrollings, wheat-harvest was a neighborhood job, and required the united help of all the men, women and children. All other work waited because the wheat wouldn't; not even on Sunday. The hands began with the ripest wheat and changed from farm to farm, day by day as the fields ripened. It took from five to a dozen men. One shocker could keep up with two cradlers and two binders. The binders tied the bundles with bands of straw. At best the harvest lasted only ten days and an untimely wet spell meant heavy loss. Three acres was a good day's work for one cradler and a squad of five men usually shocked five acres of wheat.

In the logrolling the short, stocky men had the advantage, but in the wheat-harvest the tall, deep-chested, rangy men were in their glory. Some trusty cradler set the pace, the others followed, each ten steps behind. Occasionally there were tests of endurance but sensible men would not risk the loss of a good hand by overwork to satisfy a foolish whim. Today we admire the endurance of a two- or four-mile runner but such activity is child's play compared to swinging a cradle in heavy wheat "from sun to sun."

After the spring work the winter fat was worked off and the men were in good training. The first swath in the morning sun started the sweat trickling down their faces and by ten o'clock there was little dry clothing. At the ends they met the water boy with a jug of fresh water from the spring. And how the barefoot urchin longed for the time when he could set his cradle down, reach for the jug with his left hand, flip it up on his shoulder and drink while he mopped his red, manly face with his right. "Gee! Only to be a man!" There were chicken, cake and pie on the dinner table and at ten in the morning and four in the afternoon the women brought out more pies and perhaps buttermilk for a short lunch under the shade trees. So the gay but tiresome work proceeded day by day from farm to farm until the wheat was all in shock. Then all gathered in a circle, gave the "stubble call," retired to the nearest swimming hole, performed the necessary ablution, laid aside their sweaty clothes full of prickly wheat beards, and wheat-harvest was over.

But the golden age of the cradler was passing. Already at the county and state fairs McCormick reapers were giving demonstrations before wide-eyed and open-mouthed Hoosiers. The cradle artist, who could leave the wheat stubble as level as if it had been clipped by a modern lawn mower, was disgusted but the "machine" was on his trail. The noblest art of the pioneer farmer was lost to his own sons.

In 1856, middle of the "glorious Fifties," Indiana raised 9,350,971 bushels of wheat, about ten bushels per head. This, perhaps, was as much as could be harvested by the cradle.

The farmer usually let his wheat stand in the shock until the hay was cut unless an untimely wind blew the shocks down. Then while the big hay frame was still on the wagon he hauled the wheat to the barn and stacked it. Sometimes he stowed it away in the barn but it was much easier and pleasanter to stack. Nobody wanted to get up in the barnloft under the hot roof and put away wheat, and then in a few days get up and dig it out again when the thresher men came. The days of the threshing floor and winnowing, as previously practiced, had passed, and even the "ground-hog thresher" was no longer used. The horse power separator had taken its place.

Threshing was the most spectacular event of the year. The "horse power" was a circular cog machine driven by eight teams hitched to sweeps. The power was carried to the separator by a long iron rod, perhaps four inches in diameter, called the "tumbling shaft." The crew consisted of two drivers and two feeders, working in shifts of two each. The driver and the feeder were the heroes. Every distinguished visitor had to step up and feed a shift to show that he was a real man. The envy of the young boys was the driver who stood on a central platform, a long whip, the "stalk" about five feet long, in his hand. This would crack like a rifle and that was the signal for the horses to step off. The driver never dreamed of striking a horse with the whiplash. Instead, he sang to his teams in a monotone, much as the cowboys used to sing to the "dogies." His voice had to be raised above the general hum of the machine as he sang: "Jack, Jill, Kate, Bill, up here, up here!" followed by two or three short whistles. He kept one eye on the feeder who might signal for more power or stick up a finger to stop. The other eye was on the horses. Some horses were lazy and had to be encouraged; a limp or flinch indicated a sore foot or shoulder. So long as the sweat flowed freely and the white lather formed where the harness touched the hair, all was well, but when a horse quit sweating it was time to take him out. The driver could make a hit with a boy by taking him up on the platform for a "heat."

The other hero was the feeder. He took the bundles or sheaves one by one, shook them to pieces and fed them in so evenly that the gentle hum of the cylinder was never broken. A "chug" brought everybody to attention. It might mean an uncut band or wet wheat had gone through. About once in a season someone dropped a monkey wrench into the cylinder. The result sounded like a railroad crash; a dozen or so teeth were gone from cylinder and concave and the work was stopped for a half-day or so.

On the right of the feeder stood the band-cutter; two men laid bundles on the table before him; one or two pitched from the stack. An elderly man filled the half-bushel measure and kept the tally; a man poured the wheat from the half-bushel measure and two boys carried the wheat to the bins. Four or five men who took the straw from the separator screen finished the crew. The machines of that day had no strawstackers. The threshing crowd usually numbered not less than thirty and the food exceeded in abundance that for the logrollings. The older men consulted the tally to see what the "turn out" or yield was. Apparently the average for the state was about as at present, 18 to 20 bushels per acre.

Hay-harvest was unimportant in early Indiana. Some timothy and more redtop grew on the wet lands, yielding at best one ton per acre. This hay was cut right after wheat-harvest with a light, long-bladed or mowing scythe. The mower had to bend over all the time making it tiresome on his back. An acre per day was good cutting. The scythe left the hay in a small windrow and if the mower was not careful a wisp of grass was left uncut at the end of each stroke. This made miserable work for the person who came along with a small hand or garden rake to gather the hay into bunches for the pitchfork, or to scatter it so the sun would cure it. When cured it was either built into shocks, "haycocks," or loaded on a sled and hauled to the mow. Much of it was stacked in the field, as you may yet see on many farms. Hay presses and mowing machines were coming onto the market as well as revolving horserakes. Red clover, now so common, was a novelty. It was considered good pasturage for stock cattle but would make horses "slobber" the same as white clover. If cut for hay there would be sure to be some ripe heads and the seed would "dry up" the milk cows. It was generally considered a good cover crop to turn under for wheat or corn.

The farmer had a breathing spell during the "dog days" of August. If he was "ornery" he hunted squirrels or loafed at the country store or blacksmith shop. If he was not "ornery" he "sprouted" the new ground, went through his cornfields with a hoe, or cut out the briers and weeds from his fence corners and pastures with the brush scythe. Poison ivy grew prolifically in the fence rows and those who were not immune often enjoyed a good case of ivy poison. This job of cutting the fence rows usually fell to the boys. Apparently all the hornets, "yaller" jackets, bumble-bees and wasps nested along the fences, and by the middle of the summer each nest was an enemy which no boy would pass up.

Those boys who were fortunate enough to live near the streams spent a large part of each day in the swimming hole. Curiously enough, girls were not permitted to go near a swimming hole. There were, of course, no bathing suits and if there had been the sight of a woman in a bathing suit would have caused a panic in any neighborhood and mobilized every deacon in the township. A woman who could even swim was of doubtful character. She was not supposed to go fishing with her brothers.

As soon as the fall rains had softened the ground the fall breaking for wheat began. A prelude to this was a week or so of manure hauling. The feverish rush of the springtime was over. All kinds of fruits were ripening and the women were busy making apple butter, drying apples, making marmalades, jelly and preserves. The horses were lazy from the green pastures, and all the folks were so full of food it was hard to keep in training. For two or three weeks the team or teams trudged slowly 'round and 'round the narrowing wheat field. The oxen with harrow or drag followed still more leisurely until the field was ready for the wheat drill or, more often, the sower. Many of the old farmers were still "skittish" of machinery and sowed the wheat broadcast. The children and turkeys chased the fat grasshoppers in the green meadows while the forest slowly put on its holiday dress of yellow and red. The fat frisky squirrels were cutting the hickory and beechnuts and spring chickens had passed through the frying stage. These were the "halcyon days" the poets speak of, unless the baby took the "summer complaint" or the older folks the "ager" or "fever" or granny came down with "yaller janders."

In the meantime the farmer had hauled his surplus wheat to the mill and either sold it to the "merchant miller" or had it ground and packed in barrels for the eastern or southern market. Store-keepers came back from the East about the first of October with a brand-new line of "hats, caps, boots and shoes," not to mention silks and satins, just beginning to rustle in Indiana society. A little later all climbed into the big wagon some bright morning and drove off to the big store to lay in the winter supplies. Real cash money was beginning to circulate among the folks. Homemade goods fell off one-half during the decade. "Store clothes," now ready made, soon crowded out the homespun, except with the deacons who mourned over the sinfulness and extravagance of the new times.

But the corn was ripening. The tassels and silks dried up, the "shoots" gradually bent away from the stalks and as they filled modestly bowed toward Mother Earth. If an early September frost did not play havoc, by the closing week of September the shucks were dry and corn was ready for the shock. The ordinary farmer cut eight or ten acres of fodder for his cattle during the winter. Nobody "hankered" for the job of cutting corn. It was hard, tiresome, uninteresting work. The dry blades cut one's wrists and neck until they were raw and bleeding; the big "woolly worms" crawled down under the worker's shirt and the sharp stubs skinned his shins as he staggered to the shock with a load of heavy fodder on his shoulder. No one who has not cut heavy corn all day knows how tired the left arm can become. No one came with a jug of water, no one brought pies and cakes to the field as in wheat-harvest. The long V-shaped lines of wild geese "honked" on their way to Florida, the last mellow specimens of the Rambo, Yellow Belleflower, Maiden Blush and Carolina Sweets hung temptingly on the rapidly coloring apple trees, and all nature called from the near-by woods. But still the corn had to be cut on time. It was just plain work.

With the fodder in the shock and the wheat in the ground came the fall chores. The onions and potatoes, long ago lost in the wild grass, had to be dug out and placed in a cool place until freezing weather threatened. Then they were either "holed up" in the garden or stored in a dry part of the cellar, if such a part existed. The big late Drumhead cabbages were through growing in October and a day was set aside when all hands made sauerkraut. If it were a German or Dutch family nothing less than four to eight barrels would do; otherwise a couple of barrels would answer. In any event it was at least an all-day job. The cabbages had to be pulled up, beheaded above the ears and the loose leaves carefully removed to get rid of all worms and traces of worms. Then the heads were placed in a big box which slid over three or four knives. After a few hours of vigorous "sawing" and salting and tamping one had a barrel of slaw which in time became "kraut." All of this made the mouth water profusely. Surplus cabbages, onions or potatoes were given to less fortunate neighbors. No one thought of selling them.

Every farmer had an orchard and every orchard had from eight to twenty varieties of apples. The Early Harvests, Red and Yellow Junes, Summer Queens, Pearmains and Sweet Bows ripened in summer; those named previously ripened in the fall. During October the Imperial Winesaps took on a fiery red, the Baldwins became red-streaked, the Romanites speckled, the Russets golden and the Northern Spies a golden green. All had to be picked from the trees and carefully laid away in a dry cool place to season for the cellar or apple hole for winter use. The best were sorted out for this purpose and the remainder given to the neighbors or run through the cider mill—come to think of it, a glass of sweet cider along about nine o'clock on winter nights after one had eaten a dozen hickory nuts or walnuts was considered healthful.

There remained the corn husking. It might be husked on the stalk or snapped off and husked in the crib shed—a husking bee, for instance. Whatever the procedure it has not changed with the years. Tractors and gang-plows have sent Buck and Bright to the showers; the cultivator has put the mules and double-shovel out of business; the corn-cutter and shredder have superseded the corn knife, but the champion corn husker of a century ago no doubt would walk right along with the champion of today—in fact Old Nokomis shucked Mondamin no differently. Human ingenuity has not yet invented a machine which can satisfactorily cut the weeds and grass from the corn rows or husk the ripened corn on the stalk.

The season ended—or began, according to the weather—with hog killing or "butchering." We may sing the praises of all the heroes of Indiana from LaSalle or George Rogers Clark to the present, but the prosperity of our state through the century has depended on Mr. Hog. In fat years and lean years, until his late unmerited humiliation (when he was ordered to be destroyed by the government) he has come up with his part, even though he does grunt about it considerably. The hog population of the state during the Fifties was about two and one-half millions, two for each person, or a dozen for each family. Both the day and the glory of the old "razorbacks" were passing but stock hogs in general ran at large and fed on the mast. During the summer when the range was poor for hogs the prudent farmer cultivated their acquaintance by giving them a few ears of corn; or perhaps out in the lane he prepared a slop trough where the hogs might come and get the garbage and skim milk or a basket of bad apples.

About the tenth of December hogs selected for the winter killing were penned up and fed corn for two or three weeks until they were fat enough to kill. As a rule they were two or three years old. On the appointed day three or four of the neighbors, each bringing "his old woman," gathered for the killing. Large kettles of water were heated to the boiling point, the water poured into large barrels or meat tubs set at an angle. The hogs were shot, one by one, stuck so the blood would drain out, then doused in the hot water until the hair was loosened, scraped with knives until free of all hair and dirt. Then tendons of the hind feet were raised, gambrel sticks inserted and the hog hung up on a pole so his nose was a foot or two from the ground. He was then gutted, the heart and liver hung up to dry, the leaf fat taken out for lard, the guts washed to be used as sausage casings. The Germans likely saved the blood for blood wurst which they stuffed in the hog's stomach after it was washed. As soon as the carcass dried it was carried into the smokehouse, where the head was cut off for "souse" and the body cut into shoulders, middlings (bacon) and hams, which left the knuckles, ribs and backbones for immediate use. Each neighbor returning home took enough "bones" to last a week. If the butcherings in the neighborhood were properly distributed each family might thus have fresh meat—spareribs, pigs' knuckles and sauerkraut, or backbones—for a month. During this month the men put on the weight they had lost in harvest. Coming near the Christmas holidays it was a time of feasting.

The women's work did not vary so much with the changing seasons. The kitchen program was varied only slightly by the season's menu. Bread and meat came on the tables three times each day. The first garden vegetables, onions, lettuce and radishes, came in early in June and went out with frost. The first berries came in about wheat-harvest and apples hung on the trees until November. From two to five milk cows had to be attended to morn and eve the year 'round; the milk was strained into crocks, in due time skimmed and the cream churned into butter and the skimmed milk served at table while still sweet, or made into cheese. As stated above, the wool furnished year 'round work. Early in the spring a dozen hens were set, half as many geese and a like number of turkeys. All these had to be nursed through the summer season.

Wash day monopolized one whole day each week and ironing and mending another. The children went barefoot half the year but it was no relief to mother. What time she saved in darning she lost in picking out briers and splinters and binding up misused fingers and toes. There was always someone ailing—"under the weather." Colds, sore throats, croup and winter fever were succeeded by summer complaint, sore eyes, chills and fevers. The mother was both doctor and nurse. And all this while she rocked the cradle with one foot. It took the Civil War to break this deadly monotony of women's lives but few mothers of the "glorious Fifties" lived to see the day.

THE FIRST STATE FAIR

George S. Cottman

George S. Cottman, the founder and first editor of the Indiana Magazine of History *(established in 1905), wrote many of the first articles that appeared in the journal. In 1907, Cottman, an Indianapolis journalist and amateur historian, contributed a short essay describing the first Indiana state fair at Indianapolis in 1852. As indicated, the site of the earliest fairs changed from year to year, but soon Indianapolis became the permanent home of the event. The present State Fairground on the near east side of the city above 38th Street, to which the fair moved in the 1890s, is its third location in Indianapolis. Two contemporary accounts of the 1852 state fair are in* The Diary of Calvin Fletcher, Vol. IV: 1848–1852 *(1975), edited by Gayle Thornbrough, Dorothy L. Riker, and Paula Corpuz, pp. 496–500, which also reprints a map indicating the layout of the grounds; and* The Indiana Farmer *(November 1, 1852), pp. 65–69.*

Indiana's first fair was held in Indianapolis, October 19–23, 1852, on the old military reservation, west of West street, now known as Military Park. It was largely through the efforts and influence of Joseph A. Wright, then governor of the State, that the institution was brought into being, and the hearty response when the movement was once under way showed that the time was right for the focussing of the State's industries.

The newspapers, which at that day reviewed local affairs but sparingly, devoted an unusual amount of space to advertising the fair both before and during its progress, and the following extract from an editorial shows the hopeful enthusiasm that greeted the occasion:

"A just pride in the utility and greatness of their pursuits will be generally infused among our farmers, mechanics and manufacturers. Standards of excellence in stock, of utility in machines, and of true taste in the elegant articles of comfort and luxury

---

From "First State Fair in Indiana," *Indiana Magazine of History*, III (September 1907), 144–145. Reprinted by permission of the Editor, *Indiana Magazine of History*.

will be fixed in the minds of all. Progress in their respective pursuits will take the place of indifference in their minds. A laudable ambition to have the mantel decorated with a silver cup will actuate all, and thus feeling and acting, who can calculate the ultimate result?"

The people responded no less enthusiastically. By that time railroad communication was established to Madison, Terre Haute, Lafayette and Peru, and with the eastern counties by the Bellefontaine and Indiana Central (Panhandle) roads. These admitted of easy access to the capital from the various sections of the State. Half rates were given; the plank roads let animals pass free of toll, and the exhibits and the crowds came.

There were 1365 entries, with quite a showing of improved agricultural machinery. Among the greatest curiosities of the time were three sewing-machines (the Home, Wilson, and Singer). There was much live stock exhibited, especially hogs, sheep and cattle, and of the latter the Durham were by all odds the most in evidence. By reason of this feature the attendance was augmented by many stockmen from Kentucky. According to the report of one paper, there were about 15,000 visitors the first day; on the second 25,000, and on Thursday, the third day, there were more people in town than the grounds could hold, and the other shows outside caught the overflow.

Among other features there was an address on Thursday delivered by John B. Dillon, the historian; and Friday and Saturday plowing matches were held out on Calvin Fletcher's farm. The gate receipts at twenty cents a head, for the five days of the fair amounted to something over $4,600, which, according to the local papers, not only defrayed expenses but allowed the return of $2,000 that had been borrowed of the State.

Altogether it was undoubtedly the liveliest week Indianapolis had ever known. In anticipation of the unusual crowds, side shows, great and small, flocked hither, all eager to catch the surplus Hoosier small change. The "Yankee" Robinson's "Athenæum," otherwise vaudeville troupe, gave three performances daily in a tent near the fair grounds, and Wells' Minstrels lured the crowds with time-honored jokes and burnt cork. A man named Diehl put up what he advertised as an "enormous pavilion" near the State House, where he let off fireworks a la Pain of modern pyrotechnic fame.

Toward the last came P. T. Barnum's Museum and Menagerie. Then there was a "grand exhibition of the World's Fair"—a reproduction by illuminated views of the famous Crystal Palace exposition; "Beard's Hoosier Panorama of 'Paradise Lost'," at one of the churches, and divers other catch-pennies.

Added to all this the Democrats had a big torch-light procession which was to close with speaking at the Wright House where the New York store now stands. The Whigs, however, objecting to the Democratic program, gathered in numbers to howl down the speakers, and pandemonium resulted. Out of this affair a difficulty sprang up between George G. Dunn and W. A. Gorman which all but resulted in a duel.

The original intention, out of deference to the other leading towns of the State, was to shift the fair from place to place, giving Indianapolis every third year. In accordance with this idea Lafayette had it in 1853 and Madison in 1854, but this plan proved financially disastrous, and it was finally decided to hold it permanently at Indianapolis.

5. The Era of the Civil War

The decade of the 1850s in Indiana was both a time of extraordinary progress economically and socially and a time of increasing sectional tension, a national trend that culminated in civil war. At first it appeared that the decade would be one of unprecedented prosperity and growth, with virtually unlimited economic progress the likely result of the considerable agricultural advances, transportation improvements, and number of new manufacturing establishments then under way or completed. A new constitution, hammered out by a convention in Indianapolis during the winter of 1850–1851, seemed to mark Indiana's departure from its pioneer period into a more politically and economically advanced state. The document provided for more elective offices, including a superintendent of public instruction, for biennial sessions of the General Assembly, limited in duration to sixty-one days, and for an end to the type of local and special legislation—such as divorces—that had been so time-consuming previously. It also prohibited the state from going into debt except in emergency situations such as foreign invasion. And it contained the infamous Article XIII, a Negro exclusion section prohibiting any further influx of Negroes into the state. Voted on separately by the people of the state, Article XIII was adopted with a slightly higher majority than was the remainder of the constitution; but of course the article became a dead letter in 1865 and was formally removed from the constitution in 1881. Otherwise, the Indiana constitution of 1851, with only a few amendments, is still serving as the fundamental law of the state.

The 1850s were a time of significant political as well as constitutional change. In the early years, following the Compromise of 1850 with its controversial Fugitive Slave Act, which was accompanied, as noted above, by Indiana's adoption of a Negro exclusion article in its constitution, the divided opinions in the state reflected its divided but strongly southern population. As the national antislavery movement slowly gathered momentum, Indiana remained more antiblack in its attitude than antislavery. However, events such as the John Freeman case, discussed below, helped create a distaste for the slavery system; and the distaste was stimulated even more by the Kansas-Nebraska Act of 1854. Another extremely controversial piece of legislation, this act repealed the Missouri Compromise line of 1820 and, theoretically at least, opened the territories of Kansas and Nebraska, which were created by the same act, to slavery on the basis of popular sovereignty—that is, allowing the people of the territory to decide for themselves whether or not to have slavery. There was an immediate outcry in the North against the Kansas-Nebraska Act and its potential for extending slavery into places previously closed to it. And this outcry was institutionalized by the formation of a new political party in 1854, the Republican party, an almost immediate power in the country. At first this new coalition of former Whigs, Know-Nothings, and northern Democrats was known in many states, including Indiana, as the Fusion or People's party; but the name Republican was generally adopted by 1856.

In Indiana, despite the continued domination throughout the 1850s of the increasingly southern-oriented Democrats, who had also controlled the state offices and the legislature since 1843, the late 1850s were marked by increasing political conflicts. The election of 1860 was an especially memorable one for both the state and the nation: the Republicans won in both but were immediately faced with the secession of South Carolina and then other states. President Lincoln confronted a divided nation when he took office, and within six weeks the Civil War had begun.

Oliver P. Morton, Indiana's peppery Civil War governor and one of Lincoln's most ardent supporters, directed Indiana's enormous contribution to the northern war effort. Although often officious and even dictatorial, Morton presented Lincoln with some of his earliest volunteer soldiers in 1861, and Indiana stood near the top overall among the states in both the absolute number (fifth) and in the per capita percentage (second) of troops provided. Morton also proved equal to the political challenges of the war years, which were made more difficult after the 1862 election returned a Democratic majority to the General Assembly. The majority refused to pass an appropriations bill in 1863, but the governor managed to operate the state on personally borrowed funds during 1863 and 1864. And he was able, using some questionable tactics and exploiting the presence of a small group of "copperheads," particularly the Knights of the Golden Circle, to bring Indiana back into the Republican column in the 1864 election.

The Civil War was one of the great watersheds in American history. Its fury extended beyond the great battlefields of war and reached into the homes and businesses and daily lives of almost all Americans. Its total impact is immeasurable, but the attempt to measure it must still be made, as Professor John D. Barnhart has done for one state in the essay below. Originally a part of his larger work, *Indiana: From Frontier to Industrial Commonwealth* (2 vols., 1954), written in collaboration with Donald F. Carmony, the chapters on the Civil War were recast and republished at the request of the Indiana Civil War Centennial Commission.

As Professor Barnhart indicates, the people of Indiana played major roles in almost all phases of the war. Militarily, the state provided officers, troops, and equipment, while at home the state offered political leadership, unswerving loyalty to the Union cause, and vital agricultural and industrial support. There was some concern about the true sentiments of the Democrats in Indiana and whether or not they would support the Union wholeheartedly; but that was a needless worry. Political differences over local issues continued to be aired, but Hoosier Democrats generally followed the leadership of men like Thomas A. Hendricks, a conservative Democratic senator whose devotion to the Union equaled that of any Republican.

There is an extensive literature on Indiana during the late antebellum and Civil War years. The best single source is Emma Lou Thornbrough, *Indiana in the Civil War Era, 1850–1880* (1965), part of a projected six-volume sesquicentennial history of the state, which contains an extensive bibliography. See also the work by Kenneth M. Stampp, *Indiana Politics during the Civil War* (1949); and W. H. H. Terrell, *Report of the Adjutant General of Indiana* (8 vols., 1869). Volume 1 of that report is a narrative of Indiana's role in the war, and it was reprinted by the Indiana Historical Bureau and the Indiana Historical Society in 1960 under the title *Indiana in the War of the Rebellion: Report of the Adjutant General*. See also Frank L. Klement, *Dark Lanterns: Secret Political Societies, Conspiracies, and Treason Trials in the Civil War* (1984), and Alan T. Nolan, *The Iron Brigade: A Military History* (1994). For the colorful Oliver P. Morton, see both the older study by William D. Foulke, *Life of Oliver P. Morton* (2 vols., 1899), and Lorna Lutes Sylvester, "Oliver P. Morton and the Indiana Legislature of 1863," in *Their Infinite Variety: Essays on Indiana Politicians* (1981), 121-154.

Political Developments

THE FUGITIVE SLAVE LAW IN OPERATION

Emma Lou Thornbrough

The place of the Negro in Indiana, ostensibly a free state, was an insecure one. Confronted with a legacy of slavery and involuntary servitude, and either open hostility or studied indifference on the part of most Hoosiers, the small number of Negroes in the state (approximately one per cent of the total population in 1820 and even less in 1860) lived in constant danger. According to the federal constitution, as well as an act of Congress in 1793, runaway slaves were to be returned to their owners. The worst feature of the law was its failure to protect free Negroes from illegal seizure and enslavement, something that happened many times. In Indiana such "kidnappings" occurred most frequently in the southern counties; but no area was immune and no one knows the full extent of the practice. Professor Emma Lou Thornbrough, in her fine study of The Negro in Indiana, *describes many such episodes as well as the efforts of primarily the Quakers in resisting this practice. And in a few cases, particularly in the antislavery (and Quaker) strongholds of Wayne and Randolph counties, their resistance was successful. In the passage below Professor Thornbrough describes the way in which John Freeman of Indianapolis thwarted an attempt to have him declared a runaway and sent to Kentucky. This occurred after a new Fugitive Slave Law had been enacted in 1850, something the South had insisted on, perhaps foolishly, since the attempted enforcement of its provisions increased northern opposition to the entire system of slavery.*

For a detailed account of the John Freeman case, see Charles H. Money, "The Fugitive Slave Law in Indiana," Indiana Magazine of History, *XVII (June 1921), 180–197; see also William M. Cockrum,* The History of the Underground Railroad . . . *(1915); Eugene H.*

From *The Negro in Indiana: A Study of a Minority* (1957), pp. 114–118.

Berwanger, The Frontier against Slavery: Western Anti-Negro Prejudice and the Slavery Extension Controversy *(1967); and Patrick J. Furlong, "The South Bend Fugitive Slave Case," in* We the People: Indiana and the United States Constitution *(1987).*

The procedure for the retaking of runaway slaves was modified by the Fugitive Slave Act of 1850, an amendment to the law of 1793 adopted in response to the demands of the representatives of the slave states. The principal change was that the 1850 measure relied for enforcement upon Federal rather than state officers. Federal commissioners, appointed by Federal judges, had concurrent jurisdiction with these judges in hearing fugitive slave cases. Testimony of the persons claimed as slaves was expressly prohibited from being admitted as evidence at these hearings. If the commissioner decided in favor of the claimant, he issued a certificate for the removal of the fugitive out of the state, and if the claimant had reason to fear that there would be an attempt to rescue the slave by force, it was the duty of the commissioner to give him protection in escorting the slave out of the state, the cost being borne by the United States government. The commissioner also had the power to deputize any private citizen to assist in the capture of a fugitive.

This act, which was one of the series of measures known as the Compromise of 1850, was supported by a majority of the Indiana delegation in Congress as necessary for quelling the sectional bitterness which threatened to disrupt the Union. In most parts of the state the measure did not evoke the immediate and universal condemnation which it brought forth in some Northern states. Abolitionist groups branded the "blood hound fugitive slave bill" as unconstitutional and pledged themselves to prevent its enforcement, but Governor Joseph A. Wright told the General Assembly that it must be carried out in good faith. Although Wright and most Indianans hoped for the "finality" of the Compromise of 1850 and the end of agitation on the slavery question, the operation of the new fugitive law had the effect of converting men who had heretofore been moderates into outspoken opponents of the slave system.

A notorious case in Indianapolis in 1853 caused a wave of revulsion against the system of slave catching. The central figure was John Freeman, a Negro who claimed to have come to Indianapolis from Georgia about 1844, and who through hard work and thrift had acquired some real estate, including a house and garden and a restaurant. In 1853 a Missourian by the name of Pleasant Ellington, who professed to being a Methodist minister, appeared in Indianapolis and filed a claim with the United States commissioner that Freeman was his slave, Sam, who had escaped in 1836 when Ellington was residing in Kentucky. Freeman was arrested, but before a hearing could be held friends learned of his plight and the commissioner was persuaded to allow him to have legal counsel. One of the ablest lawyers in the city, John L. Ketcham, came to Freeman's aid, and the commissioner, much to the disgust of Ellington, agreed to a delay. The case soon attracted wide attention in the newspapers, and public opinion apparently compelled the commissioner to see that Freeman was given a chance to prove his right to freedom. A postponement of nine weeks was granted for the securing of evidence. Efforts to secure the release of Freeman on bail were unavailing, although some of the most prominent men in Indianapolis helped raise the bond. The commissioner decided that bail was not permissible, and the Negro was kept in jail for nine weeks, and as an added injury was compelled to pay the cost of a special guard that was hired to see that he did not escape.

Two other lawyers, John Coburn and Lucian Barbour, joined Ketcham in the case, and the three worked tirelessly and brilliantly to secure evidence. Correspondence with persons in Georgia corroborated Freeman's claim that he had resided there and was free, while witnesses from Georgia were brought to Indianapolis to identify him. Meanwhile, the real Sam, who had escaped from Ellington, was traced to Canada. He freely confessed his identity, and witnesses who had known him in Kentucky went to Canada to identify him and brought depositions to Indianapolis. This sworn testimony showed that the physical characteristics of Sam and Freeman were quite different as to both height and color; nevertheless Ellington and three witnesses whom he had brought with him had not hesitated to swear that Freeman was Sam after compelling him to submit to a physical examination.

To clinch the case for Freeman his old guardian arrived from Georgia to identify him, and six other witnesses from Georgia arrived on the day set for the final hearing of the case. Their testimony was not called for because Ellington had given up and left the city. The commissioner dismissed the case, and Freeman was released. He was free, but the cost of proving his freedom in the face of a wanton and unscrupulous attempt to enslave him had cost him everything that he had saved from a life of hard work. The only redress which the law afforded for the financial loss and the indignities which he had suffered was a damage suit. He won an award of two thousand dollars in a suit against Ellington, but this was a hollow victory. The award was never paid since Ellington sold his property and left St. Louis to escape payment. Freeman also brought suit in the Marion County Circuit Court against the United States marshal who had imprisoned him. The case was taken to the Indiana Supreme Court which upheld the right to sue the United States official since the acts with which he was charged—assault, forcing the prisoner to strip naked, and extorting money from him for the pay of the guard—were not part of his official duties and were unlawful. But again this was only a technical victory since the court ruled that the suit should have been brought in Rush County, the residence of the marshal. In the end Freeman was able to save his home and a garden plot through the help of many persons in both Indiana and Georgia who had become interested in his case. Nevertheless, he left Indianapolis and moved to Canada at the outbreak of the Civil War, apparently because he feared a southern victory.

Freeman's case was watched with intense interest throughout the state, and there was widespread relief and satisfaction when his freedom was assured. The case showed more forcibly than all the speeches of antislavery orators the woeful inadequacy of the Federal law to protect the rights of free Negroes. As a Fort Wayne newspaper observed: "A more flagrant case of injustice, we have never seen. It appears to us in such cases, that if the person swearing to the identity of the accused and seeking to consign a free man to slavery, were tried and punished for perjury, a wholesome lesson would be given which might prevent injustice to free persons of color. The fugitive slave law evidently needs some amendment, to give greater protection to free persons of color. As it now stands, almost any of them might be dragged into slavery. If Freeman had not had money and friends he must inevitably have been taken off into bondage. Any poor man, without friends, would have been given up at once and taken away, and it was only by the most strenuous exertions that Freeman was rescued. A law under which such injustice can be perpetrated, and which holds out such inducements to perjury, is imperfect and must be amended or repealed. The American people have an innate sense of justice which will no longer allow such a law to disgrace our statute books."

Cases such as this, which were widely publicized, hastened the final extinction of slavery. But in the meantime, as the editorial observed, in spite of his ordeal, Freeman was more fortunate than many members of his race. No one will ever know how many anonymous Negroes were carried off into slavery without the benefit of counsel or a fair hearing simply because they were without friends or money.

BIRTH OF THE REPUBLICAN PARTY IN INDIANA

Roger H. Van Bolt

An insight into the confused political situation of the mid-1850s is provided by Roger H. Van Bolt of the Alfred P. Sloan, Jr., Museum at Flint, Michigan. Van Bolt's doctoral dissertation at the University of Chicago, large portions of which were published in the Indiana Magazine of History *in the 1950s, was an examination of Indiana politics from 1840 to 1856 and focused on the rise of the Republican party. In the chaos that existed after the demise of the Whig party following the 1852 election, a number of groups attempted to become the second major party in the two-party system and thus provide the opposition to the Democratic party. In the elections of 1854 the various factions in Indiana coalesced into a "Fusion" party, made up of former Whigs, Free Soilers, Americans (Know-Nothings), and northern—or antislavery—Democrats. Surprisingly, this "conglomeration of antagonisms" routed the Democrats "Horse, Foot, and Dragoon" (p. 185) but then found it impossible to carry through a legislative program in 1855. Some elements of the Fusionists then organized themselves into the People's party, and as such later participated in the first national convention of the new Republican party in 1856. But disagreements over policy positions shattered the temporary unity and paved the way for a Democratic victory in 1856. Ashbel P. Willard, a brilliant young politician from New Albany, defeated Centerville's Oliver P. Morton in the gubernatorial race, and the Democrats also regained control of the Indiana General Assembly.*

For a general overview of the political scene in the 1850s, see Emma Lou Thornbrough, Indiana in the Civil War Era, 1850–1880 *(1965); Charles Roll,* Colonel Dick Thompson: The Persistent Whig *(1948); Willard H. Smith,* Schuyler Colfax: The Changing Fortunes of a Political Idol *(1952); and Ralph D. Gray, ed.,* Gentlemen From Indiana: National

From "The Rise of the Republican Party in Indiana, 1855–1856," *Indiana Magazine of History*, LI (September 1955), 185–187, 191, 206–213.

Party Candidates, 1836–1940 *(1977), especially the essays on Julian, English, Colfax, and Hendricks. See also the recent monograph by William E. Gienapp,* The Birth of the Republican Party, 1852–1856 *(1987). His chapter on "The Confusion of Fusion," pp. 103–128, deals, in part, with Indiana politics in the 1850s.*

The fusion of the anti-Democratic elements in 1854 had been accomplished under intense heat; the resulting amalgam was yet to be tested for durability. With no elections in 1855 to keep the political fires burning, the manipulators of Fusionism were cautiously observing the cooling-down process, waiting to see what they had created. The year 1855 would reveal whether the result was a new compound or merely a mixture.

Shortly after the fall elections of 1854, while the Democrats were still smarting under their defeat by the conglomeration of antagonisms that had routed them "Horse, Foot, and Dragoon," the Fusionists called an outdoor meeting at Indianapolis for November 1, 1854, to celebrate their victory. Thomas Smith of New Albany was chairman; among the speakers were Henry S. Lane, Samuel W. Parker, Oliver P. Morton, and Godlove Orth. The theme of their speeches was by now a familiar one: to forget all past political affiliations and to forward the new movement. They declared that freedom, temperance, and pure elections should be the watchword of the party. The "people" resolved that the Declaration of Independence, the Constitution, the Ordinance of 1787, and the resolutions of July 13 were long enough and broad enough planks with which to build a platform capable of supporting all the American people.

When the meeting adjourned, the Know Nothings in the group stayed on to hold a conclave of their state council. After many arguments, they chose Godlove Orth as their candidate for United States senator and Milton Gregg of the *New Albany Tribune* for state printer. The action of the council indicated trouble ahead for the brittle new party, for the politically experienced realized that organization should come before a search for party spoils. Men like Jacob Chapman and Michael C. Garber had hoped that strong organization would be developed.

When the legislature convened in January, 1855, the new party was given its first opportunity to carry out its political promises. The first obstacle to hurdle was the election of a United States senator. Rather than permit the choice of a Fusionist, the Democrats refused to caucus. Some Fusionists who reasoned that the so-called old liners could not refuse to go into an election felt that the stalemate was temporary. As Orth wrote: "For this would, more than anything else [serve] to drive us together & Keep us together for the next campaign—nor will the Prest. Election swallow up this dereliction of duty as they confidentially hope."

A week went by, and with it went the hope of ending the deadlock. Orth's optimism was gone; now he wrote: "If they [the old liners] had the assurance that a Natl. Whig—who didn't fuse, don't fuse, and who is anti-Sam, could command the necessary strength—they would, in my opinion, give him the old line vote—and elect him." Thus in its first political skirmish with the Democracy the Fusion lost the encounter. As a consequence of this stalemate, Jesse Bright alone represented Indiana in the United States Senate until 1857. In the meantime, the legislature attempted to co-operate on other matters.

The temperance advocates of 1854 were still to be satisfied. Early in February, 1855, the general assembly approved an act which prohibited the sale of liquor in the state, following the Maine law principle. The new law passed with a comfortable majority and in the senate, where the Democrats held a slight advantage, seven members of that party supported it. Popular reaction among the "cold water" boys was spontaneous. Indiana had again joined the ranks of the reformers. Governor Joseph A. Wright's faithful correspondent, John Hunt, reported that "the people here are Laughing all over their faces on account [of] the passage of the Temperence Bill: we have had 2 illuminations. They are becoming intemperate on temperence."

The so-called Whiskey Democrats were not yet defeated, however. Within a short time, an Indianapolis saloonkeeper named Roderick Beebe opened for business. His immediate arrest made possible a test case. The Indiana Supreme Court received the case in the November term, and Judge Samuel E. Perkins, who had declared the legislation of 1853 unconstitutional, handed down the same decision on this temperance bill. Thus the door was opened once again for unhampered liquor traffic. Politically, the Democrats had won another victory, this time in the courts of the state. . . .

The adjournment of the legislature brought to an end the political maneuvers in the general assembly, but the organization of the parties continued throughout 1855. The session had revealed that the politicians were not out of the troubled waters of the previous summer. The Democrats were busy reorganizing their efforts for the coming presidential year while the Fusionists needed to maintain the semblance of political organization they already possessed, meanwhile hoping that structure could be given to the amorphous mass.

During 1855 the state Democracy was not very active, since the elections were local in nature. At a meeting in Indianapolis in April, the party reiterated its claims of 1854, with particular emphasis given to anti-Know Nothingism.

The Fusionists had more difficult problems. After the elections of 1854, the once harmonious elements became suspicious of one another. The Free Soil elements had begun to "feel quite offish" after Milton Gregg was nominated for state printer, while the temperance forces generally lost interest once the new law was in the legislative mill. Under the guidance of Joseph G. Marshall of Madison the old Whigs had aspirations of their own for senatorial nominations. Finally, there was the question of what would become of the Know Nothing movement. Among the leaders of 1854 who were in the state capital attempting to weld the Fusion more firmly was Schuyler Colfax, the congressman-elect from South Bend. Some " 'outsiders,' " he reported from Indianapolis, " 'ought to be expected to be preaching concord rather than attempting to sow disunity.' " He was not sure that the Know Nothings might not be the chief opposition of the Fusion. The ex-Whigs themselves, after the initial success, felt that instead of remaining in the background they should come to the fore to manage affairs for the Fusion. . . .

Reactions to the People's convention varied. The "South" Americans refused to stand by the nomination and a platform that was so strongly "Republican" in character. One American editor blamed William Sheets, the president of the state council, for the failure of the party. He bitterly growled: "The officiating head of the American party in Indiana is rotten to the core! He has sold us to our enemies." Such reports as these, however, were exceptional.

On the other hand, to such radicals as George W. Julian, the party had not gone far enough in its denunciations. Julian was unable to find a single true antislavery man on the whole ticket. He called the People's party a "combination of weaknesses, instead of a union of forces." One of Julian's friends, Daniel Worth, despondently described the Indianapolis convention thus: "A poor miserable truckling concern without either soul or body. . . . You will mark the fact that our wise-acres at Indianapolis ignored even the name of Republican as well as all antislavery principle. This was done for the benefit of Knownothings and old fossil Whigs who have just emanated from their old political graves where they have been 'persevering to rot,' and are now ready to take office at the hands of antislavery men provided they are not compelled to take more antislavery than they might safely take of *arsenic*." The old abolitionists who sought a political home among the factions of the new party were sorely disappointed.

The People's convention, however, was antislavery enough in sentiment to frighten away the more conservative elements of the Democratic opposition. The friends of William H. English felt that the stand of the party assured them of success in the coming canvass. One wrote confidently, "I see by the proceedings of the peoples Convention that Black Republicanism was triumphant, no elector was appointed for this District. Gregg [the local American editor] has been unhorsed, I think the whole affair a miserable abortion, the policy of nominating a broken down set of renegad Democrats, because they love niggers more than white folks will not win in Indiana. we Shall beat the whole tickett by thousands."

The tremendous importance attached to national questions in the progress of the state party brought the question of the national Republican conventions into sharp focus. The first meeting of the Republicans was held in Pittsburgh in February. The role of the Hoosiers in this initial assembly is rather vague. According to the various writings of George W. Julian, he played an important role. He did serve as chairman of the committee on organization and was one of the vice-presidents. William Grose of Henry County was appointed to the executive committee, and Oliver P. Morton was a member of the resolutions committee. Julian explained later that the Fusion had "subordinated every question of principle to its desire for political success. The situation was most humiliating." This preliminary meeting, which served primarily to formulate more solid propositions upon which a permanent organization could be established, was an impetus to the Philadelphia convention in June.

Henry S. Lane was elected president of the second convention. In his address the former Whig extolled the virtues of Henry Clay. Had the Kentuckian been alive, he would have been leading the Republican party, declared Lane. The disunion cry, he claimed, came from South Carolina "unhung" nullifiers who still had the halter of General Andrew Jackson about their necks. Caleb Smith, another ex-Whig, formerly of Indiana but at this time a resident of Cincinnati, also spoke. This retired legislator called the Republican party the true national party. He was careful to state that his party would not interfere where slavery already existed, yet since the institution was always aggressive, the Republicans were the only party that would maintain the principles of freedom. These two Hoosiers permitted the speakers who followed them to express more radical views. One was Owen Lovejoy of Illinois, who spoke of the divine inspiration of the Declaration of Independence and its mission in America. Henry Wilson of Massachusetts was allowed to shout: "Sir, our object is to overthrow the Slave Power of the country, now organized in the Democratic party of the country."

It is interesting and significant to compare the list of delegates selected at Indianapolis to attend the Philadelphia convention with the list of men who answered the roll call of the credentials committee at the convention. The first and second districts, which were strongholds of the Americans, were represented at Philadelphia by Hoosiers who lived outside these constituencies; apparently those appointed did not attend. There were also substitutions in the seventh and eighth congressional districts. The replacements were often men of prominence from other areas in the state.

The Indiana delegation was indicative of a mature party leadership. There was a sprinkling of editor-politicians: William G. Terrell of Lafayette, an ardent ex-Whig; Thomas H. Bringhurst, Whig editor of the *Logansport Journal*; Charles D. Murray of Kokomo, another Whig editor; and John Defrees, a member of the platform committee, the leader of the state press as well as of the People's party. The lone ex-Democrat was the Bright antagonist, Michael C. Garber of the *Madison Courier.*

Another significant group was made up of businessmen—merchants, bankers, and railroad promoters. Defrees was connected with the Central Bank at this time. Henry S. Lane of Crawfordsville was a banker with his father-in-law, Isaac Elston. Daniel R. Bearss of Peru, a Henry Clay Whig, was a retired mercantilist, one of the wealthiest men in the county. Benjamin F. Claypool of Fayette County was president of the state bank in Connersville. Jacob B. Julian of Centerville was a sometime banker and railroad promoter. Henry County sent Martin L. Bundy, a wealthy citizen. From Terre Haute came L. A. Burnett, a leather and hide dealer. Finally, Samuel Hanna was a delegate from the Fort Wayne district. This Allen County Whig was a frontier capitalist and one of the wealthiest men in Indiana. Hanna had begun as an Indian trader and was president of the Fort Wayne and Chicago railroad.

A few of the ardent exponents of the various isms were also represented, but they were in the minority. One of these was Jonathan W. Gordon of Indianapolis, whose law practice was such that it had given him ample time to edit the *Temperance Chart*, a publication appearing under the patronage of the Sons of Temperance. James Ritchey of Franklin County, who was named to the national executive committee, was another reformer devoted to many causes. Judge William Peaslee of Shelbyville had been an original member of the Know Nothings in the "dark lantern" stage.

Taken as a whole the membership indicated Whig entry into the leadership of the National Republicans of Indiana. The respected and prosperous of the now defunct party were gaining control of the new organization. For the most part it was a conservative leadership, replacing the more radical elements that had rushed into the Fusion in 1854. This Whig group, however, did not include the old Whigs of the river counties but came rather from the northern and central sections of the state, the areas in which significant economic and social change was taking place in the fifties. These Hoosiers, who were taking strides to secure political advantage, were to determine the character of the future Republican party of Indiana.

With the nomination of John C. Fremont, the Indiana delegation, Republican in fact if not in name, returned home to stump the state in the new party's first national campaign. Back in Indiana, as a result of the problem of the course of the Americans, the important political question was the matter of support. Before the convention met in Philadelphia, John Defrees, chairman of the state central committee, called for a ratification meeting to be held at Indianapolis on July 15, 1856. The Americans, however, decided to await the results of the People's convention before meeting; consequently they called their gathering for July 16. The decision was of some significance since it seemed to mean that no longer were the Know Nothings, now Americans, attempting to set the pattern for the Fusionists.

The People's convention on July 15 was little more than a ratification meeting. Henry S. Lane and Stephen S. Harding were among the speakers. The afternoon program included a few Kansas speeches as well as a parade of young men attired as "Border Ruffians" and "Buford's Thieves."

By the time of their state convention on July 16 the Americans had been reduced largely to the position of an irreconcilable minority of the old Whig party. The seceders of the conventions of the previous year had brought many of the Indiana Americans into the People's party; those left behind were chiefly from southern Indiana. An important leader of the party in Indiana was Richard W. Thompson, who was made permanent chairman of the state party. In June, Humphrey Marshall of Kentucky had written Thompson: " 'We must have a *separate* Fillmore ticket in Indiana. You must go to the Convention—and you must head the movement and go on the Electoral ticket—there is no time for trifling . . . *we must not fuse*.' "

The activities of Dick Thompson were reported to the People's chieftain, Henry Lane, by one of his correspondents: " 'We are peculiarly situated here [Terre Haute]. R. W. Thompson is using extraordinary means to prevent an organization upon Frémont. . . . He maintains that the Planter has the same right to occupy the territories with his slaves that the northern farmer has with his horses. Thompson is making desperate exertions to carry his points, he does what he has seldom done before; he is on the streets and at the corners in season and out of season, trying to inveigh old Whigs into his scheme of resuscitating the Whig party.' "

The convention itself was not particularly impressive as compared with the People's meeting of the day before. Only about one-fourth of the counties were represented, for the Americans had become a sectional party within the state with the chief centers in New Albany, Jeffersonville, Terre Haute, and Vevay. The Democratic pocket and the American pocket were almost the same. A last attempt to endorse Fremont was put down hurriedly, and the support of the state ticket was left open, a policy which amounted to a handicap for Morton and the People's party. With the conclusion of the meeting the battle lines of the coming presidential campaign were drawn: the Democracy, with Buchanan, had divided opposition. After the convention, Thompson labored to organize Fillmore clubs over the state; only one of these, at Lafayette, was north of the National Road. But the Americans lost more than they gained in press support. Perhaps the greatest blow was the defection of John W. Dawson of the *Fort Wayne Times*, who was also a candidate on the state People's ticket.

The campaign during the summer and fall of 1856 was a test of the new People's party. No longer an impetuous upstart nor a purely offensive party, it was now a political organization which was beginning to operate as a responsible group and which had to resort also to defensive actions in the rough and tumble tactics of the canvass. At the state level and in Congress its leaders had the opportunity to carry out the demands and promises of 1854.

In the Kansas situation the People's party in Indiana and the Republicans in the nation had a firebrand that was capable of igniting men's emotions. Jim Lane, who had promised to carry the truth to every corner of the North, dramatically rushed back to Kansas just before the campaign reached fever pitch. At the end of May, he announced to the electors of Indiana, " 'You have heard the late thrilling news from Kansas. I am hastening there, then, either to relieve, or perish with that gallant bleeding people.' " Whereupon he cancelled a series of speaking engagements that would have taken him to many corners of the state.

The numerous letters and dispatches from Kansas that appeared in the press and the speeches of those who had recently returned served to arouse the citizens. Editors gave the latest happenings high priority. Wheeler in South Bend reported to Colfax: "The subscribers were anxious for Kansas News, and I gave them Kansas news. Kansas news would spoil by laying over; Day's Speech would not." Schuyler Colfax's wife was the happy recipient of "Governor Robinson's Polka," the gift of her husband's political ally, Nathaniel P. Banks. She commented that the governor was then "suffering imprisonment in Kansas at the hands of those vile despots, the border ruffians, for the crime of loving Freedom better than Slavery." In the Whitewater Valley an even more powerful impact of the Kansas affairs was felt, for the news came that a member of a party of Hoosiers who had gone to Kansas had been killed in an attack.

The political capital in firing the emotions of those who were already enlisted in the ranks of the People's party was one matter, but when the "fagenders" began to fall under the spell of the Kansas dispatches, the Democracy began to worry. One of Governor Wright's political friends hoped the excitement would end. "The Kansas troubles afford the theme for about all the declamation of the opposition, and at this moment they effect the creation of some prejudice to our injury. May we not reasonably hope for a conclusion of those disturbances soon?" Then the Democrat expressed an interesting point of view that was not exactly high doctrine in Democratic circles. He wrote: "Anything that Congress would with propriety do ought to be done—Confidence once restored, that Kansas will probably be a free-state, and all is well with the Democracy, for the people, I am persuaded would gladly see this constant agitation of the subject of slavery driven out of the Halls of Congress."

The campaign centered about the sectional issue, and with the cry of "Black Republicanism" ringing in their ears, the excitement of the people grew as the October state election day approached. The Democrats made the most of the American People's party split as well as of the fact that most Hoosiers hated the Negro. In one Democratic neighborhood, in Dubois County, it was reported that several young ladies of the community, dressed all in white, paraded through the streets carrying a banner, " 'Fathers, save us from nigger husbands!' " Less dramatically but with effective results, the Democrats stressed the theme that the Black Republicans were plotting abolition and the bestowal of full social and political rights upon the Negro. The brunt of the state campaign was borne by Oliver P. Morton, an anti-Nebraska Democrat. He was rather evenly matched on the stump with Ashbel P. Willard, who was a brilliant speaker.

The results of the local campaign were indicative of the events to come in the November elections. Willard carried the state by almost 5,000 votes. Examination of the results in the congressional districts reveals the sectionalism of the state. Morton carried the Whitewater valley and the northern districts. The congressional election resulted in a sizeable increase in the number of Democratic victories. Indiana now had six of the old liners back in Congress, while the People's party had lost four seats.

The Impact of War upon Indiana

INDIANA IN THE CIVIL WAR

John D. Barnhart

The Civil War was the greatest challenge Indiana's democratic government had met. The war affected all of the citizens of the state, penetrated their vital social relations, and threatened their necessary and cherished organizations. The way the people met that challenge constitutes much of the history of the war years in Indiana.

That all patriots yield obedience to the voice of the people when expressed in a constitutional manner and that all citizens unite in preserving the Union and the Constitution was the message of Abraham Lincoln to the people of Indiana as he journeyed from Springfield, Illinois, to Washington, D.C., for his inauguration as president of the United States. The next day, February 12, 1861, his fifty-second birthday, he was escorted to the railway station where he entrained for Cincinnati. Lincoln's Indianapolis appearance and speech were the subject of favorable comment by the Republican *Daily Journal*, but the Democratic *Daily Sentinel* declared

From "The Impact of the Civil War on Indiana," *Indiana Magazine of History*, LVII (September 1961), 185–193, 198–201, 212–213, 221–224.

him to be a theorist, a dreamer, and an impractical man who lacked the will and purpose to be a leader.

The attack upon Fort Sumter, April 12, 1861, stunned the people of Indiana and its sister states. When the news came over the wires, small groups gathered to discuss the ominous deed. Some were gloomy because of the portent of war. Others were angry because of the insult to the flag and the threat to the unity of the nation of which the flag was the symbol.

Angry or sad, the people responded immediately. In two mass meetings in Indianapolis on the evening of the following day, the people promised to defend the government with their lives, fortunes, and sacred honor; and on Sunday, April 14, ministers of various churches gave their sanction to these same loyal sentiments. When President Lincoln and Governor Oliver P. Morton called for troops, volunteers came forward in such numbers that Indiana's quota could have been filled twice.

South Carolina had seceded from the Union on December 20, 1860, and five other states joined her on February 4, 1861, to organize the Confederate States of America. Jefferson Davis was elected president, and the raising of one hundred thousand troops was authorized. Texas soon came into the Confederacy, and after Lincoln's call for soldiers four additional states seceded.

The border states were in a difficult position, for their people were divided in sentiment, and none relished the prospect of their land becoming a battleground of contending armies. Indianans were particularly concerned about the decision of Kentucky because it was separated from Indiana only by the Ohio River and citizens of the two states had been friends since frontier days. The decision of Kentucky might determine how close the fighting would come to Hoosier soil.

A large number of Indiana citizens were natives of southern states or the children of transplanted southerners. Many of them had relatives or friends among the people of the Confederacy. Former southerners were not so numerous in the northern counties of Indiana, but they were quite numerous in the southern and central counties where the danger of invasion was greater. Richard Thompson, of Terre Haute, received letters from relatives in the South appealing to him to try to stop the war. But Hoosiers who had been born in the states on the south side of the Ohio River had helped to make Indiana a free state in 1816. They knew from experience some of the injustices involved in slavery, and they did not want them in Indiana. They did not object, however, to this institution in the southern states until efforts to preserve it threatened the unity of the nation.

War issues tended to divide the people of Indiana, to break the unity of families, to form groups with different ideals, to split political parties into factions, and to prevent representative government from functioning smoothly. A few Hoosiers who were pro-southern were willing to acquiesce in disunion. Jesse D. Bright, whose influence was dominant in the Democratic party for some years before 1860, shared these views. He was expelled from the United States Senate on February 5, 1862, because he had written a letter to "His Excellency, Jefferson Davis, President of the Confederation," in which he recommended a friend who wished to sell an improved firearm. Other Peace Democrats opposed the use of force and insisted that the Union could be preserved by concessions to the South. Included in this faction were Lambdin P. Milligan, John C. Walker, and Horace Heffren, individuals associated with the secret political societies.

More numerous were the Constitutional Union men who wanted to preserve the Union and therefore supported the war, but who opposed such measures as the tariff and the National Banking Act. Many of these Union men were willing to offer some concessions to prevent a war or to bring an early peace. When they realized that the destruction of the Union might leave Indiana a part of the interior nation—without free access to the sea and with her trade subject to taxes imposed by a southern or eastern confederacy—their nationalism increased perceptibly. Nevertheless they declared that they were unwilling to fight an abolition war.

A few War Democrats openly supported the state and national administrations and joined with the Republicans in forming the Union party. Among the War Democrats were former Governor Joseph A. Wright, James Hughes, of Bloomington, Lew Wallace, and Allen Hamilton.

The firing on Fort Sumter not only started the Civil War but made it necessary for Indiana Democrats to readjust themselves rather quickly. They had recently been engaged in state and national political campaigns with considerable intensity and had continued their criticism of and hostility toward the Lincoln and Morton administrations. After April 12, vigorous hostility began to assume the aspects of disloyalty, which the Republicans were quick to turn to their advantage. Such action only increased the anger of the Democrats and made their protests more vigorous. Although the remarks of the Democrats were often tactless, the Republicans did not prefer charges in a civil court against them, much less secure a conviction in a criminal court against anyone.

The war not only embarrassed Democrats, but it also divided Republicans. The latter differed about the concessions they would make to avoid war, but the real division came later in respect to the Emancipation Proclamation. Was the preservation of the Union the sole purpose of the war? At the beginning the answer was almost always in the affirmative. A few Republicans, however, like George W. Julian, "had no love for a proslavery Union." He regarded liberty as more desirable than the Union. Radicals of this type demanded that no concessions should be made to the South and that they were insisting that slavery should be destroyed. Julian said on January 14, 1862, that

> the disturbing element has uniformly been slavery. This is the unclean spirit that from the beginning has needed exorcism. . . .
>
> This rebellion is a bloody and frightful demonstration . . . that slavery and freedom cannot dwell together in peace. . . . I believe the popular demand now is, or soon will be, the total extirpation of slavery as the righteous purpose of the war and the only means of a lasting peace. . . . Never perhaps in the history of any nation has so grand an opportunity presented itself for serving the interests of humanity and freedom.

In the naming of his cabinet, Lincoln tried to counteract the division within the party. He chose party leaders who represented different elements and sectional groups in order that he might keep the support of all factions. For secretary of the interior, Lincoln chose Caleb B. Smith, of Indianapolis, who had been a lawyer, a newspaper publisher, and a railroad president. An advocate of internal improvements, Smith was elected to the state house of representatives from 1832 to 1842. From 1843 to 1849 he served Indiana as a member of the national House of Representatives. He was a skilled stump speaker, and his appointment came to him at least in part because of his support of Lincoln in the Republican national convention in Chicago. His appointment was also a recognition of the important role played by Indiana Republicans in Lincoln's nomination and election. It has also been alleged that the choice resulted from a pre-nomination pledge made by Judge David Davis and Joseph Medill to secure the selection of Lincoln by the Chicago convention and which Lincoln felt obligated to carry out although it was made without his knowledge. Smith remained in the cabinet for less than two years; his resignation became effective on January 1, 1863.

Indiana's congressional delegation was divided between seven Republicans and four Democrats. All of the latter were from the vicinity of the Ohio and lower Wabash rivers. William S. Holman, of Aurora, was a War Democrat who was later better known as the "Watchdog of the Treasury." John Law, of Evansville, the historian of Vincennes, was a War Democrat who vigorously opposed emancipation as a war aim. James A. Cravens, of Washington County, was also a War Democrat. Daniel W. Voorhees, of Terre Haute, has been called a Constitutional Union Democrat whose sharp tongue led many to consider him a Peace Democrat. "To him abolitionism and secession were equally hateful; and he bewailed the breaches of the Constitution and the tyranny of the war Government in terms of unmeasured [opprobrium]."

The seven Republican members of the National House of Representatives ranged from radicals to moderates. Schuyler Colfax, editor of the South Bend *St. Joseph Valley Register*, had been elected to Congress in 1854, and was re-elected until he became vice president of the United States in 1869. He was considered in 1860 for a post in Lincoln's cabinet, but was passed over for Caleb B. Smith. Colfax served as speaker of the House of Representatives from 1863 to 1869 and was known as a Radical Republican. George W. Julian, of Wayne County, already noted as a radical, had been a Free Soil member of Congress from 1849 to 1851 and a Free Soil candidate for vice president in 1852. Now he was a Radical Republican deeply interested in the abolition of slavery. Albert S. White, of Tippecanoe County, was more conservative than Julian but was very energetic in trying to secure adoption of gradual emancipation of slaves and indemnification of their owners. Albert G. Porter, of Indianapolis, had been a Democrat but had joined the new Republican party, which elected him a congressman in 1858 and 1860. After Sumter he favored a vigorous prosecution of the war. William M. Dunn, of Madison, was elected in 1860 but defeated in 1862. He entered the army and became assistant judge advocate general in 1864.

Although Oliver P. Morton had been elected lieutenant governor, he became the chief executive on January 16, 1861, when Governor Henry S. Lane resigned to accept a seat in the United States Senate. Believing that war was inevitable, Morton was foremost in preparing the state to do her part in support of the national administration. After Sumter was fired upon, he appointed Lew Wallace adjutant general, Colonel Thomas A. Morris quartermaster general, and Isaiah Mansur commissary general. The state fairground at Indianapolis was transformed into Camp Morton, where Indiana volunteers were trained, equipped, and organized into regiments. . . .

Indiana's geographical position, her large population, and her large crops of agricultural products made her support of the war important. Since the state was located between the Great Lakes and the Ohio River, railroads connected her cities, villages, and farms with Atlantic ports. Other railroads which ran from north to south were prepared to carry troops, supplies, and food to the armies which were soon located in the south central states. Indiana was a part of the great production area for wheat, corn, and hogs. Hoosier farmers raised more hogs than those of any other state and were second in the production of wheat. Only four loyal states had a larger population or more members in the national House of Representatives.

Most of the state was in the drainage basin of the Ohio River, which with the Mississippi River formed the natural outlet for her surplus products. Although the east-west railroads opened the way to other markets, commerce to New Orleans had not diminished. Consequently the outcome of secession was of vital importance because it threatened Indiana's most natural route to the markets of the world.

The state, however, lacked the funds necessary to organize and equip regiments and to send them to the front. Temporarily the need was supplied by private persons and banks, among which was Winslow, Lanier, and Company, of New York. James F. D. Lanier, formerly a banker of Madison, Indiana, and a founder and principal stockholder of the Second State Bank of Indiana, was largely responsible for the interest this firm took in Indiana affairs. Although he left the state in 1851, he was much concerned about Indiana's part in the Civil War. His company loaned Governor Morton $420,000 at this time. Since this loan and other actions required legislative approval and cooperation, Morton called a special session of the general assembly which met on April 24.

The new governor undertook the great task of guiding the state through the war years. He addressed the special session of the legislature with an appeal that politics be forgotten and that all act as patriots. The members of the assembly responded quickly and vigorously, divided legislative offices between the two parties, authorized an issue of $2,000,000 in state bonds for the defense of the state and nation, and appropriated $1,600,000 for military purposes.

The Indianapolis *Daily Sentinel*, which on April 13, hailed the firing on Fort Sumter as the "Abolition War of Seward, Lincoln and Company," and advised on April 15, "Let Them Go in Peace," promised on April 25 that "there will be no factious opposition on the part of the Democratic members." Four days later it urged: "The Legislature of Indiana should promply provide for all the requisitions of the General Government." The ultimate was reached on May 10 when it commented on the possibility of war or peace: "There is now no choice in the matter. The Government must be sustained." It actually used "Webster's Reply to Hayne" against the arguments of the secessionists. The call to action seemed to have brought unity to Indiana—at least the dissident elements became quiet, but this temporary unity was not to last long.

Since the markets for many products of southern Indiana had been in the southern states and trade continued after Sumter, the legislature appointed committees to investigate the possibility that aid was being given to the Confederacy by the continuation of trade. Acts were adopted defining treason, prohibiting correspondence and trade with the Confederacy, and providing penalties for violation of these measures. The federal government also intervened to prevent commerce with the enemy. Interference with the normal economic activity of this part of the state resulted in hardships for the people.

The governor was authorized on May 6, 1861, to organize six additional regiments from the volunteers. They were formed into a brigade under Brigadier General Joseph J. Reynolds, a graduate of West Point who had several years of military experience. The regiments were soon in federal service. To safeguard the immediate defense of the state, a militia was provided under the title "Indiana Legion." Its organization was confined largely to the southern counties, and inevitably much of the burden of local defense fell upon the citizens of this part of the state.

A debate over the purpose of the nation in waging war also revealed elements of disunity. Both houses of the general assembly adopted resolutions which declared that the men and resources of the state should not be employed to destroy slavery or the constitutional rights of the states. Some of the legislators wanted to add pledges stating that the preservation of the Union was the sole aim of the war, but radicals asserted that only the abolition of slavery would bring permanent peace. . . .

A rancorous partisan conflict without precedent in Indiana also took place in 1862. The Democratic state convention met in Indianapolis on January 8 in the midst of discouraging circumstances. Divided among themselves in respect to support of the war, their attitude towards slavery, and the methods of preserving the Union, Democrats were associated in the minds of many people with the rebellion of the South. Thomas A. Hendricks, president of the convention, promised support of the war for the preservation of the Union, but warned against abolitionists and complained about economic changes which the war stimulated and which worked to the advantage of the East. The platform promised support of a war for the "integrity of the Union under the Constitution" but opposed emancipation of the Negroes or the subjugation of the southern states. The platform was unrealistic in demanding the preservation of the Union as it had been before the war.

The Union party, a coalition of Republicans and War Democrats, met in convention on June 18, anticipating an easy victory. Governor Morton as president of the convention again urged the abandonment of party for the duration of the war. He also spoke of treasonable societies in the state and of the possibility that strong measures against them might be necessary. Another speaker likened the Democratic convention to the Hartford Convention in which the Federalist party had opposed the War of 1812 and by so doing had destroyed its own usefulness. The nominations for offices were divided between the War Democrats and the Republicans. The platform declared in favor of vigorous prosecution of the war, which should be waged for the preservation of the Union and not for the abolition of slavery.

Developments that occurred between the meeting of the Union party convention and the election caused a sharp reversal of sentiment. Economic measures of the Lincoln administration—the growth of the national debt, the Pacific Railroad Act, with its large land grant and loan of money to a private corporation, and especially the raising of tariff duties to aid manufacturers—seemed to be a return to Hamiltonian policies. Arbitrary arrests, interference by the military in civilian affairs, violation of freedom of speech and the press, and the suspension of the writ of habeas corpus for all persons charged with disloyal practices caused the people to fear that their constitutional liberties were in danger. The failure of the military to win the war was very disappointing. Hoosiers had expected the opening of the Mississippi River, but they were not prepared for the failure of McClellan's Peninsular Campaign, the call for more volunteers which followed, and the disaster at the Second Battle of Bull Run.

One of the causes of dissatisfaction in the state was the conscription of soldiers. Volunteers had enlisted in 1861, but in December the War Department, fearing that it could not equip and use so many soldiers, ordered governors to cease raising troops. When resumed in 1862 recruiting became increasingly difficult. In June urgent appeals were sent to the governors for more regiments, and early in July Lincoln issued a call for three hundred thousand additional soldiers. Fervent appeals, promises of money for the support of soldiers' families, and bounties for volunteers brought only languid recruiting. On July 17, 1862, Congress passed an act authorizing the states to resort to conscription if necessary to meet their quotas. In each county a commissioner was appointed, who in turn named a deputy in each precinct. The latter was to make a list of all resident male citizens between the ages of eighteen and forty-five. The commissioners and deputies then passed on all pleas for exemption and sent the final lists to the general commissioner in Indianapolis. The general commissioner determined whether each township had met its quota and then ordered those that had not to draw names from the list and send the draftees to the capital. Substitutes could be employed.

In conformity with this measure, on August 4, Lincoln requested another 300,000 men. Because of inadequate records, Indiana officials assumed that the state had failed to furnish its quota, although later investigation indicated that the state had furnished 8,008 more men than had been required. The draft was administered by state officials and was applied only to those townships which had not furnished the number of volunteers required of them. A total of 3,003 men were conscripted. Dissatisfied persons destroyed a draft box and delayed the officials in Blackford County for two days, while threats and misdemeanors marred the record of Fountain County. "Few events did more to strengthen the opposition [to the state Republican administration] than this first crude attempt to administer a draft." It seemed to confirm fears of arbitrary government.

The reassertion of abolitionism raised again the question of the purpose of the war and of the sincerity of the original statements of the war aims of the administration. Although Lincoln had revoked the military orders of General John C. Frémont, in Missouri, and General David Hunter, in South Carolina, both of whom sought to abolish slavery in their military districts, the President suggested that Congress pass a measure for compensated emancipation in the border states. Congress accepted this proposal only insofar as it applied to the District of Columbia and excluded slavery from the territories. After the Battle of Antietam, Lincoln issued the preliminary Emancipation Proclamation, September 22, 1862, which declared that slaves would be free in all states resisting the Union on January 1, 1863. Since the proclamation applied only to the people of the Confederacy—who would not obey the order—it was in reality only an announcement of policy and may not have freed a slave. Although very pleasing to the Radicals and to English liberals who helped prevent English interference in the American war, to many in Indiana the proclamation meant that the war had become a means of ending slavery as well as a struggle to preserve the Union. To numerous citizens who had migrated from south of the Ohio River and who were not willing to fight for the abolitionist cause, this proclamation was very objectionable.

The New Albany *Ledger*, along with many War Democrats who had been affiliated with the Union party, transferred its support to the Democrats. As the strength of the Union party weakened, its leaders resorted to charges of disloyalty and treason and to a stimulation of emotions by means of horror stories which told of cruelty on the part of Confederates. The report of a federal grand jury on a secret political society was circulated as a campaign document. Republicans cultivated the impression that only Union party members were loyal and that only their candidates could safely be entrusted with official positions.

The grand jury report just mentioned exposed the existence and activities of the Knights of the Golden Circle. This organization, which originated before the Civil War, was said to have been devoted to the conquest of Mexico and its acquisition by the United States. As secession became [im]minent, the South took the place of the nation in the organization's ritual and purpose, and the order expanded into the Ohio Valley. Castles or local chapters were organized in Indiana, but the revelation of the group's existence and the charges of its supposed treason were so inextricably involved in the efforts of the Union party to win the state election of 1862 that the grains of truth cannot now be separated from the chaff. The charges were often so extreme as to discredit themselves. Many of the people undoubtedly believed that the order was an organization of traitors, and, perhaps, some of the members were. Other observers asserted that such allegations were not only false but were made for the purpose of winning the election. The existence of the society has been questioned, but the persons said to be its leaders were critical and unfriendly towards many of the methods which the state and national administrations were using to win the war. The KGC was said to have protected individuals against arbitrary arrest and mob action, opposed Hamiltonian economic policies, and insisted that the draft was unconstitutional. Its friends asserted that it was only a harmless political club, but its enemies attributed to it all kinds of disorders, murders, resistance to conscription, and treason. . . .

In addition to alarms about secret societies, resistance to conscription, and other disorders, Indiana suffered invasion in 1863. Captain Thomas Hines, one of the officers of the famous Confederate cavalry leader, John H. Morgan, crossed the Ohio River above Cannelton, pushed northward as far as Paoli and Hardinsburg, and returned to the Ohio above Leavenworth. Most of his men were captured, but Hines swam the Ohio and escaped.

A month later, on July 8, Morgan crossed the river at Brandenburg, Kentucky, with nearly three thousand cavalry, advanced to Corydon, divided his forces and took Paoli and Greenville, united his troops again at Vienna and Lexington, moved northeastward to Versailles, and left the state near Harrison, Ohio. He had little trouble securing food, money, and fresh horses and was able to defeat the small bodies of militia that opposed him. Governor Morton called on the men of the southern half of Indiana to organize, arm, and take the field. In the northern part of the state, citizens were asked to organize military companies and hold themselves ready for action. In two days, twenty thousand men assembled in Indianapolis and another forty-five thousand were nearly ready to serve. Morgan destroyed railroads and bridges to delay his pursuers. The damage he wrought in the state has been estimated at $500,000, but in return he left a host of stories—many humorous, others tragic—that have enriched the traditions of the state. Because he feared to try crossing the Ohio River at Madison and because the militia was closing in, he fled into Ohio. On July 26 he was captured at Salineville in eastern Ohio. He had expected the people of Southern Indiana to come to his aid, but their efforts to capture him should have quieted the fears of various officials about their loyalty. . . .

Indiana had furnished 208,367 men, of which 11,718 were reenlistments. If the average family contained four persons, more than half of the families furnished one of its members to the armed forces. Almost 12 per cent of the soldiers, 24,416, were killed or died during the war. A few over 5 per cent, or 10,846, deserted from the service. Although the deserters were a blot on the state, the military record of Indiana soldiers was otherwise very creditable.

One of the near-casualties of the Civil War years in Indiana was the Democratic party, which had enjoyed an almost uninterrupted series of victories before 1860. Although badly beaten by Governor Morton and associated in the minds of many people with treason, the Democracy staged an early revival in the election of Thomas A. Hendricks to the governorship in 1872. Possibly the Jacksonian wing, which might have furnished liberal leadership, was even less popular than the party. But Jacksonian principles became more popular in the person of "Blue Jeans" James D. Williams, who was elected to succeed Hendricks. The lack of progressive leadership was also revealed in the weakness in Indiana of the Granger movement, which laid the foundations for the state regulation of railroads and utilities in four upper Mississippi Valley states, but did not produce such results in Indiana. Little progressive legislation, aside from that regarding education, was passed until near the end of the century. How much of this conservatism was due to Morton's war on the Democracy and changes which occurred during the war can only be estimated.

Economic changes of the war period also tended to diminish the influence of the old Democratic areas. The river interests were injured by the closure of the Mississippi, the destruction of southern markets, and the competition of railroads. Serious reductions were recorded in the building of steamboats, the sale of agricultural products to the South, and the distribution of goods by merchants of river towns. In general, counties south of the Wisconsin Moraine continued to grow, but at a slower rate than northern and central counties. The southern area in 1860 contained 45 per cent of the total population of the state, but five years after the close of the war the percentage had declined to 39 per cent.

On the positive side, the prosperity that accompanied the war and the rise of the new industrial order paved the way for the acceptance of the changes. During the war the Republican administration had enacted the National Banking Act of February 25, 1863, and repeatedly raised the tariff. Aided by war contracts, the tariff, and railroad transportation, a new economy in which manufacturing assumed an increasingly important role began to achieve significance. The new national banks, some of which replaced former state banks, also became a part of the new order. Railroads enlarged the markets that were available for Indiana farmers, while the feeding of the soldiers required vast quantities of supplies from western states. High prices raised considerably the standard of living in rural areas and small towns, where many new houses were built. These homes were in part made possible by the prices received from raising wheat. Whatever remained of frontier self-sufficiency disappeared along navigable streams and railroads. A less frugal way of life developed. Labor, too, gained, for recruitment of men for the armies produced a shortage of manpower. Towns and cities grew more rapidly. . . .

A conflict which lasted four years and involved so many people, either directly as members of the armed forces or indirectly as civilians who supported the armies, could not possibly have left the nation unchanged. The early promises, demanded by the Democrats and so readily given by the Republicans, that the nation should be preserved as it was appeared at the end of the war to resemble the early notion that the conflict would last only a few weeks. In addition to the casualties, the handicap placed upon the Democratic party, the growth of cities, the increase in manufacturing, and sectional fears and animosities had effected a breach in the mental and spiritual life of the nation that could not be healed quickly. The Union had been preserved, but at a terrible price! The questions of the nature of the Union and the right of secession had been answered. Although the guns became silent and the soldiers came home, politicians were unable to make peace with defeated fellow citizens for ten additional years. The reconstruction which followed the fighting was not a separate process, but the time required to check the forces released by the firing on Fort Sumter.

MORGAN'S RAID INTO SOUTHERN INDIANA, JULY 1863

William E. Wilson

The single episode of the Civil War which most directly involved Indiana, and which lives on in legend and lore, is Morgan's Raid through the southeastern quadrant of the state in July 1863. General John Hunt Morgan, a cavalry officer who had long harbored plans to operate north of the Ohio River, crossed into Indiana at Mauckport, moved northward through Cory-

---

From "Thunderbolt of the Confederacy, or King of the Horse Thieves," *Indiana Magazine of History*, LIV (June 1958), 119–130.

don and Salem, then eastward through Vernon and Versailles and on into Ohio, where he and his men were captured. The purposes of the raid have been variously explained: to relieve the pressure on Confederate troops in Tennessee, to aid General Lee in his northern invasion (Morgan had not yet learned of Lee's defeat at Gettysburg on July 3), to encourage the "copperhead" sympathizer element in southern Indiana to support the South openly, or simply to ransack and plunder the region, thereby obtaining horses and supplies. Whatever its purpose, the raid terrorized the state momentarily and brought a massive—if disorganized—outpouring of men from all parts of the state to resist the invasion. W. H. H. Terrell estimated that 65,000 citizens gathered within forty-eight hours to defend their state, and Emma Lou Thornbrough concludes that this response "belies the tradition of widespread disloyalty and sympathy for the Confederacy."[1]

In the selection below Professor William E. Wilson takes a minority position concerning both the purposes and effectiveness of the Morgan raid, but his review of the events, the opposing interpretations concerning Morgan himself, and the impact of the invasion is a useful one. For a detailed study of this episode by a participant, see Basil W. Duke, History of Morgan's Cavalry *(1867). See also W. H. H. Terrell,* Indiana in the War of the Rebellion *(1869, reprinted 1960), pp. 209–254; and Edison H. Thomas,* John Hunt Morgan and his Raiders *(1975). For a brief treatment of Morgan's Raid in fiction, see Chapter Five of Jessamyn West,* The Friendly Persuasion *(1945).*

Zigzagging across southern Indiana and Ohio in the summer of 1863, John Hunt Morgan wove a trail as raddled as turkey tracks. Although his pursuers were never more than a few hours behind him, they were never sure of the whereabouts of the man known variously as The Thunderbolt of the Confederacy and The King of Horse Thieves, until they stumbled upon him.

Today, plaques and monuments mark Morgan's route from Mauckport, Indiana, where he crossed the Ohio River on a July day almost a century ago, to Salineville, Ohio, near the Pennsylvania line, where he surrendered eighteen days later. But the modern tourist who attempts to follow that trail of some six hundred miles will find himself almost as confused as the Federal cavalrymen Morgan was dodging in 1863. The legend of Morgan's Raid along the north shore of the Ohio has grown as ubiquitous as Morgan himself once seemed to be.

At times, the vitality of the legend gives the visitor the impression that the country has not changed since Morgan swept across it. There have been changes of course, but off the main highways there is much that remains the same. If those slumbering, isolated hill-villages dream at all, they can dream now only of the past. On their quiet streets the houses where Morgan dined and slept have a certain lustre upon them, and nearby, at crossroads and along creekbanks, the old battle sites remain as they were when home guards stood and fought or, more often, dropped their inadequate arms and fled. In the back-country lanes where Morgan rode, it is possible still to imagine that distant thunder on a sultry summer day is the echo of his horsemen's passing. And all along the way there are, still living in that country, men and women whose forebears sat on rail fences in their childhood and watched the raiders gallop by.

Surviving also in southern Indiana and Ohio, almost as vital as the legend of Morgan, are the bitterness of 1863 and the contempt that was added to it when at last

1. Emma Lou Thornbrough, *Indiana in the Civil War Era, 1850–1880* (1965), p. 204.

the Confederate raider was captured and imprisoned in the Ohio State Penitentiary, head shaved and beard shorn like a common criminal's. In that country, The Thunderbolt is only The Horse Thief, and the descendants of the people he robbed console themselves, like their forebears, with the conviction that his unauthorized invasion was a failure.

Actually, it was not.

It is true that Morgan lost to the Confederacy an organization of 2,400 seasoned cavalrymen. He did fail to rally to his support the Copperheads believed numerous in the area through which he passed. He turned eastward only sixty miles south of Indianapolis, which indeed he might have captured and where he might have released and armed from the city's arsenal some three thousand Confederate prisoners. And he failed to unite with Lee in Pennsylvania, as some say he intended to do.

But the arguments in Morgan's favor are stronger.

The damage to railroads, steamboats, bridges, and public stores inflicted by the raid amounted to at least ten million dollars. The cavalry unit of 2,400 was disintegrated, but most of the men escaped and lived to fight for the Confederacy again. In contrast with their own small losses, the raiders captured and paroled six thousand Federal home guards and regulars and killed or wounded some six hundred more, they kept thousands of Yankee citizens in a paralyzing state of panic for a fortnight, and by their penetration behind the lines they immobilized 28,000 troops under General Ambrose Burnside, who otherwise would have joined General William S. Rosecrans three weeks before the battle of Chickamauga.

On only one score can Morgan's raid be truly said to have failed, and here the argument, like most of the arguments against him, must rest on hypothesis. Since Morgan was destined to disobey the orders of his commanding officer and cross the Ohio eventually, it is too bad that he did not disobey nine months earlier, when he first conceived and proposed the Indiana and Ohio raid. Then, even with the same tactical mistakes and the same losses, he might have accomplished much more than he was able to accomplish in 1863.

Nine months earlier, Morgan's men were less war-weary, less starved for luxuries, and better disciplined. Although the number of Copperheads in Indiana and Ohio was probably exaggerated by the Republican canard that all Democrats were traitors of one degree or another, what Southern sympathizers there were in the states north of the Ohio might have welcomed the raiders more warmly if Morgan had been able to keep them under control.

Of more significance was the opportunity which lay within the grasp of General Braxton Bragg in 1862 and which was never to come again. That summer Bragg invaded Kentucky. If he had joined forces with General Kirby Smith while Morgan harassed the Federals' rear on Northern soil, he could easily have taken the entire state out of the Union. All that was needed was to prevent General Don Carlos Buell's being reinforced at Louisville, and Morgan could have accomplished that, just as he prevented Burnside from reaching Rosecrans in Tennessee a year later. But Bragg said no, and Morgan obeyed him. Buell got back to Louisville, consolidated his forces, and returned to the offensive; and the Confederates' opportunity was lost.

All this is based on the assumption that Braxton Bragg would have acted swiftly and vigorously in conjunction with a raid by Morgan in 1862, and that of course is a large assumption. Still it can be soundly argued that the tragedy of Morgan's disobedience lies in its postponement. Morgan's original proposal was a good one, but when finally his patience with his over-cautious and short-sighted chief was exhausted and he took matters into his own hands, the most propitious times for insubordination had passed.

By the best accounts, Morgan was an even better strategist than tactician. Nature had endowed him with "gifts which she very rarely bestows, and which give the soldier who has them vast advantages; a quickness of perception and of thought, amounting almost to intuition, an almost unerring sagacity in foreseeing the operations of an adversary and in calculating the effect of his own movements upon him, wonderful control over men, as individuals and in masses, and moral courage and energy almost preternatural."

These are the words of Basil W. Duke, who commanded the first of the two brigades Morgan led across the Ohio. In his *Reminiscences* and his *History of Morgan's Cavalry*, General Duke regards his commanding officer always with admiration and respect. So, in *The Partisan Rangers*, does Adam R. Johnson, who commanded the second brigade. Both these men were able and intelligent soldiers and both lived after the war to become distinguished and respected citizens, Duke as a prominent lawyer in Louisville, Johnson as the founder and patriarch of a prosperous town in Texas.

Their estimates of Morgan should prove that he was neither the lawless brigand that his enemies in Indiana and Ohio called him nor the unruly hothead that some historians have concluded he was because of his insubordination on the banks of the Ohio. By all standards of military conduct there is no justification for his action of course, but if he had disobeyed Bragg earlier and achieved a greater success, the insubordination would have been more generously regarded afterwards. . . .

Although John Hunt Morgan was born in Alabama, he regarded himself as a Kentuckian. He grew up in Lexington, Kentucky, a member of a slave-owning family. After a year of service in the Mexican War, he returned to Lexington and married a young woman of delicate health who was soon to die. In business, he was a successful manufacturer of hemp and woolen goods, and he was active in many civic affairs. . . .

When Morgan embarked upon the Indiana and Ohio raid, he was thirty-eight years old, married for the second time, a brigadier general, a cavalryman of two years of arduous service raiding in Kentucky and Tennessee, and a veteran of the battle of Shiloh. By the time he reached Brandenburg, Kentucky, on the banks of the Ohio on the morning of July 8, 1863, he had completed his raiding mission under Bragg's orders. Capturing Columbia, Lebanon, and Bardstown, he had destroyed large quantities of Federal stores in Kentucky, had thoroughly confused the Union command as to the intention of the Confederates, and had already delayed Burnside's march into East Tennessee to join Rosecrans. By that time, too, he had long since made up his mind to cross independently into the rich country north of the Ohio.

Morgan's reasons that July morning were not so cogent as they had been nine months earlier when he first contemplated the raid, but they were still valid. Bragg and Rosecrans were facing each other now in Tennessee, neither ready to strike. They had already engaged in one major battle, at Stones River, and each could claim a sort of victory, Bragg's statistical, Rosecrans's strategic, but neither's decisive. Bragg's force was smaller than Rosecrans's, but it was in top condition, had the advantage of shorter supply lines, and was maneuvering on familiar terrain. If Burnside could be kept in the North, the chances of the Confederates holding their own at least were still good.

Elsewhere, conditions seemed to favor a bold Confederate action of the sort Morgan was about to undertake. Down the Mississippi, Grant was still hammering at Vicksburg and had not yet overpowered it when Morgan left Tennessee. In the East, the Confederate Army had won two major victories, at Fredericksburg and Chancellorsville, and, so far as Morgan knew when he stood on the banks of the Ohio, Lee was still marching into Pennsylvania. Finally, in the North, there were draft riots and a growing weariness of the war.

How much these last two considerations weighed in Morgan's decision is a matter for conjecture. He spoke on several occasions of joining Lee in Pennsylvania, but at the same time he was making definite plans to recross the Ohio at Buffington Island above Cincinnati. The project of union with Lee was probably only an alternative to be resorted to if the crossing at Buffington Island failed. As for the dissidence in the North, he would naturally have welcomed a large-scale revolt, but there is no good evidence that he counted on support from Copperheads, in spite of attempts to prove that he was deeply involved in "the Northwest Conspiracy." For one thing, Morgan's first raid into Kentucky the year before must have taught him not to expect recruits from Southern sympathizers. If his fellow Kentuckians would not rally round him, certainly few disaffected Hoosiers and Ohioans would do so. Moreover, his treatment of the few Copperheads who approached him in Indiana and Ohio demonstrates his lack of confidence in the Knights of the Golden Circle.

"Good," he is reported to have said to one of them, as he took the Copperhead's horse. "Then you ought to be glad to contribute to the South."

The crossing of the Ohio got off to a bad start. Although two steamboats were easily captured for the ferriage, a party of home guards were established on the Indiana side behind houses and haystacks. The raiders' Parrotts had to be put into action to silence the single Hoosier field-piece before the crossing could commence. Then, after the Second Kentucky and the Ninth Tennessee were over the river and the home guards were retiring, a Federal gunboat steamed round the bend and began tossing shells alternately at the raiders on the Indiana shore and those who had not yet left Brandenburg on the Kentucky side.

The appearance of the gunboat brought the ferrying to an abrupt halt. Worse still, it put the entire Confederate force in a hazardous position. Delay was dangerous, because pursuing Federal cavalry would soon be coming up from the south. Yet if the crossing was abandoned, half the troops would be left stranded on the Indiana shore. Morgan opened up on the gunboat with every piece of artillery at his disposal, but for two hours he could not drive her off. When the situation had come to seem most desperate, however, she suddenly turned tail and fled, her ammunition exhausted.

That night, after firing the two steamboats and setting them adrift, Morgan's men camped at Frakes Mill six miles north of the river. Behind them, one of the boats, the

"Alice Dean," did not burn completely, and until only a few years ago a part of its carcass was still visible in the water where it sank.

The next day, the raid was on in full swing,—and *swing* is a good word for describing its progress. Morgan had what the English call "a good eye for a country," but he amplified his vision and prehension by using his troops as an insect uses its tentacles. They rode usually in fours, and at every crossroad those at the head of the column fanned out, foraged and scouted for several miles on both sides of the main force, and then rejoined it in the rear. Thus was Morgan not only kept informed of any threat on his flanks, he kept the countryside in a wide area through which he passed in constant alarm and confusion as to his whereabouts and the direction he was taking.

A Canadian telegrapher named George Ellsworth, but called Lightning by the raiders, further extended Morgan's vision and his knowledge of the purposes of his adversaries. Ellsworth had the priceless skill of mimicry at the telegraph key. By watching a captured operator work or by listening to one on a tapped wire, he could soon imitate the man's style so well that he was able to deceive other operators and get information from them. Better still, he could send out false information and even false orders. His expert faking made it possible for Morgan virtually to assume command of the enemy forces surrounding him and to put them almost anywhere he wanted them.

At Corydon, once the capital of Indiana, the raiders met their first serious resistance. Outside the town, four hundred home guards barred their way. Before the defense could be broken, sixteen Confederates were killed, but Morgan was able to enter the town in time for noonday dinner at the Kintner Hotel. It was while he was dining there, on July 9, that he learned from the innkeeper's daughter that Lee had been defeated at Gettysburg almost a week before. There is no evidence that he even considered turning back when he received this disheartening information.

After Corydon, the men were in the saddle twenty-one hours out of every twenty-four for the next two weeks. They advanced to Salem, Vienna, and Lexington, but nine miles below Seymour they began to swing eastward toward the Ohio line.

When the news of the invasion came to Indianapolis, its people were panic-stricken, and if Morgan had pushed straight on from Salem on July 10, he might indeed have captured the city. In another twenty-four hours, however, it was too late. By that time, Governor Oliver P. Morton had the situation in hand, General Lew Wallace, home on leave and on a fishing trip on the Wabash, was back in uniform and on his way downstate to help General Edward H. Hobson, who was hot on Morgan's trail, and General Henry M. Judah, whom Burnside had dispatched in Cincinnati to head the raiders off if he could. More damaging to Morgan, however, than the combined maneuvers of all three of these generals was the thing that was happening to his own men. They had begun to loot and to straggle.

Horses had been taken as needed from the beginning. This was the custom of cavalrymen, both Union and Confederate. It not only gave the raiders fresh mounts along the way, it denied them to their pursuers. Morgan tried to see that the exchanges were as fair and as legal as possible under the circumstances, but in his swift, zigzag movements he lost contact with many of his men, and by the time they reached Salem, the plenitude of the shops and stores after impoverished Dixie was too much for them. To use Basil Duke's euphemistic words, they developed "the propensity to appropriate beyond limit or restraint."

General Duke could be—and was—more specific. Describing the raid for *Century Magazine* in January, 1891, he wrote:

> The weather was intensely warm,—the hot July sun burned the earth to powder, and we were breathing superheated dust,—yet one man rode for three days with seven pairs of skates slung about his neck; another loaded himself with sleighbells. A large chafing dish, a medium-sized Dutch clock, a green glass decanter with goblets to match, a bag of horn buttons, a chandelier, and a birdcage containing three canaries, were some of the articles I saw borne off and jealously fondled.

At Harrison, Indiana, twenty-five miles from Cincinnati, all detachments that could be reached were drawn in and thereafter a strong provost guard kept the stragglers under some control. They would not throw away their loot, but from there on their holiday was ended. Morgan was no longer a wolf on the prowl; he was now a fox in flight, and the hounds were baying all around him.

Still, he was able for another two weeks to dodge, turn, stand at bay, turn and dodge again, and even vanish for several hours at a time. He circled round Cincinnati in the night, the men in the rear lighting torches every few yards to pick up the trail of the vanguard in the foam dropped from the mouths of the horses and the dust kicked up by their feet. Then on to Buffington Island, in as straight a line as he dared to follow.

Halfway to the proposed point of crossing the river, he learned that Vicksburg had fallen and that Lee was retreating across the Potomac. At 1:00 P.M. on the eighteenth, he reached Chester, Ohio, eighteen miles from his destination. He knew that the river was rising and delay was dangerous, but his men were exhausted and he was encumbered with two hundred wounded so he postponed the crossing till the next morning and stopped for a two-hour rest that would allow the stragglers to come up.

This decision proved disastrous. The next morning, at the riverside, General Judah's whole force was upon him. Then came Hobson's advance under General James M. Shackelford. And after that, Federal gunboats appeared and began shelling the raiders from the river.

Duke's brigade was lost in the ensuing battle, but Morgan and Johnson succeeded in leading a thousand men out of the trap; and twenty miles farther up the river they began to cross. Johnson got over with three hundred men, but when Morgan himself had swum his powerful mount half way over, he turned back. Too many of his men were behind him, and gunboats were approaching that would cut them off. He preferred to remain with them to the end.

Yet the end did not come for another six days, during which Morgan traversed the eastern half of the state; and when finally he surrendered, he surrendered voluntarily.

He was riding along with Captain James Burbick of the Union militia near Salineville. He had persuaded Captain Burbick to guide him to the Pennsylvania line in return for his promise to leave the district unharmed. Suddenly he asked Burbick whether he would give him and his men paroles if he surrendered, and the startled militiaman agreed. When the word was passed around to the 364 men remaining with Morgan, they must have dropped from their saddles in unison, like the crew of the Ancient Mariner's ship falling to the deck, for when Colonel Shackelford came along a few minutes later, they were all sound asleep.

Shackelford refused to honor the terms Captain Burbick had granted Morgan, and Morgan and his men were taken back to Cincinnati as prisoners of war. When they were incarcerated in the Ohio State Penitentiary at Columbus two days later, they were treated as common criminals.

Four months after their imprisonment, Morgan and six of his captains tunneled their way out of the penitentiary and escaped. Morgan fought again, in Virginia, but never again so boldly or successfully. As one contemporary put it, "The plain truth is that Morgan never had a fair chance after he escaped from prison." He was given only the meanest troops to command, and his requests and proposals fell upon deaf ears in Richmond. There were many in authority there, too, as in the North, who thought him a failure; and among them, quite understandably, was Braxton Bragg.

John Hunt Morgan was finally shot dead at point blank by a Union soldier in Greeneville, Tennessee, on the fourth of September, 1864, and the soldier is said to have cried out after he fired the fatal shot, "I've killed the damned horse thief!" By that date, Morgan was indeed no longer The Thunderbolt, but it mattered little to the Confederacy then what he was. The war was already lost, and the time for such feats as he could once accomplish had passed.

Postwar Patterns

The dual nature of Indiana politics continued into the Reconstruction period, when problems associated with the Civil War dominated the scene. The loyalty of the state to the Union blended imperfectly with the program of "Radical Reconstruction" designed to bring about complete political and social equality for the former slaves. This duality is reflected in the state's two most prominent postwar leaders: Republican Oliver P. Morton, governor and then senator, who ardently supported Radical Reconstruction policies while maintaining his control of state politics; and Democrat Thomas A. Hendricks, senator and then governor, who just as strongly opposed efforts to remake the Constitution during a time of inflamed passions. As a result, Indiana offered only lukewarm support to the Radical Reconstruction program, giving successively smaller margins of victory in its ratifications of the Thirteenth, Fourteenth, and Fifteenth amendments. Then, in 1872 it elevated the conservative Hendricks to the governor's mansion. In so doing Indiana became the first northern state after the Civil War to elect a Democrat to its highest office. The gradual revival of the Democrats stemmed from a general weariness with wartime issues; dissatisfaction with Reconstruction policies, particularly regarding Negro rights; unhappiness over the growing centralization of power in Washington; and concern about economic and monetary matters.

The last issue became of even more pressing importance in the wake of the Panic of 1873 and the widespread depression that followed. A central question in national politics had long been what to do with the unbacked paper currency, known as "greenbacks," issued during the war. Some politicians, chiefly Republicans, favored a rapid contraction in the amount of currency; this would be achieved by withdrawing the greenbacks from circulation and returning to a specie payment system as quickly as possible. Others, chiefly Democrats, favored the permanent retention of the greenbacks as an aid to debtors. Obligations that had been incurred with a depreciated currency were to be paid in the same currency. The positions of the political parties in Indiana on this issue were murky, however, in that Senator Morton favored only a gradual return to specie payment. The greenback-retention idea, known as the "Pendleton Plan," did become part of the Democratic program in the 1868 election, and the issue was revived during the depression of the early 1870s. Eventually—in 1875—a political party known as the Independent party, later called the Greenback party, was organized in Cleveland, Ohio, and its first national convention was held in Indianapolis in May 1876.

The depression of the early 1870s was also the backdrop for one of the most interesting and significant elections in the state and the nation, which also coincided with the national centennial. In the first essay below, Professor W. T. K. Nugent describes the mood of the people, the nature of the centennial celebration, and the transitional significance of events at this time. The second essay, by Professor Rebecca Shoemaker of Indiana State University, is a memorable portrait of the man elected governor in 1876, a farmer-politician known as "Blue Jeans" Williams. This was also the year of the famous "disputed election" for president, in which the Republican team of Hayes and Wheeler was declared victorious over Democrats Tilden and Hendricks by an 8–7 vote of a special electoral commission. Thomas A. Hendricks, the Democratic vice-presidential nominee, was only one of several Hoosiers accorded this honor in the post–Civil War period. Schuyler Colfax was elected as Ulysses Grant's vice-president in 1868, and Hendricks himself was elected with Grover Cleveland in 1884. William H. English was an unsuccessful vice-presidential nominee with Winfield S. Hancock in 1880, as was John W. Kern, William Jennings Bryan's running mate in 1908. However, Charles W. Fairbanks was elected with Theodore Roosevelt in 1904, and, of course, Thomas R. Marshall enjoyed two full terms as Woodrow Wilson's vice-president from 1913 to 1921.

There were many other burning political, social, and economic issues of the Reconstruction period. Foremost among them were the somewhat related questions of temperance and women's rights, and state organizations for the promotion of both were established. Resolutions leading to woman suffrage never cleared the Indiana legislature, but several temperance laws were passed, and a number of temperance organizations, including the Women's Christian Temperance Union and the Prohibition party, were established during the 1870s. More positive results came in the economic field, despite the depression of the 1870s and the national railroad strike of 1877. The state's railway network was largely completed by 1880, and a beginning was made toward railroad regulation helpful to farmers and other shippers. Professor Emma Lou Thornbrough, author of the most comprehensive study of Indiana during the Civil War and Reconstruction periods, describes below the significant railroad developments of the 1860s and 1870s.

For more information on the immediate postwar period in Indiana, see Emma Lou Thornbrough, *Indiana in the Civil War Era, 1850–1880* (1965); John D. Barnhart and Donald F. Carmony, *Indiana: From Frontier to Industrial Commonwealth* (2 vols., 1954); Ralph D. Gray, ed., *Gentlemen from Indiana: National Party Candidates, 1836–1940* (1977); William D. Foulke, *Life of Oliver P. Morton* (2 vols., 1899); and John W. Holcombe and Hubert M. Skinner, *Life and Public Services of Thomas A. Hendricks* (1886). See also William G. Carleton, "The Money Question in Indiana Politics, 1865–1890," *Indiana Magazine of History*, XLII (March 1946), 105–150; Robert P. Sharkey, *Money, Class, and Party: An Economic Study of Civil War and Reconstruction* (1959); and Dee Brown, *The Year of the Century: 1876* (1966). Finally, there is an excellent analysis of Indiana politics in the so-called Gilded Age as seen through the eyes of an active participant in Charles W. Calhoun's biography, *Gilded Age Cato: The Life of Walter Q. Gresham* (1988).

THE 1870s IN CONTEXT

Walter T. K. Nugent

Professor Nugent, a specialist in late nineteenth-century American history, discussed America during the time of the centennial at an annual meeting of the Indiana Historical Society in 1972. Organized in a series of concentric circles, the lecture considered first the "Centennial Fourth," then the year 1876, a somber backdrop to the festivities in July, and finally the "broader context" of the 1870s, particularly the depression which lasted from 1873 until the end of the decade. In addition to the well-publicized events of the period, such as Custer's Last Stand and the controversial centennial election, Nugent points to many basic changes during the decade that foreshadowed the major problems and configurations of American society in its second century. In Nugent's phrase, the decade constituted a "seed time of modern conflict."

Nugent, a professor of history at the University of Notre Dame, is the author of The Tolerant Populists: Kansas Populism and Nativism *(1963);* The Money Question During Reconstruction *(1967);* Money and American Society, 1865–1880 *(1968); and* Modern America *(1973). For more information on the American centennial, see Dee Brown,* The Year of the Century: 1876 *(1966); see also C. Vann Woodward,* Reunion and Reaction: The Compromise of 1877 *(1956); and T. Harry Williams, ed.,* Hayes: The Diary of a President, 1875–1881 *(1964).*

My purpose in speaking to you this afternoon is to tell you something about the shape and structure of American society at the time when the nation ended its first century and began its second. As I shall try to show, that society was a proud and in

From "Seed Time of Modern Conflict: American Society at the Centennial," *Indiana Historical Society Lectures, 1972–1973* (1973), pp. 31–44.

many ways a confident one, yet also one which confronted some very serious difficulties. I like to regard the 1870s as Act I, scene 1, of a long epic which we can call "America in the Modern Age," in which the nineties provided Act I, scene 2 (an even more troubled time), and in which, of course, later acts are still in progress as we approach the bicentennial.

First I want to talk about the first day of the United States' second century, the Fourth of July of 1876. Then we can take up its immediate context, and then the general context of the seventies. The Fourth in 1876 was the "Centennial Fourth," and everybody seemed very much aware of that fact. In much of the country it was celebrated as a three-day holiday, a very rare thing for that time, beginning with preparations on Sunday the second, much activity on Monday the third, especially Monday evening, and climaxing on Tuesday the Fourth. Celebrations took place for three days from San Francisco to New York. The biggest affair was at Philadelphia, then hosting the Centennial Exposition: as five hundred thousand people lined the streets, a great torchlight parade of ten thousand workingmen and five thousand G.A.R. veterans, still black-haired and straight-backed only eleven years after the Civil War, passed before the presidential candidates, Hayes and Tilden; the Emperor of Brazil, Dom Pedro, and lesser foreign dignitaries; and several governors and mayors, marching beneath triumphal arches not used in Philadelphia since La Fayette was received there in 1824.

In Indianapolis the celebrating was no less intense. For weeks, L. S. Ayres & Co. had been advising ladies to buy new hats and dresses for July 4, "this day of days," and an editorial warned that "those only who wind up the day in sobriety are worthy to be citizens of a repulic [*sic*] one hundred years old." There could have been an ominous symbolism in the appearance of a bad electrical storm late in the evening of July 3, literally the eleventh hour of America's first century, and threatening weather continued until mid-morning on the Fourth. But the skies cleared, and by 2 P.M. the celebrations were enjoying fair skies, westerly winds, and (if it had been invented yet) a comfort index of about 72. The day lengthened into a delightful evening, with the temperature 70° at sunset.

Special trains had brought an estimated twenty-five thousand people into Indianapolis from out of town for the festivities, and we presume that they were not disappointed. A "monster balloon," called "America" and guided by one Professor Shotts, ascended from the Indianapolis Exposition grounds, rose to a height of three miles, and landed about an hour later north of Greenfield; while aloft a "young theatrical couple" were married in it. A gala parade brought out marchers from a long list of voluntary associations: the Schwarzer Ritter Order Band preceded the Veterans' Association, the Fraternité Française, the Emerald Society, the Liederkranz Society, the Turnverein, the Society of St. Joseph, the Männerchor, the Free-Thinkers' Society, the Beer Brewers' Association Band, and many others; it took almost a full newspaper column in six-point type to list the program and the marching order of the parade. Governor Hendricks, recently nominated for Vice-President by the Democrats, presided, while the Hon. Byron K. Elliott gave the main speech.

On the fifth, the newspapers devoted column after column to minute descriptions of the parade, of house decorations along the route, of the tableaux (the "floats" of those days), and to verbatim transcripts of all the Indianapolis speeches as well as, in five-point type for a page and a half, William M. Evarts' principal address at the Philadelphia celebration. What were they talking about? "Fourth of July oratory" has long since become a cliché, but there is no reason to doubt the sincere pride of these people when they said: *rejoice, rejoice*. A few lines from an editorial will serve: "The nations of the Old World look on in wonder at our achievements, and while there is a proud victory there, all over the land a patriotic thrill stirs the American heart, as the people gather, as prophesied by the fathers of the republic, to render grateful shouts of rejoicing over the heritage that is ours. Let the day be festal for all. Let the rich and poor, who alike enjoy the blessings of freedom, rejoice together. Let the old rejoice in the inheritance of their children. Let the young rejoice in the promises of the future. Let all render grateful thanks to the God of nations for our free and peaceful land from the Atlantic to the Pacific, from the lakes to the Gulf." Pride, indeed; and beyond that, optimism, and confidence in the future. I do not get the impression that these were a fearful people, shouting down the wind to suppress their own insecurities. Nor do I think they were being particularly naive or hypocritical; they were expressing something they believed, in a manner partly ritual, partly evangelical.

And they were not blinded by fervor. One of the most accurate and revealing sentences written on that occasion was the following, from a *Sentinel* editorial: "It was hard times yesterday, and will be to-morrow, but to-day is the Centennial Fourth of July."

Indeed there were many hints, amid the festivity, that all was not Arcadian in the America of 1876, and that the celebrations on the Fourth provided a decided contrast in mood with the run of life in 1876. The same newspapers that described the Centennial so glowingly also confirmed that a few weeks before, on a branch of the Yellowstone River called the Little Big Horn, Maj. Gen. George Custer and a sizable U.S. Army detachment had been massacred by the Sioux under their great chief, Sitting Bull. Another news story on July 4 reported that the Chicago Common Council had had to abolish the Health and Public Works Boards of that city because expenses were running $2 million ahead of tax income. A classified advertisement promised that Drs. Johnson and Laubach, of the American Opium Institute at 247 North Tennessee Street, would "cure the opium habit in ten days," with "no charge whatever until the patient says he is cured." In another and more frightening manifestation of the depression, the newspapers stated that a horde of two hundred tramps had infested and taken over Milwood, Illinois, a small town thirty miles south of Springfield, and "sundry depredations have been committed at various points," the most serious being the wreck of a passenger train because a switch was thrown the wrong way. The assumption was that the tramps did it. "The train men on the Toledo, Wabash, and Western railroad," the papers said, "are supplied with arms, and the company guarantees the legal expenses of defending any of its employees who are obliged to use force in defending the property of the company against the tramps. There is no doubt that some vigorous action is necessary to protect farm houses, small villages and railroad trains against this late development of villainy." Tramps have not been seen very much in the past couple of decades, but those of us who can recall the depression of the 1930s will remember those sometimes menacing figures.

They were no novelty in the thirties, but I suspect that they were in the 1870s—for the reason, as I will suggest in a moment, that the seventies were the first decade in which the kind of social dislocations and problems which we think of as "modern" became apparent and widespread.

During that summer which was brightened momentarily by the "Centennial Fourth," politics continued in its tawdry way. The Republican party, forced to pay attention to the reformers within it because the scandals of the Grant Administration would not down, nominated the virtuous (and empty-headed) governor of Ohio, Rutherford B. Hayes, for president. The Democrats, expecting to benefit electorally from the "Republican" hard times, and smelling their first presidential victory since Buchanan's in 1856, nominated the spotless Samuel Tilden, governor of New York. Some months later, the irony became apparent that these two paragons had headed the only presidential election in American history in which the will of the electorate was almost certainly thwarted by outright vote fraud, the inconclusive and scandalous disputed election of 1876. . . .

Thus, to summarize for a moment, we are confronted with a contrast when we look for the content of the public press and public debates of that summer of 1876. The festive celebration of the Centennial Fourth had a context. The context included unsatisfactory relations between white Americans and American Indians (especially unsatisfactory to General Custer, admittedly, but unsatisfactory also to Sitting Bull and indeed to all concerned); a disastrously poor resolution of the problems of the freedmen; financial crises in urban government; the need for opium cures, reflecting some degree of drug abuse; instances of semiorganized violence against persons and property, and a climate of fear resulting from such instances (which could be multiplied); political corruption, not only in executive agencies, tarnishing the mighty figure of General Grant, but in the presidential election itself; and finally, a profound disagreement over the future shape of society, having its specific focus in debates over the money question, but ramifying much more generally. Such was the more-or-less immediate context of the Centennial celebration.

The broader context was even less happy. The Centennial happened to take place in the middle of a bleak, severe, economic depression, the first since before the Civil War, and the longest since the late 1830s. The depression of the seventies began in the manner typical of nineteenth-century reverses in the business cycle, of which it was the fourth but not the last. . . .

Indeed, financial hardship or outright disaster struck many people between 1873 and 1879, and unfortunately the worst effects of the depression were visited upon those least able to withstand them. Thus the economic events of the seventies fortified the prevailing nineteenth-century conviction that panics and depressions, like tornadoes or crop failures, were natural, inevitable calamities—whether of an angry Deity or of a blind Nature made little difference. In addition, the depression of the seventies was felt in such a peculiar way as to disguise the crisis for some, yet make it especially hard on others. Retained profits and dividends were not greatly disturbed; total national output in mining, manufacturing, and agriculture actually increased rather than decreased; the balance of trade improved, since the depression was less severe here than in other industrializing countries; and the currency continued to stabilize, allowing specie payments to be resumed as planned in January, 1879. Consequently, two key groups—those we may classify as "capitalists" and those responsible for such national economic policy as there was—while certainly aware that trade had fallen off, could console themselves that in major respects the depression was not all that bad, and actually had a beneficial effect in shaking out reprehensible tendencies toward speculation.

But in the meantime, many farmers, industrial workers, and railroad employees were experiencing layoffs, effective cuts in wage rates, and declining farm prices. The point, therefore, is that among those who needed to know, for the middle and long-run good of society (including themselves), that productivity and wealth were being distributed unevenly, the depression did not provide that knowledge directly; while for farmers and workers the depression experience was direct indeed. Political policy makers, opinion leaders, and businessmen of some magnitude were shielded, in part, from the realization they ought to have had that a crisis was in progress.

This oddly distributed depression of 1873–78 occurred just at a time when major social and economic changes were taking place, and it was a catalyst which intensified the visibility of change, in tangible and unfortunate ways, to many Americans. But because the depression was selective in its effects, it did not help as it might have in teaching people how to cope with these changes.

What were these basic changes which the depression of the seventies intensified yet disguised, or at least did little to make visible? There are at least half a dozen that are relevant. First: Sometime during the early seventies, farmers ceased to be a majority of the gainfully employed. It would be another forty years before any other *single* group—specifically, factory workers—outnumbered farmers, and before more Americans lived in towns and cities than on farms. . . .

Second: Americans in the 1870s were remarkably mobile. We do not know as yet whether mobility was greater in the seventies than in the 1840s and 1850s; historical demography is yet a young field. But it is already clear, for areas that have been analyzed, that mobility was much greater then than it has been in recent decades. The Department of Commerce has been telling us that since World War II, roughly 20 per cent of American residences change each year. In the 1870s the figure was apparently about 50 per cent. . . .

A third change occurring during the seventies was the advent of new difficulties in achieving law and order. We have already mentioned the problem of tramps; they came back in greater force in the nineties, and a Populist governor of Kansas was damned as an anarchist in 1893 for instructing law enforcement officers to treat them more sympathetically as unwillingly unemployed people. We should also notice the retreat from Reconstruction in the South, where 90 per cent of black Americans, the freedmen, lived, a group still 80 per cent illiterate and deprived, not through their own failings but from the inanition of Reconstruction and redeemer governments alike, of land, implements, and education. The white-supremacist Bourbon regimes that followed Reconstruction created a superficial kind of order, but their policies of political co-optation and subtle repression of the freedmen were hardly a real answer to the South's problems of social order, and helped generate later and more bloody protest and repression. We should remember too the shock waves that passed over the nation in the wake of the Great Railway Strike of 1877, the first clash between labor and capital on a nationwide scale, indeed the first major occasion when, as later became habitual, the interests of capital and labor were regarded by both sides and many in between as hostile rather than basically harmonious. When the strike of 1877 erupted at Pittsburgh and state militia fired into a crowd, killing over fifty people, the response of much of the metropolitan press around the country was to approve, on the grounds that though unfortunate in its effects sometimes, armed force was the only way to deal with threats to property. Thus the gut reaction was to nail down the tops of the powder kegs even tighter; and they blew off later at Homestead, at Pullman, and again and again down into the twentieth century.

Technological change made itself felt in the seventies. A few items may be suggestive. Scholes's patent on a workable typewriter was taken out in the early seventies, and later in the decade, particularly after the depression ended, that device promoted significant changes in governmental and business office practices, such as the employment of women in clerical jobs. Developments in refining, mining, and civil engineering allowed precious metals to be brought to market far quicker than ever before, and were one basic reason why the reopening of the Comstock Lode in 1873, bringing with it the prospect of floods of silver bullion inundating the United States Mint, contributed to the fright of "sound money men" and the attractiveness of silver dollars rather than greenbacks as a reflationary device. The introduction of the Bessemer process in steel making, soon to be followed by the use of the open-hearth method, provoked an extremely sharp rise in the average size and output of iron and steel companies. Likewise, the average size of railroad firms rose markedly, as entrepreneurship by leaders like Commodore Vanderbilt and J. Edgar Thomson began to create transcontinentals, trunk lines, and other railroad combinations, and economy and efficiency dictated consolidation of such necessities as round houses, switching yards, terminals, and other elements of railroading.

These processes involved yet another, and very basic, change in the seventies and afterward: namely, a different employee-employer ratio in many occupations from what had existed earlier. Consider for a moment the case of Indiana. It was neither the least nor the most industrial state, either nationally or within the East North Central cockpit of industrialization. Looking back at the sixties, we can see in the East North Central states a doubling or tripling of the number of manufacturing establishments, and a similar rate of increase for invested capital and numbers of workers. But in the seventies, there was a *decline* in numbers of establishments, although investment and numbers of employees continued to rise. This was not simply a consequence of the depression; the pattern continued into the relatively prosperous eighties. . . .

A final change beginning in the seventies, in large part an outcome of the foregoing, and catalyzed by the depression, was in what we might call the self-image of farmers, workers, and manufacturers. Employee-employer ratios and relationships were changing; agriculture was declining in relative strength in the labor force and in share of national income; workers, farm and non-farm, often felt with some justification that they were not getting their fair share of the new wealth they helped produce; and people who owned capital—plant, equipment, or intangibles—reacted with discomfort to farmer-labor unrest and with shock to episodes like the Pittsburgh railroad riot of 1877. For all these reasons, an earlier sense of harmony among economic and social classes disappeared. Instead of a commonalty of producers, a term of self-identification which excluded almost nobody so long as he made some social or economic contribution, we begin to find expressions of polar division between debtors and creditors, capitalists and workers, indeed between rich and poor. This was a development which began very noticeably in the seventies, and was to intensify and continue for decades to come.

So American society at the centennial contained problems and changes of an unpleasant and unpromising kind, more unpleasant and unpromising than was appreciated at that time. Let us descend to a further level of pessimism. American society then possessed neither the ideological nor the institutional tools to cope with these changes. No apposite theory of large-scale enterprise, either business or labor, yet existed. In regard to government, the prevailing attitude was what can be termed "positively negative": a positive, structured belief that governments should not act as regulators or initiators of social adjustment. Institutions were ill-equipped to deal with these changes; the political parties, despite the intense loyalties they generated, were not able easily to absorb new ideas or programs, and the Democrats were even more averse to government activism than the Republicans were. The churches were split on many doctrinal and social issues, and, on balance, the churches reinforced the dominant ethic, rather than criticizing or reforming it. The schools were not yet enrolling many students; elementary education was seldom compulsory, and secondary education was very rare (only in 1874, in the Kalamazoo decision, had it become judicially clear that tax money could be spent on secondary schools, since such a small minority of the public used them).

How did this calamitous situation come to an end? The answer is that it did not end, really, in the seventies. It was alleviated by the conjunction of several events in 1879 and 1880, especially business recovery; but in the nineties it got a good deal worse. These problems, twenty years older and harder, were resuscitated by the more severe depression of 1893–97, were compounded by fears about the new immigration, the end of the frontier, further urban and technological change with consequent social dislocations, and further outbreaks of violence and disorder in the South, the West, and the North. The 1870s, the Centennial decade, were thus a preview, a warning, of a culture crisis. The warning was not heeded, but was only disregarded or temporized with. What had to occur—and did not until after 1900 and beyond—was substantial change in ideology, and substantial change in institutions in the direction of social control.

Thus I find that the seeds of many modern conflicts were sown in the seventies. The Americans of that decade, more than in most others, had reason for profound gloom. Yet we still must remember the hardy confidence, the pride, which was so evident on that beautiful summer day of the Centennial Fourth: when, eleven years after Appomattox, and in the midst of depression and even worse problems, an editorialist could still talk of the American flag as "the emblem of all that is free and noble in government, . . . by its one hundred years of permanence it has attained a proud consciousness of dignity and power that never Roman eagles bore." I submit that, in the face of such a statement made at such a time, an affirmation whose pride and optimism was justified, at least with the long passage of time, we might regard somewhat more calmly and more confidently the crisis of culture which we find before us today.

GOVERNOR "BLUE JEANS" WILLIAMS

Rebecca Shepherd Shoemaker

Professor Rebecca Shoemaker prepared an article on James D. "Blue Jeans" Williams for inclusion in a collection of essays about various political leaders in Indiana. Williams, elected governor of Indiana in 1876, was a farmer in Knox County, near Monroe City, for most of his life. Contrary to what might be expected from such a rural and agricultural state, Williams, the state's seventeenth chief executive, was, according to an earlier biographer, "the first farmer and the last pioneer" to occupy the position. He was not, however, a newcomer to politics, having served in the Indiana General Assembly, on the State Board of Agriculture and, for a single term, in the United States Congress. But he remained a Knox County "dirt farmer" all the while. In Congress, where he received both the nickname "Blue Jeans," for his customary garb throughout his life, and a well-earned reputation for frugality, he became the butt of many jokes; but this probably endeared him to his constituency even more. One comment, reminiscent of some of President Lyndon Johnson's remarks about Congressman Gerald Ford, was that Williams couldn't sign his name without biting his tongue.

Nominated for governor in 1876, he defeated Benjamin Harrison (a late replacement on the Republican ticket for a scandal-plagued Godlove Orth) in the fall election, a contest some referred to as one between "Blue Jeans" and "Blue Blood." Tall and gaunt in appearance, Williams bore a striking resemblance to Abraham Lincoln; but his gubernatorial years were undistinguished. Williams died in November 1880, only weeks before his term would have expired. The printed sources on Williams are quite limited, but see William Wesley Woollen, Biographical and Historical Sketches of Early Indiana *(1883), and the entry on Williams by Christopher B. Coleman in the* Dictionary of American Biography, *XX, 267–268; see also a sampling of the anti-Williams stories in a reminiscing article by W. R. Holloway, "Recollections of the Exciting Campaign of 1876 in which Harrison Was Defeated for Governor,"* Indianapolis *News, May 23, 1909.*

James D. Williams, often referred to as "Blue Jeans" Williams because of his lifelong habit of wearing clothing made of the homespun material, confined his speeches during his service in the 1875–1876 session of the United States House of Representatives to comments on the need for thrift and economy in government. During a debate on the report of the Committee on Accounts, of which Williams was chairman, Charles Foster, an Ohio Republican, objected to the committee's cuts in appropriations by making reference to the homespun "Kentucky jeans" statesmanship of the Democratic members in their attitude toward government expenditures.

From Rebecca Shepherd Shoemaker, "James D. Williams: Indiana's Farmer Governor," in *Their Infinite Variety: Essays on Indiana Politicians* (1981), pp. 195–222 passim.

Williams, who felt the remarks to be directed particularly at him, rose to respond. He began his rejoinder by saying, "I am not ashamed of my old Kentucky jeans. The people of Indiana are not ashamed of me because I wear it." He then enumerated some of the economies that had been instituted by the committee under his leadership, and concluded by saying:

> The trouble with a great many of our friends here, and I am sorry to see it, is that they have been here so long that looking up into those galleries they think the people there are the only constituents they have got. They forgot that they have any constituents at home. If they thought a little less of the clothes that may be worn here, whether they be of broadcloth or Kentucky jean, and looked a little less at the galleries, it would be better for them.

This incident encapsulates the two factors that can be said to have played the greatest part in the successful political career of James D. Williams: his emphasis on careful spending by the government, and his reverence for his homespun, agricultural background. These characteristics were, in the beginning, simply a part of the way he chose to lead his life. As he gained stature in the Indiana democracy, however, they began to arouse comment. Williams was often taken on first sight to be a simple old country farmer, and the nicknames "Blue Jeans" and "Old Uncle Jimmy" were originally intended to make him an object of public derision. It is indicative of the character and intelligence of the man that he was able to use these nicknames and the simplicity of his life and beliefs as political assets. His success is measured by a public career that spanned forty years, including service in the Indiana General Assembly, in the United States House of Representatives, and as governor of Indiana. . . .

A study of Williams's activities while a member of the General Assembly indicates that he was interested in a variety of issues. He is credited with being the author of a law that gave a deceased husband's estate, up to a maximum of $300, to his widow without the obligation of administration. Many of the bills he drafted were designed to benefit the farmer, such as one to fund the completion of the Wabash and Erie Canal (1857) and one to make railroad rates uniform within the state of Indiana (1871). He gave a substantial boost to agricultural education in 1865 when he guided through the General Assembly a bill designed to accept for Indiana the provisions of the federal Morrill Land Grant Act of 1862. This bill paved the way for the founding of Purdue University in 1869, an institution Williams supported later with legislation concerning its governance (1871). He supported legislation, too, to aid in the growth and perpetuation of the Indiana State Board of Agriculture (1865).

In spite of Williams's attention to other issues, however, it is clear from the records of his work in the state legislature that his main interest was always finance. Williams's biographer Howard R. Burnett comments:

> His first vote was in opposition to a House resolution providing that two copies each of the Indianapolis *Sentinel* and Indianapolis *Journal* should be provided for each member out of the general expenses of the Assembly. Thus his legislative record for economy in public expenditures, that later made him so prominent in state, and for one session of Congress, in national legislation, was begun with his first vote and remained consistent to his last one.

Williams continued to be a watchdog of state expenditures throughout his career in the General Assembly. He was severely criticized during his later life for attempting during the sessions of 1861 and 1863 to secure passage of a resolution requiring Governor Oliver P. Morton to account for all expenditures from a $100,000 contingency fund provided him for use in the Civil War effort. Some political opponents called Williams a Copperhead and accused him of trying to hamper the war effort, but available evidence indicates that he was primarily concerned with the management of Morton's wartime financial policies, of which many Democrats were critical at the time. . . .

The 1876 campaign for governor of Indiana represented the culmination of Williams's political career. He had made his name (as well as his nickname) and his stand on major issues well known throughout the state. His term in Congress had served to strengthen his commitment to careful spending by government. He claimed to favor repeal of the Specie Resumption Act of 1875, and continued to support the idea of a widely circulating paper currency. Now, with financial and economic problems evident everywhere, and the voters calling for an antidote to the extravagances of the Grant administration that were coming to light almost daily, the fiscally conservative qualities of Williams seemed to appeal to the voters as never before. The money issue, more than any other subject, shaped the speeches, debates, and editorials of the 1876 political campaign in Indiana, and each party worked hard to make its views on the subject known. The Republicans, as might have been expected, were conservative. They favored redemption on demand, in gold or silver coin, of all paper currency, United States bonds, and bank notes. Their gubernatorial candidate, Benjamin Harrison, denounced the Greenback movement and argued that it was always the debtor class that suffered from a fluctuating currency. The Greenbackers, of course, were adamantly opposed to any plan that removed large quantities of paper money from circulation. The Democrats were in favor of cheap money and generally opposed to contraction of the currency by any method; they opposed the Specie Resumption Act and demanded its repeal. . . .

The Democratic press around the state responded to the nomination of Williams with a flood of editorials praising the choice and explaining why they favored his selection. As the following representative samples indicate, their comments consistently reflected approval of the two characteristics that seemed to be his chief assets: his devotion to thrift and his plain country background.

> Williams is the soul of honesty. Simple in his tastes, economical in his habits, being in himself the embodiment of Democratic theories, he will arouse enthusiasm from one end of the state to the other. (Terre Haute *Journal*)

> . . . among the plain country folk who have become tired of the extravagance and "flummery" of the office holders, "Uncle Jimmy's" blue jeans suit will be more revered than the purple robe of an emperor. . . . (Logansport *Pharos*)

> His very appearance will give to the people the best of assurances of a return to the economy and simplicity of the past—his very presence will be a dissertation upon, and condemnation of, the ostentation, extravagance, and display which have obtained in

> high station and which, coupled with the criminal means employed to sustain them, have brought the people well-nigh to bankruptcy and the nation to dishonor. (Columbus *Bartholomew Democrat*)

The Republicans were the first of the three parties to open their campaign, with a speech by [Godlove S.] Orth at Greencastle on July 8. As was frequently the case among the candidates for governor, Orth limited his speech mainly to the Republican record in national affairs, waved the "bloody shirt," and said little about state issues. A more formal kickoff was held on July 20, with simultaneous rallies at several locations around the state. Shortly after this series of events, however, the Republican campaign effort was marked by serious accusations against Orth that eventually forced his withdrawal. The Republicans selected Benjamin Harrison to replace Orth as their nominee for governor. Harrison presented a decided contrast to the first candidate. Capitalizing on his reputation as a good lawyer and a staunch Presbyterian, as well as his record in the Civil War, during which he had attained the rank of brigadier general, Harrison seemed the answer to the Republicans' problems. His Democratic opponents quickly capitalized on his city life style and refined manners, however, labeling him the "kid gloves candidate" and arguing that his aristocratic manner indicated that he had not a shred of sympathy for or understanding of the common man. The editor of the Democratic Indianapolis *Sentinel* described him as "cold as an icicle," a man with "more brains than feeling." The Democrats also implied that Harrison's nomination would split the Republican party because of the acknowledged feelings of ill will between Harrison and United States Senator Oliver P. Morton, leader of a large faction among Indiana Republicans. . . .

Despite the pessimistic predictions of some of Williams's opponents, his years as governor brought few surprises. He was sworn into office on January 8, 1877, and his inaugural address emphasized once again the two areas that had held his lifelong interest and attention: agriculture and economy. He spoke of the value of the farmer's way of life:

> Our position, soil and climate, as well as the habits of our people, all point to that branch of labor which is devoted to agriculture as our chief reliance for lasting wealth and returning prosperity. This calling should rank with us first in respectability, as it unquestionably is first in importance.

Williams also stressed the necessity for honesty and economy on the part of public officials:

> The true principles of economy in the administration of public affairs are essentially the same as those which obtain in individual transactions. No expenditures should be incurred for official services or otherwise unless found necessary or useful, and then at the lowest amount compatible with full and intrinsic value and ample ability of performance. Tested by this rule, all unnecessary offices, if any are found to exist, should be abolished. Public officers should be held to the strictest accountability. Excessive legislation is an evil. The increased burden thereby imposed upon the treasury is but one of the evils growing out of it.

In spite of Williams's personal interests in these topics, a variety of other subjects demanded his attention in the three years and nine months during which he served as governor of Indiana. He repeatedly sought increased appropriations for the state's system of prisons and for the general expansion and improvement of a variety of social services, including the Soldiers' and Sailors' Orphans' Home near Knightstown, the schools for the deaf, dumb, and blind, and facilities for women at the state hospital for the insane. . . .

Perhaps the most widely noted achievement of Williams's administration as governor was the procurement of plans and funds for the erection of a new state capitol. The bill passed by the 1877 General Assembly for this purpose reflected Williams's emphasis on economy and accountability. It provided $2,000,000 for construction and stipulated that any work done at additional cost would be done at the architect's expense. In addition, the architect was required to post a bond of $100,000 to guarantee his commitment to the job. Construction was begun in 1878 and completed in 1888, with such close adherence to the terms of the law that $20,000 of the original appropriation were returned to the state treasury upon completion of the project. . . .

Williams died in office on November 20, 1880. A variety of physical ailments, including diseases of the kidneys and bladder, apparently caused his death, but many people, including family members, felt it was hastened by the passing of his wife the previous June. Williams died in Indianapolis, and his body lay in state first in the Marion County Courthouse, then at Vincennes on November 23. Jeve Hershey, a civil engineer who lived in Vincennes at the time, described the arrival of the body there:

> Gov. J. D. Williams was brought here to day deep snow I marched in procession. funeral at Court House Gov. Cullom of Ills. spoke—a large no of dignitaries from Ind[ian]apolis came here . . . It was snowing furiously and every bell in the City was tolling—it was the most sad and gloomy day I ever witnessed

The funeral was attended by many officials from Indiana and surrounding states, and the body was laid to rest in Walnut Grove Cemetery, the family plot near Williams's home. Friends and supporters collected more than $500 for the erection of a suitable monument for the grave site, and the stone was erected in 1883.

Thus ended the life, and the political career, of James Douglas Williams. Though he was to many during his own lifetime a source of amusement and conjecture, he also filled a definite need for the people of Indiana, especially during the 1870s. His career and his term as governor represented what was perhaps a final attempt to recapture the pioneer and agrarian ideals and traditions on which the state had been built, and which the nation as a whole seemed to be losing sight of during the last decades of the nineteenth century.

6. Into the Modern Era

The discovery of a natural gas field in Indiana in 1886 touched off a new cycle of economic growth. Major new industries, particularly glass, tinplate, and strawboard companies, were attracted to the state, and the birth of the automobile industry in Indiana was also intimately related to the development of the natural gas fields. The Indiana gas supply, however, was quickly exploited and virtually disappeared within less than twenty years; but the industrialization fostered by it continued and expanded markedly in the early twentieth century.

Accompanying the industrialization of Indiana at the turn of the century was a growing urbanization, particularly in the capital city. Indianapolis at mid-century had still been a comparatively small and unimportant city, except for its political significance; but by 1900 it had become nearly three times as populous as Evansville, then the second largest city in the state, and it far exceeded this ratio in 1920. For the state as a whole, its urban population in 1880 was only 19.5 percent of the total; that percentage reached 34.3 in 1900 and the 50 percent mark was exceeded for the first time in 1920. By that time, it was close to the national average, but the rate of urbanization in Indiana was much slower than in neighboring Illinois and Ohio. Similarly, Indianapolis did not become a huge industrial center like Chicago or Cleveland; rather, in Meredith Nicholson's words, it remained "a city of homes" with broad, shaded streets and an unfrenzied pace of life. The small-town atmosphere of Indianapolis is described below by Nicholson, a native Hoosier, who defends his city as one with charm, character, and culture as well as economic vigor.

The late nineteenth century was also a time in which the political role of Indiana was unusually prominent on the national scene. The state was large, its two major political parties were nearly evenly balanced, and both national parties frequently placed Hoosiers on their tickets as one means of attracting the state's electoral votes. The Democrats, working from their base of the "Solid South," needed only the electoral votes of New York and Indiana in the North to carry an election; and the Republicans also concentrated on these northern states in order to prevent a Democratic victory. Indiana's status as an "October" state until 1880, moreover, served to place the state in the national spotlight at election time. Between 1868 and 1916 there were no Hoosiers on the tickets of the two major parties in only three elections (1872, 1896, and 1900). However, in 1900—and in four other elections as well—Eugene V. Debs of Terre Haute headed the Socialist party ticket. Given Indiana's importance in the electoral process, both parties did everything possible legally—and sometimes illegally—to carry the state.

As Indiana entered the twentieth century, a period of unusually rapid industrial growth was under way. By 1920 the manufacturing sector had nearly equaled the agricultural sector in production. Professor Clifton J. Phillips in his comprehensive survey and analysis of the state during the years from 1880 to 1920, written for the sesquicentennial history of Indiana, examines the underlying factors involved in Indiana's somewhat belated but nevertheless significant development as a manufacturing state and then describes a basic industrial activity pursued during the early twentieth century—the processing of agricultural products. Other important items manufactured in Indiana during this time were glass, tinplate, furniture, pharmaceuticals, farm wagons and implements, iron, steel, a variety of ferrous and nonferrous alloys, and automobiles. Elwood Haynes of Kokomo introduced the automobile to Indiana, if not to the nation (only the Duryea brothers in Massachusetts had produced and then briefly manufactured an automobile prior to Haynes), as he himself explains in the concluding section of this chapter.

For more information on turn-of-the-century Indiana, see the recent and valuable study by Clifton J. Phillips, *Indiana in Transition, 1880–1920* (1968); Frances Doan and Frank H. Streightoff, *Indiana: A Social and Economic Survey* (1916); Jacob Piatt Dunn, *Indiana and Indianans: A History of Aboriginal and Territorial Indiana and the Century of Statehood* (5 vols., 1919); and John D. Barnhart and Donald F. Carmony, *Indiana: From Frontier to Industrial Commonwealth* (2 vols., 1954). The automotive work of Elwood Haynes is described in Ralph D. Gray, *Alloys and Automobiles: The Life of Elwood Haynes* (1979).

Natural Gas

THE GAS BOOM

John Bartlow Martin

John Bartlow Martin, a freelance writer and reporter at the time of this publication, built a series of magazine articles he had prepared for Harper's Magazine *into a book about Indiana in 1947. Still a useful and provocative analysis of the state,* Indiana: An Interpretation *contains interesting vignettes on individual Hoosiers, which are interspersed in a general survey of the state's historical development. Martin had frequently visited Muncie to report on "Middletown" during World War II, and in analyzing the effect of the natural gas boom on Indiana, he again used Muncie as a case study. The city was located near the center of the state's nineteen-county-wide gas field, and its offer of free gas and building sites to prospective manufacturers had induced the Ball family, among others, to remove its glass manufacturing plant from New York to Muncie. The family and company have been important in Muncie's growth ever since.*

For a time Indiana had the largest gas field known in the world. Its discovery in 1886 gave an enormous boost to the state's industrial development; at least 300 factories were built in Indiana as a direct result of the discovery. "The interest in natural gas is well nigh universal,"

From *Indiana: An Interpretation* (1947, 1992), pp. 75–81, 83–84, 86.

the Indianapolis News *reported in April 1887, and its "prospects" were a constant topic of conversation. "It's a poor town that can't muster enough money for a gas well just now," commented the reporter. Symbolic of both the interest and the problem of wastefulness were the hundreds of huge flaming torches, or flambeaux, that dotted the countryside of the Gas Belt and offered proof that gas existed in apparently limitless quantities. Pleas for less extravagant use of the resource, coupled with warnings about rapid depletion of the supply, generally went unheeded, and legislative attempts to prohibit exploitation of the gas were defeated in the courts. By 1903 the natural gas boom in Indiana was over. Years of extravagant use and simple wastefulness had taken their toll. The question was no longer whether but when the wells would run dry, and factory closings and shifts to new supplies of imported gas or to other forms of energy had already begun.*

After a distinguished career as a journalist, Martin became an advisor to presidents and presidential candidates and later a professor of journalism at Northwestern University. He served as United States Ambassador to the Dominican Republic from 1962 to 1964, an experience he has described in Overtaken by Events *(1966). He is also the author of a number of other books in the fields of prison reform, mental health care, desegregation, and regional history. His last major work was a two-volume biography of the man whom he had served as a speechwriter,* Adlai Stevenson of Illinois *(1976) and* Adlai Stevenson and the World *(1977), but see also the autobiographical* It Seems Like Only Yesterday: Memoirs of Writing, Presidential Politics, and the Diplomatic Life *(1986). Martin died in 1987.*

The complete story of Indiana's natural gas boom and bust remains to be told, but its outline can best be followed in the annual reports of the state's Department of Geology and Natural Resources from 1887 to 1903. See also Margaret Wynn, "Natural Gas in Indiana: An Exploited Resource," Indiana Magazine of History, *IV (March 1908), 31–45; and Ralph D. Gray, "The Puritan and the Robber Baron: An Episode in the Exploitation of Indiana's Natural Gas,"* Proceedings, Indiana Academy of the Social Sciences, *3rd Ser., VII (1972), 102–110.*

In 1876 men boring for coal at Eaton, near Muncie, sank their diamond drill six hundred feet into the earth, and foul fumes issued forth amid awesome noises. Word spread that their drill had bitten into the roof of the devil's cave, and in dread they plugged the well. But in 1884 gas was discovered at Findlay, Ohio; immediately manufacturers flocked there and the town prospered. Hoosiers remembered the old devil's cavern, unplugged the bore, drilled 322 feet deeper, and struck gas so strong that when they channeled it through four pipes and lit it, a ten-foot flame, visible twelve miles away in Muncie, burst from each pipe. Thousands of townsfolk hurried out by buggy and wagon. They could feel the heat sixty feet from the well. They crept close to sniff the gas and announced with pleasure that its odor was not noisome.

Gas fever swept the state. Overnight, wagon salesmen and apothecaries and even farmers became wildcatters. Developments were discussed round every courthouse square. Wells were sunk everywhere without regard to geology. When gas came in, the drillers did the obvious thing: lit it. As a result towering flames burned night and day in town and country alike. Special Sunday excursion trains carried excited citizens, burdened with basket lunches and children, to the gas field. Probably nothing else ever so captured the imagination of the people of Indiana. And no wonder—here beneath their feet all these years had slumbered a giant, and now they had wakened him. When the spectacular flambeaux blazed on the darkened countryside beside farmhouses theretofore lit only by pioneers' candles and coal-oil lamps, it was as though Indiana had suddenly burst out of her night.

And in a very real sense she had. About this same time the gas failed abruptly in Ohio, and stranded manufacturers hurried across the state line. The Indiana field lay roughly northeast of Indianapolis, with Muncie and Anderson near its center. In 1886 this was a farming section. Gas brought industry.

Signs of the new age already had appeared. Chauncey Rose, the railroader, struck oil in front of the Terre Haute House. Although iron ore was soon exhausted at Terre Haute, the iron-masters remained. The first coal mine was opened at Shelburn in 1868; geologists said coal deposits covered 6,500 square miles around Terre Haute. The Knights of Labor arose. During the great railroad strikes of 1877 (which Eugene Debs opposed), Lew Wallace laid aside his pen and once more led a company of militiamen. Robert Dale Owen died that year and so did Oliver P. Morton. The Erie Nickel Plate reached Hammond, and at South Bend James Oliver invented the chilled-steel plow. German-language newspapers were founded at Indianapolis. John Purdue and others donated two hundred thousand dollars for a university at Lafayette. Indianapolis put down its first pavements, of wood block, in 1870. Moralists across the nation denounced the Indiana divorce laws. The price of a vote in Indianapolis in 1876 was ten dollars. In 1880 Lew Wallace published *Ben Hur*, and William H. English built English's Opera House, where nearly every great actor and actress after Sarah Bernhardt appeared.

Before 1897 some 5,400 gas wells had been drilled in Indiana. Indiana's five-thousand-square-mile gas field was the nation's largest. Moreover, the flow was dependable. People thought it would last forever. At Anderson, a farming village living on memories of the canal days, citizens met in the courthouse January 25, 1887; gas had been struck at Kokomo, Marion, Noblesville, Muncie; should Anderson sit by idle? The citizens subscribed twenty thousand dollars, drilled near the Midland Railway station, and struck gas on March 31. "The people went wild with excitement" and sightseers and capitalists from all over the United States flocked to Anderson. When they dismounted from the trains at the Panhandle depot or the Big Four depot, they were confronted by a huge pine arch that spanned the street and was ornamented by flambeaux. The flame from the first well at Anderson towered a hundred feet into the night with a roar "like the running of a heavy railroad train," and for a month the people did little but gape. Finally on May 24 at another courthouse meeting, citizens organized a board of trade to deal with an inquiry from a Connecticut manufacturer as to "what inducements" Anderson was offering manufacturers to locate there. Trading in leases became brisk. Sidewalk superintendents watched the laying of mains angrily: rumors had arisen that Standard Oil was secretly behind the enterprise, and a newspaper prophesied darkly that Anderson would end in the hands of "the Octopus." A rival Citizens' Company was formed and, presumably, the secret agents of the Octopus withdrew in the night.

Even well-laid pipe lines leaked in cold weather, and explosions resulted. In 1888 a store proprietor on North Main Street smelled gas, went to the cellar, lit a match, and the gas exploded. Frequently citizens were awakened by dull booming explosions and, rising to follow after the horse-drawn fire trucks, gazed disconsolately upon a clutter of gingerbread and bric-a-brac. The When Block, symbol of Anderson's growth, was wrecked. An explosion in a house was heard two miles away, but marvelous to the pious, the Baptist church directly across the street was undamaged.

In a shower of rocks big as hens' eggs, workmen fought to control a gusher at Hartford City; fifty million feet of gas were escaping daily and "There are grave doubts about the workmen's ability to 'pack' the monster." On December 14, 1890, the Indianapolis *Journal* reported that Elwood was "the gem city of the natural-gas belt" and said capitalists were expected that week from Cincinnati, Indianapolis, Logansport, and Columbus and Coshocton, Ohio. Elwood gave a tin-plate company fourteen acres on the Kidwell farm beside the well "Vesuvius"; the company sent its lawyer out to Elwood, and soon his son, Wendell Willkie, was born there, February 18, 1892.

By 1893 some three hundred million dollars had been invested in factories in Indiana; about three hundred factories had been built directly because of gas. A historian wrote: "The efforts of the genii of old have been fairly eclipsed."

When in 1886 the well at Eaton was rebored, Muncie, a farm town, was changed forever. A few months later a syndicate of capitalists bought real estate worth $150,000, and soon people were talking of Muncie as the "Birmingham of the North"; nobody resisted the change or doubted its value. The *News* rhapsodized:

Tell me not in mournful numbers
That the town is full of gloom,
For the man's a crank who slumbers
In the bursting days of boom.

Houses were scarce, rents rising fast. One evening in the lobby of the Kirby House a newcomer complained he couldn't find a ground-floor office. Up spoke James Boyce and asked how much rent he'd pay. He said sixty dollars. Boyce pointed to a good vacant lot across the street and said: "Gentlemen, if you will rent the rooms I will have a brick building there in a week's time." He worked his men all day and by gas light all night and within the week he had erected a brick building with a ninety-six-foot front and six rooms for stores, each with a handsome plate-glass window. The Indianapolis *Journal* described Muncie as a "thriving city of eight thousand people. Though small, it is metropolitan. Here are the essential conveniences of the largest American cities, without their dust, disease and foul air. The Muncie citizen orders his groceries by telephone, his residence is lighted by artificial gas, his place of business by electric light, having choice of both systems, the Brush and Edison incandescent, his meals are cooked by natural gas; there is a good fire department and the Gamewell fire alarm system; he has three railroads, and will soon have an electric line of cable street railway; there is a first-class system of water works . . . sewerage and clean macadamized streets . . . public schools that have no superior in the state . . . a free public library. . . ." And all this in a few months. Home town pride swelled mightily. The Muncie *News* of April 12, 1887, said: "Speculators expected to find in Muncie an Indiana village like Portland, Anderson or New Castle, with a sickly natural gas flame as a curiosity," and reported that one astonished visitor said: "Why this is not a Hoosier village, but an Indiana city."

Inevitably Muncie attracted criminals and prostitutes. By 1890 Muncie had at least a score of whorehouses, and in each from four to eight girls practiced. Moralists complained that respectable men fathered bastards by loose women. In 1900 a drummer reported that a High Street theater surpassed the Bowery in New York "for downright lewdness and immorality." A local historian noted: "The 'quart shops,' low dives and other haunts of vice flourished without check . . . deemed . . . a necessary part of industrial prosperity . . . moral forces . . . had not increased apace with the material expansion. . . ."

Of all the factories that came to Muncie the most important, by any standard, was the glass factory of the Ball brothers. Their career—and it is paralleled by many others in Indiana though usually on a lesser scale—is the story of the rise of midland American capitalism, not transplanted, but a native growth. The Ball brothers were descended from an Englishman who came to the American colonies about a hundred and forty years before the War for Independence. Their father was a restless inventive farmer and trader, not notably successful. Their mother, a strong God-fearing woman, taught them to help each other, a doctrine they never forgot. They were born between 1850 and 1862 in this order: Lucius Lorenzo, William Charles, Edmund B., Frank C., and George A.

When their father died in 1878, Edmund and Frank C. began manufacturing at Buffalo, New York, small wooden tubs for fish packers. The other brothers joined them. The factory burned. They started anew, making metal kerosene cans. They began making the cans out of glass encased in metal. Soon they were also manufacturing fruit jars. Natural gas was discovered in Indiana. Fuel was a major factor in glassmaking. Moreover, the Midwest market for glass jars was growing. The Balls visited perhaps a dozen communities. Each had a newly formed and useful board of trade (later many of them became little but employers' associations designed to hold down wages). It is said that Muncie gave the Balls free fuel, $5,000 cash, and some land to locate there. George A. Ball has said that Muncie's gas promised to last and "perhaps Muncie had a better selling crowd." The Ball brothers built a plant on a seven-acre cornfield on the edge of Muncie and got into production in 1888. F. C. Ball was president, Edmund vice-president and general manager, William secretary, George A. treasurer, and Lucius director (but Lucius devoted most of his time to medicine). They stacked the jars in the field like cordwood to await summer shipment. The only other sizable factory in Muncie made bentwood products; it folded up when the wood was gone and carriages became outmoded. The Balls gobbled up one tract of property after another until they owned seventy acres. News of their success spread. Soon almost every town had its factory making hand-blown glass. Windfall, Ingalls, Yorktown, Upland, had visions of rivalling Muncie, Anderson, and Marion. But, as George Ball has said: "When the time came they had to put in enough money to buy some machinery, they just closed up their doors and went back to farming. They hadn't bought anything but some moulds."

The Balls were among the first to foresee the failure of gas. While prodigals still burned flambeaux, they installed control valves. Before long they employed more people than anybody in Muncie.

After the gas grew weak at Muncie they built factories at new gas fields in Kansas and in Texas; they established plants in Illinois and Oklahoma; they built or bought a paper mill and a corrugating plant and a zinc mill and a short railroad. They diversified—banks, real estate, a retail store, newspapers, a brewery, oil in Texas, oil pipe in Pennsylvania. Frank C. became a director of the Federal Reserve Bank of Ohio and of the Borg-Warner Corporation of Chicago. George A. became chairman of the Merchants National Bank of Muncie and a director of the Merchants Trust Company, Banner-Whitehill Furniture Company, Kuhner Packing Company, Borg-Warner; he invested heavily in the Great Lakes Portland Cement Company, the Intertype Corporation, the Dictaphone Corporation, and others. Edmund became a director of some traction companies, Warner Gear Company, Durham Manufacturing Company, Merchants Bank and Trust. And so on—the list grew longer and longer. Theirs was a family enterprise. Their leader seems to have been "Mr. F. C.," a rather impressive man, with high forehead and soft curling mustache. After two of the brothers died in the 1920's, he and George A. were the active ones. Their activities engaged the attention of Congressional committees investigating patents, holding companies, and other aspects of the concentration of economic power. One brother became a Republican national committeeman, another was mentioned as a possible candidate for Governor or Senator, at least one contributed to the Liberty League that opposed Roosevelt's New Deal. . . .

It is certainly not possible now to render final judgment on whether the Balls' influence on Muncie has been beneficial or baleful, and it may never be possible, at least not until archeologists investigate American capitalism. About all one can do is report the opinions of some Muncie people.

Most Muncie people are eager to attest the Balls' "democracy." The Lynds located a man who repeated fondly how one of the Balls borrowed an overcoat for a party in 1889 because he didn't want to buy a new one when he was just starting in business. Another man recalls: "E. B. Ball was the most democratic of them all, he'd be walking through the plant and see a fellow trying to tighten something with a wrench and he'd stop and help him." Muncie people are fond of pointing out that "G. A. and his wife and daughter go to the early show at the Rivoli just like anybody else," of telling how G. A., though past eighty, comes to work every day and uses a plain office with an old-fashioned roll-top desk and works in his shirt sleeves and has been known to take an upper berth in a Pullman car. "They were just like us when they started out," young businessmen will tell you, for the Balls represent the American dream come true.

Although at one time or another wild tales have circulated concerning members of the younger generation, the original brothers lived lives above reproach, and almost no malicious gossip has touched them, a remarkable thing when one considers their conspicuous wealth. They are described only as honest Christian gentlemen who believe without hypocrisy that unrestricted free enterprise for manufacturers, great profits, low wages, and large munificence constitute the best possible social system.

A few scoffers had said the gas wouldn't last ten years, and in truth it didn't last twenty. The 1891 legislature forbade the burning of flambeaux; during the winter of 1905 gas heat failed even at Muncie, and shortly thereafter gas gave out almost everywhere. Alexandria and Elwood declined; Matthews, a gas-lit boom town between Muncie and Marion, today is nothing but a brick street. None the less, few major factories left the state. No new gas field was discovered immediately elsewhere, and, moreover, new cities were rising, the Midwest was booming, and Indiana was the heart of the Midwest. The gas failure didn't matter; by then nothing could stop Indiana.

Life in the Capital City

INDIANAPOLIS AND MIDWESTERN CULTURE

Meredith Nicholson

Meredith Nicholson was one of Indiana's outstanding literary figures. Perhaps now the least remembered of the quartet that also included George Ade, James Whitcomb Riley, and Booth Tarkington, Nicholson was the most active of the group in defending and explicating Hoosier culture. His chief work of this type was the delightful little book The Hoosiers *(1900), a collection of essays on the people of Indiana, their land and way of living, and their literary and political achievements. The essay below, which later appeared in* The Provincial American and Other Papers *(1912), is in this genre—a defense of the little-known but often ridiculed Hoosier capital. To Nicholson it was a city of beauty and culture, a city whose virtues as a residential community were not obliterated by the growing industrialism of the period. It was also a city with an interesting origin, the grand design of the national capital, and a rich political and intellectual life. As such, it was truly "the capital of all the Hoosiers."*

Nicholson, called by literary historian Arthur W. Shumaker "one of the most rabid of Hoosiers," was a native of Crawfordsville, Indiana, but he lived and did most of his writing in Indianapolis. A versatile writer of poems, essays, and novels, his best-known works, in addition to The Hoosiers *and* The Provincial American, *were two novels,* The House of a Thousand Candles *(1905) and* A Hoosier Chronicle *(1912), and another collection of essays,* The Valley of Democracy *(1918). His total output was prodigious. Widely traveled and an entertaining speaker, Nicholson was much in demand as a lecturer. A staunch Democrat and a popular spokesman for the United States as well as his native state, Nicholson served as American envoy to Paraguay, Venezuela, and Nicaragua between 1933 and 1941.*

There is still no full biographical or literary study of Nicholson, who died in 1947; but brief summaries of his life and literary output are in Richard E. Banta, Indiana Authors and Their Books, 1816–1916 *(1949), and Arthur W. Shumaker,* A History of Indiana Literature *(1962). See also Dorothy Ritter Russo and Thelma Lois Sullivan,* Bibliographical Studies of Seven Authors of Crawfordsville, Indiana *(1952).*

From "Indianapolis: A City of Homes," *Atlantic Monthly*, XCIII (June 1904), 836–845.

The Hoosier is not so deeply wounded by the assumption in Eastern quarters that he is a wild man of the woods, as by the amiable condescension of acquaintances at the seaboard, who tell him, when he mildly remonstrates, that his abnormal sensitiveness is provincial. This is, indeed, the hardest lot, to be called a mudsill and then rebuked for talking back! There are, however, several special insults to which the citizen of Indianapolis is subjected, and these he resents with all the strength of his being. First among them is the proneness of many to confuse Indianapolis and Minneapolis. To the citizen of the Hoosier capital Minneapolis seems a remote place, that can be reached only by passing through Chicago. Still another source of intense annoyance is the persistent fallacy that Indianapolis is situated on the Wabash River. There seems to be something funny about the name of this pleasant stream, which a large percentage of the people of Indianapolis have never seen, unless from the car window. East of Pittsburg the wanderer from Hoosier land expects to be asked how things are on the Way-bosh,—a pronunciation which, by the way, is never heard at home. Still another grievance that has embittered the lives of Indianapolitans is the annoying mispronunciation of the name of the town by benighted outsiders. Rural Hoosiers, in fact, offend the ears of their city cousins with Indian*o*polis; but it is left usually for the Yankee visitor to say *Injun*apolis, with a stress on *Injun* which points rather unnecessarily to the day of the war-whoop and scalp dance.

Indianapolis—like Jerusalem, "a city at unity with itself," where the tribes assemble, and where the seat of judgment is established—is in every sense the capital of all the Hoosiers. With the exception of Boston and Providence, it is the largest state capital in the country; and no other American city without water communication is as large. It is distinguished primarily by the essentially American character of its people. The total foreign-born population of Indianapolis at the last census was only 17,000; whereas Hartford, which is only half the size of Indianapolis, returned 23,000, Rochester, with 7000 fewer people, returned 40,000; and Worcester, in a total of 118,000, reported 37,000 as foreign-born. A considerable body of Germans and German-Americans have contributed much to the making of the city; but the town has been passed over by the Swedes, Poles, and Bohemians that are to be reckoned with in many American cities. There are, however, 5000 negro voters in the city. Indianapolis is marked again by the stability of its population. A large percentage of the householders own their homes; and a substantial body of labor is thus assured to the community.

Indiana was admitted as a state in 1816, and the General Assembly, sitting at Corydon in 1821, designated Indianapolis, then a settlement of straggling cabins, as the state capital. The name of the new town was not adopted without a struggle, Tecumseh, Suwarro, and Concord being proposed and supported, while the name finally chosen was opposed for reasons not wholly academic. It is of record that the first mention of the name Indianapolis in the legislature caused great merriment. The town was laid out in broad streets, which were quickly adorned with shade trees that are an abiding testimony to the foresight of the founders. Alexander Ralston, one of the engineers employed in the first survey, had served in a similar capacity at Washington, and the diagonal avenues, the generous breadth of the streets, and the circular plaza at the monument are suggestive of the national capital. The urban landscape lacks variety: the town is perfectly flat, and in old times the mud was intolerable, but the trees are a continuing glory.

Central Indiana was not, in 1820, when the first cabin was built, a region of unalloyed delight. The land was rich, but it was covered with heavy woods, and much of it was under water. Indians still roamed the forests, and the builder of the first cabin was killed by them. There were no roads, and White River, on whose eastern shore the town was built, was navigable only by the smallest craft. Mrs. Beecher, in *From Dawn to Daylight*, described the region as it appeared in the forties: "It is a level stretch of land as far as the eye can reach, looking as if one good, thorough rain would transform it into an impassable morass. How the inhabitants contrive to get about in rainy weather, I can't imagine, unless they use stilts. The city itself has been redeemed from this slough, and presents quite a thriving appearance, being very prettily laid out, with a number of fine buildings." Dr. Eggleston, writing in his novel *Roxy* of the same period, lays stress on the saffron hue of the community, the yellow mud seeming to cover all things animate and inanimate.

But the founders possessed faith, courage, and hardihood. Too great stress cannot be laid on their work. They sacrificed personal ambition for the good of the community. Their patriotism even was touched with the zeal of their religion. For many years before the civil war a parade of the Sunday-school children of the city was the chief feature of every Fourth of July celebration. The founders appreciated their opportunity, and labored from the first in the interest of morality and enlightenment. The young capital was a converging point for a slender stream of population that bore in from New England, and a broader current that swept westward from the Middle and Southeastern states. There was no sectional feeling in those days. Many of the prominent settlers from Kentucky were Whigs, but a newcomer's church affiliation was of far more importance than his political belief. Indianapolis was charged in later years with a lack of public spirit, but with reference only to commercial matters. There has never been a time when a hearing could not be had for any undertaking of philanthropy or public education. . . .

Following the formative period, which may be said to have ended with the civil war, came an era of prosperity in business, and even of splendor in social matters. Some handsome habitations had been built in the antebellum days, but they were at once surpassed by the homes which many citizens reared for themselves in the seventies. These remain, as a group, the handsomest residences that have ever been built at any period in the history of the city. Life had been earnest in the early days, but it now became picturesque. The terms "aristocrats" and "first families" were heard in the community, and something of traditional Southern ampleness and generosity crept into the way of life. No one said *nouveau riche* in those days; the first families were the real thing. No one denied it, and misfortune could not shake or destroy them. . . .

Many of the striking characteristics of the people are attributable to those days, when the city's bounds were moved far countryward, to the end that the greatest possible number of investors might enjoy the ownership of town lots. The signal effect of this dark time was to stimulate thrift and bring a new era of caution and conservatism; for there is a good deal of Scotch-Irish in the Hoosier, and he cannot be fooled twice with the same bait. During the period of depression the town lost its zest for gayety. It took its pleasures a little soberly; it was notorious as a town that welcomed theatrical attractions grudgingly, though this attitude must be referred back also to the religious prejudices of the early comers. Your Indianapolitan who has personal knowledge of the panic, or who has listened to the story of it from one who weathered the storm, has never forgotten the discipline of the seventies: though he has reached the promised land he still remembers the lash of Pharaoh. So conservatism became the city's rule of life. The panic of 1893 caused scarcely a ripple, and the typical Indianapolis business man to this day is one who minds his barometer carefully.

Indianapolis was a town that became a city rather against its will. It liked its own way, and its way was slow; but when the calamity could no longer be averted, it had its trousers creased and its shoes polished, and accepted with good grace the fact that its population was approximately two hundred thousand, and that it had crept to a place comfortably near the top in the list of bank clearances. A man who left Indianapolis in 1880, returned in 1900—the Indianapolitan, like the cat in the ballad, always goes back; he cannot successfully be transplanted—to find himself a stranger in a strange city. Once he knew all the people who rode in chaises; but on his return he found new people abroad in smart vehicles; once he had been able to converse on topics of the day with a passing friend in the middle of Washington Street; now he must duck and dive, and keep an eye on the policeman if he would make a safe crossing. He was asked to luncheon at a club; in the old days there were no clubs, or they were looked on as iniquitous things; he was taken to look at factories which were the largest of their kind in the world. At the railroad yards he saw machinery being loaded for shipment to Russia and Chili; he was told that books published at Indianapolis were sold in New York and Boston, Toronto and London, and he was driven over asphalt streets to parks that had not been dreamed of before his term of exile.

Manufacturing is the great business of the city. There are nearly two thousand establishments within its limits where manufacturing in some form is carried on. Many of these rose in the day of natural gas, and it was predicted that when the gas had been exhausted the city would lose them; but the number has increased steadily despite the failure of the gas supply. There are abundant coal-fields south and southwest of the city, so that the question of fuel will not soon vex manufacturers. The city enjoys, besides, the benefits to be derived from the numerous manufactories in other towns of central Indiana, many of which maintain administrative offices there. It is not only a good place in which to make things, but a point from which many things may be sold to advantage. Jobbing flourished before manufacturing became a serious factor. The jobbers have given the city an enviable reputation for enterprise and fair dealing. When you ask an Indianapolis jobber whether the propinquity of St. Louis, Cincinnati, Chicago, and Cleveland is not against him, he answers that he meets his competitors every day in many parts of the country and is not afraid of them.

Indianapolis is not like other cities of approximately the same size. It is not the native who says so, but the visitor from abroad, who is puzzled by a difference between the Hoosier capital and Kansas City, Omaha, and Denver, or Minneapolis and St. Paul. It has perhaps more kinship with Cincinnati than with any other Western city. Most Western towns try to catch the step of Chicago, but Indianapolis has never suffered from any such ambition; so the Kansas City man and the Minneapolis man visit Indianapolis and find it slow, while the Baltimore or Washington or Hartford visitor wonders what there is about the Hoosier capital that reminds him of his own city.

Indianapolis is a place of industry, thrift, and comfort, and not of luxury. Its social entertainments were long of the simplest sort, and the change in this respect has come only within a few years,—with the great wave of growth and prosperity that has wrought a new Indianapolis from the old. If left to itself, the old Indianapolis would never have known a horse show or a carnival,—would never have strewn itself with confetti; but the invading time-spirit is fast destroying the walls of the city of tradition. Business men no longer go home to dinner at twelve o'clock and take a nap before returning to work; and the old amiable habit of visiting for an hour in an office where ten minutes of business was to be transacted has passed. A town is at least a city when sociability has been squeezed out of business and appointments are arranged a day in advance by telephone.

The distinguishing quality of Indianapolis is its simple domesticity. The people are home-loving and home-keeping. In the early days, when the town was a rude capital in the woods, the people stayed at home perforce; and when the railroad reached them they did not take readily to travel. A trip to New York is still a much more serious event, considered from Indianapolis, than from Denver or Kansas City. It was an Omaha young man who was so little appalled by distance that, having an express frank, he formed the habit of sending his laundry work to New York, to assure a certain finish to his linen that was unattainable at home. The more the Hoosier travels, the more he likes his own town. Only a little while ago an Indianapolis man who had been in New York for a week went to the theatre and saw there a fellow townsman who had just arrived. He hurried around to greet him at the end of the first act, "Tell me," he exclaimed, "how is everything in old Indianapolis?" This trifling incident is more illuminative of the characteristic qualities of the Hoosier capital than any pages of historical narrative.

The Hoosiers assemble at Indianapolis in great throngs with slight excuse. In addition to the sixteen railroads that touch there, newly constructed interurban traction lines have lately knit new communities into sympathetic relationship with the capital. You may stand in Washington Street and read the names of all the surrounding towns on the big interurban cars that mingle with the local traction traffic. They bring men whose errand is to buy or sell, or who come to play golf on the free course at Riverside Park, or on the private grounds of the Country Club. These cars carry freight, too, and while they disfigure the streets, no one has made any serious protest, for are not the Hoosiers welcome to their capital, no matter how and when they visit it; and is not this free intercourse, as the phrase has it, "a good thing for Indianapolis"? This contact between town and country tends to keep alive a state feeling, and as the capital grows,—as, let us say, it takes on more and more a metropolitan spirit,—the value of this intimacy will have an increasing value, making a neighborhood of a large area. The rural free delivery of mail is another factor to be suggested in indicating the peculiar position occupied by Indianapolis as the centre of state life. A central Indiana farmer's wife may take a newspaper from the country carrier at her own door, read the advertisement of an entertainment or bargain sale at Indianapolis, and within an hour or so she can be set down in Washington Street. The economic bearing of these changes on the country merchant is a serious matter that need only be mentioned here.

Unlike many other American cities, Indianapolis has never been dominated by a few rich men. The rich boss has never ruled it; the men of wealth there have usually possessed character as well. And when, in this frugal, cautious capital, a rich man is indicated, the term is relative in a purely local sense. It is probably fair to say that there are more large fortunes in the much smaller towns of Dayton or Columbus, Ohio, than in Indianapolis, where a quarter of a million dollars is enough to make a man conspicuously rich.

There is something neighborly and cosy about Indianapolis. The man across the street or next door will share any good thing he has with you, whether it be a cure for rheumatism, a new book, or the garden hose. It is a town where doing as one likes is not a mere possibility, but an inherent right. The only thing that is insisted on is respectability,—a black alpaca, Sunday-afternoon kind of respectability. You may, in short, be forgiven for being rich and making a display; but you must be good.

The typical citizen is still one who is well satisfied with his own hearth,—who takes his business seriously on week days, and goes to church on Sundays, that he may gain grace by which to view tolerantly his profane neighbor of the new order who spends Sunday at the Country Club. The woman of Indianapolis is not afraid to venture abroad with her market basket, albeit she may ride in a carriage. The public market at Indianapolis is an ancient and honorable institution, and there is no shame and much honor in being seen there in conversation with the farmer and the gardener or the seller of herbs, in the early hours of the morning. The market is so thoroughly established in public affection that the society reporter walks its aisles in pursuit of news. The true Indianapolis housewife goes to market; the mere resident of the city orders by telephone, and takes what the grocer has to offer; and herein lies a difference that is not half so superficial as it may sound, for at heart the people who are related to the history and tradition of Indianapolis are simple and frugal, and if they read Emerson and Browning by the evening lamp, they know no reason why they should not distinguish, the next morning, between the yellow-legged chicken offered by the farmer's wife at the market and frozen fowls of doubtful authenticity that have been held for a season in cold storage.

The narrow margin between the great parties in Indiana has made the capital a center of incessant political activity. The geographical position of the city has also contributed to this, the state leaders and managers being constant visitors. Every second man you meet is a statesman; every third man is an orator. The largest social club in Indianapolis exacts a promise of fidelity to the Republican party, and within its portals chances and changes of men and measures are discussed tirelessly. And the pilgrim from abroad is not bored with talk of local affairs; not a bit of it! The nation's future is at once disclosed to him. If, however, he wishes to obtain a Godkinian forecast, he can be accommodated at the University Club grillroom, where a court of destructive critics meets daily at high noon. The presence in the city, through many years, of men of national prominence—Morton, Harrison, Hendricks, McDonald, English, Gresham—further helped to make Indianapolis a political centre. Geography plays a chief part in the distribution of favors by state nominating conventions. Rivalry between the smaller towns is not so marked as their united stand against the capital. The city has had, at least twice, both United States Senators; but governors have usually been summoned from the country. . . .

The high tide of political interest was reached in the summer and fall of 1888, when Benjamin J. Harrison made his campaign for the presidency, largely from his own doorstep. For a man who was reckoned cold by acquaintances, his candidacy evoked an enthusiasm at home that was a marked tribute to Mr. Harrison's distinguished ability as a lawyer and statesman. The people of Indiana did not love him, perhaps, but they had an immense admiration for his talents. Morton was a masterful and dominating leader; Hendricks was gracious and amiable; while Gresham was singularly magnetic and more independent in his opinions than his contemporaries. William H. English had been a member of Congress from a southern Indiana district before removing to Indianapolis, and an influential member of the constitutional convention of 1850. He was throughout his life a painstaking student of public affairs. When he became his party's candidate for Vice President on the ticket with Hancock in 1880, much abuse and ridicule were directed against him on account of his wealth; but he was a man of rugged native forces, who stood stubbornly for old-fashioned principles of government, and labored to uphold them. Harrison was the most influential of the group, and he had, as few Americans have ever had, the gift of vigorous and polished speech. He did not win men by ease of intercourse, or drive them by force of personality, but he instructed and convinced them, through an appeal to reason and without the lure of specious oratory. He stood finely as a type of what was best in the old and vanishing Indianapolis,—for the domestic and home-loving element that dominated the city from its beginning practically to the end of the last century. . . .

The soldiers' monument at Indianapolis, which testifies to the patriotism and sacrifice of the Indiana soldier and sailor, is a testimony also to the deep impression made by the civil war on the people of the state. The monument is to Indianapolis what the Washington Monument is to the national capital. The incoming traveler sees it afar, and within the city it is almost an inescapable thing. It stands in a circular plaza that was originally a park known as the Governor's Circle. This was long ago abandoned as a site for the governor's mansion, but it offered an ideal spot for a monument to Indiana soldiers, when, in 1887, the General Assembly authorized its construction. The height of the monument from the street level is 284 feet, and it stands on a stone terrace 110 feet in diameter. The shaft is crowned by a statue of Victory thirty-eight feet high. It is built throughout of Indiana limestone. The fountains at the base, the heroic sculptured groups "War" and "Peace," and the bronze astragals representing the army and navy, are admirable in design and execution.

The whole effect is one of poetic beauty and power. There is nothing cheap, tawdry, or commonplace in this magnificent tribute of Indiana to her soldiers. The monument is a memorial of the soldiers of all the wars in which Indiana has participated. The veterans of the civil war protested against this, and the controversy was long and bitter; but the capture of Vincennes from the British in 1779 is made to link Indiana to the war of the Revolution; and the battle of Tippecanoe, to the war of 1812. The five Indiana regiments contributed to the American army in the war with Mexico, and 7400 men enlisted for the Spanish war are remembered. It is, however, the War of the Rebellion, whose effect on the social and political life of Indiana was so tremendous, that gives the monument its great cause for being. The population of Indiana in 1860 was 1,350,000; the total enlistment of soldiers and sailors during the ensuing years of war was 210,497; and the names of these men lie safe for posterity in the base of the gray shaft.

A good deal of humor has in recent years been directed toward Indiana as a literary centre, but Indianapolis as a village boasted writers of at least local reputation, and Coggeshall's *Poets and Poetry of the West* (1867) attributes half-a-dozen poets to the Hoosier capital. The Indianapolis press has been distinguished always by enterprise and decency, and in several instances by vigorous independence. The literary quality of the city's newspapers was high, even in the early days, and the standard has not been lowered. Poets with cloaks and canes were, in the eighties, pretty prevalent in Market Street near the Post Office, the habitat then of most of the newspapers. The poets read their verses to one another and cursed the magazines. A reporter on one of the papers, who had scored the triumph of a poem in the Atlantic, was a man of mark among the guild for years. The local wits stabbed the fledgeling bards with their gentle ironies. A young woman of social prominence printed some verses in an Indianapolis newspaper, and one of her acquaintances, when asked for his opinion of them, said they were creditable and ought to be set to music,—and played as an instrumental piece! The wide popularity attained by Mr. James Whitcomb Riley quickened the literary impulse, and the fame of his elders and predecessors suffered severely from the fact that he did not belong to the cloaked brigade. General Lew. Wallace never lived at Indianapolis save for a few years in boyhood, while his father was governor, though he has in recent years spent his winters there. Maurice Thompson's muse scorned "paven ground," and he was little known at the capital even during his term of office as state geologist, when he came to town frequently from Crawfordsville, the home of General Wallace also. Mr. Booth Tarkington, a native of the city, has lifted the banner anew for a younger generation. . . .

The citizens like their Indianapolis, and with reason. It is a place of charm and vigor,—the charm and ease of contentment dating from the old days, mingled with the earnest challenge and robust faith of to-day. Here you have an admirable instance of the secure building of an American city with remarkably little alien influence,—a city of sound credit abroad, which offers on its commercial and industrial sides a remarkable variety of opportunities. It is a city that brags less of its freight tonnage than of its public schools; but it is proud of both. At no time in its history has it been indifferent to the best thought and achievement of the world; and what it has found good it has secured for its own. A kindly, generous, hospitable people are these of this Western capital, finely representative of the product of democracy as democracy has exerted its many forces and disciplines in the broad, rich Ohio Valley.

Manufacturing and Industry

There was a significant change in the Indiana economy during the late nineteenth and early twentieth centuries. Agriculture at last gave way to manufacturing as the leading sector of the economy, and the items manufactured changed from being primarily the products of the fields and forests of the state into a much more diversified product line, often with raw materials coming in from outside the state. Perhaps the most dramatic example of the general trend would be the development of Gary, Indiana, as a major steel-producing center. Founded in 1906 as the manufacturing headquarters for the nation's first billion-dollar corporation, United States Steel, Gary arose as if overnight from marshy flatlands at the foot of Lake Michigan. Soon the Calumet region in the extreme northwestern portion of Indiana was the state's leading industrial area. As the two selections below indicate, other forms of manufacturing were also important during the 1890s and the early years of the 1900s. Professor Phillips, author of the most recent comprehensive study of the state during the forty years after 1880, describes the basic reasons for Indiana's somewhat late industrial blossoming, which nevertheless was widely scattered throughout the state and featured the use of new sources of motive power and new business consolidations, but which also continued to rely heavily on the processing of agricultural products.

In the second selection below, one of the pioneers in the development of a new industry for Indiana and the nation describes his first automobile. Elwood Haynes (1857–1925), a scientist and inventor who later discovered a number of important new alloys, including Stellite and stainless steel, was the designer and builder of Indiana's first car in 1894. Later he and Elmer Apperson, operator of the machine shop in Kokomo where the first Haynes was built, converted the shop into Indiana's first automobile factory. By 1920 automobile manufacturing had become one of the top three industries in the state.

For additional information on the industrial development of Indiana, see Powell A. Moore, *The Calumet Region* (rev. ed., 1977); and George Starr, *Industrial Development of Indiana* (1937). For information on the remarkable number of automobiles built in Indiana, including the classic Auburns, Cords, and Duesenbergs, and the once-popular Studebakers, which were manufactured in South Bend until the 1960s, see Wallace Spencer Huffman, "Indiana's Place in Automobile History," *Indiana History Bulletin*, XLIV (February 1967), 11–44, and LIII (March 1976), 35–51. The first full biography of Elwood Haynes is Ralph D. Gray, *Alloys and Automobiles: The Life of Elwood Haynes* (1979).

THE GROWTH OF MANUFACTURING

Clifton J. Phillips

The emergence of Indiana as a leading industrial commonwealth in these years is closely related to at least four major factors: (1) large quantities of agricultural and forestry products which furnish the raw materials for manufactures; (2) deposits of mineral resources, especially abundant and cheap fuels such as coal, natural gas, and petroleum—though the last played a much less significant role in industrialization than the other two; (3) excellent transportation facilities with a dense network of railroads crisscrossing the state as well as waterways for freighting (the Lake Michigan ports beginning to function just as the traffic on the Ohio River and its navigable tributaries began to decline); (4) Indiana's fortunate geographic location at or near the center of the population of the United States and directly in the path of a large share of east-west commerce, with wide access to markets. Increasing urbanization was part of this pattern, Indianapolis and a dozen or more smaller cities in the state gaining population and economic weight during this period. Indiana also enjoyed the commercial advantages of proximity to the great urban marts of Chicago, Cincinnati, and Louisville outside the state boundaries.

Several changes took place in the nature of manufacturing enterprises during the period from 1880 to 1920. One involved the types of motive power used in factory production. Steam power grew slowly, remaining the leading prime mover until challenged by electricity about 1914; water power generally declined and the internal combustion engine became increasingly important, as the following table indicates:

HORSEPOWER OF TYPES OF PRIME MOVERS
1880-1919

Year	*Steam*	*Water*	*Electric*	*Internal Combustion*
1880	109,960	21,810	—	—
1890	174,060	16,305	323	176
1900	296,926	11,964	7,903	12,295
1905	336,932	9,685	33,582	21,171
1909	449,127	7,893	233,193	109,105
1914	430,504	9,905	450,357	66,691
1919	521,446	10,162	652,754	189,271

Another important shift was from the processing and fabrication of such local raw materials as lumber, wheat, and meat to the manufacture of durable goods, many of

From *Indiana in Transition, 1880–1920* (1968), pp. 274–287.

them made from iron and steel. Even native fuels such as coal and natural gas tended to play a somewhat smaller part in the state's manufacturing industries after 1900 than before. Some manufactures flourished while utilizing little or none of the state's natural resources. The blast furnaces of the Calumet Region, for example, transformed ores from the Mesabi range in Minnesota by means of coke made from Pennsylvania and West Virginia coal, using limestone imported from Michigan for fluxing. In this case, Indiana's chief industrial advantage was its location, which, among other things, made possible bulk transportation of raw materials by water. Moreover, an industry like glass manufacturing, which used practically no local raw materials, but was drawn to Indiana by the promise of free or cheap fuel during the gas boom, was able to remain in the state after the cessation of the flow of natural gas by switching to coal or other sources of heat.

A third shift was regional. As the earlier manufacturing centers along the Ohio River declined in importance, the central and northern counties became more heavily industrialized. A northward movement of manufactures was already well under way by the seventies but was greatly accelerated in the succeeding decades. Of the seven leading industrial counties which together produced approximately half of the state's manufactures in 1879, only two—Vanderburgh and Floyd—were located in the extreme south. With the abrupt decline of New Albany in the eighties, Floyd County dropped out of the ranks of the principal industrial counties. Evansville alone among southern Indiana cities continued to keep pace as a manufacturing center. In fact, its county, Vanderburgh, held fifth place in the value of manufactured products in the state as late as 1919. Marion County, containing the capital city, Indianapolis, remained in first place until 1919, when Lake County, a newly developed area, overtook it. Other leading industrial counties in this period were Vigo (Terre Haute), St. Joseph (South Bend), Allen (Fort Wayne), and Madison (Anderson). The concentration of industry in certain regions was well shown in the 1920 census, when Marion and Lake counties together reported 48.8 per cent of the total products for the state and 33.6 per cent of the total number of wage earners.

Indianapolis was the industrial as well as political capital of the state in 1919, with 21.8 per cent of the value of its manufactured products. Using the same measure of comparison South Bend was in second place in that year, having passed Evansville in 1904, largely because of the establishment of the automobile industry in the former place. By 1914, however, the comparatively young East Chicago in Lake County was ranked second, ahead of such older industrial cities as South Bend, Evansville, Fort Wayne, and Terre Haute. Five years later Indianapolis still held its supremacy, but second place would have to be awarded to Gary on the basis of the Lake County figures, for the Federal census reports omitted statistics of the new city to avoid disclosure of individual operations. Evansville fell to sixth and Terre Haute to eighth place or lower, depending on what position should be assigned to Whiting, another virtually single-industry city whose statistics were not revealed by the Bureau of the Census. Other important industrial cities in descending order of value of manufactured products in 1919 were Hammond, Anderson, Kokomo, Michigan City, Muncie, Mishawaka, Elkhart, Marion, Richmond, and La Porte.

Manufacturing in Indiana as in the rest of the nation was moving in the direction of large-scale factory production, which had far outdistanced neighborhood industries and hand trades in value of products by 1900, though the latter remained surprisingly numerous. If all manufacturing establishments with a product of less than $500 are included, the total number in 1899 was 23,657, of which 13,396, or 56.8 per cent, represented either small shops or hand trades. Yet the value of products of these last establishments amounted to only $30,515,265, or approximately 8 per cent of the total value of the state's manufactured goods in that year. On the other hand, in 1899 Indiana boasted 16 establishments out of 443 in the whole country employing over 1,000 persons. Twenty years later manufacturing companies in the state doing over $1,000,000 worth of business accounted for only 3.8 per cent of the total number of establishments but 71.5 per cent of the gross value of products. In several industries the proportion of value of products manufactured by such concerns was much higher—agricultural implements, 87.0 per cent; automobiles, 97.0 per cent; and slaughtering and meat packing, 92.1 per cent.

In the nineties occurred a series of industrial combinations affecting Indiana which stimulated a great deal of discussion of monopolies and "trusts." The Gas Belt alone spawned combinations in the glass, strawboard, and tinplate industries in this period. Despite considerable unfavorable public opinion and some antitrust legislation by the General Assembly, the process of integration of Hoosier manufacturing into the national economic sphere continued strongly into the twentieth century. By 1919 such huge corporations as the American Can Company, American Car and Foundry Company, American Hominy Company, American Seeding Machine Company, American Tin Plate Company, General Electric Company, General Motors Corporation, International Harvester Company, Pittsburgh Plate Glass Company, Standard Oil of Indiana, and United States Steel Corporation were each represented in the state by one or more factories. In addition, corporations were increasingly replacing individuals and partnership firms. The number of manufacturing enterprises owned by corporations rose from 27.2 per cent in 1904 to 37.4 per cent in 1919, while their average number of wage earners and value of products increased from 80.6 per cent each to 91.7 and 93.5 per cent, respectively. By 1919 the proportion of corporate ownership had reached 100 per cent in such industries as railroad car construction and repair, and cement, glass, and iron and steel manufacturing. . . .

Evidence of the continuing importance of agriculture in the production of raw materials for manufacturing in Indiana was the consistently high rank of the processing of meat, grain, and other foods among the state's industries throughout most of the period from 1880 to 1920. Yet the statistical significance of these particular industries was chiefly derived from the total value of products, which necessarily included a disproportionately large sum for the value of the materials used. Thus the processing of such agricultural products, significant as they were in total value, actually added less to the state's wealth than many manufacturing industries less dependent upon local raw materials, such as iron and steel and glassmaking. Nevertheless, meat packing, flour milling, and food processing made good economic sense in a state with both abundant agricultural resources and excellent transportation facilities. While this type of manufacturing was not sufficient in itself to place Indiana in the front ranks of industrial states, it clearly played a major role in the creation of an industrial base in a primarily agricultural region.

By 1899 slaughtering and meat packing constituted the leading industry in Indiana, computed according to value of products, which in that year amounted to $43,862,273, or 11.6 per cent of the total value of the state's manufactures. Although it fell to second place in 1914 and third place in 1919, its value of products remained relatively high. But the value added by manufacture amounted to only $12,339,000 in 1919. By this standard of measurement slaughtering and meat packing could not be counted among the state's ten leading industries.

Before 1901 the principal slaughtering and meat-packing center in Indiana was Hammond, a Lake County city named for George H. Hammond, a meat wholesaler in Detroit and a pioneer shipper of dressed beef in refrigerator cars, who built a slaughterhouse in 1869 in what was then an uninhabited spot near the Indiana-Illinois boundary. In 1890, four years after the founder's death, the Hammond Packing Company was sold to an English syndicate, and its annual slaughtering capacity was enlarged to 300,000 cattle, 25,000 sheep, and 10,000 hogs. Tragedy struck in October, 1901, when a disastrous fire almost completely destroyed the plant. J. Ogden Armour purchased the Hammond holdings in an attempt to create a giant meat trust, but, when this maneuver was rejected by the Federal courts, he closed the Indiana meat-packing plant permanently in May, 1903, and moved its operations to Chicago. Not only was this a great blow to the economic well-being of the city of Hammond, but the loss meant a sharp drop in the state's meat production as shown vividly in the report of the census of manufactures in 1905, when the total value of slaughtering and meat-packing products fell by one third, to $29,352,593.

Indianapolis succeeded Hammond as the center of slaughtering and meat packing in the state. The introduction of artificial refrigeration and the "summer pack" in the seventies through the experiments of George W. Stockman of the British-owned Kingan and Company helped to give the capital city a leading position in the industry. In 1914 its value of products totaled $37,780,039 and in 1919 soared to $104,805,746, according to which Indianapolis ranked fifth among meat-packing cities in the nation after Chicago, Kansas City, Omaha, and New York. Other Hoosier cities with commercially significant facilities for slaughtering and meat packing were Fort Wayne, Evansville, Lafayette, and East Chicago. Indiana's main meat products were pork, both fresh and cured, beef, and sausage, plus lesser quantities of veal, mutton, and salted beef. Auxiliary products of the slaughtering and meat-packing industry included hides and pelts, lard, tallow, and oleomargarine, as well as glue, soap, and fertilizers, which were chiefly manufactured in separate establishments. The value of products of the entire industry rose to $51,022,000 in 1914 and $134,029,000 in 1919.

In spite of the large livestock and slaughtering interests in the state, Indiana did not rank particularly high in the tanning of leather and its manufacture into finished products. The value of tanned and curried leather, which was $2,729,000 in 1879, did not reach that large a sum again until 1914 and was only $4,730,000 in the inflationary year of 1919. Although the figures are not perfectly comparable because of the inclusion of small shops and hand trades in the earlier census returns, the manufacture of boots and shoes declined from a total value of products of $2,144,000 in 1879 to $1,278,000 in 1914, before rising to $2,854,000 in 1919. Saddlery and harness manufacture remained fairly stable until 1914, but dropped significantly with the decreased use of horses by 1919, when the value of products was $2,520,000. Glove making, which was not even reported in the censuses of 1880 and 1890, was an extremely minor industry in Indiana, with products valued at just $588,000 in 1919. The only leather industry which expanded in the state in this period was the manufacture of trunks and valises, the value of such products rising from $84,000 in 1879 to $264,000 in 1914 and $1,348,000 in 1919.

According to value of products, Indiana's leading industry in the eighties and nineties was the milling of grain, which slipped, however, to second place in 1899, fourth place in 1914, and finally, sixth place in 1919, when total output was valued at $75,111,000. Since grain was grown commercially in most of the state, mills were relatively numerous and widely scattered. Their number, however, reached a peak in 1900 with 897 reported in the census returns of that year, and then declined to 563 in 1909 and 450 in 1919. Indianapolis was the leading flour-milling city in the state, closely followed by Evansville, though large mills were also found in cities like Fort Wayne, Lawrenceburg, and Terre Haute. The Igleheart Brothers Company in Evansville created a famous brand name, "Swans Down," which it introduced in 1876. In 1895 it began packaging Swans Down Cake Flour and three years later initiated a national advertising campaign which helped to make this product a family favorite throughout much of the United States.

Wheat flour was the chief product of Indiana mills, though large quantities of corn meal and hominy were also manufactured, along with smaller amounts of rye and buckwheat flour and barley meal. More important commercially than the latter were livestock feeds—corn and oats ground together as well as bran and middlings, by-products in the manufacture of wheat flour. As the wheat belt moved northward and westward to Minnesota and Kansas, wheat-flour production declined in Indiana, as did most mill products except hominy and grits, of which the state remained the leading producer in the country through nearly the whole of this period. Indiana's "hominy king," Theodore Hudnut, founded a mill in Terre Haute just after the Civil War which became the foundation of a large corporation organized by him in that city and elsewhere in 1890. Most of his holdings outside Terre Haute went into the establishment of the consolidated American Hominy Company in 1902.

Another grain-using industry was the "wet" milling of corn in order to manufacture starch and related products. One of the earliest successful starch factories in the United States was built in Indianapolis in 1867 by a German immigrant, William F. Piel. In 1890 a consolidation of the Piel firm with several others in Indiana and elsewhere created the National Starch Manufacturing Company, which then controlled about 65 per cent of the American market, according to William F. Piel, Jr., vice-president and later president of the new corporation. The state ranked second after New York in the production of starch in both 1889 and 1899, though the total value of products declined from $1,580,543 to $989,639 in this period largely because of the closing of several plants brought about by the 1890 merger.

Other products of starch mills were livestock feeds, glucose or corn syrup, and corn oil. Indiana became a major producer of the last two products in 1906, when the American Maize Products Company, which specialized in the manufacture of salad oil, built a large plant in East Chicago. Largely for this reason, by 1909 Indiana

FLOUR AND GRISTMILL PRODUCTS IN INDIANA
1899–1919

	Wheat Flour		Corn Meal and Flour	
Year	*Pounds*	*Value*	*Pounds*	*Value*
1899	4,722,208	$20,059,135	1,987,719	$ 2,601,562
1904	5,181,906	25,282,880	909,622	2,076,266
1909	4,794,847	25,315,671	855,409	2,483,265
1914	4,526,879	21,183,688	984,239	3,030,308
1919	4,305,436	47,088,134	512,179	4,451,959

	Hominy and Grits		Bran, Middlings, and Feed	
Year	*Pounds*	*Value*	*Tons*	*Value*
1899	96,714,589	$ 715,640	376,154	$ 4,763,783
1904	182,106,165	2,147,012	374,314	6,703,490
1909	256,678,796	3,758,367	388,022	8,740,647
1914	292,131,101	4,620,892	337,627	8,412,421
1919	93,956,630	3,222,770	345,170	18,598,847

ranked fourth among the states in the total value of starch and glucose products, which amounted to $5,750,000 in that year.

Bread and other baked goods were also produced on an increasing scale in the state during this period. The industry was characterized by a comparatively large number of small and medium-sized bakeries, while Indianapolis led in value of products, followed by such other cities as Terre Haute, Fort Wayne, and Evansville. One of the most successful Hoosier entrepreneurs in this field was Alexander Taggart of Indianapolis, whose Parrot and Taggart Bakery in the capital city was merged into the United States Baking Company, later a part of the National Biscuit Company, a corporation formed in 1898 which also controlled bakeries in Fort Wayne and Terre Haute. In 1905, however, Taggart sold out his interest in the National Biscuit Company in order to organize the Taggart Baking Company in Indianapolis, which became the largest bakery in the state. The steady growth of the industry, as shown in the table below, reveals the general shift from home to factory baking which occurred during this period.

BREAD AND OTHER BAKERY PRODUCTS,
1879–1919

Year	*Number of establishments*	*Average number of wage earners*	*Value of products*
1879	155	519	$ 1,292,000
1889	264	1,025	2,282,000
1899	391	1,334	4,166,000
1909	754	2,505	10,209,000
1919	802	3,759	30,020,000

The most important food-processing industry to become firmly established in Indiana during this period was vegetable canning, which was closely related to the rapid growth of truck gardening in the central and northern sections of the state. Although pioneer canners like Gilbert C. Van Camp of Indianapolis and James T. Polk of Greenwood had begun commercial operations on a small scale in the sixties and seventies, the main advance came after 1890 with the discovery of natural gas and the subsequent rise of the domestic manufacture of tinplate. Indiana benefited particularly from the westward movement of the canning industry, which had been previously centered on the Atlantic Coast, and showed the most rapid increase among the ten leading states in the value of output in the first decade of the twentieth century. The following table indicates the growth of the industry:

CANNING INDUSTRY IN INDIANA, 1879–1919

Year	*Number of establishments*	*Average number of wage earners*	*Value of products*
1879	6	337	$ 249,000
1889	11	2,020	885,000
1899	60	2,002	2,589,908
1909	134	3,406	8,758,000
1919	166	4,170	27,823,000

Canneries proliferated in this period. They were located in large cities such as Indianapolis as well as in dozens of small communities scattered throughout the vegetable-growing districts of the state, especially in Boone, Daviess, Delaware, Henry, Howard, Johnson, Madison, Scott, Tipton, Wabash, Washington, and Wayne counties. Among the chief products in Indiana were canned tomatoes, beans, peas, pumpkin, hominy, and sweet corn. Cucumber pickles and tomato catsup as well as a small quantity of fruit were also preserved. In the early nineties Frank Van Camp, son of Gilbert C. Van Camp, initiated the canning of a popular food combining pork and beans with tomato sauce, and the Van Camp Company remained for many years the leading manufacture of that product, which was generally known to Americans as "Boston baked beans." Indiana was also the birthplace of another important innovation in the industry, the canning of hominy, which was apparently originated by Isaac V. Smith in Delphi in November, 1896. A leading canner in the southern part of the state was Joseph W. Morgan, who established the Morgan Packing Company in Austin, Scott County, and several other small nearby towns at the beginning of the twentieth century.

By 1909 Indiana was ranked first among all the states of the nation in the canning of baked beans; second in pumpkin; and fourth in both peas and tomatoes. The canning industry was moving westward so rapidly by this time, moreover, that in 1919 Indiana had taken first place in the canning of pumpkin, hominy, and tomato pulp, while retaining its premier position in baked beans, and was in second place in tomato paste and kidney beans.

A NEW INDUSTRY

Elwood Haynes

In 1890 I moved from Portland, Ind. to Greentown, Ind. where I became field superintendent for the Indiana Gas & Oil Company, which company was about to begin the construction of a pipe line from the Indiana gas field to Chicago. Litigation and defective pipe delayed its construction.

During the delay in the work of constructing the pipe line I had a great deal of driving to do, and it occurred to me again that some better means of locomotion over the highways than the horse and buggy might be procured. The great trouble with the horse was his lack of endurance and this became more apparent when he was driven day after day.

I accordingly laid plans for the construction of a mechanically propelled vehicle for use on the highway. I first considered the use of a steam engine, but made no attempt to build a car of this description for the reason that a fire must be kept constantly burning on board the machine, and with liquid fuel this would always be a menace in case of collision or accident. Moreover, the necessity of getting water would render a long journey in a car of this description not only troublesome, but very irksome as well. I next considered electricity, but found that the lightest battery obtainable would weigh over 1200 pounds for a capacity of twelve horse hours. As this showed little promise of success, I gave it no further consideration, and proceeded to consider the gasoline engine. Even the lightest made at that time were very heavy per unit of power, and rather crude in construction.

My work was confined to Greentown, Ind. in 1890 and 1891. In the Fall of 1892 I moved to Kokomo and the following Summer (1893) had my plans sufficiently matured to begin the actual construction of a machine. I ordered a one-horsepower marine upright, two cycle, gasoline engine from the Sintz Gas Engine Company of Grand Rapids, Michigan. This motor barely gave one brake horsepower, and weighed 180 lbs. Upon its arrival from Grand Rapids in the Fall of 1893, lacking a suitable place, the motor was brought directly to my home and set up in the kitchen.

When the gasoline and battery connections were installed, the motor, after considerable cranking, was started and ran with such speed and vibration that it pulled itself from its attachments. Luckily, however, one of the battery wires was wound around the motor shaft and thus disconnected the current.

In order to provide against vibration, I was obliged to make the frame of the machine much heavier than I first intended.

The "horseless carriage" was built up in the form of a small truck. The framework

From "How I Built the First Automobile," *The Haynes Pioneer* (July 1918), pp. 5–7.

in which the motor was placed consisted of a double hollow square of steel tubing, joined at the rear corners by steel castings, and by malleable castings in front. The hind axle constituted the rear member of the frame and the front axle was swiveled at its center to the front end of the "hollow square." This arrangement permitted the ends of the front axle to move upward and downward over the inequalities of the road without wrenching the "hollow square" in which the motor and countershaft were placed.

At that time there were no figures accessible for determining the tractive resistance to rubber tires on ordinary roads. In order to determine this as nearly as possible in advance, a bicycle, bearing a rider, was hitched to the rear end of a light buckboard by means of a cord and spring scale. An observer seated on the rear end of the buckboard recorded as rapidly as possible "draw-bar" pull registered by the scale, while the buckboard was moving at the rate of about ten or twelve miles per hour on a nearly level macadam street. The horse was then driven in the opposite direction at about the same speed, in order to compensate for the slight incline. This experiment indicated that about 1–75/100 pounds "draw-bar" pull was sufficient to draw a load of 100 pounds on a vehicle equipped with ball bearings and pneumatic tires. With this data at hand it was an easy matter to arrange the gearing of the automobile so that it would be drawn by the motor. Crude though this method may appear, it shows a striking agreement with the results obtained today, by much more accurate and refined apparatus.

The total weight of the machine when completed was about 820 pounds. July 4, 1894, when ready for test, it was hauled into the country about three miles behind a horse carriage and started on a nearly level turnpike. It moved off at once at a speed of about seven miles per hour and was driven about one and one-half miles into the country. It was then turned around, and ran all the way into the city without making a single stop.

I was convinced upon this return trip that there was a future for the "horseless carriage," although I did not at that time expect it to be so brilliant and imposing. The best speed attained with the little machine in this condition was about eight miles per hour.

It would hardly seem that the automobile has been in existence a sufficient length of time to justify a reminiscence; it seems, rather, to be a creation of yesterday, and the result of the development which had its beginning a quarter century ago.

I will be pardoned if I write to some extent of my own experiences in those early days, since at the time the automobile was unknown in the United States, and was just in its incipient state in Europe. When my first machine was taken out into the street on preliminary trial, people living in adjacent houses, men, women, and children, rushed out and surrounded it, leaving only an enclosed circle, perhaps twenty feet in diameter, in which to start. Under these circumstances it was manifestly unsafe to make a trial, since not one of the persons intending to operate the machine had ever seen anything of the sort before, much less having ever driven one. No attempt was therefore made to start the machine, but it was taken to the country behind a horse and carriage, and after being driven a short distance on its own power further into the country, was turned about and headed toward the city.

At that time the bicycle was very popular as a pastime, especially among young ladies. I remember as the little machine made its way along the streets we were met by a "bevy" of girls mounted on wheels. I shall never forget the expressions on their faces as they wheeled aside, separating like a flock of swans and gazing wonder-eyed at the uncouth and utterly unexpected little machine. This was in 1894. A number of these young misses are married now and have children nearly grown. To these children there is nothing new about the automobile, but many of them are intensely interested in its rapid growth, and in the convenience which it has afforded to many of them.

Shortly after this, I made a journey about eight miles into the country. On the way we were obliged to pass through some fresh gravel, which rendered our progress slow. Just at this time we were overtaken and passed by a lady and gentleman driving a horse and buggy. I suggested to the gentleman that it would be better for him to let us go ahead, as we would make better progress after we had gone through the fresh gravel. He preferred to precede us, however, and as soon as we reached the smooth road again the young man who was with me opened the cutout from the muffler, and the result was [a] succession of sharp staccato reports.

Immediately the young man driving the horse ahead of us cracked his whip and urged his horse forward at full speed. The cutout was then closed until we again came within a short distance of the horse and carriage, when the operation was repeated; again the whip was brought to bear and the speed of the horse increased, much to the amusement of the young man who was driving with me. As a matter of fact, we were only driving about eight miles per hour, but this was enough to make the driver ahead of us get uneasy, and after three miles of intermittent speeding and slowing down, he turned into a side road and let us pass.

On another occasion in driving the little machine, I met an old gentleman seated on a load of crated tomatoes. He was so interested and watched us so closely that when his horse began to shy he dropped one of the lines, and with the other, pulled the team to one side and down a slight embankment, which caused the load to overturn. Luckily, the old man was uninjured. I settled with him there and then for the damaged tomatoes and took his receipt in full.

At that time there was some question in the minds of the public as to the right of the "horseless carriage" on the highway. Lawyers were consulted regarding the matter and looking up the law, they discovered that the question had been broadly covered, not only by the lower court, but by the Supreme Court as well, and that the decisions were of sufficient scope as to unquestionably include the automobile and give it a full and unrestricted right on the highway.

I remember very well when the little machine was unloaded for the Times-Herald contest in 1895 at Englewood, a suburb of Chicago. I was riding down Michigan Avenue, intending to drive to the central portion of the city, and had scarcely proceeded more than six or eight blocks, when I was accosted by a policeman who ordered me to leave the boulevard at once, as nothing like "horseless carriages" were permitted on that thoroughfare. I remonstrated with him what harm the machine could do to the boulevard, since it was equipped with rubber tires and made but little noise. He simply replied that it was "Arders, Sir," so I could do nothing but obey. Contrast that state of affairs with the constant stream of automobile traffic over

Michigan Avenue today and you will be able to realize what vast changes have taken place since then, not only in the mode of locomotion but in public sentiment as well.

In 1899 I made a trip of about one thousand miles in a "horseless carriage" to New York City. There were many amusing incidents connected with this trip. Almost every horse shied at the "new-fangled" vehicle, and some of them even bolted from the road, endangering the lives of the occupants of the vehicle. One incident, which came near having a serious ending, occurred on the way down the Hudson River. We met a party of "Summer girls" who were evidently taking a vacation in the country. A sober, staid-looking old horse was attached to an open, spring wagon in which five or six girls were riding. About the time the horse came opposite the automobile, he turned suddenly to one side, and doubling himself, proceeded to jump over the stone wall by the roadside. It can well be imagined that there were screams and consternation on the part of the young ladies. Luckily, however, the horse considered himself safe when his forefeet were over the wall, and before I could reach him to give assistance, he had gotten back into the road and proceeded quietly on his way without doing any apparent harm.

On another occasion on the same trip we were met by an Irish woman driving a load of vegetables to market. As soon as she came within hailing distance she called for us to stop and motioned wildly with her hands. We, of course, stopped the machine, and I went forward to lead the horse, but she remarked apologetically, "I would not have asked you to stop, sir, but the horse is blind, sir." It is needless to say that I did not take pains to lead the horse by, but immediately informed the good woman that she was in no danger whatever, since a blind horse had never been known to take fright at a "horseless carriage." She seemed much relieved when we passed, and her horse paid not the slightest attention to the machine.

While perfecting the "horseless carriage" I had never lost my interest in metallurgy and introduced aluminum into the first automobile crankcase in 1895. The alloy for this crankcase was made up for the purpose and consisted of 93% aluminum and 7% copper. This was, I believe, the first aluminum ever placed in the gasoline motor, and, as far as I am aware, in an automobile. Moreover, this particular composition has become a standard for all automobile motors at the present time.

At about this time (1896) I also introduced nickel-steel into the automobile, and at a later date, I made a number of experiments in the alloying of metal, and succeeded in making an alloy of nickel and chromium containing a certain amount of carbon and silicon, which, when formed into a blade, would take a fairly good cutting edge. The metal would tarnish after long exposure to the atmosphere of a chemical laboratory.

Later, in 1899, I succeeded in forming an alloy of pure chromium and pure nickel, which not only resisted all atmospheric influences, but was also insoluble in nitric acid of all strengths.

A few months later I also formed an alloy of cobalt and chromium, and an alloy of the same metals containing a small quantity of boron. These later alloys were extremely hard, especially that containing boron.

In 1904 and 1905 I made some further experiments upon the alloys of nickel and cobalt with chromium, with a view to using the alloys for electric contacts in the make-and-break spark mechanism, and in 1907 I secured basic patents on both of these alloys.

And so it has gone. Naturally and necessarily, once the automobile began to gain favor it was necessary to enlarge our organization.

Today the Haynes car is made in a big factory—a striking contrast to the time when my first car was made in a little machine shop and when I paid the mechanics who were hired to assist in the building of it, according to my plans, at the rate of forty cents an hour.

These men had no faith whatever in the self-propelled vehicle and worked at this rate only when their regular work was "slack." But I had to guarantee them that payment.

Frankly, I did not realize on that Fourth of July, when I took the first ride in America's First Car, that a score of years later every street and highway in America would echo the sound of the horn and the report of the exhaust.

When one contemplates the tremendous industry that has grown—taking into consideration the making of automobiles, tires, carburetors, and all the varied appurtenances of the automobile, he is filled with wonder that so much as all this could possibly have come to pass in such a short space of time.

For it was years after the first car was put into practical use that the automobile industry began to develop at all.

7. The New Century

Indiana entered the twentieth century still primarily agricultural, still politically pivotal, and increasingly recognized as the "typical" American state. Muncie was selected by sociologists Robert and Helen Lynd as America's "Middletown" in the 1920s. In many ways the early decades of the century were the most productive ones for the state and most satisfying to its citizens. Indiana retained a distinctiveness since it had not yet been drawn into the homogenizing swirl created by modern transportation and communication networks; but the state also began to achieve greater recognition in economic and social matters while continuing its prominent roles in politics and literature. For many years Indiana rivaled Michigan for leadership in the production of automobiles, and even after Michigan pulled ahead in quantity, based largely on the mass production revolution achieved by Henry Ford, there was still a qualitative contest to be considered. The Indianapolis Motor Speedway, built in 1909 and home of the first 500-mile race in 1911, is an appropriate symbol of the importance of the automobile to the state.

Indiana was also a leader in another form of transportation—the interurban. The name itself was the brainchild of Charles Henry of Lafayette, who built one of the first electrified intercity railways between Lafayette and Indianapolis. By 1920 a splendid network of interurban lines had been developed, blanketing the entire state, except for the "pocket" in the southwest, and connecting all of its major population centers. Ultimately the interurban, like the passenger railroad, fell victim to America's torrid and continuing love affair with the automobile, a loss that is particularly regrettable in the face of the worldwide energy crisis beginning in the 1970s.

In addition to automobiles and interurban cars, Indiana in the early twentieth century was the birthplace of a new and extraordinarily useful and significant alloy known as Stellite. This metal, a combination of cobalt, chromium, and tungsten, was the product of years of metallurgical investigation by Elwood Haynes. He was looking for a nontarnishing metal suitable for tableware; but Stellite, while it is noncorrosive, is also so hard and both heat- and wear-resistant that it is not feasible for cutlery use. Instead, it was used initially as a tool metal, as a metal to cut other metals, and it virtually revolutionized the machine tool industry in the 1910s and 1920s. In the meantime Haynes persisted in his search for a nontarnishing cutlery alloy, and he discovered stainless steel in 1912, a few months before an English metallurgist made a similar discovery in Sheffield.

During the early part of the twentieth century, the Progressive era in American political history, Indiana was not particularly progressive. In Governor Thomas R. Marshall's phrase, he himself was a "Progressive with the brakes on," and perhaps that description applies to the state as a whole. The closest Indiana came to a Progressive governor was J. Frank Hanly, a Republican and a reformer whose lifelong advocacy of temperance eventually led him to abandon the Republican for the Prohibition party, under whose banner he ran for president in 1916. In spite of his long political career, Hanly remains a controversial and still largely unknown man, but his public service provides insight into state politics during the Progressive era.

Another feature of this era was the succession of state centennials in the Midwest, from Ohio's in 1903 through Missouri's in 1921. Indiana's celebration was marked by a profusion of activities, particularly historical pageants written for the occasion in practically every county and the appearance of a number of special centennial publications. But the most significant and appropriate state action was the establishment of a state park system. Stemming largely from the work of Richard Lieber, who served as the first head of the state park system, the Indiana state parks became some of the most outstanding in the nation.

More than parks, politics, and new products characterized Indiana in the early twentieth century. It remained not only an important agricultural state, with corn its number one crop, but it also developed important new methods of agricultural education. Purdue University's "corn school," either a short course taught to farmers brought to the campus in West Lafayette or a series of brief lectures and demonstrations presented from the back of railway cars in the farmers' own locality, introduced the latest techniques in ground preparation, hybridization, and fertilization to the agricultural community.

For a comprehensive view of Indiana in the early twentieth century, see Clifton J. Phillips, *Indiana in Transition, 1880–1920* (1968); see also the contemporaneous studies by George S. Cottman, *A Centennial History and Handbook of Indiana* (1915), and Julia Henderson Levering, *Historic Indiana* (1909). Aspects of the state's political development are revealed in three biographies: Claude Bowers, *The Life of John W. Kern* (1919); John Braeman, *Albert J. Beveridge: American Nationalist* (1971); and Ray Ginger, *The Bending Cross: A Biography of Eugene V. Debs* (1949). See also the essays on Kern, Debs, Fairbanks, and Marshall in Ralph D. Gray, ed., *Gentlemen from Indiana: National Party Candidates, 1836–1940* (1977); Cedric C. Cummins, *Indiana Public Opinion and the World War, 1914–1917* (1945); and, on urban life, James B. Lane, *"City of the Century": A History of Gary, Indiana* (1978).

Politics and Prohibition

THE RIDDLE OF GOVERNOR HANLY

Jan Shipps

J. Frank Hanly was elected as a Republican in 1904 to be Indiana's twenty-fifth governor. Born in humble circumstances in Illinois in 1863, he came to Indiana as a young man, where he taught school and did common labor while pursuing legal studies. Admitted to the bar in

1889, he entered politics at the same time, was elected to the Indiana General Assembly and then to Congress, serving a single term in Washington. Hanly was defeated for reelection in 1896 and in a try for the Republican nomination to the United States Senate in 1898; but he served as governor of Indiana from 1905 to 1909. Hanly was an enigmatic man, the victim of diametrically opposed interpretations concerning his leadership and character—largely, one suspects, because of his determined advocacy of prohibition legislation. Governor Hanly pushed a county-wide option law through a reluctant legislature in a special session late in 1908, which contributed to the Republican party loss in 1908. Hard feelings persisted when Hanly abandoned the Republican party for the Prohibition party, accepting that party's nomination for president in 1916 and continuing his moral crusade during the campaign and afterwards.

In an essay written for a collection on Indiana politicians who gained national recognition, Professor Jan Shipps has attempted to solve the puzzle of Governor Hanly's conflicting images: was he primarily a political opportunist, or was he in fact a committed moral reformer? By examining afresh the available evidence, including a previously overlooked but revealing scrapbook, Professor Shipps decides in favor of the latter view. But in evaluating his governorship during the Progressive period, she concludes that his too complete involvement with the temperance crusade lessened his effectiveness in dealing with other pressing concerns. Professor Shipps, a member of the departments of history and religious studies at Indiana University-Purdue University at Indianapolis, is a specialist in the history of American religions. Her major publication to date is Mormonism: The Rise of a New Religious Tradition *(1985).*

To recapitulate, if the opportunist is one whose social origins are not important, one who uses people and issues to achieve his ends, one whose principal motivation is self-interest, and if the moral reformer is a white Anglo-Saxon Protestant who either grew up in or moved into the middle class, who—under the impression that the perfection of society depends on it—is willing to use the power of the state to force acceptance of the moral code of his culture, does either pattern fit Governor Hanly?

A fairly elaborate protrait of Hanly as an opportunist can be constructed merely by noting that both of Indiana's leading Republicans, Charles W. Fairbanks and Albert J. Beveridge, assumed that Hanly's long-range goal was a seat in the United States Senate, and then accepting the idea that their assumption was correct. If the fact that Hanly desired a Senate seat is used as a point of departure, it is not difficult to marshal enough circumstantial evidence to support the notion that Hanly was more concerned to seize the main chance for himself than to bring about the demise of demon rum. The governor's puzzling behavior in forcing the passage of county option can be regarded as a conscious endeavor to ingratiate himself with the Indiana voters who, so he thought, were overwhelmingly opposed to the liquor traffic. His prodigious activities on behalf of the Anti-Saloon League in the years immediately following his governorship can be presented as essentially self-serving exertions designed to build enough popular support to get Hanly nominated and elected in

---

From Ralph D. Gray, ed., *Gentlemen from Indiana: National Party Candidates, 1836–1940* (1977), pp. 255–258, 263–268.

1914 when the senatorial choice would be up to the people rather than the state legislature. The organization of the Flying Squadron and its subsequent institutionalization can be construed as an attempt to construct a permanent power base from which to operate. And his acceptance of the Progressive party's gubernatorial nomination, his withdrawal from that race, and his acceptance of the Prohibitionists' presidential nomination—which, indeed, followed hard upon—can be used as the final conclusive testimony to prove that Hanly was first, last, and perhaps always, more opportunist than anything else.

On the other hand, the same circumstantial evidence can be used to present Hanly as a sincere, courageous, unselfish proponent of moral reform who was totally committed to the cause of prohibition. A good way to demonstrate this possibility is to accept at face value Hanly's claim that his decision to run for president on the Prohibition ticket represented the culmination of an evolutionary process, and then to go on and measure Hanly's story against the commitment model which was developed by Silvan S. Tompkins in connection with his study of the lives of four leading abolitionists. This theory describes deepening levels of commitment which occur in a series of identifiable stages across a reformer's adult life: the individual experiences an initial attraction to a cause, he begins to take risks for it, the risks stimulate abuse and suffering which lead to a sense of identification with other persons working for the same cause, a deeper and more profound commitment follows which, in turn, leads to the taking of even greater risks and subjection to more intense punishment, until a "point of no return" is reached and total devotion to the cause is the only possible course to be taken. In Hanly's case, the initial attraction of prohibition was present long before he became governor. The 1908 county option embroglio can be regarded as his first real risk taking for the temperance movement. The Republican party's casting their former governor from the inner circles of power can be seen as a peculiarly intense form of punishment. Hanly's developing friendships with Oliver Wayne Stewart and other Prohibition party leaders may well indicate that Hanly was identifying with those who were fighting against alcohol without hope of political "preferment." His decision to throw off his allegiance to the Anti-Saloon League's policy of working for temperance only through existing political parties can be construed as a signal that his commitment to prohibition had overridden his loyalty to the Republican party. His involvement in the Flying Squadron venture can be pictured as an emotionally satisfying experience of intimacy with those persons in the nation most completely bound up in the cause, an experience which led, inevitably, to his final break with his former political colleagues and his decision to cast his lot henceforth only with those who were willing to sacrifice everything in order to transform their vision of a saloonless nation into reality.

As useful as Tompkins's commitment theory is in extending an understanding of the governor's career, it cannot be used to solve the basic problem of missing data. That situation persists, and its seriousness is vividly illustrated by the realization that the two preceding very different pictures can be drawn from the sources by making different assumptions about what was happening, but without doing violence to the data. Given the absence of the sort of direct evidence concerning motivation which can be gleaned from diaries, letters, and other personal papers, it is important to ask at this point whether further rehearsal of the events of Hanly's life can serve a useful purpose if the inevitable result can only be an enigmatic portrait of the man. In some instances where there are simply no useful sources to work with, the answer to such a question might well be no, but here, fortunately, the answer can be yes since the private record, although it is so very thin that it can almost be said to be nonexistent, contains one key item, a gigantic scrapbook filled with Lincoln memorabilia which once belonged to Governor Hanly.

Because practically the entire Hanly collection in the Indiana State Library consists of large clipping books which were compiled by the governor's son-in-law, Harry O. Garman, this particular scrapbook is easily overlooked. Furthermore, as it contains absolutely nothing directly related to Hanly's life, the scrapbook might be dismissed as irrelevant, or at the very least, unimportant. But this is not the case. Of all the Hanly materials, this book which contains an astonishing collection of carefully—one might even say, lovingly—displayed pictures of and clippings about the Civil War president must be deemed the most private and most personal. If it is used as a clue to guide a close and sensitive reading of the published materials by and about the Indiana governor, it can diminish the inevitable ambiguity found in a published political record and illuminate the portrait of Hanly clearly enough to show that the picture of the governor as opportunist is distorted and that, while it is imperfect and overdrawn, the picture of a sincere, courageous, unselfish true believer in the temperance cause is a more accurate and realistic portrait of the man. . . .

Viewed from the legislative standpoint alone, the Hanly administration cannot be fully understood; it must be considered from the standpoint of leadership style and overall program emphasis. It must, moreover, be set inside the story of the Indiana political situation during those years, and it must not be kept isolated from the larger picture of what was happening in the United States between the turn of the century and the beginning of the First World War. Professor Wiebe describes the way historians have struggled to find a "proper angle of historical vision" from which to examine those crucial years. He concludes that the complex situation is best summarized in the concept of modernization; that an exceeding amount of backing and filling to the contrary notwithstanding, America moved out of the traditional into the modern age between 1900 and 1917. An adequate analysis should indicate the extent to which the Hanly administration participated in this process.

Noting the passage of legislation which created the Indiana Railroad Commission, placed the state's charitable and correctional institutions on a nonpartisan basis and expanded such services, called for the public monies to be deposited in public depositories, required state officers to make daily settlements with the state treasurer, established a uniform system of bookkeeping and examination of public accounts, demanded state examination of private banks, and so on, some contemporary political observers decided that Hanly's administration compared favorably with those of progressive governors like Robert M. La Follette of Wisconsin and Joseph W. Folk of Missouri. However, the balance sheet of measures passed which contributed to the state's modernization is not as impressive as it first seems if one recalls that Hanly was sent to the State House in the same election in which the popular Teddy Roosevelt was sent to the White House, and that the 1904 Republican victory in Indiana was so overwhelming that Hanly's party had a majority of more than three to one in the General Assembly. The Hanly administration's list of legislative accomplishments was actually quite a limited one, although the governor was not entirely to blame since the party was terribly divided. Nevertheless, Hanly's own conservative commitment, which put the brake on any headlong rush to establish any policy at odds with his laissez faire economic notions, was a contributing factor, as was his imperious and abrasive leadership style. Most of all, the governor's dedication to moral reform so outweighed every other possible consideration that critical issues were often neglected so that Hanly could conduct a crusade against vice.

Although the reports of speeches which Hanly gave throughout the country in the interim between the close of his governorship and his nomination for president strongly suggest that he came to see the liquor traffic as the fundamental moral problem facing the nation and saw its cessation as a panacea, this was not true during his tenure as chief executive. During these years vice assumed many shapes, and the governor's reform energies were not only employed against alcohol but energetically expended on efforts to stop state officers—and Republican ones at that—from stealing public money, to destroy gambling equipment and close the illegal but popular casinos at West Baden and French Lick, to end opportunities for placing wagers on the outcome of horse races, and even to prevent the growing of tobacco in the southern part of the state. As the laws were enforced indiscriminately, opposition developed in the General Assembly, but the crusade called for very little legislative cooperation since immorality was already illegal in Indiana. Opposition, in fact, simply seemed to strengthen the governor's determination to cleanse the Augean stables.

Opposition threw Hanly's reform activites into sharp relief, making him appear as the protagonist best able to protect the state from the frightening forces which seemed to confront Hoosierland as it moved into the modern world. He would turn the clock back and make the world comfortable and safe for Indiana's predominantly white, Anglo-Saxon, Protestant citizenry. Seen from that perspective, the path Hanly trod is not unlike the paths of certain southern demagogues whose appeal rested less on their accomplishments or programs than on their protectors' images, and whose power rested on their popularity with the people rather than on their influence with the politicians.

If the record of Hanly's administration ceased with the accounts of events which occurred before the 1908 Republican convention, the conclusion to this essay and the answer to the question posed at its beginning about motivation would have been that the available evidence is simply too ambiguous to provide much information. Fortunately, however, a full account exists of what the governor said to that convention, and in the text of that emotionally overpowering oration, further evidence of Hanly's identification with Lincoln appears. Speaking before a packed audience which included all the state's most influential Republicans and most of its press corps, many of whom had grown weary of his efforts at reform, Hanly reviewed the efforts the administration had made to deal with the problems confronting the state, and then concluded with an expression of his growing belief that the liquor traffic lay at the base of all of them: hypocrisy, commercialism, greed, avarice, corruption in politics and civic affairs, utter disregard of law, the malice in the hearts of men and grief of women. Summing up, he said of the liquor traffic:

> I hate it as virtue hates vice, as truth hates error, as righteousness hates sin, as justice hates wrong, as liberty hates tyranny, as freedom hates oppression. I hate it as Abraham Lincoln hated slavery, and as he sometimes saw in prophetic vision the end of slavery, and the coming of the time when the sun should shine and the rain should fall upon no slave in all the Republic, so I sometimes seem to see the end of this unholy traffic, the coming of the time when, if it does not wholly cease to be, it shall find no safe habitation anywhere beneath Old Glory's stainless stars.

Considered alone, this particular reference to Abraham Lincoln might appear merely as a rhetorical conceit, but if those words are treated as key words the way a detective—or a psychologist—would see them, and if the full record is once again reviewed, it becomes obvious that at some point during his struggle to rid the state of all the practices he considered immoral, Hanly came to see the situation as one which not only threatened Indiana, but one which endangered America's most favored nation status as God's promised land. As the presence of slavery had menaced the United States a half century before, so the liquor traffic seemed to threaten it in Hanly's day. Faced with the awesome responsibility of high office and the apparent disintegration of the world his forefathers made, the governor's relationship—the word is consciously chosen—with Lincoln changed. In a way more metaphysical than rational, Hanly seems to have come to regard Lincoln not only as someone to emulate, not even merely as a hero, but as a sort of principle around which the whole of the remainder of his life was organized.

After 1908 Hanly adopted a single-minded attitude toward ending the liquor traffic; that had to precede everything else. And the method of doing so had to change. His experience with local and county option in Indiana had shown him that liquor was portable as well as potable and that laws concerning liquor were rescindable as well as passable. He came to believe that even statewide prohibition efforts could do little more than split the United States asunder and leave the nation half dry and half wet. A constitutional amendment prohibiting the importation, manufacture, and sale of intoxicating beverages seemed to be the only answer, and so the ex-governor worked to that end through the Methodist Episcopal Church and the Anti-Saloon League. Then, recognizing that prohibition's own house was hopelessly divided, he was instrumental in the formation of the Flying Squadron, an organization which attempted to bring unity to the movement, one "Born in prayer, as men knelt about a table in the center of a little room in Columbus, Ohio, a room that [was] sacred because Abraham Lincoln spent a night in it." He established the *National Enquirer* in order to hasten the coming of a time "when to have owned brewery stock will be as shameful as to have held slaves." He gave up the possibility of political preferment in the nation's major political parties, and, although his acceptance speech made it obvious that he entered the race with no illusions of success, he decided to run for president in 1916 because he had come to believe that the Prohibitionists could, if elected, render the nation a service "unmatched since the days of Abraham Lincoln and the abolition of human slavery," by making America free from the evil of alcohol.

Rather than crediting the exertions of Hanly and the Prohibitionists, scholars generally conclude that the activities of the Anti-Saloon League working through the major parties plus the need to conserve grain during World War I were responsible for the passage of the Eighteenth Amendment which prohibited the manufacture, sale, and transportation of intoxicating liquors within the jurisdiction of the United States. If Hanly could not claim direct responsibility for making America a saloonless nation, he was nevertheless presented with an opportunity to keep the vision alive, and he rose to the occasion with dignity, honor, and intelligence. The addition of the amendment to the constitution had been made subject to its ratification within seven years by the legislatures of the several states. This process had been such a speedy one that the amendment was declared ratified by the necessary proportion of states less than thirteen months after it had been proposed by Congress. However, since at least thirteen states had referendum provisions in their constitutions, it appeared that enough state ratifications might be rescinded to make the amendment inoperative. When the opponents of the amendment, with careful attention to all legalities, petitioned for a referendum in Ohio, one was held and the state's ratification was invalidated. Since Ohio's ratification had been tallied in the counting which had placed the amendment in the Constitution, an effort was made to use the outcome of the Ohio referendum as the basis for ending prohibition. Appealed through the state and federal court systems, the case reached the United States Supreme Court where the temperance side of the issue was argued so effectively by Governor Hanly that the court held that a state legislature's ratification of a constitutional amendment could not be invalidated by referendum. The danger to prohibition was turned back, and the nation's "noble experiment" could proceed without legal hindrance.

More substantial obstacles stood in prohibition's way, of course, but Hanly, mercifully perhaps, did not live to see his vision besmirched by flappers, G-men, and bathtub gin. He was killed in an automobile accident on August 1, 1920, before the fundamental incompatibility between sumptuary legislation and a democratic society became evident. As was his beloved hero, Hanly was cut down in the first flush of triumph when victory seemed assured and when the cause to which he had committed himself, sacrificing his career if not his life, still seemed worthwhile. That his cause was as anachronistic as Lincoln's was prescient must not completely denigrate the governor's achievement for—as incomplete as the record is—it nevertheless reveals that, as certainly as was Lincoln, J. Frank Hanly was engaged in what he perceived to be the ongoing struggle to transfigure America and make it fulfill its destiny as the last best hope of earth, God's Promised Land.

Roads and Rails

FARMERS, POSTMEN, AND THE GOOD ROADS MOVEMENT

Wayne E. Fuller

Nineteenth-century America traveled over dirt roads, with occasional stretches of gravel-topped turnpikes or highways. These roads were used for local purposes, for infrequent—perhaps weekly—farm-to-town movements. Most intercity travel was done on the railroads. Rail mileage in America increased from 192,000 in 1900 to approximately 260,000 in 1916, the peak year, which was also the year of the Federal Highway Act and the beginnings of concrete-surfaced highway construction financed by a gasoline tax. Long years of agitation by a jostled and bruised citizenry had preceded the enactment of this legislation; and several important elements were influential in the "Good Roads Movement," which was organized in the 1890s. Although many people assume that the coming of the automobile, also in the 1890s, was responsible for the movement, two other factors, the bicycle craze of the late nineteenth century and the coming of rural free delivery in the early years of the twentieth century, were responsible for initiating the demand for improved, hard-surface roads. Much to the chagrin of the farmers, however, who were seeking all-weather routes to town for themselves, their mailmen, and their produce, the automobile lobby altered the government's first efforts in highway construction. Instead of building a network of farm-to-city roads to aid primarily the agricultural community, the major thrust was to build an intercity system which was of only incidental utility to farmers.

In the selection below Wayne E. Fuller, professor of history at the University of Texas at El Paso, describes the role of the RFD, the rural free delivery of mail, in fostering the Good Roads Movement. His book, more than a history of one branch of the postal service, is also a delightful account of rural America's transition from one-room schoolhouses, dusty or muddy roads, and horse-and-buggy travel to the modern world of automobiles, tractors, superhighways, and air-conditioned consolidated public schools. For additional information on the Good Roads Movement, see John B. Rae, The American Automobile: A Brief History *(1965) and Christy Borth,* Mankind on the Move: The Story of Highways *(1969). Indiana state geologist W. S. Blatchley published a lengthy report on Indiana's roads and its road-building needs in the* Thirtieth Annual Report *of the Indiana Department of Geology and Natural Resources (1905); see also David R. Wrone's account of early twentieth-century road improvements in a neighboring state, "Illinois Pulls out of the Mud,"* Journal of the Illinois State Historical Society, *LVIII (Spring 1965), 54–76.*

From *RFD: The Changing Face of Rural America* (1964), pp. 177–183, 189–192, 194–196.

Good road enthusiasts loved to tell about the man who reached to pick up a man's hat from the middle of a farmer's mud-soaked road and was surprised to find a head of hair beneath it. "Hold on, boss," said a voice, "don't take my hat; I've got a powerful fine mule down here somewhere if I can ever find him."

Archer Butler Hulbert, *et al.*, *The Future of Road-Making in America (Historical Highways of America,* XV [Cleveland, 1905]), 97.

The average American farmer in 1900 had few material possessions more valuable to him than the road that ran past his farm and on into his marketplace. Over this road flowed the commerce of the countryside. The cotton that would one day clothe the shopgirl in London began the first leg of its journey along this road; so did the livestock, corn, and wheat destined to feed the American nation and a large part of the world as well. Here passed the farmer's children on their way to school, the farmer and his wife to Grange, and the entire family on its way to church. And finally over this road came the rural mailman bouncing along in his buggy to bring the daily mail to the farmer and keep him in touch with the world beyond his neighborhood.

As important as this road was to the American farmer, one might have expected to find it reasonably smooth, possibly graveled, and certainly passable all year round. But the average farmer's road was almost none of these things, and a stranger visiting rural America at the century's beginning could never have accurately judged the road's importance from its appearance. As late as 1904 only 151,664 of the nation's 2,151,000 miles of roadways had been improved with gravel, shell, oil, or some other substance. The rest, nearly 2,000,000 miles of them, were dirt; rough, rutted, often impassable, these were the farmers' farm-to-market roads.

Country roads at the turn of the century were largely products of expediency. Born of necessity, they had been established with a minimum of effort and with no more planning than it took to figure the quickest route from farm to town. Skirting the banks of rivers and streams, following the floors of valleys, and going directly over mountain barriers in accordance with the rule that a straight line is the shortest distance between two points, their course had often been determined by prominent topographical features. Or else they had been built over old Indian trails which in turn had followed paths first made by animals.

Even where the government had surveyed the land and laid it out in neat square blocks, the roads were not immediately strung straight along section lines as they were later to be throughout much of the nation. Herbert Quick, that sharp observer of the scenes of his childhood in Iowa, told how the change came about. "In the beginning," he wrote, "the landscape was a glorious undulating sea of waving prairie grass, on which floated here and there a quadrangular raft of tillage. The roads were wagon tracks running diagonally from the village to the farms, and in main roads from town to town; but these were gradually crowded by tillage from their antigodlin courses to their present places on the section lines, all running north and south or east and west."

Established haphazardly, the farmers' roads were maintained in the same fashion. In nineteenth-century America their upkeep was the sole responsibility of the local government, which meant in practice that the farmers were almost entirely responsible for their own roads. True, the counties usually levied a road tax, but very little money was ever accumulated by this tax. Traditionally farmers paid the tax by working on their roads so many days a year. They might work at this as many as ten days each year, but however long they worked, it was never long enough for them, with their antiquated methods of road repair, to do much more than rearrange the dirt.

How the system worked was once described by a man with practical experience. "The first time I ever worked on the road I was the overseer," he wrote in 1902, "and my section was some 3¼ miles in length. After beating about in the usual fashion among the hills and mountains for two or three days 'warning out' my hands, the hour set for beginning work came, but the hands did not. By and by, however, they began straggling in, evidently expecting to make a short job of it. . . . The road had been 'scratched' once in the previous eighteen months, not worked at all, and was of course in desperate condition. By 11 o'clock most of the hands had come, each bringing some tool (so-called). What a conglomeration it was! Old dull axes, worn out shovels, hoes and mattocks—nothing fit to work with."

But even had they brought better tools, it would probably have made little difference, for the farmers in 1900 were nearly as innocent of good road-building techniques as their grandfathers had been. Their usual practice was to scrape the dirt in the center of the road, smooth it over with a drag or rake and let it go at that. If they knew how to grade and crown a road so that water would drain off instead of in, they rarely did so. Nor had they in many places even developed the idea of drainage ditches at the sides of the road. Culverts to carry off the water from low places were a novelty, of course, and so too were bridges in some localities. Even such a simple task as removing the weeds and brush along the roadside in the autumn to prevent snowdrifts in winter was neglected. And to change a road, to abandon part of it and build another to make it straighter or the grade smoother was unthinkable. The road had always been where it was, and there it must remain.

The net effect of the farmers' road-building efforts by 1900 had been to produce roads that served the farmers poorly in summer and left them stranded in winter. It was once estimated that in some areas as many as 27 tons of water fell each year on one mile of an ordinary road three rods wide, and when this happened to country roads improperly graded and unequipped with drainage ditches, rural America was absolutely mud-bound. As one rural postal agent surveying Macoupin County, Illinois, in the early 1900's put it, the roads at such times were "entirely out of the power of the road commissioners to remedy, and only an appeal to the Almighty can ameliorate their condition."

With no place to go, the rain and melting snow stood in puddles in the roads or saturated the soil creating marshes of mud that seemed utterly bottomless. Wagon wheels rolling over the roads at such times cut deep into the mud trying to reach bottom. Huge ruts were formed, sometimes deeper on one side than the other, so that a wagon moving through leaned heavily to one side. After a time the narrow ruts could be followed in comparative safety, but a head-on meeting with another wagon meant trouble. One wagon must leave the well-worn tracks and cut new ones. This was done only at the risk of overturning or becoming so deeply mired it was more than one team of horses could do to move the wagon.

The cost of poor country roads to the farmers was enormous. Farm spokesmen used to say in the days before World War I that a bushel of wheat could be hauled from New York to Liverpool for 1.6 cents less than it cost to haul it over 9.4 miles of a dirt road. In 1912, according to one estimate, it cost the American farmer 23 cents a ton mile to transport his harvest to market while in England it cost only 11 cents a ton mile, 10 cents in Germany, and in France 7 cents. Besides this, farmers were compelled to take their crops to market shortly after harvest when markets were glutted and prices lowest. If they waited for prices to rise, bad weather was likely to have made their roads barriers instead of boulevards. "The Iowa farmer," ran a little jingle, "cannot haul to market when the market is high; he must haul to market when the roads are dry."

But poor country roads meant poor country schools, poor churches, poor community relationships, and isolated farmers as well as financial losses. The one-room schoolhouse so common to rural America could never become a larger consolidated school as long as roads made it impossible for farm children to travel greater distances to school. Nor could farmers participate in community affairs when the roads were so bad they could scarcely leave their farms except by foot or horseback. Rather than risk their horses, buggies, and tempers on their soggy winter roads, farm families stayed away from church, neglected their neighbors, and attended but few of their community's social functions. Grandmother Brown, recalling her experiences in pioneer Iowa, remembered that though her family lived only five miles from Denmark, they could go to church there only once in a great while because the task of pulling a wagon through the muddy roads was too much for the horses who needed their rest on Sunday just as the farm family did. It was exactly this situation Grangers had in mind in 1906 when they said "Bad roads spell ISOLATION for the American farmer in giant letters which reach across the continent from ocean to ocean."

In spite of all this, the American farmers had not been nearly so concerned about their poor country roads through the years as they had been about the nation's railroads. If they were able to get their harvest to market before bad weather set in, this was all they asked. They were resigned to being isolated on their farms through the winter and spring, partly because this was the way things had always been but more because when they looked at those ten-mile strips of mud and water separating them from their marketplace and euphemistically called "roads," no salvation from their plight seemed possible.

Other people, however, besides the farmers were interested in good roads, and in 1892 a group of men, spurred on perhaps by the complaints of the bicyclists who were just then discovering the nation's poor roads and by railroad officials concerned with the high cost of moving the harvest from the farm to the railroad, organized the National League for Good Roads. The next year they prevailed upon Congress to establish the Office of Public Road Inquiry within the Department of Agriculture and endow it with an appropriation of $10,000. This was the beginning of the modern good roads movement.

The work of the Office of Public Road Inquiry was largely educational. It published a number of circulars and bulletins on good road-building techniques, and in conjunction with a private organization, the National Good Roads Association, it sponsored the good road trains that toured the nation from Buffalo to Birmingham in the early 1900's and took the latest road-building procedures directly to the farmers and other interested road-builders.

But circulars, bulletins, and good road trains built no roads. To get the farmers to work on their roads took something more than road-building demonstrations and speeches, and in the end it was not so much the work of the Office of Public Road Inquiry that induced farmers to repair their roads and mend their bridges in the early days of the new century as it was rural free delivery of mail.

The first indication that rural delivery would beget good roads came in 1899 when the Post Office Department declared that no rural routes would be established where roads were not usable the year around. True, this regulation was leniently interpreted when the RFD was young, and many a route was laid across roads fit only for mud turtles, but the regulation was still no idle threat. Literally hundreds of rural route petitions were rejected because of poor roads, and when they were, disappointed farmers came face to face with a practical, concrete illustration of the cost of poor roads for the first time in their lives.

Many of them, particularly in the South, objected indignantly against being denied rural delivery because of poor roads, and so did their congressmen. But it was so obviously impossible to have good service over roads sometimes impassable, that even hardheaded farmers could see the point. And when they realized the Department meant business, they began working their roads as they never had been worked before.

The rural agents, laying out rural routes in those years when Theodore Roosevelt was in the White House and progress was a byword, noticed the phenomenon and mentioned it in their reports to the Department. Roads that had received no more attention in the past than some farmer's hearty curse, were now being drained, dragged, and crowned in a manner virtually unheard of a short time before. Bridges were built and culverts laid. Even the weeds and trash were removed from the roadsides.

In the Midwest the farmers were helped immeasurably by the timely appearance of the King road drag. This simple device, popularized by a Missouri farmer named D. Ward King, was nothing more than a split log, one half fastened solidly about three feet ahead of the other. But if it were pulled over a muddy road especially after a rain, it smoothed the road and rounded it toward the center in such a way as to cause it to drain more easily. When the road dried it became quite hard, and farmers learned that a fairly decent road could be made if the dragging process were repeated several times. Besides, it was so cheap every farmer could have one, and so simple almost any farm boy could operate it. In 1906 King showed his drag to a group of farmers at Wellesville, Kansas, and within a week as many as 100 drags were reported within a radius of eight miles of the town and all but two miles of a twenty-five-mile rural mail route out of the town had been dragged. . . .

Of course, the RFD was only one of the pressures inducing the states to write good road laws in this period, and whether it was more influential than the Office of Public Roads, the good road associations springing up like sunflowers on a Kansas prairie, or even the rise of the automobile, no one can say. Its contribution was, at least, important. Nothing else brought the sense of urgency to the good roads movement that rural delivery did. When the Post Office Department withheld rural routes from farmers whose roads were poor, state legislatures were confronted, as President

Cleveland would have said, with a fact not a theory, and compelled to write good road laws they might otherwise have preferred merely to discuss.

Anyone wise in the American way of doing things could have guessed that once the states had begun to help build roads, it would be but a matter of time before the national government would also be asked to help. Indeed, the good road advocates were already waging a campaign for national aid while the states were still in the process of writing their road laws. But here the good road[s] movement floundered for more than a decade, blocked by the theory that such aid was unconstitutional.

This theory went back at least as far as 1817 when President James Madison vetoed John C. Calhoun's Bonus Bill on the grounds that its provision to use national funds to build roads within the states was a power not delegated to Congress. Subsequently, President James Monroe and Andrew Jackson both vetoed similar bills for nearly similar reasons; and with the Democrats in control of the government most of the time up to the Civil War and Southerners increasingly touchy about states' rights, the idea that the national government should not help states with their internal improvements, as roads were then spoken of, became firmly fixed. In fact, the Democratic party implanted this idea in their political platform in 1840 and kept it there right up to the Civil War.

After the Civil War this question was almost forgotten—perhaps because people came to believe railroads would take care of the transportation problem—until 1893 when the government was asked to appropriate $10,000 for the Office of Public Road Inquiry. What followed this request in the House of Representatives revealed the deep-seated, pre-Civil War attitudes:

CONGRESSMAN C. B. KILGORE (Texas): "Is not the purpose of that proposition to open a way to Federal supervision over dirt roads?"

CONGRESSMAN WILLIAM HATCH (Missouri): "It is not; and there is not a member on the Committee who would entertain that proposition for a moment."

That seemed to settle the matter, and for another seven years almost nothing was said about national aid for local roads beyond the piddling appropriations made each year for the Office of Public Road Inquiry.

Then, early in the new century, attitudes changed, and people began talking about national aid for local roads as if they had never been afraid to mention it before. Roy Stone, director of the Office of Public Road Inquiry, had noticed the change by 1903. In 1892, he declared, "we dared not whisper, 'National aid to road building' save in secret: now we can shout it on all the highways and byways."

What had happened in those eleven years to produce this change? The answer was clear: in 1892 there had been no rural delivery; in 1903 there was. As early as 1901 good road zealots, seeing that the RFD provided an argument for circumventing the Constitution, had latched on to it and were playing it for all it was worth. The Constitution, said they, gave Congress the power to establish post offices and post roads; the government was already building and maintaining post offices, so obviously "establish" meant "build and maintain"; hence, the government had the right to build and maintain post roads as well as post offices, and since every country road used by the RFD was a post road, the government had the right to build and maintain country roads. It was that easy to demolish, at least by argument, a precedent more than three quarters of a century old.

This was the beginning. And for fourteen years a steady stream of bills with national aid for state roads their object, poured through congressional hoppers. Some were bills to improve rural route roads only; and some, like the one Tennessee's Walter Brownlow first proposed in 1902, were broader in scope. But always rural delivery remained the heart of the argument for national aid, and one wonders how federal support for roads would ever have been won had there been no RFD. Like Aladdin's lamp, the good road people found that the RFD could be rubbed again and again, and the genie would always produce some good reason why the national government should help finance local road improvement.

The twentieth century had no more than reached its first birthday, when the nation heard that because of rural free delivery it was the national government's duty as well as its constitutional right to help the states with their roads, and this made so much sense that even a man like Alabama's Colonel J. M. Faulkner, who had fought for states' rights in the 1860's, saw the light. "Though . . . I am a strict constructionist of the constitution of the United States," said he, "still wherever it is clear that a duty is of a public nature, I am strongly in favor of having that duty performed by the Government. Now, it is a fact . . . that good roads and rural mail delivery go hand in hand. We cannot have rural mail delivery without having good roads, and, believing that we are entitled to both . . . , I believe that we should leave nothing undone to secure these as rights which belong to the people."

Just how much influence automobile interests had had in the good roads movement up to this time is not easy to determine. Because the automobile and the good roads movement appeared on the American scene about the same time, it has been easy to assume the former inspired the latter. The trouble with this easy assumption is that it puts the horseless carriage before the horse, so to speak. The good roads movement had already begun by the time Charles Duryea drove the first American gasoline automobile on its maiden run in 1893, and people were already talking about national aid for roads in 1901 when there were only about 15,000 automobiles registered in the whole country.

But in the beginning the good roads movement was essentially agrarian and had nothing to do with automobiles. The very fact that the Office of Public Road Inquiry, later called the Office of Public Roads, was attached to the Department of Agriculture, indicates the nature of the movement. True, the farmers had neglected their roads shamefully until the 1890's, but after the inauguration of the RFD they had become the heart and soul of the good roads movement. And why not? Good roads meant not only free delivery of their mail, but cheaper transportation of their crops from farm-to-market, better churches and schools, and an end to isolation, and it was only logical that they should have taken the lead in the fight to win government aid for road building. Their support of the Shackleford bill was also logical, for it provided for the upkeep of the very kind of roads the farmers were interested in.

The automobile people, however, who had up to this time played no conspicuous part in the campaign for national aid, now stepped in to wreck the farmers' bill. It developed that they had no particular interest in improving farm-to-market roads. If federal money was to be spent on roads, they wanted it spent on hard-surfaced, interstate, and transcontinental highways that stretched from coast to coast so that Americans might "see America first." They did not want the money wasted, as they said, on roads that began "nowhere and ended nowhere."

Merciless in their attack, they dubbed the supporters of the Shackleford bill "Knights of the dirt roads," and the *Washington Times* fulminated against following "the rural mail carriers . . . to erect a road system without any plan nor purpose." And by the time the bill reached the Senate, the American Automobile Association had written senators urging them to vote against the bill.

The Senate did reject the measure perhaps because of the American Automobile Association, as some of its members claimed. But the bill had no friend in the White House, and this must have been a factor in its defeat. As a matter of fact, President Taft was not only opposed to this bill, he was opposed to the principle of government aid for roads, and even the approaching election of 1912 was not enough to make him change his mind. Invited to attend a good road[s] convention in the autumn of that year, Taft gave his answer to his private secretary. "I am not going to the Good Roads Convention," he wrote, "for the reason that I would make more enemies if I went than if I stayed away because I would have to tell the truth. I do not believe in involving the Federal treasury in a weight of obligation to build roads that the States ought to build."

And that was that. The best Congress could do that year was to appropriate $500,000 to be used jointly by the Post Office Department and the Department of Agriculture to improve certain rural route roads and to study the economic effects of such improvement. Of course this was only a stopgap measure passed to relieve pressure and stall for time while the problem was studied, but it turned out to be important. It established the principle, later called dollar matching, of forcing the states to share with the national government the expense of road repair, and proved that cooperation between the national government and any unit of government below the state level would not work. Both these bits of experience proved valuable when Congress finally got around to working out its final road-building bill.

INDIANA'S INTERURBAN SYSTEM

Jerry Marlette

There was once, according to William D. Middleton, an interurban railroad "wrapped around nearly every Indiana county courthouse"[1]—an exaggerated statement, to be sure, but not by much. By 1920, with almost every major city in the state touched by at least one interurban line, the state boasted one of the finest interurban systems in the country. Indianapolis, with a huge interurban station, a barn-like structure covering nine tracks over which 400 cars a day entered the city, was at the center of the "largest peripheral interurban network in the United

1. *The Interurban Era* (1961), p. 140.

States."[2] *More than 2,400 miles of main track electric railway lines crisscrossed the state, providing fast and convenient service at a reasonable price. Much intercity travel was by "the cars" long into the automobile era; but eventually the competition of that era proved fatal. Some of the larger interurban companies survived the difficult decade of the 1920s only to collapse during the Depression of the next decade; and soon the interurbans, with one exception, were little more than a memory. In the northwestern part of the state the South Shore Line connecting South Bend, Michigan City, Gary, and Hammond with Chicago has survived into the 1990s and continues to serve a loyal commuting public.*

Jerry Marlette, an electric railway aficionado from Indianapolis, compiled a history of the Indiana lines in 1959. The passages from his book reprinted below provide a rapid overview of the construction, operation, and eventual decline of the interurbans. As in all forms of travel, accidents occasionally occurred on the interurbans and brought forth demands for new safety legislation. The worst accident record was compiled in 1910, when five head-on collisions occurred. In 1911 the Indiana General Assembly enacted a number of laws governing interurban operations, and in 1913 the Public Service Commission, with broad powers over electric railway services and rates as well as other forms of transportation and public utilities, was established. For additional information on the interurbans, see William D. Middleton's two books, The Interurban Era *(1961) and* South Shore: The Last Interurban *(1970); see also George W. Hilton and John F. Due,* The Electric Interurban Railways in America *(1960), and a second book by Marlette,* Interstate: A History of Interstate Public Service Rail Operations *(1990).*

The first day of the new century was indeed a big one in Indianapolis; the first interurban car entered the capital city. The Indianapolis, Greenwood, and Franklin Railroad ran its first car from the Greenwood shops, 12 miles south of Indianapolis, although the handrails had to be removed and the passengers shifted to the outside in order for the car to squeeze by the overhead wire poles, which were at that time located in the center of the streets. The car also had to jump the Belt Railroad rails, as the crossing had not yet been put in. However, these were minor matters, and the citizens of Indianapolis rejoiced at this sign of progress. Regular service between Indianapolis and Greenwood began ten days later.

Other lines opened in 1900 were those between Indianapolis and Greenfield, LaPorte and Michigan City, Terre Haute and Brazil, and Aurora and Cincinnati (Ohio), while local service was expanded in Marion by the entry of another company upon the local scene. The end of 1900 found 678 miles of electric lines operating 671 motor and 308 trail cars, while 7 miles of mule line operated 13 cars.

Expansion continued at a rapid rate through the early years of the new century, with a hundred miles being built on paper to every one laid on the ground. Probably in no other state in the country did the interurban strike the popular fancy with such force as it did in Indiana. While the state saw nearly two hundred companies achieve operating status, another two hundred and fifty plus filed papers of incorporation, with as many more organized and funds solicited but not incorporated. To these must be added unknown hundreds which never got beyond the planning stage. Of course, planning traction empires was a popular luncheon subject and parlor game for a number of years, but many of these unfinished dreams were the plans of hard-

---

2. Clifton J. Phillips, *Indiana in Transition, 1880–1920* (1968), p. 256.

From *Electric Railroads of Indiana* (1959), pp. 6-20.

headed businessmen which did not pass the paper stage for some mighty good reasons, among which were the depression of 1893, the business recessions of 1907 and 1913, and the first World War. . . .

Another great obstacle was that of securing franchises. Many times a company would be able to obtain franchises and rights-of-way for all but a small strip of land, and would then be stymied either by high prices or city objections. In some cases court relief was obtained, some land was donated by persons and towns anxious for traction service, while in others some high strategy was necessary. Such was the case when the Indiana Northern Traction Company was stopped by a cemetery south of Wabash: fearing an injunction, the company built through and beyond the cemetery between sunset one evening and sunrise the next morning. Although the city authorities were rather unhappy and threatened to force removal of the track, nothing was ever done, and the company completed its line without further incident. At other times and places, traction companies were forced to resurvey their proposed lines in order to meet demands of the various city councils that they enter cities only upon certain streets.

The most violent of these incidents ended in a free-for-all in Crawfordsville. The Indianapolis and Northwestern Traction Company, after being granted a franchise in that city and depositing the necessary bond, had its franchises revoked by the city council. Nevertheless, the company moved laborers and materials into town and prepared to lay track on Main Street. The city council ordered out the police and fire departments, and they formed battle lines just south of the Court House. When the first pick hit the pavement, the firemen turned on their water, and the fun began! The company laborers used pick handles and bricks, the firemen their hose, and the police their nightsticks. After some of the company men started to puncture the fire hose with their picks, the police arrested several of them and the city filed a suit of contempt against the company. However, over a thousand Crawfordsville citizens petitioned against the suit, and it was dismissed, allowing the company to go ahead with its work unmolested, although it had to fight a couple of other court battles before it finally secured all necessary franchises. . . .

One of the greatest steps forward was the opening of the Indianapolis Traction Terminal on September 12, 1904. Besides combining all lines in one station, allowing easier transfer between cars, the Terminal provided much needed office space for the various lines, along with express and baggage offices, ticket counters, etc. It also was a great help to the city cars in Indianapolis. Before the giant train shed was available the interurbans loaded and unloaded at various points on the city streets, thereby causing many delays to the local service. Another boon to the weary traveler was the opening of the Indianapolis Joint Ticket Office, the first interurban joint agency in the country, on July 1, 1905.

Frequency of service was constantly increasing, and rose from less than 100 trains per day in and out of Indianapolis in 1902 to nearly 400 per day in 1910. Granted, some suburban terminals in larger cities had more trains per day than did Indianapolis, but it should be remembered that the great majority of the trains serving Indianapolis made runs of 40 miles or more, with some running as high as 170 miles in length. All types of service were offered, from the small lightweight local cars to the big limiteds with their smoking and baggage compartments, and the all-chair parlor cars. The first interurban sleeper service in the country was offered on September 15, 1903, when a Holland Palace Car operated over the four lines connecting Indianapolis and Columbus, Ohio. Trains were exceedingly popular, being offered both locally by the individual lines and, in connection with steam roads, to points as far away as Niagara Falls.

One of the biggest headaches of the interurban lines was that of express and freight service. At first, the companies did not want to handle it, feeling that the steam roads, with their already complete facilities, were more fully equipped to handle this type of business. However, the interurbans more or less backed into hauling freight; since the baggage compartments for passengers' luggage were not always filled, they started carrying small express shipments. This led to freight, in small quantities, and then to larger amounts requiring special equipment. Since the average interurban line was too short to profitably handle any long-haul, car-load shipments, and the steam roads were naturally reluctant to interchange with such competition, the interurbans were forced to rely for most of their freight income on less-than-car-load shipments which were more expensive to handle. Some of the larger companies began to work out interchange agreements among themselves, and, as interstate connections were completed, a healthy freight business began to develop. Freight revenue in 1910 accounted for some 7% of the roads' gross earnings. . . .

After the initial problems of construction and untried equipment, most of the lines were fairly free of any worries other than how to make a profit. Among the miscellaneous troubles was that of the Indianapolis and Eastern, which ignored a smallpox quarantine in Knightstown despite arrests and track blockades and almost lost its franchise as a result; complaints against frightening horses (a switch occurred when a Marion city car was hit by a runaway Marion Fire Department ladder truck, whose horses had bolted when the ladders were removed at a fire!); various squabbles over excursion rates and destinations; and a court order forcing the Winona Interurban Railway to offer Sunday service (the railroad was controlled by a church assembly and refused to run trains on Sunday until the court threatened loss of its franchise).

There were a number of accidents during the early days, and most of them were bad ones. Among the more serious were an Indiana Union Traction car rolling through Alexandria at 40 miles an hour with the brakes out, finally stopping after hitting the passenger station and burying 2 persons in the wreckage; a Union Traction Limited and a UT freight colliding at Ressler Crossing north of Tipton, killing 6 and injuring 12; and a Marion, Bluffton and Eastern collision just east of Marion which killed 6 and injured 60. The greatest disaster of all was the head-on collision north of Kingsland on the Fort Wayne and Wabash Valley, September 21, 1910. This wreck, which claimed 42 lives, was caused by a south-bound extra passing a siding while running ten minutes late, then meeting a northbound local (loaded with fair-going passengers) on a curve. The resulting damage claims forced the reorganization of the company.

Nature played a hand in the havoc, too. The Toledo and Chicago saw part of its newly constructed line between Auburn and Garrett sink 38 feet into a peat bog. The Cincinnati, Lawrenceburg and Aurora was probably the hardest hit of any interurban company in the country during the great Ohio River flood of 1913. When the flood had passed, the C L & A assessed its damages at over $145,000, and went into receivership shortly thereafter.

On July 1, 1914, interurban mileage in Indiana totaled 2318, of which 2137 was first main. Over this trackage were operated 1229 passenger, 363 freight, and 78 mail, baggage and express cars. Electric service was operated in 67 of the state's 92 counties. The only cities of more than 5,000 population not served by electric railways, either city or interurban, were Bedford, Bicknell, and Bloomington, all in the southern part of the state.

The Long Decline—World War I to World War II.

Although not immediately apparent, the coming of World War I was the beginning of the end for the electric railway industry. In itself, the war was not wholly to blame, although material shortages played a big part in the decision to abandon at least one line, and rising prices made several more increasingly unprofitable. Ironically, they were worth almost as much as scrap as in their full operating condition!

The basic troubles of the interurban in Indiana can be traced to two factors: they were designed at first as short haul lines; and they featured largely untried equipment. Of course, as the years went by both of these conditions were corrected. The shorter lines expanded or merged, and better equipment became available. By that time, however, more than one line had gotten in so deep financially that it never recovered, although the final reckoning might be deferred for years.

Probably the prime factor which led to many failures and subsequent reorganizations, consolidations, and receiverships was overcapitalization. As an example, the 62 mile Indianapolis, New Castle and Toledo initial capitalization was $9,000,000 ($4,500,000 in bonds and a like amount in stock), a rate of some $144,000 per mile. Needless to say, such a figure would require practically the entire year's income to merely pay the interest on the funded debt, leaving nothing to pay the operating expenses. Dividends? They were practically unheard of after the early years. As a result, stocks and bonds dropped drastically, and it became harder and harder to attract desperately needed new capital. The common stock of the Union Traction Company dropped from $24 per share in 1904 to $2 per share in 1922, and the preferred from $71 to $20, with bond prices in proportion. Of course, during reorganization, many of these companies dropped their capitalization to more realistic figures—the Indianapolis, New Castle and Toledo, for example, dropped to $2,200,000, or around $35,000 per mile.

While the companies were struggling with the financial structure, another and greater menace to their future entered the picture—the automobile. The post-war auto, after four years of accelerated development, was vastly improved over its pre-war ancestor, and found ready acceptance by the American public. The highway system was much better, too, with constant additions and improvements to the pre-war mileage. Along with the private automobile, with its greater freedom of movement and pride of possession, came two additional competitors—the motor bus and truck. While not too strong for several years after the war, by the mid-twenties they were firmly entrenched on the transportation scene, and caused the abandonment of several lines in Indiana. Some lines converted to buses and trucks themselves and continued operations for years. A few of them are still in service today (Indiana Railroad, Indianapolis and Southeastern, Evansville and Ohio Valley, and several city lines).

Other factors contributed to the decline. There was a lack of connections to permit long hauls (Indiana and Illinois, for instance, were never connected). Many roads were built alongside steam roads, which caused constant and bitter competition (the steam roads, being firmly entrenched before the interurbans came along, usually won out, except for short haul passenger service). Hasty promotions were undertaken in many areas which would never be able to support any kind of line and collapsed at the first rough going. The exhaustion of the natural gas supply in the Gas Belt meant the end of inexpensive fuel for power, and the delays caused by operation in dense city traffic, which also prohibited the use of more than three or four car freights, seriously hampered freight service.

In spite of these apparently insurmountable obstacles, most of the lines rolled right along until November, 1917. In that month two companies gave up: on the 3d, the Goshen, South Bend and Chicago (the first section of the Chicago-New York Air Line) achieved the dubious honor of being the first interurban line in Indiana to abandon service. It was followed shortly by the Bluffton, Geneva and Celina. In April, 1918, the second city line quit, the Madison Light and Railway abandoning local service in Madison on the 30th. The Lake James Railroad also abandoned its line after the summer season closed on October 15. This pattern continued for the next few years, with several of the smaller companies being reorganized or abandoned, and the larger ones abandoning unprofitable branches and city services.

The picture was not entirely gloomy, however. The larger companies, being still very much alive, inaugurated new services to attract business, and in many cases did very well. Working through the Central Electric Railway Association, which included practically all companies in its membership, the lines initiated new ticketing and baggage handling procedures, and introduced an immensely popular ticket called the "2,000 Penny Coupon Ticket." This book, which contained $20 worth of transportation although selling for $17.50, was honored by all members of the CERA, and was immediately acclaimed by commercial travelers, who up to that time had been faced with the problem of different rates and tickets when changing lines. With this book, the traveler simply handed the book to the conductor, who tore out the fare needed, and the ticketing was accomplished, saving much time and trouble for all concerned. Tickets were also sold in ten-day, twelve-ride form, and in monthly commutation books. . . .

Equipment was being constantly improved, too. The all-steel car was seen more and more, and special cars, such as parlor-diner (Interstate, 1923) and sleeper (Interstate, 1924) were put into service. Several of the smaller cities saw the erection of new stations, usually combination passenger and freight buildings. . . .

Accidents continued to claim many lives. Among the worst were a head-on collision between two motor and trailer trains at Alfont, just east of Fortville, on the Union Traction, which took a toll of 21 in the crash and ensuing fire; and a Honeybee (Indianapolis, New Castle and Eastern operated by Union Traction) car which hit a truck and trailer at 21st and Emerson Avenue in Indianapolis, killing 20 and injuring several more. The trailer, filled with Sahara Grotto members, was on its way to Fort Harrison (northeast of Indianapolis) when the car struck. The truck pulling the trailer was untouched, thereby probably saving another 20 or more from death. A major disaster was narrowly averted in Edinburg on the Interstate, when a Pennsylvania freight struck a trainload of 500 Mile Race fans returning to Louisville. Scores were shaken up, while a dozen were injured slightly.

With the prosperous years of the mid-twenties contributing enormously, the Hoosier interurban and city lines were making progress toward financial stability when Black Friday struck late in 1929. The effects of this day and its subsequent wave of financial failures were soon felt by the electric railways and their parent, the electric power industry. Early in 1930, the managements of the larger interurbans in Indiana took under consideration a proposal of Midland United Company (Samuel Insull's holding company) to consolidate all the principal lines into one giant traction empire.

Arrangements were quickly made, and on August 1, 1930, Indiana Railroad, the largest interurban company ever operated in the United States, began operation over the properties of Union Traction Company, Indiana Service Corporation, Interstate Public Service Company, and Northern Indiana Power Company. Prior to this consolidation of management, Union Traction abandoned 74 miles of unprofitable lines, and shortly afterward Indiana Railroad dropped 44 more and discontinued parlor-dining service. Also that fall, Terre Haute, Indianapolis and Eastern abandoned 188 miles of line.

Several more abandonments followed in early 1931, and then, on June 29, Indiana Railroad assumed operation of 214 miles of THI&E properties, giving it a grand total mileage of 956, by far the largest in the country. By the end of 1931, however, IRR abandoned 70 miles, and 205 more in 1932, in addition to discontinuing sleeper service between Indianapolis and Louisville. Other major abandonments in 1932 included Indianapolis to Connersville and Greensburg (107 miles), and Fort Wayne to Lima (65 miles).

Indiana Railroad was not thinking of quitting, however, as was shown by the placing in service, during 1931, of 35 deluxe, all-steel, high-speed coaches. These cars, of latest design and comfortably furnished, were assigned to limited service between Indianapolis and Louisville and Indianapolis and Fort Wayne. In 1935, 10 lightweight cars were purchased from Northern Indiana Railway, and, after some shifting around, were permanently assigned to Indianapolis-Fort Harrison and Muncie-New Castle runs. Railway Post Office service was inaugurated between Indianapolis and Peru and Fort Wayne and New Castle, using three former Indiana Service Corporation all-steel combination cars. Other changes were in converting all suitable steel cars except RPOs to one man operation in 1936, and a general revamping of power facilities.

After abandoning several other unprofitable lines and selling the local properties in the New Albany-Jeffersonville area, IRR again expanded by purchasing, for junk, the Dayton and Western Traction Company. Extensive rebuilding was undertaken in order to maintain limited service between Indianapolis and Dayton. However, in the 1937 recession, the IRR was brought to its knees, due mainly to labor troubles, when the line was hit by a six-week strike among its own employees, and the company never completely recovered from the blow. It was forced to abandon 150 miles of line, including the recently purchased Dayton and Western, and began to plan substitution of buses and trucks for the rail service. The first division to be so changed was the Indianapolis-Peru-Fort Wayne run, converted in September 1938.

Other companies around the state felt the pinch too. Several small abandonments took place during the early and mid-thirties. Then, immediately prior to World War II, most of the remaining lines gave up, including several routes of Gary Railways, and complete cessation of local service in Evansville, Vincennes, South Bend, Mishawaka, Anderson and Terre Haute occurred. Many of the routes in Indianapolis had also been converted from street car to trackless trolley by 1940. Only the South Shore, with its heavy suburban traffic, managed to show a profit, but even it went into bankruptcy before reorganization in 1938.

The cruelest blow of all was delivered by the Public Utility Holding Company Act of 1935, which, among other things, required holding companies to restrict their operations to a single integrated system and to "reasonably incidental or economically necessary activities." As interpreted by the Securities [and] Exchange Commission, this required the separation of power and railway operations. Although fought off for several years, the Supreme Court upheld the act. The beginning of the end for IRR was in sight, since Midland United naturally preferred to retain its more lucrative power service. Implementing this plan of separation, IRR abandoned the line from Seymour to Louisville and prepared to convert most of the remainder of the system to bus and truck operations.

In the face of rising costs and another war in Europe, this conversion was inevitable, and January, 1940, saw the end of operation between Indianapolis and Terre Haute. Then, in January, 1941, IRR ceased rail operations by abandoning the Indianapolis-Muncie-Fort Wayne and Muncie-New Castle lines, and turned the Indianapolis-Seymour line back to the Public Service Company of Indiana, its lessor, for operation under the terms of a 999 year lease between Interstate and Indianapolis, Columbus and Southern Traction executed in 1912. However, a collision in September, 1941, damaged most of the line's rolling stock, causing cessation of service. PSC bought out of its contract for $2,125,000, and the line was scrapped just a few weeks before the outbreak of World War II. Ironic—another few months of operation and this line, the first into Indianapolis and the last one out, might be in operation yet.

Inventions

STELLITE
"Not Steel but Its Master"

Ralph D. Gray

A less well-known but truly remarkable industrial achievement in Indiana during the early years of the twentieth century was the development of Stellite by Elwood Haynes. The non-

ferrous alloy, heat-resistant, corrosion-free, and incredibly hard, was used initially in the machine tool industry. It replaced high-speed steel as tool bit material in most severe service applications, both speeding up and cheapening the cost of manufacturing; and a number of other valuable uses were found for it as well. Haynes is best known as an automobile pioneer, having manufactured Haynes automobiles for thirty years. But his singular and most significant achievement in a lifetime full of accomplishment was the development of Stellite and related alloys over the course of a number of years and hundreds of experiments. The account below describes the long process involved in developing the metal, ascertaining its properties, obtaining patents, and embarking on its manufacture. For further details on the alloy company Haynes established in Kokomo in 1912, see Ralph D. Gray, Stellite: A History of the Haynes Stellite Company, 1912–1972 *(1974). A contemporaneous account of Haynes's life, corrected and approved by Haynes personally, is in Jacob Piatt Dunn,* Indiana and Indianans *(1919), III, 1215–1219.*

A newspaper reporter wrote of Elwood Haynes: "He is never happier than when shut off from the outside world in a laboratory, immersed in the mysteries of chemistry." Haynes's daughter agreed with this assessment: "Father hated business, deciding who should do what," she remarked in 1970, "he much preferred his research." Before 1905, however, his time for metallurgical research in improved laboratories was very limited. His occupations had required most of his energies for more than a decade after his graduation from Worcester Free Institute in 1881. Then, in the middle 1890s, when he settled into a somewhat routine job as manager of the Indiana Natural Gas and Oil Company's Kokomo plant, he had devoted his evenings and weekends to developing a horseless carriage. When this in turn led to the formation of a manufacturing company, Haynes had found little time for metallurgical research, even though Elmer Apperson took charge of manufacturing the Haynes-Apperson cars. Haynes had been needed to handle other aspects of the business, especially the promotional work and arranging for new financing as necessary. He also sought both mechanical and metallurgical improvements in the Haynes-Apperson automobiles. The seven automobile patents Haynes obtained, either singly or with others, indicate some of this mechanical work; he seemed equally proud of his metallurgical work, never failing to point out that he had introduced the use of aluminum in automobile engines in 1895 or that he had used nickel steel in the automobile built in 1896. Indeed, it appears that the need for alloy steels in the automobile industry prompted Haynes's return to the laboratory and led, at least indirectly, to his most significant metallurgical discovery. It was while Haynes was searching for a suitable alloy for use as the contact points on spark plugs that he discovered the alloys he patented under the name Stellite. The name derived from the Latin word for star, *stella*, which Haynes considered appropriate because of the bright, nontarnishing surface of his cobalt-based alloys.

Haynes's interest in metals was one of long standing. In his youth, fascinated by an older sister's college chemistry book, he had conducted a number of experiments using makeshift equipment, including a homemade furnace in which he melted

---

From *Alloys and Automobiles: The Life of Elwood Haynes* (1979), pp. 117–126.

whatever bits of scrap metal he could find. He had been able to continue and develop his interest in metallurgy in college; his senior thesis had been "The Effect of Tungsten upon Iron and Steel." In the course of this work he had made some of the first "high speed steel" in the United States, an alloy later patented by J. Maunsel White and Frederick W. Taylor that had important applications in the machine tool industry. There was no connection between Haynes's work and that of White and Taylor—i.e., the two research efforts were done independently and had different goals—but their achievement indicates the potential significance of the work Haynes was doing on his own. He also began to investigate the influence of chromium on steel and steel alloys, a combination Haynes later discovered produces stainlessness; he had been prevented from exploring this field in Worcester because he had not included chromium in his original thesis proposal. His college research, limited initially to the influence of tungsten, nevertheless proved to be significant in Haynes's later metallurgical accomplishments.

The year's study at Johns Hopkins University in 1884–1885 had been an extremely important supplement to his previous work. His instructors, especially the outstanding chemist Ira Remsen, were eminent researchers as well as dedicated teachers. Haynes had learned new experimental techniques and laboratory procedures at Johns Hopkins; in later life he credited his Baltimore experiences with his eventual successes in metallurgy.

During the 1890s Haynes had conducted his metallurgical experiments in a small laboratory that the INGO Company had permitted him to build on the floor above the gas company office. He installed a small furnace there, operated by natural gas, in which he melted his ingredients in tiny crucibles—"about the size of a coffee cup," according to his daughter—and the alloy samples he produced there were sometimes quite tiny, making subsequent analysis difficult. He persevered in these experiments, usually conducted in the evenings after the children's regular bedtime story, and by the end of the decade he was obtaining very promising results. Eventually two companies would be established based upon his metallurgical discoveries of Stellite and stainless steel.

These were the tangible results of a search Haynes had undertaken tentatively as early as 1887 for a nontarnishable metal suitable for table cutlery. The family legend is that Haynes wanted to relieve his wife of the drudgery of polishing the silverware. In a biographical sketch approved by Haynes and published in 1919, Jacob P. Dunn reported that in 1887 Haynes began a series of metallurgical experiments in search of an alloy that "would resist the oxidizing influences of the atmosphere, and . . . take a good cutting edge." At first he tested various copper alloys but "after some years of trial" rejected them as unsuitable. He next worked with various rare metals, including tungsten, nickel, chromium, cobalt, molybdenum, and aluminum. Haynes made his fusions then in "small graphite crucibles, which were heated in a blast furnace of the Fletcher type, operated by natural gas." The first alloys that he produced in the late 1890s contained considerable amounts of carbon and silicon as impurities. But by 1898 he finally obtained a carbon-free alloy of nickel and chromium, having combined "the pure mixed oxides of the two metals with powdered aluminum, in a crucible lined with pure oxide of aluminum."

As Haynes reported it, when these ingredients were heated sufficiently "the reaction was so violent that most of the metal was thrown from the crucible." Only a "few small pellets" could be recovered. One suspects his family and business associates had reservations about these periodic explosions, but the experiments continued. The nickel chromium alloy possessed a "fine color," and when polished "exhibited a luster." Shortly afterwards Haynes also produced very small pellets of a cobalt-chromium alloy. This alloy, similar in appearance to the other, also was hard and could [not] be scratched by a file. It occurred to Haynes that the metal might be used for cutlery, but just at the point of significant discovery in 1901 Haynes was obliged to assume full-time management of his automobile business and consequently lost his laboratory at the gas company.

This hiatus lasted until September 1, 1905, when Haynes turned over the direction of his company to new managers. Then, for the first time since his graduate school days, he was free to engage in long periods of uninterrupted metallurgical research. The results were impressive.

He worked in a laboratory behind his house. There he repeated his previous experiments with nickel, chromium, and cobalt, hoping to find an alloy suitable for "electric contacts in the make-and-break spark mechanism" of his automobile. By then, he was able to produce his alloys in small bar castings, five or six inches long, either a quarter or a half inch square. Carefully analyzing and testing these bars, Haynes was able to acquire a fuller understanding of the "very tough and malleable" alloys he had produced. He shaped some of the bars into razor, pocketknife, and table knife blades, and found them to be free of corrosion after months of constant use. "One of these table knife blades has now been in use for more than two years in the kitchen," Haynes reported in 1910, "where it was used for all sorts of purposes, such as cutting bread, turning griddle cakes, peeling and paring vegetables, and for various other purposes such as are known to the culinary arts. After all this use and abuse, the knife shows not the slightest trace of tarnish, and has held its luster so well that when exposed to the sun it shows a reflection which dazzles the eyes."

Haynes attempted to modify the properties of his alloys by varying the composition percentages and adding other substances. He learned to make alloys of extreme hardness, including one which he formed into a small lathe tool. It showed cutting qualities comparable to that of high-speed steel and even surpassed this standard tool metal in light, rapid cuts when intense heat was generated. He emphasized in 1910 that he did not recommend this material as yet for lathe tools. Later, however, this became one of the most important early uses of Stellite, after Haynes had modified its composition through the addition of tungsten.

On April 25, 1907, after he felt sufficiently knowledgeable about their chemical and mechanical properties, Haynes applied for patents on two binary alloys. He engaged the Chicago firm of Poole and Brown, which had handled some of his previous automobile patents, to make the application. The allowance notice was dated November 7, and upon payment of the $20 fee for each one, the patents were issued on December 17, 1907—No. 873,745 covering the cobalt-chromium, No. 873,746 the nickel-chromium alloy.

The initial petition for the former combination described a "novel metal alloy" of high and durable luster and sufficient hardness to make it suitable as a substitute for mild tempered steel in manufacturing "edge tools, . . . as table and pocket cutlery, physicians' and dentists' instruments, or standards of weight, measures, etc. etc." The alloy would take an "extremely lustrous polish, rivaling silver in this respect," and would "resist oxidation and all forms of corrosive fumes commonly occurring in the atmosphere." Similarly, it showed "no tendency to tarnish when exposed to the atmosphere of a chemical laboratory for a long period of time, and even retained its brilliantly polished surface when subjected to boiling nitric acid."

Haynes in his patent application then described three methods of producing the alloy before listing the required specific claims for the invention: he specified a chromium content of between 10 percent and 60 percent, the remaining 40 to 90 percent of the alloy being cobalt. The application on the nickel-chromium alloy was similarly worded, specifying an anticipated use of the alloy "in the manufacture of tools and implements requiring a moderately sharp cutting edge" and, because of its desirable luster and other permanent qualities, in the production of "standards of weight, measures, and like uses." The chromium content of this alloy was specified as from 30 to 60 percent, and again three methods or processes of manufacture were outlined.

These applications were initially rejected by Patent Office Examiner William J. Rich, on the ground that A. L. Marsh's patent (No. 811,859, issued February 6, 1906) anticipated Haynes, but Haynes overcame this objection by an affidavit to the effect that he had produced his alloys prior to the filing day of Marsh's patent application (March 15, 1905) and by submitting dated samples. Moreover, while the Haynes and Marsh alloys were of similar composition, their intended use was considerably different, since Marsh anticipated a use for his discovery not in edge tools but in electrical apparatus. There is some evidence that Haynes and Marsh subsequently made an agreement that Haynes would develop only the cobalt-base alloys, Marsh the nickel-base. No such agreement has been found, but Haynes dropped all experimental work with nickel alloys and went on to develop his cobalt-base tool metal. In a question and answer session following a paper Haynes gave in December, 1919, "Stellite and Stainless Steel," he was asked if Marsh's work with "Nichrome" was earlier, later, or simultaneous with his own. Haynes replied:

> I suppose I would be telling secrets out of school if I told that. I discovered the alloy and he discovered the resistance qualities in it. He uses it for resistance wire. We made a gentleman's agreement that neither would go into the other's field. That is better than to have a law suit.

Stellite, as Haynes termed his patented alloys, was announced to the scientific and industrial world in 1910. In that year he attended the San Francisco convention of the American Chemical Society to read a paper. Entitled "Alloys of Nickel and Cobalt with Chromium," it opened with a brief résumé of the history of each metal. Haynes then recounted some of the details of his long years of experimentation with them and reported on the chemical properties and possible uses of his alloys. Although he noted that such promising items as chisels and lathe tools had been produced and tested, he was not yet ready to recommend his alloy for these uses. For the moment he predicted only that the uses of Stellite would include pocket and table cutlery, surgical instruments, chemical laboratory equipment, and standard weights and measures. He was unable to project the probable cost of Stellite on a manufactured basis but thought it would be only slightly higher than steel. At the conclusion of his talk, Haynes displayed several samples of Stellite to the audience.

The paper aroused considerable interest in Stellite. One San Francisco newspaper featured the remarks of Haynes in its story of the American Chemical Society meeting, which was said to have been "jolted clear out of its rut of technical discussion" by Haynes's account of a new alloy. Another newspaper headlined its story: "New Alloy Dooms Steel in Making of Cutlery," the subhead reading "Elwood Haynes, Father of the Automobile, Erects Factory to Utilize Process." Strangely, no mention of the Haynes address appeared in the Kokomo newspapers, but other editors picked up the story, including the misleading reference to the factory, and Haynes was soon inundated with calls for the metal, which he was unable to supply. One such request came from a Dr. Repin, head of the Pasteur Institute in France, who was seeking a suitable metal for surgical instruments. Haynes also received a number of letters from owners of mining properties offering him chromium, nickel, and cobalt ores. The most significant contact of this type came from Thomas Southworth, an official of the Deloro Smelting and Refining Company near Cobalt, Ontario. The Deloro firm was seeking an outlet for its vast supplies of cobalt, then considered a nearly worthless, unsalable by-product in the production of silver. Its primary use prior to the development of Stellite was as a coloring agent in the manufacture of ceramics.

Southworth explained in 1918 the roundabout way by which he first learned of Stellite. In 1910 a business associate in Wales sent him a clipping from an English newspaper that had reprinted an account from an Australian paper referring to Haynes's San Francisco address. Southworth immediately contacted Haynes directly, who thereupon visited him in Toronto and arranged to obtain a supply of cobalt. At the same time Southworth obtained a license from Haynes to produce Stellite in Canada and certain other countries. Apparently Haynes made these arrangements in exchange for, in addition to the customary royalty, assistance in developing Stellite cutlery. Some of this developmental work was done in Sheffield, England, although the cutlers there learned, as did Haynes and the American firms he engaged to produce pocketknives, that Stellite's hardness made it very difficult to work with in this way.

Manufacturers in both Ohio and Massachusetts worked on the production of Stellite knives in 1910 and 1911. Haynes himself made the necessary quantities of the alloy in his laboratory, where he was assisted by his brother-in-law Harry Lanterman, but he sent the castings to other firms for completing the knives. As early as 1911, Haynes sold a few Stellite knives, of which he was extremely proud, and gave a number of them as Christmas gifts in 1911, delighting the recipients. In April, 1912, he was accepting quantity orders from sales agents, although difficult manufacturing problems still remained. Even Thomas Southworth of the Deloro firm, in consultation with his colleagues in Sheffield, found the existing Stellite composition impossible to process, and appealed to Haynes to make "new experiments in melting." The

Sheffield cutlers had been "unable to drill" the necessary rivet holes because the alloy's "temper is so high."

Fairly regular sales occurred during the year, nevertheless, and Haynes was unswervingly optimistic in the face of the production difficulties. Confident in the future of Stellite, he realized that new manufacturing procedures perhaps would be required but believed the results would be worth it. Although forced to reject many requests for purchases, he began to advertise through small printed circulars, in anticipation of planned expansion.

In March, 1912, he had to refuse a request for a quantity of Stellite, pointing out that "thus far, I have not made it for sale at all except in the form of table and pocket cutlery." Most sales were by mail order, which he handled personally, although in April the George W. Claffin Company of Providence, Rhode Island, temporarily served as the sales agent for Stellite knives in New England. In May, Haynes described one of the Stellite products he manufactured as a "Gentleman's light three blade pearl handle pocket knife," but pointed out it was "not suitable for tough use. The large B[lade] of this K[nife] measures 1¾″ from shank to point, & 2¼″ over all. I expect shortly to make up a larger size . . . (2¼ × 2¾″) @ $2.50 each. The metal used is hard, [but] will neither rust nor tarnish under any natural conditions whatever."

In the winter of 1911–1912, while initiating the manufacture and sale of his Stellite knives made according to his original formula, Haynes was actively involved in seeking ways to improve the alloy. During this time Haynes made what, in retrospect, must be regarded as his most significant metallurgical discoveries. On the one hand, he learned that the addition of tungsten to his basic cobalt-chromium alloy rendered the metal incredibly hard without affecting its heat-, stain-, and corrosion-resistant qualities. This discovery eventually earned millions of dollars for Haynes. On the other hand, he became aware of the effect of chromium upon iron and steel—that is, he discovered that chromium in the proper proportions would render iron and steel rustless, or stainless. Patent applications on both discoveries were submitted, but only one was granted immediately. That the stainless steel idea would encounter difficulty was evident from patent attorney C. C. Poole's reaction to it. Haynes spent many hours during March and April, 1912, in correspondence with Poole, trying to convince him that he had made a patentable invention. Poole had hesitated in submitting the application because "chrome iron" and "chrome steel" were not new. Both had been known in the nineteenth century and various combinations had been patented. Haynes eventually persuaded his attorney that he had made new discoveries and a patent application was made, but, as Poole had anticipated, the patent office rejected "all claims of [the] chromium steel patent." Characteristically, this failed to discourage Haynes, who promised "additional experiments" and then "we will make new application."

Although most of his attention at the moment was devoted to making Stellite according to his new formulae and testing the results, he informed Poole that "some very interesting things are developing just now from my experiments with Stellite and chrome steel." A week later, he added, "I am very busy just at present with

Stellite but as soon as I have finished the work in which I am now engaged I will take up the chrome steel matter again with you." This later work led to a patent application in 1915 for stainless steel, but first he would explore those "very interesting things" in the development of Stellite.

The laboratory notebooks in which Haynes carefully recorded his experimental work were copied in the 1920s. These data were used in an important court case, *Haynes Stellite Company* v. *Chesterfield Metal Company*, which upheld the validity of Haynes's Stellite patent No. 1,057,423. The typescript of this record, now in the possession of the Cabot Corporation's Stellite Division in Kokomo, Indiana, reveals the slow, laborious process by which Haynes developed and then improved Stellite. It also indicates, by reading between the lines, some of the excitement and sense of discovery Haynes experienced as various tests were conducted on the sample bars.

As early as October 3, 1908, in fact, an alloy of tungsten, cobalt, and chromium was made, but he noticed nothing significant about it at that time. In 1911, in the course of a careful experimental program Haynes returned to these three ingredients, making in March of that year a cold chisel from the "very hard" bar he had cast. It "showed most remarkable cutting qualities," was difficult to roll or forge, and its very fine grain helped to give it an appearance "rivaling that of the finest tool metal." New combinations were made in April and tested for hardness, elasticity, and resistance to acid. By February 16, 1912, he had an alloy of cobalt and chromium, with traces of tungsten, silicon, and molybdenum, which he thought would "make an excellent material for chisels," and added, "I am inclined to think it will make good lathe tools as it is." He continued making slight modifications in the composition, and on April 25 made a ternary alloy of cobalt, chromium, and tungsten. The bar was "*very hard* and brittle," took "a good polish," and would "readily scratch quartz"; "I believe it to be one of the *hardest* alloys I have yet made." He immediately tested these and similar combinations in lathes at the Haynes Automobile Company. The results were striking. Operators were able to turn out a normal day's work by midafternoon, approximately a 50 percent increase in efficiency. William A. Wissler, a Union Carbide Corporation metallurgist who once worked for Haynes at the Haynes Stellite Company, wrote in 1939, "These and other tests showed that these cobalt-chromium-tungsten cutting tools were much superior to any then available, and in 1913 they were placed on the market."

Haynes himself communicated the dramatic results of the lathe tool tests to his Canadian associates in May, but for reasons he explained he was unable to make any public announcements about the breakthrough. "I have some information regarding Stellite which I am sure will be very pleasing to you," he began. "I have been experimenting quite industriously on other uses [besides cutlery] for the alloy & have recently succeeded in producing some most remarkable results from lathe tools made of this material." He then described the tests, and speculated upon their economic significance. The $11.00 per pound "high speed steel" used in the lathes at the automobile plant was not very satisfactory. In making some articles, such as "semi-steel wheels," the lathes had to be turned slowly and "even then the tool must be ground at least once for each wheel." After inserting a tool of Stellite made according to the new formula, the machine turned "just about twice as fast & completed 41 wheels without becoming dulled." In another test, an operator completed 26 wheels in ten hours with a steel tool; using Stellite he produced 24 wheels in five hours. He concluded that a Stellite tool "showed 41 times the endurance of the steel tool & did nearly twice the work in a given time," but he asked Southworth not to publicize any of this because "I am to read a paper before the International Congress of Applied Chemistry next September on Cobalt & its alloys" and "I am under obligations not to publish any data which is to appear in the paper previous to the time."

Haynes then noted that the automobile plant had already decided to replace all its steel tools with Stellite ones (paying a price of $3.00 per pound). "It must not be supposed," Haynes cautioned, "that ordinary Stellite will give these results. This is a special alloy but its composition will be made known to you as soon as I am at liberty to disclose it."

A month later Haynes reported again to Southworth on the enthusiastic, if initially incredulous, response to Stellite tools within the trade. Many high-speed steel salesmen refused to believe the men at the Haynes plant about Stellite's capabilities as a tool metal but changed their opinions after seeing the tools in service. Two men, in fact, solicited Haynes "most earnestly" to be allowed to sell Stellite, but he refused since no production facilities existed and his own plans for manufacturing and marketing Stellite were not yet formulated. He assured Southworth that when the time came Stellite tool metal "in large lots" would "sell readily at from $3.00 to $5.00 per pound" and offered to come to Deloro "just before or just after I read the paper" on Stellite. He proposed to "show some trustworthy person how to make the metal on a *small scale* just as I make it in Kokomo. I expect to make some rather exhaustive experiments upon turning tools within the next 2 or 3 weeks, & will let you know the results."

By this time Haynes was ready to seek a patent on his improved Stellite alloys. The initial application submitted July 20, 1912, specified two ternary compounds—one of cobalt, chromium, and tungsten, the other of cobalt, chromium, and molybdenum; it also described a quaternary compound of all four metals. Rich, the patent officer, required separate applications on the ternary and quaternary alloys but promptly allowed them when received. The allowances were made on September 5 and 6, 1912, with the patents issuing on April 1, 1913. Patent No. 1,057,423 covers the cobalt-chromium-tungsten combination (with the tungsten ranging from 5 to 60 percent); Patent No. 1,057,828 covers an alloy of cobalt, chromium, tungsten, and molybdenum, again with the chromium group metals (tungsten and molybdenum) ranging from 5 to 60 percent.

When notified in early September, 1912, that the patents would be forthcoming, Haynes immediately began to arrange for manufacturing Stellite. By strange coincidence, at the time of his notification of allowance by the patent office, he was in New York presenting his paper on the new alloys before a session of the International Congress of Applied Chemistry. In his talk Haynes referred to his paper of 1910, delivered in San Francisco, in which he had described his basic cobalt-chromium alloy. The alloy now "is modified to such a marked degree by the introduction of other substances," he reported, "that I have felt justified in reading another paper on this subject." He reviewed his experiments carried on since "1907 or 1908," when tungsten, molybdenum, and other elements were added. He still used a natural gas furnace for this work (although in 1912 he purchased an electric one for further experimentation), making his fusions at first in graphite crucibles. The carbon in the graphite, however, contaminated the metal, so he constructed special crucibles for his later tests.

Haynes then made his first public announcement on the lathe test results in machining the cast-iron wheels. Using high-speed steel, twenty-six wheels had been turned out in a ten-hour day; with a Stellite tool, forty-nine wheels had been completed. The steel tool, moreover, had been ground fifty times during the day; the Stellite tool "was dressed slightly by a carborundum whetstone, after its day's work was completed." With Stellite cutters in the boring-head of a cylinder-drilling machine, ten hours of work had been performed in three hours and twenty minutes. Haynes predicted that Stellite "will not fully supersede high speed steel in the machine shop, but in cases where rapid work is the main consideration, it will doubtless replace high speed steel." Haynes's prediction proved correct, although exceedingly modest. No one could have anticipated the broad range of uses to which Stellite has been adapted. This, the widespread utilization of Stellite, was to be the legacy of the little business, the Haynes Stellite Works, Haynes established at the end of 1912.

The State Centennial

Indiana had been the first state to enter the Union after the War of 1812, a conflict, part of a general world war, that ushered in a century free of world wars. The century ended for Europe in 1914; three years later the United States also became involved in World War I. Against the somber backdrop of war abroad, and amid a growing debate concerning the United States' preparedness and possible involvement in the war, Indiana celebrated its centennial in 1916. The occasion was marked by a series of programs, historical pageants, and public festivals throughout the state. The theme of the centennial clearly was the progress achieved since the state—with only fifteen sparsely settled counties hugging the Ohio River—had been admitted into the Union. Homage was paid to the courageous pioneers, some of whom were still remembered by the 1916 celebrants, who had carved out the foundations of a prosperous and progressive state a century before.

The centennial coincided with a strong conservation movement developing throughout the country, fostered in large part by President Theodore Roosevelt's interest in it. A few farsighted people in Indiana recognized the opportunity to make a lasting contribution to conservation and to create a fitting legacy of the centennial. As Harlow Lindley pointed out in 1916, many communities desired to make the state centennial memorable by erecting permanent memorials such as libraries, schools, churches, bridges, and parks; but only one movement had been undertaken to memorialize the state as a whole. Not only would a series of state parks be a "dignified and worthy permanent memorial," since it would preserve tracts and buildings associated with state history as well as spots of scenic beauty and pristine charm, but it would also provide the citizens of the state with much-needed recreational opportunities.[1] No individual deserves more credit for creating an Indiana state park system, however, than Richard Lieber, a businessman and social activist who promoted the idea of the parks for four or five years before it was authorized by the legislature.

Lieber, a German emigrant to Indianapolis in 1891, enjoyed a brief and successful business career in that city before he devoted himself to public concerns and finally—from 1917 to 1933—to public service as the first director of the Department of Conservation (later renamed the Department of Natural Resources). For a sympathetic but reliable study of Lieber, the national conservation movement, and the development of Indiana's state park system, one of the best in the country during Lieber's long period of leadership, see Robert A. Frederick, "Colonel Richard A. Lieber, Conservationist and Park Builder: The Indiana Years" (unpublished Ph.D. dissertation, Indiana University at Bloomington, 1960). See also the report on the innumerable activities undertaken as part of the centennial celebration in Harlow Lindley, ed., *The Indiana Centennial, 1916. A Record of the Celebration of the One Hundredth Anniversary of Indiana's Admission to Statehood* (1919), part of which—Richard Lieber's report for the park committee—is reprinted below.

CENTENNIAL LEGACY
The State Park System

Richard Lieber

I herewith beg to submit my report as Chairman of the Committee on Indiana['s] State Centennial Memorial.

The first meeting of the Committee was held March 18th, 1916, since which time our activity has never lagged. We were spurred on to immediate action by the fact that sixty days later one of the garden spots of Indiana, namely, Turkey Run, was to be sold at public auction. Turkey Run is a paradise of rocky gorges, glens, bathing beaches and waterfalls, a retreat for song birds, and a garden of wild flowers. It has hundreds of magnificent black walnut, oak, poplar, and other stately trees, all grow-

1. Harlow Lindley, ed., *The Indiana Centennial, 1916* (1919), p. 45.

From "Report of Park Committee of the Indiana Historical Commission," in Harlow Lindley, ed., *The Indiana Centennial, 1916* (1919), pp. 50–55.

ing in a primeval forest which the Lusk family carefully preserved from the lumberman's axe.

We immediately began an extensive campaign for funds and in this were materially assisted by the press of the State. We sought the opinions of leading Americans concerning our enterprise and received most encouraging replies from such men as President Wilson, Governor McCall of Massachusetts, Theodore Roosevelt, Vice-President Marshall, Senators Kern and Taggart, Stewart Edward White, Ellery Sedgwick, Editor of the Atlantic Monthly, Lyman Abbott and others.

The actual work of gathering funds commenced in April. A joint Committee of the Indianapolis Board of Trade and Chamber of Commerce was appointed and this Committee held daily meetings during the period of active solicitation. By proclamation of Governor Ralston the week beginning April 24 was designated for the purpose of making contributions to the State Park Fund. This resulted in the organization of some volunteer committees in the State at large. I am pained to acknowledge, however, that the citizens of the State generally did not respond in a manner which can possibly be compared to the liberality of the citizens of Indianapolis. I believe, however, that this was due to the fact that the Committee was in closer contact with Indianapolis than other communities in the State, and that with a better knowledge of the facts and circumstances in connection with the Park movement, adequate funds can still be raised throughout the State.

Upon the day of the sale of Turkey Run, the Committee became a bidder and continued to bid until it came to the conclusion that it was useless to compete with a commercial bidder. As a result the property was sold to the Hoosier Veneer Company of Indianapolis for $30,200. The Committee, however, did not allow this disappointment to curb its activities and then and there determined to acquire Turkey Run notwithstanding its apparent failure. Negotiations with the Hoosier Veneer Company continued all summer and fall and finally on the 11th day of November, the property was purchased for the sum of $40,200. Figuring taxes and interest charges the profit of the Hoosier Veneer Company was approximately $9,000. On the other hand, the Committee after making very careful investigations of the timber and land values, concluded that the property was worth all they had paid for it.

While the Committee was negotiating for Turkey Run, a Committee of citizens from Owen County informed us that McCormick's Creek Canon was about to be sold by the administrator of the estate of Dr. F. W. Denkewalter, the latter having spent a lifetime in acquiring the various portions of this scenic tract. The appraisement of the property fixed its value at $5,250, and after viewing this bit of scenery, the Committee determined to buy the same provided that the citizens of Owen County would raise one-fourth of the purchase price among themselves and would guarantee that the cost would not exceed the appraisement. Due to the enterprise and civic spirit of the citizens of Owen County, this property was acquired and will go down into history as the first link in the chain of parks to be established. It is due these people to acknowledge that if the citizens of all the counties in Indiana would show an equal interest in this movement, the State would before long be assured of one of the most magnificent systems of State parks in the country.

The failure to acquire Turkey Run at the time of the auction sale interfered with the campaign to gather funds, but we were assured at that time by the gentlemen constituting the Board of Directors of the Indianapolis Motor Speedway Association that if we would persist in our efforts, they would eventually aid us financially. These men more than redeemed their promise. The Indianapolis Motor Speedway Association donated the sum of $5,065 and Mr. Arthur C. Newby, whose share of that contribution was one-fourth, gave us in addition thereto the sum of $5,000. Furthermore, he has aided the Committee actively in the collection of funds to an extent that would have meant failure except for that assistance.

During all our work we were supported by the active and sustained interest of Governor Ralston, and I wish to take this occasion to extend to him the thanks of our Committee. Furthermore, I am particularly pleased to acknowledge the most valuable assistance rendered by your acting chairman, Dr. Frank B. Wynn, who has made the work of our Committee his own and who actively participated in all our activity. Much of the success of the work of our Committee is due to his great zeal and circumspection.

I feel that this report would be incomplete without giving the views of our Committee on State Parks generally. Established upon a broad and substantial basis, Indiana State Parks would not only memorialize the past but would build for the future by practical conservation. They would distinctly point out the desirability of preserving trees, of protecting birds and animal life. They would constantly be a great public lesson in conservation and show the folly of prodigal waste of Indiana's superb natural resources. They would impress upon the public mind that wastefulness of Nature's beauties and treasures is out of harmony with the spirit of the time, progress and the needs of Indiana's new century.

The United States Government long ago won widespread popular approval in setting aside large scenic tracts, preserving them for all time against commercial vandalism and providing immense recreational grounds. They are on a very generous scale and show what Indiana might do on a smaller scale in the accomplishment of similar ends. National Parks like the Grand Canyon, Yellowstone, Yosemite and Glacier, because of their remoteness, are available only to those Indiana people who have time and means to visit them, but a system of State Parks would bring recreation grounds close [to] home to practically all our people.

While State Parks present a new idea to Indiana, there are successful examples to be found in other states that place the proposed Indiana system beyond experiment. Massachusetts awoke to the importance of State Parks a score of years ago, and has since been preserving scenic seashore, river banks and wooded hilltops that had previously been privately owned. Massachusetts now has many parks from six to fifty acres in extent.

Maine has made a beginning in the same direction. A still more notable achievement in the State Parks is found in New York, especially in the preservation of Niagara Falls, in the great gorge of the Genesee River, a great reservation in the Adirondack mountains, and the Palisades along the Hudson River.

Not content with the National Park reservation within her borders, California has invested $250,000 in ten thousand acres at Boulder Creek to preserve a forest of redwood trees.

But Wisconsin doubtless holds the lead in State Parks. In the beginning park enthusiasts of that State made a systematic examination of Wisconsin's scenic resources with a view to placing the ownership in the public. One of Wisconsin's State Parks is in Door county, including 3,800 acres. The acquisition of five or six thousand acres of forest around Devil's Lake is under way and the Dells of the Wisconsin River, and another tract of some 2,700 acres along the Mississippi River are to be added to the State's system.

In all of these States, as it would be in Indiana, the chief purpose of State Parks is to refresh and strengthen and renew tired people, and fit them for the common round of daily life.

Other States, as doubtless will Indiana, have found that there is also a cash value in scenery, an income to be derived from excursionists, from special commercial privileges and concessions, and from fish and game, an income that can be turned toward the cost of maintenance.

In Boston's elaborate Metropolitan Park system is an example of possibilities within the reach of Indiana cities which they might follow on a small scale. The Boston system includes its own and that of thirty-seven surrounding cities, the system having established both parks and connecting parkways, and highways for motor and other traffic. The Blue Hills reservation, twelve miles from the state house, has 4,700 acres; Middlesex Falls, five miles from the state house, contains 3,200 acres, this park being bordered by five cities; Mystic Valley Parkway, along lake and river of the same name, is a third of the larger areas in the Boston system. Many miles of rocky and wooded tracts are included, as well as great stretches of seashore. About $7,000,000 has been spent for lands for this system and as much more is going into development, the money being raised by State, city and town taxation.

Density of population in Europe does not permit the creation of extensive parks. But every scenic spot, large or small, has been beautified, giving whole provinces the aspect of one large park in which are nestled villages, towns and even cities themselves.

The European long ago learned the material value of scenery. The ubiquitous red Baedecker is an eloquent testimonial thereof. Take little Switzerland, for instance. It has 16,000 square miles compared to Colorado's 104,000 square miles. We do not have to read "Tartarin on the Alps" to know that it is the most superbly ordered and highest dividend paying scenery in the world. It is well enough to speak of Nature's hygienic value, of its recuperative and recreative strength, but when one reflects for a moment that Americans alone—not to mention all the other nations—have left annually $50,000,000 in that little country, it is realized that scenery has an inherent cash value and that the so-called "Lungs" of a people have from a given viewpoint a most convincing resemblance to a fat purse.

In conclusion, I hope and trust that the small beginning we have made will have laid the foundation for a comprehensive system of State Parks which will not only stand forever as a token of the past, but which will bring health, wealth and happiness to our own generation and the many that will come after us.

8. Indiana Writers

Indiana has long enjoyed its reputation as the home state of an outstanding group of writers—novelists, poets, dramatists, essayists, historians, even politicians. The tradition stretches far back into the pioneer period, despite the lack of general literacy in the state during antebellum days; it reached its peak during the late nineteenth and early twentieth centuries, when perennial bestsellers by such authors as Lew Wallace, James Whitcomb Riley, Gene Stratton Porter, and Booth Tarkington were turned out regularly. Between 1895 and 1945, according to the now famous analysis of librarian John H. Moriarity, Indiana ranked a close second only to New York as a source of "best sellers" published in the United States. In recent years the literary tradition of the state has remained strong, with such Hoosier-born writers as Jessamyn West, Kurt Vonnegut, Dan Wakefield, and more recently James Alexander Thom enjoying a wide national audience.

In the first selection below, Professor Howard H. Peckham assays an answer to the question of why Indiana has had so many prolific writers whose works continue to be well received by the public. He finds both a series of historical reasons and the self-perpetuation of the momentum established as possible explanations. The remainder of the selections in this chapter provide either articles about some of Indiana's best-known writers or examples of their prose.

Two excellent collections of Indiana writing that serve to introduce many of the state's best authors with excerpts from their most famous works are Richard E. Banta, ed., *Hoosier Caravan: A Treasury of Indiana Life and Lore* (rev. ed., 1975); and A. L. Lazarus, ed., *The Indiana Experience: An Anthology* (1977). There is also the fairly recent monograph, Arthur W. Shumaker's *A History of Indiana Literature* (1962); see too the useful brief overview of the subject by Richard A. Cordell, "Limestone, Corn, and Literature: The Indiana Scene and Its Interpreters," *Saturday Review*, December 17, 1938, pp. 3–4, 14–15; the older study by Meredith Nicholson, *The Hoosiers* (1900); and four biographies: Fred Kelly, *George Ade: Warm-Hearted Satirist* (1947); James Woodress, *Booth Tarkington: Gentleman from Indiana* (1954); Richard Crowder, *Those Innocent Years: The Legacy and Inheritance of a Hero of the Victorian Age, James Whitcomb Riley* (1957), and Judith Reick Long, *Gene Stratton-Porter: Novelist and Naturalist* (1990).

Practitioners of the Art

HOOSIER AUTHORS
Who and Why

Howard H. Peckham

Howard H. Peckham, formerly professor of history and director of the William L. Clements Library at the University of Michigan, served as director of the Indiana Historical Bureau and the Indiana Historical Society from 1945 to 1953. During this time the sesquicentennial of Indiana Territory was celebrated, and the editors of the new illustrated journal American Heritage *devoted most of an issue to a series of articles on Indiana. Peckham contributed this useful essay on Indiana literature, underscoring the validity of the state's reputation for literary output and then attempting to suggest reasons for it. Professor Peckham is also the author of* Pontiac *(1963),* The Colonial Wars, 1689–1762 *(1963), and* Indiana: A Bicentennial History *(1978).*

When that perennial Chautauqua lecturer, the late Opie Read, first appeared in Fort Wayne, he announced that he was aware of Indiana's literary reputation and therefore if there was an author in the audience would he please stand? Whereupon the audience rose en masse. Mr. Read recovered himself in time to notice one old man still seated and called attention to him as one Hoosier who was *not* an author.

"Oh, no, he writes, too," someone said. "He's just deef and didn't hear your question."

The story was told by George Ade and others with such variations that it may be a piece of folklore. Indiana's literary productivity is one of those phenomena that is easily exaggerated. Two or three best-selling authors become a dozen; a poet in every county becomes a poet in every town. Investigation, however, has revealed some startling statistics. Books have been a major product in this state. Writing is all out of proportion to the population.

Wabash College recently has issued a bio-bibliography of Indiana authors. To whittle down the project even to king size, the sponsoring committee set certain limitations. The hundreds of magazine and newspaper contributors were not admitted unless they had also published a book. Writers of textbooks and law books were also omitted, eliminating generations of college professors. The study was further confined to Indiana's first century as a state; consequently anyone whose first book was published after 1916 was left out. Even with this generous sloughing, the committee wound up with more than 950 eligible writers! That means an average of ten

From "What Made Hoosiers Write?" *American Heritage*, II (Autumn 1950), 24–27, 59–60.

new book authors a year for a hundred consecutive years. Moreover, almost no one was a one-book author. All this in a state whose population had grown to about 2,800,000 in 1916.

Yet it is not simply that so many Hoosiers wrote that gave the state its reputation; it is the indisputable fact that a score of those writers produced one best-seller after another which compelled national attention to Indiana. The librarian of Purdue University examined the authorship of the ten best selling novels each year from 1900 to 1940. By allowing ten points for the number one best-seller, nine points for the second best, and so on down to one point for the tenth book on the annual list, he totaled up a score of 213 points for Indiana authors in this period. That score was exceeded only slightly by New York's 218 points—from a population four times larger! The next ranking states hardly offered competition: Pennsylvania 125 points, Virginia 102, Kentucky 94.

If readers find these comparisons difficult to credit, here are the names of some popular authors claimed by Indiana, both before and after 1900: George Ade, Charles and Mary Beard, Albert J. Beveridge, Claude Bowers, Mary Hartwell Catherwood, Elmer Davis, Lloyd C. Douglas, Theodore Dreiser, Edward and George Eggleston, Martha Finley (of Elsie Dinsmore fame), John Hay, Kin Hubbard, Annie Fellows Johnston (the Little Colonel series), George Barr McCutcheon, Charles Major, William Vaughn Moody, George Jean Nathan, Meredith Nicholson, David Graham Phillips, Ernie Pyle, Gene Stratton Porter, James Whitcomb Riley, Booth Tarkington, and Lew Wallace.

This writing started early in Indiana. The first author is shared with Kentucky. Jesse Lynch Holman was born there, but he migrated to Indiana in 1811 when he was twenty-seven. In the state of his adoption he became a member of the Territorial Legislature and later a state and federal judge, a Baptist minister, and a founder of Franklin College and of the Indiana Historical Society. He died in 1842. The year before he came to Indiana he had had published a novel, *The Prisoners of Niagara*, and later in life he wrote much poetry for Indiana newspapers. From that date the race began. Production increased slowly in the 1830's and 1840's with poets now largely forgotten, essayists writing on religious questions, scientific articles from New Harmony, and first-person "confessions" of criminals and alcoholics. An anonymous novel about Indiana was published in the state in 1845, along with a few other examples of fiction. Not until the late 1850's did Indiana's literary lights attract Eastern attention. Meredith Nicholson believed that Mrs. Julia Dumont, the teacher of the Eggleston boys, was the first to attain this distinction, with her *Life Sketches from Common Paths: A Series of American Tales*, published in New York in 1856. These stories had already appeared in western periodicals; indeed, Mrs. Dumont's first story was published in 1824.

There was a lull in writing during the 1860's, doubtless occasioned by the war. Then in 1871 appeared Eggleston's *The Hoosier Schoolmaster*. He was followed by Lew Wallace and Riley, and the literary bloom was almost an explosion. If there was a Golden Decade, it was the period 1900 to 1910. At that time Riley, Major, Thompson, Tarkington, Ade, Nicholson, Moody, Phillips, McCutcheon, and Mrs. Porter were turning out one best-seller after another. Indiana's literary reputation was indestructibly established. The furious pace was maintained for another two decades, which was remarkable endurance. If American literature may be said to begin about 1820 (Bryant's *Thanatopsis*, 1817, Irving's *Sketch Book*, 1819, and Cooper's *Spy*, 1821), then it took the East two centuries to "flower." Indiana bloomed within one century after American settlement.

All this literary activity has been noticed before. A contributor to the *Cincinnati Daily Gazette* for December 7, 1876, reviewed the library of Indiana authors collected by one Daniel Hough and was impressed to the extent that his commentary filled three columns. Meredith Nicholson devoted a book to his fellow writers in the state in 1900—*The Hoosiers*. Prof. Robert Cordell of Purdue appraised the Indiana writers for the *Saturday Review of Literature* in 1938. But the motives have escaped analysis.

The fact that an unusually large number of people born and educated or long resident in Indiana have turned to writing, and that a respectable percentage have achieved great popularity has to be accepted as truth. But why did they? Why did so many Hoosiers take to their pens? What caused this widespread urge to communicate?

There is no magic answer. It can only be speculation from a few relevant facts. Those must include the geography of the state, the people it attracted, the character and institutions it developed, and the opportunities it provided. Examining the state's history with this inquiry foremost in mind, some suggestive approaches to the answer can be uncovered.

Indiana's boundaries, except for the Ohio River and part of the Wabash, are not natural. Therefore it is not a distinct locality differing suddenly from the adjoining territory of its neighbors. Nevertheless, a distinguished geographer calls the area that constitutes Indiana "one of the most fortunate areas in America." Not in totals, but in proportion to its size and population, it is perhaps the richest of all the states. Most of the state has deep, fertile soil; the climate is favorable to lush crops; natural resources are rich; crops are heavy in yield and dependable; sources of income are diverse; and the location in the United States is advantageous.

Admittedly the pioneers faced a harsh existence, clearing the land, resisting disease, fighting the Indians on occasion, and establishing a civilization. But such is the geography of Indiana that hard work was almost certain to be rewarded by a comfortable standard of living. Moreover, agricultural work is seasonal, periods of heavy work alternating with periods of light work. Throughout the nineteenth century Indiana was predominantly an agricultural state. Recognition must be given the fact that Hoosiers pursued an occupation and achieved a standard of living that allowed a certain leisure.

It is all very well to talk of literature being born of agony and struggle. But the actual writing is done in peace and quiet, in hours that can be snatched from the toil for existence for the pursuit of an art. As a professor of English assured me, writing is like whittling: it presupposes a certain amount of leisure time on the part of the practitioner. My contention is that the resources of Indiana gave many of its people that time to write. It may also explain the lack of tragic themes in Indiana literature.

Of course, the opportunity is not the performance. Not everyone with leisure turns to writing. Why did Hoosiers? . . . They did, I believe, because they developed into a highly articulate people. If tragic themes are lacking in Indiana literature, so are "cults of unintelligibility"—the obscure self-expressionists, and the experimental schools and movements. There were no synthetic literary centers like Greenwich Village or Santa Fé. Hoosiers wanted above all to communicate, to be understood by their contemporaries.

Indiana had only 2500 inhabitants in 1800, made up of Frenchmen at Vincennes, frontier veterans of George Rogers Clark's campaign settled on their bonus lands around Clarksville, and a few fur traders and squatters. When Indiana entered the Union at the end of 1816, the population had multiplied to about 75,000. By 1820 it had doubled again.

In 1860 the total population numbered 1,350,000, and Indiana ranked sixth among the thirty-three states. Over 57 per cent of the people were already true Hoosier, having been born in Indiana itself, compared to 20 per cent in 1840.

The Ohio River was the great highway of entrance to the state, and it was natural that the southern part of the state should fill up first. Settlers pushed up the river valleys and northwestward across the state. Southern states had supplied a large portion of Indiana's first immigrants and continued to pour them in. Indeed, Indiana became the home of more Southerners than any state north of the Ohio. The wave from Ohio, Pennsylvania, and New York started a little later, after the Erie Canal and the National Road were opened, but grew rapidly in volume and surpassed the southern contingent. New Englanders were a relatively small portion, but they often came in groups and influenced particular towns. There were some 11,000 Negroes in the state in 1860. On top of the few French who were already there and who came later were added a number of Germans and Irish. Indiana has been called the first melting pot in the country, and the assertion is true. The foreign element amounted to only 9 per cent in 1860 and then decreased, but Indiana was the first state to receive immigrants from the two different sections of the United States in proportion to their relative numbers.

This mixture of nationalities and sections was successfully amalgamated into a Hoosier type, but the process made lively politics. The Southerners brought with them a Democratic political tradition, a satisfaction with private education, and a leisurely attitude that found time for great hospitality, social gatherings, endless conversation, and reading. It is not correct to assume that they were pro-slavery. In fact most of them moved to Indiana because they were not in sympathy with slavery. A strong contingent of Quakers from North Carolina came for that reason. The central states of Ohio, Pennsylvania, and New York, with their admixture of New England forebears, plus the sprinkling of New Englanders who came directly to Indiana, carried the Whig banner, an interest in public schools and cultural pursuits, and an energetic distrust of leisure.

The politics bear some relation to the literature, because both activities stem from articulateness. It is said that the first words uttered by Hoosier infants are: "I'm not a candidate for any office, but if nominated I will run, and if elected I will serve." Since lawyers are prone to enter politics, it is significant to recall how much encouragement was given these expressionists. Written into the state constitution of 1851 was the provision that "Every person of good moral character, being a voter, shall be entitled to admission to practice law in all courts of justice." And that remarkable section was not stricken out of the constitution until 1932.

The various religious denominations provided another field for polemics. Catholicism was firmly established here first by the French, a situation duplicated in Michigan and Illinois. It was strengthened by the Irish who came to dig the canals in the 1830's and by many of the Germans who came after 1848. The Baptists organized first among the Protestants, but were soon followed by the Methodists and Presbyterians. The Quakers formed an influential minority. After the revival of the Second Great Awakening, the followers of Alexander Campbell won many adherents, and the Church of Christ's Disciples eventually became the second largest denomination. The Protestant Germans were mainly Lutherans, but they also introduced the United Brethren, Dunkers, and Mennonites. Yet all of these people were able to make the kind of life each enjoyed—the Southern aristocrat in the river towns, the Ohio farmer, the Pennsylvania trader, the foreign laborer, the faithful Catholic, the foot-washing Baptist, the simple Quaker. Indiana was rich enough to provide a good living for all and eliminate a jealous competition for security.

The Hoosiers' intellectual achievements were uneven and unorthodox. Free public schools were shamefully lacking. Although the Constitution of 1816 called for "a general system of education, ascending in regular graduation, from township schools to a state university," the people allowed the latter to be established but sturdily resisted taxation for local schools. The Supreme Court supported them. A few families hired tutors in the Southern tradition; a few individuals and churches conducted private schools. Denominational colleges were opened until the educational system was top heavy and the colleges had to provide their students first with a high school education. In 1840 Indiana stood sixteenth among the 26 states in the illiteracy of adults, surpassed by every northern state and by three southern states. The population was over 14 per cent illiterate. When the question of whether to raise taxes for free schools was referred to the voters in 1848, the proponents of free schools won a narrow victory. But it was a victory delayed by the drafting of a new state constitution in 1850. By this date Indiana ranked twenty-fifth among the 31 states in illiteracy. The first General Assembly under the new constitution enacted a public school law, only to have it vitiated by adverse Supreme Court decisions. Appropriation of local taxes for tuition was forbidden. Not until 1885 did the Supreme Court reverse itself.

The absence of an adequate free school system had three interesting effects. Folklore, largely brought in by Southerners, was preserved, embroidered, and disseminated. Even today Indiana is recognized as having a larger body of folklore, collected and uncollected, than any other Midwestern state, with the possible exception of Illinois. The existence of the Hoosier Folklore Society, with its quarterly magazine, is one attestation. Moreover, Indiana is the home of the "tall story." There was a recognized "liar's bench" in many towns, and the leading story teller was admired for his talent rather than derided for his wanderings from the truth. Story telling was a recognized form of social intercourse and entertainment. The best story tellers collected loyal audiences and elevated loafing to a fine art. That is, men were wont to spend their free evenings or free hours during the day "loafing" at a hospitable shop. There was no social stigma attached to this inert use of leisure unless, of course, one never worked at all. The men traded news and they gossiped, but they also told stories simply for the sake of telling a good story. The practice has disappeared fast since the introduction of the automobile, the movie, and the radio, but is by no means extinct. The earlier Hoosiers sharpened their imaginations by perpetuating and enlarging a great corpus of folklore.

The second effect was on the language. Archaisms of speech were retained and colloquialisms developed because there was no leveling and refining process provided by the standardized public school. Peculiarities of usage and pronunciation remained to enrich and vivify the Hoosier speech. It is this speech that Riley appropriated and reported. As Professor Cordell has pointed out, Riley was not a dialect poet because there was no real dialect in use in Indiana; rather he utilized "the uneducated Hoosier's bad grammar," as found in the central part of the state, it should be added. Eggleston collected and reported Hoosier usage of a generation earlier. Left to his own resources for descriptions and comparisons, the Hoosier coined some apt and striking metaphors. He was a sharp observer. He seemed to have what Aristotle called "an eye for resemblances," which is the very essence of expression. The close relation of a rich language in Elizabethan England to the wealth of Elizabethan literature has been established, and Dr. I. A. Richards of Harvard University emphasizes that the skilled use of metaphor in that age is a "fact which made Shakespeare possible." Some Indiana farmers today retain an original and graphic way of expressing comparisons.

The third effect of the paucity of schools was a hunger for knowledge that sought satisfaction through libraries and cultural or literary clubs. Vevay was founded in 1814 by a Swiss group who believed they could cultivate grapevines there. Three years later Andrew Miller found 84 dwellings, 34 shops, 8 stores, 3 taverns, a court house, jail, church, market house, and school; "two lawyers, two physicians, a printing office, a library of 300 volumes, and a literary society in which are several persons of genius and literature." Governor William Henry Harrison was one of the founders of the Vincennes Historical and Antiquarian Society in 1808. Vincennes also boasted a Thespian Society that gave plays from 1806 to about 1830. Frances Wright founded the Female Social Society at New Harmony in 1825. The Edgeworthalean Society at Bloomington was a women's literary club founded in 1841. Another was the Clionian Society of Vernon, organized in 1858. The oldest women's club still to survive in Indiana is The Minerva of New Harmony, founded by Robert Owen's granddaughter in 1859. All of these organizations were forums where members were obliged to offer papers.

The Constitution of 1816 provided for county public libraries, to be supported by ten per cent of the proceeds from the sale of town lots in the county seat. Libraries were opened in a majority of the counties, but they were poorly provided for. Semi-private libraries organized by individuals flourished better. One was started in Vincennes in

1807, another in New Harmony in 1825. William Maclure was instrumental in forming the Workingmen's Institute and Library at New Harmony in 1838. Upon his death in 1840, he left $150,000 for the establishment of workingmen's libraries in other towns. At least fifteen towns availed themselves of the bequest. Then in 1852 the General Assembly provided for township school libraries, with books purchased from a state tax. There were certain limitations that prevented every township from obtaining this grant, but over two-thirds of the state's 938 townships secured libraries. Books were selected by the state, and the first distribution sent an average of 321 volumes to each library. Each year new volumes were added. With the levy of 1855 the tax for libraries ceased for ten years, and the institutions declined. Nevertheless, a respectable beginning had been made and the books were widely read; in some townships circulation ran six to ten times the total number of volumes. Their effect on the generation that matured in the next decade must have been considerable. Tom Marshall, Hoosier vice-president under Woodrow Wilson, attributed the literary fecundity of the state more to these libraries than to any other single cause.

By the time of the Civil War a Hoosier character was emerging, with traits derived from the geographical and population factors. He was rustic because of his closeness to the soil, but not socially crude. He was hospitable and friendly because of his Southern background, the abundance of nature, and his rural isolation. His neighborliness was founded on a strong belief in equality and his experience of pioneer co-operativeness, as well as his loneliness and ability to share. Poet Joseph D. Welsh noted this characteristic in his "Indiana Georgicks," published in 1839, and emphasized it with a footnote. The Hoosier was independent in thought and proud of it, because in a mixed political and religious atmosphere he had been forced to define his position and maintain it. George Ade said he was "a puzzling combination of shy provincial, unfettered democrat, and Fourth of July orator. He is a student by choice, a poet by sneaking inclination, and a story teller by reason of his nativity."

There was a kind of tolerance to be found in his sense of humor, because he had learned to get along with people who differed from him. With his humor he even punctured his own pride from time to time. The word "Hoosier" was originally an epithet of opprobrium, a fighting word to the native Indianan. But in the last fifty years he has adopted it as his own label and now beats his chest and declares proudly that he's a Hoosier. There was the veteran of the Civil War home guard of Salem which was called out to stop Confederate General Morgan on his famous raid. He was proud of his military service as a youth. "What did you do when you saw Morgan's men ride down the hill into town?" he was asked. Honestly if ingloriously he replied: "I run like hell, jes' like ever'body else did!" Or take another Hoosier who on his one hundredth birthday was asked the inevitable question to what he attributed his longevity. He said he thought it was because "I always had sort of an aversion to hard work."

Despite his independence, the Hoosier was gregarious, a joiner of lodges, political parties, and clubs. Indianapolis is still the best market for fraternal jewelry in the U.S. Talk was the social medium, the common entertainment, and the democratic denominator open to all. Hoosier pride in his state took root early, after defeating the Indians, writing a constitution, laying out a capital in the wilderness, and providing for a state university. By 1830 a group of citizens looked back proudly on their handiwork and decided to preserve the story of it by forming the Indiana Historical Society, the oldest continuous state historical society west of Pennsylvania.

There remains to be considered the opportunities that early Hoosier writers had to achieve publication. This factor alone is a powerful stimulus of the muse. Artistic creation, as Shücking points out in his little-known essay on *The Sociology of Literary Taste*, is not necessarily something that erupts, forcing its way out, but is dependent to a large degree upon recognition and encouragement. The literary center of the West was first Lexington, Kentucky, and then Cincinnati. Early Indiana was orientated around Cincinnati; Indianapolis having been placed in the geographical center of the state, it was on the northern fringe of population for a long time. The first literary periodical in the West was *The Medley*, a monthly begun at Lexington in 1803. It lasted hardly a year. Lexington tried again in 1819 with the *Western Review*, a monthly that survived for about two years. The monthly *Western Censor* was started in Indianapolis in 1823 and lasted a little more than a year.

Then Cincinnati assumed literary leadership in more ways than one. It entertained authors like Dickens, Mrs. Trollope, and Harriet Martineau, and produced its own. Its publishing offices turned out books as well as periodicals. The *Literary Gazette* was a weekly of 1824. The *Western Review* was a new monthly started in 1827 which ran for four years. It was followed in 1831 by the semi-monthly *Cincinnati Mirror*, which lasted till 1836. James Hall edited the *Western Monthly Magazine* from 1833 to 1837. Prof. Ralph L. Rusk calls it the most important magazine on the frontier. The *Western Messenger*, a monthly devoted to religion and literature, began in 1835 and ran for six years. In 1841 the famous *Ladies' Repository* was started and continued for the next thirty-five years. All of these periodicals invited contributions of poetry, essays, and moral fiction. Whether they paid little or anything, the ambitious editors provided a vehicle for many an aspiring author—without competition from the superior talents of New England.

Anthologies were another outlet. W. D. Gallagher of Cincinnati issued the first anthology of Western poetry in 1841 in his *Selections from the Poetical Literature of the West*. Thirty-eight writers were represented, of which three were from Indiana. When W. T. Coggeshall published his *Poets and Poetry of the West* at Columbus in 1860, he drew on 152 writers. Thirty-six were residents of Indiana or had been born here.

Printing in Indiana began at Vincennes in 1804. For the first few years it was confined largely to legal, Masonic, and denominational pamphlets and volumes. The first literary work in the state was ventured by two printers in Salem in 1818. It was an anonymous *Life of Bonaparte*, probably reprinted from an earlier Philadelphia edition. The next literary work to come from an Indiana press was a local edition of Joel Barlow's *Vision of Columbus* in 1824; its popularity in the West was exceeded only by the works of Scott and Byron, according to Prof. Ralph L. Rusk. Thereafter local printers began to take risks on local authors.

The influence of the New Harmony experiment on literary production in the state is difficult to analyze. Robert Dale Owen later described the colonists as a "heterogeneous collection of radicals, enthusiastic devotees of principle, honest latitudinarians and lazy theorists." Nevertheless, there were a few talented men who could write—the Owens, Maclure, Say, Josiah Warren —and certain dissenters from the experiment who vented their spleen in print. These invaders of the state were by no means typical; they were regarded as queer, godless, and even ridiculous by the ordinary Hoosier. Still, they provided a yeast. They had ideas and intellectual curiosity; they showed that they valued self-expression and the printed word; they had their own press. All this was stimulating, and some of the leaders stayed on in Indiana. The New Harmony press turned out some respectable pamphlets in the 1830's and 1840's.

Of course, Indiana was not isolated from the national temper. Indeed, Hoosiers were more cognizant of the East before the Civil War than the East was of Indiana. Undoubtedly the "flowering of New England" had some effect in stirring the creative impulse in Indiana. At least the Eastern writers were considered to have failed in attempting to picture frontier scenes. The ferment of reform nationally, 1830 to 1850, in the fields of antislavery, temperance, benevolence, women's rights, industrial working conditions, penology, revival religion, etc., as well as a rash of fads, like phrenology, health foods, Greek Revival architecture, co-operative living schemes, and cure-alls was felt in the West. This was the great era when men had limitless faith in their ability to improve society; Utopia was just around the corner. "Internal improvements" was the cry of the politicians, and Indiana embarked on a ten-million-dollar program in 1836 when the state revenues amounted to $50,000 a year. Along with others, Van Wyck Brooks has observed that "there is a vital connection between the phenomenon of literary energy and the phenomenon of human belief in the possibilities of the individual man." Indiana believed it had emerged from the wilderness and created a respectable culture. The West regarded the Eastern literary lights with some envy and impatience, complaining that the literature of the Ohio Valley was being ignored in the East. Hoosiers began to flex their cultural muscles self-consciously.

Altogether these multiple factors—the geography of the state, the mixture of inhabitants, the emergence of an articulate Hoosier, the development of a rich language, the temptation of literary clubs and periodicals, the New Harmony stimulation, the example of New England's literary output, the faith in progress, the hospitality of the nation to new ideas—all these prepared Indianans for a literary splurge. Had it not been for the Civil War, the movement probably would have blossomed earlier.

Once a few Hoosiers began to achieve success in writing, momentum gathered rapidly because of the number of latent writers who simply needed the spur of an example. Some took up their pens to attack the picture of Hoosierdom presented by Edward Eggleston in 1871. A few tried to follow the pattern of historical fiction set by Lew Wallace in *The Fair God* (1873) and *Ben Hur* (1880). But it was Riley who unloosed a horde of imitators. His poems began to appear in newspapers in 1877, and his first book, *The Old Swimmin' Hole* and *'Leven More Poems*, went through two editions in 1883. He seemed to demonstrate that an education was not necessary for writing and that homely subjects were fit topics for poetry. All the stored up observations on domestic life and nature were poured out in rustic bad verse by unsuspected harborers of the muse—not merely housewives and farmers, but lawyers, bankers, physicians, teachers, and ministers.

There is something to be said about the interchangeability of the arts. Persons with talent in one field often have some competence in another. Men who might have developed their aptitude for music or painting turned to writing instead, because they saw their friends doing it and achieving success. "If Jim Riley can make money writing poems like that, then by golly I can!"

Immediately more outlets were provided than the periodicals and daily press. A new crop of literary societies were organized, male as well as female, not to listen to outsiders but to hear papers written by members. And they did not meet just once a month, with a long summer recess. The Indianapolis Literary Club, a men's organization that is still flourishing, was founded in 1877 and meets weekly. The Terre Haute Literary Club, also for men, was established in 1881. The Ouiatenon Club was formed at Crawfordsville ("the Hoosier Athens") in 1883. Thirty-seven women's literary clubs that were organized before 1890 are still going.

Another curious development was the organization of the Western Association of Writers at Indianapolis in 1886. Although writers in other states were eligible for membership, it was monopolized by Hoosiers, mainly on the level of those who contributed verse to newspapers. But Riley, Nicholson, Catherwood, Thompson, Wallace, Major, and Tarkington were early members. The Association held annual meetings, but these gatherings of fifty to one hundred members became week-long literary festivals at a lake resort in June. Members read their own effusions and listened in turn to others. They met and conversed in smaller groups. Regardless of the quality of the programs, the stimulation to the writers of this fellowship was as great as life at Brook Farm to its select clientele. The Western Association lasted about twenty years.

Something else was happening too. In 1890 the center of population of the United States was found to be in eastern Indiana. That mythical center has moved slowly across the state in succeeding decades, but is still within Hoosierdom. Indiana elections were going the way of national elections. The state began to be cited as a reliable average or as a barometer of national temperatures. Hoosiers developed a sense of their own typicalness, a feeling that here was an area of real Americans. It reinforced their state pride, and one effect was a boosting spirit toward their own writers.

A final aspect of the momentum was that the second printing of Riley's first book in 1883 marked the first venture into publishing of the Merrill, Meigs and Company book store of Indianapolis. In 1885 the company absorbed another book store and became the Bowen Merrill Company, publishers as well as book sellers. In 1898 the name was changed to Bobbs-Merrill, and it became exclusively a publishing house in 1910. The existence of a publishing company in Indiana that could market its products nationally was a great stimulus to Indiana writers, and employees of the firm kept an eye out for budding local authors. It was a Bowen-Merrill salesman who brought in a manuscript from a Shelbyville attorney named Charles Major. *When Knighthood Was in Flower* appeared in 1898, and it became a best-seller for fourteen consecutive months. Riley remained a Bobbs-Merrill property, and Tarkington and Mrs. Porter started with them.

The momentum of Indiana literary production appears to have slackened in the last fifteen years. Possibly a depression and a war have interfered, and the authors whose names were household words in the first three decades of this century are no longer living. The stimuli that affected the earliest generations of writers are no longer effective. Although the geography is the same, the wilderness is gone and that great leveller, industrialism, is increasing. The newspapers give less space to literary contributions than they used to, although each Indianapolis daily prints such a column; the regional periodicals are gone or have become academic. Language differences have been ironed out by the free public school system. Faster and more widely accessible means of communication and travel have depleted the distinctiveness of Hoosier life; it conforms more and more to the pattern of life nationally. A noticeable amount of ancestor-worship prevails among readers; the two houses in which Riley lived and Mrs. Porter's two sylvan retreats are preserved as memorials, and the former homes of Eggleston, Wallace, Moody, Ade, and Tarkington are pointed out to visitors. Whether the "crop" of popular writers is giving out is uncertain, but the soil seems to have lost some of its fertility, although the Indiana State Federation of Poetry Clubs had a membership of 250 active poets in 1948. Perhaps the taste of the rest of the country no longer conforms to the fare that is offered or could be offered by more recent Hoosier authors.

A CARTOONIST AND A HUMORIST

George Ade

George Ade, himself one of Indiana's most popular writers, a humorist and a dramatist, was also a journalist who took great pride in his home state and his fellow Hoosiers. His career began in Chicago, where he and John McCutcheon, also from Indiana, roomed and worked together on a newspaper. Both subsequently became famous in their respective fields. McCutcheon's classic "Injun Summer" cartoon is still republished annually by the Chicago Tribune, *and Ade's "Fables in Slang" continue to entertain new generations of readers. Another Indiana humorist, both a journalist and a cartoonist, whose work continues to appear regularly long after his death is Kin (McKinley) Hubbard. While working for the Indianapolis* News, *Hubbard created his timeless character Abe Martin, a rural philosopher and observer of human nature and the passing scene. Hubbard's drawings and epigrams are still run regularly in the Indianapolis* News *more than fifty years after their first appearance there. In 1910 Ade did the following portraits of his two fellow newspapermen for the* American Magazine. *Additional information on McCutcheon is in his autobiography; on Kin Hubbard, see the brief appreciation by J. Harley Nichols published in the* Indiana Magazine of History, *XXVII (March 1931), 1–9.*

John T. McCutcheon.

In these days of factory journalism, with the Archimedean lever being worked by motors and the "department" displacing the old-time editor, it means something when a regular, day-by-day newspaper worker attaches to himself a real following of

From "Interesting People: John McCutcheon," *American Magazine*, XLIX (April 1910), 759; and "Interesting People: Kin Hubbard," *ibid.* (May 1910), 46, 49–50.

faithful believers. Many a brash young specialist can do the mushroom act. He bounds into the Sunday supplement with a brand-new conception entitled "Tikey the Tuff" or possibly "The Brutal Twins" (the ones that fire the buck-shot into their grandmother) and for a few weeks he is a vogue; then he dwindles from a necessary evil to an unmistakable pest and winds up as an unpleasant reminiscence.

Most of the geniuses who make pictures for the newspapers are so funny they cannot last. Furthermore they seem to think that the cranial angle of the regular subscriber corresponds to that of the African ant-eater. It is a relief to find a newspaper artist who is not straining to be irresistibly comical—who is content to catch the tableaux from the passing show and submit them to us in a mood that is simple, kindly and human.

John McCutcheon began making cartoons for Chicago papers about fifteen years ago. He has taken long jumps into all parts of the world since then, but whenever he can be strapped down in Chicago he is good for a daily contribution to the first page of the *Tribune*. Some say that he is a habit; others that he is an Institution, the same as Hull-House or the Board of Trade. There is no denying that his work is immensely popular and that his sermonizing, though genial and apologetic, is most effective. Politicians sigh for the favoring stroke of his crow-quill pen and the faithful who are working to lift up and cleanse and beautify Chicago hail him as their most valuable ally. He has the courage to find his topics among the little events that make up existence instead of hammering away at huge issues or fussing with public men who are already advertised beyond their merits. He never loses his temper and he has the rare gift of directing a cartoon at an opponent without tacking on a personal insult.

A good many thousands of people in the Middle West wait every day for McCutcheon's cartoon and miss him when he goes traipsing off to Africa to hunt big game. No cartoonist since Nast has had such a steadfast and loyal following. His salary, as newspaper salaries go in Chicago, is so large that many people refuse to believe it.

Abe Martin of Brown County.

Kin Hubbard is a young man on the staff of the "Indianapolis News" who ladles out a small portion of home-made humor every day of the year. His tabloid contributions are supposed to be the meditations of one Abe Martin, who lives down in Brown County, Indiana, where small fields of nubbin corn nestle between the clay hills, but where the persimmon, the pawpaw and the 'possum make amends for agricultural shortcomings. Nature smiles in Brown County, and anyone who has visited that part of our common inheritance will know why.

Abe Martin is as quaint and droll as Josh Billings and Artemus Ward ever dared to be in their respective periods. Their homely paragraphs are now fossil remains of what was supposed to be amusing at the time. But Abe Martin is up to the minute. He takes in the traveling troupes at Melodeon Hall, is an impartial critic of moving-picture shows, has looked with cold disapproval at red touring cars, and knows people residing in Indianapolis. His comments on men and affairs prove him to be a grim iconoclast, an analytical philosopher, and a good deal of a cut-up.

His daily offering consists of two parts which are totally unrelated, but which are wedged together in one paragraph, apropos of nothing in particular. For instance:

> "There's a' unusually big crop o' girls with bulgin' foreheads and retreatin' chins wearin' turbans this fall. The streets er so wide at Crawfordsville th' neighbors hev t' use opery glasses to keep a line on one 'nother."

Or this one:

> "Newt Plum's married dorter up at Indynoplus is savin' up to get a spring chicken. Friday was Tipton Bud's birthday annyversity and his wife gave him a straight-handled umbrella so he wouldn't leave it hangin' on some bar."

There will always linger in the memory Mr. Martin's sage observation that "Some girls are born with big feet and others wear white shoes." Only a few weeks ago he called attention to the fact that "Ez Pash's son-in-law has written from South Dakota for a home-seeker's ticket."

However, these fragments fail to give a true notion of the quality of Mr. Hubbard's delightful humor. He has collected his best stuff into several little books and almanacs which will be a joy to anyone who likes homespun truth trimmed up with tomfoolery. James Whitcomb Riley says of him:

> "Abe Martin—dad burn his old picture!
> P'tends he's a Brown County fixture;
> A kind of comical mixture;
> Of horse sense and no sense at all."

The funny man who comes to bat daily cannot knock a three-bagger every time, but Kin Hubbard has a high percentage and shows no signs of letting down. He has an abiding popularity in the Hoosier state for the reason that he deals in truth, maintains a kindly mood and never hesitates to go after make-believes and shams with a good stout hickory.

Sayings of Abe Martin.

In this month's "Interesting People" Mr. Ade's little article about Kin Hubbard whets the reader's appetite for a taste of Abe Martin's foolishness. Following are a few extracts:

Ole Ez Pash started t' whitewash his chicken coop Saturday but he didn' have terbacker enough t' finish it.

Miss Germ Williams wuz t' spend th' day in Morgantown yisterday but she fergot t' have it put in th' paper, so she didn' go. . . .

False teeth er all right in ther place.

Nothin' a little man says ever sounds probable. . . .

All things come t' him that waits—if he knows where t' wait.

If prosperity will jist return no questions will be asked.

A feller don't have over two er three real friends in a lifetime. Once in a while you meet some one that's nice an' clever, but he generally turns out t' be an agent for somethin'.

You won't meet any autos in th' straight an' narrow path.

Uncle Ez Pash says his new hired man is so dinggasted lazy thet he hed t' sharpen all th' stumps on th' farm t' keep him from settin' down. . . .

A friend that hain't in need is a friend indeed.

Lafe Bud has resigned his job at th' sawmill 'cause it took up too much o' his time.

What is worse than havin' some one try t' tell you about a play they saw?

You never hear nothin' 'bout "th' money father used t' make."

Tabitha Plum ran her peek-a-boo waist through th' pi-an-oley last week an', by ginger, it played a medley. . . .

I got a letter from Rushville sayin' thet ther wuz a Uncle Tom's Cabin troupe up ther' last week an' thet th' dogs were good, but thet they hed poor support.

Elder Berry an' wife hev gone to Wapakoneta, Ohio, t' live with ther son, Stephen. Aunty Berry will be greatly missed ez we hev no newspaper here.

A couple o' strangers wuz here this week talkin' up a cannin' factory. One wuz dressed like a Dimmycrat an' th' 'tother looked like he wuz in ordinary circumstances too.

It's all right t' be close-mouthed an' cool-headed if you kin be thet way without lookin' stupid.

Opportunity only knocks once, an' then we're generally in th' back part o' th' house.

It'll soon be time fer Christmas jewelry t' turn green.

Ther' doesn't seem t' be no effort made t' curb th' sale o' plug hats t' irresponsible an' commonplace people.

Dock Marsh an' th' boys er back from a huntin' trip in Arkansas. They killed eight quarts.

Nobuddy kin talk as interestin' as th' feller that's not hampered by facts er infermation.

Once in a long time you find enough relatives on speakin' terms t' hold a family reunion.

Autobiographical Excerpts

GRANDFATHER'S PANTS

Booth Tarkington

Booth Tarkington (1869–1946) is Indiana's most popular and prolific writer, the best known of the "Big Four" during Indiana's "Golden Age" in literature, and the tireless recorder of life on the right side of the tracks in America during the first decades of the twentieth century.

*Twice awarded the Pulitzer Prize for the novels he set in his native Indianapolis (*The Magnificent Ambersons*, 1918, and* Alice Adams*, 1921), Tarkington also wrote plays, historical romances, and widely appealing stories about young people, particularly his Penrod and Sam stories.*

Tarkington was born into an upper middle-class family in Indianapolis, and his novels, even the stories about childhood, reflect the life-styles and values of cultured, cultivated, and genteel America. Following a sheltered childhood, Tarkington completed his secondary education at Phillips Exeter Academy and then enrolled in Purdue University, where he was a friend of George Ade and John McCutcheon; he later attended Princeton University but earned no degree there. Instead, having immersed himself in the literary and dramatic activities available there, he left Princeton in 1893 to take up a career as a full-time writer. Unpublished after more than five years of effort, Tarkington finally broke into print with his highly successful novel of the rural Midwest, The Gentleman from Indiana *(1899). In a short time some of his previously written stories were also published, and Tarkington's reputation as a novelist and dramatist was established. In 1902, following a family pattern (his uncle and namesake, Newton Booth, had been governor of California), he was prevailed upon to run for the Indiana General Assembly, was elected, and served a single term. But Tarkington discovered that public service was not for him. The experience did give him material for several short stories about political life on the local level, which were collected and published under the title* In the Arena: Stories of Political Life *(1905).*

*Because of the enormous productivity of Booth Tarkington and the popularity of his major works of fiction, the selection chosen to represent him here comes from the less well-known collection of letters he wrote to his nephews while traveling abroad in 1903 and 1904. Already a successful novelist (*The Gentleman from Indiana*,* Monsieur Beaucaire*,* The Two Vanrevels*,* Cherry*) and a retired politician, Tarkington was in a light-hearted mood as he traveled with his parents and his young bride through Italy and France. He wrote the letters, often illustrated with humorous line drawings, to his elder sister's three sons, to whom the later Penrod stories were dedicated. They reflect Tarkington's ebullience, his wit and charm, the teasing yet loving relationship he had with the boys, and his need to write stories constantly. The best introduction to Tarkington, his life, and his literature is the excellent biography by James Woodress,* Booth Tarkington: Gentleman from Indiana *(1959); see also William E. Wilson,* Indiana: A History *(1966). A perceptive literary critic, Wilson contrasts the life and literary style of Tarkington with that of his equally prolific contemporary, Theodore Dreiser.*

Capri, Dec. 15

My dear Men:

From up here, 500 feet above, the sea looked fairly quiet, so Auntie Lou, Cousin Eleanor and I walked down the road that Krupp, the cannon man, made a present to Capri, to the Picolo Marina, a tiny fishing village at the foot of the rocks, with a tiny bay, behind a big flat rock, and a church and a tiny beach. We got some boatmen and descended some old stone steps that go down into the water and climbed into the boat. Then we were rowed by four men under the lee of the cliff that goes straight down into the deep, deep water. They don't row, hereabouts (in fact from the north

---

From *Your Amiable Uncle: Letters to His Nephews* (1949), pp. 147–161.

of Switzerland down it's different), as we do at home. They stand up in the boat and *push* the oar—like a gondolier—against a thwart. You never see an oarsman *pulling*.

When we came out from the lee of the cliff we struck the open Mediterranean and the swell that came all the way from Florida. Our boat seemed very small and we were most squeamish, p'tickerly Me. We would go sailing up into the air four and a half miles (precisely), then we would go down (the same distance—exactly), but my insides wouldn't keep to the measurements. By and by we turned into the cliff and entered the Green Grotto. This is an arched rock, slightly cavernous, about fifteen feet above the sea on the inner side of the arch, and about a hundred on the upper. The arch is about thirty feet wide, and the water underneath is luminous, fiery green—like emeralds made liquid—as green as the Blue Grotto water is blue. The rocky ceiling takes on the green light, but it is not a comfortable place in a running sea, because you can't tell when a big wave will lift your boat up and smash your hat against the roof. The waters roar and thunder, and you hear a wild, helpless, despairing calling—calling—calling, a wail that says, "Oh, take me home! Take me *Home*!" This comes from your stomach.

We rowed to a place just beyond the arch, and tried to get into a low hole in the cliff which is the entrance to the *Red* Grotto; but the waves were too high. But we saw something just as queer. It was an uncanny thing in an uncanny place—queer and wild and desolate. Far over the "turbulent swirl" the sun was going down; overhead the cliffs of cold stone towered up sheer to Mount Solaro, almost 2,000 feet. The sea was roaring and groaning in all the caves and swiping the huge rocks and flying into foam in consequence. Right by us was the spout, of which we'd never heard. If they had it on the Jersey or New England coast, they'd have a summer resort built round it in two months; they'd give it a fancy name and an Indian Legend and sell sody-wotter, pop and cigarettes at a stand ten feet away. But they have so many wonders on Capri that it passes unnoticed and unadvertised. All the cliffs are cavernous, full of grottoes and are undermined by the sea. The spout is a small hole in the rock, not as big as this sheet of paper, and about two feet above the sea line. About twice a minute it begins to holler and take-on and squall and beller and puff and pant and roar. Then comes out of it a grea'-big jet of water blown into fine spray; it looks like an engine letting off steam. It comes out horizontally—and makes a pow'ful thrilling noise. It isn't a geyser. It is simply the end of a narrow passage in the rocks, the other end of which is under water. When the sea is running the air inside gets compressed, and, when the pressure is relaxed with the dip of the wave, explodes, carrying the water with it.

I'm sure you envy us, seeing such things—and yet those I've written of are *nothing* to those I *could* tell you! The reason I don't tell you the latter is that I still have hopes of going to heaven. Besides, I don't believe in *much* lying, anyway. . . . We found on the little beach a queer stone, a big pebble, like amber coated with flour—you might take it for the old kind of candy called jujube paste. It is translucent; when you hold it to the candle, the light shines through it. This isn't a lie. . . .

I think I have written you about the coral and tortoise shell of this neighborhood. The different specialties characterize each of the European cities; for instance: in

Geneva and Lucerne, wood carving, which the mountaineers do in the "long winter evenings"; Milan, silk; the mulberry trees spread everywhere about the city—the silkworms feed on mulberry leaves, you know; Venice, glass, pre-eminently; Venetian glass has been esteemed for centuries; Venice also exports beautiful furniture, of fine woods, stained and carved to imitate the antiques; Florence, mosaics and gilt-work, for picture frames, tables, mirrors, chairs, etc.; Rome for ruins, churches and pensions; Naples for coal, tortoise shell, silk and smells; Munich for art and beer; Vienna for the ladies' dressmakers, health foods, and a fast life; St. Petersburg for the other kind of skates; Berlin for soldiers and sports; Paris for eating, theaters and gay shops; London for men's tailors, traveling bags, hansom cabs and chops and ale and multitudinousness and silversmiths.

This is the *instructive* part of a letter, sneaked in like a dry piece of ham in a sandwich. But don't let it bother you; you can forget it—easily.

Papa John has been three days hunting a New Testament! *Aren't* any in English on the island. The few there are, are in Latin, though the priest has one in Italian. Books seem to be hard to get here anyhow; maybe not enough people know how to read. P. J. wanted to find out what mention the Scriptures make of Tiberius, the emperor under whom Christ was crucified.

Tiberius lived here as I've said, and the natives still call the cliff on which his principal palace was built "Timberio" or "Tiberio." This is because it has been called that "from-father-to-son" for 1800 years. They haven't got it from *savants*, or archaeologists; they've just always known it as Tiberius's place; that's all.

When you get a little older and foolisher, and read some silly English novels, and Thackeray, maybe, and Walter Scott and the "society gossip," you will *maybe* go through a phase of talking about "old families," and "best people" and "good families" and other funniments of that sort that young people and new people nearly always go through at home. You should remember, when the fit comes on you, that *all* families are old; how can they help it? When you speak of an "old" family you mean that it's an unenterprising family; sticks like a mud turtle to one place, because it's too fat, or too stupid, or too timid, to try any other place. Columbus was a *new* family man. The Aztecs had the only old families in America. Here in this hotel are members of old families, older than Boston, Philadelphia, New York or French Lick ever dreamed of. Their families have lived in the same houses on Capri for 2,000 years. Now and then the houses had to be patched and rebuilt but the people remained. And yet these aristocrats are not proud. They bow humbly and gratefully and hopefully (of tips) when we pass. They are dishwashers.

So don't be upset or have your heads turned by the fact that your two G'fathers came to Indianapolis when there were only a few acres of shanties and boardwalks and mud, and Fall Creek ran through the Columbia Club and the legislature met in a woodshed. It isn't to your credit. And don't be proud that your family was respectable even before the improvements on the new house were begun. Think of the Caprisian dishwashers and be humble. Leave it to them and the Aztecs and the Biddles and Winthrops and Stuyvesants to talk of old families. The Caprisians and Aztecs probably *won't*, being genuinely "old." The others may, though they'll probably take most of it out in thinking—which is a more disastrous way of puffing oneself up with hallucinations. (Get out the dictionary again, with-a-pleasant-smile.)

We have been gone three months—and probably will be away four more, because you have to stay in Papa John's and Nana's house. It is a great sacrifice we are making for you; I hope you appreciate it. How would you like it, this sort of a life, nothing but music and sea and cliffs and flowers—and scenery and lying abed till ten or eleven in the morning, and the warm sun of Italy? We shall have to bear it—and I believe that you needn't worry *too* much about our comfort. And it is far from unpleasant to think of you in the old house where you belong; where your mother grew up, mostly, and your pa courted her; and where, on the spot now occupied by the Hanna cathedral, your uncle was caught by Nana smoking cigarettes in the barn, accompanied by Albert Goepper and three of the Chapman boys, the youngest aged five.

The rooms have different names now: Papa John's room was all pink dotted out in crimson and was called "Hauté's room"; my room, the front room, was called "Uncle Newton's" room; Nana's room was called "Gran'ma's room." The big bathroom was my room. Papa John used to sleep up in the attic. He *said* he liked it, even in winter. They didn't heat that bed with hot-water bags; he carried a hot iron with him. Henry George slept in the barn and he had hot irons, too; set the barn on fire with 'em once. Your mother embroidered many pretty things and gilded up old office chairs till they looked like Louis Quinze. That's different from *quince*—doesn't mean fruit and is pronounced almost like "*Kazz*." It means the style of furniture in vogue in France during the reign of Louis XV. Your mother could take some of her embroidery and a dime's worth of gilt and make a $1.15 chair look like $19.65 at wholesale. Some of 'em are there yet, and they look nice to this day.

By the way, tell her to look up some of a month ago's *Harper's Weeklys*—there's a little article of mine in one of 'em, written in London, on the difference between American and English audiences and actors, which she might care to see. It isn't a good article; wasn't *meant* for an article—I *gave* it as an interview, but *they* treated it as an article and paid for it, a very mixed blessing, like a wormy nut, or taffy with lemon in it.

Goodness, aren't this the longest letter! How can it have happened? But "Satan always finds some work for idle hands to do." I wonder if the hours hang heavy in Shortridge—they used to be pretty dolesome for me. But your ma makes it up to you when you come home, I "expect." You probably gorge yourself from the sideboard and pantry, Sir John; and you, Laird Donald, most-like hit up a few of the same when you return from your own labors. And I believe that's not so bad, after all. I suppose you have your agonies, but I can't believe they were as great as mine, because, for one thing, your parents fond-and-dear have made you such gorgeous swells that you never went through the tragedy of Grandfather's Pants, as I did.

That was when I was about 13–14 or 12–13 some score of years ago. Perhaps I never told you. To begin with: never say "pants" for trousers—because it has come to mean something else, most often. I had just got into high school and I suffered because I was still kept in knickerbockers, the only boy in my class who still wore them. I spoke of this at home without intermission, but P. J. and Nana gave me the Deaf Ear. Then Uncle Newton came, I "complained a good deal" and hinted round considabul; he sympathized, and one day, when we were downtown together, said: "I'll get you some long breeches—two pairs of them and a new overcoat, to boot. Where's a good clothing store?" Then I was conscience-stricken; I didn't want that good uncle to spend much money on me, so I led him to the cheapest store I knew, "The Old Original Eagle"; I think it still exists. And in my humbled state—while he waited in front—I picked out the two cheapest pairs of trousers I could find and a flimsy overcoat and bore them away, rejoicing. They were $1.50 apiece and the overcoat was $8.00—I remember the amount was $11.00.

For a week I was a proud and lofty youth. *Then* both pairs of trousers gave way in various places—important places. I *could* not go back to the indignity of the discarded knee breeches after having appeared at school in "long pants." You know how that would be; I just couldn't think of it. None at all would have been better. But the decencies of the state—let alone etiquette—necessitated a soon change from the Original Eagle garments. I could not face the morrow in them, from day to day; and it was well for me that I was never paddled, for the knout would have struck home, in truth.

Uncle Newton had gone but Grandfather Booth was there, in his old room; with the little open stove fire, coughing cheerily and reading the *Banner o' Light*. He was a gentleman and hearkened unto a voice crying in the wilderness, never having grown very far from his own boyhood. He ramped about in his wardrobe and haled forth two pairs of trousers, saying: "Surely, of these two, one pair could be made for you." My eyes glistened with hope and gratitude; I folded the trousers to my happy heart, as he continued: "And here is a dollar for the tailor."

I got me upon the back of our then horse and sought and *found* a tailor who would do the deed for a dollar; making over the two pairs of G'ther's Pants into one pair for me. It would take a week's hard labor, he said. Then was I puffed up—mighty with expectancy—and happy beyond precedent. If a damsel looked askance at my legs during that week, I bore it manfully, though, i' faith, the Original Eagles were very near the parting of the ways; for I thought: "Aha! Next week and you shall succumb!" And I was proud, for G'ther wore only broadcloth; and of that same rich texture were the trousers in store for me. I should be the richly clad Earl's son, the princeling of the school. And if there were churlish youthen that betimes mocked me of my Original Eagles, I bore it easily that week, picturing to myself their coming envy and humility.

That night I bore those trousers home, ahorseback—I still remember. My heart beat high with expectation of the morrow's triumph and I nursed the burden tenderly. I arose early, donned my treasures and set forth to school.

It was a brisk, sparkling morning and I stepped high. My bosom swelled with joy and pride, swelled 'way up. I passed a stranger who looked strangely indeed—not so much of himself but in the way he gazed at my legs in the act of passing. There was something about his eye that misliked me—something unexpected. A little farther on I looked over my shoulder at him. He had stopped and was leaning against that sycamore in the sidewalk, exhausted with laughter. This was my first puncture; I couldn't understand it. I know that the trousers had held—they seemed to be all right. Yet mysterious alarms assailed me; my confidence was gone. I could discover nothing the matter, and hoped that the stranger had private food for mirth of his own. Still, I lingered not in the schoolyard but hastened to my own desk in the back row.

When I was called up by the teacher, for some reason, just after school tuck-up and went forward to her desk, there was a sudden whispering about me—"*Look at Newton's pants!*" As I passed down the aisle I left behind me stricken and waving forms, my comrades choking and collapsing—and by the time I reached the front, those on the outside aisles were bobbing up and down and even *standing*, to see my legs. I was not disappointed in *one* way, at least; I certainly made a sensation. After the first flush of excitement had subsided and I had got back to my desk, I whispered to Henry Ditmer, who sat next to me, and asked him to tell me what was the matter. He was holding his head low over his desk and trying to stop his snorting by holding his handkerchief over his mouth; but he wrote a note and slipped it to me: "Your difernt colors—I mean your pants."

It was the terrible truth. The texture and shade of each of the pairs of trousers G'ther had given me was different; my $1.00 tailor had used one pair for the front and the other for the back; also the nap of the front ran down and the nap of the back ran up. In front I was sober black; behind, I was a frolicsome gray!

Next day I resumed my Original Eagles.

AN ERNIE PYLE SAMPLER

Ernie Pyle

Ernie Pyle, a newspaperman and columnist, found his special niche in life and in the hearts of Americans during World War II. He became, through his daily columns, the chief interpreter of the war from the viewpoint of the common soldier. Ernie lived with the G.I.'s, ate the same food, slept in the same places, and underwent the same hardships as they did, and then wrote unadorned first-person accounts of these day-to-day experiences, good and bad. Two brief examples of his writing follow, one describing life on board a small ship, an LST, the other describing the experiences of an infantryman from Indiana. In both cases, following his usual practice, Pyle gives the name and hometown of his comrades and treats mundane matters in a simple yet powerful fashion.

Pyle was born in 1900 near Dana, in Vermillion County, Indiana. He attended Indiana University and then started newspaper work. Eventually he became a roving columnist who submitted a daily column from wherever he happened to be. This suited his bohemian life-style and served as valuable training for the type of writing he came to do during the war. After extensively reporting on American participation in the war in Europe, Pyle insisted on a tour of duty in the Pacific. He was killed by a Japanese sniper's bullet on the island of Ie Shima in April 1945. Pyle was the author of five major books, basically collections of his newspaper columns: Ernie Pyle in England *(1941);* Here is Your War *(1943);* Brave Men *(1944);* Last Chapter *(1946); and* Home Country *(1947). There is a good biography of Pyle by a friend and fellow newsman, Lee G. Miller,* The Story of Ernie Pyle *(1950). See also* Ernie's War:

The Best of Ernie Pyle's World War II Dispatches, *edited with a biographical essay by David Nichols (1986).*

LST Cruise.

A correspondent who wanted to go to Anzio simply drove to the dock where the ships were loading, told the Army captain in charge, and the captain said, "Okay, get on this boat here." Since it was a very front-line kind of war at the beachhead, isolated and horny-handed like the early old days in Tunisia, there was little red tape about it. Our troops were supplied and replaced by daily ship convoys.

I went on an LST (landing ship tank)—a type of vessel being considerably publicized at home then and probably the outstanding ship of our amphibious forces.

It was the second time I had been on one. The first time was the previous June at Bizerte, a few days before we took off on the invasion of Sicily. At that time I was living on a warship, but took a run around the harbor one day going aboard various types of landing craft, just to see what they were like. I spent about half an hour on an LST that day, and had never been on one since.

So imagine my surprise when I climbed aboard for the Anzio trip, checked in with the captain, and suddenly realized that it was the very same LST, still commanded by the same man. He was Lieutenant Joseph Kahrs, of Newark, New Jersey—a 37-year-old bachelor and the product of two universities. Before the war he was a lawyer in practice with his father in Newark. After Pearl Harbor he went into the Navy. His sum total of seafaring had been several trips in peacetime.

Exactly one year to the very day after he enlisted, Lieutenant Kahrs and a crew just as landlubberish as himself took over a brand-new LST and pointed her bow toward Africa. Only two men of the crew of more than sixty had ever been to sea before.

Just before my Anzio trip, they celebrated their ship's first birthday and everybody aboard had a turkey dinner. In that one year of existence their LST had crossed the Atlantic once, taken D-day roles in three invasions, and made a total of twenty-three perilous trips between Africa, Sicily, and the Anzio beachhead.

They were almost blown out of the water once, and had had countless miraculous escapes, but they were never seriously damaged. Most of the original crew were still with it, but instead of being green landlubbers they were tried and true salts.

Long lines of soldiers, loaded down with gear, marched along the dock to enter adjoining ships. They were replacements to bolster the fighters at Anzio. A person could tell by their faces that they were fresh from America. They carried a new type of barracks bag, which few of us over there had seen before. The bags were terrifically heavy, and it was all the boys could do to handle them.

One of the passing replacements remarked, "Hell, I've got more clothes than I had when we left America. I don't know how we accumulate so much."

Italian children scampered along with the marching soldiers, insisting on helping with the heavy bags. Some soldiers shooed the children away, but others accepted their help.

We were due to sail a few hours after I got aboard, but at the last minute there came a warning of a storm of gale force brewing in the Mediterranean. We laid over for twenty-four hours.

Some of the sailors took the opportunity next day to go ashore, and asked if I didn't want to go along. But I said, "What for? I've been ashore for three months already." So I stayed aboard, and just killed a full day doing nothing.

We were tied up along the waterfront street of a small port city near Naples. All day long the dock was a riot of Italians grouped below to catch cookies and chocolates and knickknacks the sailors and soldiers threw down to them. There must have been two hundred people on the dock, either participating in the long-shot chance of actually catching something or just looking on. Many of them were children, boys and girls both. Mostly they were ragged and dirty, but they were good-natured.

Every time a package of crackers went down from above, they scrambled and fought over it like a bunch of football players. Now and then some youngster would get hurt, and make a terrible face and cry. But mostly they'd laugh and look a little sheepish, and dash back in again after the next one.

All Italian children called all American soldiers "Hey, Joe," and all along the dock was a chicken-yard bedlam of "Hey, Joe, bis-ueet," each boy crying at the top of his lungs to call attention to himself, and holding up his hands.

The soldiers' favorite was a stocky little fellow of about eight, with coal-black hair and a constant good humor. He was about the only one of them who wasn't ragged, the reason being that he was entirely clad in military garb. He had on a blue Navy sweater and the biggest pair of British tropical shorts I ever saw. They came clear below his knees. His legs were bare, with gray Army socks rolled down to his shoetops which must have been at least size eight. To top it all off, he had a beguiling grin with a tooth out in the middle of it.

This youngster was adept at walking on his hands. He spent hours walking around the muddy stone street on his hands, with his feet sticking straight up in the air. The soldiers and sailors were crazy about him, and every time he finished his little performance he'd get a flood of crackers. I finally figured out that he walked on his hands so much because it was easier than walking in those gigantic shoes.

Pretty teen-age Italian girls in red sweaters came and stood at the edge of the throng watching the fun. The sailors and soldiers at the rail were quick to spot them, and the play for them was on. Reluctant and timid at first, the girls finally obeyed the sailors' demand that they try to catch something too, and in they went battling for broken crackers.

Most Americans were touched by the raggedness and apparent hunger of the children. But it was hard to feel sorry for those kids, for although maybe some of them really were hungry, the rest of them were just having a wonderful mob-scene sort of good time.

It was the old women in the crowd that I could hardly bear to look at. Throughout the day there must have been a couple of dozen who came, tried for half an hour to catch something, and finally went dejectedly away. They were horrible specimens of poverty and uncleanliness. They were old and pitiful and repulsive. But their hunger most surely was genuine.

One elderly woman, dressed in tattered black and carrying a thin old shopping bag on her arm, stood at the far edge of the crowd, vainly beseeching a toss in her direction. Finally one sailor, who had just started on a large box of Nabiscos, piece by piece, changed his mind and threw the entire box toward the old woman.

It was a good throw and a good catch. She got it like an outfielder. But no sooner did she have it in her arms than the crowd was upon her. Kids and adults both tore at the box, scratched and yelled and grabbed, and in five seconds the box was empty and torn.

The poor old woman never let go. She clung to it as though it were something alive and precious. And when the last cracker was gone she walked sort of blindly away, her head back and her eyes toward the sky, weeping, her face stricken just like that of a heartbroken child, and still gripping the empty box.

It was a spectacle, watching that foreign riot of childish emotions and adult greed that day. But some of it was too real—greed born of too great a necessity—and I was glad when word came that we would sail that night.

The sailors aboard the LST had the same outlook on life as the average soldier overseas—they devoted a good part of their conversation to home and to when they might get there.

They were pretty veteran by then, and had been under fire a lot. They had served the hot beaches of Sicily, Salerno, and Anzio. They knew a gun fired in anger when they heard one. On the whole, although the boys who manned those beachhead supply ships were frequently in great danger, they did live fairly comfortably. Their food was good, their quarters were fair, and they had such facilities as hot baths, new magazines, candy, hot meals, and warmth.

An LST isn't such a glorious ship to look at. It is neither sleek nor fast nor impressively big—no bigger than an ocean freighter—and yet it is a good ship and the crews aboard LSTs are proud of them.

The sailors slept in folding bunks with springs and mattresses. The officers slept in cabins, two or so to a cabin, the same as on bigger ships. The engines and crew's quarters and bridges are all aft. The rest of the ship is just a big empty warehouse sort of thing, much like a long, rectangular garage without any pillars in it.

Two huge swinging doors open in the bow, and then a heavy steel ramp comes down so that trucks and tanks and jeeps can drive in. The ships can land at a beach for loading and unloading, or run nose-first to a dock.

They have flat bottoms and consequently they roll when there is no sea at all. The sailors said, "They'll even roll in drydock." They roll fast, too. Their usual tempo is a round-trip roll every six seconds. The boys said that in a really heavy sea they could stand on the bridge and actually see the bow twist, like a monster turning its head. It wasn't an optical illusion either, but a result of the "give" in these ships. The sailors also said that when they ran across a sand bar the ship seemed to work its way across like an inchworm, proceeding forward section by section.

My LST had handled every conceivable type of wartime cargo. It had carried a whole shipload of fused shells, the most dangerous kind. Among the soldiers of many nationalities that had been on the ship, the crew found the Indian troops of

Johore the most interesting. The Indians were friendly, and as curious as children. The Americans liked them; in fact, I've found that Americans like practically anybody who is even halfway friendly.

The Indian soldiers base practically every action on their religion. They brought their own food, and it had to be cooked by certain of their own people. They made a sort of pancake out of flour that was full of weevils and worms. But it was sacred, and if an American cook tried to help out and touched the pan, the whole batch had to be thrown away. Even going to the toilet was a religious ritual with them. They carried special toilet-seat covers previously blessed by some proper person, and would no more think of using an unblessed toilet than you would think of committing murder.

Lieutenant Joseph Kahrs told me of one touching incident that happened when the Indian troops were put ashore. One of them had fallen ill and had to be taken back to Africa. He was the only Indian left on the ship. The tragedy of his pitiful case was that the poor unfortunate was caught without a sacred toilet seat, and he had dysentery.

"What did he do?" I inquired.

"I never did ask," Lieutenant Kahrs said. "I couldn't bear to know. To me it is the most frightful incident of the war."

It was after dark when we backed away from the dock. We nosed out to sea for a mile or so, then dropped anchor for a couple of hours—waiting for other ships to finish loading and join us.

There was always the danger of submarines, and once off the beachhead the ships were frequent targets for aerial bombing and shelling from the land. Quite a few had been hit by all three methods, yet the supplies kept going through, and were often piled on the beachhead a day ahead of schedule.

One night the Germans hit a gasoline dump and burned up some five thousand gallons. An officer said, "At home, where gas is rationed, that would seem like an awful lot, but up here it's just a drop in the bucket and makes no difference at all."

Our fleet of supply ships was manned by Americans, British and Greeks. As we lay at the dock before sailing, a British LST was on one side of us and a Greek on the other.

When we finally got under way for good, I went to the open-air deck just above the bridge to see how a convoy formed up at night. On LSTs the bridge is completely enclosed with heavy armor plating which has little slits of thick, bullet-proof glass to look through. Since visibility is thus limited, the officer in charge stays on the open-air deck above and calls his instructions down through a tube to the bridge.

The moon was swathed in clouds, but it gave a faint light. I could see landmarks silhouetted against the horizon, but not much more.

"Have you ever looked through night binoculars?" the captain asked. "Try these."

The view was astonishing. Those binoculars seemed to take twenty-five per cent of the darkness out of the night. With them I could see several ships in line, where I could see none before.

Far ahead of us, directly out to sea, we saw occasional flashes of gunfire. I asked what that could be, but no one knew. It seemed unlikely that a naval battle could be going on out there, and yet there were the flashes.

"That's one of the things I've found out about the sea," Lieutenant Kahrs said. "You're always seeing and hearing things which are completely mysterious and unexplainable. You go on your way and never do find out the answer."

Hedgerow Fighting.

Soldiers are made out of the strangest people. I made another friend—just a plain old Hoosier—who was so quiet and humble you would hardly know he was around. Yet in a few weeks of invasion he had learned war's wise little ways of destroying life while preserving one's own. He hadn't become the "killer" type that war makes of some soldiers; he had merely become adjusted to an obligatory new profession.

His name was George Thomas Clayton. Back home he was known as Tommy. In the Army he was sometimes called George, but usually just Clayton. He was from Evansville, Indiana, where he lived with his sister at 862 Covart Avenue. He was a front-line infantryman of a rifle company in the 29th Division. Out of combat for a brief rest, he spent a few days in "Exhaustion Camp," then was assigned briefly to the camp where I worked from—a camp for correspondents. That's how we got acquainted. Clayton was a private first class. He operated a Browning automatic rifle. He had turned down two chances to become a buck sergeant and squad leader, simply because he preferred keeping his powerful B.A.R. to having stripes and less personal protection.

He landed in Normandy on D-day, on the toughest of the beaches, and was in the line for thirty-seven days without rest. He had innumerable narrow escapes. Twice, 88s hit within a couple of arm's lengths of him. But both times the funnel of the concussion was away from him and he didn't get a scratch, though the explosions covered him and his rifle with dirt. Then a third one hit about ten feet away, and made him deaf in his right ear. As a child, he had always had trouble with that ear anyway—earaches and things. Even in the Army back in America he had to beg the doctors to waive the ear defect in order to let him go overseas. He was still a little hard of hearing in that ear from the shellburst, but it was gradually coming back.

When Tommy finally left the lines he was pretty well done up and his sergeant wanted to send him to a hospital, but he begged not to go for fear he wouldn't get back to his old company, so they let him go to a rest camp instead. After a couple of weeks with us (provided the correspondents didn't drive him frantic), he was to return to the lines with his old outfit.

Clayton had worked at all kinds of things back in the other world of civilian life. He had been a farm hand, a cook and a bartender. Just before he joined the Army he was a gauge-honer in the Chrysler Ordnance Plant at Evansville. When the war was over he wanted to go into business for himself for the first time in his life. He thought he might set up a small restaurant in Evansville. He said his brother-in-law would back him.

Tommy was shipped overseas after only two months in the Army, and when I met him he had been out of America for eighteen months. He was medium-sized and dark-haired, and had a little mustache and the funniest-looking head of hair I ever saw this side of Buffalo Bill's show. While his division was killing time in the last few days before leaving England, he and three others decided to have their hair cut Indian-fashion. They had their heads clipped down to the skin, all except a two-inch ridge starting at the forehead and running clear to the back of the neck. It made him look more comical than ferocious, as they had intended. Two of the four had been wounded and evacuated to England.

I chatted off and on with Clayton for several days before he told me how old he was. I was amazed; so much so that I asked several other people to guess at his age and they all guessed about the same as I did—about twenty-six. Actually he was thirty-seven, and that's pretty well along in years to be a front-line infantryman. It's harder on a man at that age. As Clayton himself said, "When you pass that thirty mark you begin to slow up a little."

This Tommy Clayton, the mildest of men, had killed four of the enemy for sure, and probably dozens he couldn't account for. He wore an Expert Rifleman's badge and soon would have the proud badge of Combat Infantryman, worn only by those who had been through the mill. Three of his four victims he got in one long blast of his Browning automatic rifle. He was stationed in the bushes at a bend in a gravel road, covering a crossroad about eighty yards ahead of him. Suddenly three German soldiers came out a side road and foolishly stopped to talk right in the middle of the crossroads. The B.A.R. has twenty bullets in a clip. Clayton held her down for the whole clip. The three Germans went down, never to get up. His fourth one he thought was a Jap when he killed him. In the early days of the invasion lots of soldiers thought they were fighting Japs, scattered in with the German troops. They were actually Mongolian Russians, with strong Oriental features, who resembled Japs to the untraveled Americans. Clayton was covering an infantry squad as it worked forward along a hedgerow. There were snipers in the trees in front. Clayton spotted one, sprayed the tree with his automatic rifle, and out tumbled this man he thought was a Jap.

Do you want to know how Clayton located his sniper? Here's how! When a bullet passes smack overhead it doesn't zing; it pops the same as a rifle when it goes off. That's because the bullet's rapid passage creates a vacuum behind it, and the air rushes back with such force to fill this vacuum that it collides with itself, and makes a resounding "pop." Clayton didn't know what caused this, and I tried to explain. "You know what a vacuum is," I said. "We learned that in high school."

And Tommy said, "Ernie, I never went past third grade."

But Tommy was intelligent. A person doesn't have to know the reasons in war—he only has to know what things indicate when they happen. Well, Clayton had learned that the "pop" of a bullet over his head preceded the actual rifle report by a fraction of a second, because the sound of the rifle explosion had to travel some distance before hitting his ear. So the "pop" became his warning signal to listen for the crack of a sniper's rifle a moment later. Through much practice he had learned to gauge the direction of the sound almost exactly. And so out of this animal-like system of hunting, he had the wits to shoot into the right tree—and out tumbled his "Jap" sniper.

Clayton's weirdest experience would be funny if it weren't so filled with pathos. He was returning with a patrol one moonlit night when the enemy opened up on them. Tommy leaped right through a hedge and, spotting a foxhole, plunged into it. To his amazement and fright, there was a German in the foxhole, sitting pretty, holding a machine pistol in his hands. Clayton shot him three times in the chest before you could say scat. The German hardly moved. And then Tommy realized the man had been killed earlier. He had been shooting a corpse.

All his experiences seemed to have had no effect on this mild soldier from Indiana, except perhaps to make him even quieter than before. The worst experience of all is just the accumulated blur, and the hurting vagueness of being too long in the lines, the everlasting alertness, the noise and fear, the cell-by-cell exhaustion, the thinning of the surrounding ranks as day follows nameless day. And the constant march into eternity of one's own small quota of chances for survival. Those are the things that hurt and destroy. And soldiers like Tommy Clayton went back to them, because they were good soldiers and they had a duty they could not define.

The Tradition Continues

Two contemporary writers, both expatriates from Indiana with thousands of devoted—perhaps cultic—followers throughout America, are Kurt Vonnegut and Jean Shepherd. Vonnegut's stock in trade is an existentialist view of the present and a science fiction vision of the future, told in a comic narrative style that mixes pessimism, irony, and black humor. Shepherd, on the other hand, deals in nostalgia; his view of life in middle America during the middle third of the twentieth century blends his near total recall of the world of his youth with his equally remarkable comic sense. The selections that conclude this section are analyses and appreciations of the two writers rather than selections from their prose.

KURT VONNEGUT

Dan Wakefield

Dan Wakefield, as his essay on Vonnegut makes clear, is also an Indiana author of growing reputation, whose works have taken him to Hollywood as a movie and television scriptwriter, and most recently back to the East Coast. Formerly a contributing editor of Atlantic Monthly, *he is the author of, among other works,* Island in the City *(1959),* Between the Lines *(1966),* Going All the Way *(1970), a novel set in Indianapolis during the 1950s, and*

From "In Vonnegut's Karass," in Jerome Klinkowitz and John Somers, eds., *The Vonnegut Statement* (Delta Books, 1973). Reprinted by permission of Dell Publishing.

Home Free *(1977). His most recent works include* Returning: A Spiritual Journey *(1988), and* New York in the Fifties *(1992).*

Vonnegut's best-known book is Slaughterhouse-Five, or The Children's Crusade *(1969), a powerful if highly unusual retelling of the Allied bombing of Dresden late in the war, an event Vonnegut had experienced as a POW. More recently he has written the novels* Breakfast of Champions, Slapstick, *and* Jailbird, *and the play* Happy Birthday, Wanda June. *For additional information on Vonnegut, see Peter J. Reed,* Kurt Vonnegut, Jr. *(1972); see also the candid interview with Vonnegut published in* Playboy, *XX (July 1973), 57–74, 214–216.*

The first time I read anything by Kurt Vonnegut, I was sitting in a barbershop in Indianapolis, leafing through a dog-eared copy of *The Saturday Evening Post* while waiting to have my favorite barber give me one of those kind of haircuts that prompted jocular fellows to quip, "Hey, I see you got your ears set out!" Har, har, har. (People said "Har, har, har" then to let you know something was funny; it was one of those doldrum years like 1953 when people seemed especially self-conscious and wanted to be what was called "One of the boys.")

To return to Vonnegut's story: I hardly remember it, but vaguely recall that it was about a little boy who played a large musical instrument, a tuba I think. It was not so much the story itself that impressed me as the fact that it was written by Kurt Vonnegut, Jr. The impressive thing about *that* was that Vonnegut, like me, was born and raised in Indianapolis, and also like me had gone to Shortridge High School and written for the Shortridge *Daily Echo*, the first high-school daily paper in the entire United States of America!

Vonnegut had graduated from Shortridge ten years before me, but his name was known to all of us aspiring writers who worked on the *Echo*. He, like us, had first been published in those pages, no doubt starting out like all other neophytes by covering meetings of the Stamp Club or freshman wrestling matches or the appointment of new officers of the ROTC. And, from such humble beginnings, he had gone on to be a professional writer, a writer whose stories were published in the Big Magazines, meccas of literary success like *Collier's* and *The Saturday Evening Post!* And if *he* could do it, maybe it meant—well, there was just the hope that perhaps we too could aspire to such glory. (As a matter of fact, glorious or no, a remarkable number of former writers for the Shortridge *Daily Echo* have gone on to make a career as authors of some sort or other, including Vonnegut, me, the novelist Jeremy Larner, the sportswriter Bill Libby, *Newsweek* correspondent and political author Richard T. Stout, *Life* staff writer Wally Terry, former *Life* staff writer and now editor-publisher of *Earth* magazine, Jim Goode, journalist John Bartlow Martin; and I'm sure there are others.)

If, as a young man in Indianapolis, you were so bold and reckless as to let anyone know that you hoped to become a writer when you grew up, it was usually regarded with the same seriousness as a little kid's expressed desire for a career in the Fire Department. Of course, there *had* been writers who came from Indianapolis, Famous Men like James Whitcomb Riley and Booth Tarkington. But they were dead. Sometimes, though, if you spoke of the dream of authordom, a knowing citizen would stroke his chin and say, "Well, I understand the Vonnegut boy does some writing. Even gets paid for it sometimes."

It was not known, however—to me or my Indianapolis informants, anyway—

whether he got paid enough to live on. I heard somewhere that he worked for one of those big corporations, like Western Electric or General Electric, one of those corporations that everyone seemed to work for in the fifties. It was said that he worked in their public-relations department, and wrote his stories and things for magazines at night. It was said that he was married and had a lot of children to support. At odd moments, looking out of train windows, or drinking a beer, or studying for a test in my cubicle at Columbia in New York City, I would think of this guy Kurt Vonnegut, Jr., and wonder how he was making out. I was rooting for him, in my own mind, mostly from selfish motives; in some superstitious way it seemed to me that if one guy who came from Indianapolis and had gone to Shortridge High School could make a living as a writer, then another guy could too (the other guy being me).

Sometimes during that hazy period—I think we are still in the early fifties—I heard he had published a novel, and somehow I got ahold of it. The novel was called *Player Piano*, and was set in the future. It was about this fictional town of Ilium, New York, where the corporation owned everything, and people were divided along very stratified lines of work and leisure, all of which was planned out by the corporation. It expressed the way a lot of people felt in the fifties about the way things were going; about the kind of life we were all going to end up with, a sort of American version of *1984*, with the corporation as Big Brother. None of us could foresee then that though the corporations would remain powerful, a time would come when great masses of young people would refuse to go to work for them anymore, would simply pretend that they didn't exist, and would invent other styles of life that they found more suitable. In this sense, *Player Piano* is the only one of Vonnegut's books that I think seems a little "dated" when read in the seventies; it was so accurately and spiritually a vision borne of the frustration of the fifties. But it was, and is, a good book—it was believable and sad and also very funny.

I was cheered not only because I liked the book but because this Indianapolis guy had written and published it. I thought that meant he had it made. Like many people, I assumed if you got a book published that meant you were an established writer and you lived off your royalties. Little did I know that in the vast majority of cases the publication of a book meant that you got a couple of reviews here and there and a thousand-dollar advance. (I didn't learn that till 1959, when I had my own first book published.)

It was difficult then to "follow Vonnegut's career," because nobody in the literary world mentioned him. Your best bet was to get a lot of haircuts and see if you could find any new stories he had written in the copies of *Collier's* and *The Saturday Evening Post* that were lying around the barbershops.

The next word I got about Vonnegut's career came from my mother. My mother had met his mother-in-law. There must be a special bond between mothers of writers, as well as mothers of girls who are married to writers. These mothers are long-suffering ladies whom fate has dealt an unkind blow. The mother just wants her child to be happy, and have a nice life, a good income, and be in good health. It is possible for a writer to turn out that way, but not likely. Their incomes are unsteady, at best. They tend to drink more than other people, which is bound to affect their health. (A psychologist's recent study showed that of the seven Americans who won the Nobel prize for literature, five were alcoholics and one "drank heavily"; the other was Pearl Buck.) My mother accepted her (or my) fate with courage and a spirit of helpfulness. She was always managing to meet the relatives of writers, to find out whatever tips they might have for me (and her). During my years in college, my mother managed to meet Kurt Vonnegut's mother-in-law, journalist John Bartlow Martin's mother, and Ralph McGill's sister.

But the news from Vonnegut's mother-in-law was dire. According to what Vonnegut's mother-in-law told my mother, who told me, Vonnegut might decide to give up writing altogether. His stories at that time weren't selling, and he was very discouraged, according to this third-hand account.

Sometime later, when I was living the wine-and-spaghetti life in Greenwich Village and managing to eke out an existence writing pieces for *The Nation* magazine, I heard from someone that Vonnegut had become a "science-fiction writer." That seemed dire to me also, science fiction then being a category that was very unfashionable, and smacked of "commercialism," whatever that might mean in terms of writing.

In 1963 I escaped New York for a period in Boston and New Hampshire, and around those environs I heard that Vonnegut was living on Cape Cod and teaching English at a grammar school. I don't know if that is true, as I never asked him, but that was "the word" then on Vonnegut. There was also a more cheering word, in the form of a novel he had written called *Cat's Cradle*, that a lot of people were talking about. They said it was quite wonderful. I read it, and agreed. In the book, Vonnegut invented a new religion (he is always inventing new religions) called Bokononism, with a prophet named Bokonon. One of the concepts Bokonon gave the world was the *karass*, which Vonnegut explained like this:

> Humanity is organized into teams, teams that do God's Will without ever discovering what they are doing. Such a team is called a *karass* by Bokonon. . . . "If you find your life tangled up with somebody else's life for no very logical reasons," writes Bokonon, "that person may be a member of your *karass*."

Not long after reading about that, I met Kurt Vonnegut, Jr., for the first time in my life. It was at a very nice dinner at the home of some friends in Cambridge, Massachusetts, in 1964. There were eight people at the dinner, and I didn't get to say much to Vonnegut, nor he to me, as everyone there had a lot of things to say to everyone else. There were only two things I remember him saying. One was that during the treacherous period when he quit his corporation job and devoted full time to writing, there came a particular year that seemed to him like a "magic year" when all his stories sold and his writing went very well and he figured he could really do it. The other thing was private, and I won't tell you that, but I liked both things I remember him saying, and I liked *him*. He laughed a lot, and was kind to everyone.

The following year I finished writing a book called *Between the Lines*, and I asked the publisher to send a set of galleys to Vonnegut in case he would be so kind as to want to make a comment about it. The book was essentially a collection of magazine articles and essays, but I added a personal, autobiographical narrative to it that explained something of what was happening to me when I was writing those things. The introductory part was all about how I grew up in Indianapolis, and how my dreams of athletic stardom were smashed when I found that I could not break the seven-minute mile. I got back a wonderful letter from Vonnegut about the book. He confessed that he, too, had been unable to break the seven-minute mile, and that we had had so many of the same teachers and same experiences as I described that, as he put it, "I almost feel that there shouldn't be two of us."

I was grateful for his nice letter, and elated by it. I began to feel guilty that I had not read all of his works, so I set about trying to find the ones I had missed, which were the ones in between *Player Piano* and *Cat's Cradle*. It wasn't easy, in those days, to just walk into a bookstore and get any book you wanted by Kurt Vonnegut. *Cat's Cradle* was a growing "underground" success, "underground" meaning that the publisher never told the public much about it, but that a lot of people who read it urged it upon their friends as an experience not to be missed. I was able to get *Mother Night* in a paperback edition, but *The Sirens of Titan* was out of print, and I finally was able to borrow a private copy of one from an editor of the house that had published it.

I liked these very different books very much. Now, you may think this was due to dumb prejudice because Vonnegut had liked *my* book, but I assure you that I am perfectly capable of not liking books written by the dearest of friends, or books by reviewers who have said nice things about books of mine. If I don't like a book written by a friend, I don't lie and pretend I like it; I just don't say anything at all. And, in turn, I have friends who do the same for me. Silence, in this area, is indeed golden. If you know a friend has read your book, and he hasn't commented to you about it, just don't ask. Stay friends.

Vonnegut is the sort of writer whom you either like a lot or dislike a lot; if you like one of his books, you are likely to enjoy the others. If you read one or two and don't like them, you might as well stop and accept the fact he's not for you. But even if you like them all, you have favorites. One of my favorites turned out to be *The Sirens of Titan*, and that surprised me, because it was supposed to be the most "science-fiction" type of all his books, and I don't like science fiction. By that I mean I don't like books that have green monsters with five arms, and lost tribes that are ruled by electronic lizards.

But Vonnegut's "science fiction" wasn't like that at all. It was about people, doing things that people might do if things had just turned out a little differently; or maybe if we *knew* more of what was really going on. One of my favorite lines is in *The Sirens of Titan*. (I have quoted it to explain many things that have little or nothing to do with science or fiction.)

In this book as in others, Vonnegut has invented another religion; in it, a man is supposed to fall from space and say a particular holy piece of scripture that will mark him as the long-awaited prophet. Well, this man falls out of the sky, and the believers gather around, and he knows he is expected to say something of great import, but he doesn't know what it is, so he just says the truth: "I was a victim of a series of accidents, as are we all." The believers cheer; that is indeed the exact thing he was supposed to say. So I wrote Vonnegut telling him of my pleasure in these books of his, and another just out called *God Bless You, Mr. Rosewater*. A lot of that one takes place in Indianapolis. In all of Vonnegut's books there is at least one person who is from Indianapolis; it is like Alfred Hitchcock always making a walk-on appearance in each of his movies.

I heard in a year or so that Vonnegut had gone out to Iowa to teach at the Iowa Writers

Workshop. Then I heard he was back at Cape Cod. We kept in touch by means of our books, which we sent to each other, and wrote friendly letters about. In 1968 I went out to California to try to write a novel I had been trying to write for most of my adult life. That winter, maybe over into 1969, his novel *Slaughterhouse-Five* came out. He didn't send me a copy, probably because he didn't know where I was, but I eagerly bought one, and thought it a marvel of a book. I wrote him about it, saying that in some strange way that had nothing to do with the subject matter, it reminded me of *Walden*; that it was the first book I had read since I read *Walden* while living in New Hampshire in 1964 that gave me a feeling of "lights coming on" in my head as I read it. He wrote back saying he thought I had overestimated the book, but thanked me anyway. He mentioned he had gone to Indianapolis for an autographing party at the bookstore of the L. S. Ayres department store. "I was there for three hours," he reported, "and sold eleven copies. All of them to relatives, I swear to God."

By that time Vonnegut was a hero on most college campuses in America, his book was a best seller, he was being written up in every magazine under the eye of God, he was asked to give graduation addresses, launch ships, and bless babies, but in good old Indianapolis, his hometown, his personal appearance drew only a handful of relatives. A third-string astronaut's wife from Hackensack, New Jersey, would have been a bigger draw. I guess it figures. The old "prophet-in-his-own-country" routine. So it goes.

But I see I have gotten ahead of the story, have jumped an important part of the plot. Which is, when Vonnegut left the Iowa Writers Workshop, and went back to Cape Cod to work on *Slaughterhouse*, the book that finally "hit" for him, how did he support himself? Vonnegut himself tells us, in *Slaughterhouse:*

> And somewhere in there a nice man named Seymour Lawrence gave me a three-book contract, and I said, "O.K., the first of the three will be my famous book about Dresden."

The way I heard it—not from Vonnegut himself or from Sam Lawrence, but the way writers hear these things about other writers and publishers' advances and so on—I heard that when Sam Lawrence first met Vonnegut he said to him, "How much money do you need to live on for the time it will take you to write your book?" And Vonnegut figured out the sum, and told Sam, and Sam gave him the sum, in advance of royalties. Which is something like a gamble or an act of faith, or both, on the part of Sam as the publisher. It turned out to be a good gamble and an intelligent act of faith.

I *do* know how Sam Lawrence happened to meet Vonnegut, because Sam told me the story himself. It was like this. Sam, who had been the director of the Atlantic Monthly Press and published *Ship of Fools* and the first J. P. Donleavy books and many other distinguished writers, had set up his own company in Boston, in conjunction with Dell Publishing, in New York. Sam was of course looking for authors. One day he read a review in *The New York Times* of the new Random House dictionary by Kurt Vonnegut. It was an astute and humorous review about dictionaries, and Sam liked it a lot and wrote to Vonnegut saying he liked it and if Vonnegut were ever in Boston, why didn't he drop in to Sam's office. And one day, without previous plan or announcement, Vonnegut dropped in. And it all began, the very nice relationship of Vonnegut as author and Sam as his publisher.

When I finally finished my own lifetime-in-progress novel, I had my agent submit it to ten publishers, one of whom was Sam Lawrence. I was living in Boston at the time, and I was nervous as hell wondering who, if anyone, would like my novel. Early reports came in: some people loved it and some people hated it. I heard early on from Sam that he was reading it and liking it. One night, pacing my fabulous book-lined study on Beacon Hill and trying not to jump out of my skin with nervous dread and anticipation, I did the very unbusinesslike thing of calling up Sam at his home and asking if he would send a copy of the novel to Vonnegut and see what *he* thought of it. The novel was set in Indianapolis, and Vonnegut is a native of that place and he probably could give a good estimate of whether the novel was any good or full of crap. Sam said O.K., he'd do that if I got him an extra copy to send to Vonnegut on the Cape, and I found an extra and had another shot of bourbon and ran down the hill to deliver the damn thing to Sam, by hand. I honestly didn't know what in the world Vonnegut would think about my novel. I had, as you know now, met him once in my life and exchanged nice letters with him. He had liked my journalistic books, but a novel is of course a different and more delicate kettle of fish.

The next thing was I got a telegram from Vonnegut that congratulated me on "your very important novel." Then Sam showed me a letter Vonnegut sent him, saying of my very own book that it was "the truest and funniest sex novel any American will ever write."

Wow. As it turned out, happily, Sam published my novel, and Vonnegut let him use that terrific quote on the jacket, and I couldn't have been more pleased. Also, before publication, Sam asked Vonnegut if he would make any editorial suggestions or criticisms of the book, and Vonnegut wrote a very intelligent two-page letter about it, making about seven suggestions of minor changes or possible additions, and I think I did about four of them.

Sam also asked Vonnegut if he could help us think up a good title for the book. My working title had been *Sons and Mothers*, and Sam pointed out that this was too confusing, there being so many other books that sounded like that, such as *Sons and Lovers*, *Mothers and Sons*, just plain *Sons*, and so on. So we all tried to think of titles, and Vonnegut sent in a long list of potential titles. . . . We finally ended up with *Going All the Way*, which I felt was faithful to the fifties tone and spirit of the book. Titles are very hard.

A month or so after all that, Vonnegut said he was coming up to Boston for the day and perhaps we could have lunch. I looked forward to that, because I had never really had a chance to sit down and talk to Vonnegut alone. We met at Jake Wirth's, which is Vonnegut's favorite restaurant in Boston. It is an old authentic German place, very plain, with lots of wurst and potato salad and thick honest sandwiches and steins of beer. The lunch was very pleasant, and like Vonnegut himself, low-keyed and kind of ironically amusing. The only thing I really remember him saying was, when he first saw me as I came in: "That's quite a head of hair you've got."

I had let my hair get long, all right, down over my ears. His comment didn't seem critical, just observational. I think we talked some about Indianapolis, and some people we knew in common there. Writers rarely, if ever, talk about writing. Maybe we did just a little, concerning some of his suggestions about my novel.

Later that spring I heard that *Life* magazine asked Vonnegut if he would like to review my novel. He said he would, but insisted on saying in the review that he was a friend of mine. This was a revolutionary thing to do—I mean, to *say* that. Most reviews are written either by friends of the author or enemies of the author, but they never admit it in the review, they pretend they just came upon this book out of the clear blue sky and are making a wholly objective judgment on it. But Vonnegut wouldn't make that pretense. He started his review by saying: "Dan Wakefield is a friend of mine. We both went to Shortridge High School in Indianapolis. . . . His publisher is my publisher. He has boomed my books. So I would praise his first novel, even if it were putrid. But I wouldn't give my Word of Honor that it was good." He went on to give his Word of Honor that it really was good.

So then everyone knew I was a friend of Vonnegut, which was fine with me, I am proud to be so counted; the only trouble was a lot of people started asking me for his address or his phone number or an introduction to him and all I would say was I knew he lived on Cape Cod, which was public knowledge from various articles about him. I knew he was being bombarded with requests and letters and queries about his life and work, and people just showing up on his doorstep, and wanting him to go ZAP or something and tell them the secret of the universe.

What was happening, especially with his adoption of the youth cult, reminded me of a story I had heard in New York about another writer who in my day was popular with children. That was the marvelous sports writer John R. Tunis, who wrote terrific sports books for boys, like *The Iron Duke, The Duke Decides*, and *A City for Lincoln*. Anyway, this friend in New York told about a kid from his hometown who, around the age of twelve, ran away from home. And where did he go? He went to the home of John R. Tunis, hoping to live there. Mr. Tunis of course had to call the boy's parents and send him back home.

Today the same kid probably wouldn't be reading sports books, and if he were precocious, he might have read Vonnegut and run away from home in hopes of living at *his* house. Anyway, a lot of kids showed up at his house, till it got to the point where he said publicly something to the effect that he really didn't *like* kids. It was similar in a way to the plight of Eugene McCarthy; Vonnegut didn't go looking for the kids, they adopted *him*.

I was especially uneasy when some very nice young friends of mine who lived on communes in Vermont and Massachusetts told me they wanted to go visit Vonnegut. I liked them, and I figured Vonnegut would like them too, but I said they would have to do whatever they wanted on their own, as I just didn't feel I could aid in what he might well construe as an invasion of his privacy.

They went ahead anyway, and it turned out O.K. One of them, Steve Diamond, gave me an account of what happened. There was Steve, a young writer, and his writer buddy Ray Mungo, and their friend Verandah Porche, "Queen of the Bay State Poets for Peace," and a few others. They went to Vonnegut's house, and he came to the door and said, "What can I do for you people?" Steve said they didn't want him to "do anything" for them, and they feared he thought they wanted some favor. Anyway, Vonnegut suggested they take a walk, and he led them out to a very beautiful spot near his house, and they all sat down on the ground. They talked, with some uneasiness, and then Steven suddenly said to Vonnegut, "Actually, there is a real reason we have come here. We are forming an organization called 'The Old Farts.' To belong, you have to smoke a lot of Pall Malls, and you have to have a porch to sit on. We would like you to be President."

All that was an allusion to Vonnegut's self-description in *Slaughterhouse-Five*, and he laughed and they laughed, and everything was O.K. They invited him, Sam Lawrence, and me to come to the May Day Festival that they and their neighboring communes were holding in 1970. We all went up, and it was a pleasant but rather restrained day, less festive than I had expected.

The main thing I remember was Vonnegut talking to Ray Mungo, who had founded the commune where the event was being held. Ray was explaining their future plans, and said that they had lived on that farm for three years now, had learned how to survive on it, and they felt they should pass it on to some of the throngs of younger kids who were coming up that way in escape from the cities; and they, as pioneers, should go farther north, where it would be more difficult, and they would learn how to survive under more primitive conditions. "You see," Ray explained, "we would like to be the last people on Earth."

Vonnegut pondered that for a moment and then asked, "Isn't that kind of a stuck-up thing to want to be?"

I don't think I had heard the term "stuck-up" since high school, but it seemed to apply quite nicely to the situation. Ray is no phony—he is in fact a remarkable young man and a very gifted writer—but he does have a real "prophetic" streak in him. Vonnegut does not, though some people assume it from his work.

Some friends of mine out here in Los Angeles, where I am living at the moment, were a little surprised about that very thing when they had dinner with Vonnegut on a trip he made out here in the spring of 1971. Both of them are writers, and mutual friends got them together for this dinner with Vonnegut. The next day my friends called me up and said how terrific Vonnegut was, and how frankly they had been afraid they wouldn't like him and were so glad they did.

"Why," I asked, "were you afraid you wouldn't like him?"

There was a silence, and then my friend said, "We were afraid he would be—'prophetic.' "

"But he's not," I said.

"Not at all," said my friend. "He's really a listener—he listened very closely to what everyone else was saying, and every once in a while he would make some wry, very funny, and pertinent comment."

No, he is not the prophetic type, and it is just another one of the ironies he finds in our weird existence that he should have been adopted as a kind of prophet by so many people, in so many places.

Excepting, of course, Indianapolis.

JEAN SHEPHERD

Joseph F. Trimmer

This section concludes with a perceptive essay on a writer of books and short stories who began his career as a radio and television personality. Jean Shepherd, a product of "The Region" in northwestern Indiana, rode his vivid memories of childhood—complete with brand names, advertising slogans, and adolescent fantasies—to broadcasting fame as he recreated for his audiences scenes of stunning realism and sidesplitting humor. His early career is detailed in the pages below, which also analyze Shepherd's In God We Trust, All Others Pay Cash *(1966), a book that uses the same techniques that made Shepherd a radio celebrity. Other books by Shepherd include* Wanda Hickey's Night of Golden Memories and Other Disasters *(1971) and* The Ferrari in the Bedroom *(1973). Joseph F. Trimmer, a professor of English at Ball State University, is a co-author of* American Oblique: Writing About the American Experience *(1976). In Professor Trimmer's view, Shepherd is keeping alive the good-natured midwestern humor of George Ade, a man whom Shepherd greatly admires. Shepherd's first book, in fact, was an edition of George Ade writings,* The America of George Ade (1866–1944): Fables, Short Stories, Essays *(1960). Like Ade too, who was a playwright as well as a humorist, Shepherd has branched out into television and movies. His hilarious full-length movie,* Christmas Story, *also loosely autobiographical, bids well to become a yuletime classic, his PBS series, "Jean Shepherd's America," is also memorable. See, in particular, another holiday-oriented episode, the timeless "The Great American Fourth of July and Other Disasters."*

The Midwest is one of our country's most complicated jokes. As with all the gags in the American jokebook, the Midwestern joke plays upon the delightful confusion of appearance and reality. To the outsider, the vast land between the mountains appears as flat and forlorn as the lives of the people who seem content to endure a feckless existence there. To the resident, however, the land that rolls away to the horizon conjures a life of ironic complexity. Loyalty and self-esteem require that the Midwesterner defend his world in public, but in private he admits to a gnawing hunger for an existence of greater substance and significance. In fact, the desire to escape the mocking suspicion of non-being may well be the most distinguishing feature of the Midwestern psyche. Yet once he does escape his environment, the Midwesterner discovers that he is haunted by the desire to return, to relive the rich fulfilling life he once perceived as futile. Ironically, his imagination has transformed a bleak landscape into a blessed memoryscape—the Midwest has become his "heart-land."

No one appreciates the twists and turns of the Midwestern joke better than Jean Shepherd. Born in Chicago in 1929, Shepherd grew up in Hammond, a mill-town in northwest Indiana that "clings precariously to the underbody of Chicago like a barnacle clings to the rotting hulk of a tramp steamer." Confronted by the "icy, detergent-filled waters" of Lake Michigan to the North, the "mile-after-mile monotony" of

---

From "Memoryscape: Jean Shepherd's Midwest," *The Old Northwest*, II (December 1976), 357-363.

the Indiana cornfields to the South, and the "thin, drifting coat of blast-furnace dust and refinery waste" everywhere, Shepherd festered into manhood amidst the ennui of the Midwestern depression (*In God We Trust*, pp. 16–17). He was briefly a student at the University of Maryland and Indiana University before serving a hitch in the Army Signal Corps. In 1951, following attempts at sportscar racing and a Volkswagen dealership, Shepherd began what would eventually become a very successful career in radio broadcasting with that prominent dispenser of Midwestern culture, radio station WLW in Cincinnati. After several years of "running a hillbilly jamboree and interviewing wild animal acts," Shepherd moved on to a sojourn with station KYW, Philadelphia, before moving finally, in 1958, to station WOR, New York. There, surrounded by the "partly completed and already eroding towers" of Manhattan, Shepherd played records and mused all night about his mythical Indiana boyhood. These nostalgic stories fascinated New York's night people—"cabbies, students cramming on No-Doz, transatlantic pilots flying in on WOR's 500,000 watt signal"—and they soon made Shepherd an "underground" celebrity. And when Marshall McLuhan mentioned him in *Understanding Media* as the creator of a new radio art form, Shepherd seemed destined to escape the vacuity of the Midwest and late night radio and emerge at last into the world of "official people." But he was quick to recognize the joke behind his new fame—his official reality in New York rested on his ability to recreate the unofficial, unreal kingdom "out there" in Middle America.

When Shepherd began a career as an author in the early sixties, it was evident that he not only understood the Midwestern joke but also intended to exploit its comic complexities. For his first book, he edited a collection of the writings of George Ade, another Indiana humorist who, in the early decades of the century, had escaped the Midwest for momentary fame in New York. In his introduction to the volume, Shepherd reminds his readers that despite the national preference for happy endings, most American writers have been preoccupied with the ideas of impotence and doom. The Midwestern writer has been particularly obsessed with such notions because "the midwest has been swimming in the turgid sea of futility. It is dotted with cities and towns that have never quite made it. Toledos that want to be Detroits, Detroits that want to be Chicagos, and Chicagos that forever want to be a New York. And they all know they are running in a fixed race." (*George Ade*, p. 10). While some writers weep over this state of affairs, others find the situation humorous. George Ade clearly belongs in the latter category because of his bemused preference for chronicling "the Great Un-chronicled. Those who are totally unimportant. So profoundly insignificant that they hardly exist in so far as literature is concerned. Those to whom nothing ever really happens. No tragedy or comedy. No romance or Great Loves. Those who settle for what they get and quietly move on" (*GA*, p. 14).

Ade's great virtue as a humorist was that he obviously loved the Midwestern people he wrote about. He portrayed their frustrations and failures with the "deep compassion of a man who had been there" (*GA*, p. 14). His people were real people, not elaborate fictions. And Shepherd insists that this is the "key to Ade as well as any other true humorist. Ade always maintained that he was not a humorist but a realist. He reported on what he *saw* in life and not what he imagined" (*GA*, p. 15). In fact,

Ade finally returned to Indiana to live because he preferred its grim reality to the insubstantial glitter of Gotham.

The qualities Shepherd underlines in Ade's work—a recognition of the futility of the Midwestern experience, a deep affection for those engaged in this fated struggle, and a belief that such experiences are somehow more *real* than the romanticism of most fiction or the surrealism of Manhattan—emerge as dominant characteristics in his own first novel, *In God We Trust, All Others Pay Cash* (1966). This collection of fifteen stories and sixteen bridge chapters concerns "The Return of the Native to the Indiana Mill Town" to do a story for an Official magazine. Ralph, the writer-narrator, reveals that his editors expect him to research the changing realities of Indiana's social landscape, but a few minutes amid the terrain of vacant lots, American Legion Halls, high tension wires, and gas stations, convince him that nothing has changed. Thus, rather than research present realities, Ralph stops at a neighborhood tavern, owned and operated by a boyhood crony named Flick, to spend the afternoon engaged in "some really good, solid Whatever-happened-to . . . ?, Did-she-ever-marry . . . ?, When-did-they-put-in-the-bowling-alley-down-at . . . ?" (*IGWT*, p. 19). Such reminiscing prompts Ralph to refashion the rubbish in his memory into stories that alternate careful cataloging of realistic detail with heavy doses of comic hyperbole.

Most of what Ralph remembers takes place in the Depression during the yeasty years of his pre-adolescence. This world is organized by ceremonial events such as Christmas and the Fourth of July or semi-significant events such as trips to the candy store and the neighborhood theater. The cast of characters includes his family, in particular his Old Man, and an assorted collection of boyhood friends and enemies with names such as Junior Kissel, Scut Farkas, and Wilbur Duckworth. The plots usually detail the quest to claim a piece of childhood junk as an official badge of belonging. Most of these quests end in failure, however, thus establishing their common theme as the destruction of romantic expectations.

Ralph's account of his attempt to outwit his fate is the subject of "Duel in the Snow." At the age of eleven, he develops an absolute mania for the most impressive item advertised in the seven-pound Christmas issue of *Open Road for Boys*—an Official Red Ryder Carbine Action Two Hundred Shot Range Model Air Rifle. Even though he reports that there are bears loose in the neighborhood, his parents do not seem to acknowledge the practicality of his Christmas gift request. Worse, his mother appears to predict doom for his dream when she says that "you'll shoot out one of your eyes" (*IGWT*, p. 30). This delphic curse follows Ralph everywhere. Atop the snow-frosted throne in Goldblatt's toy department, Santa listens while Ralph begs for his heart's desire, but he only chortles "Ho-Ho-Ho! You'll Shoot Your Eye Out, Kid" (*IGWT*, p. 38). When Ralph feels inspired to write a theme on "What I Want for Christmas," Miss Bodkin returns his blue-lined Indian Chief tablet paper without the usual "Watch margins" or "Check Sp." Instead, she writes, "You'll shoot your eyes out. Merry Christmas" (*IGWT*, p. 40). The drama ends as one might expect. Ralph gets what he wants and then almost gets it in the eye. On Christmas morning, as he practices with his new air rifle and authentic Red Ryder target in the backyard, one of the B-Bs ricochets off the target and slashes across the left side of his face. Although he is able to concoct another explanation of the accident for his parents, Ralph is sure that his wound is a sign from the gods who fix the lives of Midwestern mortals.

A series of similar experiences leads Ralph to ponder what he calls the two streams of life theory. Apparently, we all start out together, but one group of people "goes on to become the official people, peering out at us from television screens; magazine covers. They are forever appearing in newsreels, carrying attaché cases, surrounded by banks of microphones while the world awaits their decisions and statements. And the rest of us go on to become . . . just as . . . office boy[s] in the Mail Room of Life" (*IGWT*, p. 58). Ralph suggests that the major difference between Them and Us is "how we react to those moments that forever seal our fate. One crowd merely puts on its sunglasses, lights another cigar, and heads for the nearest plush French restaurant in the Jazziest section of town, sits down and orders a drink, and ignores the whole thing. While we, the Doomed, caught in the brilliant glare of illumination, see ourselves inescapably for what we are, and from that day on sulk in the weeds hoping no one will spot us" (*IGWT*, pp. 59–60). In a crazy way, their indifference to reality authenticates them as officially *real*, while our recognition of the way things are guarantees our continued non-existence.

Ralph demonstrates the hypothesis by telling us about a blind date he had with one Junie Jo Prewitt. He prepares for the evening reveling in the "warmth of Sweet Human Charity" that prompted him to accept the date. He was doing his friend Swartz a real favor. To his utter amazement, Junie Jo turns out to be "the greatest looking girl I ever saw in my life" (*IGWT*, p. 63). But the evening does not go well. None of Ralph's sure-fire stories works. Not even the one about how "Uncle Carl lost his false teeth down the airshaft" (*IGWT*, pp. 63–64). Then comes the epiphany. As Ralph edges closer to Junie Jo on the streetcar seat, he notices overhead an advertisement that speaks directly to him: "DO YOU OFFEND?" (*IGWT*, p. 64). Ralph suddenly realizes that HE is the Blind Date. "A Blind Date that didn't make it" (*IGWT*, p. 65). His silence for the remainder of the evening suggests that Ralph is no longer blind and that he is looking desperately for a patch of weeds.

In "Hairy Gertz and the Forty-Seven Crappies" Ralph remembers one of the few times that he did conquer his sense of insignificance. The occasion is a night-time fishing excursion with his Old Man and several of his beer-drinking cronies to Cedar Lake, a muddy, mosquito-infested pond fed by some unknown form of seepage. From one side of the lake he hears the hiss of skates from the roller rink; from the other side, he recognizes the whining saxophone of Micky Isley as he and his Moonlight Serenaders play "Red Sails in the Sunset" for the couples at the dance hall. In the middle of the lake are "17,000 fishermen, in wooden rowboats rented at a buck and a half an hour" (*IGWT*, p. 71). As they glide slowly over the submerged mountain of Shell and Sinclair oil cans, the men slurp Atlas Prager and troll for that infamous Midwestern fish, the Crappie. Suddenly, Ralph's bobber goes under and then everyone begins reeling in fish. But Ralph's real victory does not occur with this jackpot catch of forty-seven crappies; that must wait until the crew returns to his mother's kitchen for sandwiches and more beer. When she allows him to stay up with the men and hear Hairy Gertz's legendary story about the Hungarian bartender, his cross-eyed daughter, and the bowlegged dachshund, Ralph knows he has made it.

Unfortunately, success is a fragile thing in the Midwest. In the very next story, Ralph's Old Man, an ardent follower of the Chicago White Sox and trivia contests, is notified that he has actually made it through all the preliminary rounds of Nehi's Great Figures from the World of Sports contest and will soon receive a major award. When the box arrives, the family uncovers a "life-size lady's leg, in true blushing-pink flesh tones and wearing a modish black leather pump with a spike heel" (*IGWT*, p. 90). The leg is actually a lamp—"the definitive lamp"—complete with a Lingerie pink shade. The Old Man spends the rest of the evening "in honest, simple Peasant admiration for a thing of transcendent beauty" (*IGWT*, p. 94). But Ralph's mother is visibly upset by the "soft glow of electric Sex" that emanates from the living room window (*IGWT*, p. 94).

The stage is thus set for a real-life drama. According to Ralph, the neurotic battle of the sexes, as portrayed by Edward Albee or Tennessee Williams, is a terrible distortion: "My mother thought 'emasculation' had something to do with woman getting to vote" (*IGWT*, p. 95). *Real* family battles concern "where to go on vacation . . . what kind of car to buy . . . or who is going to take out the garbage" (*IGWT*, p. 94). In this case, the battle begins once Ralph's mother, who was "always jealous of that lamp," inadvertently breaks it one day while dusting. When the Old Man's heroic attempt to restore his symbol of victory fails, the Great Freeze sets in. For three days, the only sound in the house is the "sucking, gargling, choking retch" of the sink (*IGWT*, p. 99). Eventually, the Old Man relents and admits that such dramatic symbols of victory are probably "too jazzy" for his world. Disappointed but undefeated, the perpetually resilient Old Man takes the family to the movies.

And so it goes with all the other people in this world: Ludlow Kissell, the neighborhood drunk, while attempting a spectacular Fourth of July fireworks display, blows up his front porch; Wilbur Duckworth, the high school drum major, while attempting to perform the ultimate trick in the annual Thanksgiving Day parade, throws his baton into the streetcar high-tension line knocking out "generators as far south as Indianapolis" (*IGWT*, p. 195); and the whole community, while attempting to acquire a "magnificent set of Artistic Delux Pearleen Tableware, the Dinner Service of the Stars," at Leopold Doppler's neighborhood theater, is outraged when it discovers that Leopold has only gravy boats to give away (*IGWT*, pp. 252–53). Euchred beyond human endurance, the theater audience bombards the screen with gravy boats and continues to riot until pacified by a battalion of "blue-jowled policemen" carrying nightsticks (*IGWT*, p. 260). Nobody ever wins. But that is because, Shepherd insists, "futility, and the usual triumph of evil over good . . . is [simply] another name for realism" (*GA*, p. 12).

9. Hoosier Life after 1920

The two decades following the triumphant end of World War I, a searing event now commemorated by the huge Indiana War Memorial in downtown Indianapolis, proved to be difficult and tempestuous ones. After the expected temporary economic dislocations resulting from the transition back to peacetime production, many Indiana citizens shared in the general prosperity America enjoyed during the "roaring twenties." Hoosier farmers, however, failed to regain their relatively favorable status of the prewar period, and their position deteriorated again as the "agricultural slump" of the 1920s merged with the "general depression" of the 1930s.

There were other areas in which Hoosiers had difficulty adjusting to the new conditions of the postwar world. The Ku Klux Klan had greater success in no other state than Indiana during the early years of the 1920s; its appeal there was based as much on the xenophobic fears and anti-Catholic prejudices of the WASP-ish nativists as on the white supremacy ideology of the Klan's founders. And, as Kenneth T. Jackson has ably demonstrated in his book *The Ku Klux Klan in the City, 1915–1930* (1966), the Klan was not exclusively a rural phenomenon but also had a significant urban clientele. In 1924 the Indianapolis Klan had an estimated 50,000 dues payers, second only to the much larger city of Chicago in the total number of its white-sheeted and hooded members. At that time, the Klan in Indiana reached both its peak and its nadir, the latter stemming from former Grand Dragon D. C. Stephenson's dramatic and lustful fall from power. Even before Stephenson's conviction on second-degree murder charges, however, the Klan, which was torn by internal dissensions, had been unable to enact its legislative program following the 1924 elections.

In the meantime, Hoosiers and other Americans were involved in the social and sexual revolutions sweeping the nation, with much of the change stemming from the ready availability of such new technology as radios and motion pictures, automobiles and airplanes. Organized sporting events, ranging from college football to the Indianapolis 500, acquired a new popularity and brought fame to individuals particularly skilled in playing or coaching. A less well-publicized but far-reaching portent for the future during these decades was biologist Alfred Kinsey's decision to begin teaching a "marriage and family" course at Indiana University in 1938.

By the thirties, of course, the country was in the throes of its most severe depression. Before the Great Depression had run its ten-year course, political changes of permanent significance had taken place. The Republican party had continued to dominate Indiana politics during the 1920s, despite the forced resignation on criminal charges of one governor and widely recognized Klan ties on the part of another; but its power ended abruptly following the onslaught of the Depression in 1929. In the 1932 election the Democrats swept into office, controlling the legislature by a 91–9 margin in the house and by 43–7 in the senate. This led to many changes of considerable magnitude in Indiana, pushed into place by Governor McNutt even before the New Deal programs of President Roosevelt, also elected by an enormous margin in 1932, changed both the political and physical landscape of the nation. Particularly noticeable in the latter category, as indicated in the selection from the pen of Glory-June Greiff, were various construction and restoration projects of the WPA and the CCC. In the latter part of the decade, however, the Republican party was assisted by a growing disaffection for New Deal programs at home and its internationalism in diplomacy, and by the timely support of an opportunistic and imaginative businessman named Homer E. Capehart. It rebounded to win the state elections in 1940, with only the exception of the governor's office—a big exception.

Most of these trends will be explored in the readings that follow, including as a final selection an "oral history" narrative of life during the Depression by a tenant farmer's wife. This selection is taken from the sizable collection of oral history transcripts in the Indiana State Library. Although interviewing, the basic technique of oral history, is not new, the production of verbatim transcripts of the interview for deposit in research libraries has resulted in a relatively new form of historical document, again based on new technology. The oral narratives at the state library and in a growing number of other local and university library collections are particularly rich on the decades of the 1920s and 1930s.

For additional information on this period in the state, see James H. Madison, *Indiana through Transition and Change: A History of the Hoosier State and Its People, 1920–1945* (1982), vol. 5 of the *History of Indiana* series undertaken by the Indiana Historical Society. It is an excellent overview of Indiana during a critical period in its history. See also John D. Barnhart and Donald F. Carmony, *Indiana: From Frontier to Industrial Commonwealth* (2 vols., 1954); John Bartlow Martin, *Indiana: An Interpretation* (1947; 1992); Irving Leibowitz, *My Indiana* (1965); William E. Wilson, *Indiana: A History* (1966); and Howard H. Peckham, *Indiana: A Bicentennial History* (1978). See also Frederick Lewis Allen, *Only Yesterday: An Informal History of the Nineteen-Twenties* (1931); David A. Shannon, ed., *The Great Depression* (1960); and Studs Terkel, *Hard Times: An Oral History of the Great Depression* (1970).

The Ku Klux Klan in Indiana

The Ku Klux Klan, a northern as well as a southern organization, had no greater following in any state than it did in Indiana during the early 1920s. Feeding on the xenophobic, religious, and racial fears and prejudices of the predominantly white, Protestant, and highly nativistic population of the state, the Klan entered the state as early as 1920 and by 1924 had become a potent political force. Both the governor of Indiana and the mayor of Indianapolis—as well as scores of local politicians—owed their seats to Klan support in that year. Klan leader D. C. Stephenson was then considered, perhaps most of all by himself, the most powerful man in the state; but he disgraced himself and the organization in 1925. Following his sadistic attack on a young Indianapolis woman while aboard a train en route from Indianapolis to Hammond, which resulted in her death, Stephenson was convicted of second-degree murder and spent many years in the Indiana State Prison at Michigan City. Paroled in 1956, he dropped from public view but not from public memory. In 1978, after years of rumor and speculation concerning the former Grand Dragon, it was learned that Stephenson had died in 1966 in Tennessee. Fortunately, there is now a volume that deals with the life of Stephenson, especially his sensational murder trial in Noblesville in 1925. See M. William Lutholtz, *Grand Dragon: D. C. Stephenson and the Ku Klux Klan in Indiana* (1991).

Two selections below reveal various aspects of Klan activity and influence in the state during the 1920s. In the first, Professor William E. Wilson provides a vivid personal account of the 1924 election, in which his father, Congressman William E. Wilson of Evansville, went down to defeat because of his opposition to the Klan. The second selection is the work of a veteran journalist, John Bartlow Martin, describing the evil genius of the charismatic Grand Dragon Stephenson and the events that led to his downfall.

The Indiana Klan, crippled but not destroyed by the Stephenson episode, lived on into the Depression years of the 1930s, but its influence had waned. Recent efforts in the late 1960s and 1970s to revive the Klan here and elsewhere have met with a limited response; studied indifference or an amused curiosity are the prevalent attitudes in the former Klan stronghold. Among the most important and valuable recent publications that relate to the Klan in Indiana and to its leader for a brief period are Leonard J. Moore, *Citizen Klansmen: The Ku Klux Klan in Indiana, 1921–1928* (1991), and Lance Trusty, "All Talk and No 'Kash': Valparaiso University and the Ku Klux Klan," *Indiana Magazine of History*, LXXXII (March 1986), 1–36. See also the reminiscences of a reporter who covered the Klan story, Harold C. Feightner, "Vignettes of the Twenties," in *Dateline: Indiana*, edited by James E. Farmer (1958), and John L. Niblack, *The Life and Times of a Hoosier Judge* (n.d.), as well as the more comprehensive histories by Kenneth T. Jackson, *The Ku Klux Klan in the City, 1915–1930* (1967), David M. Chalmers, *Hooded Americanism: The History of the Ku Klux Klan* (1965), and Wyn Craig Wade, *The Fiery Cross: The Ku Klux Klan in America* (1987).

THE KLAN AND A CONGRESSMAN

William E. Wilson

When I think of the nineteen twenties, I think of the heat of summers in southern Indiana where I spent my vacations from Harvard. They were mostly happy summers, but there was one that was not—the summer of 1924, which came at the end of my freshman year. It glows luridly in my memory, an ordeal by fire through which I had to pass in the process of growing up.

We drove home to Evansville that year from Washington, D.C., in mid-June, my father and mother and sister and I, in the family Hudson. I had taken the Federal Express down from Boston as soon as my exams were over, and the next day we left the capital, where my father had just finished his first term as a congressman from Indiana. I was pleased with myself, secretly but no doubt obviously, for surviving the year at Harvard fresh and green out of a midwestern high school, and I was proud of my father for *his* record as a freshman in Congress.

We sweltered all the way home, across Maryland and Pennsylvania and Ohio and on into Indiana, the sun burning bright little braziers of blinding fire all around us on the nickel trimmings of the Hudson as we raced across the countryside at my father's touring speed of thirty-eight miles an hour. "Is it hot enough for you?" the filling-station men invariably said when we pulled up for gas; and in the tourist homes where we stopped, we kept the electric fans going all night. But I did not mind the heat. A Hoosier boy, I had been miserably cold in New England all winter, and homesick too. When we crossed the state line east of Richmond, I remember, we all sang "Back Home Again in Indiana," unashamedly sentimental.

On our arrival in Evansville, there was the old house on Chandler Avenue to explore and readjust to, and there were all my stored possessions to sort over and reappraise: adolescent love letters hidden in the secret compartment of my roll-top desk, minutes of the club I had belonged to in high school, yearbooks, dance programs, my rock collection, and even a bag of marbles from grade-school days, with an agate mooned by many battles. I thought I had outgrown them all but discovered I could not throw anything away. Eighteen is an age that looks both ways. There were also those first home-cooked meals after a year of institutional fare, and there was the impatient waiting, all that long first day, to see an old high-school friend whom I shall call Link Patterson. Link had not gone to college and had a job, like any grown man; he would not be home till suppertime.

After supper I walked over to Link's house. The moist, hot air was fragrant with the smell of the Ohio River and new-cut grass, and catbirds mewed in the bushes under front porches, where people sat in swings and rockers and said "Good evening" as I passed. But I was thinking of Link Patterson. Four years before, Link and I had bought our first long pants on the same day. We had double-dated in his father's car and in my father's as soon as we were old enough to drive. We had survived Miss Long in Latin together, and Mr. Baldwin in trig. We had tried out for the senior play and failed, and tried out for basketball and made the squad, though never the team. We had even had one glorious, bloody fight and afterward, for six weeks, walked to high school and back together without speaking to each other. We were the best of friends.

But the Link Patterson who met me on his front porch that night was not the Link Patterson I remembered. He looked the same and he greeted me in the old way, by cracking me hard on the biceps with his fist as I came up the porch steps. But he was not the old Link Patterson. Nor were his parents the same. I had loved his mother almost as much as I loved my own, and his father—garrulous, bawdy, and uninhibited—had always given me a man-to-man feeling that I had never shared with

---

From "Long, Hot Summer in Indiana," *American Heritage*, XVI (August 1965), 57–64.

my own more dignified father. But that night Mrs. Patterson was restrained and formal and seemed only half-glad to see me, and Mr. Patterson said almost nothing at all. I remember especially how they watched me, as if they were waiting to accuse me of something that they knew about but I did not.

The four of us sat on Link's porch for a while exchanging banalities. It was hot; we all agreed on that. In Boston, I told them, the winters were very cold. Yes, Harvard played basketball, but it wasn't Indiana basketball, and I bet our old team at Central could beat the Harvard varsity without half trying. Did I know they were building a new high school out on Washington Avenue? And what did I think of Tunney's chances against Carpentier? But we never got down to fundamentals, like girls or whether Billy Little's new band was as good as Hoagy Carmichael's up at Indiana University, and at the end of a half hour, Link said, "I'm sorry, Bill, but Mom and Dad and I have to be somewhere at eight o'clock," and I left and walked home, disappointed and puzzled.

My sister said I had outgrown Link Patterson, and that made me angry because it implied that I had become a snob or something. But my mother said it was sometimes hard to renew an old acquaintance, and she was sure Link and I would be back on the old basis soon. My father said nothing. He sat in the porch swing drumming his fingers on the arm of it in the way that made my mother nervous, until my mother finally said, "Will, I wish you wouldn't do that," and he got up and said he had to go down to the office, and wouldn't I like to come along?

We drove down Chandler to Fourth and down Fourth toward Main. As we approached a large vacant lot we saw that a crowd was gathered under floodlights, and a fiddlers' contest was in progress on a platform in the blue haze of a pit barbecue. My father said, "That's probably where the Pattersons are tonight. The Agoga Bible Class is raising money to build a tabernacle on that lot. They outgrew the Strand Theatre and moved into the Victory Theatre, and now they've outgrown it. They gave the preacher an automobile last month."

"But the Pattersons aren't Baptists," I said.

"Those aren't all Baptists, by any means," my father said, gesturing toward the crowd as we passed. "There aren't that many Baptists in Vanderburgh County."

"Aren't you going to stop?" I asked, remembering the church socials we had attended during his campaign two years before, when I had eaten chicken and dumplings of every Christian denomination.

My father shook his head.

"I'm afraid it wouldn't do any good. Harry Rowbottom has priority in that crowd." Harry Rowbottom was my father's Republican opponent. He had come to Evansville from Cincinnati eleven years before, had worked as a clerk in an oil company, and served three terms in the Indiana House of Representatives. He was not yet forty that summer, fourteen years younger than my father. I had never seen him, and I would not have a glimpse of him in his public life until 1928, when I was a newspaper reporter in Evansville. From that later period I remember him as a bombastic and platitudinous speaker, a vigorous man with large bovine eyes set wide apart in a heavy dark face.

"But Grandmother Cook is a Baptist," I said.

"I said they aren't all Baptists!" my father said, almost angrily.

He parked the car on Main Street and went into his office, leaving me alone to ponder his irritation about the Bible class barbecue. He was a man who seldom lost his temper. When he returned to the car, he did not start the motor but sat in silence for a minute or two watching the Saturday-night shoppers pass on the sidewalk. Finally, without preface, he said: "Son, I'm not going to be re-elected in the fall."

"You're joking," I said.

He shook his head.

"A lot of people have turned against me," he said, "a lot of good, honest, but misguided people like your friends the Pattersons. I decided I'd better tell you tonight, before you begin to hear it from others."

"Why, Dad, you can't help winning!" I said. "As many Republicans vote for you as Democrats. You've always said that yourself. And there are all those things you've done in your first term—the Ohio River bridge and the tax bill you wrote with Mr. Garner and ——"

"It isn't what I've done that counts," he said. "It's what I have refused to do."

"What is that?"

"Join the Ku Klux Klan."

In Cambridge I had read newspaper stories about the Ku Klux Klan that was being revived from the ashes of Nathan Bedford Forrest's old Klan of Reconstruction days, but college students in those days read newspapers very superficially. I did not take the modern Klan seriously.

"But of course!" I said. "A man like you isn't going to dress up in a sheet and make a fool of himself!"

Father shook his head again.

"It's a very serious matter out here this year," he said. "Senator Ralston warned me about it when he came back from a trip to Indiana last Christmas, and when I came out here in the spring for the primary, I was told to join the Klan, *or else*. I refused, of course, and now they're out to beat me, if they have to steal votes to do it. Your mother and sister don't know yet. I wish I could send them away during the campaign, but of course your mother wouldn't leave me in an election year. This summer is going to be an ugly business, son. I wish there were some way I could spare all three of you."

I felt his loneliness in that moment and was proud he had chosen to take me into his confidence. But I still thought he was mistaken. He was my father. He was invincible.

"Those people know your worth," I said, nodding toward the crowds passing on the sidewalk, "and they will vote for you."

"Too many of them have been bamboozled into a sense of self-righteousness by a bunch of demagogues," he said. "We've gone a long way in this country, but apparently we still haven't freed men and women of their suspicion of each other, their prejudices, their intolerance. I think that is going to be the big battle of this century. My little fight here in Indiana is just a preliminary skirmish and my practical political sense tells me I'm going to lose it. I'm not a crusader by nature, but, God help me, I'm not going to budge one inch from where I stand!" . . .

On Monday, still incredulous, I went out to the Willard Library on the other side of town and did some long-neglected homework among the bound newspapers on the political situation in Indiana.

There was a man named D. C. Stephenson who had come to Evansville from Texas two years before and entered the Democratic primary but, without explanation, had not campaigned and had lost the nomination to my father by an overwhelming majority. D. C. Stephenson was now, in 1924, Grand Dragon of the Ku Klux Klan in Indiana, which had a half million members, and he was ruling his Invisible Empire from a luxurious suite of offices in Indianapolis. "I am the law in Indiana," he was saying. Although he was only thirty-three years old, he signed his letters "The Old Man." In April, 1924, Governor Warren T. McCray had been sentenced to federal prison for using the mails to defraud, and Stephenson was supporting McCray's secretary of state, Ed Jackson, as the Republican candidate to succeed him. Jackson had given the Ku Klux Klan its charter to organize in Indiana three years before, and Stephenson had become the organizer in 1922, dropping his campaign in the primary race that spring against my father. Rumor had it that Stephenson had made over two million dollars in eighteen months from the sale of Klan memberships and Klan regalia. A congressman's salary in those years was only $7,500.

Stephenson was also supporting my father's Republican opponent now. But whether men like Harry Rowbottom and Ed Jackson on the Klan slate were actual members of the Klan was a question that could not be answered, for in 1924 no one except Klan officials was publicly professing membership. After all, candidates for office did not have to make an issue of the Klan; the Klan's support was enough. In the spring of 1924, Stephenson was quoted in the newspapers as saying, "God help the man who issues a declaration of war against the Klan in Indiana now." This meant any man, like my father, who refused to go along with their intolerance.

The times were ripe for the Klan's views in the mid-Twenties. Woodrow Wilson's internationalism had been repudiated; provincialism was the order of the day. Corruption had been the order of the day during the Harding administration, and his successor was the apostle of mediocrity and laissez faire. America was in the doldrums of a vulgar prosperity from which any kind of "crusade" would be a relief. White Protestant Americanism was the "ideal" the Ku Klux Klan set up for the smug and self-righteous who shared in the nation's prosperity and for the malcontents who had no share in it. If you were rich you could attribute your riches to your God-given right as a one-hundred-per-cent American to be rich and to be suspicious of anyone not of your kind who wanted to share the wealth with you; if you were not rich, you could at least be proud that you were not a Catholic who worshipped in Latin, a Jew who had a foreign-sounding name, or a Negro whose skin was black. Complacency and boredom, combined with an unacknowledged sense of guilt, can demoralize a nation as much as division or dissension.

Although I had promised my parents to take some vacation before I looked for a summer job, I set out from the library at once to find one. I wanted to return to college in the fall, but I knew that my father, out of office, was going to have a hard time keeping me there. Within an hour I was signed up to work for the Crescent City Refining Company in one of their filling stations. I was to work weeknights from five o'clock to nine, with one night off, and twelve-hour shifts on Saturdays and Sundays, and my pay would be fifteen dollars a week. That was not much toward a Harvard education, even in those days, but it was something. I went to work that evening.

I had been assigned to a station at the edge of the Negro district, and at quarter to five I appeared for work in oversized khaki coveralls that my father wore when he tinkered with the Hudson.

"I'm the new helper," I said to the man who sat in a chair tilted against the one shaded wall in the sunbeaten waste of the station. "Schelhaus" is as close as I can come to remembering his name.

He looked me up and down slowly, chewing on a matchstick. A long, oily nose drooped over his thin mouth. His black eyes were set close together. Finally he dropped the front legs of the chair sharply to the concrete.

"College boy, ain't you?"

"Yes, sir."

"What's your name?"

"Bill Wilson."

"Wilson? You the Congressman's son?"

"Yes, sir."

"I heard they hired a couple of boys today and you was one of 'em." He looked at the hand he had raised from a grease-stained knee. The hand was wrinkled, oily, and brown. He studied it uncertainly for a moment and then let it drop back upon the knee. "Well, you're on time. That's something. Name's Schelhaus. You take your orders from me."

"They told me downtown that you were the boss here, Mr. Schelhaus," I said.

"You're goddam right I am!"

At that moment another man came round a corner of the station, and Schelhaus said, "Here's the new helper, Dave. We got the Congressman's son." He stood up then, went inside, and shut himself in the toilet.

Dave looked friendlier than Schelhaus. He was younger, thirty maybe, with a wide mouth and yellow hair and blue eyes. He kept taking off his cap and putting it back on, like a baseball player.

"Schelhaus is an s.o.b., kid," he said. "You 'n' me'll stick together."

"Apparently he doesn't like my father's politics," I said. "Or maybe it's because I'm a college student."

Dave took off his cap and put it back on.

"Are you a crossback, kid?"

"A what?" I said.

"Catholic."

"No," I said. "Why?"

"I heard your old man was one."

"Well, he isn't," I said. "But what difference would it make if he was?"

"We don't want no crossbacks or kikes around here," Dave said. "Politics is different. Nobody's a Democrat or Republican any more. Hell, I used to be a Democrat myself! And you being a college boy is O.K.—with me anyhow. I wouldn't've minded going to college myself." He repeated the ritual of the cap and, afterward, clucked his tongue. "All them flappers! You tell 'em, saxophone!"

I knew by then what I was up against, but I was resolved to make the best of it. As the evening wore on, however, nothing more was said about my father, and I began to think my biggest problem would be to remain neutral in the tension between Dave and Schelhaus. There was not much to admire in Dave, but there was even less in Schelhaus. He was not only disagreeable; he was lazy. He often went to the toilet when there were cars in the drive, and after Dave and I had done all the work, he was critical. "Can't you clean a windshield better than that?" he would say to me; or, to Dave: "The nozzle nearly fell out of that tank while you were filling it. You better watch yourself, or I'll have to report you."

The first Negro came into the station about an hour after I started working. He was driving a Ford truck, with "Hauling" painted crudely on the panels. I wiped the windshield and filled the radiator while Dave stood at the back cranking out the gasoline. It was not until the truck drove off that I saw the dark, rainbow-streaked puddle of gasoline on the concrete. Dave must have spilled at least a gallon. I was sure that before long Schelhaus would lash out at him for his carelessness, and there was an awkward silence among us when I sat down between him and Dave and tilted my chair against the wall.

"What the hell did you mean, doing that?" Schelhaus said, finally.

I glanced covertly at Dave, who remained silent, his gaze fixed on the cars passing in the street.

"You a Bolshevik or something?" Schelhaus said.

Still Dave did not speak, and then I saw that Schelhaus was addressing me.

"You mean me?"

"Who the hell else would I mean? What did you think you were doing back there?"

I turned in appeal to Dave. But Dave continued to stare straight ahead.

"I don't know what you mean," I said.

"Oh, yes, you do!" Schelhaus said. "You know damn well what I mean. Giving that nigger radiator service and wiping off his windshield."

"But you said ——"

"I never said you was to give free service to a goddam black nigger!" Schelhaus shouted, sweat popping out on his oily forehead. "There ain't no job in this country can make a white man wait on a nigger! This is still a free country, and you'd better learn that pretty quick—you and your old man both!"

At the unexpected inclusion of my father in the tirade, I lost my temper.

"If it's a free country, then the Negro should get the same service as everybody else," I said.

"The *Nee*gro!" Schelhaus mocked, almost screaming. "Listen to him, will you? the *Nee*gro!"

Before I could speak again, he got up and went into the toilet and slammed the door behind him.

I was trembling, and when Dave reached over and laid a hand on my shoulder, I jerked away.

"I don't have to listen to that kind of talk," I said, "and if he says anything about my father again, I'll punch his nose!"

"O.K., O.K.," Dave said, trying to quiet me. "Schelhaus is an s.o.b., and I don't blame you. But you got to think of the principle of the thing too, kid. If you give a nigger an inch, he'll walk all over you. Schelhaus is right about that. It's a matter of self-respect, kid. A guy has to keep his self-respect or he ain't worth a damn. It's just a matter of self-respect. See?" . . .

My summer wasn't all misery. Link Patterson and I restored a kind of basis for our old friendship; we played tennis, took steamboat excursions, and sometimes, after my work hours, had double dates. But more often than not the Pattersons were off somewhere at a "meeting." They never said what the meeting was or where, and although Mr. Patterson was a Democrat and had supported my father ardently in 1922, he never mentioned the race for Congress that year. It was a strange contrast to the previous campaign of two years before, when Link and I had travelled about the congressional district with my father and eaten chicken and barbecue and applauded all the speeches. Now, whenever I suggested going to a rally, Link always had something else to do.

I found a new girl that summer and for a while we thought we were in love, but I never learned where she or her family stood on the issue of the Klan. She would not talk about it. Almost every time I took her out, my car was trailed by the Horse Thief Detective Association, which was the police force of the Klan. It was always the same car that did the trailing, and I finally got used to it. It would pick me up about a block from our house, follow me to my girl's house, and wait while I went in to get her, and then follow us to the movies or wherever we were going. When we came out, it was there waiting and would follow us home. One night, when I eluded its shadow and parked on a country road with her, a farmer pulled up beside us and said, "If you kids know what is good for you, you'll move along. The Kluxers are patrolling this road tonight, and God knows what they'll do to you if they catch you here."

I knew. At least I had read and heard stories of what the Horse Thief Detective Association was doing to others. They entered homes without search warrants and flogged errant husbands and wives. They tarred and feathered drunks. They raided stills and burned barns. They caught couples in parked cars and tried to blackmail the girls, or worse. On occasion, they branded the three K's on the bodies of people who were particularly offensive to them. And over in Illinois there had even been a couple of murders. I took my girl home.

No violence befell me or anyone in my family that summer. Not even a fiery cross was burned in our yard, although I saw crosses burning on hillsides near the places where my father spoke. But there was always the threat of violence around us in the hot and humid air of those breathless months. By chance I answered a number of the anonymous telephone calls we got at our house. "Hi, nigger-lover," the calls often began, and thereafter were so obscene they were unprintable. I am sure that my father got plenty of them, at his office and at home. Contrary to his former custom of sitting unmoved beside a ringing telephone and letting someone else in the family answer it, he always leaped toward it ahead of the rest of us that summer. Often he hung up without a word and returned to his chair. "Wrong number," he would say, if we asked him who it was. I suppose my mother answered some of those calls too, and my sister. But we never mentioned them in the family.

There were also anonymous letters in my father's mail—threats, innuendoes, scurrilous abuse, obscenities. He never spoke of them, but years later, after he died, I found a collection of them shoved into the back of his safe-deposit box at the bank. I don't know why he kept them. Maybe he forgot they were there. A couple were informing letters which, if he had chosen to use them, might have ruined some of his political enemies.

There were continual petty annoyances, pranks mostly, not intended to do us any harm but designed to create an atmosphere of anxiety and dread. More than once, when Father was at a meeting or when I had a date, the air was let out of the Hudson's tires or the battery was disconnected. Our window screens were soaped with the three K's. In the middle of the night the telephone would ring and when we answered, no one would be there. One sneak enjoyed a particularly annoying practice of partially unscrewing the light bulbs in our garage, so that when we drove in at night we could not turn them on. It was like a perpetual Halloween in midsummer.

As July wore on into the dog days of August, the Klan came more into the open—as an organization, that is. The lay members and politicians did not unmask or make themselves known, but the Klan leaders became bolder. The Evansville Klavern bought full-page advertisements in the Evansville newspapers announcing a public meeting in the Coliseum. The advertisement said: "Joe M. Huffington of Evansville, nationally known Klan leader, will discuss the Klan from a local viewpoint." I went down to the Coliseum that night when my work was finished and found the big municipal auditorium packed with people. A program, handed to me by a hooded usher, gave the title of Joe M. Huffington's speech: "Here Yesterday, Here Today, Here Forever." In the course of the speech, Huffington explained (inaccurate in his date): "The original Klan of 1861 was organized to deal with a bad system of local government. The present Klan was formed to preserve the best system of government in the world." The multitude cheered.

Making the rounds of the county fairs had been one of the pleasures of the campaign of 1922, but not in the summer of 1924. The Klan took over with a Konklave at each of them. At New Harmony, in Posey County, they publicly initiated a class of three hundred new members on the fairgrounds and afterward paraded, several hundred strong, through the village that a century before had been the scene of Robert Owen's experiment in social equality. At Boonville, in Warrick County, where Abe Lincoln used to come afoot from his father's cabin on Little Pigeon Creek to hear the law trials, three thousand of them gathered in the anonymity of their robes for an all-day outing and a big parade and speeches about the need for One-Hundred-Per-Cent Americans to take the law into their hands, while an airplane circled overhead dragging a twenty-foot cross. They even turned up at the fair in Dubois County, where the population was predominantly Catholic.

Klantauguas, or lectures on the principles of the Ku Klux Klan, were common at club meetings and semipublic gatherings. Processions of robed Klansmen marched into churches on Sunday mornings in the middle of services and laid sums of money on offertory rails, and some preachers were suborned and spoke in support of "the Klan ideal" thereafter. One who did not, in the northern part of the state, was taken across the Michigan line and branded. The Klan licensed bootleggers, and the Horse Thief Detective Association raided those who did not pay. Kiddy Klaverns were organized, Konsorts gathered in auxiliary clubs, and an abortive plan was launched to make Valparaiso University, upstate, into a Klan Kollege. The Klan's *Kourier* solicited the membership of native-born, white, Protestant Hoosiers and offered Klectokons, the Klan regalia, for sale.

By mid-August they were parading in Evansville. I stood one steaming August noonday at the corner of Seventh and Main and watched them march past, men on horseback, men in cars, men on foot, women, children, all in robes, all hooded, some carrying flaming crosses on long poles, silent except for the hum of motors and the clop of hooves and the soft shuffle of shoes on the half-molten asphalt. Afterward, the newspapers said there were more than five thousand of them. I wondered whether the Pattersons and my girl's family were among them. I wondered how many of them were our neighbors on Chandler Avenue.

People still were loath to talk about the Klan. Suspicion sealed everyone's lips. My father told me once he felt as if he were campaigning in a vacuum. He was not an orator and, for the most part, hammered away methodically at the issues. A member of the House Rivers and Harbors Committee, he advocated a badly needed program of flood control along the Ohio River. Although he did not drink, he was a "wet," opposed to Prohibition. He was an old-fashioned low-tariff Democrat and a strong believer in the principle of the graduated income tax, still a fairly new venture in taxation. But it was almost impossible to make the Klan an issue in that year of its beginnings; with no focal point for attack in the shadows of the Invisible Empire save a few acknowledged leaders and organizers, he could speak only in generalities on the subject of tolerance and decency, asserting his contempt for the forces that worked in secret against him.

Sometimes, when he and I were alone, he would shake his head in dismay and say, "I would never have believed that a thing like this could happen to Indiana. Hoosiers have always been generous, friendly, and kind. A poison has got into their blood." But when my mother and sister were around, he would not talk about politics. He still tried to joke and tease occasionally, but the attempts were feeble failures. I could tell from the troubled look in my mother's eyes that she knew the reason. Even garrulous and uninhibited Mr. Patterson, Link's father, continued to hold his tongue—until the very last day I was in Evansville.

An hour before train time on that day in mid-September, I went over to the Pattersons' house to say good-bye. It was a Sunday, and they were all at home. They shook my hand and wished me well.

"Write, now," Link said; and I said I would.

Mrs. Patterson told me to be a good boy, and Mr. Patterson advised me not to do anything he wouldn't do; and I promised.

But it was an awkward and stilted farewell, and we all knew it.

At the very last, as I was going down the porch steps, Mr. Patterson pushed Link aside and followed me out to the sidewalk. There he moved close and, holding up three fingers between his face and mine, said, "Tell your dad it's not too late." That was all he said. But I knew what he meant. Those three fingers were for the three K's.

I did not tell my father. I knew he would not change, and I did not want him to.

My parents drove me up to Terre Haute to catch the Southwestern Limited, and I returned to Harvard and began my sophomore year. For the next six weeks my father sent me clippings from the Evansville *Courier* almost daily so that I would be informed without his having to write long letters. I watched the rest of the campaign in print. But the print was not very illuminating. The newspaper gave little space to the Klan and was noncommittal editorially. But on the day before the election, the *Courier* did publish on its front page a prediction that Congressman Wilson, alone among Democrats, was sure to win, and by at least 10,000 votes. That clipping arrived in Cambridge the day after the election, and I already knew that my father had lost, by 3,500. I remembered what he had said in the car on Main Street in June: "They're out to beat me, if they have to steal votes to do it."

That morning after the election I talked with my family on the telephone. My mother and sister wept a little, but my father's voice was strong and clear. He sounded almost cheerful. "Next time, son," he said. "Next time." He was overoptimistic. He was defeated again in 1926; and two years later, when the Klan was at last collapsing and the Indianapolis *Times* and its editor, Boyd Gurley, won a Pulitzer Prize for campaigning against the organization, he had to step aside for younger men in his party. But that morning in the fall of 1924, my father's voice on the telephone gave me the confidence and courage I needed. I knew that as long as there were men like him in Indiana, the Ku Klux Klan too would pass. . . .

THE RISE AND FALL OF D. C. STEPHENSON

John Bartlow Martin

On April 2, 1925, D. C. Stephenson was arrested. It is almost impossible twenty-odd years later to recall how incredible that seemed. David C. Stephenson, Grand Dragon of the Ku Klux Klan in Indiana, had said with reason: "I am the law in Indiana." Less than a year earlier the Klan had won political control of the state. It claimed a membership of nearly half a million. On occasion it took over good-sized cities to hold its awesome parades, it burned its fiery crosses almost nightly, it made the laws in Indiana, and it enforced them. Its ruler was Stephenson, a man probably without precise counterpart in American history.

But a determined, outraged father, George Oberholtzer, swore out a warrant for the arrest of Stephenson, charging him with assaulting Madge Oberholtzer. Twelve days later Madge Oberholtzer died, and the charge became first-degree murder. With this

---

From *Indiana: An Interpretation* (1947, 1992), pp. 184–199.

indictment began the end of Indiana's experiment in home-grown dictatorship. By a wonderful irony Stephenson, leader of an organization sworn to uphold virtue and smite immorality, was brought to trial for a crime involving gross moral turpitude.

Madge Oberholtzer was the daughter of a thoroughly respectable family in Irvington, an upper middle-class section of Indianapolis. Her father was in the railroad mail service. She had attended Butler College in Irvington and a business school, and she had taught in a rural school and had done secretarial work for a couple of Indianapolis business houses before going to work "at the Statehouse," as her father put it. In Indiana the Statehouse is Mecca for ambitious folk of all kinds. Madge worked for the State Superintendent of Public Instruction. In 1924 she was a rather pretty girl of twenty-eight, unmarried. She once had been engaged but "the young man had to go to the war." She was five feet, four inches tall, weighed about 145 pounds, and her father testified: "I don't think there ever was a more healthy looking girl than she was."

She was murdered in March 1925, not long after she had met Stephenson. He was then about thirty-three years old, though most people thought he was much older, an impression he encouraged by asking his followers to call him "The Old Man." He was handsome, with blond hair, thin, plucked eyebrows, a thin mouth, narrow, steady blue-gray eyes, and a ready smile. He was squat and powerfully built. He dressed conservatively and looked like, say, a banker. Most people seem to remember him as a suave man of the world, a behind-the-scenes manipulator, but one man recalls the day when, folksy as any baby-kissing candidate, he walked coatless into a resort hotel dining-room in northern Indiana and joked heartily with vacationing Hoosiers. Then, that evening he distributed fistfuls of ten-cent tickets at the lakeside dance hall and stood beaming on the sidelines while the young people danced. (But later that night, long after the folks had gone to bed, Stevie, as his intimates called him, came roaring into the hotel grounds in a fast car, and he needed the assistance of his bodyguards to get upstairs. The Klan raided blind tigers relentlessly, but Stevie liked a drink, indeed, evidence hinted that he once had been treated for alcoholism.)

When he met Madge Oberholtzer he had been in Indiana only three years, but his rise had been spectacular. A few months earlier he had managed Ed Jackson into the Governor's office and he was the most powerful man at the inaugural banquet at the Athletic Club on January 12, 1925. Madge, in her controverted deathbed statement, claimed she met Stephenson at the banquet, and it is easy to see why, young and ambitious and on the fringe of politics, she did not refuse flatly when the great man asked her for a date. After all, they had been properly introduced. He telephoned her insistently and she dined with him at the Washington Hotel where he had a suite; he called for her in his Cadillac. Later she attended a party at his house "with several prominent people when both gentlemen and their ladies were present." This house, only a couple of blocks from the house where Madge lived with her parents, was "one of the show places of Irvington." It was here that the party which ended in murder began. On Sunday evening, March 15, 1925, Madge returned to her own home about ten o'clock. Her escort departed and her mother told her that somebody had been telephoning for her from Irvington 0492. Madge called the number and Stephenson answered and, telling her he was leaving for Chicago, urged her to come to his home on a matter of great importance. He sent his bodyguard for her—Earl Gentry, a big ex-cop who smoked cigars. He and

Madge walked to Stephenson's house. "I saw Stephenson and that he had been drinking. . . . So soon as I got inside of the house I was very much afraid." The housekeeper was not there. Stephenson was not married at that time. They took Madge to the kitchen and Earl Klenck came in. He was a deputy sheriff and another of Stephenson's henchmen. "I said I wanted no drink but Stephenson and the others forced me to drink. I was afraid not to do so and I drank three small glasses of the drink. This made me very ill and dazed and I vomited."

Stephenson told her he wanted her to go with him to Chicago, but she refused, being "very much terrified." He told her: "You cannot go home." The men selected guns from a dresser drawer. Gentry arranged for a drawing-room on the midnight train to Chicago. They all got into Stephenson's automobile and drove to the Union Station, stopping en route at the Washington Hotel to pick up the tickets.

They took her into the compartment (or drawing-room) and Gentry climbed into the upper berth, her deathbed statement continued. "Stephenson took hold of the bottom of my dress and pulled it up over my head. I tried to fight but was weak and unsteady. . . . What I had drunk was affecting me. Stephenson took all my clothes off and pushed me into the lower berth. After the train had started Stephenson got in with me and attacked me. He held me so I could not move. I . . . do not remember all that happened. He chewed me all over my body, bit my neck and face, chewed my tongue, chewed my breasts until they bled, my back, my legs, my ankles and mutilated me all over my body."

The next thing she remembered was being wakened next morning. "Stephenson was flourishing his revolver. I said to him to shoot me. . . ." They took her off the train at Hammond about 6:15 a.m., just before the train crossed the state line into Illinois. They walked the block from the depot to the four-story Indiana Hotel. Stephenson was wearing a cap, a pair of laced boots, khaki trousers, and a closely fitting black sweater. He needed a shave. The party was assigned to rooms 416 and 417, adjoining rooms but without a connecting door. In room 416 Stephenson gave the bellhop a half dollar and ordered breakfast. The boy left. Madge begged Stephenson to send a telegram to her mother. He dictated it: "We are driving through to Chicago will take train back tonight," and Gentry said he would send it.

"Stephenson lay down on the bed and slept. Gentry put hot towels and witch hazel on my head and bathed my body to relieve my suffering. . . ." Stephenson wakened and "said he was sorry, and that he was three degrees less than a brute. I said to him, 'You are worse than that.' " The bellhop brought up their breakfast and Stephenson, standing shirtless beside Madge, who sat dazed on the edge of the bed, tipped him a dollar. Stephenson ate heartily, Madge only drank coffee.

Stephenson's chauffeur, "Shorty," came in; he had driven Stephenson's car up from Indianapolis. "I said to Stephenson to give me some money that I had to buy a hat. 'Shorty' gave me $15.00 at Stephenson's direction and took me out to the car." She bought a small black silk hat for $12.50. Then "I said to 'Shorty' to drive me to a drug store in order that I might get some rouge. We drove to a drug store near the Indiana Hotel and I purchased a box of bi-chloride of mercury tablets."

Back at the hotel, the men got some more liquor, and Madge asked permission to go into room 417 to rest. Stephenson said: " 'Oh no . . . you are going to lie right down here by me.' I waited awhile until I thought he was asleep then I went into room 417 [alone]. There was no glass in room 417 so I got a glass in 416 . . . I laid out eighteen of the bi-chloride of mercury tablets and at once took six of them. I only took six because they burnt me so."

Now she lay down on the bed "and became very ill . . . vomited blood all day." About 4 p.m. Stephenson found her, and she told him what she had done, adding: "If you don't believe it there is evidence on the floor and in the cuspidor . . . the cuspidor was half full of clotted blood." He made her drink a quart of milk and told her they would have her stomach pumped at a hospital, where she could register as his wife. "I refused to do this as his wife. . . . Stephenson said that the best way out of it was for us to drive to Crown Point and for us to get married . . . I refused. Stephenson snapped his fingers and said to 'Shorty,' 'pack the grips.' Stephenson helped me downstairs. I did not care what happened to me."

On the 175-mile drive to Indianapolis they removed the license plates. "All the way back to Indianapolis I suffered great pain and agony and screamed for a doctor. . . . They refused to stop. I begged and said to Stephenson to leave me along the road some place . . . Stephenson said he thought I was dying . . . I heard him say also that he had been in a worse mess than this before and got out of it. Stephenson and Gentry drank liquor during the entire trip. I remember Stephenson having said that he had power and saying he had made $250,000. He said that his word was law."

They reached Stephenson's house in Irvington late that night, and Madge's mother was at the door. One of them stalled her and they concealed Madge in the loft above the garage. (Stephenson ordinarily slept there, a friend of his has said, avoiding the house out of fear of attack.) Stephenson told Madge: "You will stay right here until you marry me." She remembered little more until the next morning when, about eleven o'clock, Klenck took her home. He carried her into her house and put her on a bed. Coming downstairs alone, he met a woman, Eunice H. Shultz, who lived with the Oberholtzers. She asked him who he was and he said: "My name is Johnson, from Kokomo . . . I must hurry. . . ."

Upstairs, Madge "was groaning, very pale, could hardly speak. . . . She said 'Oh I am dying, Mrs. Shultz.' " Her alarmed parents, who had been out hunting her, returned home and called the family physician, Dr. John K. Kingsbury. They already had consulted their attorney, Asa J. Smith; it was he who later took from Madge the dying declaration that wrecked the Klan in Indiana. Several physicians attended Madge, and her brother gave blood for a transfusion; but she died April 14, and her father charged Stephenson, Gentry, and Klenck with murder.

D. C. Stephenson's origin is clouded. Probably he was born in Texas in 1891 and spent some of his boyhood in Oklahoma. A printer's apprentice, he became a second lieutenant during the 1914–18 war. Beautiful women were important in his life (he married at least two before he was thirty). Honorably discharged from military service, he moved to Evansville where he took up his life work.

Now, the original Ku Klux Klan, organized in 1865 by bored Civil War veterans and perverted into an instrument of Negro terrorization, was dead by 1872. The Klan of the 1920's owed its tenets to Know-Nothingism, and its name, regalia, and some of its outlandish terminology to the Reconstruction Klan. Founded in Georgia in 1915 by Colonel William J. Simmons, the modern Klan didn't amount to much until 1920 when two press agents took it in hand. The original leaders were replaced in 1921 by Hiram Wesley Evans, a Dallas dentist who as Imperial Wizard was by turns D. C. Stephenson's mentor and his implacable enemy. Under Evans, Klan membership rose to an estimated six million in 1924. That year the tide of the national Invisible Empire reached high watermark. The date coincides precisely with the high watermark of Stephenson's own career in Indiana.

Indiana—perhaps because it represented a cross section of the United States—was fertile ground for the Klan. The war's backwash favored its growth, but so did other conditions. There was the boredom of the small towns. There was the old tradition of intolerance—before the 1914–18 war you could hear whispers that every Catholic church was fortified and built on a hilltop to command its town with firepower, and you could see roadside signs at village outskirts: "Nigger, Don't Let The Sun Set On You Here." Although thousands of Europeans had come to work in the steel mills and coal fields, Catholics, Jews, and foreigners were oddities in central Indiana. The old stiffbacked yeomanry, the farmers and the small-town merchants, were set in their ways, resentful of outsiders. In 1918 Mark Sullivan watched the revered G.A.R. come down to the railroad station at Peru to see draftees off to another war, and when a fellow passenger asked in a foreign accent: "Who are them old guys?" Sullivan understood hundred-per-cent Americanism. And now in 1920 the postwar scramble for jobs was on, with foreigners and Negroes competing with returning veterans. Hoosiers were sick of world problems, they were hell-bent for normalcy. Any organization sworn to uphold hearth and fireside and womanly virtue, "Americanism" and law and order, was assured of welcome. The Klan waged righteous war on Bolsheviks, Catholics, Jews, Negroes, bootleggers, pacifists, evolutionists, foreigners, and all persons whom it considered immoral. It worked closely with the potent Anti-Saloon League and it revived the moribund Horse Thief Detective Association, a Civil War "regulator" group that now became the Klan enforcement arm, a formidable vigilante organization that entered private homes without warrant and got to be the bane of petting parties on lonely country roads.

In Evansville, D. C. Stephenson set about organizing the war veterans and entered the 1920 Congressional primary as a wet Democrat. The Anti-Saloon League licked him; he promptly became bone-dry and Republican. He joined the burgeoning Klan, taking with him his beloved veterans. He was a personable man and an eloquent speaker. Hiram W. Evans may have met Stephenson earlier in Texas. In 1922 he gave him the job of organizing the Klan in Indiana, and before long Evans added twenty other states from Maine to Nebraska. For a time Stephenson maintained headquarters at Columbus, Ohio, but soon he moved to Indianapolis, where meanwhile he had gone into the coal-and-gravel business. He sold Klan memberships for ten dollars each, of which he kept about four dollars. The white robes and peaked caps, manufactured for a dollar and ten cents, cost the members from five to ten dollars. In eighteen months, it has been estimated, Stephenson made between two and five million dollars. He hired full-time organizers, some of them stock-and-bond salesmen or Florida real-estate promoters, and he encouraged rank-and-file Klansmen to obtain new members by giving them a split of the initiation fee extracted from each "alien" admitted to the Invisible Empire. Among his most diligent proselytizers were Protestant clergymen. People of all kinds joined eagerly—power-hungry ward heelers and men from the criminal classes, prominent businessmen and bankers. Your nextdoor neighbor might be a Klansman and you never would know it even after an application for membership had been mailed to you at his instigation. The application, on stationery bearing pen and ink sketches of Klansmen on white-shrouded horses and headed "Imperial Palace, Invisible Empire (incorporated), Aulik of the Imperial Wizard," contained twenty questions, including these: "Are you a gentile or jew?", "Do you believe in White Supremacy?", "What is your politics? . . . religious faith?"

The Klan had more than the usual amount of the abracadabra common to secret orders. It suited the Hoosiers fine. The klaverns might meet once a week, the local leaders might meet almost nightly. Many of their meetings were simply poker sessions in the clubroom above the store overlooking the square, but many were more serious. Every now and then posters would appear mysteriously on telephone poles at rural crossroads, posters announcing a konklave, or a klavalcade, a parade. At the appointed time, usually just at dusk, the robed and hooded marchers formed near the outskirts of one of the small cities on the Indiana plain. They came from miles around. In orderly procession they marched into town, and the street intersections were patrolled by brother Klansmen who had usurped the police function. Why could they get away with this? Simply because they were in truth the law. The mayor was Klan elected; so were the city councilmen; so were the sheriff and the prosecutor. No one viewing a parade could laugh at the Klan's absurd posturings. There they were, the hundreds, perhaps thousands, of marching men, all clad in white from head to foot, no leaders, no flags, no drum-and-bugle corps, nothing but silent men marching in the dusk—that, and a silent, awed crowd of onlookers. Through the town they moved, perhaps pointedly passing the Negro district or the home of the Catholic priest, and on out to the side of the country road where in the gloom of the evening they set up their wooden cross on a hillside and soaked it with kerosene and fired it for all to see. Perhaps they took in new members, who, kneeling before this blazing symbol of terror, swore secrecy and obedience until death.

The Klan seemed omnipotent and omniscient. Its armed investigators, some of them thugs from Herrin, Illinois, raided blind tigers. Klan members issued warnings to nonmembers who, neighborhood gossip said, were cheating on their wives. It warned that the Pope was on his way to America. Once a mob of fifteen hundred, exhorted by a Klan speaker, actually met a train at North Manchester and forced the single frightened passenger who alighted to prove that he was not the Pope. The Klan spread fast. By 1924 it claimed from a quarter- to a half-million members, more than a tenth of Indiana's total population.

Stephenson, an adroit opportunist, seized on Governor McCray's conviction as proof that the duty of the Klan was plain: to purify, to purge Indiana politics. A former Exalted Cyclops of the South Bend klavern said that he understood the Klan was building a political machine to control the United States, that "we planned to extract Catholicism from the schools as a dentist would extract teeth," that at least one local klavern broke up when the Klabee, or treasurer, could not account for the funds, that Klansmen who had been planted on every newspaper in one of the state's largest cities regularly furnished to Klan leaders advance proofs of editorials and news stories before publication.

Thus while the rank and file played ghost, their leaders had more serious aims: money and political power. They got both. Stephenson maintained an expensive yacht and owned interests in various business enterprises. Did a Knight who was a chiropractor by day want to get his profession legalized? Stephenson would put a bill through the legislature. When a bill that would have abolished Madge Oberholtzer's job came before the legislature, Stephenson killed it for her.

He could be a man of the people when he chose. Once at a downstate farm home he "got down on the floor and crawled around with the baby"; he had come dressed in hunting clothes to arrange for a rabbit hunt on Thanksgiving, almost an annual rite on Indiana farms. He promised to go fishing with one of his downstate organizers, and when in the summer evenings he drove through his realm, he would park his Cadillac slantwise at the curb on the square and chat about crops with the klavern leaders who left the corner drugstore to stand with one foot on the running board.

But he also moved in a fast circle in the capital city—a circle of cocktail parties in hotel suites and dinner parties in the hotel roof garden above the city, a circle that met in a smoke-filled room when the Legislature was in session. A circle, in short, that he must have denounced many times in flaming speeches to the rank and file in the country districts.

And he also could be spectacular. When, on July 4, 1923, two years after he joined the Klan (his phenomenal career was surprisingly brief), he assumed office as Grand Dragon of the Realm of Indiana, he arranged at Kokomo the greatest konklave ever held in Indiana. After the Knights had assembled two-hundred-thousand strong (his estimate), he swooped down from the sky in a gilded airplane, stepped from it clad in resplendent robes, and pledged his unfaltering leadership. When he departed majestically, the hysterical multitude threw at his feet coins and jewelry.

He knew all the tricks. He called himself the foremost mass pyschologist of his time—a claim that cannot be dismissed lightly—and he kept before his desk a bust of Napoleon. His ambition was to be President of the United States. He had his eye on the Senate seat of Sam Ralston, whose health was failing fast in 1924, and on the 1928 Republican presidential nomination. Who dares say with certainty he would have failed? No one had laughed when he explained to the throng at Kokomo that he was late because he had been consulting with President Harding on high matters of state, nor when, frequently, he kept callers at his office waiting on the pretext of speaking long distance with the White House.

Having built his organization, Stephenson led it into the political campaign of 1924. Already he had made deals with some of the bosses. The Klan crossed party lines. It voted for its own members and its friends, whether Democrats or Republicans. But by and large the Klan won power by using the Republican Party, probably because the Republicans were already in control of Indiana, and Stephenson, instead of trying to lick 'em, joined 'em.

Before the polls had been open long on that primary day in May 1924, it was apparent that something new had come into Indiana politics. Negro leaders had double-crossed their race and thrown support to Klan candidates. The Klan was supporting Ed Jackson (Republican) for Governor. He was nominated. Stephenson dominated the Republican Party.

But only four days after the primary it became known that Stephenson and the Klan leaders were at odds. The leaders claimed he was banished from the Klan for conduct "unbecoming a Klansman" and involving a manicurist. Stephenson said he had resigned earlier because he didn't like the way the national leaders stirred up religious and racial hatred and used women to frame their political enemies on Mann Act charges. On April 7, 1924, that is to say: "On the Deadly Day of the Weeping Week of the Appalling Month of the Year of the Klan LVII," His Lordship, H. W. Evans, Imperial Wizard, had signed an edict ordering the Evansville Klavern number one to try Stephenson and had addressed it to "All Genii, Grand Dragons and Hydras, Great Titans and Furies, Giants, King Kleagles and Kleagles, Exalted Cyclops and Terrors, and to All Citizens of the Invisible Empire, in the name of the valiant and venerated dead."

Could such stuff be taken seriously? Indeed, it was the opening of a fight for big stakes involving ultimately, perhaps, the fate of the nation. To Cadle Tabernacle at Indianapolis, Stephenson summoned Klansmen from every Indiana county in an effort to sever the Indiana realm from the "domination" of Evans and Walter F. Bossert, who was an imperial representative and a Republican politician. Stephenson said: "God help the man who issues a proclamation of war against the Ku Klux Klan." The gathering elected him Grand Dragon. (Grand Dragons always had been appointed at national headquarters.) He said: "We're going out to Klux Indiana as she's never been Kluxed before."

Everybody was politicizing in this crucial election year. Indiana Klansmen had rival Grand Dragons, Bossert and Stephenson, and the politicians were nervous. Who really controlled the Klan vote? One night late in May the Klan paraded in strength through Indianapolis, starting on Indiana Avenue, heart of the Negro section, and thousands of citizens watched soberly. Nationally, the Klan claimed the power that blocked Al Smith's nomination. Ed Jackson stumped Indiana in Stephenson's car. Strife within the Klan became vituperative and deadly. The campaign ground on to election day. On that day the Klan elected "most everyone that was elected."

Now to Stephenson's elaborately appointed eight-room office suite on the third floor of the new Kresge Building, came a steady stream of legislators and other state dignitaries. Stephenson himself rarely was seen in the halls of the sepulchral Statehouse, but his men were there. He was desperately busy. For years criminal prosecutions and frame-ups had been common in Indiana politics. But now matters were approaching the flash point. Stephenson said the Klan leaders from Atlanta were trying to frame him on a morals charge. A woman who said she was his first wife from long ago came to Indianapolis and sued him on March 18, 1925, for desertion and nonsupport, and it was said that her expenses were paid by Stephenson's Klan enemies. Curiously, only the day before, Madge Oberholtzer had taken poison in the hotel room at Hammond.

Madge Oberholtzer's father said: "Neither faction of the Klan is mixed up in this. I am going through with this uphill fight for the sake of humanity—for the sake of other fathers and their daughters." Stephenson's secretary, Fred Butler, said: "We've always landed on our feet, haven't we?" Stephenson, in a dark suit and pearl-gray hat with turned-up brim, told a reporter: "I'd give anything if I could get away from the Ku Klux Klan."

Friends of Stephenson have argued that he, a shrewd man fully aware of the many enemies who confronted him that critical spring, would not have been indiscreet enough to get drunk and assault an innocent maiden. With what glee his enemies must have read the newspaper accounts of his arrest! As the trial began Stephenson declared that the murder charge was part of a gigantic conspiracy fostered by the Imperial Wizard. Was it a frame? Well, the chief evidence against Stephenson was Madge Oberholtzer's "dying declaration." Asa Smith took it from Madge, and he was a reputable lawyer with a substantial civil practice.

But was it possible that Smith was made an innocent party to a conspiracy? That would mean that Madge Oberholtzer lied in making her dying declaration. This Stephenson's partisans charged. A booklet published in his behalf in 1940 attacked the dying declaration at various points. For instance, why did Madge make no outcry or effort to escape? Again, although "terrified" and "very ill," she was able to note such details as the fact that Stephenson's revolver was pearl-handled but did not recall that the Pullman porter (as he testified) brought sandwiches to the compartment. Again, the newspapers reported she bought the hat and the bichloride of mercury at stores in the hotel building, which she would not logically have used a car to reach, as she said she did. (And it is a curious fact that the state introduced no witness to testify he had sold her either poison or a hat.) The pamphlet questioned, among other things, whether in those days in Indiana a woman of the virtue claimed for Madge Oberholtzer would have gone voluntarily to a bachelor's home at ten o'clock at night, whether she could have been "forced" to take three drinks. The pamphlet asked whether she would have gone unguarded from the hotel room where her abductor slept to an adjoining room to take poison instead of escaping and whether she would have swallowed the poison and vomitted all day alone in the room without seeking aid. Nevertheless, Judge Will M. Sparks admitted the declaration and said: "[Its] credibility and weight are wholly for the jury." And this Indiana judge told this jury of ten farmers, a businessman, and a truck driver: "The certainty of the declarant's belief that he or she is *in extremis* and that in a very short time, those immortal and spiritual elements which inhabit the body will forsake it, to encounter the dread possibilities of the unknown and supernatural world beyond the grave, is deemed to furnish a sanction equivalent to that of a solemn and positive oath administered in a court of justice." As to the statement's details, one must remember that when she made it, Madge Oberholtzer was in pain and she was dying. Of course Madge's statement was not subject to cross-examination.

But the question of Stephenson's guilt involves broader issues. For certainly this was no ordinary murder case—that is, death did not immediately follow the act of violence charged, and indisputably Madge took a deadly poison by her own hand. This raised the question: what, precisely, killed the girl? The state's medical experts contended that she died of a pneumonia infection caused by the bites on her breast, that she would have recovered from the mercury poisoning and ensuing nephritis, and that Stephenson's delay in providing medical treatment contributed to her death. The defense claimed simply that she had committed suicide. This had been the verdict of the coroner, Paul F. Robinson, and he testified for the defense at the murder trial.

The trial was venued to Noblesville, a small county-seat town not far from Indianapolis. Thus Stephenson, charged with heinous crime, came back from the wicked capital city to the country folk whence sprang his original power. Neither Stephenson, Klenck, nor Gentry took the witness stand. The defense established an alibi for Klenck (he was discharging his duties as deputy sheriff at the time of the attack). Its witnesses testified that Madge had known Stephenson a little longer and a little better than her dying declaration indicated, but that was all. The court refused a defense offer to prove that Madge had visited a married man at police headquarters and that his wife had caught them. Attacking the point in the dying declaration where she related that Stephenson and Gentry had stopped at the Hotel Washington to pick up the railroad tickets, one witness testified that he had seen her sitting alone in the car and that she seemed under no duress.

The trial lasted more than a month; the transcript covers 2,247 pages. Judge Sparks, charging the jury, said it was possible for one person to drive another by fear to suicide, and that this would amount to felonious homicide. But in such cases the suicide must have been a reasonable step taken in well-grounded fear of immediate violence and must have been the natural consequences of the "unlawful conduct" of the person who caused the fear. These questions were for the jury, which also had to consider Madge's past relations with Stephenson and her chances of seeking help during the abduction, for the question of whether she went to Hammond willingly was crucial. If she assented to the "humiliation" that drove her to suicide, then of course no homicide had been committed. But if she had been assaulted forcibly, then the jury had to determine whether suicide was a logical consequence, that is, whether, to a virtuous woman, death might be preferable to dishonor. If it so determined, it should convict. If the defendants, having abducted Madge forcibly, willfully kept her prisoner in the Stephenson garage and withheld medical attention, they were guilty of murder. Judge Sparks defined second-degree murder as unpremeditated homicide committed "purposely and maliciously," and he defined malice as not simply ill will but as "any wicked or corrupt motive." It was of second-degree murder that the jury convicted Stephenson. Klenck and Gentry were acquitted. And Stephenson was sentenced to life imprisonment.

What would happen now, politically? Stephenson went to prison boasting that Governor Jackson would pardon him. He didn't. Ordinarily Klansmen went on holding their meetings as always, but the professional politicians were quick to read the omens. They who so recently had welcomed Klan support now shunned it desperately. The Democrats feared that the Klan would move in on them. A Democratic boss said: "We don't want the poisonous animal to crawl into our yard and die." Democrats sensed a new political weapon. Clearly the political machinery that had controlled Indiana so tightly was flying apart. For years to come "Stephensonism" would be a label fatal to any Indiana politician. They all knew it; they scurried to cover. The fearful politicians heard rumblings from the penitentiary at Michigan City. Stephenson, embittered by Governor Jackson's refusal to act, was going to blow the lid off. Finally the storm broke. Stephenson disclosed the location of two "black boxes" containing his private papers. The Indianapolis *Times* launched a crusade. Stephenson played ball: "I have been railroaded to prison to protect others." It became plain that Stephenson for years had collected evidence against the politicians he corrupted. Three Marion County grand juries conducted the investigation. Witnesses disappeared. The black boxes disgorged. Mayor John L. Duvall was indicted for violation of the Corrupt Practices Act; February 4, 1931, he began serving a thirty-day sentence. Six members of the Indianapolis council, indicted for receiving bribes, paid small fines on minor charges and resigned. The entire city administration had been overturned. The *Times* produced a $2,500 check (among others) drawn by Stephenson in favor of Ed Jackson during the 1924 campaign. "After three weeks deliberation" Governor Jackson explained that the check was payment for a riding horse named Senator which had choked to death on a corncob. Finally came evidence purporting to show that Jackson, while a candidate, had offered a bribe of money and immunity to Governor McCray, then under indictment. Jackson was indicted; he pleaded the statute of limitations and was saved. The former Republican State Chairman went to Leavenworth on a conspiracy charge. Other officials were indicted. Judge Clarence W. Dearth of Muncie was impeached; he had once threatened a newsboy peddling an anti-Klan paper; he barely escaped removal from office.

The pot had boiled over. For its part in building the fire under the Klan, the Indianapolis *Times* won the Pulitzer Prize in 1928. By 1928 the Klan claimed only four thousand members in Indiana. Is the Klan dead in Indiana? Probably only a few local groups survive. On July 2, 1934, a fiery cross burned at Kokomo. Throughout the 1930's—the Democrats were in power—the Klan was political poison. Among the men washed into local offices by the Republican tides of 1940 and 1942 were a number of Klan holdovers. In 1944 Robert W. Lyons, a millionaire chainstore lobbyist, was elected Republican national committeeman, and a member of his own party denounced him as a onetime Klan intriguer; he resigned.

Stephenson in 1947 was still in prison, having carried his case unsuccessfully through more than thirty appellate actions. He has claimed that Klan death threats prevented him from presenting an adequate defense and, recently, that he has been kept a "political prisoner" by "the machinations of Robert W. Lyons." One newspaperman has said: "Stephenson is the hottest thing at Michigan City—if you paroled him it'd be worse than getting caught stealing ten thousand dollars." Stephenson himself once wrote this note to a newspaperman: "I should have been put in jail for my political activities but I am not guilty of murder." Many Hoosiers agree.

Higher Education

Indiana college life in the 1920s and 1930s and beyond involved much more than intercollegiate athletics, fraternity parties, and the antics of stereotypical students during the flapper, tin lizzie, and Depression eras. These years, despite the economic conditions and declining student enrollments of the 1930s, witnessed significant new departures in the field of higher education. Governor Paul V. McNutt can be credited with stressing, even in 1933, the necessity of continuing state support to the physically handicapped and to students at all levels:

> There are certain obligations which the state cannot deny even in periods of greatest stress: the care of its ward[s] and the education of its children. In the one, the obligation runs to the unfortunates themselves. In the other, the obligation runs to society as a whole. The hope for future prosperity and leadership lies in trained men and women. Children are born and grow up in periods of depression as well as in periods of prosperity. It is impossible to arrest their development. They have but one chance, which cannot be postponed. Roads and buildings may wait, but not the children.[1]

The legislature responded, and support for higher education and other public services continued, followed by numerous innovations.

The reading below reflects the willingness of the administration at Indiana University to support new ideas and approaches in scientific studies. The newly installed president of Indiana University, Herman B Wells, recruited outstanding new faculty, recognized research as a vital ingredient in the life of a university, and helped foster a climate of intellectual and academic freedom within the state despite increasingly strident criticism, particularly concerning the activities of a young biology professor, Alfred C. Kinsey.

PROFESSOR KINSEY AT INDIANA

Thomas D. Clark

This selection comes from a comprehensive history of Indiana University written by Thomas D. Clark, a distinguished professor of history at the University of Kentucky and the author of several historical works. His writings include histories of Kentucky, the western movement, the frontier, and the South. Professor Clark was visiting professor of history at Indiana University in Bloomington from 1965 to 1970.

No university in all of creation had ever been called upon to defend the freedom of investigation and publication in the highly personal area of human sexual behavior as Indiana University had to do in the 1940s and 1950s. Research in this sector of human life involved not only a deeply intimate matter but since the days of the

1. Quoted in John D. Barnhart and Donald F. Carmony, *Indiana: From Frontier to Industrial Commonwealth* (2 vols., 1954), II, 505.

From *Indiana University, Midwestern Pioneer*. Vol. III: *Years of Fulfillment* (1976), pp. 247–257, 262–264, 289–291.

ancient Hebrews had been spoken of in muted whispers. The Institute for Sex Research in Bloomington was in time to deal with most of the ancient moral and social mores in an open and statistically analytical fashion. Reports of the institute opened cracks in the heavily insulated wall of human reticence, and lifted the shades of hypocrisy. Institute researchers called into sober reconsideration moral and civil laws men had lived by, and revealed how in a startling percentage of the population archaic laws were violated in face of the realities of human behavior.

The organization, financing, and defense of the Institute for Sex Research in Indiana University was to become an ultimate test of academic freedom, freedom of investigation, and of publication. This was made even more trying by the location of the university in a conservative community and state. Progress of the institute from the outset was fraught with enormous emotional reactions if not actual resistance, a testing of university administrative courage, and the trauma of establishing at least two important landmarks in American intellectual freedom. Constantly Dr. Alfred Charles Kinsey, and his able associates, Wardell B. Pomeroy, Clyde E. Martin, Paul H. Gebhard, and William Dellenback, were accused of setting back sex education in America, and in all civilization, for that matter. They were charged with frivolity, licentiousness, lack of proper scientific methodology, and social irresponsibility. To more frugal-minded Hoosiers they were charged with wasting the university's economic substance.

Few if any American universities ever faced such a delicate challenge of public relations, of public exposure, and of protecting the freedom of research and investigation. Almost constantly after 1945 President Herman B Wells and his senior administrative colleagues were called upon to justify the existence on the campus of the Institute for Sex Research. There is no reckoning of the time these officials spent in connection with the defense of the institute, and even in settling internal university staff wrangling. Alfred C. Kinsey was a strong-willed and dedicated man who had already established himself as an able entomologist before he became interested in human sexual behavior. His personality and private moral habits were tough shields against attacks upon him for frivolity or lasciviousness.

The defense of the institute would have been difficult enough in ordinary times, but the period of the 1940s and early 1950s was one of the most explosive in the history of American bigotry and public fears. It was an age charged with enormous anxieties, made tremendously more sensitive by the fulminations of Senator Joseph McCarthy against communism in and outside the context of the Federal Government itself. Both the press and the public were ready to capitalize on any departure from what was considered the social norm. The Kinsey research came within the scope of threat to the social status quo. Neither the critics of the McCarthy ilk nor the general public which had an inkling of the Kinsey Institute were able to differentiate between what was believed to be the threats of communism and threats of overturning folk mores and ancient beliefs and traditions.

Kinsey had a long association with Indiana University. Carl Eigenmann wrote William Lowe Bryan on May 12, 1920, that Alfred C. Kinsey, a New Jerseyman, a graduate of Bowdoin College with a B.S. degree in 1916, and a doctorate from Harvard University, 1919, would be hired as an assistant professor in biology at a salary of

$2,000. His duties would be to take charge of biology for home economics classes, and to teach entomology. The Graduate Dean explained that young Kinsey had been a laboratory assistant at both Radcliffe College and Harvard University. He had worked under the direction of M. W. Wheeler in the famous Bussey Institution, and there was a hint that he would be a safe instructor because he had been active in Boy Scout work, and had ten years' experience with boy's camps. Eigenmann was impressed by the fact that the new instructor was "studying a group of insects in Florida to California." This was reminiscent of his own hunt in this territory for blind cave fishes. To assist Kinsey in his pursuit of gall wasps the Department of Biology set aside $800 with which to purchase entomological equipment.

Bryan told the Indiana Board of Trustees on May 29, 1920, that he concurred "that Dr. Alfred C. Kinsey be elected to the position of assistant professor at $2,000 for the year 1920–1921." These were matter-of-fact recommendations for the employment of a lower-level professor. Not one of the three men in that centennial year of the university could possibly have envisioned the impact this slender young scientist would have on the university and on mankind in general.

Kinsey was reared in a conservative New Jersey family. The boy had a good high school record, but there was conflict between him and his father over the choice of a career. The father wanted Alfred to become a mechanical engineer; he, however, went away to Bowdoin to become a scientist after two years of distasteful technological study. At the time of his appointment to the Indiana University faculty Alfred C. Kinsey was an intense and dedicated young scientist who pursued fervently the answers to several genetic-mutation-evolution and biological questions in an extensive investigation of oak gall wasps. During the summer and early fall of 1920 he held a Sheldon Traveling Fellowship to go on a collecting trip from Florida to California, a project which took him into thirty-six states. On October 20, 1920, the *Indiana Daily Student* reported that the new professor was in Bloomington with "an immense amount of material." There is no doubt that Kinsey impressed Eigenmann most favorably. His collecting trips had already yielded literally thousands of specimens of wasps and oak galls. At the end of the second semester in June 1922 Eigenmann wrote Bryan, "In regard to Dr. Kinsey, we all feel that he is a success as a teacher and investigator and if any promotions or increases in salaries are made for the coming year he should receive favorable consideration."

Kinsey's devotion to his research gained him a reputation early. In October 1923 he received as a gift a hundred specimens of gall wasps from Professor A. Trotter which had been collected along the Pacific Coast in California and Mexico by Dr. F. Silvestri, an Italian scientist. Of equal importance Kinsey's reputation continued to grow on the Indiana campus. In his final year as Dean of the Graduate School, Eigenmann wrote President Bryan at the end of the semester May 31, 1924, "I consider Dr. Kinsey one of the most brilliant of the younger men in the University," and he was happy the young professor had refused a seductive offer from the University of Illinois.

Not only did the tiny boxes and cases containing oak galls and wasps multiply by leaps and bounds as Kinsey went on annual searches for new materials; he was busy with the preparation of a 600-page textbook *Introduction to Biology*. When the manuscript was in an advanced stage of preparation, he submitted it to twenty-six biologists and to a number of experienced high school teachers for critical appraisal. He included illustrations and photographs from 300 artists. Kinsey told a reporter, "The most distinctive feature of the book is the style. I have attempted to employ the high school student's own language, and to use it in the same way that it is used around the camp fire or in the woods." He felt he had made a new approach to presenting physiology, heredity, ecology, distributive biology, and some of the other sciences.

At the moment when evolution and anti-evolution arguments swept the country, and fanatics, especially in Tennessee, Arkansas, Mississippi, and North Carolina, made capital issues of the subject, Alfred Kinsey was positive in his belief in the evolutionary processes of animal life, including man. He told the Indiana University Psychology Club in December 1926, that reflexes, tropisms, instinctive behavior, memory, and reasoning were traits which should be studied in lower animals in order to understand the complex behavior of humans.

Within a decade the young scientist had traveled 32,000 miles and had collected a phenomenal number of wasp specimens. In February 1930 he published his *The Gall Wasp Genus Cynips: A Study in the Origins of the Species*. Almost immediately he was off again on a semester-long expedition with Ancil Holloway and Donald McKeever, graduate students, to gather gall wasps in Mexico. Despite horrible roads and other handicaps these collectors were able to bring back to Bloomington a large and varied collection. By this time three distinctive traits characterized Professor Kinsey. He was a complex personality, a dedicated scientist, and a prodigious worker. Kinsey placed stress on quantitative statistics; for instance, on November 6, 1934, the *Indiana Daily Student* said he had returned from a seventeen-day trip of 3,200 miles in which he collected six bushels of galls; in all, he had traveled 66,000 miles. A year later he was to add 10,000 miles more in travel with James H. Coon and Osmond P. Breland to southern Mexico, Guatemala, and El Salvador on a National Research Council grant and university funds in search of the origins of the species. This journey yielded 400 new insect species, and 50,000 specimens. In 1936 he published *The Origins of Higher Categories in Cynips.*

The passing years brought honors to Kinsey. In 1937 his name became a "starred" entry in *American Men of Science.* By that time his collection of wasps had grown to more than 4,000,000 specimens, representing a thousand species, and he boasted, "The annual additions to our collection exceed the insect collection of the National Museum at Washington or at the American Museum at New York." Despite the fact Kinsey's collection grew at the rate of 60,000 additions a year, and new evidence of mutations and species was constantly being revealed, there was evidence the scientist was becoming somewhat disenchanted with Indiana University.

It is difficult from available documentary material to fit Alfred Kinsey into the Bloomington campus scene. He had a Methodist background, as did many southern Indiana Hoosiers, but this fact was scarcely discernible as compared with the zeal of his academic neighbors. He did, however, fix a part of his attachment to Indiana when he married Clara Bracken McMillen of Brookville in 1921, an Indiana graduate of that year. Kinsey enjoyed good recorded music, and later almost made a fetish of his "music nights." He was an avid gardener, taking special pride in his extensive iris beds. He perhaps had very few close friends in the university community, and most of his colleagues either did not know him well or regarded him with some degree of mixed feelings. He was often outspoken in faculty meetings, and frequently regarded committee meetings and many aimless faculty debates as a waste of time.

Before William Lowe Bryan retired, Kinsey was rather strong in his belief that Indiana University had reached a point of stagnation. Cornelia Vos Christenson has quoted a confidential letter on this subject in her *Kinsey: A Biography* (1972). "The President is seventy-five years old," he wrote, "and unwilling to settle any question, large or small. The whole University is in a mess; we get nothing done apart from the ancient routine—I would leave at the first opportunity offering comparable recompense and research opportunities." Bryan obviously did not suspect Kinsey's attitude when he wrote the entomologist after his retirement in June 1937, saying, "I have rejoiced always in what you have the ability to do and what you do. It is an extreme satisfaction for a man in my position to aid such a man as you to do his work." Even in 1938 when Wells became president, Kinsey was uncertain which way the university would go. No doubt part of his problem was that after the publication of his book the gall wasp project had lost some excitement and challenge.

Somewhat fortuitously a new challenge arose early in the Wells presidency which was to have significant impact on both men and the University. Kinsey never really forgot his scoutmaster concern for youth. As a biology professor and high school text author he naturally invited youthful confidences. The *Indiana Daily Student*, June 22, 1938, announced that a non-credit course of twelve lectures would deal with the legal, economic, sociological, psychological, and biological aspects of marriage during the forth-coming summer session. Men and women seniors and graduate students would be admitted to the lectures.

Almost from the outset of the marriage course, Kinsey and his colleagues faced parental, ministerial, and even medical opposition. When a Bloomington matron protested to young President Wells about the course, he admitted he knew little of its content and asked her to register for it and give him a report. She came away enthusiastic about Kinsey's lectures. Not so Dr. Thurman Rice of the Indiana University School of Medicine, and one of the lecturers. Throughout the rest of Kinsey's life Rice was to prove an irritant if not a nemesis.

Some faculty wives took the course and complained bitterly to Dean of Women Kate Mueller, but not about the content. They accused Kinsey of using the course to gather research materials for his private use. In a sense they were right because this was the beginning of long years of gathering sex histories to be used as basic information for several major studies on the subject.

By 1940 Kinsey had had enough of carping and complaining about the marriage course. He faced the alternatives, partly because of administrative prodding, of either toning down the boldness of the course, or of giving full time to sexual research apart from the general university program. Kinsey chose the latter, telling President Wells, "No scholar will voluntarily waive his right to disseminate information in the field in which he is especially qualified." Already he was embarked upon the sexual habits and behavior of the human animal. Even beyond this he concerned himself with the broad legal and social implications of human sexual behavior. Speaking in a Columbia University forum on crime, he was pessimistic that any appreciable modernization of sex laws would occur "in our life time" because of our persistent holding of ancient prejudices. He startled even his liberal audience by saying that only 5 percent of sex crimes were really dangerous, the others were simply breaches of custom dating back three or four thousand years.

In the spring of 1941 Kinsey was informed that the committee for research in problems of sex of the National Research Council had given him a grant of $1,600 to enable him to get under way the program of the newly formed Institute for Sex Research in Indiana University. By that time Kinsey had recorded his 200th case of sex history and was aiming at 10,000 before he published his first study. To date the largest number of case histories taken in the field was 290. Half of the Kinsey cases filed by May 1941 were those of college students representing 140 institutions.

A year later the Research Council's special committee comprised of Robert M. Yerkes, George W. Corner, and Lowell J. Reed recommended a grant of $7,500 for 1942–43. In the meantime Kinsey had taken a thousand new sex histories. The three distinguished scientists of the committee visited Indiana University in December 1942 to determine the degree of future support needed to carry on the work of the institute. Already the public was beginning to get a severely perverted notion of the existence of Kinsey and his institute and there was some restiveness.

Alfred C. Kinsey sought sex histories from all levels of human society with a zeal seldom exhibited by even the most dedicated researcher. He was frequently oblivious to the necessity for establishing some degree of rapport with both people and the institution. President Wells' correspondence files reflect this fact. Dr. George N. Shuster, president of Hunter College, wrote Wells on February 4, 1943, that a problem had arisen on his campus. It had been discovered that a young woman was inducing students to meet with a Professor Alfred C. Kinsey to discuss their sex histories. The "procuress" received a dollar a head for each interviewee she brought the professor. Shuster said, "The problem which now presents itself to us is one of public relations. If girls who have been drawn into this project talk about it, we may very well have a story for some of the more sensational papers. They would undoubtedly try to suggest that Hunter is delving into the private lives of its students and that we are no doubt teaching love, etc." He asked President Wells to find out from Kinsey what actually went on. If he knew the facts he could better deal with any repercussions which might occur. Wells replied, explaining Kinsey's work, and saying he was certain the scientist would be glad to give Shuster the precise information he sought. In the meantime he felt the facts would offer no basis for scandal-mongering. This was only one of many times when the president was called upon to explain and defend the Kinsey project.

Kinsey had difficulty on this score at home. Mrs. Fred Hugill of Chicago wrote Dean Kate Mueller in February 1945, that her daughter Shirley had told her parents when she was at home for Christmas vacation that Kinsey had interviewed the members of a psychology class. Mrs. Hugill expressed no objection to the interviews, but she opposed Kinsey imparting voluntary sexual information, such as telling students "a very large percentage of college girls were not ignorant of sexual experience." Dean Mueller informed President Wells in a memorandum of February 19, 1945, that Kinsey always asked positive questions such as "When is the first time you have had such and such experience?" She said he refused to accept a negative reply. Wells noted on the memorandum "I am to see Kinsey when he returns."

Nothing, however, deterred the work of the institute. The medical division of the Rockefeller Foundation through the National Research Council upped its grants to $23,000 in June 1943, to $25,000 in 1944, to $28,000 in 1945, to $35,000 in 1946, and in 1947–48 it gave $40,000. By the latter date Kinsey had attained 3,000 personal sex histories. Now the problem was that of breaking the news of his research to the public. This he began to do locally when he addressed the Bloomington Rotary Club in September 1946. He told the service club that his study was then in its eighth year of research. He claimed 11,000 personal sex histories had been accumulated, but his objective was to take 100,000 histories. This latter number seemed to become an obsession with Kinsey. He announced that within a year the first volume, that on the sexual behavior of the male, would appear.

On December 30, 1946, the *Indianapolis Star* repeated Kinsey's report on his work, but added the sensational announcement that the human female matured much later than the male, shaking irrevocably an ancient folk belief. Females, he said, did not reach full sexual development until age 28, while males were mature at 16 years of age. This statement was to be repeated countless times by the American press. Kinsey told newsmen his was "a fact-finding survey, and there is no attempt to make any moral or social examination of the data." He felt people told him and his colleagues, Pomeroy and Martin, the truth because they believed the scientists would observe their obligation of confidentiality.

Kinsey's paper before the American Association for the Advancement of Science in Boston in late December 1946 was to bring his project much broader national publicity. While sex, he said, was important to marriage, personalities of husbands and wives were vital to lasting unions. If a marriage lasted until couples were forty or fifty years of age, it would last the rest of their lives, because the differing ages of sex maturity was a minor fact in middle-age adjustments. Some children began sexual activities at a very early age, patterns of sex behavior underwent few changes after adolescence, and mating ages showed a greater differential among better educated people. These statements were to receive wide news coverage, a fact which brought the university almost a frightening amount of publicity. Early in 1947 *Newsweek* said, "For 2,000 years, the belief has persisted that women mature at an earlier age than men. But last week Dr. Alfred C. Kinsey of Indiana University upset this theory with a scientific report, the first of its kind on an eight year study of sex behavior." The magazine then repeated the age differentials of 16 and 28 between the sexes. In this way the Indiana University administration got a foretaste of what both the institution and its professor of sex would face when the first volume of the institute's report was published.

Kinsey and his impending report on the sexual behavior of the human male had become highly newsworthy. This moment in fact was one in which the entire society of civilized man was emerging from an age of sexual muteness, if not secrecy, into one in which the subject would become a matter of extremely bold and open conversation. The New American Library published a $.25 paperbook entitled, *About the Kinsey Report: Observations by Eleven Experts on Sexual Behavior in the Human*

Male. A 75,000-copy edition was sold in ten days, and the press gloated, "When new records are made, sex will make 'em." President Wells addressed a memorandum to the University's Executive Committee on October 30, 1947, in which he said the publication of the first Kinsey volume was near at hand; there would be eight reports in all. The national magazine and newspaper press would doubtless give the Kinsey material wide publicity. The first book would be published by one of the oldest and most reputable medical houses and it would prove of use to physicians, psychiatrists, social workers, and others of kindred professional interest. The president predicted the book would be controversial, but it was the product of scientific exploration, and "It seems to me it is essential that we stand firm in our support of the book and the research. We are not called upon to endorse the findings, but we are called upon to stand firm in support of the importance of the project and the right to publish it. Any less than that would be fatal. We would lose the respect and the services of our best faculty men and the respect of the scholarly world generally." Wells then expressed the belief that the work would be of fundamental importance and in time would be accepted as such by the public. He reminded the committee that Pasteur's researches had stirred controversy when they were publicized.

A month after President Wells had made his declaration to the Executive Committee, the *Indianapolis Star* revealed how much sensation could be generated by Kinsey's work. The paper said the Indiana University scientist had found that 50 per cent of all married men were unfaithful to their wives; men in the armed services were less active sexually than the civilian male at home, and slightly less than three-fourths of the male population were potent at seventy years of age, and the more education a man had the less apt he was to have premarital experience.

The selection of the publisher for Kinsey's books was undertaken with as much care and foresight as possible. Three topflight commercial publishers were considered, but Herman B Wells urged Kinsey to seek an established medical publisher. In fact, throughout the early years Wells had tried to keep the scientific-medical aspect of the work in the forefront. Somewhat by fortuitous circumstances Kinsey met Laurence Saunders, president of the prestigious Philadelphia medical publishing house, and publication arrangements were made. When a contract was signed with this house, Helen Dietz, a senior editor, was given the task of working with the obstinate author. The editing of Kinsey's books became something of an epoch in publishing history. He was a determined cocksure man so far as his style and method of presenting his work were concerned, and he turned off editorial suggestions with great assurance.

The Saunders house, accustomed to issuing slow-selling professional books, had counted on selling an edition of 10,000 copies; this figure was arrived at after the report of what the company believed was a sophisticated market survey. Within two months after publication, the volume on male sexual behavior had sold 200,000 copies, and in time it had eleven printings. In Bloomington the campus bookstore sold out its first order on the afternoon of January 5, 1948, the day of publication.

True to Wells's prediction, the book was widely reviewed and commented upon by both the news and magazine presses. Kinsey told Henry Butler of the *Indianapolis Times*, "People have wanted a book of this kind. I think scientists have completely underestimated the public's desire to get a really unemotional, scientific book on sex." The *Army Times*, February 7, 1948, said, "Believe it or not department . . . that best selling . . . and well-nigh impossible to get *Sexual Behavior in the Human Male* by Dr. Alfred S. [*sic*] Kinsey . . . was originally planned as a scientific textbook. In fact, the dignified Philadelphia publishing firm . . . W. B. Saunders Co. . . . is knocked on its scientific heels by the overwhelming demand for the book." . . .

Reactions to the first study no doubt caught Kinsey and everybody else by surprise. Wisely the university administration prevailed on the scientist to seek a medical publisher, but even they were startled by the report of sales. Laurence Saunders told W. B. Rogers, the Associated Press editor of "Books and Art," that even the professional market survey service had told the company that "Its considered scientific opinion was 'that this best seller would not sell at all.' " Kinsey, however, had predicted a big sale. Wells made the modest statement in his *Annual Report*, 1947–48, "With the publication of the first volume of the Kinsey Report, the significance of at least one of the research programs associated with the University has become known to the public, here and abroad."

The president surely did not know just how widely known this published material would become. Neither the university nor Professor Kinsey counted on the razzle-dazzle of publicity or on the humorists and cartoonists. When Peter Arno published his famous cartoon, "Is There a Mrs. Kinsey?" in the *New Yorker Magazine*, May 1948, reporters scurried off to Bloomington to interview Clara McMillen Kinsey. Henry Butler from the *Indianapolis Times* published an extensive account of the Kinseys' courtship, marriage, and home-life. The June Issue of *McCall's Magazine* contained an article about Mrs. Kinsey, Wardell B. Pomeroy, and Clyde M. Martin. President Wells visited Julian Huxley, then director-general of UNESCO, in his Paris office, and the conversation turned to the Kinsey research. Huxley knew Kinsey slightly, but under the influence of Peter Arno, he asked Wells, "Is there a Mrs. Kinsey?"

Not only was Professor Kinsey's volume on male sexuality subjected to intense scrutiny by scientists, but he was adjudged by more esoteric sex experts. The *Cosmopolitan Magazine* asked "a number of weighty Americans to comment on 'this Kinsey business.' " One of these, Mae West, said, "I supposed it would be dangerous to admit that at the best sex is fun." Miss West felt that Kinsey's defenders did not make enough allowance for romance. The daily press reported her as saying she was not surprised at anything in the Kinsey book. She too had made a more or less close study of the human male and agreed with the professor's findings. She had, however, used somewhat different approaches in her study because "I am afraid the only figure I employ is my own." She told Robert Ruark, the columnist, "I had the field licked before Kinsey ever saw it."

It was said erroneously that Kinsey asked Tallulah Bankhead if he might ask her a number of very personal questions. She readily agreed to be interviewed if in turn she could ask Kinsey equally as personal questions; and gossip had it, the Indiana professor departed at once. Martha Raye produced a phonograph record entitled, "Ooh Dr. Kinsey!" which was banned by the big broadcasting companies. Jack Lait, Jr., commented that people always did what they were told they should not do, and

Martha Raye's record sold 500,000 copies. Kinsey no doubt stirred up some of this gossipy sex linkage when he went in search of sexual histories among the females of Hollywood in September 1949.

There was almost no end to the incidents and public chatter about the Kinsey report aside from the scientific comment. In Winston-Salem, North Carolina, lawyer Phil Horton was threatened with mayhem at the hands of enraged local women. They thought he had said that 75 per cent of the town's women lacked virtue; that is, the local newspaper said he had made the statement. What he actually said was that Kinsey was quoted as saying 75 per cent of college and high school girls were lacking virtue. By November 1949 many people must have come to agree with the Bloomington *World-Telephone* reporter who wrote, "Dr. Kinsey will go down in history as the first writer to give a successful nitroglycerin transfusion to a statistic." . . .

In historical perspective two side results of the Kinsey studies were significant. There can hardly be any doubt that the two earlier volumes (*Sexual Behavior in the Human Male* [1948] and *Sexual Behavior in the Human Female* [1953]) lifted the veil on sex both as a scientific and social topic of primary interest, and engendered an openness of discussion of the fundamentally important procreative drive of the human animal. For the first time in the history of civilization this became a fact. This was eloquently documented by newspaper and periodical presses, by numerous lateral studies, and by an unestimated amount of public discussion. There is accumulated in the Institute for Sex Research on the Indiana University campus one of the most voluminous collections of press clippings, articles, personal correspondence, public addresses, and cartoon materials pertaining to any revolutionary movement in science history, with the possible exceptions of the nuclear bomb and the lunar explorations.

Amidst the noisy public fury stirred up by the first two volumes, American newspapers and periodicals themselves experienced movements of sharp revision of social attitudes and approaches in dealing with the Kinsey studies. In fact, press treatment of the subject was almost as significant a documentation of changes in American cultural and social history as were the basic conclusions of the Kinsey researches themselves. The decade, 1947–57, was a traumatic one in which none, including Alfred C. Kinsey, the Indiana University administration, or the American organs of publicity could comprehend with certainty the dimensions of the current social revolution. Certainly no one of these escaped the innate pains of this transitional era.

From the perspective of the 1970s, it is somewhat startling to realize how reluctant the public, including a good portion of the academic community itself, was to accept with dignified calmness the results of an objective scientific investigation. In even clearer fashion the publicizing of the Kinsey story brought about considerable changes in the reporting of scientific findings by the press. It is interesting that the Rockefeller Foundation financed a project of the National Association of Science Writers to study science reporting and its effect upon public reactions, and to bring about changes in this field of writing.

Nowhere in this chapter has it been a purpose to evaluate the work of Professor Kinsey, his staff, or the institute in any manner so far as their scientific contributions were concerned. The existence of the Institute for Sex Research on the campus of a public university was indeed a striking fact in the history of American higher education. The

Indiana University administration experienced all sorts of soul-searching, public pressures, scientific sniping, and constant exposure by the American press. All of this tested administrative and Board of Trustees courage. Reflective of this fact is the sentence that appeared in the publisher's foreword to *Sexual Behavior in the Human Male* in which it said, "It is based on surveys made by members of the staff of Indiana University . . . " rather than by an integrated department of the university.

The frequent defenses made by President Herman B Wells, and Deans Herman T. Briscoe and Fernandus Payne were within themselves landmarks in the battle for academic freedom and the right to publish scientific findings. Earlier mention is made of the McCarthy era, but more than this, the 1950s were years in which most Americans at heart sought social stability if not social complacency. For a Middle Western university to support such a socially explosive and intimately personal program of research was indeed to adventure into an unexplored cavern of many unpredictable labyrinths—the most threatening of which was loss of institutional prestige and vital financial support.

On May 16, 1955, and after two jolting periods of public relations challenges, Herman B Wells wrote W. F. Pommeranke of the University of Rochester, "Indiana University stands today, as it has for fifteen years, firmly in support of the scientific project which has been undertaken and is being carried on by one of its eminent biological scientists, Dr. Alfred C. Kinsey." The president knew full well what the emotional cost of this resolution had been, and his colleagues on the Indiana faculty no doubt appreciated the dividends the university's stand returned to them in genuine academic freedom to do research and to publish objective findings.

Politics and Society during the Depression

The decade-long Great Depression of the 1930s had a profound impact on the people, their way of life, and their institutions. No one who lived through the Depression emerged unchanged, and the memory of its variegated impact still informs—if not haunts—all persons over the age of sixty in 1990. On the national level, the Depression is associated with the New Deal agencies and programs established in response to the economic crisis after March 1933. On the Indiana level, the period is associated with Governor Paul V. McNutt and his equally vigorous response to the needs of the people beginning in January 1933.

In the first selection below, Professor I. George Blake describes the first hectic months of Governor McNutt's administration. A sympathetic narrator, Professor Blake provides a glimpse of conditions in Indiana at the time and describes the remarkably complete—even highhanded—changes in state government and in the powers of the governor's office that McNutt instituted. These included an extensive reorganization of the executive branch of state government; new taxing proposals; the formation of the "Two Percent Club," which required all government appointees to contribute two percent of their salaries to the Democratic party; the establishment of the state Alcoholic Beverages Commission, a controversial agency then and now; and an old-age pension program. Like Roosevelt with the U.S. Congress, McNutt had an overwhelmingly Democratic legislature to work with and was able to get almost everything he requested. The work of a major New Deal program, the Works Progress Administration (WPA), in transforming public accommodations is described below in the selection by Glory-June Greiff.

Not everyone, of course, agreed with the programs and actions of the New Deal or of the politically ambitious McNutt, who was barred from succeeding himself immediately, but who had his eye on higher office anyway. During the tense general strike in Terre Haute in 1935, McNutt called out the National Guard to keep matters under control. This action caused Norman Thomas to label the governor a "Hoosier Hitler" and persuaded a Terre Haute historian that McNutt's strong antilabor stance destroyed whatever chance he had for national elective office. Still, President Roosevelt took few chances and appointed McNutt to an administrative post in the Philippines during the late 1930s before naming him Federal Security Administrator prior to the 1940 convention. Furthermore, Roosevelt specifically rejected McNutt as a running mate in 1940, preferring instead his Secretary of Agriculture, Henry A. Wallace.

While the Democrats enjoyed their enormous electoral majorities in the 1930s, the Republican party in Indiana staged a strong comeback in the latter part of the decade, a surge that resulted in a near Republican sweep in 1940. Buoyed by the presidential candidacy of native son Wendell Willkie, Indiana Republicans carried the statewide elections, excepting only the governor's race (where the popular and folksy Lieutenant Governor Henry F. Schricker defeated Kokomo attorney Glen R. Hillis); and the Republicans won eight of Indiana's twelve seats in Congress.

As Professor William B. Pickett explains below, the Republican revival owed a great deal to the promotional work of a southern Indiana supersalesman, Homer E. Capehart, a political neophyte as well as a recent Republican convert. Capehart's famous Cornfield Conference in 1938, held on his Daviess County farm outside of the small town of Washington, revitalized the party, brought in much-needed campaign contributions, and paved the way for success at the polls in 1940 and afterward. Capehart eschewed an immediate political reward, preferring to work behind the scenes for a time; but he later served three terms in the United States Senate between 1945 and 1963. William Pickett, a professor of history at Rose-Hulman Institute, completed his doctoral studies at Indiana University with a dissertation on the remarkably successful business career of Homer E. Capehart prior to 1945. Pickett's biography of the businessman-politician, *Homer E. Capehart: A Senator's Life, 1898–1979*, was published in 1990.

The final selection, a portion of an oral history transcript by Mrs. Julia Hedge, provides a vivid picture of life for a tenant farming family in southern Indiana during the Depression. The Hedges and their five children then lived near Vincennes on the property of John Brevoort, and were one of eight tenant farm families there. With men's wages at ten cents an hour, life in the 1930s for the Hedges and thousands like them was an "intense struggle," but it also had its lighter moments and its rewards, and ultimately the indomitable courage of the people prevailed.

Mrs. Hedge was interviewed by Thomas Krasean, then director of the Lewis Historical Library at Vincennes University and a pioneer in developing a formal oral history program there and earlier at the Indiana State Library. This excerpt represents but a tiny sample of a vast and rapidly expanding new resource for the historian. Major oral history collections are located at the Indiana State Library, Indiana University at Bloomington, Vincennes University, and Wabash Public Library, and there are others at a number of colleges, universities, historical societies, and local libraries throughout the state.

DEPRESSION GOVERNOR

I. George Blake

Paul Vories McNutt was inaugurated Indiana's thirty-third governor in an outdoor ceremony on January 9, 1933, the fourth Indiana University man to be elected head of the state. He presented a most striking personal appearance as he took the oath of office. His six-foot frame was crowned with a mass of silver-white hair, and his facial features were those of a Greek god. Some even thought he looked like a movie matinee idol. Judge Walter E. Treanor, chief justice of the Indiana Supreme Court, administered the oath.

When McNutt assumed the reins of office it was generally thought that even he, with all his dash and verve, never would be able to achieve the changes in state government he had promised in the campaign. His party had been almost demoralized during the long period of Republican rule, and the spirit of defeatism seemed to have permeated its ranks.

Many students of Indiana politics believed that McNutt would be forced to spend most of his term getting rid of holdover officials named by his predecessor for four-year terms. Because of the tremendous patronage difficulties which faced him, there was no guarantee that he would be able to effect a workable administration. There was also the uncertainty as to what course the new legislature would pursue. It was almost solidly Democratic, but its lack of experience made it most unpredictable.

Indiana, perhaps as much as any state, felt the full force of the depression which had followed the stockmarket crash of October 29, 1929. There was widespread suffering as the result of business failures, and extensive unemployment. Farmers lost their land due to their inability to repay loans or to pay taxes, and general economic chaos ran rampant throughout the state. Savings accounts dwindled to nothing in

---

From *Paul V. McNutt: Portrait of a Hoosier Statesman* (1966), pp. 124–126, 129–134, 137–143.

many cases, and with the loss of jobs and income, real economic hardship ensued. Indiana had her share of bread-lines and soup-lines. Mobs often congregated on the steps of the Statehouse. Schools were closed and the teachers were unpaid. Every problem which faced the nation faced the new government in Indiana.

The prestige of the state of Indiana was at a low ebb. Political scandals had rocked the state. Governors and other public officials in high places had been accused of corrupt practices in government. Departments of government were so disorganized and costly that the taxpayers were spending hundreds of thousands of dollars for services that did not benefit them. No one was responsible for the conduct of state government, and the "buck" was passed in every crisis. All of this was reflected in curtailed tax income for the state and municipal governments.

Such was the situation in Indiana when McNutt became governor. His inaugural address stressed the theme of economy for his administration. His speech was considered a masterpiece in statecraft. "The change in government," he said, "for which we have prepared, is here. It carries with it tremendous responsibilities and the possibility of far-reaching consequences. It offers an opportunity to prove that government may be a great instrument of human progress. It is a ray of hope which heartens us as we follow a path dark with ominous shadows." Under such circumstances, he said, "I assume the great office of Governor of my native state with unaffected humility, conscious of limitations but sincere in my desire to serve all of the people according to the best of my skill and ability. I pray God that I may be given the wisdom, the courage and the strength to perform the duties of the office and to lead the way toward the satisfactory completion of the important tasks to which all of us must now set our hands." . . .

From the very beginning McNutt insisted that economy in the cost of government and the simplification of operation would be the goal of his administration. He demanded that the chief executive be given strong powers to cope with the emergency facing the state. To accomplish his purposes he formulated a wholesale executive reorganization bill for the consolidation of overlapping departments, bureaus and commissions, reducing the number from several scores to about eight. Its purpose was not only to reduce the cost of government, but also to promote greater efficiency of operation. Its real purpose, however, was obviously to give McNutt a much greater control over the patronage, by creating a truly formidable political machine entirely dominated by him.

McNutt's executive reorganization bill and other centralizing measures were recognized by the legislators as "must" bills, to be passed by both houses under suspension of the rules, so well drilled was the Democratic majority. His critics and even his friends were amazed at the rapidity with which some of the bills were enacted into law. Often an important bill would appear seemingly from nowhere, be introduced into the House, sent to the Senate, passed again and signed, all on the same day. (It must be remembered that the Democrats outnumbered the Republicans 43 to 7 in the state senate, and 91 to 9 in the House.) It was said that often the legislators had to await publication of the bills to know what they had actually passed. Such unorthodox methods were bound to cause voices to rise in protest. Some of the anti-McNutt Democrats strongly objected to this slow centralization of power as being foreign to the principles of the Democratic party.

The executive reorganization bill was probably the most important and far-reaching of all McNutt's "must" proposals. Its title is interesting:

> A bill for an act concerning the executive including the administrative department of the government of the State of Indiana; repealing all acts and laws in conflict herewith and declaring an emergency.

This so-called "Mussolini" bill provided for the consolidation of all 168 of the state governmental agencies into the following departments: executive, state, audit and control, treasury, law, education, public works, and commerce and industry. The governor would be given absolute authority over the departments. The "ripper" provision of the bill allowed him to discharge any employee or officer at his discretion. He was given the power to appoint or commission all officials except the deputies of the six elected officials. This meant that the governor could remove at his pleasure and discretion all but twelve officials in the entire state administrative organization. Only officials holding constitutional offices, and their deputies, were immune from the governor's power.

Such sweeping dictatorial powers were justified by McNutt as being necessary "to simplify the laws providing for the operation of the executive, including the administrative department, to eliminate duplications of activities, to effect radical reductions in personnel of officers, employees, and servants of the state of Indiana, to concentrate responsibilities in the elective offices, and to reduce the costs of executive and administrative government."

There seemed to be at first general approval of the measure. The Indiana State Chamber of Commerce, the Indiana Farm Bureau, the Indiana Manufacturers' Association, and the State Federation of Labor were among the many organizations indicating their support. They believed that such a measure would create more efficiency and economy in government by eliminating overlapping functions and duplications. The support of such organizations assured the immediate and favorable attention of the legislature.

Not everyone, however, was so enthusiastically in favor of the proposal. Some of McNutt's political opponents, even in his own party, considered the proposed legislation a device to cripple them politically. Frank Mayr, Jr., who had long been jealous of McNutt's meteoric rise to power, was again the secretary of state, and he realized that if enacted into law, the bill would deprive him of his great patronage power over the automobile license division. A three-man board, composed of the governor, the lieutenant governor, and the secretary of state, would make all decisions affecting the Department of State, in which case Mayr would be in the minority. Nevertheless there was such universal approval of the measure that Mayr could not cause its defeat, and it passed both houses with little opposition.

About the only real opposition to the bill came from a group of one Democratic and seven Republican senators who challenged McNutt to show how greater economies would be effected under his plan. They charged that the bill would "build up the greatest machine ever known on the face of the earth unless it was Nero's." Several attempts were made to amend the bill, but all failed. McNutt persuaded his many friends, including McHale, who was not even a senator, Anderson Ketcham, the Democratic floor leader, Virgil Simmons, another non-member, and Pleas Greenlee, his executive secretary in charge of patronage, to use their influence among the legislators.

As a consequence of their activities the bill passed the House 80 to 15 on February 2, 1933, after the third reading, and it cleared the Senate 39 to 7, in spite of Republican charges that it would cause an increase in expenditures and "the development of the greatest political machine in politics." Others warned that it was invalid and contrary to the Constitution of the United States. The final passage with some slight amendments was completed on February 3. McNutt immediately signed the bill into law the same day, although he said there would be no immediate sweeping changes in the present governmental set-up, as he had until June 30 to regroup the 168 divisions of the state government. It had taken only a week to accomplish the bill's introduction, passage, and signing.

As a part of his own "executive" department, Governor McNutt retained control of the division of safety, including the state police department, the automobile theft fund, the bureau of criminal investigation and identification, the fire marshal's department, the dry cleaning department, the state athletic commission; the adjutant general's division, including the armory board, battle flag commission, Grand Army of the Republic, the naval militia, Soldiers and Sailors Monument, Spanish War Veterans and Veterans of Foreign Wars; the state board of accounts, the budget department, the board of clemency, the board of state charities, poor relief commission, industrial aid for the blind, the free employment commission, Governor's yearbook publication, the state probation department and all state institutions. Thus, directly the governor controlled some of the most important features of the state government. . . .

By April 14 the entire state government had been reorganized into eight central departments. Governor McNutt was branded by some as a Fascist dictator, but he insisted that the state government must be run as a business, and the people of Indiana had made him the business manager of the State. Some of his supporters claimed that the office of governor had formerly been so limited in its powers that gross inefficiency had resulted. In the election of 1932 the people had demanded a change, and this change had been accomplished through the election of a general manager, and therefore McNutt's activities were justified by the decision of the voters.

As stated previously, Governor-elect McNutt, shortly after his election, had visited all the state institutions and made a detailed study of their problems. Just before he was inaugurated, he met with the newly elected Democratic members of the legislature and outlined the recommendations he intended to propose for consolidations and transfers of departments in the statehouse. The executive reorganization act was the result. But the increased powers which it gave the governor created serious problems. There were 35,000 applicants for the 3,000 jobs to be filled. Under the circumstances, it was virtually impossible to satisfy every jobseeker, even the most loyal among the Democratic party workers. Many members of the 1933 General Assembly were rewarded for their services by being appointed to lucrative state and federal positions, while Republicans were dismissed, although in some few instances the boards were made bipartisan. An attempt had been made to have the reorganization act declared unconstitutional, but this failed, and organized Democratic opposition to McNutt dwindled to nothing, although Republican opposition was still quite strong. By the end of his first six months in office, McNutt had practically completed his reorganization of the state government. . . .

Governor McNutt's reorganization program was not the only piece of legislation he had introduced early in his administration, although it did act as a portent of future important recommendations which were later enacted into law. Even before President Franklin D. Roosevelt inaugurated his so-called "New Deal" program of relief, recovery, and reform, Governor McNutt had begun such a program in Indiana. Indeed, many of the federal measures which were later enacted into law had their origin in Indiana, and nearly all of them required state action before they could be implemented for the benefit of the people. The McNutt administration supported the Roosevelt policies enthusiastically.

One of the most controversial laws passed in the 1933 session of the General Assembly was the Gross Income Tax. It was bitterly attacked by the Republican Party and the Retail Merchants Association of Indiana. There is no question that McNutt did use dictatorial powers in having this act passed. The bill embraced over one hundred typewritten pages, and not more than ten members of the legislature out of 150 had read or studied the measure. But the day it was laid on their tables at 9 a.m., the retailers' association sent out wires to all the merchants in the state and promised to march upon the Statehouse the next day—5,000 strong.

Meantime McNutt had suggested that this bill be presented to a caucus of the Democratic members of the House and Senate. Senator Chambers, who owned the two newspapers in New Castle, was to present it and explain it to the members of the legislature. But unfortunately the merchants in his home town advised him that if he did not withdraw his support, or if he took an active part in support of the legislation, they would start a new newspaper. So on the morning that the caucus was to be held, Chambers notified McNutt that he would not appear at the caucus.

McNutt then contacted McHale and asked that he explain the bill to the legislature. McHale, of course, was not an employee of the state or of McNutt, but he had volunteered his services to McNutt. He had almost complete charge of the legislative program, and worked on the eighth floor of the Indianapolis Athletic Club, which was commonly referred to as the "Bill Factory." He appeared before the legislature and spent two hours presenting the bill and answering questions from all those present. He read the wire from the merchants' association and stated that the bill would have to be enacted into law before midnight of the day it was introduced.

Ordinarily a bill that size and so controversial and so much an innovation would take six or seven weeks, but because the Democrats had such a large majority, they were asked to pass it and enact it into law under suspension of the rules, without changing a word or punctuation. The result was that the bill became law and was signed by McNutt the same day. The next day over 3,000 marched on the Statehouse in protest, but the following day 7,000 farmers appeared at the Capital and cheered McNutt for giving them the first relief they had from the heavy tax burden.

The Republican Party in the next campaigns attacked the gross income tax law, but in the meantime it became so popular that no party or individual has attempted to advocate its repeal.

Even before the national government acted, Indiana under McNutt's leadership passed a measure calling for the legalization of the sale of beer and wine. The bill, which repealed the "Wright Bone-Dry" prohibition law of 1917, passed on March 2, 1933, and was to become effective on the repeal of the federal prohibition laws, such as the Volstead Act and the Eighteenth Amendment.

Shortly after Roosevelt became President, the national Congress modified the Volstead Act permitting the sale of 3.2 beer and wine in states that had repealed their own prohibition laws and had provided for such sales. Thus on April 7, 1933, beer and wine became available in twenty states, including Indiana. . . .

Under the 1933 law, all out-of-state beer was channeled through ten importers who were licensed by the excise commissioner. The latter was appointed by the governor. These importers were chosen from the ranks of sturdy Democrats and loyal McNutt Republicans. McNutt therefore had complete control over the patronage. The 1935 legislature changed the name of the importers to Ports of Entry, and provided for the licensing of from fourteen to one hundred.

Naturally there was considerable opposition to the 1933 law and those that followed. Many people were violently against the return to the manufacture and sale of intoxicating liquors, while others opposed it because it denied the rights of local option, even though the "open saloon" and the tavern in rural areas were eliminated. Still others resented the very close alliance between the Democratic party and the liquor traffic, and Governor McNutt himself was severely criticized for his part in the enactment of the legislation, especially because it increased his power over the patronage.

Another measure which became law in Indiana before the federal government acted was the one providing for an old-age pension system. McNutt had promised such relief in his pre-election campaign, and the general assembly of 1933 enacted it into law. It provided payments up to $180 per year for indigent citizens over 70 years of age. The following year a special session of the legislature brought the payments in line with the national program, with compensation for the unemployed, the blind, the dependent, and the aged provided by the federal, state, and county governments.

McNutt's political power was augmented by the city skip-election bill, introduced into the General Assembly on February 27, 1933. This called for the postponement of the 102 city elections from 1933 to the following year. Its purpose was to extend the terms of the city administrations, sixty percent of which were Democratic, for an extra year, thus insuring the continued predominance of the party in municipal affairs. It would also give McNutt additional power over the patronage so that he could further dominate the party and control subsequent elections. Naturally the Republicans bitterly attacked the proposed legislation, but McNutt cited several precedents to justify his demands. He estimated that the one-year postponement of municipal primaries and elections would save the taxpayers nearly a quarter of a million dollars. The bill passed the house on March 1, 1933, by a vote of 73 to 13, and the Senate approved it the same day. McNutt affixed his signature immediately. The Republicans challenged the constitutionality of the law in the courts, but it was upheld and remained on the statute books until 1941, when it was finally repealed by the

Republican majority in both houses of the General Assembly, during the administration of Henry F. Schricker, the Democratic governor.

The Reorganization Act of 1933 and the Skip-Election Law of the same year proved to be politically shrewd moves on the part of Governor McNutt. He was now firmly entrenched in power, and was in a position not only to control the Democratic party in Indiana, but also to implement his ideas of government. Yet such an ambition would cost money, and he began to effect schemes to increase the funds of the party for such purposes. As a consequence the Hoosier Democratic Club was organized. This was an organization made up of all the Democratic state and local appointive and elected officials for the purpose of securing their active political cooperation in McNutt's program. This immediately was dubbed the "Two Percent Club" because each member was required to contribute that percentage of his salary each month to the organization or "machine."

There seemed to be a difference of opinion as to whether membership in the club was voluntary, or required of all those holding state or local political jobs. It was said that if an employee failed to "contribute" he would be dismissed summarily. Thus McNutt could at once rid himself and his administration of any "disloyal" appointees, and cause the defeat of "reluctant" elected workers at the next election. Yet Pleas Greenlee, who was in charge of the patronage, claimed that many employees did not belong to the Hoosier Democratic Club, and that no one had ever been disciplined for failure to "kick in." There is no doubt, however, that McNutt knew who were members and who were "disloyal."

Although the Democratic State Committee refused to assume any responsibility for the Two Percent Club, it willingly accepted the benefits of its treasury. The money was used to reduce party deficits and to aid the party in financing its political campaigns, as well as to assist in carrying out the party's program. It was the feeling of the leading Democrats that it was much better to have the rank and file of loyal Democrats pay their share toward the activities of the party, than to depend on the support of big business interests.

THE WPA IN INDIANA

Glory-June Greiff

In the selection below, Glory-June Greiff describes the immense impact of various New Deal work programs, particularly those of the oft-maligned Works Progress Administration (WPA), upon the physiognomy and cultural resources of the state of Indiana. Greiff has made a special study of the activities of both the WPA and the CCC (Civilian Conservation Corps) within the state, particularly in the state parks and in various urban parks. A state and local historian as well as an ardent voice in the historic preservation movement, she has prepared a number

---

From "Roads, Rocks, and Recreation: The Legacy of the WPA in Indiana," *Traces of Indiana and Midwestern History*, III (Summer 1991), 40–47.

of multiple property nominations for inclusion on the National Register of Historic Places, thereby obtaining special recognition for such places as Washington Park in Michigan City and the downtown area of New Carlisle, both in northern Indiana, and for CCC- and WPA-related structures within the original fourteen Indiana state parks.

The Great Depression gripped the United States during the years following the stock market crash of 1929. By 1932, the American people eagerly listened to a man who appeared to have some answers and swept Franklin D. Roosevelt into the presidency. He wasted no time in effecting his innovative battle plans. Roosevelt and his advisors created numerous "alphabet agencies" to launch an amazing number of programs during the administration's first hundred days. Among them was the Federal Emergency Relief Administration (FERA) to aid the unemployed. So great was the emergency that a large portion of FERA money had to be doled out as direct relief, but Harry Hopkins, a former social worker whom Roosevelt had appointed director, had other ideas. He believed from the start that the government had a responsibility to provide jobs to those who were unemployed through no fault of their own, and so FERA included a rudimentary work relief program. By the fall of 1933 it was clear the government was not getting men back to work fast enough, so Hopkins convinced Roosevelt to establish the temporary Civil Works Administration (CWA), designed to carry the unemployed through the winter with work programs. CWA was criticized by some as make-work, although its mission was simply to get a lot of men working in a short time. Others labeled CWA as insufficient because the program ended in March 1934. FERA, still in effect, established a stronger work relief program after the CWA experiment ended. Several major projects begun under FERA or CWA, especially those concerned with parks and roads, would later be continued by the Works Progress Administration. Fall Creek Parkway in Indianapolis was one such long-term, multiphased project. . . .

Roosevelt in 1935 was ready to put Hopkins's work-relief program into effect. In his State of the Union address Roosevelt told Congress that the dole was "a narcotic, a subtle destroyer of the human spirit" and added the following: "I am not willing that the vitality of our people be further sapped by the giving of cash, of market baskets, of a few hours of weekly work cutting grass, raking leaves, or picking up papers in the public parks. The federal government must and shall quit this business of relief." In other words, the administration of direct relief—the dole—was to return to the states and local governments. But the federal government now offered an alternative to handouts—the Works Progress Administration, which began in the summer of 1935 with Harry Hopkins in charge. Its mission was to provide work to employable persons in need, and by so doing reduce the relief rolls. Whenever possible the skills of the jobless person were matched to the job. With Governor McNutt's New Deal-style state agencies already in place, Indiana's WPA program took off immediately with projects sponsored by local governments. Indiana was the first state in the nation to fill its quota, and soon the number of formerly unemployed workers who now earned wages greatly reduced the county relief rolls.

So widespread was WPA activity that it is difficult to comprehend that large segments of the public were apparently unaware of its impact even as it was going on all around them, although negative or silent press must have played a part. The largest expenditure of WPA money and manpower in Indiana went to roads in the farm-to-market program, state highway expansion and improvement, and streets and sidewalks in the towns. Today one may still find stretches of pavement stamped "Built by WPA," in downtown Lafayette or Terre Haute, for example. Fairgrounds, including the State Fairgrounds in Indianapolis, were improved or expanded to accommodate the larger crowds that now could attend from outlying areas. All the roads the WPA built suggested the need for a new concept, the roadside park. Indiana was among the nation's leaders in developing this type of facility, largely with WPA or CCC labor, or with workers from the National Youth Administration.

The Works Progress Administration in Indiana built or improved waterworks and sewer systems, fire stations, school buildings, armories (several fine Art Deco examples remain), city halls, airfields—all manner of public buildings. They conducted classes in arts and crafts as well as training programs in various vocational skills. The WPA Women's Division employed thousands in their sewing projects, and the fruits of their labor went to those on relief who were needier still. Most counties set up canning programs that employed women. WPA workers re-bound books in libraries that had been unable to buy new volumes because of lack of funds. Those unemployed with clerical skills collected county records and organized them into more usable files, a boon to latter-day genealogists. No skills were ignored; actors, directors, and theater technicians produced plays and took them on the road to people who had never before seen live theatrical performances. Musicians, too, were employed in this manner. (The WPA built the stages and bandstands for their performances as well.) Music and theater also played a large part in the WPA's recreation program. Writers worked in public relation jobs in the WPA and in every state produced a guidebook. *Indiana: A Guide to the Hoosier State* is among the best of these, over five hundred pages of still fascinating reading. Researchers went into the field to collect folklore that likely would have been lost without the WPA. For perhaps the first time, the government supported art for the masses; art about the people came to the people in murals painted in public buildings and in sculptures that graced their lobbies and courtyards.

And the Works Progress Administration met the recently voiced needs of the people for a more satisfying life through recreation. Because of labor laws that had created shorter hours, even those who were employed had more leisure time than ever before. A burgeoning recreation movement urged that this time be used "advantageously." The WPA complied with this notion, converting old buildings or constructing new community recreation centers where classes for all ages were offered, plays and concerts performed, and indoor sports enjoyed. These buildings ranged from purely functional gymnasiums to attractive structures in contemporary styles. Imaginative uses of native materials were frequent, for the bulk of the federal money granted to projects under the WPA was to be used for wages; the sponsor generally provided the land, tools, and materials. Therefore, around Bloomington and Bedford one finds abundant limestone and sandstone construction; native timber was used extensively throughout southern Indiana. Up north in the rolling prairies, glacial fieldstone walls and buildings are common in WPA construction. . . .

The WPA fulfilled people's need to play. Recreational projects were among the most successful of their efforts because, as Joseph Baker, head of the WPA Recreation

Section, declared, "recreation projects are flexible and can offer employment where there is greatest need; most of their expenditures go directly to local unemployed labor; they do not compete with private enterprise, and most important of all, they make permanent contributions to better living conditions and increased opportunities for more abundant living." The WPA constructed every possible kind of recreational facility, even such delights as skating ponds, ski slopes, and snow slides for children's sledding (one is still used in North Judson). WPA workers expanded zoo facilities; many parks sported new duck ponds or monkey islands. Community centers nearly always included—or were little more than—gymnasiums, especially if they were attached to schools. The WPA built hundreds of athletic fields in Indiana for softball, baseball, and football, from simple graded spaces to elaborate stadiums, frequently, but not necessarily, adjacent to high schools. Some sports previously considered the domain of the country club set gained wide public access as WPA workers built or expanded tennis courts, golf courses, and swimming pools in towns all across the state. Many of the bath houses erected for these were quite attractive and still stand. Unfortunately, many are abandoned and subject to vandalism. South Bend's Walker Field pavilion is one of the finest, and particularly handsome structures still serve Connersville and New Castle. Most WPA park developments included a concrete wading pool for children, but these are difficult to find today. The polio scare of the 1950s caused most to be closed; subsequently they were torn out. A few abandoned examples remain in Indianapolis, Mishawaka, and New Albany. All these increased recreational opportunities and facilities combined to make parks for the people—as opposed to the more formal green spaces of previous years—that were great sources of community pride. . . .

All in all, it is difficult to comprehend the intensity of some of the criticism leveled against the Works Progress Administration, especially in Indiana where it was generally—and visibly—so successful. The *Fort Wayne Sentinel*, for example, consistently printed anti-New Deal political cartoons, yet that city today boasts a beautiful park and boulevard system that was constructed by the WPA. While it is true that compared to direct relief the WPA cost more per unemployed person in actual cash outlay, there is really no comparison. Unlike the dole, the WPA provided the government with a return in labor for its investment; the local community benefited directly and indirectly; money was circulated, and some returned to the government via taxes; and the workers' pride remained intact. Nothing else fulfilled all those needs so well. As WPA director Harry Hopkin's enthusiastically maintained, "only a work program can answer . . . all aspects of the unemployment problem. Only a job can answer the problem of a jobless man; only a wage will increase purchasing power, for a basket of groceries starts no dollars circulating; only through work can these people make their contribution to our national well-being." Certainly one may argue points of administration, wages, hours, and eligibility, but the logic behind such a program was sound.

In Indiana, the WPA contributed extensively to the built environment. The many structures that remain are sturdily built, often designed in the attractive styles of the

1930s. Indeed, it is unlikely that any Hoosier throughout the course of the day does not enter, use, or pass a structure built by the Works Progress Administration.

THE REVIVAL OF THE REPUBLICAN PARTY

William B. Pickett

The Cornfield Conference of 1938, held on Homer E. Capehart's farm in southern Indiana, demonstrated a new unity and purpose in the national Republican party and marked the beginning of a more conservative era in American politics. It was also a turning point for Capehart. From that moment on he devoted much of his time to selling both the Republican party and himself as the embodiment of its ideals. These activities culminated in his election in 1944 to the United States Senate where he remained for three terms, longer than any Hoosier Republican before him.

Capehart personified the success story of the American dream. As the son of a frugal Indiana farmer he experienced strong doses of family affection, Christian teaching, and back-breaking work on a small farm in Pike County and in Daviess County where his family moved to a tenant farm when Capehart was thirteen years old. His childhood instilled in him a restless drive to succeed. Although his formal education stopped with his graduation from high school in 1916, Capehart continued to learn. As a young baking powder huckster and later as an army supply sergeant during World War I, he gained self confidence. Following the war he sold farm implements and commercial popcorn and peanut toasting machines, and in 1927 he founded the Capehart Automatic Phonograph Corporation in Huntington, Indiana. The company manufactured coin operated phonographs for use in commercial locations such as sweet shops, drug stores, and dance halls—the first such devices with the capacity to play twenty-eight records continuously, automatically turning each one over to play the other side. Renamed the Capehart Corporation, the company moved to Fort Wayne where it produced an expensive record player for use in fashionable homes, yachts, and hotels.

The world wide business collapse which followed the Wall Street crash of 1929 temporarily shelved Capehart's career as an entrepreneur. The Capehart Corporation had been expanding production in 1932 when a drop in sales, a decision to stop dividend payments, and subsequent disagreement with his board of directors—a group which held the controlling preferred stock—resulted in Capehart's removal as president and loss of all equity in his own company. Drawing upon his experience as

From "The Capehart Cornfield Conference and the Election of 1938: Homer E. Capehart's Entry into Politics," *Indiana Magazine of History*, LXXIII (December 1977), 251–254, 258–266, 270–272.

a successful salesman and business promoter, Capehart decided that the Depression had occurred because Americans, like his board of directors at the Capehart Corporation, had become needlessly pessimistic. What the country needed, he thought, was an attitude of optimism, individual self discipline, and willingness to produce and to sell goods.

It was this simple, even naïve, set of beliefs and his enormous determination that Capehart took to Farny Wurlitzer, chief executive of the Rudolph Wurlitzer Company in North Tonawanda, New York, in the summer of 1934. Capehart convinced Wurlitzer that he could lift the New York company out of its desperate financial difficulties. Wurlitzer hired Capehart, and in four years Capehart fulfilled his promise. He supervised the manufacture and sale of the colorful and popular Wurlitzer juke boxes of the 1930s—activities which made Wurlitzer prosperous and made Capehart a millionaire. With some of his new wealth Capehart in 1936 had the satisfaction of purchasing several acres of farm land in Daviess County next to the Graham Farms where at age fourteen he had helped his father plow. . . .

The Hoosier Republican party, as Capehart had already discovered, was in no less disarray than its national organization. Indiana had a history of strong two-party competition, but Paul V. McNutt's entry into the governor's office in 1933 marked a new dominance for the Democratic party. McNutt pushed through the Reorganization Act of 1933 which centralized the administration of state government and placed almost complete control of expenditures and patronage in his hands. Indiana Democrats added to their power through administration of such relief programs as the Works Progress Administration, the Public Works Administration, and farm subsidy payments. By the mid-1930s the party had become relatively prosperous from McNutt's famous "two per cent club," which collected that amount annually from the salaries of state patronage job holders. During these years Hoosier Republicans had disintegrated into factions occupied with squabbles for control of the state organization and appointments to the national committee. The rank-and-file was apathetic. Older members wanted a return of the golden years of Coolidge and continued their support for former Senator James E. Watson—pro-business spokesman for Indiana Republicans for over sixteen years and Senate majority leader during the Hoover administration. By early 1938 a dispute over who would be the next state chairman had caused Muncie manufacturer George A. Ball to resign as national committeeman, and it was uncertain where the state committee would find money for the upcoming congressional campaign.

Fortunately for the Indiana GOP, Hoosier Democrats began experiencing even greater difficulties in 1937. Roosevelt's plan to increase the number of justices on the Supreme Court (which had become a major obstacle to New Deal reforms) and the apparent failure of his economic program in mid-1937 caused serious cracks in the Hoosier Democratic machine, by that time under the leadership of McNutt's protégé, Governor [M. Clifford] Townsend. The first break occurred when the independent minded Democratic Senator Frederick Van Nuys of Indiana became one of ten senators who signed the majority report against Roosevelt's Supreme Court measure. Governor Townsend went to Washington, and after conferring with Roosevelt told the press from the White House steps that he did not know who would be the 1938 Democratic nominee for the United

States Senate from Indiana. "There is nothing certain," Townsend remarked, "except that it will not be Senator Van Nuys." From that moment the Democrats were in a turmoil. Indiana leaders pressed for party harmony, but they could not find a suitable alternative to Van Nuys, who had decided to run for reelection to the Senate against the wishes of the party if necessary. The Republicans had their first good chance for a comeback since the onset of the New Deal.

Acting on his desire to help revitalize the Republican party and the nation's economy, Capehart in February, 1938, suggested a mid-term Republican conference to be held on his Daviess County farm in the following August. Recalling a successful company picnic which he had organized the previous year at North Tonawanda—a festive celebration for Wurlitzer juke box salesmen and their wives—Capehart presented the plan for a cornfield rally to State Republican Chairman Arch Bobbitt. Bobbitt told Capehart that the party was down, that workers were discouraged, and that he had been hoping for a statewide meeting of precinct committeemen and women. Capehart replied, "Why not have a clambake on my farm?" And he gave Bobbitt a contribution check for the state GOP—a check Bobbitt remembers as "Much larger than I had received from anybody for a long time." The motives were uncomplicated, the approach spontaneous and direct. Before it was over Capehart had personally paid out some $25,000.

In the months following the meeting with Bobbitt, Capehart's interest in the party and participation on the Frank committee attracted the attention of the Republican leadership. In July National Chairman Hamilton announced that a Hoosier Republican rally to be held on August 27 at the Capehart farm in Daviess County would open the GOP national congressional election campaign. To give party leaders an opportunity to meet and discuss problems, Hamilton arranged for attendance of Representative Joseph W. Martin, chairman of the Republican congressional campaign committee; Capehart's recent acquaintance, Glenn Frank; and Marion E. Martin, assistant chairman of the national committee in charge of women's activities. Former Senator James W. Wadsworth of New York agreed to give the keynote address, and invitations went to national committee members, state chairmen, senatorial, congressional, and gubernatorial candidates in twelve midwestern and plains states. Capehart was to be general chairman.

When asked later how his suggestion had become so important, Capehart responded in his typical salesman's hyperbole: "I handled it exactly like I'd have handled the introduction of a new musical instrument or an automobile or any new product. . . . Keep writing your name in the sky and if you've got a good product it will be successful, it will draw people to it and they'll buy it." There were, of course, other reasons; the opportunities offered by the Democrats' problems, the need of the Republican party for an attractive program and new money, plus the facts that Capehart made good news copy and had experience staging successful sales conventions. Early in July the state Republican committee began publishing advances about the Cornfield Conference and its host, who personified the farm boy to riches aspect of the American dream. "A country that permits a poor boy to work his way up is good enough for me," Capehart would say. "If they [presumably the New Deal administrators] keep on monkeying with it, they're going to make it impossible for a kid to do what I have done." Reporters enjoyed pointing out the unity in Capehart's progress from boyhood on a neighboring farm to the realization of his dream to own an "agricultural showplace." The amusement industry periodical, *Billboard* magazine, reported: "Capehart plans to 'put up the biggest circus tent ever and show the boys some good entertainment in the way of circus acts'. . . . His able showmanship in presenting this type of affair is well-known and is attested to by thousands of coin-machine operators and distributors."

Early on the morning of August 26 the site of the conference on Capehart's farm was ready. Twenty-eight blue and white striped tents were arranged according to Capehart's blueprint on a 120 acre freshly mowed alfalfa field bordered on the east by the Big Four Railroad tracks and on the south by a county road. Corn had grown in the field other years, and, for those who would insist on accuracy, an adjacent field was filled with green eared stalks in full tassle. The large tent would accommodate ten thousand people seated at tables. There were tents for each of the twelve Indiana district Republican delegations, four for kitchens, one for headquarters, and one each for radio broadcasters, the press, and Republican literature. Small tents sheltered the first aid station and soft drink concessions. The parking area could hold thousands of cars.

GOP festivities began that morning in Gary, where the pied piper of the affair, the Wurlitzer Military Band—a hundred piece ensemble which had won the "best band in the United States award" at the national band contest in Chicago in 1937—left their headquarters on a zigzag southward route. Riding in three sign covered buses, the band traveled from Gary to the Capehart farm, stopping for brief concerts in South Bend, Fort Wayne, Indianapolis, Bloomington, and eight other communities. At Indianapolis a crowd of placard carrying Republicans and a huge live elephant rented from a circus met the band on Monument Circle and held a pep rally. Arriving that evening at the Capehart farm, band members barely had time to eat before they were again playing a two and a half hour concert for a crowd of fifteen thousand. After the concert thousands of citizens from miles around listened as Frank and United States Senate candidate Raymond E. Willis gave the opening addresses of the Cornfield Conference. Meanwhile in Indianapolis, politicos from the thirteen "breadbasket states" gathered at the Columbia Club to meet national leaders and plan strategy for the election. The busy senatorial candidate from Ohio, Robert A. Taft, found time to hurry to Indianapolis to meet the other Republican candidates and get "what advice I could from John Hamilton, Joe Martin and Senator [John G.] Townsend, [Jr.]."

The next morning, August 27, 1938, a summer haze veiled the sun's first rays, and a gentle cooling breeze caused the blue and white canvas tents on the Capehart farm to sway gently. Cooks and waiters were at work steaming clams and barbecuing chickens over huge charcoal pits in the four kitchen tents. Out on the road Capehart's Daviess County neighbors gave parking directions to the first of the thousands of cars they would handle that day. A short time later special trains began to arrive, including one from New York, carrying Capehart's associates from North Tonawanda and Buffalo.

By midmorning lines of automobiles were stirring clouds of dust as they converged on the parking area. More visitors arrived by special train. When Capehart rang the noon dinner bell, his guests—twenty thousand precinct committeemen and county chairmen and their families and dignitaries from out of state—ate at tables filled with barbecued chicken, relishes, mashed potatoes and country gravy, corn on the cob, watermelon, rolls and butter, iced tea, and coffee. The main tent resounded with clinking silver and the din of midwestern politicians devouring more than five thousand chickens, seventy thousand steamed clams, and three tons of corn on the cob. Outside, shuttle trains from Petersburg and Evansville to the south and Terre Haute to the north arrived with more party faithful and the curious who wanted to see a real Indian chief, watch stuntmen, and listen to yodelers, guitar players, a German band, the Wurlitzer Military Band, and thirty-two individual drum and bugle corps from the surrounding area. Overseeing this "Homeric feast" (as *Time* magazine called it) was the tireless Capehart in floppy canvas sun hat, white long sleeved shirt, long checked tie, tan cotton trousers, and cigar in the corner of his mouth. Reporters observed him in perpetual motion, shaking hands with Hamilton, standing with arms around Willis and Frank, talking with his assistants. No detail was too minor for his concern, no county committeeman too unimportant for his warm greeting and handshake. He even supervised the decoration of the speakers' rostrum.

When the delegates had finished lunch, Republican State Chairman Bobbitt opened the public meeting from the platform at the middle of the main tent where, among others, former Senator Watson sat. As late as 1936 Watson still believed Coolidge instead of Hoover should have been the party candidate in 1928. He watched quietly now as more youthful and energetic GOP members sought to adapt the party to the "new circumstances of American life." Representative Charles A. Halleck, Indiana's only Republican member of the House of Representatives, introduced each speaker until Hamilton, Wadsworth, Willis, Capehart, and five other party officials had spoken. The only hitch was when Wadsworth went over his allotted time, and Halleck had to ask him to hurry up and finish. . . .

Capehart's maiden political address, perhaps the most thoughtful of the day and an oratorical success, revealed certain weaknesses. Like the unpublished Frank committee report it confronted the perennial problem of modern industrial societies—how to provide both economic security and incentives to work and produce. But Capehart's speech contained no proposals about how relief could be better administered and no specific program for obtaining the expansion of private enterprise necessary to eliminate unemployment and the need for public relief. Taking a position which he would in later years label "political realism," he endorsed the best features both of the experiment he condemned and of the pre-Depression Republican policies under which the United States had achieved industrial leadership of the world. No more than had Landon did Capehart tell how a Republican political leadership would bring the economic recovery necessary to American capitalism, but like Landon and Hoover he expressed his eternal optimism that it could. Finally, his resort to partisan name calling, while perhaps politically useful, revealed an unfortunate willingness to join the party in its appeal to the blind emotions of the fearful rather than to the constructive proposals of the thoughtful.

The immediate response was less to Capehart's address, however, than to the fact that the Republican rally had taken place. No one could deny the national impact of the Capehart Cornfield Conference. It made front page news in the New York *Times*, the Chicago *Tribune*, and local newspapers from Pawhuska, Oklahoma, to Walla Walla, Washington, to Concord, North Carolina. Most papers reflected the sentiments of a New York *Times* editorial which suggested "a real elephant under the main tent after all, instead of the skeleton of a prehistorical animal that lost his hide with his shirt in 1932." The Newark *Star Eagle* believed that the Republican protest "shows signs of cohesion. A militant minority has spoken with a voice of confidence in its destiny." Newspaper coverage was so intense that Charles Michelson, director of publicity for the Democratic National Committee, wrote a special article to play down the affair. Published in newspapers across the country, Michelson's response asked if the five thousand chickens which Republicans consumed at the Capehart picnic had any relation to the two chickens in every pot promised by Hoover. He predicted that the Democrats could stop campaigning and still have a majority of eighty or ninety votes in the House of Representatives after the November election. The "utmost variation" in the Senate, he said, could not involve more than "a seat or two."

It is impossible to know the effect of the Cornfield Conference upon the national election of 1938, but to Michelson's probable dismay the opponents of the New Deal made important gains in November. The election increased GOP representatives by eighty, from eighty-nine to 169, and the number of Republican senators by eight, from fifteen to twenty-three. Most of the defeated Democrats were liberal New Dealers from industrial sections of the East and Midwest. Some eighty other House Democrats were at best unenthusiastic about the New Deal. Of the sixty-nine Democrats remaining in the Senate as many as thirty were now hostile to Roosevelt's programs. Forty-five of the eighty new Republican representatives were from the Midwest. Democratic National Chairman James A. Farley called it "the great turnover."

In Indiana Capehart's financial support and skills as an impresario gave an energetic boost to the Republican party. After the Cornfield Conference, he campaigned hard for the party. Hoosier Democrats recognized clearly the danger of a resurgent GOP. Meeting at French Lick the day of the Capehart Cornfield Conference, they announced the end of their factional struggle and united behind the candidacy of Senator Van Nuys. In a campaign speaking tour for Willis and other Republican candidates, Capehart continued the drum beat sounded by his Cornfield Conference speech. He attacked government spending, cutting of production in time of scarcity, appeals to class hatred, relief without restored opportunity, and failure to increase farm prices. As the election neared, he and Willis repeated their message to almost four thousand Indiana Republican precinct meetings simultaneously in a radio broadcast originating from the Capehart farm.

Despite Capehart's efforts Willis narrowly lost to Van Nuys in the November election. But Indiana Republicans won seven of twelve congressional races and elected their candidate for secretary of state. The state senate remained Democratic but house Republicans gained a slight majority. The total vote was second largest in Indiana history. Republicans carried every rural congressional district except one and 85 percent of the rural counties. In their report to the national chairman state Democratic officials spoke of conservative farmers disillusioned with the crop control program, of the WPA make work programs which helped make farm labor scarce, and of the wages and hour law which hurt businessmen running small factories. The Democrats complained that government leniency toward sit down strikes, government spending programs which antagonized independent voters, and the so-called Democratic purge gave the Republicans "effective ammunition" with conservative elements. While they did not mention the Capehart Cornfield Conference, the Democrats prophetically concluded that "if the momentum gained by the Republicans . . . which the election more or less set in motion is not checked through co-operation by our party, Indiana indeed will be a doubtful state in 1940."

TENANT FARMING LIFE DURING THE DEPRESSION

Julia Hedge

KRASEAN Now these houses that you lived in, you didn't rent them, did you?

HEDGE No, we didn't pay anything on them. They were furnished us.

KRASEAN What about the furniture in the house itself?

HEDGE No, you had your own furniture. These houses were very crudely built.

KRASEAN Can you describe what one of these houses was like?

HEDGE The outside of them was like you would think of a barn. Wide panels of wood, and it was just sawmill wood, you know, not finished. The boards ran up and down this way, on the outside of the house.

On the inside was a narrow board like what we used to call a ship lap—tongue groove, I think, they call it now. It ran cross-ways on your walls on the inside and on the ceiling. The doors were just boards nailed together with cross pieces on them.

In our house, we had two windows in our kitchen. We had one in the living room and one in the bedroom, and that's all the rooms we had.

KRASEAN You had three rooms.

HEDGE We had three rooms and the bedroom was very small. It was narrow. It wasn't near as long as this room and it was, I imagine, about 7½ to 8 feet wide. That's all we had.

The floors were wide boards—for the floors. The house that we lived in wasn't on a foundation, it was on big round blocks, sawed out of logs—for corner blocks. We

---

From Mrs. Julia Hedge Interview, Lewis Historical Library, Vincennes University. Reprinted by permission of Mr. Thomas Krasean and the Director of the Lewis Historical Library.

had a little old porch in front—just enough to get in out of the rain—the same thing, and a back one the same way. We had three steps to go down at the back or the front either one, to get out on the ground. The roofs were tin. Tin roofs.

KRASEAN It made it pretty warm in the summer, didn't it?

HEDGE It made it awfully warm in the summer, and awfully cold in the winter, because there was big cracks around the windows all the way around. They were old, see, and the weather had done that.

We would tear up rags and take us a knife—table knife—and poke those rags in the cracks clear around and tighten up those the best we could. After our work was done, of an evening, and we were all in the house so the doors didn't have to be open, we would take toe sacks—we would call them, they call them gunny sacks now, anyway they're a mesh bag like you get 100 pound of potatoes in—we would stuff them under the bottoms of the doors. If you didn't do that, and it come up a snow during the winter, you had snow all over your floors.

We had no carpets. We did have a linoleum—a 9x12 linoleum, but that didn't cover the floor and it didn't come to the wood work. There was no quarter round around the wood work, to keep out the cold air from coming in like that. It got awful cold in the winter.

We had a heating stove in the living room and in the kitchen we had an old fashioned wood range. We burned wood in that all the time. Perry would go to the elevator and get big loads of cobs—we had an old shed out here that he would put them in—and we used those for kindling. We would get up of a morning and he would tear some paper up and put it in the bottom of the stove, put some cobs in there and pour a little coal oil on your cobs, set that afire and stack your wood in on that.

If your wood was real green—in the winter time, you couldn't cut dead wood—you cut down green maples for the cook stove. We would have that split into about 2 inch squares or something like that and about 16 inches long. They were sticks of wood and we used to pile the oven full of that wood when we had a fire in the cook stove and dry that out to have the next morning to start a fire, so that we could get breakfast on time for the children to be off to school and Perry to be to work.

KRASEAN Is this pretty much like all the houses around?

HEDGE They were all practically the same. Some were bigger. Most of them were all just about alike.

KRASEAN How come some were bigger?

HEDGE The foreman's house was a little larger. Now, Doad Hall was our foreman. There was about eight families on that. He called his ground #1, #2, and #3 farms down there, see. Doad Hall was our foreman. Now, his house had seven rooms in it. It had an upstairs to it, see. There were three bedrooms upstairs. It would get so cold in the winter time. Just the one heating stove downstairs wouldn't heat those seven rooms. Then sometimes those children would come downstairs and sleep on a cot or whatever they had to sleep on.

KRASEAN So the foreman really didn't have much better than . . .

HEDGE He didn't have too much better, only he got a little more money, and occasionally he could buy a little coal, and we couldn't.

KRASEAN Where did you get your wood?

HEDGE Brevoort had woods on his ground and we could go out there and cut all the wood we wanted.

KRASEAN They didn't provide it for you, you had to cut it.

HEDGE No, you would go out and get it yourself. He had a team and a wagon. We could always use the team and wagon. They would work through the week, when they had a full week's work. On Sunday Perry and I would go out and cut poles—small trees—about like that, and load them on to the wagon and bring them on in. Then we had what we called saw bucks built. They were two by fours that run something like this, see.

KRASEAN Crossways.

HEDGE Uh huh. You would set your pole in there. One would get on one side and one on the other with a cross cut saw and you sawed that off into blocks. If you could get a pretty good size tree, you also sawed it into blocks, then took the ax and split it. If it didn't split with the ax, we had an iron wedge that we put in there and pounded that iron wedge. If they were real hard to split, you broke your ax handle. Then you had to drive clear to Vincennes to get a new ax handle.

KRASEAN And again, all of this you had to provide yourself?

HEDGE Yes, you had to provide all that yourself. The only thing you got free was your house and your garden spot. He did let you pasture your cow. You was supposed to buy your loose feed, but he did have pasture for your cow.

KRASEAN In other words, you think the landowner tried to make it as easy for you as he could—or as comfortable?

HEDGE Everybody was the same. He didn't show no partiality. Every person had the same amount, except the foremen. They got a little more. The Halls had two cows. We could have one. Of course, they had quite a few kids too. At that time, most people had big families. They didn't have big doctor bills, in a way, because the doctor bills weren't so high then. Another thing we didn't have the money, so you had to doctor your own child whatever was the matter with them. If it had a loose tooth, you pulled it. If it had a cut on its head, you pulled it together and put adhesive tape on it and disinfected it. If you didn't have anything else you put on salt water or boric acid water and disinfected the wound with that, and then closed it up yourself.

KRASEAN So it really wasn't a matter of going to the doctors, you tried to do it yourself?

HEDGE You tried to do it yourself all you could, because we didn't have a car then, in the early days. Now later on we got a little model-T car. But you had to take the team and wagon and drive about 8 miles to town and maybe the doctor would be out somewhere else. There you were. Besides, a man would have to take off from work, and he couldn't afford to do that.

KRASEAN There was no such thing as vacation or any kind of leave.

HEDGE You got no vacation whatsoever. You were off on Saturday afternoon. Every two weeks you got a Saturday afternoon off that was pay day. Then you got Sunday off. But in real bad weather, you got plenty of vacation, because you couldn't work. Those days, we had big snows. If it would come a big snow and maybe sleet on top of it, the mules couldn't be gotten out, and you would get a vacation.

KRASEAN But they would still continue to pay.

HEDGE No. You got paid for the days you worked. If you worked two days of the week, you got $2.00. When it came down to a dime an hour. When we first moved there, we were getting a dollar and a quarter. Two days would make you $2.50.

If one of the family got sick and you just had to take off, if you didn't have anybody—any of your relatives willing to work in your place, like a boy 14 or 15 or something, you lost that too. Besides, you had to pay your own bills.

We had some insurance with Western & Southern—a death benefit insurance. People didn't have sick and accident then. Most all of it was death benefit.

KRASEAN What kind of work did you do in the winter, then?

HEDGE In the wintertime they broke the stalks and in the late fall they would plow the ground for the coming wheat crops. They would get hay out of the stacks that was stacked in the field and haul it in and put it in the hay-loft, up over the barn. Just things like that. They would trim brush, along the levee and along the ditches and banks, and just do whatever they could do.

KRASEAN Do you recall any time in which Mr. Hedge couldn't work for quite a lengthy period during the winter, when it really got pretty bad?

HEDGE Well, I've seen times when he wouldn't make over $4.00 or $5.00 for a month's time. We had three children then. Clora Ethyl, Walter, and Clarence. It was pretty rough—specially when the cow went dry it was rough. You didn't have any milk.

Doads had two cows, as I said, and if we could go down there and get milk, I could get milk for a dime a gallon—but that was a hour's work to get a gallon of milk—if they had enough to go around. Of course, we did have eggs, most of the time.

KRASEAN You say you had chickens?

HEDGE We had three dozen hens—if the minks didn't carry them off before hatching time—the next time to raise some more. We hatched our own chickens. We would set a hen on 15 eggs, and she would probably hatch around 11 or 12. We would shell some corn and we had a hand grinder, like an old-fashioned mill. We would grind that for our chickens' feed. For the real little ones—I would cook that sometimes like a cornbread and crumble it for the real little chickens, to get them started. They had a lot of territory to run around in and they could catch a lot of insects in the spring, when they had the little ones.

KRASEAN I am kind of curious. Now you talk about perhaps a time when you might not have made more than $4.00 or $5.00 a month, what was your diet at that time? What kind of food could you buy?

HEDGE Beans and potatoes and rice and oats, mostly—dry food. We had milk and if we could get a little sugar, why the children would eat quite a good deal of rice. We would have oats and I made quite a deal of soups, because in vegetable season I canned an awful lot of food—vegetables. What I could.

KRASEAN Now this would be from your garden?

HEDGE Well, from my garden or from the wild. We picked wild grapes and made wild grape jelly and we picked blackberries, and we could gather greens in the spring and we canned those. Then Brevoort would give us some corn. We were supposed to eat what corn we wanted, in the corn season. We canned that. Then Perry had a cousin that worked for Simpson Orchard, where they had apples, and they would pick those dropped apples up and haul them out. He would bring us down apples, and I would can apples and make apple butter. Of course, I made all my own jellies, and made our salad dressing and things like that.

KRASEAN So it really was a sort of simple sort of diet.

HEDGE It was a home thing. We didn't have any meat to amount to anything at all.

KRASEAN That was my next question.

HEDGE No, we didn't. One year Perry and Milt Hall went together and bought a hog from Seldon Montgomery, and we had that. But that's about the only time we had our own meat—just that one hog and we divided between two families.

Oh, occasionally we could get a little bologna or something like that, but not too much. A little jowl bacon or something.

KRASEAN This was what you bought in town?

HEDGE Well, we would buy it at the Liberty Meat Market. We usually bought our bread there, because we could get six loaves of bread for a quarter. They were pound loaves of bread. They would have a special on it usually on Friday and Saturday and we could get six loaves for a quarter. We just went every two weeks to town, see. Then when we ran out of that bread, we made our own biscuits and our own cornbread. If I ran out of cornmeal, I ground some corn and sifted it. I would give the chickens the heavy and used the thin meal to make cornbread.

KRASEAN Apparently there was no real loss, I suppose, in not having meat to eat.

HEDGE Well, we substituted beans for meat. We had navy beans every day.

KRASEAN This you could buy?

HEDGE We could buy navy beans. We would get the split ones. We would get 10 pound for 29¢. . . .

KRASEAN You say you had chickens. What about having some chicken once in a while?

HEDGE Oh, sure. We tried to raise enough chicken to have chicken along in the summer time. See, the hens didn't start hatching until about late March or something like that. Then your chickens had to be about two months old or something of that sort, before you could fry them. We would have fried chicken. We ate an awful lot of gravy and biscuits, too. . . .

KRASEAN And pay day was how often?

HEDGE Once every two weeks.

KRASEAN Every two weeks on Saturday?

HEDGE Every other Saturday afternoon. That's when he would let men have the team to go to town with their families. We always went, because that was the only time we got to go—unless it was real, awful cold and we couldn't take the children out.

We would get the wagon out and put straw in the wagon and then we had a big old comfort that we would throw in on that and wrap the children up and put them in there and throw another comfort over them. Maybe they would be asleep before we got to town. I tried to go to town with Perry all the time. Of course, I've always went with Perry wherever he went, and he's always went with me—unless he went to work or I went to work.

KRASEAN Now when the time came to go down town, when you could on the wagon, you didn't try all eight families to go at once?

HEDGE Everybody went the same day. You would see them lined up like a string of cars for a stop sign. They would come in if their wives had their children ready. We always had to have the coal oil can in the wagon and the lard bucket in the wagon, and things that we needed, because we had to have our coal oil for our lights and in the summer time we burned a coal oil stove, instead of cutting wood for a cook stove. It made it awful hot in there, too.

We would have our children dressed and have our meal on the table, and have the children fed, usually. Then when Perry would come in he would eat and then we would start to town.

KRASEAN You said the landowner would give you a wagon, but he couldn't possibly give eight wagons.

HEDGE Yes, each man could take a wagon if he wanted to. The teams he drove to work he could use to go to town in. Behind Will Bey's there where that little red rooster thing is, there, you know, that used to be a lot there, with a hitch post. There was a horse-shoeing place right on the corner. Then behind that we would take our teams in there and tie them up back there. Then we could get our groceries and put them in the wagon from there.

Where the parking lot is now—between Busseron and Buntin, there between First and Second—that was what they called a hitch lot. People would take their teams and wagons there and tie them up. Then down below where the Memorial Bridge is now, on First Street, there was a delivery barn there. If you wanted to, you could take your teams there and tie them up, too, if they had extra space.

KRASEAN So this was really the big afternoon—Saturday afternoon?

HEDGE Yes, it was, because you would look forward to it. You would be out of this, or would be out of that, or something, and you looked forward to going to town on Saturday afternoon.

Going to town, and going to church on Sunday was the only recreation we had. Of course, the children enjoyed going to town, because Mr. Bey had a big store in there and he had chairs around the heating stove, back in the back. We could take our children in there and they could see the neighbors' kids, you know, and people that maybe we had known before. A lot of people came in there just for conversation, and to get their groceries too.

You didn't pick up your groceries in a shopping cart. They had counters in front and groceries were stacked on the shelves behind. We went in there with our grocery list written down and we could either hand it to the clerk or we would read it off and they would write it on their sales pad. They would put the groceries all in a box and we would be ready to go.

Us mothers could go in there with our babies and it was nice and warm. We could dry our babies and feed them their bottles and things right in there where it was warm and comfortable. He was a wonderful man to all the poor people.

KRASEAN He was the main man you bought from?

HEDGE He owned the store and he was a wonderful man to people. He had come up the hard way, himself, and every once in a while, he would give little kids a cookie or a sucker or something like that. He liked to do that.

Then after we moved to town, I worked for Mr. Bey for five years in the store. I think he is the most wonderful man that ever hired people in this town. He wasn't cross. He didn't complain. If you made a mistake, you had all the chance in the world to correct it. He didn't complain. Anything in the store that you wanted to eat—like a cookie, or candy or pop—it was yours free, when you worked for him. . . .

KRASEAN Your duties, as a wife, was mostly indoors and getting sewing and cooking and washing done. But you also helped to some extent outside with the chickens and . . .

HEDGE I took care of the chickens, I milked the cow, I put the feed in for the mules—the corn in the box and the hay in the manger, for the mules. I took the cow to the pasture, I churned my own butter, I carried all the water in from the well—we had to carry water in buckets and I washed the clothes on the board. I ironed the clothes with irons we would set on the stove and get them hot. Then you had a handle that clamped over it. Some did and some had the handles built on. You had a hot pad that you picked them up with and ironed until the iron was cold. Then you would put it back and pick up another one. We usually had three irons, or at least two irons.

I done the sewing and I scrubbed the floors and took care of the baby, canned the food. That was the big problem, was canning a lot, too. And go pick the berries. I hoed in the garden, and pulled weeds and in the thirties, in the summertime, after my oldest daughter got twelve years old, I would let her watch the little ones and I worked in the tomato field. It belonged to the canning factory up here. They had rented some ground from Brevoort and they planted tomato seeds to raise plants to ship to different places in the country—the plants. I worked in that, in the fields.

I would go to work at 7:00 and I would work until about 5:00 or 6:00 in the field. Then I would do my washing at night—when I done that, I would wash at night. I would light the old lantern and take it out and hang up the clothes, so they would be there for the next morning—so I could go to work.

I didn't put heavy work on Clora Ethyl. I never did let her do a washing by herself or anything like that. The ironing—I wanted to be there when that was done, because there was danger of getting burned. Both in fixing the fire, and with the iron—especially with the little children.

KRASEAN During the Depression period, when the children were small, what would you do in an evening, say, after Mr. Hedge got home?

HEDGE Well, it usually was almost dark. We would have supper ready when he got home, then we would eat supper and do the dishes. Then I would help the children with their lessons—what they had to do. Of course, we would play with the little kids.

If we had one learning to walk, we would sit down and say, "Come to me," and we would teach them to walk like that. We usually gathered walnuts and hickory nuts in their season and we would have them out in the shed in an old gunny sack, hanging up. We would get walnuts and set us an old quilt out behind the stove and take an iron and lay it on our lap, and a hammer, and crack our nuts and pick them out for the little ones and let the others pick them out. We would sing songs. Perry read a lot. He liked to read—when he had the time—and we would read the paper—if we had a paper. We didn't take any magazines, much, only "Prairie Farmer" or something like that. Of course, during the daytime, there was plenty of work to take care of the entire time—during the daytime. . . .

KRASEAN At any time did Mr. Hedge's salary or hourly wage go up at all during the Depression?

HEDGE Well, not until it commenced to lift. Perry got around a dollar or a little better than that a day, up until he got on W.P.A., in '38. Now that's when we got lifted a little. He got on W.P.A., and as I said, he got $48.00 a month for that. He got paid every two weeks for that. They didn't have to work every day. They worked until they had worked so many hours in the week, then they were off until the next week to put in so many hours. I can't recall the number of hours they put in, but we got $24.00 every two weeks on W.P.A.

That work consisted of going out and mowing weeds on the highways and repairing roads and things of that sort. All road work that he done. Then in 1940 they put him in the commissary down here. They would send you a card and you would go where they sent you—the government. They would come out through the regular W.P.A. office. They gave him a card to report to the commissary, which was set up in town. The government issued food like what we call surplus food today. . . .

HEDGE I got me a new cook stove when Roosevelt got to be President and Perry got on W.P.A. I was really proud of that. That was pretty. It was a coal-burning stove, but it was a cream color and trimmed in nickel-plate. I always loved to polish that thing and make it shine. I used to get out in the back yard and I could see it through the kitchen door. I would just back off and look at my beautiful stove.

KRASEAN How were you able to get this?

HEDGE I bought it on payments. Then, later on, I bought a living room suite on payments at Mitchell's. We bought an awful lot of things from Mitchell's—furniture. It started out as Vincennes House Furnishing. Then they moved over there at the Mitchell's store. Then I just built up as I could on those things. Roosevelt is the man that made it possible.

The day we got the W.P.A. card for Perry to go on W.P.A., I was crying. Walter said, "Mother, why are you so happy?"

"Son, that means food on the table. That means shoes for you kids to wear." My boys had gone to school in the wintertime with overshoes and no shoes under them at all. I was just thrilled to death! (Breaks down)

I guess I'll always have a praise for Roosevelt.

10. War, and Cold War

The mood of the people of Indiana was strongly isolationist during the 1930s. Even Elmer Davis, who emerged from his Ohio River hometown to become a Rhodes scholar, *New York Times* reporter, and CBS Radio news commentator, was an isolationist until he visited war-torn London as the guest of Edward R. Murrow during the "blitz" in 1940. Then he became an internationalist who was convinced that America would—and should—enter World War II eventually. Most Americans, however, and most Hoosiers, were unpersuaded until the Japanese attack on Pearl Harbor united the country and led to an unrestrained war effort against the Axis forces in Europe and Asia.

The impact of the war on the country, of course, was enormous, fully as complete in its own way during the 1940s as that of the Depression had been during the 1930s. In Indiana the impact of the war was particularly heavy. Nearly 10 percent of its population, 340,000 men and women, entered the armed services, some 10,000 of whom never returned. At the same time, there were massive changes going on at home from 1940 on. Hundreds of industries received war production contracts and converted to the manufacture of war materiel; a few new factories, particularly ammunition and ordnance plants, were established; unemployment was virtually eliminated; and numerous military installations of all kinds—training facilities, prisoner of war camps, proving grounds, and air fields—were developed. Large military contractors within the state included General Electric of Fort Wayne, International Harvester of Fort Wayne and Indianapolis, Studebaker and Bendix Aviation of South Bend, Servel of Evansville, the steel companies of northwestern Indiana, Allison and Curtiss-Wright of Indianapolis, even Eli Lilly of Indianapolis (producing blood plasma and various medicines). All areas of the state, except, for the most part, Terre Haute, perhaps because of the radical labor image it earned in the 1930s, participated in the economic boom.

Other ways in which the war was brought home to the American people were price controls; food, clothing, and gasoline rationing; and various civil defense programs. War bond, scrap iron, and paper drives were common, and news of the war's progress was eagerly followed while people on the home front labored grimly to provide the necessary tools and equipment for the men "up front." The attitudes of the soldiers abroad are best related in a letter from a member of the Indiana General Assembly to the Speaker of the House in January 1945:

> At the present time I am serving as a line sergeant in the 3d Army, 5th Division, on the snow-covered western front. All of the G.I.'s in the infantry, as they march thru the mud, slush, and snow have but one goal in mind—that is, to get the task com-

> pleted and return home to our families and friends. I wish to assure the members of the House and people of the State of Indiana that our fighting men are making sacrifices of life, limb, and physical and mental discomfort that are beyond the conception of soldier or civilian who has not actually undergone such experiences. They make these sacrifices and take that one step forward when every bone and muscle in their body tells them they cannot go forward—in order that our country might have an everlasting peace.[1]

For the American black the war had a second purpose as well. While fighting against totalitarian and racist governments abroad, blacks reflected on their own lack of complete freedom at home. Consequently, they desired the war experience to end not only despotism abroad but also racism and discrimination at home. Some black newspaper editors used a "double-V" symbol to represent the dual battle going on, and in some respects the civil rights movement of the 1950s and 1960s stemmed from changes within the military occasioned by the war. A selection below traces the history of race relations in Indiana through World War II and analyzes the changes that occurred during the war years.

The immediate concerns of most Hoosiers in the late war and postwar years were economic and political, and there was a strong desire to get things back to normal as soon as possible without sacrificing the economic gains of the period. As journalist John Bartlow Martin discovered in 1944, "middle America" as represented by the working people of "Middletown" (Muncie) was far more interested in tomorrow's paycheck than in the postwar settlement, internationalism, or the United States' future relations with Russia and China. There were latent currents of hostility toward both Communism and government interference, however, and both attitudes were strongly reflected in Hoosier politics and policies during the Cold War era.

Senator William E. Jenner of Bedford, a man selected by Irving Leibowitz as the typical Hoosier of his generation, reflected the state's distaste for massive federal spending programs—often to the state's own economic loss—and for accommodations of any kind with the Soviets. He was an ardent supporter of Senator Joseph McCarthy during the latter's heyday and was critical of both the Democratic opposition to McCarthy and the moderate Republicanism of President Eisenhower during the 1950s. But as Elmer Davis indicated in a 1950 address, portions of which are reprinted below, there was another Indiana view in those days as well.

For a good account of home-front America during World War II, see Richard Polenberg, *War and Society: The United States, 1941-1945* (1972). For a perspective on Indiana during the war years, see especially the series of books issued by the Indiana World War II Commission, the work of which is partially described below by Professor Lynn W. Turner; see also a special issue of *Traces of Indiana and Mid-*

---

1. Gene Eckerty to Hobart Creighton, January 8, 1945, in *Letters from Fighting Hoosiers* (1948), ed. Howard H. Peckham and Shirley A. Snyder, p. 169. Staff Sergeant Eckerty was killed in action in Germany in February 1945.

western History for Fall 1991, which contains a series of articles on Indiana and World War II "50 Years Later."

The Urban Home Front

INDIANA'S MOBILIZATION FOR WAR

Lynn W. Turner

Lynn W. Turner, when the essay below was written, was both an associate professor of history at Indiana University and director of the Indiana War History Commission, established in 1942. He describes the work of the commission, which led to the publication of a number of extraordinarily useful volumes about Indiana's role in the war, and summarizes some of the findings of the commission's scholars regarding life, economic development, and the extensive home-front mobilization that occurred after 1940. Turner also compiled, with the assistance of Heber P. Walker, one of the books issued by the commission, Indiana at War: Civilian Directory *(1951). Subsequently Turner became president of Otterbein University in Westerville, Ohio. Among the books published by the commission were Max Cavnes,* The Hoosier Community at War *(1961), Bernard Friedman,* The Financial Role of Indiana in World War II *(1965), Howard H. Peckham and Shirley A. Snyder, eds.,* Letters from Fighting Hoosiers *(1948), and Dorothy Riker, comp.,* The Hoosier Training Ground *(1952). For additional information on Indiana at this time, see, in addition to James H. Madison,* Indiana through Tradition and Change: A History of the Hoosier State and Its People, 1920–1945 *(1982), volume 5 of the state sesquicentennial series, the special issue of* Traces of Indiana and Midwestern History, *III (Fall 1991). The entire issue is devoted to exploring Indiana's role in the war, both on the home front and at the battle fronts in Europe and the Far East. See especially the essays by Darrel E. Bigham on Evansville and by Stephen G. McShane on the Calumet region. Elsewhere Patrick J. Furlong has written on South Bend's contribution to the war effort. See his "Arsenal of Democracy: South Bend Factories during World War II,"* Indiana Military History Journal, *VI (October 1981), 15–21.*

The basic reason for the organization of the Indiana War History Commission in 1942 was to guarantee, so far as humanly possible, that history would tell no lies in recounting Indiana's part in World War II. Its immediate concern during the war years was the preservation of records—a task which it attempted to perform so thoroughly that no gaps would be left as open invitations for the myth-makers. The end of the war brought the collecting phase of the commission's work to a virtual close. It then turned to the other indispensable part of its mission, embodied in the 1947 act of the general assembly which made it an independent state agency to "write, publish and sell a comprehensive history of the state's war activities." The commis-

---

From "Indiana in World War II—A Progress Report," *Indiana Magazine of History*, LII (March 1956), 1–20. Reprinted by permission of the Editor, *Indiana Magazine of History*.

sion subsequently decided that the execution of this mandate required the production of a ten-volume series to which was given the general title *Indiana in World War II*. Three of these proposed volumes—a gold star honor roll, a book of letters from Hoosiers in the armed services, and a history of military installations within the state—were to cover the purely military side of Indiana's war effort. A fourth was to be a general survey and personnel directory of civilian war service in federal and state agencies and private organizations. Four of the remaining volumes were to deal respectively with the industrial, agricultural, financial, and social history of Indiana during the war years. Another book was to cover the story of civilian defense in all of its ramifications, and the final volume was planned as a popular summary of the entire series. Of these ten projected volumes, three have been published and are on the market, two are now ready for publication, and three more are in various stages of advanced preparation. Thus it is apparent that the research has been finished for eight of the ten volumes and the entire project is rapidly nearing its original goal. The work is far enough advanced that its final impact can be estimated: the rough outlines of the picture are clearly visible and the details have been filled in for a great portion of the canvas. To some degree this paper may serve as the forerunner of that last volume—the summary of the series—by attempting to evaluate the results of more than a decade of research.

The services of a special commission were not required to measure Indiana's participation in the war effort statistically. It is well known that the state furnished approximately 363,000 men and women to the armed forces of the nation and that more than 10,000 of these gave their lives in their country's service. Federal statisticians declare that Indiana's manufacturers produced $3,200,000,000 worth of war goods and that new war factories, costing more than a billion dollars, were erected within her boundaries. Agricultural production in Indiana increased by 49 per cent during the war years, the annual production of the coal mines almost doubled, and the number of employed grew by more than 66 per cent. Hoosiers purchased $3,085,000,000 worth of war bonds, while, at the same time, paying nearly two and three-quarters billion dollars in taxes. These figures are imposing, but their significance is clarified only by comparisons with national totals or with the accomplishments of neighboring states. It is instructive, for example, to learn that while Indiana contained 2.6 per cent of the male population of the United States in 1940, she contributed only 2.5 per cent of the men in the armed forces and only 2.2 per cent of those who enlisted voluntarily, while Californians, who made up 5.3 per cent of the population, comprised 5.9 per cent of the armed forces and 7.4 per cent of the volunteers. A more flattering comparison is that Indiana, which ranks twelfth among her sister states in population, raised herself during the war from ninth place to seventh in the total value of industrial products and that she ranked no less than third in the nation in her ratio of war production to population.

What conclusions may be drawn from these facts? It is dangerous enough even for experts to venture interpretations of contemporary history, but what this paper attempts is doubly perilous, since it proposes to generalize upon others' interpretations. Doubly distilled deductions usually either lose the original qualities of the brew entirely, or emerge as concentrations too potent to be exposed to the public. Whichever this may be, here are some of the things worth remembering that may have been discovered through the commission's studies of Indiana's participation in World War II.

First of all, the war offered some proof that the proud boast "INDIANA—The Center of Almost Everything" is not simply Chamber of Commerce propaganda but reasonably demonstrable fact. Whether because of her geographical location at the center of population, her unique combination of distance from the coasts but proximity to markets, her natural resources, her transportation network, her skilled labor, her diversified industry, her educational system, the skill of her politicians, or a judicious mixture of all these factors, it is certainly apparent that Indiana was attractive both to military officers planning the location of key installations and to governmental officials searching for the placement of war contracts. "They like us down in Washington," Governor M. Clifford Townsend reported after a visit to the capital as early as December, 1940. Nor was this just a politician's statement for home consumption. Already by that time Du Pont had nearly finished construction of the gigantic Hoosier Ordnance Plant at Charlestown, contracts had been awarded for the Kingsbury Ordnance Plant at the other end of the state, the Navy had taken over half of Martin County for the development of a billion dollar ammunition storage depot, and the Army had announced plans for developing a fifty-six thousand acre proving ground in the hills behind Madison. When World War II began there were only two major military installations in Indiana—Fort Benjamin Harrison and the Jeffersonville Quartermaster Depot. Before it ended there were thirty-one—ten ordnance plants, seven air bases, six storage depots, five training camps, two great general hospitals, and the Army's largest proving ground. The military contribution made by these installations was considerable, but the economic and social consequences of their presence in Indiana were even more significant.

The story of the role which Indiana industry and labor played in the war is fundamentally the same although the chronological pattern is different. Principally because no Indiana city plays the dominant role in any major industry which Detroit, for example, exerts in the automotive world, Hoosier factories were backward about getting into defense production during 1940 and 1941. To some extent this was a matter of deliberate choice, reflecting an isolationist attitude toward world affairs and a Republican distrust of New Deal politicians. But it soon became a cause for alarm—the major contracts were going to the great metropolitan centers and Indiana was not getting her share. Curtailment of purely civilian goods such as automobiles and washing machines by government fiat, shrinking stockpiles of strategic materials, and "priorities unemployment" actually brought a serious threat of depression to Indiana during the months just preceding Pearl Harbor. American entry into the war and a vigorous campaign of protest in which Hoosier congressmen and industrialists took a leading part soon brought Indiana from somewhere near the rear of the industrial parade to a front rank. Evansville, for example, turned from the production of refrigerators and automobiles to bullets, airplane engines, and LST's. In 1941 she was facing a problem of severe unemployment: by 1943 she was listed by the War Manpower Commission as an area of critical labor shortage.

One of the finished manuscripts in the possession of the War History Commission is a history of Indiana's war production record by George M. Blackburn, a former research assistant. Much of this five-hundred-page manuscript is devoted to a recital of simple but incredible facts. There is the story of Kaufman T. Keller, president of Chrysler Corporation, who was asked by Army Ordnance if his Plymouth assembly plant at Evansville could produce .45 caliber cartridges by the billion. His answer was simply, "Yes," and when the startled Army officer asked if decisions of this magnitude were always so readily made, Keller replied, "Not always, Colonel, but we have been hearing more and more about billions in recent years. I still can't imagine what a billion is like, so I'd like to make billions of something and find out." The Evansville plant obliged Keller by turning out 3,264,281,934 cartridges—96 per cent of all the .45 caliber ammunition fabricated for the armed forces.

There was similar drama behind the 70,000 liquid-cooled airplane engines produced by the Allison plant in Indianapolis, and behind Studebaker's stepping up production of her B-17 engines from ten a month to twenty-three hundred. The Indiana Ordnance Works made one and a half billion pounds of smokeless powder, the Bridgeport Brass plant in Indianapolis produced more than a billion pounds of its product, Guide Lamp at Anderson turned out thirty-six million shell cases, Pullman-Standard at Hammond built thirty-nine hundred tanks, Jeffersonville Shipyard, a thousand miles away from the ocean, launched one hundred thirty-three LST's. Such figures could be continued ad infinitum. Indiana furnished 30 per cent of the electronics gear for the armed forces, 75 per cent of their forty millimeter armor-piercing shells, 92 per cent of their needle bearings, 60 per cent of the extruded aluminum, and 98 per cent of the solenoids. There were also unique contributions: Bloomington RCA's variable time fuse, which the navy regarded as second only to the atom bomb as a wartime scientific achievement, the Indianapolis Naval Ordnance plant's Norden bombsight, Studebaker's amphibious weasel, and even an improved pancake turner created by a modest New Albany manufacturer who admitted that "none of the Generals have mentioned in their memoirs that this played a substantial part in any of their campaigns.". . .

A second generalization which emerges very clearly from each of the commission's studies is that the war effort in Indiana had a pungent grass-roots flavor. So much emphasis has been placed by both friend and foe upon the federal bureaucracy in recent years that one gets an impression of monolithic government at Washington crushing out all local initiative and self-direction. This was certainly not true in Indiana. The record, in fact, showed that to a surprising degree, Indiana civilians fought the war in their own way, sometimes with better and sometimes with worse results than when it was entirely directed by national officials.

Civilian defense is an excellent illustration of this point. Indiana did not wait for directives from the federal government to begin organizing in this field; in fact, Hoosiers were somewhat overeager in their forming of early vigilante groups without legal authority. It was partly to channel this enthusiasm that Governor Townsend created an Emergency Defense Council on May 30, 1940, fully a year and a half before the United States became a full-fledged belligerent, and well before either the federal government or the other states had given much thought to this activity. The General Assembly replaced this rudimentary committee on March 10, 1931, with a combination of advisory and administrative councils, which worked so smoothly that it became a model for many other state defense organizations. Under the energetic leadership of Clarence A. Jackson, the Indiana State Defense Council posted a brilliant record of accomplishment in coordinating the myriad facets of civilian defense and civilian services. Many of its activities were unique, an excellent example being the Indiana Plan of Bi-Racial Cooperation which attracted nationwide attention and received a special citation of merit from the national Office of Civilian Defense. The plan was itself a testimony to the state's sturdy independence, for it was conceived as a means of warding off compulsory fair employment decrees in Indiana by accomplishing the same objective through voluntary agreements. Headed by Theodore Cable of Indianapolis, a member of the State Advisory Defense Council, and J. Chester Allen, the Negro Activities Coordinator in the State Defense Council, the plan set up a number of biracial committees throughout the state. Their chief function was to bring management, labor, and Negro representatives together to plan for the equitable integration of the Negro labor potential into war industry and to mitigate racial discrimination in employment, housing, schools, and recreation. Success in the first of these objectives, at any rate, was indicated by a rise of 82 per cent in the number of Negroes employed by Indiana industries within a year.

One of the earliest problems tackled by the Emergency Defense Council was the chaotic situation at Charlestown, Indiana, produced by the building of a $150,000,000 powder plant employing more than 13,000 construction workers on the edge of a slumbering village of 900 inhabitants. Charlestown became the earliest "boom town" of World War II, a prototype of hundreds to follow in nearly every state, including at least a dozen more in Indiana, and something of a national guinea pig for all the social experiments that were devised to meet the staggering problems of such overnight growth. With "powder workers" jammed into every garage and chicken coop, stacked four deep in the town's two restaurants and ten deep in its single tavern, congesting traffic all the way to Jeffersonville and crowding the natives off the village streets, the mere details of policing, sanitation, garbage disposal, schooling, and recreation became nightmares to the harried local officials. Neither the Du Pont Company nor the War Department assumed responsibility for anything beyond the plant's gates, and it was still too early in the defense program for any of the federal agencies which later multiplied like rabbits to offer advice. The state government came to the rescue by sending a defense co-ordinator to the aid of the bewildered town fathers. According to one of the priceless definitions that emerged from the war "A co-ordinator is a man who brings organized chaos out of regimented confusion." It would be foolish to pretend that anyone could have done more than impose a slight degree of organization upon the chaos at Charlestown, but something was accomplished. At the suggestion of an Indiana University professor, for example, an official census was taken, thereby almost tripling the amount of a gasoline tax refund to which the town was entitled. When federal agencies stepped in later with plans and money for sewer construction, recreational facilities, housing, and schools, the majority of Charlestown's citizens were duly grateful. The township trustee, however, upheld Indiana's ancient tradition of rugged individualism by abruptly canceling plans for a new $600,000 school building which was being financed by the Public Works Administration—after eight months of work had gone into it.

Race Relations in Indiana

The history of white-black race relations in Indiana is often a grim story, originating in the ill-disguised slavery known as indentured servitude in the early nineteenth century and continuing through years of discrimination, exclusion, and general hostility. In the latter third of the nineteenth century, however, as Professor Emma Lou Thornbrough indicates below, there was "substantial, if uneven, progress for the colored population." Always a small minority in the state, blacks in Indiana constituted a scant 1 or 2 percent of the population throughout most of the nineteenth century. Following a substantial movement into the state from the South during and following World War I, the black population stood at 4.4 percent of the total in 1950, and at 7 percent in 1970, compared to 11 percent for the nation as a whole.

Professor Thornbrough is the leading authority on the history of blacks in Indiana. She is a professor of history at Butler University in Indianapolis and the author of *The Negro in Indiana: A Study of a Minority* (1957), *Since Emancipation: A Short History of Indiana Negroes, 1863–1963* (1963), *Indiana in the Civil War Era, 1850–1880* (1965), as well as biographies of two black leaders, Booker T. Washington and T. Thomas Fortune.

Additional information on this topic may be found in *The Hoosier Community at War* (1961), by Professor Max Cavnes of Centre College, Kentucky. His account provides a careful review of the economic plight of blacks in Indiana on the eve of the war, the legislative struggle to eliminate discrimination against blacks in defense plants, and various forms of social discrimination also encountered.

A SUMMARY VIEW

Emma Lou Thornbrough

The years between the Civil War and the end of the century were a period of sub-

From *The Negro in Indiana: A Study of a Minority* (1957), pp. 391–396.

stantial, if uneven, progress for the colored population, especially in the legal and political realms. Although equal treatment was not always maintained in practice, in the eyes of the law Negroes were recognized as citizens entitled to equal protection. While the adoption of the Fifteenth Amendment was bitterly resisted, once political rights were granted there was never any movement to take them away. Although some Negroes might be ignorant and venal and blindly partisan, and although white politicians might seek to exploit them, they voted openly and freely. The state, which before the Civil War had denied colored children any schooling at public expense, assumed responsibility for educating them and in theory, at least, for giving them the same schooling afforded white children. In spite of the fact that many communities maintained separate schools which were inferior to those for the white race, and in spite of economic conditions which prevented many colored children from taking advantage of the opportunities open to them, the race had made impressive progress in education by the end of the century.

In private relationships which were not regulated by law racial patterns changed less markedly. Economic opportunities did not keep pace with educational progress. Negroes continued to be barred from skilled occupations and, regardless of their qualifications and ambitions, were relegated for the most part to menial, unskilled, low-paying jobs. Socially there was almost no mingling of the races, and Negroes were denied accommodations in most public places which white patrons frequented in spite of the adoption of an innocuous civil rights law. In the social and economic realms there was evidence that barriers were hardening rather than relaxing at the end of the century and that race feeling was stronger than it had been a few years earlier.

The most striking change after 1900 was the great migration from the South, beginning during the First World War and continuing to the present. During the period from 1910 to 1920 the Negro population of the state increased by about 50 percent. The rate of increase fell off slightly during the twenties but rose again during the thirties, until by 1940 there were 122,473 Negroes in the state or 3.3 percent of the whole. The years of the Second World War and the postwar period saw the most spectacular increase. By 1950 Negroes numbered 175,785 or 4.4 percent of the whole. The new arrivals headed for the industrial centers, by-passing the older Ohio River communities except for Evansville, and moving northward to Indianapolis and the newer cities in the extreme north, especially the steel centers in the Gary area. The last city, which did not even appear in the census in 1900, had reached a population of more than one hundred thousand by 1930, including 17,922 Negroes. By 1950 the number of Negroes had reached 39,326 or almost 30 percent of the total population. However, the largest number continued to be found in Indianapolis, where by 1930 there were 43,967 Negroes or 12 percent of the total. By 1950 the number had reached 64,091 or about 15 percent of the whole. Meanwhile, the number of Negroes in some of the smaller cities in the southern countries had declined, and the movement from the farm to the city which had begun before 1900 continued until the Negro farmer had all but disappeared.

The great influx during the First World War led to a temporary increase in racial intolerance, one manifestation of which was the Ku Klux Klan, which was especially powerful in Indiana in the twenties. The last spectacular race disorder in the state occurred in 1930 in the city of Marion in Grant County, which had acquired a reputation for lax law enforcement. Two Negro youths, who had confessed to robbing and killing a white man and assaulting his young woman companion, were taken from the jail by a mob and hanged. Although race feeling was strong among much of the white population, the resort to mob violence was universally condemned, and the Marion incident was an isolated one. Probably most of the population of Indiana today would be startled to know that a lynching had occurred in the state so recently.

In the economic realm there was very real progress and a marked increase in material well-being for many members of the race. More and more Negroes found employment in industry, although in general only the menial and unattractive jobs were open to them. It still remained true that Negroes were the last to be hired and the first to be fired. No other group was so adversely affected by the Great Depression. But the industrial booms of the years of the Second World War and thereafter opened new opportunities for employment to thousands. However, the census figures of 1950 show that only about one eighth of Negro male workers were classified as craftsmen or foremen in industry, while the number in professional, managerial, and clerical positions was much smaller. The largest number remained in the unskilled categories whether in industrial or service jobs. Among women the largest group remained private household workers, with large numbers listed also as service workers and operatives in such businesses as laundries and dry cleaning establishments. Smaller numbers were found in manufacturing and clerical positions.

The economic position of some workers was strengthened by the rise of the Congress of Industrial Organizations, which, unlike most of the unions in the American Federation of Labor, not only admitted Negro members but actively fought against discrimination on all fronts. In some member unions Negroes attained positions of leadership, and through the activities of the C. I. O. some were able to exercise a more effective role in politics. In 1945 a noncompulsory Fair Employment Practices Act was adopted by the legislature. The preamble declared that it was "the public policy of the state to encourage all of its citizens to engage in gainful employment, regardless of race, creed, color, national origin or ancestry" and to discourage discrimination. The act authorized the State Labor Commissioner to make studies of discrimination, to receive complaints, and make recommendations, but no penalties were provided for noncompliance.

In the social realm Negroes continued to be a group apart. The civil rights act adopted in 1885 remained on the statute books without any strengthening amendments and was seldom invoked. The segregation of the races in such places as restaurants, hotels, and theaters remained almost complete until the years of the Second World War, when a gradual relaxation of racial barriers began. Fortified by their stronger economic position and an increased awareness of their legal rights, Negroes gradually began to invade establishments heretofore regarded as exclusively for a white clientele, but proprietors continued to discourage their patronage. Although the old patterns have not changed rapidly, they are changing. Evidence of the persistence of racism in popular thinking is reflected in the fact that Indiana alone of Northern states east of the Mississippi retains in her laws a ban against interracial marriages, a law which was enacted before the Civil War.

In the field of education the school law of 1877, which provided for permissive but not compulsory segregation, remained unchanged for almost three quarters of a century. In the southern counties and in many of the cities throughout the state separate schools continued to be maintained. During the twenties, when the influence of the Klan was powerful, racial lines began to be more sharply drawn. For example, in Indianapolis, where heretofore there had been some all-colored and some mixed elementary schools, the school board ruled that all colored children must attend separate schools. In 1927 for the first time a colored high school was opened in the city, and thereafter colored students were excluded from the other high schools. It was not until 1949 that the state legislature adopted legislation banning segregation in public schools. The act provided for the completion of integration of pupils of both races by 1954 and provided that state funds should be cut off from any school system which practiced segregation or which discriminated on account of color in the hiring, upgrading, or tenure of teachers.

The unquestioning allegiance to the Republican party which had marked the entry of Negroes into politics continued well into the twentieth century. In spite of their increasing numbers Negro voters continued to be ignored for many years so far as elective offices were concerned. From 1897 to 1933 no Negro sat in the state legislature. During the late twenties defections from the Republican party began because of the close alliance of the leaders of that party with the Ku Klux Klan. The trend continued during the years of the Great Depression and the New Deal until a veritable revolution had occurred in Negro voting habits. A group which had been solidly Republican for generations became almost as solidly Democratic. The change that was taking place was reflected in the election of the first Negro Democrat to the General Assembly in 1932. Since that date there have been colored lawmakers at every session, some of whom have been generally recognized as being among the most able members. There has always been at least one member from Indianapolis while others have been elected from the industrial center of South Bend in the north and one from Evansville in the south. Most of them have been Democrats but some have been Republicans. The only Negro to serve in the state Senate is a Republican. Although in national elections in recent years most Negroes have voted for Democratic candidates, the vote is not solid. While Negro voters have continued to fail to receive elective offices in proportion to their numbers, their political strength and maturity have steadily increased, and their votes are cultivated assiduously by both parties. By the mid-twentieth century, in politics, as in education, patterns which had been established in the nineteenth century were drastically altered, while in the fields of occupations and social relationships, although they were changing, they were changing gradually.

Political Issues following 1945

The basic conservatism of the Hoosier state welled up in the immediate wake of

World War II, a fact perhaps best illustrated by Indiana's choice of senators during the latter 1940s and throughout most of the 1950s. Both William E. Jenner and Homer E. Capehart were elected to the United States Senate in 1944, and both were conservative—if not reactionary—Republicans. Jenner took office immediately, filling the vacancy created by the death of Senator Frederick Van Nuys; but he served only until Senator Capehart took his seat for a full six-year term early in 1945. However, after a stormy Republican state convention in which the incumbent Republican Senator, the decent but aging Raymond E. Willis, was refused renomination, Jenner became the Republican nominee in 1946. He served two full terms in the Senate, from 1947 until 1959, when he retired voluntarily.

To Irving Leibowitz, a distinguished newspaper editor and columnist and the author of a lighthearted but perceptive survey of the Hoosier state in the 1960s, Bill Jenner was the true "symbol" of Indiana during the Cold War era. Called the "defender of Senator Joseph McCarthy and defamer of General George C. Marshall" by Howard H. Peckham,[1] Senator Jenner was also a spokesman against big government and the welfare state.

In the first selection below Leibowitz reviews Jenner's public career, the consistency of his views, and his acerbic personality. A transplanted easterner who became an ardent booster of the Hoosier state, Leibowitz served as managing editor of the Indianapolis *Times*. When the newspaper ceased publication in 1966, Leibowitz served in a similar capacity in Lorain, Ohio, where he died in 1978. His enthusiastic book *My Indiana* (1966) was based in part on a series of his newspaper columns for the Indianapolis *Times*.

Jenner's antigovernment stances were reinforced in 1947, when the Indiana General Assembly went on record in opposing the principle of federal aid to states and localities. "Indiana needs no guardian and intends to have none," declared the legislators. "We Hoosiers—like the people of our sister states—were fooled for quite a spell with the magician's trick that a dollar taxed out of our pockets and sent to Washington will be bigger when it comes back to us. We have taken a good look at said dollar. We find that it lost weight in its journey to Washington and back." Consequently, the legislators concluded that "there is no such thing as 'federal' aid. We know that there is no wealth to tax that is not already within the boundaries of the 48 states. So we propose henceforward to tax ourselves and take care of ourselves. We are fed up with subsidies, doles and paternalism. We are no one's stepchild. We have grown up. We serve notice that we will resist Washington, D. C. adopting us."[2]

Democratic State Senator Charles F. Fleming, then the minority leader in the upper chamber, has written about this "historic resolution," ridiculing its philosophy and describing his efforts either to defeat the resolution directly or to force a literal interpretation of it and thereby bring about its defeat indirectly. However, the action struck a responsive chord within the state and among conservatives throughout the nation. It is not by accident that Indiana, a major industrial and agricultural state—among the top ten states in both categories—ranked dead last in the amount of fed-

1. Howard H. Peckham, *Indiana: A Bicentennial History* (1978), p. 151.
2. *Laws of the State of Indiana, 1947* (1947), II, 1509–1510.

eral funds received as late as 1975.[3] The passage from Charles F. Fleming's biography of Henry F. Schricker, the Hoosier "Mr. Democrat" during the 1940s and 1950s, concerns itself with this issue.[4] Fleming, a labor leader in northern Indiana, worked closely with Governor Schricker during his second term of office (Schricker, uniquely in Indiana, was governor from 1941–1945 and again from 1949–1953); Fleming served as Indiana's Secretary of State from 1949–1951. Later, while completing his biography of the governor, he taught government and sociology at North Central High School in Indianapolis, where he is now living in retirement.

The final selection comes from the sometimes acerbic pen of Judge S. Hugh Dillin, a former president *pro tem* of the Indiana Senate, who describes some adroit political maneuvering in 1961 that led to the repeal of House Resolution No. 2. It was at about this point too that Indianapolis Mayor John J. Barton decided that the capital city would accept federal aid if and when it was offered.

SENATOR WILLIAM E. JENNER

Irving Leibowitz

How can Indiana produce a Wendell Willkie and a Gene Debs and then elect to the United States Senate a William E. Jenner?

Willkie and Debs lit up the skies everywhere and warmed men's hearts. But Jenner was Indiana's shooting star. No one ever represented the thinking and feeling and heart of Hoosierland with more fidelity than Bill Jenner. He is arrogantly proud of his state, suspicious of strangers and fearful of new ideas. This provincial and patriotic attitude—"more Hoosier than thou," Robert Benchly once said—is patently peculiar to Hoosierland.

"We want Willkie! We want Willkie!" the Willkie cult chanted in 1940 at the Republican national convention in Philadelphia. "One World," he preached. Before Dwight D. Eisenhower ever cast his first ballot, before he even knew he was a Republican, Willkie had reshaped the image of the Republican Party from isolationist to internationalist. He took the Grand Old Party down the middle of the road, for which his fellow Hoosier Republicans never forgave him.

"Debs! Debs! Debs!" the immigrant railroaders and coalminers used to cry. Eugene Victor Debs battled and went to jail for them. In the 1890's, he was the social conscience of the nation. He wrote: "While there is a lower class I am in it; While there is a criminal element I am of it; While there is a soul in prison I am not free." He was a Socialist.

---

3. *New York Times*, December 21, 1975.

4. See also the interview of Carl M. Dortch (1979) at the Indiana University Oral History Research Project Office in Bloomington. Mr. Dortch was head of the Indianapolis Chamber of Commerce for many years.

From *My Indiana* (1966), pp. 15–30. Copyright © 1964, 1992. Used by permission of the publisher, Prentice Hall/A Division of Simon & Schuster, Englewood Cliffs, N.J.

People everywhere, except Indiana, showered affection, love and respect on Willkie and Debs. The overwhelming majority of Hoosiers was opposed to their policies and principles. Willkie and Debs never represented Indiana. But Bill Jenner did.

William Ezra Jenner was—and is—pure Indiana. To understand the state, it is worth taking a longer, more careful look at him.

Why pick Jenner, who no longer is in the United States Senate? Why not Congressman Charles Halleck, who was President Eisenhower's good right arm on Capitol Hill?

Halleck's dalliance with Eastern Republicans takes him out of the typical Indiana class. Jenner is the Indiana symbol. And what a symbol! He pounds the desk. He cusses. He dramatizes. He shouts. He whispers. He can be warm and gregarious. He can be ice cold. He can turn his emotions on and off.

Jenner has been described variously as a southern Indiana hillbilly, a demagogue, a wild and woolly vigilante, a witch-hunter, a grand inquisitor and a fascist firebrand.

His political associates picture him as one of the last of the great patriots, a courageous and militant battler for American sovereignty, the preservation of the U.S. Constitution and the uprooting of the Soviet fifth column.

His is both loved and hated as passionately as if he were still in the United States Senate, which he voluntarily quit to come back home to Indiana to raise his only son, Billy, as a Hoosier. What makes Jenner tick would make an engrossing study for any psychiatrist, writer or student of political history.

It is a standing joke that when traveling he carries more medicine in his suitcase than clothes. He is an incurable hypochondriac. His wife Janet simply cannot get sick because once she does, he gets the same thing—"only worse." Janet tells friends the only time she was able to "suffer alone and in peace" was when she gave birth to Billy.

"Bill didn't know how to cope with that," she says.

When you question Jenner about this he shrugs his shoulders and says, "It runs in the family. I used to hear my daddy and mom complain from the minute they got up in the morning."

According to his Indiana friends, Jenner is loyal, extremely thoughtful, kind and generous. According to his enemies, Jenner is a "hater."

Lisle Wallace, grain merchant of Sheridan, Indiana, and an old political pro who once managed Robert A. Taft's campaign for President in Indiana, puts it this way: "If you're his friend, Jenner'll lead you through hell. If you're his enemy, he'll push you through hell."

Hugh Gray, fishing pal, confidant and adviser to Jenner, says, "Bill never forgets a friend—or an enemy."

At Republican rallies, receptions, parties and conventions, Jenner once was the undisputed king of applause. Today, though no longer in public life, he still gets a bigger ovation from Indiana Republicans than any politician, except Senator Barry Goldwater, champion of the right wing.

In 1956, at the Republican state convention in Indianapolis, Jenner's bitter factional foe was Governor George N. Craig. The Craig machine had charge of decorations, bunting and seating. Huge, blown-up pictures of President Eisenhower, Governor Craig and Senator Capehart looked down on delegates in the State Fairgrounds Coliseum, but there was not one single poster of Senator Jenner.

Yet, when Jenner's chum and protégé Harold Handley won the nomination for Governor and the balloting was over, the delegates, weary and tired from an exciting full day of voting in hot and humid weather, whooped and hollered, "We want Jenner!"

Flushed with victory after four years of bickering with Governor Craig, Jenner marched dramatically from his inconspicuous box to the rostrum, his face wreathed in one big crease of a smile.

"This," he said, "is the end of a perfect day." The ovation that followed was one of the most exciting, and sentimental, in the long and turbulent history of Indiana's political conventions.

How does Jenner react to such adulation?

He eats it up. This is when the "ham" in him comes out. He's liable to embrace, hug or kiss the nearest person. He'll throw both hands up into the air over his head in the shape of a giant "V" and shout, "God love you."

In 1952, when Eisenhower was campaigning in Indianapolis, he stood on the same platform with Jenner in the Butler University fieldhouse. They received a tumultuous reception. Tom Stokes and other Washington correspondents were aghast, they said, at the undisguised act of Senator Jenner clasping Eisenhower's hand high in the air in the traditional political salute. Some of the newspapermen wrote about "the ugly display" of coattail riding by Jenner. Jenner says the newspaper photographers in front were pleading and yelling, "Hold up his hand, Jenner."

What Stokes and the others couldn't understand apparently was that Jenner was doing what comes naturally to a politician acknowledging a warm reception. It is a wonder the effervescent Jenner didn't do cartwheels across the stage.

With the death of Senator Joseph McCarthy of Wisconsin, his close friend, Jenner automatically inherited some of McCarthy's pals and all of his enemies.

In one important respect Jenner differed from McCarthy. All the time McCarthy was probing Communists, his fellow Senators rarely went along. It was usually a one-man investigation. On the other hand, every committee report on subversion submitted by Jenner, as chairman, was unanimously adopted. Jenner's subcommittee report, "Interlocking Subversion in Government," almost sold as well as the Kinsey Report in Washington and was a monumental work of spotlighting Communist influence in our own government. He named the men and women who pledged allegiance to the Soviet Union.

Even Jenner's critics took notice. The *Richmond Times-Dispatch* editorialized:

> Senator Jenner is not one of our favorite statesmen (it was he who termed the career of General George C. Marshall 'a living lie'), but it must be conceded that the report he and his Senate subcommittee have unanimously made on the subject of Interlocking Subversion in Government Departments is one of the most startling documents of the decade. . . . All in all, the Jenner subcommittee has done an effective and important piece of research.

Jenner's enemies say he is brutal. When President Eisenhower had a heart attack before his second election, a colleague asked Jenner in the Senate cloakroom what would happen to Republican chances if the President died.

"If necessary, we'll stuff him and run him and still win," Jenner said, jokingly.

To understand Bill Jenner, who comes from the hills of southern Indiana (Marengo, population 800), you've got to know him as a baby, boy, collegian and businessman.

Jenner was born July 21, 1908 to L. L. Woody and Jane McDonald Jenner in a two-room "smokehouse" shack close to the tracks of the Southern Railroad. He was a sickly infant and nearly died a couple of days later. His father was a country fellow who later ran a general store where you could buy feed, food or a Ford. It is still operated today by the oldest son, Donald (Donnie) Jenner. A third and youngest son, Loren, is in charge of a hatchery at Shelbyville.

"Bill was a little puny as a kid, but just a regular fella like the rest of the kids," says Donnie. "He got into the same trouble the other kids did."

Jenner doesn't know where he got his flair for dramatics, but he recalls that a woman he called "Auntie" back in Marengo taught him elocution lessons—"where to place the emphasis." He also remembers performing as an actor and singer in the deep Marengo Cave, a regional attraction that was illuminated by carbon lights. He received $1.50 for each ten-hour day. His specialty was singing "When I'm Big Like My Daddy" and reciting "Barefoot Boy."

Although Jenner and his Scotland-born and Indiana-reared wife, a stunning sight in taffy-colored hair, shunned the glittering social whirl when he was in the Senate, they did occasionally step out to parties and dinners with intimate friends. At one affair given by the late Senator Styles Bridges of New Hampshire, "the Marengo kid" went to town. He got out in the middle of the floor and did a classy Charleston with Ruth Montgomery, a Hoosier who is a top Washington correspondent for Hearst newspapers. When the orchestra struck up "Back Home Again in Indiana," Bill got up again and sang a solo.

Jenner's favorite relaxation is with an intimate circle of hometown friends who call themselves "the mutual admiration society." A rule of each party is that everyone present must perform at least once—sing, dance, tell a story or recite a poem. Jenner is always the center of attraction, always the star.

At Indiana University, Jenner was fascinated by politics, dramatics and singing, in about that order. He got good grades, but was considered "lazy." Once, his father paid a surprise visit to the Bloomington campus. He went to the classroom on twentieth century drama, where young Jenner was supposed to be, but Bill wasn't there. Woody Jenner finally found his son upstairs in his room at the Delta Tau Delta fraternity house—sleeping.

He threw him out of bed, hit him a couple of licks on the head, booted him on the backside and pushed him down the stairs, hollering, "You bum. You're not going to sleep when I pay money for you to go to school."

"Dad, don't embarrass me in front of all my friends," Bill pleaded.

The more young Jenner protested, the angrier his father became. "Dad was an emotional fella," Jenner recalls.

This was an occasional, but not typical happening in the Jenner household. Bill revered his father. As a youngster he sat around a potbellied stove in the Jenner general store and listened to his father, Republican chairman of Crawford County, spin tales of the Republican heroes of yesterday—men like Speaker Joe Cannon, Senator Albert J. Beveridge and Senator Sunny Jim Watson. Woody Jenner was forever teaching Bill. Just before he died in 1950 he was playing cards in a rustic cabin Bill owns with Hugh Gray on the east bank of the White River near Shoals. Woody borrowed forty dollars from his son. After the game, Bill reminded his father about the loan.

"Let that be a lesson," his father said. "Never lend money to a gambling man."

In the depths of the Depression, Jenner received his law degree and was admitted to the Indiana bar. He couldn't get a job, but his father wouldn't let him come back to work in the store.

"I sent you to college," Woody Jenner admonished him. "Don't you come back to these poor hills."

When the late Indiana Supreme Court Justice Frank Gilkison was elected a Circuit Court judge, Jenner took over his law office—two tiny rooms over a grocery store and a barbershop alongside the B & O railroad tracks in Shoals, Indiana. The rent was six dollars a month.

At about this time one farmer became so enraged with another that he shot him right between the eyes with a Spanish revolver. Jenner got the case. The colorful jury trial, involving heated accusations on both sides, provided a perfect setting for the now-famous Jenner histrionics.

Bill made a legal plea of self-defense (although eyewitnesses said the victim was driving a team of horses at the time). The principal argument advanced by barrister Jenner was that the victim was a rotten character who "needed killing." Apparently the all-farmer jury agreed. They acquitted the defendant in a matter of minutes.

The judge was furious. "This is the first time I ever heard of a legal killing," he fumed.

In 1934, in a Model A Ford that cost $125, Bill campaigned for State Senator in Lawrence, Martin and Orange counties—the craggy hill country of southern Indiana. He was elected, and has never since been defeated in a general election.

Jenner's plunge into politics didn't cause a ripple in the State Legislature in Indianapolis. At the insistence of his father, he went to see Harry Fenton for advice on how to act in the Senate. Fenton, a political genius, was secretary of the Republican Central Committee, and considered "the most conservative Republican in Indiana."

Fenton was unimpressed with Jenner. "Son, I know your type. You're another one of those young smart-aleck know-it-alls. You sit your ass down in the Senate and don't say a damn word for thirty days."

Jenner didn't open his mouth. Once he dozed off and fell out of his chair. He would have kept silent for the entire sixty-one-day session, except that one day the presiding officer in the Senate, Lieutenant Governor M. Clifford Townsend, addressed a statewide women's meeting at the Athletic Club. His topic was the Senate and he gave a humorous word picture of all the Senators. Jenner, he saved for last.

"I can't tell you a thing about Jenner," Townsend told the ladies, "he's been asleep for thirty days."

The quote was printed in the Democratic newspaper the *Indiana Sentinel* and widely distributed around the state. Jenner was mortified. When he went home for the weekend his neighbors laughed at him. "That's a helluva way to represent us, Jenner," they said. "What are we payin' ya fer, to sleep?"

Bright and early Monday morning, Jenner was waiting for Fenton to come to work at Republican headquarters. He was blazing. When Fenton entered, Jenner threw a copy of the *Indiana Sentinel* at him and cried, "That's what I get for listening to you. You made a buffoon out of me."

Fenton calmed him down. "I hear you make a pretty fair country speech," he said. "Don't do it today or tomorrow, but you wait for a good opportunity and take the floor on a point of personal privilege and then you let 'er rip."

Jenner didn't have long to wait. Jacob Weiss, the Democratic Senate leader, wasn't content to have one of his bills pass. He picked it up, waved it while he turned to the galleries and pompously boasted, "This is just another promise of the Democratic platform being fulfilled for the people."

Jenner was on his feet. "Mr. President! Mr. President!" he screamed.

Lieutenant Governor Townsend couldn't believe his eyes. Finally he said, "The chair recognizes the wide-awake Senator from Orange, Martin and Lawrence counties."

Jenner poured it on. All his pent-up rage and humiliation came flooding out in a torrent of abuse at the Democrats. He blasted them for what they promised and what they delivered. Today, Jenner still calls it the best speech he ever made. It was widely reported. From that emotional outburst on, Jenner was marked for greater service by the Republican high command. Fenton, who lost his own son, practically adopted him.

In 1937 and 1939, Jenner served as Republican minority leader of the State Senate. In 1941, when the Republicans captured control of the State Senate, he was elected President Pro Tempore.

After the outbreak of World War II, Jenner resigned from the State Senate and volunteered for the Army Air Force. While still overseas, he was nominated and then elected to the United States Senate to serve the unexpired term of the late Senator Frederick Van Nuys.

In later campaigns, Jenner was an indefatigable worker. Like his Senatorial colleague, Homer Capehart, Jenner would do most anything to attract a crowd—sing, dance, act or ride an elephant down Main Street, as he once did in Danville, Indiana. Even his most bitter factional foes concede he is one of the shrewdest strategists in a convention or a general election. He is a team player who places loyalty and discipline above other traits.

"He likes to carry the ball," a close friend said. "But he'll carry the water, too. The important thing to Bill is that he wins."

Jenner came up in politics when the Ku Klux Klan influence was dying. Nevertheless, political foes have accused him of sympathy with the Klan or friendship with men who were Kluxers. There is no question that Jenner knew politicians who were Kluxers. There was scarcely a figure in the Republican Party who wasn't in the Klan in the 1920's.

Jenner went to the funeral of Robert Lyons, onetime Klan treasurer. He sat in the front row, deliberately. He said he wouldn't turn his back on a friend. (Lyons had engineered the maneuver to make Jenner the Senator for the unexpired term of Van Nuys.)

Jenner was a boy when the Klan was in its heyday. He was growing up at a time when the Indiana Klan was not alone in making righteous war on Bolsheviks, Catholics, Jews, Negroes, pacifists, evolutionists, foreigners and others considered "immoral." It was the Hoosier way. Although thousands of Poles, Hungarians, Italians and Czechs had come to work in the steel mills and coal fields, Catholics, Jews and foreigners were oddities in many parts of Indiana.

The isolation and boredom of small towns made them fertile ground for suspicion and bigotry. Jenner was exposed to all the traditions of intolerance.

He rang the rafters with blood-and-thunder political speeches in the Billy Sunday style. He damned the Bolsheviks. In Congress, opposing the Marshall Plan, he cried that we were pouring American money down the rat holes of Europe. He "wrapped" himself in the American flag and charged that mysterious people in high places were undermining and subverting the country.

All the time, Jenner was saying out loud what the people were whispering in the hills of southern Indiana—in Marengo, Paoli and Shoals. Jenner said it with tears streaming down his face, with his voice breaking. He said it with indignation and ridicule. He said it with thunder in his voice and lightning in his eyes. He peppered his words with earthy and colorful (sometimes purple) prose.

I used to wonder how he managed to work himself up, to make himself angry enough to bring real tears. He told me, "I always build a straw man and then I tear hell out of him."

This is not to evaluate whether Jenner was right or wrong. Later historians will do that. Jenner was earnest, sincere and believed in what he was doing. What he said was pure Hoosier. He is more a "made in Indiana" product than the Indiana limestone that is blasted out of the rock quarries of Bedford, his present hometown.

But whatever his prejudices, Jenner is no Kluxer, no bigot.

When Indiana high schools would not allow Negro schools to participate in the state basketball tournament, Jenner helped push through the State Senate a bill opening the tourney to all public and parochial schools, regardless of race or religion. State Senator Robert Lee Brokenburr, son of a slave, who rose to become an alternate delegate to the United Nations, is one of the most respected Negro civic leaders in Indiana. He credits Jenner with helping to break down the Jim Crow barriers in Indiana sports.

Nor can any politician in Indiana forget the tremendous battle Jenner waged and won, over the powerful protest of publisher-politician Eugene Pulliam, to get Cale J. Holder, a Catholic, appointed a federal judge.

It seems to me that Jenner always was trying to prove, to himself and the world, that what he stands for represents a real and permanent value. He doesn't believe, as former Defense Secretary Charles Wilson was quoted as saying, that what is good for General Motors is necessarily good for the United States. Jenner has his own yardstick on complicated foreign and domestic policy: "Is it good for Billy?"

Jenner believes that if it is good for his only child, William Edward, it will be good for the millions of other Billys in America.

Just where does Jenner stand politically today? He is about as far to the right as you can get and still stay inside the Republican Party. Jenner summed up his political feelings in his farewell message to the Senate:

> You know how it (the Republican Party) was taken over by Paul Hoffman and his kind, the modern Republicans, and the men in the shadows behind them. . . . You know how the Democratic Party was transformed from a party accepting Franklin Roosevelt's temporary reforms, but still committed to the Constitution, into a party managed by Harry Hopkins, Dean Acheson, Walter Reuther and the men in the shadows behind them.
>
> . . . [A] government with too much money to spend destroys the society it governs, in two ways. A spending government corrupts the weak with the current equivalent of bread and circuses. Today we call them Federal aid and summit conferences. More important, a spending program must destroy the strong.
>
> I say the American people are being pushed in the direction of catastrophic inflation by wild-eyed Socialists, ambitious intellectuals, power-seeking demagogues and hidden Communists.

Some of Bill Jenner's best friends, as the saying goes, are Democrats—conservative Southern Democrats who share his philosophic views. Jenner is flattered by right-wingers who want to run him for President on extreme third-party platforms. He has shied away from all splinter parties. His intuitive political sense tells him that they do not have the broad base to succeed.

From time to time, Jenner has been on intimate terms—politically and socially—with Richard Nixon. Yet, when John F. Kennedy defeated Nixon for the Presidency by an eyelash, Jenner said privately, "The only difference between Kennedy and Nixon is that it would take Nixon eight years to take us down the same road to socialism that it takes Kennedy four years to do. Nothing can stop us now. Jumpin' Jez-sus H. Christ, we're headed for socialism."

Jenner evaluates Nixon as "an astute politician, no better or no worse than the average politician . . . an opportunist with no courage."

About Goldwater, Jenner says, "I'd rather see him President than any other man I know." President Eisenhower never was an idol to Jenner.

"He (Eisenhower) had the greatest opportunity to reverse the trend of government spending and utterly failed," Jenner says. "Ike was popular, but he could never transfer his popularity to the party. He left his party in a weakened position. He didn't understand politics. He didn't care about politics and he didn't work for the party. He was made by Wall Street and the international bankers."

Jenner, now out of politics (for good, he says), speaks darkly of the future. He doesn't think there is a man in the Republican or the Democratic parties who can save the country today.

"We're broke," Jenner says. "We're bankrupt. There's no stopping. No reversing now. You could have Jesus Christ himself as President and you couldn't change it. Ever since (Franklin D.) Roosevelt, we've been accelerating toward centralization of government, one world, socialism.

"It won't be men who'll change it. It'll take a calamity, a disaster, fiscal collapse, something worse than the Hoover Depression. They talk about Social Security. How much Social Security will you have after a fiscal collapse? Out of the ashes of ruin, a man might come along who would help us. If we're lucky, it'll be a man like Goldwater. It could be a man like Walter Reuther. What would we do then?"

It is uncertain at this point whether Jenner ever will make a comeback in Indiana politics. He is well established in a profitable law office and has little regard for the Hoosiers running the Republican Party today. The feeling is mutual. Yet there are some Republicans who are concerned that in a normally Republican state, in 1963, Indiana had a Democratic Governor (Matthew Welsh) and two Democratic Senators (Vance Hartke and Birch Bayh.)

"At this stage of the game," said former Republican State Chairman Robert Mathews, "the Republican Party needs Bill Jenner more than he needs it."

There are those who contend that Democrat Henry F. Schricker, and not Bill Jenner, is the real symbol of Indiana. It is possible that the quiet and soft-spoken Schricker might be the "gentleman from Indiana" at his best.

He doesn't arouse strong emotions in anybody's breast as Jenner does. Hoosiers either admire Jenner or hate him. They generally like Schricker.

A Democrat close to Governor Welsh insisted that I was wrong in picking Jenner over Schricker as the Indiana symbol. He painted a convincing picture.

Schricker, he said, was "nice people, corny, basically honest and everybody knows it . . . he gives a strong feeling of standing on his own feet and doesn't want to try anything for the first time. He has a distrust of change. Hoosiers just don't get as excited and concerned about things as Jenner. They're calm, like Schricker. You get the idea that Schricker won't set the world on fire but in his own way he's pretty slick."

William Madigan, former Statehouse correspondent for the Associated Press, used to call him "Slippery Hank" because (1) it was difficult to pin him down, (2) he kept everyone guessing about where he stood and (3) he could change his mind often. The Democrats called him "The White Hat." They used his white hat as the party's emblem of purity.

Schricker was born in North Judson, Indiana, August 30, 1883. He took a home-study legal course, passed the bar, practiced law, was a small-town banker at twenty-three, and later became editor of a good weekly newspaper, the *Starke County Democrat*. He likes to remind people that his parents were poor immigrants from the old country (Germany).

Schricker plays the part of a country fellow to perfection. He probably has eaten more chicken dinners and attended more church socials and fish fries than any politician in Indiana. He is proud of membership in his hometown volunteer fire department and his work with the Boy Scouts.

He made a name for himself all over Indiana when he was State Senator and later Lieutenant Governor. "If Henry says it's good, I'm fer it," was a typical comment in the Legislature.

In Indiana, a Governor cannot succeed himself. Yet Schricker twice was honored with the highest office in the state. In 1940 his personal popularity put him into the

Governorship. No other Democrat went to the Statehouse with him, as Republicans swept every other state office. In 1948, Schricker led the Democrats back into the Statehouse while President Harry S Truman lost the state.

Twice Schricker ran for U.S. Senator and lost. It is almost as if Hoosiers trusted his judgment and honesty to run the state, but wanted a much more outspoken conservative in Washington. The Republicans who defeated him for Senator were Bill Jenner and Homer Capehart.

The interesting dilemma over which is the Indiana symbol, Jenner or Schricker, is that both men are basically conservative.

An Eisenhower Republican who has had political run-ins with both Schricker and Jenner summed up the argument this way: "We all like to think of Schricker as the Indiana symbol, but Jenner really is."

HOUSE RESOLUTION NO. 2

Charles F. Fleming

Early in the Eighty-Fifth General Assembly, it was rumored that the Republicans were going to introduce a resolution that would definitely establish a State policy in regard to Indiana's future position on Federal Aid. This rumor had Lothair Teetor, an industrialist and legislator from Hagerstown, Indiana, and George Henley, an attorney and legislator from Bloomington as authors. All the Democrats could do was wait and see if the rumor crystallized.

On January 13, 1947, House Concurrent Resolution No. 2 was introduced in the Indiana House of Representatives by Teetor and Henley. Senator Fleming immediately called a minority caucus of both the Senate and the House Democrats.

In caucus it was determined that the minority, in both the House and the Senate, would attack the resolution by trying to incorporate a literal interpretation into the document by amendments. The appropriate amendments were drawn and the members returned to their respective chambers. Representative Robert Heller, of Decatur, the minority floor leader, was to lead the fight in the House; and Senator Fleming, of Hammond, would lead the debate in the upper chamber. The strategy planned by the Democratic minority was the result of daily consultations with Schricker and his attitude toward the proposed resolution. The former Governor also believed the efforts of the minority, in their efforts to defeat the resolution, should be incorporated in both the *House* and *Senate Journals* as a matter of record.

House Concurrent Resolution No. 2 read as follows:

> . . . Indiana needs no guardian and intends to have none. We Hoosiers—like the people of our sister states—were fooled for quite a spell with the magician's trick that a

---

From *The White Hat. Henry Frederick Schricker: A Political Biography* (1966), pp. 108–115. Reprinted by permission of the estate of the author.

> dollar taxed out of our pockets and sent to Washington, will be bigger when it comes back to us. We have taken a good look at said dollar. We found that it lost weight in its journey to Washington and back. The political brokerage of the bureaucrats has been deducted. We have decided that there is no such thing as "federal" aid. We know that there is no wealth to tax that is not already within the boundaries of the 48 states.
>
> So we propose henceforward to tax ourselves and take care of ourselves. We are fed up with subsidies, doles, and paternalism. We are no one's stepchild. We have grown up. We serve notice that we will resist Washington, D. C. adopting us.
>
> Be it resolved by the House of Representatives of the General Assembly of the State of Indiana, the Senate concurring: That we respectfully petition and urge Indiana Congressmen and Senators to vote to fetch our county courthouse and city halls back from Pennsylvania Avenue. We want government to come home. Resolved, further, that we call upon the legislatures of our sister states and on good citizens everywhere who believe in the basic principles of Lincoln and Jefferson to join with us, and we with them to restore the American Republic and our 48 states to the foundations built by our fathers.
>
> Teetor-Henley Representatives

. . . The Republican majority pushed the measure through the House with very little difficulty on the same day of its introduction. However, the resolution was vigorously attacked by the Democratic minority. Minority leader Heller inquired "What would Indiana do next year without federal aid for its highway, conservation, and school lunch programs?" Representative Teetor's reply to Heller was that even though the federal aid programs could not be eliminated immediately, what was contained in the resolution ought to be "a general objective of all legislators."

On January 14, the Democratic minority in the House again attempted unsuccessfully to revive House Concurrent Resolution No. 2. Heller moved that "the Speaker of the House appoint a committee to inform the members of the State Budget Committee and the House Ways and Means Committee, which reimbursements from the Federal Government will not be accepted by the State of Indiana," in 1947. In his discussion of the motion, the minority leader stated: "I do not know whether this resolution was offered with serious intent or for political reasons. If the former we must decide which of the Federal grants we will accept or which we won't." Representative Henley, co-author of the measure, defended the Republican-endorsed resolution. Henley explained:

> We are serious about the resolution, but as long as 47 other states are obtaining Federal handouts Indiana must accept them or else be in the position of paying taxes for Texas, or any of our sister states.

It did not take the overwhelming Republican majority very long to indefinitely postpone Heller's motion.

On January 17, the *Indianapolis Star* editorialized on the resolution passed by the House. The title of the editorial, "So Spoke Our Rugged Pioneers," gave evidence of the *Star's* ability of being able, through imaginative projection of one's own consciousness into another being, such as a rugged pioneer, to attempt to sway public opinion. The editorial reflectively stated that:

Initiative and resourcefulness of Hoosier pioneers have been rekindled by the G. O. P. majority in the Indiana House. In scoring the pabulum of subsidies, doles, and paternalism, the representatives issued a proclamation of independence from Washington bureaucracy.

The resolution they adopted demanded, in effect, that the state's congressional delegation 'fetch our county court houses and city halls back from Pennsylvania Avenue.'

. . . The Indiana State Chamber of Commerce, taking practically the exact position of the *Star*, noted that the House-passed resolution might "turn out to be the most important legislation of the 1947 General Assembly." On January 17, the issue of the Chamber's legislative bulletin advocated that House Concurrent Resolution No. 2 would initiate a movement for the restoration of "states rights." The bulletin further commented that the resolution would be the fuse for a nationwide battle to return to the states the rights and responsibilities which have been relinquished in recent years to the Federal government. The Chamber bulletin further pictured House Concurrent Resolution No. 2 as Indiana's declaration to "stand on her own feet and resist Federal domination through doles, subsidies, and paternalism." The bulletin further stated "even though it would be difficult to live up to the spirit of House Concurrent Resolution No. 2," Indiana could make "a start toward proclaiming its independence in matters that pertain to Indiana."

Thus supported by the entire majority of the Republicans in the House of Representatives, the *Indianapolis Star*, and the Indiana State Chamber of Commerce, House Concurrent Resolution No. 2 came to the Senate on Jaunary 21, and was handed down by the President of the Senate on January 22.

Senator John W. Van Ness, Republican President pro tem of the Senate, proceeded to inform the Senate of the very fine features and principles incorporated within the resolution, and closed with the following:

Any person who votes against this resolution is voting against home rule, against the people of Indiana governing themselves.

Senator Charles F. Fleming, minority caucus chairman, inquired if the majority floor leader would yield the floor for questioning. When the Senator from Valparaiso consented to yield, Senator Fleming wanted to know if the members of the majority party had prepared the necessary bills for introduction to replace the monies that the State Budget Committee had included in the biennial budget for the State Board of Health, the State Conservation Department, for Indiana's extended program of Flood Control, for the hundreds of miles of highway construction planned by the Indiana Highway Commission, and for the many townships, towns, and cities, who really knew of "home rule" and who desired to participate with the Federal government for local improvements. The majority floor leader answered in the negative. Senator Fleming then offered the following amendment and recommended its adoption:

Mr. President: I move that House Concurrent Resolution No. 2 be amended by adding the following:

Be It Further Resolved, That in the event of the passage of this resolution that the State Budget Committee be and is hereby instructed to leave out of the budget submitted by it all considerations of financial assistance from the Federal Government and replace the same with State of Indiana funds and increase the budget accordingly.

Senator Mitchell, of La Porte, immediately moved that the motion to amend be laid on the table. On a voice vote the motion to table prevailed.

Senator Fleming's amendment was an attempt to force the literal interpretation of the resolution. By the addition of his amendment, the Republicans would have faced a dilemma. If they had been sincere in their belief of "home rule" and the rejection of all Federal grants of aid, they would have accepted the amendment and made the necessary legislation for additional new taxes, or increases of tax revenues already in the statutes.

After the Democratic amendment was tabled, the Republican-controlled Senate adopted the House Concurrent Resolution No. 2 with a straight party-line vote of 34 to 11. The Lieutenant Governor, Richard T. James, announced the vote in an unusual manner by saying: "Thirty-four have voted in favor of Indiana and eleven in favor of Washington."

Following the adoption of the resolution, Senator Fleming asked for the floor on a point of personal privilege. He lectured the Republican majority on the progress made in the United States since the ratification of the National Constitution. He asked "Why do you want to regress to the stature of the states under the Articles of Confederation?" He pursued this line of reasoning by inquiring, "Would you, all of you who voted in favor of this resolution, want the legislatures of the several states to again assume the powers they possessed in colonial days, providing a weak Congress, and no separation of powers?" The Senator chided the majority party, saying "Today you are flush with the temporary elations of a political victory accomplished in 1945. Your actions in the Eighty-Second General Assembly, when by 'ripper bill legislation' you made an attempt to destroy Constitutional government in Indiana, and now this resolution of secession from the Union, will not go unnoticed by our people. Elections are temporary, and emotions are but fleeting moments of man's desires; enjoy your moments of today's irrationalism, for the day of reckoning is not far off. We of the minority in this Senate shall watch each piece of proposed legislation, and if there is one bill that even remotely refers to any attempt to obtain Federal aid in any form, we shall call you to task."

Interestingly, House Concurrent Resolution No. 2 continued to be a news story in many of the conservative newspapers in the State. The *Indianapolis Star*, after the adjournment of the General Assembly, proudly continued to "declare" that Indiana would be better off without federal "handouts" as it kept parroting its cliche to "let the states run their own affairs."

Since a concurrent resolution does not have the power of the law, it simply means that the State is petitioning its delegation in the Congress to do something about the particular situation contained in the subject matter within the resolution. House Concurrent Resolution No. 2 was received by the Congress, read on the floor of the House by Congressman Raymond Springer, Republican from Connersville, on February 10. It aroused some comment from Mid-Western Congressmen; but more important, *not one of the eleven Congressmen from Indiana, ten Republicans and one Democrat, came forward to defend the resolution*. This lack of response rather concretely supported the Democratic position; for if a Congressman supposedly keeps his "fingers on the pulse of his constituency," the ineptness and complacency on the part of the ten Indiana Republican Congressmen indicated there was no great enthusiasm on the part of their people for the rejection of Federal grants.

REPEAL OF THE RESOLUTION

S. Hugh Dillin

S. Hugh Dillin, a young lawyer from Pike County at the time he first entered the Indiana General Assembly in 1937, served in the House of Representatives from 1937–1942; later, following service in World War II, he returned to the House in 1951, and was a member of the Indiana Senate from 1959 until his appointment to the federal bench in 1961. The selection below, originally an appendix to Governor Welsh's book about events during his gubernatorial term, describes the convoluted process by which Senator Dillin and others in his party were able to secure a quiet repeal of the infamous anti-federal aid resolution. This selection serves not only to clarify an obscure event in the state's history, but also reveals the true nature of politics in Indiana and elsewhere. For further information on the subject of Indiana and federal aid, see James H. Madison, "The American Constitution and the Old Federalism: Views from the Hoosier State" (1985), a Poynter Center lecture in the Bicentennial of the U.S. Constitution Lecture Series. There is also a brief but delightful account of Indiana politics in the 1970s as told by an insider, Representative Richard Watham. See Watham's Law: The Hang-ups of an Indiana Politician *(1981).*

During the summer of 1960, I had occasion to attend certain meetings of the Wabash Valley Association, and in this connection frequently encountered United States Senator Homer Capehart, who was actively interested in flood control projects. The senator and I discussed how difficult it was to obtain flood control appropriations in Congress because of a resolution passed in 1947 by the Republican-controlled General Assembly denying any need for federal aid in Indiana. This position of the Congress was confirmed by Congressman Mike Kirwan of Ohio, chairman of the Public Works Subcommittee in the House of Representatives, who in a speech at Vincennes during the summer of 1960 ridiculed Indiana for its position and stated, in effect, that the state could look for few federal funds from his committee as long as the resolution remained on the books.

I asked Senator Capehart if he would permit me to use his name in the legislature as favoring the repeal of this resolution. I further inquired if he would confirm to

---

From "How Federal Aid Finally Came to Indiana: Or, the History of House Concurrent Resolution No. 2, 1961 General Assembly," Appendix B of Matthew E. Welsh, *View from the State House: Recollections and Reflections, 1961–1965* (1981), pp. 238–241.

Republican leaders in the General Assembly that, in his judgment, the resolution should be repealed. He gave affirmative answers to both questions. Accordingly, shortly before the beginning of the 92nd General Assembly in 1961, I approached Lieutenant Governor Dick Ristine, Senator Wendell Martin, and two or three other Republicans, and suggested that we quietly scuttle the old resolution, citing Senator Capehart as substantial Republican authority for this position. They seemed willing to give the matter serious consideration, and Ristine even stated flatly that the old resolution was silly and should be repealed. They all said, however, that they needed to check with higher headquarters. Some days later, presumably after having checked with the Republican high command, these gentlemen informed me regretfully that they could not cooperate.

This matter was discussed with Senate Democrats in caucus, and they were advised that Republican cooperation would not be forthcoming. It was apparent that we could repeal successfully in the Senate at any time, but without House concurrence this would amount to nothing but a few lines in the newspapers. So I suggested that we hold our fire and see what came along.

A young Republican from Miami County, Kermit O. Burrous, had been elected for the first time to the House in 1960. He was so new that he had probably never even heard of the old federal aid resolution. Burrous lived in the fifth congressional district, which at the time the legislature convened was without a congressman because of an election contest. Burrous was interested in flood control along the Mississinewa and Wabash rivers in Grant, Huntington, Miami, and Wabash counties; and on January 10 he introduced House Concurrent Resolution No. 2, memorializing Congress to enact legislation to provide relief from flooding on these rivers. Burrous was able to get his resolution out of committee, and it came up for third reading on January 23. He made a speech in support of the resolution to the effect that the dirty Democrats in Washington had prevented the seating of the duly elected Republican congressman from the fifth district, that the fifth district therefore had no voice in Congress, and that accordingly he had introduced his resolution so that Congress might be advised as to the needs of the fifth congressional district of Indiana. This rabble-rousing speech secured the votes of the Republicans in the House, and the Democrats went along because the resolution called for federal aid. The resolution passed the House 85–0.

When the resolution arrived in the Senate it was referred to the Committee on Natural Resources and Conservation. Senator Kenneth Reagin, a member of the committee, called it to my attention as possibly providing the vehicle for bigger and better things. I quickly agreed with Reagin and completely redrafted the resolution, including the title.

At this time John Van Ness, former Republican majority leader of the Senate, was actively lobbying for passage of the Port Authority Bill on behalf of Midwest Steel Corporation, and Senator Ruel Steele was urging another large appropriation for the continuation of the Monroe Reservoir project. I called these gentlemen into my office and handed them my redraft of House Concurrent Resolution No. 2. They read it and opined that it was a fine resolution but would never pass. I advised them that if it did not pass there would be no port bill and no money for the Monroe Reservoir.

They said that both of these projects were on the governor's program and would pass whether I wanted them to or not. But I pointed out that I would be appointing all conference committees from the Senate, and would positively guarantee that neither of their pet projects would pass unless I had their wholehearted cooperation on House Concurrent Resolution No. 2. They agreed to cooperate. I then suggested that they sell the revised resolution to the Senate Republican caucus on my promise that no Democrat would make a speech of any kind, and especially would make no speeches, comments, or news releases castigating the Republicans for being such a bunch of idiots for the past several years. I further agreed that the amendment could be offered by Senator Steele. Van Ness and Steele were successful in selling this package to the Republican caucus after several days of deliberation, and on February 16 Steele offered the amendment that was adopted on voice vote without explanation or comment by anyone. Immediately after the adoption of the amendment, the resolution was placed upon passage, again without speech, comment, or explanation, and passed 44–0.

A day or two before the amendment and passage of the resolution, Steele, Van Ness, and I took Representative Burrous and House Speaker Richard Guthrie to lunch at the Columbia Club and explained what we were doing, invoking the holy name of Senator Capehart, and assuring them that what was being done was for the greater good of the great state of Indiana. It was suggested that immediately upon passage of the amended resolution in the Senate it would be returned to the House, and that if Representative Burrous would make a motion to concur with the Senate amendment as soon thereafter as possible, without explanation, and preferably at a time when the boys were shuffling their feet just before the noon or evening recess, that Speaker Guthrie could gavel it through without incident.

This plot succeeded and the amendment, on motion of Representative Burrous, passed the House on February 17. The printing of enrolled copies was given priority, and on February 20 copies were delivered in Washington to all members of the Indiana congressional delegation, to Congressman Kirwan, and to his opposite number in the Senate, Senator Robert Kerr, both of whom then approved federal appropriations for Indiana's flood control program.

In addition to the concurrent resolution, the following language was inserted into the operating appropriations bill: "The Governor is hereby authorized to accept on behalf of the State of Indiana any and all federal grants-in-aid, available to the State of Indiana, and such grants-in-aid so received are hereby appropriated for their purposes."

So far as I know no newspaper ever ran a story on this occurrence, and I really doubt that any of them ever found out what was going on.

11. Recent Trends

Indiana has come a long way from its rural and even backward character of the early nineteenth century, when it trailed its neighbors in most of the important indices concerning economic, educational, and cultural development. At the present time the state ranks as one of the leading industrial-manufacturing-agricultural components in the Union. Its economy is strong and diversified, and it does not have a dangerous reliance on one or even a small number of types of industry. In the northern part of the state iron and steel manufacturing dominate, but there are also a number of strong and efficient smaller industrial companies, especially in the South Bend-Mishawaka, Elkhart, and Fort Wayne areas. In the central and southern sections of the state, pharmaceuticals (Lilly, Miles), prefabricated housing (National Homes), and automobile parts and accessories are the leading industrial activities; but a pattern of small-scale manufacturing permeates this part of the state also, particularly in Indianapolis, Richmond, Connersville, Terre Haute, Batesville, Cannelton, and Evansville. Mineral resources, especially coal in southern and west-central Indiana but also limestone, gypsum, and small amounts of gas and oil, are now an increasingly important element in the economy. At the same time, Indiana still ranks high in its overall agricultural production of corn, soybeans, wheat, and popcorn, as well as in various kinds of livestock and all sorts of fruits, melons, and berries.

Particularly noteworthy is the development of Indiana's transportation facilities during the past two decades. Indianapolis is the convergence point of no fewer than seven interstate highways, all of which are connected by the interstate loop around the city, making the capital city of the state also the interstate highway capital of the nation. Complementing the highway system, which also features an interstate across southern Indiana and the Indiana Toll Road across the north, two new Ohio River ports were opened in the late 1970s and 1980s; a large new port on Lake Michigan, the Burns Harbor facility, was opened in the early 1970s; and the Indianapolis International Airport, formerly known as Weir Cook, has undergone extensive enlargement and remodeling preparatory to introducing direct international flights.

Indiana's modern image is perhaps also reflected by its participation in the space program: three members of the first two generations of astronauts, including Virgil I. ("Gus") Grissom of Mitchell, Indiana, received their technical training at Purdue University. Indeed, the educational innovation within the state during the third quarter of the twentieth century, particularly the development of regional campus systems by the major state universities and the inauguration of a statewide system for providing vocational and technical training, have revolutionized the opportunities for education available to most Indiana residents. The number of private colleges has remained stable during these years, although the raising of private funds to support small liberal arts colleges has become more difficult.

A final point of Indiana development concerns two seemingly contradictory but actually quite complementary developments: the urban revitalization programs in several Indiana communities and the growing interest and action in the field of historic restoration and preservation, including the adaptive reuse of many valuable and irreplaceable structures. A number of Indiana communities have redesigned their center cities using the mall concept. The opportunity to do this came to Richmond dramatically, if tragically, when a 1968 gas explosion destroyed the heart of the old downtown; but the Richmond citizens seized the chance to make progress out of chaos. Other cities and towns undergoing significant modernization include Columbus, Huntington, Evansville, Madison, and Indianapolis.

The readings below analyze some aspects of modern Indiana's economy, the changing political scene—Indiana's entry into world commerce on a large scale via its three public ports on Lake Michigan and the Ohio River, unified city and county government in Indianapolis, a more moderate if still right-of-center political stance, the reluctant adoption of legislative reapportionment, as required by Supreme Court mandate, the important place of high school and college athletics, and finally, the Indiana character.

Economic Issues

The selection below describes some aspects of the bitter struggle for a deep-water public port in Indiana. Opposed by environmental groups, particularly the Save the Dunes Council organized in 1957, and Senator Paul Douglas of Illinois (who had a summer home at Ogden Dunes, Indiana), the Burns Harbor project had virtually unanimous long-term support from the state political and business leadership. Ever since 1937, when the legislature established the Indiana Board of Public Harbors and Terminals, a body that was superseded by the Indiana Port Commission in 1961, all of the governors, the state's congressional delegation, and many others had pushed for an Indiana public port on Lake Michigan, something all other Great Lakes states already had. The major breakthrough came in the mid-1960s when the momentum started by Governor Welsh was carried on by Governor Branigin, who, as described below, presided at groundbreaking ceremonies in October 1966. His successor, Governor Edgar Whitcomb, was the proud master of ceremonies at the port's somewhat premature dedication and opening festivities in 1970, but since then Burns International Waterway/Port of Indiana has been an economic engine of sizeable proportion; various import-export companies occupy space on the port property and some two million tons of goods pass over the docks there annually. This tonnage is exclusive of the huge ore and iron and steel shipments through the port that are handled by the Bethlehem Steel Company's enormous ultramodern plant located adjacent to the port. The pages below come from a forthcoming historical study sponsored by the Indiana Port Commission on the occasion of its thirtieth anniversary. For an account of the origins of Burns Harbor, told from the perspective of environmentalists, see Kay Franklin and Norma Schaeffer, *Duel for the Dunes: Land Use Conflict on the Shores of Lake Michigan* (1983). See also the earlier Indiana Port Commission-sponsored account by Lawrence M. Preston, *The Port of Indiana: Burns Harbor Waterway* (1970), a booklet first distributed upon the occasion of a gala opening ceremony in July 1970.

THE STRUGGLE FOR BURNS HARBOR

Ralph D. Gray

During the early 1960s, the Indiana Port Commission did what it could to persuade the federal government to embrace and offer federal funding for its customary portion of the construction projects. Clinton Green [Governor Welsh's administrative assistant and the first secretary-treasurer of the Indiana Port Commission] became a familiar figure in Washington as he moved between 1600 Pennsylvania Avenue and Capitol Hill to conduct his lobbying activities. He attended the Senate committee hearings on the Douglas and Hartke park bills in February 1962, which led to another round of arguments regarding the merits of the port project. Senator Douglas repeated his intentions, if the park bill failed, to "fight them to the death" in opposing appropriations for the port. In addition to his concerns about increased pollution, he said the park was needed as recreation for seven million urban dwellers in the expanding metropolitan corridor from Gary to Milwaukee. The need to save the dunes, he concluded, "had become a regional and national concern rather than purely a state matter."

Rather than engaging in public debate at this time, Green focused on getting Bureau of the Budget and executive branch approval of the Corps of Engineers recommendations. In July he accompanied Governor Welsh to the White House, where they met with President Kennedy and several advisers. When Kennedy was asked at a news conference the next day if he was going "to help Governor Welsh," his answer was an immediate "No." He added that the governor was there to explain his views. The issue for Kennedy was whether the proposed economic development would adversely affect the national park, and he promised a decision and a recommendation to Congress on the matter soon.

The reticence on the part of the Kennedy administration to support the port project openly led to unusually harsh rhetoric from two normally reserved men. Lieutenant Governor Richard Ristine charged that Kennedy's actions were a payback to the Chicago politicians for his thin electoral margin in 1960, and Governor

---

From *Indiana's Public Ports: A History of the Indiana Port Commission* (forthcoming, Indiana Historical Bureau).

Welsh, only a bit more circumspect, vowed that the state would go ahead with the project, with or without federal assistance.

In the meantime, the debate within Indiana and the adjacent states of Illinois and Kentucky escalated. The Save the Dunes Council called for a massive letter-writing campaign to senators and representatives, urging approval of the Douglas park bill (which would kill the port project) rather than the Hartke bill (which would let both projects proceed). The Chicago *Tribune* also weighed in with a heavy editorial barrage against the port, as did Len O'Connor, a respected newsman who aired a nightly commentary on the NBC-TV affiliate in Chicago. O'Connor's "editorial" of October 11, 1962, contained many misstatements of fact and brought forth a stinging, five-page rebuttal from James W. Chester, a Valparaiso attorney and son of the man who had broached the idea of a Burns Harbor port to George Nelson initially [in 1932].

It is interesting to note that Kentucky and Illinois newspapers, particularly the Louisville *Courier-Journal* and the Chicago *Tribune*, as well as writers for the New York *Times* and the *Christian Science Monitor*, supported the conservationist position while ignoring, downplaying, or simply misstating the position of the port proponents. [Port historian] Lawrence M. Preston's comment that the port side favored both a port and a park, but that the other side insisted on a park only in the area concerned is a valid point. . . .

The sale of sand from the Indiana lakeshore to Northwestern University provoked another outcry against the port, even though the transaction was between Bethlehem Steel and the university. The arrangement involved land that was targeted for port acquisition soon, and a large protest resulted. Even the Chicago newspapers complained about the supposed violation of the dune lands in question, although they had acquiesed earlier when Indiana sand was used as fill material for Lakeshore Drive. This time the sand was to be used to create an area for university expansion lakeward, and both the school officials and the state of Indiana were roundly denounced. It mattered not, in the minds of the complainers, that the port site would soon be leveled or excavated in any case, either for a public or a private port. Preliminary removal of the sand saved an estimated $1,750,000 in future construction costs.

The problems and disappointments of 1962—Washington inaction, internal bickering, criticism from conservationists—continued into 1963. They began with the 101-day session of Indiana General Assembly that convened in January, an historic legislative gathering that veteran political reporter Edward Zeigner has called the most memorable of all time. When the regular session opened, Governor Welsh proposed the creation of an Economic Development Fund of $35,400,000, to be funded primarily through an increase in the cigarette tax. The fund would be used for two long-overdue bridges over the Ohio River at Cannelton and Mauckport, improvements in the state park system, a water reservoir in Monroe County, and for building a port in Porter County. The port project was to receive $25,500,000 of the money, thus enabling construction to begin, but it was expected that most of this money would be repaid to the state eventually by the federal government.

There was, of course, opposition to the governor's plan, from Lake County Democrats and others. At one point, to counter false information and to familiarize key legislators from around the state with the project, the governor and the IPC arranged a flying tour to and around the Lake Michigan site, but in the end these efforts were wasted and the Economic Development Fund did not materialize. Important tax restructuring measures were adopted (although it required a special session, convened immediately following the stalemated one to achieve them), including the imposition of a two-percent sales tax, the first in the state's history, and a cigarette tax increase. The latter permitted construction of the two bridges (completed in 1964), but port construction money was not provided at this time. Significantly, however, the legislature at this time authorized the IPC to expend up to $600,000 (from the $2,000,000 appropriated in 1957) in order to permit engineering and design studies to continue, and to authorize additional financial studies.

Although disappointed in the failure to get full funding, release of some of the previously appropriated money was enough to activate the IPC. It had already identified and entered into preliminary discussions with an engineering and consulting firm of some prominence in St. Louis, known as Sverdrup and Parcel and Associates (S&P). This firm had done work for the state of Indiana previously, and Clinton Green recommended that the commission approach them again. Lieutenant General Lief Sverdrup, senior partner in the firm and a former member of the Corps of Engineers who had served directly under General MacArthur in his Far Eastern command during World War II, personally responded to the IPC overture in June, stopping in Indianapolis en route home from New York City. The next month, while flying to a meeting with other officers of S&P, the commission voted, if no problems emerged during the meeting, to engage S&P as the engineering company to plan and design its deep-water port on Lake Michigan. It proved to be a wise choice and marked the beginning of a long, harmonious, and mutually advantageous relationship covering the construction of not one, but all three of Indiana's public ports.

[In the meantime, while this] showdown in the Senate between Douglas and the two Indiana senators, Bayh and Hartke, was developing, the House of Representatives prepared to consider the dunes park bill already passed by the Senate and related legislation. J. Edward Roush, in whose district IPC chairman and newspaper owner, James R. Fleming, lived, had mobilized House Democrats in favor of both the park and the port bills. Charles Halleck, minority leader on the other side of the aisle, was still undeclared regarding the park bill, but of course he was a longstanding advocate of the port. Moreover, Indiana's veteran congressman from Gary, Ray Madden, was "back in the fold" on the Burns Harbor issue. The Gary *Post-Tribune* welcomed his return, pointing out too that the Gary and East Chicago mayors who had opposed it were now both out of office. Moreover, the paper surmised that Madden "now sees through" Senator Douglas's efforts—their effect would be to restrict Indiana's development in favor of Chicago. Madden's return also meant that all of Indiana's state leaders were united in opposing the Douglas plan. As a result, the Indiana delegation in Washington expected action during 1965, but they looked for "an intense legislative battle on both measures before they are sent to the President."

It proved to be intense, indeed, and drawn out, with a major confrontation coming in a closed-door Senate committee meeting, wherein Senator Douglas tried to keep the park and port bills linked together. By September, however, Charles Halleck succeeded in separating the bills in the House, so that approval of one project was not dependent upon the fate of the other. This continued to be the case, despite heated debate on the matter. The final version of the bill, as agreed to by a House-Senate conference committee on October 18 and as passed by both houses of Congress on October 27, 1965, authorized up to $25 million in reimbursement payments to the state of Indiana, subject to satisfactory assurances to the Secretary of the Army that water and air pollution sources would be controlled. On the key point, however, rather than park *approval*, no appropriation was to be authorized until the Indiana Dunes National Lakeshore bill has been *voted* upon "in both house of Congress during the same Congress." This was a highly unusual procedure and wording, but represented still another major step forward for the port, for it permitted work on the project to get under way.

Although a few preliminary construction steps had already been taken, such as aerial surveys and test borings, both on- and offshore, the first construction contract for building Burns Harbor was let in November 1965 to the Walsh Construction Company of Gary. A sizable contract, it involved grading the site and building both a terminal railroad and a construction access road for the harbor construction crews. Later, following final Corps of Engineers approval in June 1966 of S&P's design memorandum, based upon its *Interim Report* of 1964, the IPC contracted with Peter Kiewet and Sons of Omaha, Nebraska, to begin actual construction of the port. Kiewet was to build the outer breakwater, dredge the harbor, and fill in (and compact) the lakeward portion of the land between the two harbor arms. During 1966 more than $20 million in contracts were let by the port commission and the steel companies, the latter having agreed to build the east and west bulkheads marking the east and west boundaries of the harbor and providing docks for their own ships and barges.

Actual construction did not await formal groundbreaking ceremonies in the fall—indeed, at Governor Branigin's suggestion, Kiewet Company men were told to be on the job during the midday program, and the planners hoped as well to have the workers unloading a barge, bringing stone in for the huge outer breakwater. Nevertheless, an elaborate celebration to mark the start of construction was held on October 10, 1966. Clinton Green and George A. Nelson, the port commission's chief actors over the years in getting the port under way, were in charge of arrangements and presided at the festivities. "A 150-Year Old Dream Come True" was the heading they gave to the press release announcing the program.

The crowd of some 650 people that came to Burns Harbor on the appointed day included dignitaries from industry, labor, and all levels of government as well as one unwelcome guest—Mother Nature in the form of winds estimated at 40 to 50 miles per hour. Master of ceremonies Nelson interrupted Senator Bayh just as he began to speak, asking the audience to move because the tent they were in was about to be blown away. Upon resuming his remarks, Senator Bayh suggested that wind at that time was appropriate, because there had been so much of it in debate over the project. Governor Branigin, not to be outdone, also remarked about the tent, saying that it represented the bipartisanship of the port project—it came from the governor's hometown of Lafayette, but was owned by a GOP precinct committeeman. The governor then reflected upon the state's 35-year-long struggle for the port, and what it would mean in the future for the state's economy. He also complimented Midwest

Steel and Bethlehem Steel for their roles in the project, and thanked the New York Central Railroad for building its classification yard there. The governor then gave the signal for the USS *Portage* to fire a salute to the occasion, but the wind prevented the noise of the 3-inch guns from reaching land. The crowd did witness puffs of smoke repeatedly, marking what the governor called the quietest shots he had ever *seen*.

Others who spoke during the proceedings were IPC Chairman James R. Fleming, who particularly praised the Indiana governors from McNutt through Branigin for their unswerving support, and Congressman Charles A. Halleck, in whose district the project was located. Appropriately, given the length of time he had battled to bring this event about, Halleck made the most extensive remarks of the day. He reviewed the major events since the 1930s leading to the port, suggesting that congressional approval would have come in 1962 "except for certain roadblocks I have already mentioned enough times" elsewhere, meaning of course the work of Senator Douglas to get a national park established in Porter County.

INDIANAPOLIS ON THE REBOUND

Robert G. Barrows

Having previously edited a volume containing a series of essays on southern cities that he called Sunbelt Cities: Politics and Growth since World War II *(1983), Richard Bernard in 1990 issued a companion volume on northern cities titled* Snowbelt Cities: Metropolitan Politics in the Northeast and Midwest since World War II. *Robert G. Barrows, managing editor of the forthcoming* Encyclopedia of Indianapolis *as well as an urban historian who teaches at Indiana University-Purdue University, Indianapolis, contributed the chapter on Indianapolis to Bernard's second volume. His essay, although generally upbeat about recent economic developments within the city, also takes an unblinking look at its larger culture.*

No event since World War II has so dramatically altered the spatial organization of Indianapolis as construction of interstate highways around and through the city. Indeed, the interstates have added a new layer of meaning to two of the city's nicknames: the "Circle City" and the "Crossroads of America." It is near the city's two circles—Monument Circle at the center and the beltway around the capital—that most development has taken place during the past fifteen years.

The Indianapolis interstates are typical of the hub-spoke-rim pattern of many urban freeway systems. The Indianapolis "rim" or beltway (I-465), a 57-mile loop, was completed in 1970 following a decade of construction. An "inner loop," finally opened in 1976, encloses the downtown on three sides and serves as a "hub" for the "spokes" of east-west I-70 and northwest-south I-65. Three other interstate "spokes"—I-69 heading northeast and I-74 to the southeast and northwest—

From "Indianapolis: Silver Buckle on the Rust Belt," in Richard M. Bernard, ed., *Snowbelt Cities: Metropolitan Politics in the Northeast and Midwest since World War II* (1990), pp. 137–157.

intersect the beltway, and six U.S. highways also radiate from the city. Thus, as it was for the railroads and interurbans, Indianapolis remains a "crossroad" for a great deal of the automotive traffic traversing the Midwest. Because of its strategic location, an increasing number of warehousing companies, distribution centers, and motor and air freight firms call the city home.

The I-465 beltway has become the city's Main Street, serving as a magnet for development. Motels, hotels, shopping centers, industrial parks, condos, apartment complexes, office parks—all are firmly anchored on the "outer loop." In Indianapolis, as elsewhere, interstate highways built to relieve central city congestion by diverting through traffic have helped to suburbanize the city's residents, businesses—and congestion. The city planners and consultants who studied the city's future in the late 1940s and early 1950s, and who warned against continued "decentralization" of the city's population, were already fighting a rear-guard action. The automobile and the limited access highway would quickly change the nature of the urban environment, transforming the city's focus, at least for many of its residents, from "downtown" to a peripheral, homogenized "no town.". . .

The 1950s also saw some tentative steps in the direction of educational equality. Since the late 1920s the Indianapolis Public Schools (IPS) had been almost entirely segregated, a result of both residential patterns and official policy. When the legislature adopted a desegregation law in 1949, however, the school board abolished separate school districts for black and white children. A majority of the city's elementary schools soon had mixed enrollments (although in many of these schools the enrollment remained *predominantly* one race or the other), and by the late 1950s most of the formerly all-white high schools had undergone at least token integration. There were a few protests by white parents, some of whom headed for the suburbs, but there were no serious incidents. "On the whole," wrote one observer in 1963, "the school authorities appeared to carry out the announced purpose of the school desegregation law in good faith."

Soon, however, it had become apparent that IPS was perpetuating rather than eliminating racial segregation. In 1964, two of the city's high schools enrolled no black students; the traditionally all-black high school enrolled no whites; and teaching and administrative staffs remained largely segregated. In May, 1968, the Justice Department, acting under authority of the 1964 Civil Rights Act, filed suit against IPS in United States District Court—the first step in a complicated and protracted case that would take over twelve years to resolve. The district court's decision in 1971 found IPS guilty of *de jure* segregation, enjoined the system from further discrimination on the basis of race, and outlined several steps to implement the decision. In an effort to prevent resegregation, the court also raised the possibility of involving the outlying school corporations as part of a lasting solution. (The 1969 consolidation of city and county quite pointedly rejected a merger of IPS and the county's other school systems.) At a second trial, in 1973, the court ordered several suburban school corporations in Marion County to begin accepting black students from IPS.

Appeals went on for years, but in the fall of 1981 one-way busing of IPS pupils to the suburban schools finally began. An advisory council with the acronym PRIDE (Peaceful Response to Indianapolis Desegregation Education) worked hard in the preceding months to ensure an orderly implementation of the court order. There were a few ugly incidents during the subsequent years—including the predictable cross burning—but no organized, sustained opposition. Black students have periodically complained that they are subject to more stringent disciplinary action than their white counterparts, and logistics remain a problem for inner-city students who wish to participate in extracurricular activities at their suburban schools, but, on balance, the program seems to have been a success. In fact, the parents of bused children sought and achieved the right to vote in township school elections—a rare if not unique situation.

In early 1969, as the school desegregation case was just beginning and after several summers of explosive racial confrontations in northern cities, an Indianapolis radio/television station commissioned a study of the city's black community. When black residents were asked by black interviewers to name "the three major problems of people living in Indianapolis," four major concerns emerged: inadequate housing; limited job opportunities and unemployment; poor schools and education; and crime, violence, and delinquency. Significantly, in light of what was happening in other cities at that time, the study reported that "even in the presence of Negro interviewers specific concern by Negroes over segregation, discrimination, or racial tension is voiced as a major community problem by only 17 percent."

The four major concerns identified by the report in 1969 are, to varying degrees, still issues today—most notably, the lack of decent low income housing and the difficulty finding employment. Residential segregation still predominates in the Hoosier capital but has certainly become less ironclad during the past fifteen years as middle-class black families have moved out of Center Township (though seldom out of Marion County). Black unemployment, especially among young men, remains a serious concern. As the Indianapolis Urban League has noted, the city's economic growth has been of limited benefit to blacks since many of the new businesses are setting up on the fringe of the city—too far out for employment of inner-city residents reliant on public transportation. On the other hand, a recent analysis of the "economic well-being" of blacks in large SMSAs ranked the Hoosier capital eleventh out of forty-eight communities examined.

Though certainly not viewed as epochal turning points at the time, several events in the mid-1960s marked the beginning of a watershed in the city's history: Bill Book died, Democrat John J. Barton was elected mayor, and a faction of the county Republican party took steps that eventually transformed not only the county GOP but the governmental structure of the county itself. Book's death removed an implacable foe of federal aid, and Barton, though a relatively conservative Democrat, had no qualms about seeking repatriation of Indiana's tax dollars from Washington. During the mayoral campaign in 1963 he argued that the city should seek federal monies for important projects. His administrative practice mirrored his campaign rhetoric and set an important postwar precedent. Barton and his staff revitalized the city's Housing Authority after years of desuetude and secured assistance from HUD for many units of new public housing. The John J. Barton Apartments, the capital's first major public housing project since the New Deal, were completed just about the time the mayor was defeated for a second term.

Barton's election presaged a Democratic sweep of Indiana in 1964, which in turn led to a shake-up in the Republican party. A group of young Marion County Republicans, disappointed with their party's showing, styled themselves the Republican Action Committee and sought to oust the party's leadership. Winning decisive victories for their slate of candidates at the primary of May 1966, they installed one of their own, L. Keith Bulen, as chairman of the county GOP. The next year they orchestrated the nomination of Richard G. Lugar as their mayoral candidate, and Bulen directed a well-managed campaign that led to victory over Barton by a margin of 9,000 votes.

Lugar, an Indianapolis native, brought something of a "new look" to the mayor's office. He was youthful (35), bright (class valedictorian in high school and college), very well educated (a Rhodes Scholar at Oxford University), and a good extemporaneous speaker. Following a stint in the navy he returned home, entered the family business, and became active with local civic groups. His election to the Indianapolis school board in 1964 was the first step of a political career that led to two terms as mayor and, in 1976, to the United States Senate.

Lugar consciously brought a private enterprise approach to the administration of municipal government—especially in the areas of long-range planning and fiscal control. But following the Barton administration's precedent, Lugar and his aides also actively pursued Washington's largess. One of the few Republican chief executives of a major urban area, Lugar became known in the early 1970s as "Richard Nixon's favorite mayor." Very successful in obtaining grants from a variety of urban-oriented federal social programs (Head Start, Model Cities, Community Action Against Poverty), Lugar also made extensive use of revenue sharing funds. Brick-and-mortar projects completed or placed under construction during Lugar's tenure include Market Square Arena (home for the Indiana Pacers basketball franchise), a Convention-Exposition Center, the Indiana National Bank Tower (at 37 stories, then the tallest building in the state), and Merchants Plaza, a combination hotel-office building-bank headquarters. Beginning this serious revitalization of the downtown area was, he later said, one of the proudest achievements of his administration.

Lugar and his successor, William H. Hudnut III, have been highly successful in energizing what they are wont to call a "public-private partnership" on behalf of the city. The premier mechanism used to accomplish this feat has been the Greater Indianapolis Progress Committee (abbreviated GIPC, pronounced "gypsy"). A private, not-for-profit, nonpartisan organization, funded by foundation grants and private contributions, GIPC is self-described as "an action-oriented advisory arm to the mayor's office."

Unlike the Indianapolis Civic Progress Association, which it quickly supplanted, GIPC has had from the beginning a formal, structural relationship with the city's executive branch. GIPC had its origins in the fall of 1964 when Mayor Barton appointed an advisory committee of business and civic leaders to "formulate a program of progress that makes use of the city's full potential." Frank McKinney, Sr., one of the *Times*'s "inner circle" in 1964, served as the first president, and his address to the members in June 1965 outlined many of the major projects that were to be undertaken by the city during the next two decades.

Although established by Democrat Barton, GIPC grew and prospered under Republicans Lugar and Hudnut. In its early years the organization worked for development of a park and reservoir on the city's far northwest side and led the drive for the convention center. More recently, GIPC has been involved in various downtown revitalization projects. The organization's strength has been an ability to marshal the talents of private sector leaders and volunteers in support of public endeavors. A broad-based group—there are now approximately seventy-five on the mayor-appointed board of directors and over 300 members—it includes representatives of business, education, labor, government, religious bodies, social service organizations, and neighborhood groups. In spite of this diverse membership, GIPC has been subject to criticism that it is controlled by a downtown business elite unable to see beyond the Mile Square. Some also view GIPC as a sort of unelected "shadow government"—an institution with tremendous influence over the city's agenda, but accountable to neither the electorate nor the City-County Council.

John Barton, in a recent interview, called the formation of GIPC the greatest legacy of his administration. Lugar, when asked to make a similar assessment near the end of his tenure, identified a government reorganization scheme enacted by the General Assembly in 1969 as his major accomplishment. Dubbed "Unigov" (a contraction of "unified government") by local headline writers, the acronym became the popular name for an arrangement that consolidated some, but by no means all, aspects of Indianapolis and Marion County governments. Most recent observers of the Indianapolis scene have agreed with Lugar's appraisal: Unigov is the single most important political and governmental change to have been effected in the Hoosier capital since World War II.

The concept of a unified city-county government did not emerge suddenly in the mid-1960s. The issue had been discussed, off and on, for over fifty years. The Committee on Post-War Planning considered the problems of government in Marion County; a "building authority" created in the early 1950s was charged with planning and constructing a joint city-county office building; and a Metropolitan Planning Commission, created in 1955, consolidated city and county planning and zoning functions. Still, the multiplicity of governments extant by the late 1950s, with overlapping jurisdictions and duplication of functions, prompted the Indianapolis League of Women Voters to title their 1959 study of local government *Who's in Charge Here?*

Although Lugar had made no specific recommendation regarding governmental reorganization during his campaign, he soon became frustrated by the dispersion of responsibility and duplication of functions he encountered, concerns shared by the Republican presidents of the Indianapolis City Council and the Marion County Council. As government officials, party leaders, and prominent businessmen attended a series of informal policy meetings in 1968, Mayor Lugar recruited a legal team to prepare tentative drafts of the legislation required to effect government reorganization. The mayor went public with the proposed plan immediately after the general election of November 5, 1968, when he announced the creation of a Task Force on Improved Governmental Structure for Indianapolis and Marion County—a group whose primary function was to rally support for the already well-developed plan.

The Unigov bill was introduced in the 1969 General Assembly. Lugar lobbied tirelessly for the measure while other proponents successfully prevailed upon local organizations to contact legislators and express "support for the *concept* of metropolitan government while avoiding arguments on the fine points of the bill. . . ." The measure passed by substantial majorities in both houses and went into effect on January 1, 1970. The entire public debate on the proposal had taken place remarkably rapidly, in just over four months. Among the reasons most often cited for the successful passage of the measure at this time was the fact that Republicans controlled both executive and legislative branches of government on the city, county, and state levels. This is not to suggest that the Unigov proposal encountered no Republican opposition; indeed, some of the most compelling arguments raised against the measure (at least in its initial version) originated within GOP ranks. But the final votes in the General Assembly—67 to 28 in the House, 28 to 16 in the Senate—were virtually straight party line ballots and reflected the Republicans' ability to dominate Unigov's legislative consideration.

In spite of the implications of the name, Unigov is by no means a complete consolidation of all governmental functions within Marion County. As one knowledgeable observer notes, "its actual impact is as much psychological as structural." Four "excluded" cities and towns retain their own governments (although their residents pay county taxes and vote in Unigov mayoral elections and elections to the City-County Council). The Indianapolis police department and the county sheriff's department operate side-by-side, and the Indianapolis fire department coexists with semiprofessional "volunteer" departments in the townships, towns, and excluded cities. Indianapolis city schools are surrounded by the county's ten other independent school districts.

"The establishment of Unigov," note its two closest students, "was much less an act of geographic centralization than of administrative integration." The measure combined the executive offices of city and county government into six major departments and reorganized the legislative functions into a City-County Council of 29 members (25 elected from single-member districts, 4 elected at-large). The mayor appoints the six department heads; the council makes appropriations, levies taxes, passes ordinances, and confirms many mayoral appointments. Unigov thus "provides a single executive and a central policymaking council with dominant power over what had previously been many largely independent and autonomous governmental units and agencies." Perhaps more important than the (partial) integration of local governments has been the increased coherence in countywide policy formation. Indeed, some observers credit the reorganization, and especially creation of the Department of Metropolitan Development, with making possible the downtown revitalization initiatives of the late 1970s and 1980s.

Unigov has not, however, received universal approbation. At the time of its passage there was some complaint that the measure had not been subjected to a popular referendum. Proponents argued, accurately, that state law did not require a referendum. This was, however, somewhat disingenuous; though not *required*, the Unigov legislation *could have* contained a provision making its operation contingent upon approval by a popular vote in the city and county. Unigov advocates obviously "wanted to avoid the difficulties, controversy, cost, and effort of a referendum campaign." They felt, in Lugar's words, that "to throw an issue which has tested the wisdom of the best constitutional lawyers in the state to persons who have not the slightest idea about what government was before or after is not wise." And they believed, again accurately, "that they had the political muscle needed to pass the bill without a referendum provision. . . ." Unigov thus became the only metropolitan consolidation in the United States during the twentieth century effected without a local referendum.

Democrats then and since have viewed the consolidation as a Republican power play ("Unigrab"). The incorporation of suburban, largely Republican voters into the city electorate, it is claimed, has ensured decades of Republican domination in the mayor's office and council. Even Lugar, who promoted Unigov as a governmental reform, admitted in the aftermath: "I know this is good for the Republicans. That is how I sold it to the legislators statewide." Republican county chairman Bulen boasted that the consolidation was his "greatest coup of all time." Motivations aside, the practical political results speak for themselves: Nine of the twelve men who served as mayor between 1930 and 1968 were Democrats. Since Unigov's enactment, however, Republicans have won every mayoral contest and have generally dominated the City-County Council (where the division following the 1987 elections was 22 Republicans, 7 Democrats).

Blacks, too, have tended to view Unigov as a dilution of their political influence—if only because it turned a usually Democratic city in which blacks were developing some political leverage in the 1960s into a Republican stronghold. In 1970 blacks comprised approximately 27 percent of the "old" city's population but only about 17 percent of the entire county. Thus, in strictly numerical terms, black political weight declined when the city's boundaries expanded to the county lines. But, as a recent analysis notes, the City-County Council's single-member district system now gives blacks "a voice in suburban affairs, sometimes giving them voting leverage that can be used to bargain for support for their own programs." Whether "blacks now play significant roles in the new government," as these same analysts claim, is open to debate depending on how "significant" is defined. Blacks (and women) do currently hold high administrative positions under Unigov, however, which was seldom the case prior to consolidation. The Hudnut administration has also fought, in opposition to the Reagan Justice Department, to retain affirmative action guidelines in city hiring and promotion.

Political Issues

Indiana politics in the 1960s and 1970s became more volatile and perhaps more polarized. Overall, the state made a decided swing to the left in the late 1950s and early 1960s, when it elected liberal Democrats to the United States Senate and to the governor's office in 1958, 1960, and 1962, and supported President Lyndon Johnson in 1964. Subsequently Indiana shifted back to the center or even right of center. In the late 1980s and early 1990s, however, political leadership within the state was shared by the two major parties but elections continued to be fiercely contested. The Democratic party not only gained control of the lower house in the legislature and elected as many as eight of Indiana's ten congressmen, but also controlled the executive office after twenty years of Republican governors; nevertheless, during this time the Republican party continued to hold both of Indiana's seats in the United States Senate, even though one of its senators, Dan Quayle, was elected vice president in 1988. Perhaps the shared leadership posture of the 1990s is just one more example of what Professor James H. Madison has described, in a book of that title, as "the Indiana way" of moderation, of middle-of-the-river navigation, and of evolutionary, not revolutionary change.[1]

In 1964, however, despite the state's image as a former stronghold of the Ku Klux Klan and still "an enclave of seedy bigotry and corruption,"[2] Alabama Governor George C. Wallace's entry into the Indiana presidential primary was decisively rebuffed. Indiana Governor Matthew E. Welsh, standing in for President Johnson when no other prominent Indiana Democrat would do so, made a vigorous campaign effort that resulted in a smashing defeat of Wallace. Governor Welsh's first-hand account of the 1964 primary, later incorporated into the book he wrote about his administration, is the first selection below.

Still another unusual political development in the 1960s was the establishment of unified government for Marion County and the city of Indianapolis, a concept referred to as Unigov. The political innovation of a bright young politician, Indianapolis Mayor Richard G. Lugar, who in 1976 became the junior United States Senator from Indiana, its purposes seem to have been less a desire to bring about greater economy and efficiency, the major selling points to the state legislature and the public, than simply political.

Political change has come to Indiana in other ways also. The Indiana General Assembly, which had been since 1851 limited to only one regular sixty-one-day session each biennium, now meets in annual but still limited sessions. In a related act, the legislature gave the incumbent governor the opportunity to succeed himself for the first time in 1976. Thus the popular and benevolent physician-politician, Governor Otis R. Bowen, was reelected for a second term in 1976. Both of his immediate successors, Robert D. Orr and Evan Bayh, also enjoyed two consecutive terms as governor. Moreover, as described below by Justin E. Walsh, the state legislature finally adopted a reapportionment act that satisfied legal and constitutional requirements. Too, in 1975 Indiana reinstituted the direct primary as a nominating device for governor, lieutenant governor, and senator, thus depriving the party conventions of this privilege and the opportunity for more political maneuvering. Finally, there is a di-

1. James H. Madison, *The Indiana Way: A State History* (1986), p. 231 and passim.
2. Edward H. Ziegner, "Indiana in National Politics," in *Indiana: A Self-Appraisal*, ed. Donald F. Carmony (1966), p. 36.

minishing amount of patronage available, because organizations like the Democratic "Two Percent Club" (which the Republicans copied with a club of their own) were outlawed by an act of Congress.[3]

For a brief introduction to Indiana politics in the twentieth century, see Edward H. Ziegner, "Indiana in National Politics," in Donald F. Carmony, ed., *Indiana: A Self-Appraisal* (1966), pp. 35-54. There are, in addition, a few biographical studies of leading Indiana politicians. Furthermore, all recent governors of Indiana have been interviewed by members of the oral history office at the Indiana State Library; of course, many other oral history transcripts relating to these years are in the collection.

THE 1964 PRIMARY ELECTION

Matthew E. Welsh

On Tuesday, April 7, Wallace captured one third of the Democratic votes in "liberal" Wisconsin. Editorialists across the nation called it a "stunning" total. More than a quarter-million Wisconsin voters had marked their ballots for the Alabama governor. On Friday, April 10, Bill Jones, press secretary to Wallace, told Indianapolis newsmen that Hoosiers could expect an "intensive campaign throughout the state." Wallace, he said, would arrive in Indiana the next week and would open his campaign headquarters at the Claypool Hotel. He had accepted an invitation to speak at Butler University the following Wednesday.

Although our work to set up a campaign in opposition to Wallace's had been carried on at an increasingly heated pace, very little had showed on the surface. We had made hundreds of contacts within the party organization and among church and civic leaders at the state and local levels. We had made it plain to these people that we felt the potential damage to Indiana's image as a state during the Wallace campaign was great. What were the stakes in the primary election? We explained to party members and Hoosier leaders that the most important consideration was the possible damage that Wallace could inflict upon the real progress in human relations that we had experienced in Indiana. Undoubtedly, Wallace's presence and his militant call for a stand against alleged incursions by the federal government would encourage hatemongers to new activity. He would uncover, if only for a short time, the latent bigotry held in check by the new social pressure for equality among all people. Politically, by a strong showing, he could do real harm to the Civil Rights Act of 1964, then awaiting congressional action. Although the historic legislation was virtually assured of passage, there remained the possibility of damaging amendments. Finally, should Wallace win and, thereby, claim Indiana's fifty-one votes at the Dem-

3. Howard H. Peckham, *Indiana: A Bicentennial History* (1978), pp. 152–153.

From "Civil Rights and the Primary Election of 1964," *Indiana Magazine of History*, LXXV (March 1979), 8–11, 13–20, 22–27.

ocratic National Convention, Indiana law required that we support him on the first ballot. We were determined to avoid *that* national embarrassment, whatever the cost.

The day after the Wisconsin primary election, reporters' interest in our reaction and preparation for the coming test increased considerably. I had released a short statement on April 8 saying, in part: "We do not underestimate the challenge and we intend to conduct a vigorous campaign in Indiana." That same day Core revealed publicly that he had scouted the Wallace campaign. He said: "The results of yesterday's election there do not surprise me. I was told by political strategists in Wisconsin that we in Indiana would have much more difficulty than they did. We are now making plans for a vigorous campaign. Our slogan is: 'Clear The Way for LBJ. Vote For Welsh The 5th of May.' "

Our campaign was beginning to take shape. We had assurances from church and union leaders that they would undertake to make their own responses to the Wallace candidacy. The Democratic State Central Committee had met, heard Chairman Core's report, and had given him their full support in mounting whatever response was necessary. We had commissioned an advertising agency to begin creative work on radio, television, and newspaper announcements. [Core's assistant, Don H.] Radler, obtained the services of Robert Davis, assistant to Thomas March, director of public relations of the Department of Conservation, on a leave basis. Davis, a former broadcast-time salesman, quickly purchased all available prime time in the entire state. A meeting with black leaders from several metropolitan areas was scheduled. We had begun to pick up momentum.

However, among those who had not been taken into our confidence as we organized our attack, the tension apparently was intolerable. As the day approached for Wallace to begin his campaign in earnest, our switchboard became increasingly clogged with calls pledging support and asking when we were going to get started. One top broadcast executive, widely known for his deep commitment to the progress of Indiana, called McManus in some honest agitation, asking if we were *doing* something or if we were asleep at the switch. Assured that we were gearing up a large effort, the caller pointed out that his stations could not ignore the Wallace campaign, but he had been haunted by the thought that there would be no effective rebuttal at hand.

Irving Leibowitz, columnist for the Indianapolis *Times*, reported that the John Birch Society had been caught in the middle, hung on the horns of a dilemma, by the coming primary election. Leibowitz wrote: "Members of the Society want Goldwater for President, but they also want to register a strong protest against the Civil Rights Bill in Congress." The columnist quoted Frank Thompson, a chiropractor at Greenwood, as saying: "I'd like to help Wallace, but I'm registered as a Republican. I didn't know a Republican could vote in the Democratic primary. I don't know what I'll do." We were to learn later that the John Birch Society and other right-wing extremist groups worked hard for Wallace in Indiana and that many Republican voters crossed party lines to sign his original petition and to vote for him on May 5. There were also a number of Republican voters who felt strongly enough about the principles involved to ask for a Democratic ballot in order to vote for me.

The Indianapolis chapter of the National Association for the Advancement of Colored People issued a statement which said in part: "We hereby protest the entry of Gov. Wallace into the presidential primary of the State of Indiana because he has advocated, spread and disseminated hatred by reason of race and color, which is against the public policy of the state."

Racial hatred was unquestionably counter to the public policy of Indiana. Despite a clinging reputation as a "Copperhead" state during the Civil War and a more deserved black eye for the scandalous political strength of the Ku Klux Klan during the early 1920s, Indiana had come a long way since the Constitution of 1851 had barred Negroes and mulattoes from entering the state. A report, prepared for me by the Civil Rights Commission after I left office, said:

> It is difficult to assess accurately the progress that has been made in improvement of the lot of the Negro in Indiana since 1960. We do know that in state government an example was set of what could be done. Likewise in local government and in private companies thousands of new job opportunities have been opened recently to Negro job seekers—some of them requiring high skills and carrying great responsibility. Literally thousands of public places throughout the state have extended their services and facilities on a nondiscriminatory basis for the first time since 1961. School administrators have doubled their efforts to reduce segregation and increase opportunities for Negroes both as employees and as pupils. A much greater awareness of the extent and critical nature of the problem exists over the state. In 1960 only four cities had official Human Relations Commissions, while in December, 1964, there were 20 such commissions.
>
> At the beginning of 1961 one could hardly find a northern state in which the Negro citizen had as little protective legislation and state programs in his behalf as in Indiana. But, during the next four years, three Legislatures enacted a set of civil rights laws as comprehensive as any other state has enacted in a 16-year period.
>
> It probably is no accident, therefore, that Indiana apparently was the only large industrial state which did not have a single disorderly racial incident occur during this entire period of national turmoil.

This, then, was the Indiana that Wallace came to mine for votes in the spring of 1964; not a state bound by the past, ensnarled in political dogma and fearful of social change, but a state that was showing the way for much of the rest of the nation in a renewed search for equal opportunities for all its citizens.

There was another, more personal, irony for me. While Governor Wallace traveled north to excoriate the federal government and its "interference" in the lives of citizens and the rights of states, I was completing a series of personal diplomacy trips into eight of the states of the Confederacy as part of the Civil War Centennial observance, returning to their governors captured Confederate battle flags found in the Indiana World War Memorial. Graciously accepting the flags in appropriate public ceremonies, the governors each had spoken of the bonds of common purpose that now held us in union as one people and a great nation. There would be no opportunity to return the battle flag to Alabama. . . .

A division of opinion developed among our group as to whether I should personally and openly carry the attack on Wallace. Several debates produced no clear decision on the matter, but it seemed to me that any attempt on my part personally to ignore the Wallace presence in Indiana would be foolhardy. I was the stand-in candidate and the logical person to carry the attack. And, as a practical matter, it would be impossible to maintain silence throughout the campaign because of daily contact with newsmen.

Before the Wallace campaign began officially, Core had told reporters that our strategy would be to knock down any voter attraction to the Alabama governor by attacking him as an overt, active racist. "Wallace contends he's running as a states' righter, but this is phony," Core said. "He really is a racist. There's nothing for him to gain in Indiana. . . . He's getting in here purely to embarrass the Johnson Administration." The state chairman pointed out that we would closely identify with the president. He emphasized that I was not a classic "favorite son" candidate, that my name would *not* be entered before the national convention.

An early April public opinion poll, conducted statewide by a professional firm, confirmed our worst predictions. If the election were held then, the polltaker said, Wallace would win 45 percent of the Democratic vote. Clearly our first task was to awaken the party organization. Although the Democratic party was united and well financed, the cumulative fatigue of more than three years work, much of it in the face of harsh public criticism, had taken its toll. We had to sound the alarm and make certain every Democrat understood that the Wallace challenge was not a political sideshow, that it had potentially grave consequences, and that we would be required to execute in a few days the kind of intensively conducted campaign that normally would require months of preparation. Fortunately, we had already begun a series of speaking engagements at party district rallies. We had been recounting the administration's accomplishments and the political workers' role in our service to the people in an attempt to invigorate the organization at the grass roots. There were several scheduled appearances remaining, and they would offer excellent public platforms.

Meanwhile, [Jim] McManus and Radler were organizing the advertising effort. They discussed the coming campaign with church and civic organizations and with Negro leaders from urban areas, collecting background material on the Wallace record in Alabama. Although we made contact with the Democratic National Committee and the White House, there was no practical service they could render, and we asked for none.

Core had established a liaison with United States Senator Daniel B. Brewster of Maryland and his staff in Washington, promising to deliver to them all the information we might consider helpful in their campaign organization opposing Wallace in Maryland's primary. Through the Brewster staff Radler met Charles Morgan, formerly a lawyer in Birmingham, Alabama, who had gained national publicity when he told a group of that city's business leaders that *all* Alabamians shared guilt in the church-bombing deaths of four Negro girls in Birmingham. Sitting in Brewster's office, Radler asked Morgan if he would come to Indiana and campaign against Wallace, whom he had once actively supported for the governorship of Alabama. Morgan said he could not afford that much time away from his work, but he would consider making a television and radio program and perhaps a trip to Indiana if it would help our cause. Radler quickly accepted, placed a call to a Washington television station, and arranged for a taping session.

That same evening Morgan sat in front of the cameras and ad libbed one of the most remarkable political talks I have ever witnessed. Speaking entirely without notes, he recounted earlier days in Alabama when he was a supporter of Wallace, then a man who preached a moderate brand of politics. He told how Wallace lost his first bid to be governor and later said simply: "I was out-segged." Morgan, recalling that Wallace once served in the Air Force, said the defeated candidate then decided to ride the political "tail winds" of Alabama. " 'Tail Wind George' became a changed man," said Morgan. "And he was never out-segged again." Morgan continued his spellbinding talk until the director stepped alongside the camera to signal that only a minute remained. Expertly, the large-jowled lawyer finished his statement. He had fashioned one of the most effective tools we were to use on radio and television.

Leaving Washington, Radler flew to South Carolina where he found James McBride Dabbs, the courtly six-term president of the Southern Regional Council, relaxing at his farm. Dabbs, who was the 1958 winner of the brotherhood award of the National Conference of Christians and Jews, agreed to come to Indiana and show the citizens that Wallace did not speak for the entire South. From South Carolina Radler went to Montgomery, Alabama, where he continued efforts to find a professional photographer who would shoot a picture of the Confederate flag flying atop the statehouse while the Stars and Stripes was relegated to a staff on the lawn. It wasn't easy, but he found one.

Back in Indiana, Radler joined us as we began to review the broadcast spot announcements and newspaper advertising layouts hastily drawn by our advertising agency. In addition, Core had called a statewide meeting of all Democratic county chairmen and vice-chairmen for the following Saturday. Radler called and got Morgan to agree to join us that day for a news conference and a closed-door speech to the party leaders.

The Wallace campaign in Indiana began on April 15. The Alabama governor had flown into Indianapolis the night before in the Lockheed Lodestar, owned by the state of Alabama and bearing the printed slogan, "Stand Up For America." He called a 9:30 a.m. news conference at his Claypool Hotel headquarters while a group of black pickets representing the local chapter of the National Association for the Advancement of Colored People and the Indianapolis Social Action Council paraded outside. Later he was scheduled to attend a student meeting at Butler University where his speech would be taped for replay on the school's radio station, WAJC. Wallace aides also had contracted for the session to be filmed by sound movie cameras, thus immediately and cheaply giving them a ready-made half-hour television program with a Hoosier setting.

Before the day was out, we were to see again the basic modus operandi of the Wallace campaign. At his news conference he said that he did not object to parts of the pending federal Civil Rights Bill because "I'm opposed to all of it. It's all bad." He was quoted as saying, "I do not believe legislation should be forced on the American people that will destroy our free enterprise system and property ownership in the name of so-called civil rights." When a reporter asked a tough question about the Birmingham church bombing, he replied: "We have an unsolved dastardly crime in every state, including Indiana. . . . When we find the person, we're going to find it's not someone who cares about Negroes or whites or America, but someone with universal malice in his heart for all mankind." On integration of the races, he was quoted as saying, "Integration is a matter to be decided by each state. The states must determine if they feel it is of benefit to both races."

At Butler University, near downtown Indianapolis, Wallace was greeted by another group of peaceful pickets expressing their disagreement with his views and his campaign. About three hundred students and newsmen filled a lecture room to overflowing for the speech and question and answer session. Once again Wallace proved his ability to handle an audience. When it appeared he was pinned by an embarrassing question, he adroitly turned it against the questioner, usually with southern humor. He got applause and laughter. Outside the room one student was quoted as saying, "It certainly makes you think. He sure is a shrewd one."

That same morning, April 15, we launched our campaign. Before a gathering of newsmen at the statehouse, I read a prepared statement that left no doubt we intended to attack Wallace the man and his racist politics as vigorously as we knew how. In part, I said:

> This is the man who stood by while dogs were set upon human beings and fire hoses were turned on groups of peaceful demonstrators. . . . His arguments for states' rights, coming from him, does [*sic*] nothing more than point to the futility of relying on states' rights when there is no respect at the state level of constitutional rights. . . .
>
> This is the man whose beliefs were responsible for the deaths of innocent children in the bombing of a Sunday school class in Montgomery [*sic*]. . . ."

This was harsh language indeed! But I felt we must let our troops know how I really felt about this campaign, and time was short. Here was a governor trying to promote a dangerous and divisive intolerance as a major principle of the Democratic party, and he was attempting to use Indiana—which had recently made great progress in this area—as a launching pad. If he succeeded, a lasting stigma would become a part of Indiana's history. I was determined to prevent his making a good showing in the Hoosier state. Frankly, I was furious—and I guess it showed. Several reporters commented on it.

The Indianapolis *Star* reported the next day: "And while Governor Welsh lashed out with words against the southern governor, he provided him two state policemen to accompany Wallace when he is in Indiana." We also had provided Wallace with a less obtrusive escort; Gordon St. Angelo, 8th District Democratic chairman, and Royal Stauffer, a friend of mine and former agent for the Federal Bureau of Investigation, watched the Wallace performance carefully and called reports back to Core at state Democratic headquarters. Their firsthand reports were helpful in determining our tactics to take whatever edge was possible off the Wallace public appearances.

The first day of the actual campaign had been a whirlwind of activity. This intense pace was to become routine. The Indiana presidential preference primary, normally a dull and colorless political event, was to become a continuing news story of national significance. One by one, out-of-town reporters began drifting into Indianapolis. Some of their names and faces were household words in much of the nation.

Each of them would check into a hotel, drop by McManus' statehouse office, and be ushered immediately into my office where we would give them a thorough briefing. Often we would find ourselves reciting the history of civil rights in Indiana. Most of the reporters wanted to hear the story of D. C. Stephenson and his Ku Klux Klan. Among those who came to Indiana to cover the election were Walter Cronkite of CBS; David Broder, Washington *Evening Star*; Herb Kaplow and Frank McGhee of NBC; Austin Wehrwein, New York *Times*; William Lawrence, ABC; Tony Ripley, Detroit *News*; Joe Cumming, Jr., *Newsweek*; Robert Hollingsworth, Washington Bureau, Dallas *Times-Herald*; Charles Bartlett, Washington Bureau, Chicago *Sun-Times*; Stan Henden, *Newsday*; Robert Baker, Washington *Post*; Richard Madden, New York *Herald Tribune*; and many other fine newsmen.

Many of the newsmen traveled with us and the Wallace entourage. Others ranged the state, talking to Indiana citizens. CBS moved its entire news broadcast organization to a store front at Washington and Pennsylvania streets in downtown Indianapolis. Across the street a pastry shop hung on its marquee: "Welcome Walter Cronkite." All of the reporters stayed to watch the campaign unfold in those final hectic weeks. On April 25 they joined us at the annual Indiana Jefferson-Jackson Day dinner where our speaker was Senator Edward M. (Ted) Kennedy, who told reporters at a statehouse news conference and later in his speech that he strongly supported my effort in behalf of President Johnson.

The president himself, who had by design remained aloof from the campaign, as he did all primaries in 1964, suddenly announced that he would make a flying tour of part of the Midwest and Appalachia on April 29. I flew to South Bend and joined him on a visit of job-training projects designed to ease that city's economic crisis, which had been brought on by the closing of Studebaker Corporation plants. We claimed virtually all the headlines in Indiana that day.

Back in Indianapolis, Marion County Republican Chairman H. Dale Brown and his Democratic counterpart, Judson F. Haggerty, issued an unprecedented joint statement urging voters to ignore Wallace at the polls. And Methodist Bishop Richard C. Raines, in a public statement, urged voters to reject the "unwholesome philosophy" of George Wallace.

> Gov. Wallace has made the proposed civil rights bill the central issue of his campaign. He has described it as a bid for expanded federal authority by power-mad bureaucrats. I find nothing in the proposed bill to justify these accusations. On the contrary, the bill seeks to guarantee for all Americans the liberties spelled out in the Bill of Rights. It is actually in the finest American tradition.

Meanwhile, the Indiana Council of Churches had begun an aggressive campaign directed at its one million Protestant church members. The Louisville *Courier-Journal* reported on April 30 that Dr. Grover Hartman, council executive secretary, had characterized the effort as the "biggest drive we've had in the five years I've been here." Actually, we had cooperated closely with the Indiana council, asking them to do whatever they felt was a practical possibility. Hartman and the Reverend Ernest Rueter of West Lafayette, who was chairman of the council's Legislative Department, threw their energies into the campaign immediately. And they did more than merely talk. A packet of information on the nature of the Wallace campaign was put together, and 1,500 of them were mailed throughout the state. Recipients reproduced another estimated four thousand. Denomination executives suggested that their pastors speak from the pulpit in support of the Civil Rights Bill, that they point out the significant moral issue involved, and that they cite Wallace's distortions of the bill's provisions. Rueter personally went on radio and television to attack the Wallace campaign.

In the days that followed, newspaper headlines reflected the cant and pace of the campaign:

"WALLACE RUNNING POLICE STATE, WELSH SAYS"
"WALLACE HITS FEDERAL RULE IN VOTE BID"
"GOVERNOR WELSH CHARGES WALLACE BENT ON PARTY DESTRUCTION"
"WALLACE RAPS COURT RULING ON PRAYER"
"WELSH STEPS UP WALLACE BLASTS"
"WALLACE MEETS WITH JEERS"

Later, former Governor Schricker, the Indiana Democratic party's patriarch, issued a fighting endorsement of my candidacy. My good friend Lieutenant Governor Richard O. Ristine, a Republican, "leaked" to newsmen his hope that I would win. "I hope Matt clobbers him," newsmen quoted him as saying. Dallas Sells, president of the Indiana AFL-CIO, who had belabored me publicly for many months because I had accepted the sales tax levy in the 1963 tax package, came forth to bury the hatchet. At a morning news conference in my office he pinned on a Welsh button and issued a statement supporting me. . . .

Perhaps the most perceptive picture of Wallace the campaigner was written by Jules Loh of the Washington office of the Associated Press. He found the Alabama governor nervous, sometimes apparently frightened by the crowds of pickets he met at his speaking engagements. He also found Wallace a master on the speaker's platform:

> On a speaker's platform, George Wallace is in his element. He can assess an audience quickly, and he has an uncanny knack of putting an unfriendly group somewhat on the defensive.
>
> On this occasion [Terre Haute speech], for example, he said:
>
> "As you know, I'm opposed to the civil rights bill now pending in the Senate, and today I'd like to tell you why. But first, how many of you are in favor of the bill?"
>
> A forest of hands shot up.
>
> "I see. And how many of you have read the bill?
>
> "About four or five. You think I'm a racist because I oppose this bill. What am I to think of you, who support it without knowing what's in it?"

It was an effective trick he used again and again.

The Welsh campaign now pulled out all the stops. We scheduled a ten minute videotaped statement by me, titled "A Solemn Appeal to Decency," on television stations around the state. We ran 240 television spot announcements, full-page advertisements in Sunday and Monday newspapers, and two dozen more showings of Morgan's "Tail Wind George" talk; we scheduled press conferences and an Indianapolis telethon for Morgan and Dabbs, who had flown to join me in an 11th District rally at the Indiana Roof ballroom, and literally dozens of speeches by Democratic officeholders and candidates.

Our "paper" committee, the Indiana Committee for Responsible Government, continued to issue daily press releases explaining the lack of truth behind the Wallace statements. The Indiana AFL-CIO bought full-page newspaper advertisements urging members and others to support me against Wallace. Our propaganda had become a veritable flood. Each Wallace spot announcement, program, or advertisement was either preceded, followed, or joined by our messages. On Friday, May 1, David S. Broder wrote in the Washington *Evening Star:*

> The Indiana Democratic Party has committed its full prestige and over $75,000 from its treasury to defeating Gov. George C. Wallace in Tuesday's primary election.
>
> Church and civic leaders, virtually all the state's newspapers, top Indiana union officials and even some Republicans have joined a well-coordinated drive to minimize the Alabama states' rights spokesman's vote.
>
> What is clear is that here in Indiana every bit of political muscle in one of the Nation's most effective Democratic organizations and every bit of respectable opinion that could be marshaled has been thrown into the fight against Gov. Wallace.

In the closing days of the campaign it became apparent that we were making headway, that Wallace had failed to build up the momentum he had achieved in Wisconsin and had expected to gain in Indiana. He was smarting especially from the Morgan television show, and he tried to discredit Morgan personally in a last-ditch Indianapolis news conference. A final poll by Louis Harris and Associates confirmed that we had turned the tide. Wallace would have gained 33 percent of the Democratic vote if the primary had come less than a week earlier than May 5. But he was losing ground rapidly.

Eugene J. Cadou, dean of Indiana's political writers and a mainstay of United Press International, had written: "There is no legal way to prevent any number of Republicans from voting for Alabama Gov. George C. Wallace in Indiana's presidential primary." It was true. A Republican voter wishing to cast his vote for Wallace needed only to ask for a Democratic ballot at his polling place. If challenged by a Democratic official, he could retain the Democratic ballot simply by signing an affidavit that he would vote for a majority of the Democratic nominees in the fall election. We were concerned about the possibility of a Republican crossover vote against me and already had advised the party organization that the poll workers should be especially alert and ready to challenge any suspected voters.

Wallace did not ignore the potential crossover either. In a final news conference he dropped a strong hint for the Republican vote when he declared that a voter crossing party lines, then supporting his own party in the fall, would be doing "nothing morally wrong."

Christian Freedom Fighters, a right-wing organization with a post office box address in Milwaukee, thought so highly of the crossover vote it bought paid advertisements in Indiana newspapers and printed a facsimile of the affidavit necessary to avert successful challenge at the polls. The appearance of a paid advertisement sponsored by an extremist right-wing organization did not surprise us. There had been many rumors of right-wing financial support for Wallace. He was careful not to discourage support from the John Birch Society. More specifically, we knew his campaign had stirred up bigots and hate organizations inside Indiana and elsewhere. For example, the Christian Freedom Fighters sent one of their members to Indiana to participate personally in supporting the Wallace campaign. This person appeared in a meeting in Elkhart in which he urged support of Wallace. The meeting was held in the home of a clergyman whose wife was an active member of the John Birch Society. Present at the meeting were a number of active members of the South Bend unit of the American Nazi party. Furthermore, perennial hatemonger Gerald L. K. Smith sent an emergency message to a list of Hoosier supporters asking for the support of Wallace, whom he called "this great, good, fine fearless, patriotic, Christian young man." We also knew that some Republicans and members of the John Birch Society had signed the original Wallace petition while they were at the same time running as delegates to the GOP national convention. Other Birch Society members helped with the busywork in the Wallace headquarters in Indianapolis.

The campaign drew to a close at the tiny hamlet of St. Anthony in Dubois County before a rally of 8th District Democrats. We finished the campaign with great relief. My staff and I were physically and mentally exhausted.

May 5 was a beautiful day for an election, and a record number of voters turned out. Core and his staff suggested a contest, and we wrote our predictions of Wallace's percentages of the Democratic and total votes, then dropped them into a hat. By evening, more than twenty reporters had gathered in our statehouse offices. We watched as the television networks began their coverage; CBS from its downtown store front, ABC from our own WLWI studios, and NBC from the local Time-Life Broadcast outlet, WFBM. By 9:00 p.m. it was clear that we had won, with only the final tabulation of total votes and percentages to be reckoned. I called the reporters together and submitted to their questions. Then I drove to the three television election headquarters and appeared with newsmen. There was no jubilation in our camp that night—only relief that it was all over and that we had held our ground.

As for Wallace, he told his supporters gathered in the Claypool Hotel: "We shook the eye teeth of the liberals in Wisconsin and you folks have shaken their wisdom teeth here."

The Indianapolis *News* reported:

> Wallace was buoyant, even cocky, early in the evening as first returns appeared to give him as high as 35 per cent of the Democratic vote.
>
> As the evening wore on and his share of the tally settled around 30 per cent or slightly lower, he maintained a high humor and insisted that "anything over 25 per cent will be a real victory."

The next day he again publicly claimed his "victory" and flew back to Alabama where he prepared to plunge into the primary campaign in Maryland. There he was to gain his greatest vote total and percentages in his three-state northern foray.

When the official canvass was made, it showed that I had won by 203,377 votes.

The total primary vote was 978,718, just short of the million voters most of us had predicted. I had received 376,023 and Wallace 172,646. Daly got 15,160 and Latham 8,067. Carpenter-Swain won 7,140 votes. Core increased his reputation as a seer when it was discovered that he had predicted Wallace would get 29.8 percent of the Democratic vote and 17.8 of the total. The actual computation showed the final percentages were 29.8 and 17.6.

Wallace emerged strongest, as we had expected, in Indiana's northwestern Lake and Porter counties. He carried Lake County, which comprised the 1st Congressional District, by 1,300 votes. He also won Porter County, one of ten counties in the 2nd Congressional District, by a vote of 3,160 to 2,697. Although his 1st District victory would have given Wallace three Indiana votes at the Democratic National Convention, we decided instead to invoke the unit rule procedure and send our delegates in an "at large" status. This decision later brought criticism from newspaper editorialists, but the controversy was slight and soon forgotten.

It was all over. Only a few short weeks before, we had been most concerned about our last few months in office, the question of who would be our party's gubernatorial nominee, how should we work toward a successful statewide campaign in November, and could we find new and more effective ways to hand over the reins of political power within the party organization and within the government to the next administration. All that had been put aside when we found ourselves in the national spotlight, faced with an adversary wholly new in American politics.

In retrospect it seemed to have been everybody's campaign. Civic, fraternal, and religious organizations had found themselves suddenly and uncharacteristically caught up in a heated political campaign. Support for a lame-duck and generally unpopular Democratic governor had come from Republicans as well as members of his own party. Newspapers and radio and television stations had given intensive coverage to the campaign, and they did a superb job under most difficult circumstances, for they too felt the emotional turmoil that the Wallace incursion created.

In the days and weeks that followed almost everyone had his say about the *what* and the *how* of it. Pundits scratched their heads over such oddities as the Wallace victory in the city of Gary, where he carried every all-white precinct, although Dr. Alexander Williams, a black, won the nomination for a major Lake County office and State Representative James Hunter, an East Chicago Negro, again led the county's legislative voting. On Capitol Hill southern senators claimed that Wallace had run up amazing vote totals, clearly indicating a revolt in the North against civil rights legislation. The Civil Rights Bill supporters replied that, if the two primaries were to be regarded as a test of sentiment on the measure, they would be more than satisfied with the 70 percent of the total Wisconsin and Indiana votes cast against the Alabama governor.

In a May 6 news conference President Johnson commented mildly on the outcome of our race in Indiana: "He [Wallace] got 24 per cent of the vote in Wisconsin and a little less than 20 per cent of the vote in Indiana. I wouldn't think that . . . would be any overwhelming endorsement of a man's record." Writing in the Indianapolis *Times*, Tom LaRochelle saw the election this way:

Gov. Matthew Welsh won the nationally significant Indiana Democratic primary over Alabama Gov. George Wallace because:
—He made the decision to get tough and lash out at the smooth-talking Alabaman, who was grabbing laughs and applause as he refused to talk about segregation.
—He put civil rights in terms of a moral issue, and quickly drew widespread support from churchmen and labor leaders.
—He worked hard to illustrate that Hoosiers on the whole are not as opposed to granting civil rights as Wallace backers thought.

ONE PERSON, ONE VOTE?

Justin E. Walsh

A state legislature is at the epicenter of state politics. In 1975, in anticipation of the 100th session of the Indiana General Assembly, members of a bipartisan committee composed of legislators from both houses recommended the preparation of "a comprehensive, professional study . . . a complete detailed history" (vii) of the Indiana General Assembly. This recommendation was adopted by the legislature in 1976, and, in 1979, Indiana historian and former college professor Justin E. Walsh was appointed to write the history. A magnificent volume resulted from his nearly eight years of work, revealing, for each of four nearly half-century periods, information not only about the legislators themselves and the major issues with which they had to contend, but also the "constitutional and political context" in which they worked. A major political issue in the recent period, from 1930 to 1970, was legislative reapportionment, which was finally resolved in 1972. Since completing his work with The Centennial History, *Walsh has become the head of the Indiana State Archives Division. He is also the author of* To Print the News and Raise Hell: A Biography of Wilbur F. Storey *(1968) and other historical works.*

The rural-dominated legislatures between 1927 and 1961 refused to act on reapportionment. By 1963, however, action appeared mandatory if the General Assembly were to escape the oblivion suggested by the 1961 Marion County Superior Court decision. Although [Senator Nelson] Grills was not a member at the session, the reapportionment act of that year was a monument to him and his cause just as surely as if he had authored the measure and steered it through to final passage. Instead of ending a decades-long controversy, however, the circumstances surrounding passage of the act confused the question further. In 1965, following several adverse federal court decisions, the Indiana General Assembly faced the greatest of what seemed an unending series of apportionment crises. There were additional enactments between 1965 and 1971, interspersed with a series of conflicting federal court decisions, before the crisis was resolved. Only in 1972, after a successful ap-

---

From *The Centennial History of the Indiana General Assembly, 1816–1978* (1987), pp. 500–505.

peal to the United States Supreme Court, did the General Assembly enact an apportionment law that withstood all constitutional challenges.

The federal judiciary became involved in Indiana's apportionment crisis on August 2, 1961, when a class action complaint (*Stout et al.* v. *Hendricks, Secretary of State*) was filed in the United States District Court for the Southern District of Indiana. Briefly, this complaint stated that, by reason of population shifts and the passage of time, the 1921 apportionment acts had resulted in under-representation of voters living in certain counties. Thus, the acts violated both the state and federal constitutions. On August 14, 1961, at the request of the United States District Court for the Southern District of Indiana, a three judge panel (hereafter designated as the court of appeals) was appointed by the chief justice of the United States Court of Appeals for the Seventh Circuit to hear the case. In August, 1962, Nelson Grills filed an action (*Grills* v. *Welsh, Governor, et al.*) in the court of appeals based upon his Marion County Superior Court judgment declaring the 1921 apportionment unconstitutional and denying the *de facto* authority of the General Assembly. On November 27, 1962, three weeks after the general election, the court of appeals consolidated all actions before it regarding apportionment of the Indiana legislature. After that date, all motions, pleadings, and briefs by any of the parties, and all entries, rulings, and opinions were to be considered as continuing developments of the consolidated action.

In light of the Marion County Superior Court judgment and the intervention of the United States Court of Appeals for the Seventh Circuit, both political parties promised in their 1962 platforms to reapportion the legislature. Democrats pledged to do so on the basis of the 1960 federal census; Republicans promised to apportion the House on the basis of population and the Senate on the basis of districts. In November, 1962, Republicans won the House by a 56 to 44 margin. They also held a 25 to 24 margin in the Senate with one seat vacant. Thus, Republicans organized both houses and passed a Republican reapportionment bill on the last day of the regular session of 1963. . . .

Faced with this situation, the court of appeals ruled that the only apportionment acts in existence in mid-1963 were those of 1921. On November 8, 1963, after the state attorney general admitted that there was no longer any rational basis for the 1921 statutes, the court of appeals declared them unconstitutional "as being invidiously discriminatory under the Fourteenth Amendment of the Constitution of the United States." The judges enjoined the 1921 statutes' use in conducting any election after the 1964 general election but declined to order an "at-large" election in 1964. The court of appeals also declined to void the 1962 election of members of the General Assembly, suggesting instead that the 1965 session could provide relief by passing a new apportionment act. In effect, it appeared the 1964 election would be held under the 1921 apportionments.

On February 10, 1964, however, the Indiana Supreme Court ruled that the 1963 apportionment act and two other laws vetoed by Governor Welsh were law because the governor had waited too long to veto them. The ruling meant that the 1964 general election would be conducted under the 1963 apportionment and left clouded the impact and future of the suit pending in federal court. Nelson Grills was pleased with the decision, but said the job was only "half done. My case . . . now apparently concerns only reapportionment of the Senate." Grills singled out the Senate apportionment because he believed it reflected a substantial discrimination against urban groups in favor of rural groups. By way of example, he said that on a strict population basis Marion County should have eight Senate seats, a gain of two-and-one-half over the total granted in the 1963 act.

When the Democratic party captured both houses of the legislature and the governorship in the 1964 election, the way seemed open for the legislature in 1965 to reapportion both houses on the sole basis of population. Action on reapportionment once again seemed mandatory when the court of appeals decreed on February 26, 1965 (while the General Assembly was still meeting), that the 1963 apportionment act was unconstitutional under both the federal and state constitutions. This decision came in the wake of rulings by the United States Supreme Court in 1962 (*Baker* v. *Carr*) and 1964 (*Reynolds* v. *Sims*) that state legislative districts nationwide must be apportioned on the basis of "one man, one vote" under the equal protection clause of the Fourteenth Amendment. . . .

The 1965 apportionment was certainly a partisan Democratic product. But Democratic plans and computerized projections notwithstanding, the Republican party swept every general election held under the plan. (Republicans controlled the House 66 to 34 in 1967; in 1969 they controlled the House 73 to 27, the Senate 35 to 15; in 1971–1972 they controlled the House 54 to 46, the Senate 29 to 21.) These results led to additional challenges in court. Senator Patrick E. Chavis, Jr., from Marion County, a black, a lawyer, and a lifelong civil rights activist, was one of the Democrats defeated for reelection in 1968. After the election, Chavis filed a federal suit challenging the constitutionality of the 1965 apportionment laws. The suit claimed multi-member legislative districts as allowed in the acts were unconstitutional on grounds that the vote of minority blocs was diluted in at-large contests. Chavis pointed to blacks who lived in Center Township of Marion County as an example of such a minority bloc. The reapportionment problems of the Indiana General Assembly began anew with the filing of Chavis' suit early in 1969.

The United States District Court for the Southern District of Indiana ruled in Chavis' favor on July 28, 1969. The court, in imitation of the threat of the court of appeals in 1965, said it would redistrict the state if the General Assembly had not done so by October 1. When Governor Edgar D. Whitcomb refused to call a special session on the matter, the District Court issued its own map decreeing single-member districts and ordered the election of all 150 legislators in 1970 under its plan. The plan threw dozens of incumbents into the same districts with one or more other members. The court also ordered the twenty-five holdover senators from 1969 to run for reelection in 1970 if they wanted to keep their seats. The state appealed the decision to the United States Supreme Court, which, on March 16, 1970, stayed the District Court decision and agreed to hear the case. This action ensured that the 1970 general election would be held under the 1965 apportionment acts.

Though the legislature won temporary relief until the Supreme Court rendered a final verdict, the 1971 session reapportioned both houses according to the "single-member district" formula spelled out by the lower court. Jack N. Smitherman of

Mooresville, chairman of the House committee on apportionment, articulated the feeling of most legislators of both parties: "My thinking is that we are crazy if we don't do it. . . . We have 1970 figures available. If we don't do it, someone could file suit and knock all of us out of our seats for 1972." Smitherman hailed "the beginning of a new era" when bills establishing single-member districts became law. Although the acts pitted several incumbents in Marion and Lake counties against one another in 1972, House Majority Leader Richard A. Boehning of Lafayette was also pleased: "It is the best that man can do or a machine could put out."

Alas, Smitherman's "new era" lasted less than one year. On June 7, 1971, the United States Supreme Court ruled 5 to 3 that Indiana's multi-member districts under the 1965 apportionment acts were constitutional. "Multimember districts have not been proved inherently invidious or violative of equal protection," said the majority. Also, said the court, it was not clear that single-member districts were the remedy "to insure representation to all sizable racial, ethnic, economic, or religious groups." At its 1972 short session, the General Assembly repealed the 1971 apportionment acts and enacted bills that kept multi-member districts in the House. . . .

The 1972 acts ended for a decade Indiana's half-century controversy over reapportionment. For thirty-five of those years the General Assembly had refused to enact a redistricting plan every six years as required by the state Constitution. This failure led to intervention by federal courts in the early 1960s, eventuating in apportionment acts in 1963, 1965, 1971, and 1972 that were based upon the decennial federal census and the formula of "one man, one vote" as decreed by *Baker* v. *Carr*. Although the state Constitution's requirement that the General Assembly reapportion every six years was not rescinded until November 6, 1984, when voters approved an amendment removing archaic language from the document, the requirement had been moot since at least 1965. In retrospect, and in light of its continuous nonfeasance until 1963, the General Assembly was fortunate that no court or court-appointed commission forced a reapportionment plan upon lawmakers that was not enacted by the legislature. Although court-decreed districting had twice been a near thing, every general election in the state's history has been based upon districting plans enacted by the General Assembly.

High School and Collegiate Sports

The past quarter century has been important in the development and expansion of athletics throughout Indiana. In addition to Title IX requirements concerning equal opportunities and funding for male and female athletes at all public institutions, new sports facilities have been opened, and a number of sports relatively new to the state have become popular among young people, including soccer, ice hockey, and volleyball. Golf and tennis, once the province of the affluent few, are more and more a pastime of the masses. But football and basketball are still the top spectator sports in Indiana. Recently the Indiana High School Athletic Association instituted a three-tier statewide postseason competition in football, similar to the one-tier or classless state basketball tournament. (Statewide competitions are also held to determine individual or team champions in baseball, track and field, tennis, golf, swimming, and other sports.)

That football is still a popular and important sport, that it lends itself to many forms of sideline inanities among the fans on so-called football weekends, and that it maintains an appeal beyond the high school level and outside the nationally ranked and televised performances of the top collegiate teams is evident from John Underwood's slightly incredulous account of the football game between traditional small-college rivals and neighbors, Wabash and DePauw. Underwood, a gifted sports reporter, is a senior writer on the staff of *Sports Illustrated* magazine; he is also the author of four books, including biographies of "Bear" Bryant and Ted Williams.

Phil Hoose, the Indiana-based author of the first item, is also a writer for *Sports Illustrated*. His book on Indiana high school basketball, titled simply *Hoosiers*, is not related to the film of that title, both of which appeared in 1986.

INDIANA'S CINDERELLA BASKETBALL TEAM

Phillip M. Hoose

Phillip M. Hoose, a writer of sports and children's books in addition to his history of Indiana high school basketball, was born in South Bend, Indiana, but grew up in Speedway, Indiana. His personal dream of wearing the brown and white uniform of Speedway High School on the basketball court failed to materialize, but his continuing love for Hoosier hysteria is equaled by his ability to paint vivid word pictures about its heroes and its dramatic moments over the years. Currently an environmental scientist and active in various programs for children, Hoose lives and works in New England. He is also the author of Necessities: Racial Barriers in American Sports *and* It's Our World, Too: Young People Who Are Making a Difference (and How They Are Doing It) *(1993). In his book on Indiana basketball, Hoose has written a highly personal but valuable account of the sport through a series of vignettes, including (in the selection below) perhaps the single most memorable event in the one-class basketball tournament that has been played in Indiana since 1911. Even James Naismith, the acknowledged inventor of basketball in 1891 during his years as director of the YMCA in Springfield, Massachusetts, stated in the 1930s that "Basketball really had its origins in Indiana, which remains today the center of the sport" (10). And earlier, after witnessing an Indiana state finals game in 1925, "he could not believe what had happened to the diversion he had started with two peach baskets. 'The possibilities of basketball as seen there were a revelation to me,' he wrote when he returned home" (44). Perhaps, then, Naismith would not*

From *Hoosiers: The Fabulous Basketball Life of Indiana* (1986).

be shocked by Hoose's revelation that "you can find eighteen of America's twenty biggest high schools gyms" (9) in Indiana.

In the selection that follows, Hoose describes the improbable story of tiny Milan High School (with several of its players, including star Bobby Plump, from nearby Pierceville) winning the Indiana State High School Basketball Tournament in 1954. This event, of course, storied among Hoosiers ever since, provided the basis for the highly successful movie Hoosiers, *starring Gene Hackman as the team's coach, produced in 1986.*

Many Hoosier kids discover their roots at the Indiana Basketball Hall of Fame, a blocky limestone shrine in downtown Indianapolis.* Each year busloads of schoolkids from Muncie and Anderson, Plymouth, Gary, Fort Wayne and South Bend race around the rooms full of trophy cases and yellowed headlines. They laugh at basketballs stretched and laced like corsets over inflated bladders, gawk at primitive shoes that once held calloused feet—and in which only a god could have dunked—and argue about which championship game film the group ought to watch. . . .

At some point, at least one kid usually stumbles into a room that is different from all the others. "Hey, what's this . . . there ain't nothin' in here but a TV set." The children are drawn deeper into the carpeted sanctum, which indeed contains nothing but a huge mahogany console with a small screen near the top. Below the screen are strips of red plastic tape that bear the words: "1954 State Final: Muncie vs. Milan. Bobby Plump's Famous Game Winning Shot. Press Button to Start."

Captured in those few seconds of scratchy, silent film is the Hoosier dream. It is there to remind all Hoosiers that old-fashioned values—hard work, boldness and imagination—will still prevail in a fair fight. And if the world no longer seems a fair fight, the tourney comes around each March to remind everyone what it used to be like before the deck was stacked.

All other states but Delaware and Kentucky have divided their state basketball tourney into classes by enrollment. Typically, big-city schools play in one tourney, medium-sized and rural schools in events of their own. In Indiana, little country schoolhouses confront great city institutions named Washington and Central and Lincoln in the same tournament. Not as many kids get trophies in Indiana, but, if you can win, you wake up not as the champ of Division II-A but as the ruler of all Hoosierland.

But only once have Hoosiers had a chance to savor the upset the event was designed to produce. That was in 1954, when Milan High School, with an enrollment of 161 students—seventy-three boys—brought down Muncie Central High School, a school ten times as big, to win a tournament in which 751 schools were entered. The game was won on a shot with three seconds left by a kid named Bobby Plump.

It has been estimated that on that day in March, 90 percent of all Indiana families were watching or listening to the game. Along with the events of World War II and the births, deaths and passages of loved ones, it is one of the most remembered events in the lives of many Hoosiers. Milan struck a blow for the small, the rural, the

*This Indianapolis facility closed in 1987, and in 1989 an imposing new Indiana Basketball Hall of Fame Museum was dedicated in New Castle. —Ed.

stubborn; Milan stopped the highway, saved the farm and allowed many to believe that change was just an option.

By hitting a fifteen-foot jump shot, Bobby Plump delivered the dream to which many Hoosiers still cling. That is why . . . one moment in his adolescence is enshrined in Indianapolis in a room all its own.

Bobby Plump grew up in Pierceville, Indiana, population 45, about thirty miles northwest of Cincinnati. He is the youngest of six children, raised by his father and eldest sister after his mother died when he was 5.

It was not an easy life, but the Plumps were not the kind to complain about what they didn't have. Bobby's father taught school for a while, but when the Depression hit he took on a chicken route to Cincinnati, selling eggs until he found factory work in Lawrenceburg.

There was a roof over their heads, but nothing unnecessary under it. There was never running water, and no electricity until Bobby was 12. Four years later they were finally able to bring home a refrigerator, but phones and television sets were always to be for others. It was a warm and supportive family, and Plump today recalls his as a wonderful childhood. . . .

Even in a community of 45, it was easy to get ten or twelve players up after dinner, when everyone came home. You played with the older kids, your brothers, fathers and in-laws. The games were rough, especially on a gravel surface; "No blood, no foul" was the Pierceville court motto.

Bobby and Glenn [Butte] and two other pals named Gene White and Roger Schroeder played together constantly. After a while, they developed a common experience of each other, each one understanding what the others were going to do on the court, the way voices in family quartets seem to reach for each other and blend. . . .

Entering the tourney [in 1953], everyone in Ripley County knew Milan had a fine team. They'd had to move their last few home games to a bigger gym, and, for the first time in a long while, the school had had to raffle sectional tickets to meet the demand. Chris Volz, Milan's GM dealer, stood up at a rally and promised the team a fleet of Chevies to drive to the sectionals. There was a lusty cheer. Hold it, Volz said, that's not all. It's gonna be Pontiacs for the regionals, Buicks for the semistate and Cadillacs for the finals. The Caddies must have felt secure in their showroom: Milan had never won even a regional game.

Milan breezed through the sectionals and headed off in Pontiacs to the Rushville regional tourney. There they got lucky. In a cliffhanger against Morton Memorial, Milan fell behind by two points with twenty-eight seconds left. The ball went out of bounds, and while it was being retrieved the timekeeper forgot to turn the clock off. When play resumed, Milan's Bill Jordan was quickly fouled, and when he looked at the clock, he was amazed to see that there was no time left. Calmly he hit both free throws and tied the game. Morton appealed without success. Plump won the game for Milan with two free throws in a second overtime.

Milan went all the way to Indianapolis before losing to South Bend Central in the afternoon semifinal game. Plump had a great tournament, scoring nineteen of Milan's thirty-seven points against Central. It had been an unbelievable season, highlighted by one of the most remarkable coaching jobs in Indiana high school history: a rookie coach had taken a school with seventy-three boys to the state finals. . . .

The 1954 group bolted off along the same path as their predecessors, losing only twice during the regular season. Seven hundred fifty-one schools entered the tourney that year, and again few took Milan seriously. A schedule that included Rising Sun, Napoleon, Aurora and Montezuma simply did not excite the Indianapolis sports writers, whose hearts were hardened against the favorite-son teams which dissolved annually before big crowds in exotic cities.

But this team was for real. Milan rolled through the sectional and regional rounds of the tournament, flattening its first five opponents by an average of nineteen points. In Chris Volz's big Buicks, they cruised into Indianapolis for the semistate tourney with something to prove.

They beat Montezuma 44–34 in the afternoon semifinal, then went back to the Pennsylvania Hotel for a nap before the night game against Indianapolis Crispus Attucks, an all-black high school. . . . Crispus Attucks was led by the great Oscar Robertson, who in 1954 was a 6′3″ sophomore forward. Attucks was a strong, savvy and spectacular team, a year away from invincibility. Milan raced to a strong first-half lead, but the effort exhausted Plump. At halftime he was seized by cramps in both legs and broke into a cold sweat. Wood wrapped him in a blanket and told him to stay in the locker room. The others would hold the lead. When Wood walked upstairs for the second half, Plump was already out on the floor warming up. His twenty-eight points led Milan to a 65–52 victory.

The next weekend, when the team fired up the Caddies for the state finals in Indianapolis, 900 of the town's 1,100 residents went with them. Milan swamped a fine Terre Haute Gerstmeyer team in the afternoon game but still entered the evening showdown against Muncie Central as definite underdogs.

Muncie Central was—and still is—a big school with an intimidating tradition. The Bearcats had won the state championship four times, more than any other school. Muncie played its home games in a gym that could hold seven times the entire population of Milan. But the pressing problem was that Muncie's front line averaged 6′4″; by contrast, Milan's Gene White jumped center at 5′11″.

Wood thought carefully about the job ahead. Nervousness would not be a problem. These kids had played together since they'd worn braces, and they weren't the kind to scare anyway. And nobody had taken them seriously enough for the fear of failure to enter in. But there was just no way a conventional approach could offset Muncie's height and muscle. Wood decided, for the first time, to try to spread offense, the Cat and Mouse, for a whole game.

The strategy worked like a charm for the first half, and Milan took a 25–17 lead into the locker room. Now all they had to do was stay calm and hit the shots that surely would come once Muncie started to press. But the third quarter was catastrophic: Milan failed to hit a single field goal and entered the final eight minutes of the game tied 26–26.

Most Hoosiers over 40 can tell you where they were during the final period of that game. Statewide television coverage of the finals had begun only three years before, but there had been a sophisticated radio network since 1921, and of course Butler

Field House was jammed with over 15,000 Hoosiers. The state stood still that Saturday night, and the dream shimmered.

Muncie pulled ahead by two points in the opening seconds. Gambling that his veteran team would prevail in the frenzy that was sure to come, Wood stuck to his game plan. He told Plump, just as if they were playing Osgood for bragging rights to Ripley County, to stand there and hold the ball until someone came out to get it.

So for four minutes and thirteen seconds Plump stood with the ball cradled under one arm, the other hand on his hip, staring at Jimmy Barnes, the player assigned to guard him. Barnes stared back, knees flexed, arms extended in a defensive position.

Most of Indiana thought Wood was insane, and many Hoosiers were furious. As the clock wound down, it sounded for all the world on the radio like Milan was *quitting*; Wood seemed to be mocking everything that every father told every son. They were *behind*, for Christ's sake, and they weren't even *trying* and the dream was ticking away. . . .

With about two minutes left, the frenzy began. Wood let Plump shoot for the tie. He missed, and Muncie got the rebound, but then Milan's zone press forced a turnover and Ray Craft tied it at 28-all. Muncie coughed the ball up again, and Plump put Milan ahead with two free throws. Muncie's Gene Flowers retied the score at 30. With all of Hoosierland on its feet, ear to the radio, eyes on the tube or in the berserk field house itself, Plump and Craft brought the ball downcourt very slowly for the last time.

With eighteen seconds left, Wood called time out. In the huddle, Gene White suggested that everyone move to one side of the court and let Plump go one-on-one against Barnes. Plump was a little surprised since he was having a terrible game, having made only two of ten attempts so far. Wood agreed. Plump was the shooter and it was time for a shot.

Ray Craft was supposed to inbound the ball to Plump, and then the entire Milan team was to shift to the left side of the court, out of Plump's way. But Plump, who had felt jittery in the huddle, nearly blew the play right away. He took the ball out of bounds himself and threw it in to Craft, who somehow found the presence of mind to catch it and toss it back.

Then the nervousness disappeared. After all, it was the play [previous coach] Snort Grinstead had told him to perfect years before, and he had done it a million times out back and at Schroeder's and against Osgood and Cross Plains and Aurora.

Alone and with nothing to do but what he knew how to do better than anything in the world, Plump slowly worked the clock down to five seconds. Then he suddenly cut across the lane, stopped quickly at the top of the key, leaped into the air and flung the ball over Barnes's fingers and toward the hoop. As the ball sailed through, Goliath buckled, Excalibur slipped free from the rock and Indiana's dream came true.

When it was over, the 200 folks left in Milan rushed out to start a bonfire. It is fortunate that the blaze did not burn out of control, since twenty-one of Milan's twenty-four firemen were at the game.

To keep his team from being crushed by celebrants, Wood permitted a brief Cadillac parade, backwards, as it turned out, around the Indianapolis War Memorial

Monument and then sequestered the boys in the Hotel Pennsylvania while joyous fans maintained a vigil outside.

They fired up the big Caddies for the last time and headed for Milan after breakfast on a bright Sunday morning. The caravan was led by Pat Stark, an Indianapolis motorcycle cop assigned to the team. They were expecting a celebration in town, maybe a brief homecoming in the Square, and then some sleep at last.

They were tickled to see the curbside crowds in the Indianapolis suburbs and thrilled by the fire trucks from Greensburg and Shelbyville that fell behind them on two-lane Highway 101. There were flags in all the little towns. Planes circled overhead. Officer Stark could not believe what was forming behind him, or ahead, for that matter.

About thirteen miles out of Milan, at Penntown, the team began to notice cars parked along the two-lane highway and met the first hikers waving and cheering and carrying picnic baskets. The motorcade had become a convoy, and they were losing speed. It took thirty-five minutes to go the eight miles from Batesville to Sunman. This was unreal.

When Officer Stark, flanked by American Legion cars, nosed into Milan, there were 40,000 people waiting. He turned off the Caddie and they all climbed onto a makeshift stage across from the park. From the stage, looking straight ahead, there were people as far as the eye could see. Kids dangled from the boughs of the sycamores in the park.

Everyone got to speak, even Stark. The big-city cop dissolved into tears. Marvin Wood repeated the four characteristics of a champion, the ones he had listed before every Milan game. They were: determination to win, self-confidence, alertness and luck. Mary Lou Wood, Marvin's wife, concluded her brief remarks with a line Bobby Plump was to use in the many speeches he would give after that day: "It's nice to be important," she said, "but it's more important to be nice."

SMALL COLLEGE RIVALRY
Wabash vs. DePauw

John Underwood

When Tommy Mont coached at the University of Maryland he experienced all the thrilling things that attend a college football coach when he is up to the noose line of his neck in the big time. Mont knew important people; he had his picture taken with Queen Elizabeth. He knew large enthusiastic crowds. He knew huge, pressing budgets and cutthroat recruiting, and blue-chip athletes whose talented hands itched to

---

lay hold of professional contracts. He knew glad hands as well, and eager-beaver alumni and friends who were faithful when he won.

Mont had succeeded the late Jim Tatum, a Maryland legend. As head coach Mont proved to be a man of intelligence and wry good humor, virtues that could not save him when his Maryland teams began to lose. Which they did, too soon. Barely had he put his ear to the ground to catch the rumblings when he was out on it.

It was my impression that Mont had quit coaching after that, but in fact he had gone—presumably under cover of night—to Greencastle, Ind. to become head coach, and eventually athletic director, at DePauw University, where a man could lose in peace. At DePauw the crowds are small, and television coverage nonexistent. A few lines in *The Indianapolis Star* on Sunday morning is the apogee of exposure for a DePauw team. The white-chip athletes who come to play there do not drive complimentary convertibles, and the alumni are not spoiled by offers to go to the Orange Bowl.

Neither do offers from professional teams turn the heads of DePauw players. Mont had a punter who signed with Denver but did not stick. The punter was distinguished by his sandals and shoulder-length hair (DePauw is a conservative Methodist school, which only recently was willing to concede that a bottle of beer on campus might not evoke God's wrath), and used to debate the length of his punts with team publicist Pat Aikman, trying to get 39-yarders stretched to 41.

Coaching at Maryland did not, as it may have seemed, make an old man of Mont. He is one of those large gray men with droopy eyelids who look as if they were born old and who can often be seen in the shadow of a scoreboard, looking up despairingly at the figures there.

At DePauw he was granted a golden twilight. If his losing seasons—since 1959—outnumbered the winners by almost 2 to 1, he was respected for his virtues and was much in demand as an after-dinner speaker. He told his audiences that DePauw football had everything Notre Dame football has except parking problems. He placed the picture of Queen Elizabeth on his desk and settled down. In time he was even given tenure, which would have been unheard-of at Maryland or any of those schools where football is too important to chance a coach's complacency.

Prim, proper little Greencastle—pop. 8,852—is not a town with an unlimited capacity for excitement, but what it gets it appreciates. John Dillinger robbed a bank there 40 years ago and townspeople are not over talking about it. A breathtakingly incongruous German World War II buzz bomb is on permanent display in the town square.

Mont, in turn, brought to DePauw football (in lieu of unremitting victories) a certain flair that could be appreciated. In the key game with archrival Wabash in 1960, DePauw scored a last-minute touchdown to cut Wabash's lead to 13–12. Mont had said if it ever came to this—a decision to go for one extra point to tie, or two to win—he would leave it to the fans. True to his word, at that turgid moment Mont turned to the stands and spread out his hands like a tent preacher. (In the press box, an assistant coach named Ted Katula, thinking Mont was signaling *him* to make the decision, dived for the floor.)

The crowd shouted "Go!"

DePauw went, and won 14–13.

"I could never have done that at Maryland," Mont said.

It was not Mont I had come to Indiana to see, however. Mont was a bonus, like finding a first-edition Melville in the quarter bookrack at the Goodwill store. It was the game—DePauw vs. Wabash—that had drawn me, through the clouds of my own doubts that college football could still get by in the kind of small-town incubators that spawned it so many decades ago.

Wabash had been playing DePauw in the privacy of western Indiana since 1890, which makes it (orchestra up) "The Oldest Continuous Rivalry West of the Alleghenies." The schools' propagandists cling to this designation as though it were a lifeline, the way other places vaunt their right to be "The Bell Pepper Capital of Kansas" or "The Birthplace of Truman Seymour." There is, nonetheless, a certain cryptic glamour to being the oldest anything, and that is what DePauw-Wabash has enjoyed, "The Oldest Continuous, etc., etc."

Any persevering self-respecting rivalry has to have pains to grow on, of course, and the seeds of a loving enmity were sown early in this one. DePauw claimed a forfeit of the 1891 game because Wabash didn't show. Wabash has no record of it, but has been unable to get it off the books. When DePauw lost in Crawfordsville one year, its student newspaper reported that "the best team cannot win when playing against 13 men, two of them the officials . . . [who] were personal friends of the Wabash coach." Wabash backed out of another game because of an incident the year before when Wabash fielded a black player. When DePauw records showed a victory over Wabash that year, Wabash officials conducted a "scrupulous investigation" and found that the losing team was actually Wabash High School.

It was not unusual in those days for DePauw and Wabash to engage such teams as Purdue and Notre Dame, but there were even bigger nuts to be cracked. DePauw played the great Illinois team of 1924 and lost 45–0. Red Grange appeared on the field once during the game to pose for a picture. After the game the DePauw coach "was granted a leave of absence."

Wabash managed to drum up a piece of business with superpower Michigan. Outweighed 30 pounds to the man, Wabash succumbed 22–0. It was considered a moral victory. "Little Giants," someone called them, and the Wabash nickname was born. DePauw's athletic teams are called Tigers. There are no romantic stories about that, but a Wabash professor says that every time the DePauw mascot—a student dressed in a $300 tiger suit—gets near the Wabash stands he loses his tail. Or worse.

By the '30s the rivals seemed to settle at their moorings like aging ships, taking on only routine passage and finding in each other the best reason for existing. In 1932 the Monon Railroad, which ran through the towns of Greencastle and Crawfordsville, donated a 350-pound bell off one of its locomotives as the winner's prize, and most of the intrigue since then has centered on the stealing of and the fighting over the Monon Bell. The series slogged along. It was remarkably even, 36 victories for DePauw, 35 for Wabash and seven ties, when I first heard of it a year ago.

I made my headquarters the week of the game at the General Lew Wallace Motor Inn in Crawfordsville, motoring in from Indianapolis through a misting rain and

33°. The Indiana sky was caked in layers of gray, like an elephant's hide. The sun had made three spot appearances since September, and the bone-chilling dampness had taken root.

Crawfordsville is 30 miles due north of Greencastle on U.S. 231. The tie line is not exactly the labyrinth at Knossos, however, so it is reasonable to say that the towns are compatible. Crawfordsville has a few more people and apparently not as many funeral homes. My first impressions were reassuring. John Wayne was playing at the 88-year-old Strand Theater. A whistling mailman was making his rounds on foot. The police wore American flags on their sleeves.

One of the latter obligingly led me in his patrol car to the Lew Wallace, which I had missed on the first pass through. Wallace was the Civil War general who wrote *Ben Hur*. His study is now a museum near Wabash, which he attended in 1840. For six days. Nevertheless he remains the school's most famous matriculator and the only name I recognized on the lists of Wabash alumni.

The Lew Wallace Motor Inn was formerly a coffin factory. The restaurant there serves an appetizing brand of canned chili that the Wabash coaching staff takes in every now and then. The coaches love it. They think the chili is homemade.

Wabash was a short walk in the rain to the western edge of town, the tiny campus spotted with huge piles of decaying leaves, the only color left on it by the advancing winter. The campus is a throwback. The original building (1832) is still in use, and additions contribute to the vaguely forbidding, bleakly exciting quality of the place. The unmistakable aura of an all-male institution.

I had been told that if you scratch the backgrounds of most Wabash and DePauw students you would find little to distinguish them—middle-class, Protestant, conservative, white. But college students wear their identities like overcoats and tend to adapt to the styles at hand, causing a school's character to harden along certain fashionable lines, and it was here that Wabash and DePauw were said to be antipathetic.

Wabash (from the short DePauw view) is a monastery for the uncouth. Wabash does not have a code of conduct for its men, only that they "behave as gentlemen," which gives them license to develop low brows and manners. You can tell a Wabash student by the way he staggers on weekends. He is the one to be found face down in the wedding cake. He does not know a Windsor knot from the Windsor Castle and never gets the part straight in his oil-slick hair. Wabash men are called Cavemen (they enjoy the image), and you wouldn't let your sister touch one with a 10-foot cattle prod.

DePauw, on the other hand, is a rest home for sissies. DePauw men are called "Dannies" and are a hankie-waving bunch. Nevertheless, they are not particularly keen-witted. A Dannie carries an umbrella when the sun is out and puts it down when it starts to rain. How does a Dannie get in shape for the big game? The coach dumps him off the bus at Wabash, and he runs like hell for home.

Dannies adhere to a strict school moral code, which is to say they sneak their drinks. When given more freedom than they can handle they are pictured running naked across the pages of *Playboy* magazine. DePauw's student body is 45% female. Wabash students therefore consider DePauw a nice place to visit, but they wouldn't want to enroll there.

These differences are mostly symbolic, of course, but it is true that DePauw is a larger, more socially tailored school (2,257 enrollment to 850) with a surer financial base, and it *does* have girls. Wabash made a two-year cost study of going coeducational some time ago and decided that girls did not belong in college. . . .

I cannot pinpoint the moment I lost my objectivity and began to care—in Wabash's favor—but I can reconstruct the reasons for it. Something as expressive and unaffected as Wabash vs. DePauw felt at ground level for a spell is quite impossible to resist. If you think you know college football by knowing Texas-Oklahoma or USC-UCLA you are as wrong as you would be if you thought you knew the United States by knowing New York.

I think the realization struck with a punt that landed on the railroad tracks at practice the next afternoon. The ball slid off an enthusiastic but inexpert Wabash foot, flew up into that grieving Indiana sky and over the fence at an erratic angle and down onto the tracks that split the field into upper and lower levels, and caromed and spun there among the ties, and I heard the train and said to myself, "Well, there goes the budget."

The Wabash coach had told me how the balls popped when the trains passed over them, an ordinance of physics he could do nothing about. But it was the economics that touched me. Football at Wabash is deficit spending, and the pops are never music to the coach's ears. "Every time we open the doors for a game," the coach said, "we lose money." What thrilled me about the remark was that Wabash had no intention of *closing* its doors, as others have, for that reason.

We watched the ball disappear, and I said to the coach, a part Cherokee Indian named Dick Bowman, that this was no place for a penny-pinching outfit to practice. To which he wisely pointed out that the cost of moving the field vs. the sacrifice of a few hunks of leather to the railroad was no contest.

Actually, he said, if I really wanted to see the budget at work I should go on a road trip, like the 300-miler to Sewannee when his wife packaged 120 homemade pimento cheese sandwiches only to find out the players preferred bologna. Leftovers don't lie. . . .

Later, over cocktails at Wood's house, a group of them—Bowman, Athletic Director Max Servies and a couple others—ganged up on me. I don't know what I said to start it, something about intercollegiate football at a small college being as impractical in today's world as a truck farm, but they swamped me with rhetoric. They said football was not there to make money; where had I been?

"Our budget's less than $100,000," Bowman said. "Gate receipts average about $7,000 a year. We can seat 4,200, and the only time we fill the stadium is for DePauw. No way to balance out."

"Athletics are for the kids, not the other way around," one of them said. "Athletics contribute to the educational experience."

"I like that," I said. "I remember a Dartmouth. . . . "

"Fifteen percent of the student body is out for football," I was interrupted. "Eighty percent participate in some form of athletics."

"Tell *that* to your Notre Dames and your Michigan States."

"And your Alabamas."

"The austerity bothers some of them," Bowman said. "I had one boy sneak out the first night. There's a high attrition rate, too, because of the academics. I'll start 11 freshmen against DePauw, including the quarterback."

"Maybe you oughta pay 'em under the table," I said, casually dipping into the peanuts.

"Are you kidding? Semipro athletes? That'd be a catastrophe. Where would we get the money? Besides, they're too close as a group within the student body. It'd be bad for morale."

"DePauw has one slight advantage. They can promise their athletes the chance to wait on tables at the sorority houses."

"They used to get an extra day off at Thanksgiving if they beat us."

"There's always a money problem here," Wood said. "You oughta see President Seymour. He'll tell you. I think he collected a million bucks last year in a door-knocking campaign.

"Old Thad Seymour. And he's an Ivy Leaguer, too."

"It's really not so critical," Bowman said. "The coaches were able to scrape up enough pin money to go out to an authentic Chinese restaurant last year."

The next day I went around to see President Thad Seymour, tracking mud onto the carpet of his office, which smelled of pipe smoke. The laminated handbill announcing the 1907 Wabash-Michigan game was on his wall. Seymour is a large man with a hearty voice and a ruggedly constructed nose that does not precede him so much as it leads his interference. He had been the dean of men at Dartmouth, and until he came to Indiana—by train—three years ago he "didn't think places like this still existed."

He reveled in it. He had participated in the faculty intramural program and he had been caught up in Wabash vs. DePauw. He said last year at the annual pre-game Monon Bell Stag Night in Indianapolis, when rival alumni and officials get together and live it up, he had, in the course of performing magic tricks for the crowd, broken an egg in President Kerstetter's lap. He thought it great fun.

Neither was he above leading the Wabash student body in a cheer or two, he said. His first year, wearing a red-and-white freshman beanie, he went onto the field to get one going. The score was 14–7 DePauw. Almost immediately after his cheer Wabash scored. "Unfortunately, we went for two points and missed. If we'd made it, it would have changed my life. I could have sat at my desk and never done another thing."

On my way out I lifted from an anteroom chair a discarded copy of the annual racy newspaper put out by Wabash journalists for the big game. This one was called *The DeBauch* and featured a nude man partially covered with a DePauw pennant lounging across the front page. President Kerstetter's head was superimposed on the man's shoulders. The headline said, "DeBauch Pres. Desires Strong Student Body." I stuffed the paper under the seat of my rental car and drove the 30 miles to Greencastle.

It was raining there as well; God was playing no favorites. Pat Aikman filled my arms with indoctrination material and arranged for me to see Tommy Mont. The DePauw newspaper he gave me was crammed with pictures of coeds, indicating to prospective students that the place was *crawling* with good-looking girls in short skirts. There was one pointed reference to the football program: "Victories are not purchased at the expense of scholarship."

Aikman said, indeed, that football was kept in perspective at DePauw, but scholarships were available to football players and they were proud of the accommodation Tommy Mont had made. The squad had a higher grade average than the student body, and 33% of the varsity were pre-med or pre-dent students. Tommy Mont's job did not depend on beating Wabash. "But, of course, we would like nothing better," Aikman smiled thinly.

We dropped in on Mont. One of his assistant coaches, a pale young man with a red crew cut, looked me over carefully and then disappeared. Mont said one thing he enjoyed about the rivalry was how well everybody got along, especially the two coaching staffs.

Ted Katula said I shouldn't listen to too much of that, because old Tommy always pulled out the stops for Wabash. He said a few years ago Mont changed DePauw's jersey colors at halftime. The ploy enraged Wabash, but it had a salutary effect on the DePauw quarterback who suddenly became Sammy Baugh.

"But the real story was Tommy's halftime talk that day. We were behind 10–0 and looking hopeless. In the middle of his talk he turned and pointed at me. 'Now you fellas know Ted here. He's been with me 10 years. I hate to say it, but he's leaving us. This is his last game at DePauw. Frankly, fellas, I'd consider it an honor if we won it for Ted.' "

"Geez, they almost tore the door down getting back out there. We won 13–10. And as you can see, I had no intention of leaving DePauw."

What, I asked, did Tricky Tommy have cooking this time?

Mont smiled without showing his teeth. "Oh, you never know," he said. "Neither team is exactly overloaded [DePauw's record was 2–6; Wabash's 3–6]. Did they tell you we haven't lost up there in 18 years?"

On the morning of the game I was up early and over to the student snack shop for breakfast. I ran into two of the players, an end named Hiatt, who had six vials of experimental fruit flies stuffed in his fatigue jacket, and a safetyman named Haklin, the team captain. Hiatt said he had played in the game last year with a separated shoulder, "but there was so much infighting and name-calling going on I didn't realize it."

Haklin was having his team meal, a carton of milk and a blueberry Danish. He said a professor had told him all the games up to DePauw were "scrimmages," and "He's right. Last year when the seniors talked to the team before the game it was like war. They said, 'You better prepare yourselves. And you better win. For your sake, not ours. You'll take a lot of crap if you don't.' "

Haklin looked down at the empty milk carton he was squeezing.

"Next year I'll be in grad school, trying for a Rhodes scholarship. But I don't know what I'll do without football. I couldn't have made it at a big school, so I came here. I'm sorry it's over."

Upstairs, Dick Bowman looked out at the elephant-gray sky over Little Giant Stadium. "Damn rain," he said. "I hope it stays away." He said he planned no gimmicks for DePauw. A basic Oklahoma defense, the fashionable triple-option offense. "Fundamentals are about all we have time to teach."

He said he had four bottles of champagne on ice for the victory party. He said he realized it wasn't enough to get high on.

A Veteran's Day Parade in downtown Crawfordsville was the only competing event at game time. Despite the threatening weather, the Wabash crowd arrived early and filled its side. The DePauws were late coming and did not fill theirs. "They don't wanta see any more than they have to," a young humorist standing next to me on the sidelines said.

The Monon Bell came clanging into the stadium on the back of President Seymour's swaying 1938 Packard, eliciting a ponderous cheer. The DePauw band was thumping overhead as Tommy Mont faced his black-and-gold-clad warriors in the dressing room and offered them clemency for a "bad season." He beseeched them to play "the doggonedest football game you ever played." They whooped and crowded the exit to the field.

It might not have been that—the doggonedest football game ever played—but it was a fine one, lacking neither skill nor drama. I stood with Mont's coaching staff in the first half in a vortex of partisanship. A guard named Dalesandro came off shaking his head in wonder. "It's euphoria, man," he shouted, wide-eyed. "I think I'm moving like hell, but I ain't moving worth a stick."

On an out-of-bounds play, a pileup occurred at my feet. Mud flew, and bodies, and a near-hysterical voice at my elbow screamed, "Crack his head off!"

Wabash, meanwhile, had unleashed a treacherous attack of orthodoxy that overshadowed Mont's more imaginative football. Coach Bowman's freshman quarterback, Cogdill, got over a case of the flutters (a fumble, an intercepted pass) and put his team in for two touchdowns in the first quarter.

Then DePauw came alive. A 92-yard touchdown march made it 14–6 just before the half. The extra point was botched. "*Dang*," Mont said, turning sharply on his heel. "We've been doing this 13 weeks, now we're dumb." But as we moved off the field he winked at me and said, "Helluva college game, isn't it?" It was, too.

I offer, in somewhat expurgated form, as a classic of its kind, Coach Bowman's halftime talk to his Wabash players: "Gentlemen," he said, "you have 30 minutes to play. For some of you, it's the last 30 minutes. DePauw hates your guts. You hate their guts. You got 30 minutes to put together all that hate and all the courage you can and kick their tails. Now relax and have a good time."

On the Wabash side I had difficulty deciding which action to follow. The Sphinx Club, those redoubtable rowdies, made a human pyramid that collapsed wildly in the grass. They also offered their own refinements in cheer lyrics:

"Rah rah ree, Kick 'em in the knee!

"Rah rah rass, Kick 'em in the wee-knee!"

Thad Seymour, a vision in red and white, came out of his president's box to lead his annual cheer. "Gimme a W!" he shouted, waving his arms.

"*Duba-ya.*"

"Gimme an A!"

"A . . .

Wabash scored again on the first series after the kickoff, lightening some of the suspense. But a Tiger named Simpson scored his second touchdown on a 71-yard run, and a two-point play cut the difference to 20–14 in the fourth quarter.

Tempers shortened as the end drew near. Hiatt grabbed a rival after a pileup, and a player close by me yelled, "That's what we need, a good fight." But the fight did not materialize. The game ended with Wabash in control at midfield.

I don't know what I expected to happen then, but nothing riotous did. Champagne flowed (briefly) in the Wabash dressing room. Dick Bowman gave me a bearhug. I went over to the DePauw dressing room to extend condolences to Tommy Mont. He was sitting on a bench, settled there as heavily as nut pudding on an unaccustomed stomach, and didn't seem eager to talk.

One of his assistants was outside and I made a few gestures of commiseration. He had the look of a man who has seen a cow break loose and kill the butcher. The series was tied, he said.

"Geezus, after all these years we gotta start over."

The Hoosier Character

Is there a distinctive Hoosier character? Assuming that the answer to that question could once be answered with an unqualified yes, even as late as the 1920s and 1930s, can the same answer be given today? The increasing homogeneity of American society, its mobility and its instant exposure to national developments via television have taken their toll on regional differences, dialects, and dress. Nevertheless, many believe that certain distinctive traits remain among the native Hoosier people, and that characteristics ingrained in the people of the Midwest, and particularly in the people of Indiana, are less prevalent or not present at all in other regions.

One view of how Hoosiers appear to outsiders is provided by Hugh Willoughby (a pen name for Nigel Harvey), a witty young Englishman who was a graduate student in agriculture for a year at Purdue University. The letters he wrote home from America were collected, edited, and published by Joseph L. Martin in 1958, two years after Harvey had returned to England. They make for a delightful and instructive view of Hoosier life "amid the alien corn" and reveal that the visitor from England was indeed impressed with certain basic Hoosier traits of friendliness, openness, a guarded optimism, and a sometimes shallow sophistication.

A second and more recent view comes from the distinguished American historian, Howard H. Peckham of the University of Michigan, who has an intimate knowledge of the state. This is based not only on several years of residence while serving as director of both the Indiana Historical Society and the Indiana Historical Bureau, but also on many years of research into the state's development. Professor Peckham is among those convinced of a distinctive Hoosier character, a distinctiveness that is formed by the unique blend of people and their respective cultural inheritances. This final selection, which was also the final chapter of Professor Peckham's history of Indiana written for the national bicentennial, summarizes the Indiana experience and the Indiana character.

INDIANA IN THE 1950s

Hugh Willoughby

10 September 1955

The university, with handsome and superb buildings, is scattered over several hundred acres. The dream of Wells come true. The engineering school is one of the biggest, if not *the* biggest, in the world. In addition to the beautiful structures there is a factory with a great dirty Battersea power-station-type chimney which is floodlit at night—very fine. The students also have a mile or so of railway of their own to play with, including one of those ferocious-big American diesel engines. The university is a spacious city of its own.

I speak of the physical plant, grounds and the rest that goes to make up a Midwestern university. I have not seen anything of the intellectual side of the campus.

There are 12,000 students at this university, with an annual intake of about 3,500. The administration has to be efficiently organised. It is.

You start the academic year with an Orientation Week. You begin by collecting in the Hall of Music (they call it Music Hall—for obvious reasons I transpose) which is—inevitably—the largest in the world. The new students about half filled it. The show opened with a funny man, sort of a court jester. He had us singing community songs, asking the chap next to us his name, girls singing against boys—damn near changing hats. Then he introduced the professors, Alf, Bill, Bert and Tom—or the U.S. equivalents. He assured us that they were nice guys. Looked just like everybody else in their underpants (these were his actual words). Then a band played us light music and the Glee Club sang.

My mind sped off to the grey Divinity Schools and the Sheldonian, took a deep breath and returned. This, of course, was folly. This job was designed for backwoods farm boys who had never been away from home (no boarding schools over here) and were a bit scared of what must be one of the greatest experiences of their lives. They loved it and it did them a lot of good. It was well done and kindly done. Sort of a Welfare State line—you know what I mean: relax and let the university take care of you now that you are here.

Then the representatives of the local churches, some thirty, came on to the stage

---

From *Amid the Alien Corn: An Intrepid Englishman in the Heart of America* (1958), pp. 16–25, 34–37, 49–55, 139–143.

and were introduced, and they asked us to separate parties they had arranged for the new students. I went. We played games and sang songs and everybody was very matey and I had a jolly good time. All of this may sound rather childish—it was not, or at least not with these people.

Orientation includes briefing and documenting. I filled in forms; I joined in queues ("lines" over here); I got things stamped; I took various forms first to this office and then to that office and then to another office. But it had to be done and it was very well done. It was a very nice case of applied bureaucracy.

Later we had a similar do, also in the Hall of Music. More bands, more Glee Club. (This university prides itself on its music. The Glee Club has sung to Queen Mary and President Eisenhower as well as to me.) Then the president of the university delivered an address. Plain suit, no pomp and circumstance, no academic splendour. But suddenly the atmosphere changed and you knew there were some really good minds behind all this frivolity. (Perchance my prejudice is showing a bit; he is a fellow Oxonian.) He didn't say anything particularly spectacular, but he said it well and truthfully, talking about scholarship. A special word to foreign students, whom he asked to refrain from judging until we knew the background and causes of things. It was like looking at the engine-room of a liner after spending a merry week eating, drinking and dancing aboard her. Possibly a rather small engine-room for such a large and rather pretentious ship. But it is there all right.

17 September 1955

Bridget and I moved into a very comfortable flat. It was pure woman's-magazine stuff come to life. Insulated, air-conditioned, a "fridge" like a chest of drawers, ample, built-in cupboards, washing machine with a dryer. Painless, hygienic, packaged—the lot. After we settled down, we had a chance to meet some of the natives. Friendly folk, very pleasant.

They are also highly picturesque. Campus clothing is a course of rich and varied delight. Generally a shirt, or windcheater affair, in most cases heavily badged or frankly thermo-dynamic—bright, loud, unharmonious, crude, picturesque-in color, and slacks or jean-slacks often coloured, too. The freshmen wear little green caps, and there are various other colourful badges of rank. The senior men wear beards. The general effect is Elizabethan. I greatly care for it.

I have adopted protective colouring. The campus is pretty broadminded over clothes, but I feel a suit and tie would be regarded as bourgeois, feudal and generally reactionary. Consequently, I wear a windcheater and fawn trousers.

Crew cuts are the usual hair style. Gives a curious air of toughness—which, I imagine, is also in the best of Elizabethan traditions.

There is a very high average of looks and, above all, an excellent turnout of girls. But very few of them seem to get far beyond the average. My eyeballs rotate cheerfully but haven't sizzled yet.

So far I have found no trace of any anti-Britishism, though this area is not traditionally famed for excessive admiration of England and her works. That delightful saying, "I were twenty years old afore I learned that damnbritisher was two words," is said to have originated in this part of the Middle West. As a matter of fact, we are a long, long way from Europe. People take you for what you are and you are expected to leave your European background behind you—as everybody else has. You start from scratch. They seem to regard you, instinctively, not as an Englishman but as a potential American. One might even say, sort of a member of the club pro tem. Europe gets very little space in the papers, and it is clearly assumed that the Middle West is its own empire, with its own future pretty clearly marked before it.

24 September 1955

We attended our first gladiatorial exhibition of American collegiatism, a football game. It was a match against a California university which opened the season. American football is very different from ours. Psychologically, it is a cross between a cup tie, pools and the boatrace.

Preliminary pep session on previous evening. Two bands march around campus, banners, floats, revolver shots, funny hats, general morale-boosting. Great cheer meeting, complete with cheer-leaders. Songs, wild cries (sounds like the cries of African aborigines or the war cries of a Scottish clan), promises of what we should do to them. Loud Noise Brigade organised for the next day, but, astonishingly, no alcohol. *Query:* How do they do it on Coca-Cola?

Stadium is a vast place. Harringay with the lid off. Astonishing variety of clothes. Glory, I wish I could draw. Jeans, thermo-dynamic shirts, weirdest caps. Massed bands from 135 (repeat, a hundred and thirty-five) local high schools turned up, wearing uniforms each one more fantastic than the last. Complete with drum majorettes, whose uniforms were even more outlandish, but briefer. Quote more navel than military unquote. The armies of the world must have been ransacked to create these uniforms. They all paraded into the stadium, which they filled—about three and a half acres of solid band—and played under a conductor on a tall stand. I felt my senses had been taken out one by one, beaten over the head with clubs and put back. But it *was* effective.

The game was violent and incomprehensible. Chaps in armour and helmets, average weight about seventeen stone (literally), looking rather like men from Mars, jumped at, on and over each other. There was also a ball, but it didn't seem to matter much, except when somebody ran with it, which wasn't often. Not knowing the rules, I regarded it as I regarded a bullfight, purely as a spectacle, like a film. I didn't think much of it as a game because there were far too many stoppages, but the Americans loved it. Bands, cheerleaders, drum majorettes, streamers (lavatory paper thrown high with an end loose makes a superb streamer). The whole treatment. Fifty thousand people in the stadium rooting like crazy. Oh, yes, we do see (and hear) life.

25 September 1955

"A church on Sunday to attend will serve to keep the world your friend."

After yesterday's pagan rite it was necessary to attend church today to cleanse our souls. Quite uncanny; it is our Church of England service word for word. I could join all the responses and prayers. But all slightly different, in a Hoosier accent—sort of a twang. Made me feel quite homesick, thinking of village churches and our local church, where we take our little boy.

The only difference is interesting. Over here they carry the American flag in the procession, along with the cross. *Query:* Is this a relic of revolutionary times? Do the Episcopalians wish to emphasise that, though they may worship as the King of England does, they are true-blue Americans?

After services Bridget and I went to the Student Union Building. Imagine a really good hotel with a huge lounge, multiplied by ten, bug in a few libraries, two or three restaurants, a very low-grade newsstand (insulting the intelligence of any university student—any student), there you are—where we had breakfast with two sophomores (second-year men) and one freshman, whom we met quite by accident. Average age, approximately eighteen years. All were local boys, rural type; in fact, farmers' sons. They answered my queries about local farming conditions and then they began to query me.

Oh yes, one of them had heard of Oxford. The other two knew we had a queen called Elizabeth. One of the chaps was astounded when I answered his question affirmatively and assured him that Americans could read English books.

Curiously, they knew something about the Empire and weren't surprised to know that the Dominions, including Canada, were virtually independent. In general, they seemed to regard us as sort of horse-and-buggy relatives. Quaint, picturesque, but not quite of this world.

Remark of the day. "You *are* like us, aren't you? You do have television and things, don't you?"

All this bears out the general view—that the young American college student is about equal to a sixteen-year-old schoolboy in England. The lads' views on the Empire were remarkable or even unique in an area not traditionally famed for undue admiration for Britishers or Britishism.

I have noticed again and again how at first the younger students are a bit nervous with me, but when I have been around a bit they seem perfectly matey. I am probably the first Englishman they have met and they have in mind the traditional caricature of the superior, up-stage, rather arrogant Englishman. Our accent sounds rather clipped and brusque to them, but they seem to understand me all right. I, however, had some difficulty understanding them, which I tried carefully to conceal.

After our late breakfast one of the friendly natives—a very hospitable chap—invited Bridget and me for a drive in the country. At first sight (ours was from the railroad window), the Hoosier countryside looks rather like ours—sort of an unkempt Suffolk. But when you get amongst it, it is very different. Most of the crops are strange; this is equally true of the trees and (pardon the old cliché) even the birds and the bees. Much to my astonishment even the weeds are different. These Americans change everything. There is the general air of untidiness, poor wire fences, gates of an almost Anglesey dereliction. General "extensiveness"—as if somebody had started to farm it and had then gone away for a holiday. The roads, by our standards, are poor. But it doesn't matter; cars get along and if you leave the main roads, well, what do you expect? Indiana is a big place and has only got four million people in it.

13 October 1955

I have been out twice with the Outing Club, in both cases to state parks. The parks are supposed to be primaeval woodlands, though I suspect much of them must have been cut over by the early settlers. All hardwoods, turning in the fall—superb greens and yellows, some reds, even this early. Though the full glory has not yet come, it puts the English autumn out of the way already. I can't describe it; you must see it. There are few places in England where you find a stretch of hardwood land as big as these parks.

At Pokagon Park in the north they have bison in an enclosure. Ferocious-looking beasts. There used to be millions (literally) of bison in the prairie areas of this state—the "brown sea" the early surveyors described, rippling and rising and falling. They were nearly exterminated and the few survivors were artifically preserved. One instance of the manner in which the Americans dealt with their natural resources.

The area in which Pokagon Park stands was sold to the United States Government by the last chief of the Potawatomi Indians in 1831 for three cents an acre. It includes the land on which Chicago now stands, much of which must now be worth at least twenty cents an acre.

On the way out on one expedition, we went through a Mennonite area—a "primitive brotherhood" type of sect. They wear beards and don't use tractors or any other modern inventions. You see chaps like Paul Kruger, the Boer leader, riding around in little buggies with lovely sleek horses. Apparently, however, the American Way of Life is too much for some of the younger men. We saw one in a lovely sleek car.

14 October 1955

Today I became a Yellow Dog. My department runs an initiation ceremony. It takes place after a fish fry and general get-together. Professors, graduate students, undergraduates all collect and there is a lot of back-slapping and introducing and general matey-ness. This goes down well. It may not be our way of doing things, but then we aren't the folk who are doing them. The chaps who do do them seem to like them. And so do I.

I am, of course, under oath to tell nobody about the initiation ceremony. But I can say it included blindfolding, horseplay and water, much, much water. (Though even here the American love of comfort came out—the water had been warmed!) The general tone of the proceedings can be judged from the motto of the Yellow Dogs: "Aim high and stick to your post." My mental age, when I am in the mood, is about twelve. I had a fine time.

The professors, or most of them, stayed. Indeed, one read the ceremonial. This, too, is the American way. And it is arguable that you get on better with the senior members of the club when the initiated members have emptied a bucket of water over you. United in a common experience, you know. Shows that the profs are the same sort of folk as you are. You must remember the whole time that we are thinking in terms of chaps who have never been away from home before and whose home may be a backwoods farm thirty miles from anything we English should even class as a village. Just other farms around them, with the same sort of people on them.

27–31 October 1955

Just back from one of the most pleasant and interesting weekends in my life. The couple who has the flat across from Bridget and me took us out to see their family—his parents and her sister, who has married a farmer. It is about a hundred miles south of here.

Jim's father is an elderly man, very like our older type of farmer in ways and looks. His wife is a granddaughter of the original homesteaders, the Germans from the Rhineland who first settled here. She told us some very interesting family stories of the first-comers, who cleared patches in the wilderness forest. There were wild turkeys in the forests at the time. Part of their modern home was once the original cabin and their original barn was burnt down only two years ago—much to my regret as well as theirs. I would like to have seen it. This part of Indiana was settled about 1840, I should say. Over the brow of the hill is a very rich, flat area which was once the Fourmile Swamp, where the settlers hunted ducks. All of this reclamation was done by manual labour. I have been concerned with enough reclamation by tractor and bulldozer to appreciate what that means.

In the afternoon I went with the old squire to a cattle auction. It was held in a tin barn. All small farmers from near by were in attendance—mostly wearing peaked caps and leather or coloured short-coats, blue jeans. Gave them the air of a very tough irregular army gathered to take hell out of somebody or other. But I soon forgot that and, blow me down, I was back in some East Anglian market. Same dull, glazed look when the cattle came in; same stolid powers of contemplation; and behind it were very shrewd, careful professional minds weighing the job up to the last cent. I know that look; I have had it tried on me sometimes by farmers who wanted to know what sort of chap I was. You feel as though you are being weighed in a very ponderous and deliberate balance by someone who, whatever his limitations, does know how to weigh. The auctioneer made the same jokes as they do at home and got the same laughs.

Jim showed Bridget and me around the local town, which is comparable to our village. We spent half an hour chatting in the local store. Straight cracker-barrel job, pure homespun; complete with the traditional Liar's Bench. All are concerned with local business conditions and local politics. Same as with us, but a different accent. Also, everybody has a car. Otherwise, just the same. Halesworth, Adderbury, Bampton—how like Greentown they are!

People here are Methodists, so Bridget and I went to chapel on Sunday. Delightfully informal. The preacher was in a windcheater and check shirt. Welcomed us all; the young couple from England got a special welcome. Everybody turned round; the young couple from England grinned. I didn't see anybody light a pipe, but it wouldn't have surprised me in the least if somebody had. Just that sort of atmosphere. Then we split into groups for a sort of discussion after readings. I wanted to show willing, so I told them about Oxford, where Wesley was "at school," and the prison (the Castle) where he preached to the prisoners, and the Kingswood Miners and the manor-house at Stanworth which he visited. Everybody very friendly. All very simple and just plain farm folk.

Of course, it is all very well to say that these people are parochial and ignorant. But I doubt if they are more ignorant than our village store-assistants and back-woods farmers and minor insurance agents and the general "business men" on a village scale. One of the most striking things about the westward movement in this area was the passion of the early settlers for education, for something to give the children who were brought up in the bush. Witness J. S. Wright, witness the spate of local farming and general uplift societies which flourished in Indiana in the middle nineteenth century. They value education over here. We may laugh in our superior way at their universities. But a degree means a lot to these people and that is surely a Good Thing.

In any case, we can't talk about ignorance. I, an Oxford M.A. and the author of three books, had to look up the state I was coming to on the map when I first heard that this trip was a possibility. I had no idea where it was. Further, this university has the largest engineering school in the world, and some of the European engineers here whom I know tell me it is pretty good. (I believe they are good judges because they have attended both European and American engineering schools.) But in six months among educated English people I never met one who had even heard of it.

To return: then we went to spend the night with Jim's sister-in-law. A 250-acre farm, equivalent in England to perhaps 100 acres. It is a family farm, run by father, son and wife, who in England in a mixed farming area couldn't cope with much over 100 acres. So it is quite a small farm. Mind you, it is good land and it is well farmed. But listen to what I found.

Single-storey house, about six years old. Central heating, real hotel-style comfort, sofas, fine rugs, TV, of course, magnificent woman's-magazine kitchen, white enamel, stainless steel double sink, lashings of cupboards, fluorescent lighting, the works. Fridge like a couple of trunks and a deep freeze and a couple of lockers in the local store where they put away the odd bullock. We ate real Ritz—including fresh strawberries.

We were welcomed by the daughter of the house who had apparently dropped in from Bond Street, sleek and smooth, with a very beautiful hairdo. This time I really did goggle. She would have stood out on the cover of any magazine, fully fashioned in all the right places and, I imagine, highly habit-forming. I put her Englishwise at eighteen, recollected this was America, and put her at sixteen. Actually it was fifteen—age of the terrors of St. Trinian's.

In the evening we had a party with some of our host's friends and played euchre. All were small farmers or their families. Out of working clothes and in their normal evening housewear they looked like prosperous business people. One of the sons has an overall-type job with an electricity concern. You wouldn't have known he wasn't a £1,000-a-year office worker or, more probably, an up and coming young salesman. He had an appropriate blond wife, also beautifully arranged and groomed. The farm has two cars.

I don't say this is normal. But it certainly isn't very abnormal. I have had a lot of rural hospitality in England but never anything near this—this sort of way some agricultural playboy, a tycoon shedding income tax, would entertain you. And they are a working farm family.

Why such luxury, such air of leisure? Well, I can think of several probable reasons. For one thing, the domestic organisation is really efficient. The house and equipment are new and designed by men who meant to end all unnecessary labour.

With agricultural mechanisation and the application of technology to farming the Americans have produced an efficient farming system so there is not so much of the pure drudgery and traipsing around as we have. They work hard, but they can work cleaner and with less exhaustion than we do. The farm I visited has pretty heavy soil and the annual rainfall is just under forty inches per year, which is a little over that of most of Oxfordshire.

And of course, there is a background of a decade of great prosperity as partial explanation for the appearance of such luxury. Jim's father vividly remembers the depression, when they had nothing to eat but everlasting cornbread (home-grown maize) and bacon. But the sons and daughters know nothing of such poverty and the elders are determined that the sons and their sons will never know of it.

As I sat there playing euchre, a magnificent dinner inside me, a can of beer at my right hand, a cigar in my face, a lush blond on one side and on the other this girl with Esquire shape and Regent Street clothes, I thought to myself, "Glory, if Establishment Division could see me now!"

12 June 1956

I spend a lot of time bushwhacking, taking certain time-studies on dairy farms. The general procedure is to turn up, a complete stranger and unannounced, and tell them who I am and what I want. In all cases I have been received with open arms, long chats and shoptalk, meals and general kindness. I am thinking of becoming a professional farm-visitor. The farmers will feed me and I shall sleep in the car. If only I could get somebody to pay for the gas—for which at present the university pays—I could travel around the country free. So far as I can see, I could do it indefinitely.

I got caught in one of these storms recently—an Indiana storm can be described as a vertical flood. Tropical. You expect to see fish swim past the windows any moment. My windscreen wiper broke suddenly, so I pulled up by the side of the road, half blind, and went into a ditch. (Cars are wide over here, which is good for girl-fun, so I am told, but confusing for English-trained drivers in heavy storms.) I threw myself on the mercy of the nearest farmer, who took it all as a matter of course, and pulled me out with a tractor. No fuss, just the sort of thing neighbours do. Plus an invitation to a meal, of course.

I was on one farm when lightning put the electricity out of action. The whole farm and house seized up, just like that. Fridge, deep freeze, water (because of electric pump), lights, milking machine, phone, everything died. Nobody minded particularly—great joke. The cows had to wait an hour or so to be milked, but even they didn't seem to mind. They are cheerful folk over here and I like them immensely.

29 June 1956

A friend took two other Englishmen and myself to the State Republican Convention at Indianapolis. The function of the convention is the election of party candidates and party officials. In practice, it is largely a fight for control of the party machine and is full of picturesque skulduggery.

One gets the impression that it is very like an indoor fair: general activity, comic hats, colours, favours, streamers, Scots bagpipe band suddenly descending the stairs; crowds of people drifting around, looking in on the candidates who lived in separate rooms, like animals on exhibition in booths—you want the best treasurer, we have him, come and see. Much back-slapping, free drinks, general fun.

The professional politicians, the party organisers, are a race apart. Many just look like the middleman in the cruder type of cartoon—fat, rubbery, smiling, loaded with cigars and automatic bonhomie.

The real dirty work was done in the traditional smoke-filled rooms. It seems to depend largely on personalities, connections, bargaining. There are no major issues. Happy is the country with no major issues; it does not really much matter who governs Indiana—the place is indecently prosperous, anyway.

I met Jenner. I had expected a sort of Malan, for he represents the Bible-thumping backveld, the small, family farmer, Protestant, "Nordic" (as opposed to "Bohunk"), isolationist, limited, dislike of city slickers, America for our type of American. But no. He was younger than I thought, not in the least patriarchal, and as rubbery and intolerably genial as the rest of them.

The general picture was that of eighteenth century English politics. Walpole, Pitt and, curiously, North would have been quite at home in this atmosphere. No real issues of principle, division by faction and personal loyalties, "men, not measures," extensive use of patronage and jobs for the boys who chose right and, inevitably, lots and lots of fun.

As a relief from the political convention, my American friend took us to the Indiana Historical Bureau. There was a *real* professor in charge. I haven't met many of the "literary scholarship" type of American, being at the wrong sort of place for it. The professor was one of the most brilliant and interesting men I have met in America. I was impressed by the usual lavish "apparatus," beautiful building, good staff, excellent library and files. The general tone and office atmosphere was pure Oxford; I recognised the type of outlook at once and was surprised to see, out the window, not spires, but a carpark.

The scope of work, which includes a lot of minor publications for schools, is very well done. The major publications were Oxford-standard—Rouse, Oman and A. J. P. Taylor would be right at home here. I would have liked to spend a long time there.

30 June 1956

We get the impression in England of America as a rather unstable society. Is this true?

It is certainly a competitive society and competition makes for strain as well as for efficiency. But, apart from the pressure on academic folk to produce, I haven't seen much of this. In any case, a prosperity in which almost anybody can get a fairly decent job blunts the edge of competition. I haven't struck anything like the atmosphere of *The Hucksters* or *The Man in the Grey Flannel Suit*.

It is certainly a highly mobile society. People shift around from place to place, from job to job, from trade to trade, far more than we do.

It is also a society which believes with a positively Victorian enthusiasm in "progress," in things getting bigger and better. They aren't very much interested in static efficiency.

It is also a highly equalitarian society, in which people are distinguished not so much by class, education or trade as by standard of living—anyway, far more than we are. So the physical standard of living is more important than with us.

As a result, people operate under rather greater strain than we do. "Getting on" is more important. One instance of this, I imagine, is the importance of the car as an index of position. But from what I have seen in the Mid-west it certainly is not an unstable society. If you don't believe me, come to Indiana and meet my American friends.

A BICENTENNIAL VIEW

Howard H. Peckham

Are Hoosiers today as distinctive from other Americans as they were? If not, when were they most distinguishable? And what are they now?

Indiana, in the middle of the eighteenth century, contained Indians, Frenchmen, and Negroes. Then came Anglo-Americans, a trickle at first that grew to a steady torrent. Although these new arrivals were from the South and the East, and sectional feelings colored their difference of outlook, they forged a new life in a new state and absorbed a modest number of foreign-born. By the time of the Civil War, Hoosiers were an identifiable lot. Travelers, visitors, and newcomers readily noticed certain traits. Hoosiers were self-reliant, self-assured, attached to the land, and used to hard work. But so were a lot of the inhabitants of other western areas. More distinctively, Hoosiers were known for their hospitable friendliness, their treatment of one another as equals, their good humor, and their shrewdness in judging character. Dependent as farmers were on weather, they committed themselves to Providence with humility and hope. Specifically, at that time, Hoosiers detested slavery, Negroes, state indebtedness, drunkenness, laziness, and horse thieves. They were mildly suspicious of Catholics, foreigners, public schools, and government interference in local

---

From *Indiana: A Bicentennial View* (1978), pp. 187–195. Reprinted by permission of The American Association for State and Local History.

affairs. They were indifferent to the political rights of women (in common with many citizens of other states) and to higher education at state expense. They supported state care of the needy and the growth of manufacturing. Optimistic, they were already boosters of their state's future.

After the shock of the Civil War, Hoosiers continued their rural life, participated intensively in politics, tolerated corrupt practices, saw fewer European immigrants than most other states, encouraged factories, and grew increasingly self-conscious of their own typicalness. Looking back from 1926, Mark Sullivan observed in *Our Times* that the typical American of 1900 more nearly resembled a Hoosier than he did the inhabitant of any other state. Surveying 1900 contemporaneously, Meredith Nicholson said that "Indiana has always lain near the currents of national life." It is strange that Hoosiers settled for typicality, as if they relished being average, rather than reaching for superiority. Possibly it was that typicalness that encouraged intolerance: for if I consider myself typical, then you who are different from me must be atypical—that is, radical or reactionary, perhaps inferior, not to be admired but ignored or opposed. It seemed appropriate that the center of population in the United States was located in southern Indiana in 1890, and in its slow westward course remained within the state until after 1940, longer than in any other state. It contributed to the self-appraisal that Hoosiers must be average.

Without boundary barriers and stretched between Lake Michigan and the Ohio, Indiana was athwart the main routes by which the East filled up the great West, making the state a constant witness to that national expansion, or manifest destiny. The state has never been plundered by outsiders, carpet-baggers who came in to mine or cut timber and then move on. What wealth and power were acquired were acquired by natives; usually by natives who were poor or middle-class to begin with.

From a retrospectus of Indiana's history one cannot help feeling that Hoosiers were most distinctively their own people in the period from 1900 to 1920. They were rural in background and outlook, without being rustic or uncouth. By then they were pleasantly mature but not sophisticated or urbane. They read their own authors (so did everyone else) and patronized their own painters. Since hard work, perseverance, thrift, and honesty seemed always to be rewarded, they clung to the old virtues. They were materialistic. Gregarious, they gathered at their own lodges and clubs and churches. They enjoyed their politics, their church suppers, their family reunions, their school exercises, their folklore, their recreations—in short, life as they found it. Perhaps their horizon was low. Those young men who went east to college frequently came back to live in Indiana. "Making it" in New York City was no more challenging than making it in Indianapolis. No one was ashamed to be known as a Hoosier; in fact, it was a badge of honor. They knew who they were and what they were, and thus they were stable.

After 1920, influences appeared that tended to mould Hoosiers into the national pattern and chip away their distinctive traits. Mobility, from automobiles and good roads, loosened inhabitants from their isolated localities and encouraged travel to the cities and out of the state. Yet Americans focused on their own problems and pleasures, ignoring the rest of the world. As much as any other factor, increased mobility undermined the country church and church affiliation in general. With movies and radio and amusement parks and auto racing, entertainment became commercial and the same for all, all over the country. The Depression was a common experience, and unions spread out from the Calumet industries. There was a turn to state government, and then to the federal government for relief. It was a blow to self-reliance and to the faith that the economic environment, unlike the weather, was not capricious and not without corrective laws.

The second World War was another sad, anxious, unifying experience. Isolationism was reduced. The united effort to serve and win brought together the people who had been parted by the Depression. Employment was general and rising. Indiana was doing something visible and significant; the old feeling of equality returned. Rising confidence brightened the postwar horizon. College enrollments ballooned here as elsewhere. New industries moved into Indiana, bringing both managers and workers from other states, diluting the native population. The spread of television had everyone watching the same network shows, familiar with the same entertainments, hearing the same songs and jokes. With a stronger economy, optimism reasserted itself.

In the early 1950s, when Senator Joseph McCarthy's witch hunt for Communists was echoed by former Communists beating their breasts over having seen the true light at last, when liberals were mourning the passing of freedom, and British historian Arnold Toynbee was concluding a pessimistic appraisal of the survival of Western civilization, the clear, cool Hoosier voice of Elmer Davis was raised. He was disgusted by all extremists. The country was not doomed this way or that, because the extremists were blind to the vast indistinct area between the clear-cut choices they insisted upon. Davis knew there were numerous people in between who subscribed to neither doctrine. They believed simply in trying to find a way, hoping to do their best; not just muddling through, but holding the fabric of society together. But neither Communists nor former Communists have any patience with experimental thinking; they want a final truth and they insist that they possess it. Davis was speaking for the unimpressed: the Hoosiers—and the millions of people like them in other states—who had grown tired of Senator Jenner's support of McCarthy and who knew empty rattling when they heard it. And they did prevail over the doom-sayers.

President James Conant of Harvard once said that the right to think and question and investigate is the basic difference between the free world and the totalitarian world. Hoosiers have always known that, though they forgot it briefly under the spell of the Klan. Most of the time, they think for themselves. Because of surviving differences between north and south, there are always countervailing forces at work. What one area or one type of worker wants, another opposes. Conflicting interests, different aims, variant energies not only provoke discussion, but prevent the state from moving firmly or swiftly in a given direction.

All of these external and internal influences have operated to homogenize the inhabitants of Indiana. They are more exposed to common experiences than they used to be. Those who contend that north and south are growing alike mean that southern Hoosiers are becoming more like those in the north. If the differences seem to have diminished, they have by no means disappeared, and a few observers believe that they have actually increased. There is still evidence of more energy and quickness and impersonal detachment in the north. A revival of interest in the history and traditions of southern Indiana has made that area more conscious of its distinctive heritage. The people remain friendly to visitors, but time is required for new residents from "outside" to gain acceptance by the old elite. The growing number of retired people moving into southern Indiana is giving a new cast to the region, not matched by a similar age group entering the north.

The growth of industry has attracted probably as many southern laborers into northern cities as there are northerners; what it has done in southern Indiana is to introduce labor unions that did not exist earlier. Mediators find the new unionists in the south a tumultuous bunch, likely to turn violent, and as unwilling to obey their elected officials as they are to accommodate their employers. Contract negotiations do not proceed with the same civility that they do in the north. So a flat declaration that Hoosiers are growing more alike cannot be made without challenges. Yet, to select a typical Hoosier today, one would look for him in southern Indiana, simply on the ground that there are fewer "outsiders" in that part of the state.

If Hoosiers feel a state loyalty like that of the inhabitants of Maine, Virginia, and Texas, it is because generally they know something of their own history. National patriotism is more critical. It is rooted in a feeling for land, for the expansive nation, for the continental potential, rather than enthusiasm for the federal government. Hoosiers actually don't care much for their Uncle Sam: Indiana newspapers carp about the extravagance of the government in Washington, its welfare generosity and foreign aid, its foolish programs and bumbling bureaucracy, which intrude on state and private affairs. Indianans complain about contributing a dollar in federal taxes and getting back only seventy-three cents in federal expenditures. Only four other states obtain less, while states in the South and Southwest receive more: Arizona gets back $1.41, and New Mexico $1.93. The notion of being plucked for the benefit of others rankles most Hoosiers, year after year. Yet they also resent offers of federal grants to education and housing, because of strings attached. They observe November 11 as Veterans Day, not the October Monday decreed by Congress. They have opposed the imposition of seasonal daylight-saving time. They prefer to go their own way.

One reason they can afford to pursue their own course is that Indiana has been singularly blessed by the philanthropy of a few local families, as much as any state and more than most. Not that those families were so extraordinarily rich, but they affectionately confined their bounty within the state. Without that private help, Indiana would be straitened, especially in higher education.

Chauncey Rose (1794–1877), who came to Terre Haute in 1818 and made a fortune as a railroad builder, gave money to the local Normal School, to Wabash College, and finally to a local technical school founded in 1874, the first private engineering college west of the Alleghenies. After his death, the school was renamed Rose Polytechnic Institute. His generosity has been matched by gifts from Anton Hulman, Jr., Terre Haute businessman and owner of the Indianapolis Motor Speedway. Today the college is known as the Rose-Hulman Institute.

John Herron's bequest to the Art Association of Indianapolis has been mentioned.

The Indianapolis Foundation began quietly in 1916 as a local trust fund to which anyone and everyone might contribute. It received a large increase in 1932 through incorporation of the William E. English Foundation under the same trustees. The English bequest was used to construct a building that houses twenty-seven charitable agencies and pays for depreciation and part of maintenance. As a result, those agencies have only small overhead costs for office space. The Indianapolis Foundation has handed out more than $13 million to local agencies, while it continues to grow from bequests and gifts. Its present assets are $16 million.

The Ball brothers of Muncie established a foundation in 1926 with current assets of $19 million. It concentrates on local giving, with emphasis on Ball State University, hospitals, churches, and civic improvements.

The Irwin-Sweeney-Miller Foundation in Columbus has a capital of $23 million and devotes the interest to programs in racial and social justice, religion, education, and the arts. The Krannert Charitable Trust in Indianapolis is nearly as large and has been especially generous to Purdue University (the Krannert Graduate School of Management), the University of Evansville, Hanover College, the Indianapolis Museum of Art (Krannert Pavilion), the Indiana University Hospital, and the Methodist Hospital of Indianapolis.

Then there is the Lilly Endowment, which made grants amounting to $53 million nationally in 1975. Since its modest establishment in 1937, it has expended $150 million in Indiana alone on the private colleges, the Indiana Historical Society, the Lilly Library, New Harmony restoration, church programs, charities, and recreations. This huge sum is quite apart from the enormous benefactions of members of the Lilly family on local projects, which far exceed that figure.

Taken all together, this munificence has enabled Indiana institutions to achieve stability, to reach more people, to serve more effectively, and to be independent in whole or in part of government grants. Hoosiers prefer to look after themselves. There is a noticeable lack of flashy, personal extravagance among wealthy families. Wealth is often indiscernible, for the richest seldom flaunt it. Such persons invariably consider themselves as middle-class, part of the general effort to be average, rather than exceptional. It is that attitude that causes Hoosiers to resent arrogance and not allow temperament among the most talented. Although they like gadgets, yet the things that man makes do not seem to take charge of his life. What a person *is* still counts for more than what he has or what he does.

Today some Hoosiers consider themselves liberals—yet, may not be. Others do not hesitate to call themselves conservatives. Both are contemptuous of radicals and reactionaries. Both are vaguely aware that the difference between them is primarily one of degree. Basically, both types prize individualism, even while viewing each other with suspicion. That is, the liberals accuse the conservatives of favoring the strongest individuals at the expense of community interest. The conservatives counterattack by accusing the liberals of sacrificing the good of the community to protect the oddest, most irresponsible members. Actually, both antagonists distrust society, blaming it for corrupting individual members or forcing them toward collectivism for the common good.

If Indiana exhibits a conservative stance in politics, economics, religion, and social concerns (and some astute observers insist that moderates have recently routed the conservatives), she has not come to that position from ignorance or innocence, but from broad experience. This explanation of the present as shaped and sustained by the past is not well understood, even in Indiana. She has witnessed an educative procession of novel, varied, and experimental communities and political parties. She has tolerated illiteracy, bigotry, and political dishonesty longer than she should have before making corrections. She has endured wars, panics, and depressions. Once she spent money wildly. These experiences have been largely forgotten by the current generation, but they all helped to sharpen Hoosier values and choices. Experimentation ultimately lost its appeal and came under suspicion; was it really necessary to try everything anyone suggested? Folk wisdom seemed more reliable: the tried and true was more comfortable. It was not a case of bitter disillusionment and rejection of change, but of deliberate discrimination, a sign of growing sophistication that non-Hoosiers seldom perceive.

Admittedly, it is difficult today to sell a new idea to the general assembly, a chamber of commerce, a newspaper, a church congregation, or a union. Hoosier minds are not closed, but they are wary. Changes are effected only by small steps. Whether this cautious pace may be ascribed to ingrained skepticism or to penetrating intelligence is for someone else to argue. Let me only suggest that it may be owing to a dim recollection of having tried something similar long ago.

That unhurried way of looking at things is significant in the 1970s in the face of the sociological "futurists." They are alarmed at the rate of change in our culture. It is moving too fast, they say; people cannot adjust, there will come a "future shock." The academics are attracted to this cheerless diagnosis. What Alvin Toffler and his sort overlook, however, are people like the Hoosiers. They don't swing with the fads, they don't rush to adopt new concepts or accept new techniques. They don't panic, but serve as national stabilizers and as a powerful brake on change. They can live in juxtaposition to new notions for a long time, until those views that don't founder become as familiar as their own homes. Gradually and belatedly, Hoosiers adjust. Though they disgust impatient reformers, they avoid cultural shocks. They are not passengers in a car careening out of control, but sit in the driver's seat and slowly roll along.

Perhaps they have the vices of their virtues. They may, for instance, be a little too self-satisfied in their conservatism, a little too shallow in their materialism, somewhat undiscriminating in their taste for literature and art, a little too undemanding in their standards of education. But over the long haul, I will bet on them to survive—with grace.

Index

RALPH D. GRAY is Professor of History and Adjunct Professor of American Studies at Indiana University–Purdue University at Indianapolis.